Fourth Edition

MANAGEMENT:
Principles and Applications

Leonard Bierman
Mays Business School at Texas A & M University

O.C. Ferrell
Auburn University

Linda Ferrell
Auburn University

Academic Media Solutions
Affordable - Quality Textbooks, Study Aids, & Custom Publishing

Len —To my family, Risa, Joshua, and David
O.C. & Linda—George Ferrell

Paperback (black/white):   ISBN-13: 978-1-942041-69-6
                            ISBN-10: 1-942041-69-1

Paperback (color):   ISBN-13: 978-1-942041-72-6
                            ISBN-10: 1-942041-72-1

Loose leaf version (B/W):   ISBN-13: 978-1-942041-70-2
                            ISBN-10: 1-942041-70-5

Online version: ISBN-13: 978-1-942041-71-9
                            ISBN-10: 1-942041-71-3

Printed in the United States of America by Academic Media Solutions.

BRIEF CONTENTS

CONTENTS

2 History of Management Thought 31

4 Ethics and Social Responsibility 93

5 Managing in a Global World 129

PART 3   PLANNING 159

6   Planning and Strategic Management   159

9 Human Resource Management 265

10 Organizational Change and Innovation 295

PART 5   LEADING 325

11   Effective Leadership in the Organization   325

14 Communicating in Organizations 421

16 Managing Operations and Increasing Productivity 481

Appendix Entrepreneurship and Small Business 511

Preface

INTRODUCTION

Management: Principles and Applications provides engaging, comprehensive coverage of contemporary management. This student-friendly text and teaching package embraces the latest perspectives on traditional concepts, newer concepts, and the challenges that managers face in business today. Our focus is the understanding and application of the concepts students will need to be successful. We have minimized complex explanations and illustrations to maximize straightforward understanding and application. Most students will need to utilize management knowledge in their entry-level job, and our goal is to prepare them to be grounded for more advanced management courses and career success.

Our research indicates that the organization and chapter content that we have selected are an excellent fit for how most management principles courses are taught. Management professors want to cover the development of management thought, but this knowledge has to be placed in the context of today's environment and challenges. Today, technology issues, global connectedness, cultural diversity, and social responsibility are changing the manager's environment. For example, in the technology area, the Internet and social media have had a revolutionary impact on the conduct of global businesses. Businesses that were once at the heart of day-to-day life, like the daily local newspaper, are going by the wayside. New business models are changing how management develops and implements strategies. For example, the sharing economy has provided a new business model that created Uber and AirBnB. Internet giants, such as Amazon and Alibaba, are challenging traditional retail stores. Artificial intelligence has the potential to transfer the business environment and create the need for new strategies and protection. Social responsibility issues such as sustainability, corporate governance, consumer protection, and other social issues are changing the manager's responsibilities. This revised edition addresses the movement for equal treatment and respect in the workplace. We specifically address current issues related to gender discrimination, sexual misconduct, and abusive and intimidating behavior in the workplace.

This text is organized into six parts and 16 chapters, plus an appendix on entrepreneurship. To facilitate learning, each chapter contains an opening vignette that provides examples of the real world of management, as well as *Business Dilemma* and *Management Insights* features to familiarize students with managerial decision making. End-of-chapter summaries help students to review important concepts in the chapter, while the learning tools and cases make the text come alive for students. Students are placed in a decision-making setting and learn how to apply management concepts through engagement exercises. Students can use these tools to relate to the types of environments and issues faced in any organization.

FEATURES OF THE BOOK

Management: Principles and Applications is structured to excite students about the field of management. This text will help students learn essential management concepts and how to apply them practically. We have structured the book in a format that helps students learn effectively and efficiently:

- A *chapter outline* at the beginning of each chapter provides a blueprint of the chapter.

- *Objectives* at the start of each chapter indicate what students are expected to learn as they go through the content.

- Every chapter begins with an opening vignette titled *Inside Management*. This feature provides examples of the real world of management that relate to the chapter topic. After reading the vignette, the student should be motivated to learn more about concepts and strategies that relate to the varying topics. Students will learn about businesses such as Dollar General, Alibaba, Timberland, Best Buy, Chick-fil-A, and King Arthur Flour.

- Boxed features—*Business Dilemma* and *Management Insights*—help students to think through the challenges and decisions that face managers daily.

- The *Business Dilemma* boxes ask students to take on the role of the manager in a hypothetical business dilemma. After reading the content, students will answer three questions about how they believe the manager in the scenario should proceed. These scenarios will help students develop their critical-thinking skills in approaching management dilemmas.

- The *Management Insights* boxes introduce students to such topics as decision making in different cultures, virtual corporate cultures, sustainability, and social entrepreneurship. Featured companies include Rebecca Ray Designs, the Rainforest Alliance, Facebook, SeaWorld, Yammer, and ATA Engineering.

- *Key term definitions* appear in the margins to help students build their business vocabulary.

- Figures, tables, and photographs increase comprehension and stimulate interest.

- A complete *Summary and Review* covers the major topics discussed and is organized based upon the chapter objectives.

- The list of *Key Terms and Concepts* provides another end-of-chapter study aid to expand students' management vocabulary.

- *Ready Recall* requires students to answer questions about the chapter content. This section helps students review their understanding of what they have read.

- *Expand Your Experience* encourages students to practice their newfound knowledge in a real-world setting.

- *Strengthen Your Skills* provides exercises related to the chapter content to help students expand their knowledge.

- Each chapter has an end-of-chapter case to help students understand the application of chapter concepts. All of the cases represent real company situations and are new to this book. Companies highlighted in the cases include Apple, Whole Foods, Zappos, Starbucks, Wells Fargo, and New Belgium Brewing.

- An *appendix* discusses the topic of entrepreneurship, including the types of industries that attract small businesses, why small businesses succeed or fail, and how to go about starting a small business.

TEXT ORGANIZATION

We have organized the six parts of *Management: Principles and Applications* to give students a theoretical and practical understanding of managerial decision making.

Part 1 An Overview and History of Management In Chapter 1, we discuss the nature of management and explore several key concepts, including management decision making, management roles, and situational differences in management activities. In Chapter 2, we look at the history of management. This chapter reviews the evolution of management as well as the key thinkers and theories that have contributed to the field of business as we know it today.

Part 2 Environmental and Social Issues in Management In Chapter 3, we examine the environment of management, including the task environment, general environment, internal environment, and the stakeholder view of the environment. In Chapter 4, we discuss the importance of management ethics and social responsibility. This chapter examines the process of ethical decision making and the growing concern for corporate social responsibility. Chapter 5 describes managing in the global environment, an essential topic in today's global and interconnected world.

Part 3 Planning We examine the planning process and the different levels of strategy in Chapter 6. The differences between corporate and business-level strategy are explained in this chapter. In Chapter 7, we explore decision making in management, including the decision-making process, decision-making models, decision-making styles, and group decision making.

Part 4 Organizing In Chapter 8, we introduce the importance of organizing jobs, departments, and the overall company. We define human resource management in Chapter 9, including recruiting, selecting, training, appraising, and compensating employees. In Chapter 10, we consider organizational change and innovation. Because change and innovation are essential for firm survival, different models of planned change and organizational development are examined.

Part 5 Leading In Chapter 11, we look at employee leadership. This highly significant topic examines different approaches and models of leadership as well as emerging trends in the leadership field. Chapter 12 explores employee motivation, including different motivational theories and how to include motivation in job design. In Chapter 13, we study effective team management. The definitions of groups and teams are provided as well as how to enhance their effectiveness. Chapter 14 considers the importance of communication in organizations.

Part 6 Controlling We discuss the management control process in Chapter 15. Controlling the activities and processes of an organization is a critical requirement for managers. In Chapter 16, we analyze how to manage operations and productivity. Quality, productivity, and inventory control are discussed in detail.

Appendix The Appendix covers the topic of entrepreneurship. Specifically, it discusses the importance of small businesses and steps for starting a small business.

ONLINE AND IN PRINT

This fourth edition of *Management: Principles and Applications* is available in multiple versions: online and in print as either a paperback or loose-leaf text. The most affordable version is the online book, with upgrade options including the online version bundled with a print version. What's nice about the print version is that it offers you the freedom of being unplugged—away from your computer. The people at Academic Media Solutions recognize that it's difficult to read from a screen at length and that most of us read much faster from a piece of paper. The print options are particularly useful when you have extended print passages to read.

The online edition allows you to take full advantage of embedded digital features, including search and notes. Use the search feature to locate and jump to discussions anywhere in the book. Use the notes feature to add personal comments or annotations. You can move out of the book to follow Web links. You can navigate within and between chapters using a clickable table of contents. These features allow you to work at your own pace and in your own style, as you read and surf your way through the material. (See "Harnessing the Online Version" for more tips on working with the online version.)

HARNESSING THE ONLINE VERSION

The online version of *Management: Principles and Applications*, 4e offers the following features to facilitate learning and to make using the book an easy, enjoyable experience:

- **Easy-to-navigate/clickable table of contents**—You can surf through the book quickly by clicking on chapter headings, or first- or second-level section headings. And the Table of Contents can be accessed from anywhere in the book.

- **Key terms search**—Type in a term, and a search engine will return every instance of that term in the book; then jump directly to the selection of your choice with one click.

- **Notes and highlighting**—The online version includes study apps such as notes and highlighting. Each of these apps can be found in the tools icon embedded in the Academic Media Solutions/Textbook Media's online eBook reading platform (http://www.academicmediasolutions.com).

- **Upgrades**—The online version includes the ability to purchase additional study aids and functionality that enhance the learning experience.

A COMPREHENSIVE INSTRUCTIONAL RESOURCE PACKAGE

In addition to the student-friendly features and pedagogy, the variety of student formats available, and the uniquely affordable pricing options, *Management: Principles and Applications*, 4e comes with the following teaching and learning aids.

- Test Item File—An extensive set of multiple-choice, true/false, and essay questions for every chapter for creating original quizzes and exams.

- Instructor's Manual—The Instructor's Manual contains a chapter outline as well as guidance for end-of-chapter materials, including case notes. The Instructor's Manual has been developed to facilitate a quick review of the chapter and provide insights to using all of the teaching devices.

- PowerPoint Presentations—Key points in each chapter are illustrated in a set of PowerPoint files designed to assist with instruction.

- Online Video Labs with Student Worksheets—A collection of high-quality, dynamic, and sometimes humorous video segments (contemporary and classic) produced by a variety of media, academic, and entertainment sources, accessed via the web. Organized by chapter, the video segments illustrate key topics/issues discussed in the chapters. Each video segment is accompanied by a student worksheet that consists of a series of discussion questions that help students connect the themes presented in the video segment with key topics discussed in the specific chapter.

- Lecture Guide—This printable lecture guide is designed for student use and is available as an in-class resource or study tool. Note: Instructors can request the PowerPoint version of these slides to use as developed or to customize.

- Quizlet Study Set—Quizlet is an easy-to-use online learning tool built from all the key terms from the textbook. Students can turbo charge their studying via digital flashcards and other types of study apps, including tests and games. Students are able to listen to audio, as well as, create their own flashcards. Quizlet is a cross-platform application and can be used on a desktop, tablet, or smartphone.

- Study Guide—A printable version of the online study guide is available via downloadable PDF chapters for easy self-printing and review.

YOUR COMMENTS AND SUGGESTIONS ARE VALUED

As authors, our major focus has been on teaching and preparing learning materials for introductory management students. We have traveled extensively to work with students and to try and understand the needs of professors of introductory management courses.

We invite your comments, questions, and criticisms. We want to do our best to provide materials that enhance the teaching and learning of management concepts and strategies. Your suggestions will be sincerely appreciated. Please email Len Bierman at LBierman@mays.tamu.edu, O.C. Ferrell at OCF0003@auburn.edu, and/or Linda Ferrell at LKF0009@auburn.edu.

ACKNOWLEDGMENTS

Like most textbooks, this one reflects the ideas of many academicians and practitioners who have contributed to the development of the management discipline. We appreciate the opportunity to present their ideas in this book.

We wish to thank Robert D. Gatewood and Robert R. Taylor for their contributions to fundamental concepts that were provided in an earlier work on principles of management. We acknowledge that their contributions provided content and substance, and permitted us to focus on contemporary management advances and applications. Their work has been invaluable in making this textbook a reality.

We thank Jennifer Sawayda for her research and editorial assistance in the revision of the chapters, cases, and boxes. We also wish to thank several individuals for assisting in developing boxes and cases. Mark Zekoff is responsible for the New Belgium Brewing, Chipotle, and Patagonia cases. Diann Kronke completed extensive research on Appledale Farms, Ford Motor Company, and Warren Buffett and Berkshire Hathaway. Shelby Wyatt was responsible for editing TOMS and assisted in research on the boxes. Lauren Grantham helped to develop the Eaton case and did significant research on the Louisville Slugger box. Kelsey Riddick assisted in developing cases and boxes. We are grateful to Brett Nafziger of A.B. Custom Solutions for his assistance with various aspects of the text. We express appreciation for the support and encouragement given to us by our colleagues at Texas A&M University and Auburn University. We are also grateful for the comments and suggestions we received from our own students, student focus groups, and student correspondents who provided feedback through the website.

A number of talented professionals at Putman Productions and Academic Media Solutions have contributed to the development of this book. We are especially grateful to Victoria Putman and Dan Luciano. Their inspiration, patience, support, and friendship are invaluable.

Leonard Bierman
O.C. Ferrell
Linda Ferrell

About the Authors

Leonard Bierman is a Professor of Management at Texas A&M University. He has published widely in journals such as the *Academy of Management Journal*, the *Strategic Management Journal*, *Harvard Business Review*, and the *Academy of Management Review*. He has considerable real-world experience in the fields of international business and human resource management, including having worked earlier in his career at the U.S. Department of Labor, the U.S. International Trade Commission, and the Equal Employment Opportunity Commission.

O.C. Ferrell is the James T. Pursell, Sr. Eminent Scholar in Ethics and Director of the Center for Ethical Organizational Cultures at Auburn University. He has served on the faculty at Belmont University, the University of New Mexico, University of Wyoming, Colorado State University, University of Memphis, Texas A&M University, University of Michigan, Illinois State University, and Southern Illinois University. Dr. Ferrell holds a Ph.D. from Louisiana State University in Marketing, an M.B.A. in Marketing, as well as a B.A. in Sociology from Florida State University. Dr. Ferrell is President of the Academy of Marketing Science. He was formerly Vice-President of Publications for the Academy of Marketing Science and was Past President of the Academic Council of the American Marketing Association. He received the AMS Cutco/Vector Distinguished Educator Award for contributions to the marketing discipline. Additional recognition includes being the first recipient of the Marketing Education Innovation Award for the Marketing Management Association, Lifetime Achievement Award from the Macromarketing Society and special award for service to doctoral students from the Southeast Doctoral Consortium. He has chaired 13 dissertations with his former students currently serving as Deans, Associate Provost, CIBER Directors, journal editors, among others. Dr. Ferrell is co-author of several leading textbooks including *Business Ethics: Ethical Decision Making and Cases* (13th edition), *Marketing* (20th edition), *Marketing Strategy* (6th edition), *Business and Society* (6th edition), and *Introduc-*

tion to Business (12th edition). He has published in the *Journal of Marketing, Journal of Marketing Research, Journal of the Academy of Marketing Science, Journal of Business Ethics, Journal of Public Policy & Marketing, AMS Review, Journal of Business Research,* as well as others. He writes weekly business ethics summaries and reviews for the *Wall Street Journal* with over 6,000 subscribers. Dr. Ferrell has served as an expert witness in some high-profile ethics, legal, and marketing cases.

Linda Ferrell is Professor and Chair of the Marketing Department in the Harbert College of Business. She served on the faculty at Belmont University, University of New Mexico, University of Wyoming, University of Northern Colorado, Colorado State University, and University of Tampa. She co-managed a $2.5 million grant for business ethics education through the Daniels Fund Ethics Initiative at the University of New Mexico. Dr. Ferrell earned a Ph.D. in Business Administration-Management from the University of Memphis. She holds an M.B.A. and a B.S. in Fashion Merchandising from Illinois State University. She has published in *Journal of the Academy of Marketing Science, AMS Review, Journal of Business Ethics, Journal of Public Policy & Marketing, Journal of Business Research,* as well as others. She has co-authored numerous books including *Business Ethics: Ethical Decision Making and Cases* (13th edition), *Business and Society* (6th edition), and *Introduction to Business* (12th edition). Professionally, Dr. Ferrell served as an account executive in advertising with McDonald's and Pizza Hut's advertising agencies in Houston, Indianapolis and Philadelphia. She has been recognized as the Innovative Marketer of the Year for the Marketing Management Association. Dr. Ferrell is on the Board of Directors of Mannatech, Inc., a NASDAQ-listed health and wellness company. She serves on the Executive Committee and Board of the Direct Selling Education Foundation. She is past president of the Academy of Marketing Science and the Marketing Management Association. Dr. Ferrell also serves as an expert witness in ethics and legal disputes.

An Overview of Management

CHAPTER 1

Source: Rawpixel/Shutterstock

Chapter Outline

After reading this chapter, you will be able to:

- Define management and describe its purpose in organizations.
- Determine the effect that management actions have on the manager and others in the organization.
- List the major functions of managers.
- Explain the importance of decision making in management activities.
- Describe the many roles managers play in an organization.
- Specify why different managers perform different job activities.
- Identify some emerging trends in management.
- Review what you can reasonably learn from a textbook about how to perform management activities.
- Evaluate a small business owner's management skills and propose a future course of action for the firm.

Chick-fil-A Excels at Managing Success

From the day it was founded, Chick-fil-A has served communities differently than other fast-food chains. The founder, Truett Cathy, established his first restaurant in 1946, called the Dwarf Grill. It was the roots of the first Chick-fil-A restaurant that opened in 1967. Cathy used his resources both efficiently and effectively to reach objectives, illustrating the importance of management to an organization. He engaged in the four management functions of planning by setting performance goals, organizing by designing jobs for employees, leading by motivating employees to achieve management objectives, and controlling by collecting and analyzing information about work performance.

Truett Cathy once said, "We should be about more than just selling chicken. We should be a part of our customers' lives and the communities in which we serve." This inspired the need for high standards of customer service at Chick-fil-A. Chick-fil-A believes it has such consistent customer service because it invests more in employee training than comparable companies and helps its employees to advance.

The company's strong employee orientation demonstrates that it supports the concept of social responsibility, or obligations to maximize its positive impact and minimize its negative impact on society. To this date, Chick-fil-A has provided $35 million in college scholarships to Chick-fil-A team members wanting to pursue higher education. Managers of Chick-fil-A restaurants across the United States have found that employees are more motivated when the company demonstrates that it cares for their well-being.

Having previously worked in the restaurant industry, Cathy decided that he did not want his restaurants open seven days a week or 24 hours a day. He saw the importance of being closed on Sundays so that employees could set aside one day to rest or engage in religious activities if they desire. This practice continues today. The management decisions made by Dan Cathy, current chief executive officer (CEO)/president and son of Truett Cathy, are still based on this same foundation. The business is not about being a part of the food industry; it is about the people who are a part of Chick-fil-A. This includes both the customers and the employees.

Chick-fil-A also takes a different approach to the prep work method of its food: "Cook less, more often." Quality is emphasized over quantity. This allows their

Source: Jonathan Weis/Shutterstock

chicken sandwiches to stand out from the competition. The restaurant's name has a hidden meaning to show they are the best in quality. The name is a take on *chicken fillet* with a capital *A* at the end. The *A* stands for top quality.

Although it still holds true to its founding principles, Chick-fil-A recognizes the emerging trend of e-business, or the use of digital technology to achieve management goals. To better connect with customers, the company created an app called Chick-fil-A One. The app allows customers who may be in a hurry to pre-order their meals and bypass the line to receive their food. The app also allows customers to pay at the counter by scanning their phones for a fast and easy experience. Chick-fil-A's foray into mobile technology is just one of many initiatives it has adopted to provide top-notch customer service.

As Chick-fil-A has grown, management roles in the areas of information technology and interpersonal communication have advanced significantly. This has resulted in the need for different levels of managers. At companies like Chick-fil-A, first-line or lower-level managers operate the restaurants, middle managers implement the strategy, and upper-level managers develop policy. The ability of the different management levels to work together cohesively to achieve management goals has contributed to Chick-fil-A's current status as the eighth-largest fast-food chain in the nation. Today Chick-fil-A's success can be seen with more than 2,100 restaurants all over the country and $5.1 billion in sales.[1]

Introduction

The different skills and the creativity that Chick-fil-A founder Truett Cathy possessed illustrate the diversity in management activities, which is one reason why management seems difficult to teach and learn. We believe that general principles or concepts exist that can be applied to all these different activities. Not surprisingly, our purpose is to share with you these general principles, which are important for understanding and learning management.

Our basic idea in this chapter is that, in order to understand what management is, it is necessary to know how it is similar and different across organizations. There are a number of similarities. All managers make decisions about the use of organizational resources to reach organizational goals; engage in the same basic activities of planning, organizing, leading and controlling; and act in the same general roles for their organizations. On the other hand, the specific task activities of managers can vary greatly due to differences—such as size and industry—in the characteristics of the organizations to which they belong.

The Nature of Management

Management is a set of activities designed to achieve an organization's objectives by using its resources effectively and efficiently in a changing environment. Resources are used to accomplish the manager's intended purpose. **Effectively** means having the intended result; **efficiently** means accomplishing the objectives with a minimum of resources. Both are part of good management—reaching objectives with a minimum of cost. On the other hand, reducing costs without considering the impact on customers and the organization will not permit reaching goals effectively. One factor that makes management difficult is that the work situation constantly changes. That is, such factors as employees, technology, competition, and cost vary greatly. This requires managers to be flexible and adapt to the environment. **Managers** are individuals who make decisions about the use of the organization's resources, and are concerned with planning, organizing, leading, and controlling the organization's activities so as to reach its objectives.

Although it may seem that management activities are quite diverse, they share some common characteristics. First, all activities occur within the context of an organization. **Organizations** are groups of individuals who work together to achieve the goals or objectives that are important to these individuals. For example, the New York Yankees is an organization that tries to win baseball games and is in the sports and entertainment business. The Red Cross tries to attract donations and volunteers to assist with disasters. General Motors makes and sells vehicles that satisfy customers. Thus, these organizations must have managers who are essential to their success.

Second, managers are in charge of the organization's **resources**—people, equipment, finances, data—and of using these resources to help the organization reach its objectives. How well managers coordinate organizational activities and use resources determines not only how well the organization accomplishes its objectives but also how the manager will be judged in terms of job performance. Firms such as Google, Apple, and Walmart are examples of companies where managers made good decisions and created success.

The Impact of Management

The management practices of an individual affect more than just one person. Management is characterized by leadership, decision making, and the implementation of work tasks. Because such activities are not carried out in isolation, management reaches several different groups connected with the organization. Like a well-synchronized athletic team, most decisions could be viewed as a team sport. Everyone has to carry out his or her responsibilities. When management is an effective team, positive performance outcomes occur. On the other hand, poorly coordinated managerial decisions often lead to organizational failure.

Leadership is the process of influencing the activities of an individual or a group toward the achievement of a goal. Howard Schultz of Starbucks envisioned a coffee chain that would be the third most common place to go after home and work. With this vision in mind, he led employees toward creating a customer-centered culture that makes customers feel special through customized drinks and a comfortable environment. Decision making is the process of choosing among alternative courses of action to resolve a problem.

management: A set of activities designed to achieve an organization's objectives by using its resources effectively and efficiently in a changing environment.

effectively: Using resources in a way that produces a desired result.

efficiently: Accomplishing the objectives with a minimum of resources.

managers: Individuals who make decisions about the use of the organization's resources, and are concerned with planning, organizing, leading, and controlling the organization's activities so as to reach its objectives.

organizations: Groups of individuals who work together to achieve the goals or objectives that are important to these individuals.

resources: People, equipment, finances, and data used by an organization to reach its objectives.

TABLE 1.1 Three Management Dimensions

Characteristics	Definition	Example
Leadership	Influences the activities of individuals toward achievement of a goal	Manager sets a common goal and gets employees to work toward achieving it.
Decision making	Choosing among several courses of action to resolve a problem	Manager decides to delete a product line because it is no longer profitable.
Implementation of work tasks	Carrying out the work decision	Manager gives an assignment to the marketing department, which then proceeds to carry out the assignment.

Leadership is important in management.

During the recession, Starbucks was hit with financial difficulties. When Howard Schultz returned as CEO, he made the difficult decision to eliminate many stores across the nation to cut down on costs. The implementation of work tasks occurs when the manager or subordinates carry out the decision. Often this requires careful deliberation and planning before action is taken. For instance, Starbucks removed the word Coffee from its logo to emphasize that the company is more than just a coffee shop. Table 1.1 explains these three management practices in more detail.

It is important to recognize that all management decisions have consequences. Three groups that are especially impacted by management activities are the manager, the manager's immediate subordinates, and the manager's organization. You can probably think of others, based on your own experiences. From the manager's perspective, those who manage well are distinctly successful. Successful managers will be given the opportunity to manage more resources and will be asked to make decisions that have even more impact on the organization.

Obviously, a manager's subordinates are directly affected by his or her actions. If the work process is organized well, everyone performs better, which is reflected by the performance appraisals of individual workers. Good performance appraisals can result in increased financial rewards and advancement opportunities. Research also suggests that employees' relationships with their manager strongly affect their work attitudes, such as commitment, satisfaction, and work involvement.[2] Managers are role models for employees and need to maintain integrity in their personal behavior and relationships with employees.

Managers lead by influencing the activities of an individual or a group toward the achievement of a goal.

By its very nature, management affects the number and the quality of the organization's products. As we have said earlier, managers coordinate the organization's resources to help it reach organizational objectives. If the manager coordinates poorly or makes poor decisions, the organization's objectives will not be met as well or as quickly. Kodak depended on film development without recognizing that digital photos were the future. Now that the firm is out of bankruptcy, it is focusing on imaging, photographic equipment, materials, and services. Its managers must make better decisions and be more innovative if the company is to survive.

We have mentioned the impact that management activities have on the manager, subordinates, and the organization. However, management activities also have a profound impact on other people and groups that have an interest in the organization. A **stakeholder** is a person or group which can affect, or is affected by, an organization's goals or the means to achieve those goals. Stakeholders include employees, customers, shareholders/owners, suppliers, government regulators, communities, and more. Consider the impact a managerial decision might have on different stakeholders involving a faulty product. If a manager notices a product is faulty or dangerous, he or she must make the decision whether to recall it. A massive recall would cost the organization, affecting everyone within the organization including investors/owners and employees. The recall of Chobani yogurt after mold in some of the products made people sick negatively impacted the firm's reputation.[3] However, failure to recall the product could harm consumers and warrant government action. Every managerial decision impacts a stakeholder to some extent, and many decisions affect multiple stakeholders. Figure 1.1 shows some of the more common stakeholders necessary for business.

A good example of the impact of management decisions is Southwest Airlines. Herb Kelleher, the co-founder of Southwest Airlines, conceived of the business by writing the idea out on a napkin. As CEO of the company, Kelleher came up with a novel idea at the time for the airline industry. The company would offer low fares by eliminating extra services deemed unnecessary. The company prided itself on getting passengers to their

stakeholder: A person or group that can affect, or is affected by, an organization's goals or the means to achieve those goals.

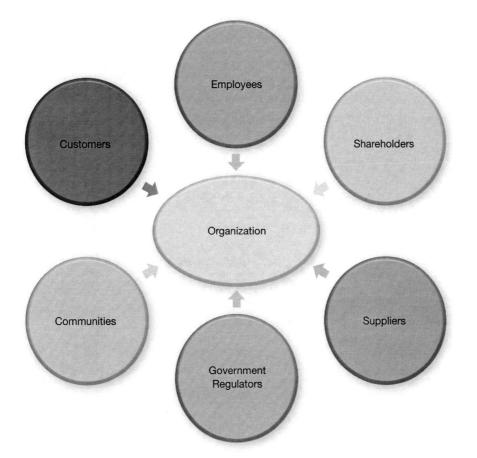

FIGURE 1.1
Primary Stakeholder Groups

destinations on time. From the onset, Kelleher made the managerial decision to develop a corporate culture that cared for its employees and created a fun environment for passengers. Subordinates showed enthusiasm at their jobs, often singing in-flight songs, and Southwest has consistently ranked as one of the world's most admired companies. Southwest is the only airline that has made a profit every year since its founding.[4] In 2010 Southwest acquired the airline AirTran, which gave the airline greater access to larger cities. Up until that time, Southwest had adopted a "keep-it-simple" strategy. However, current CEO Gary C. Kelly believed that it was time to make major changes to spur growth. The acquisition allowed Southwest to become a greater competitor to Delta Airlines.[5] This illustrates the impact of management decisions on the growth and success of Southwest Airlines.

The Functions of Management

All management activities can be classified into four major functions: planning, organizing, leading, and controlling. We will discuss these separately, but they usually occur simultaneously in management activities. Table 1.2 describes these four functions.

Planning

planning: Determining what the organization will specifically accomplish and deciding how to accomplish these goals.

Planning involves determining what the organization will specifically accomplish and deciding how to accomplish these goals. How to use the resources at the command of the manager is the objective of planning.

For example, the manager of the New York Yankees baseball team has to plan the type of players and resources needed for each season. Then there are plans for the strategy and player lineups for each game. At Pizza Hut, an individual store manager plans ahead by anticipating the next week's demand for food, which may be affected by variables such as weather and holidays. She then plans a work schedule of employees, orders supplies, and inspects all equipment, including delivery vehicles, to try to meet that demand.

Organizing

organizing: The activities involved in designing jobs for employees, grouping these jobs together into departments, and developing working relationships among organizational units/departments and employees to carry out the plans.

Organizing refers to the activities involved in designing jobs for employees, grouping these jobs together into departments, and developing working relationships among organizational units/departments and employees to carry out the plans. Some organizing activities, such as forming committees, developing work teams, and staffing for special projects, occur frequently. Others are more periodic. For example, the departmental structure that results from the organizing function is retained until something suggests that a

TABLE 1.2 Characteristics and Examples of the Four Functions of Management

	Characteristics	Retail Example
Planning	Determining appropriate goals for the firm and deciding how to accomplish these goals	Retailers set sales goals and plan inventory needs. All merchandising efforts and promotion are linked to objectives.
Organizing	Assigning responsibility to employees for task achievement to collaboratively achieve goals	Establishing a retail structure to accomplish tasks and creating collaborative ways to reach objectives.
Leading	Influencing and motivating others to achieve set goals	Performance incentives and team building exercises lead to goals.
Controlling	Monitoring, evaluating, and maintaining desired performance	Monitoring the results of merchandising and promotion efforts and making changes when necessary.

Part 1 An Overview and History of Management

Organizations engage in planning, organizing, leading, and controlling activities to be successful.

change in structure is needed. Within the New York Yankees baseball organization, for instance, there may be departments for scouting, player development, ticket sales, and promotion. The Yankees' manager can use all these departments to carry out his plans for leading the team to success and financial profits.

Leading

Leading refers to influencing others' activities to achieve set goals. Leading is based on knowledge of the principles of human behavior. Basically, a manager attempts to organize the work environment to obtain high work performance from employees. Even though there is much more to be learned, we already understand a lot about how to influence individuals' performance. For example, there are ample data to indicate that selection, training, and communication along with goal-setting levels, compensation, and work design are among the organizational factors that managers can use to significantly affect an employee's job performance.[6] The manager of the Yankees, for example, must lead and motivate highly publicized athletes who often earn millions of dollars. They also maintain the support of the fans and other stakeholders. On the other hand, employees at a Pizza Hut restaurant, for the most part, are students working part time for minimum wage and who do not view the work as part of their careers. In each organization, the manager attempts to influence the level of employees' work performance by applying principles of human behavior. Table 1.3 describes ten tips managers can use in exhibiting successful leadership.

leading: Influencing others' activities to achieve set goals.

TABLE 1.3 Ten Tips for Successful Leadership

1. Support employee participation and creativity.
2. Develop effective teams.
3. Listen as much as you speak.
4. Encourage employee feedback.
5. Identify and guard against ethical risks.
6. Act as a role model for employees.
7. Build solid relationships.
8. Clearly communicate company expectations.
9. Align employees behind a common vision.
10. Never rest on your laurels, but always look for improvement.

Controlling involves collecting and analyzing information.

Source: bleakstar/Shutterstock

The management activities that we have described so far establish future goals, specify how to reach these goals, and attempt to motivate organizational members to work toward the attainment of these goals. If all these functions are carried out properly, goals should be attained. However, recall the popular expression, "the best-laid plans of mice and men." The management function of **controlling** refers to those activities that an organization undertakes to ensure that its actions lead to the achievement of its objectives. It involves collecting and analyzing information about work performance and taking corrective action if this information indicates that performance is not contributing to goal achievement.

controlling: Those activities that an organization undertakes to ensure that its actions lead to the achievement of its objectives.

Returning to the Yankees baseball team, the manager will examine batting averages, pitching records, and other data and make changes in the lineup accordingly to try to win more games. Baseball is far more than a game, however. It is a big business. Management must take into account and analyze revenues statistics related to ticket sales, concessions, sales of team-related retail products, and other promotional items.

Management Decision Making

Along with the four basic management functions, all managers engage in the decision-making process—gathering information, using information to reach a decision, and implementing the decision. Each of the four management functions requires a manager to make decisions. Planning, for example, requires gathering information about future objectives, assessing the organization's ability to reach those objectives, and drawing up specific actions needed to guide the organization toward achievement of its objectives. In essence, processing the appropriate information is the key to planning.

As another example, leading—influencing employees' performance—also requires a lot of information gathering. The manager must understand the principles of human behavior and the factors that positively and negatively influence performance. He or she must also be familiar with employees' characteristics such as job skills, desire for achievement, and work commitment because these are linked to individual work performance. CEO of Xerox Jeff Jacobson must have a good grasp on employee skills, company performance, and progress toward company goals. Moreover, the manager should know what characteristics of the work situation influence performance, such as the level of difficulty of operating the technology and the time allowed for completing each task. Obtaining this information should precede the manager's evaluation of what alternatives are available in a particular situation, as well as the implementation of the chosen alternative.

While this decision-making process may sound easy to carry out, it is very difficult. The difficulty lies in the complexity of the information gathered and the uncertainty of the decision process and the methods of implementing the decision. For example, account managers in computer software firms have a number of important decisions to make with very little certain information. Typically the account manager comes in after the sales representative has made the sale and has promised services and programs to the new client. In a short time, the account manager must prepare a service plan that includes a schedule of events such as training, on-site visits, trials of the software programs, and quality-control test runs. To do this, the account manager must make specific commitments of personnel, products, and equipment. These commitments, in turn, become the milestones upon which the software company is judged by the client. Yet, these decisions are often made with only limited data about the expertise of the client's employees, the condition of the necessary company data and records, and the accuracy of the client's own judgment of needs.

Effective Management at Rebecca Ray Designs

Rebecca Yuhasz Smith's thriving retail and wholesale company grew out of an interior design business she started in 1998 in Chagrin Falls, Ohio. In her spare time, Rebecca designed handbags based on her love of animals and the sporting lifestyle. These handbags were often equestrian-themed and were created to be works of art. Soon Rebecca found that demand for her handbags was growing so rapidly she could hardly keep up. After happening to meet with a member of the Amish community, Rebecca decided to work with Amish communities in Ohio and Pennsylvania to create and sell her bags.

As the manager and founder of Rebecca Ray Designs, Rebecca had to plan the organization's goals, organize the different job functions, lead others to develop and sell the products, and control the activities needed for achieving firm objectives. It was decided that the company's organizational culture would center on the founding principle, "A company can do well by doing good." Under Rebecca's leadership, Rebecca Ray Designs chose to sell American handmade luxury items (known as American Couture). Bags are hand-sewn by Amish women with pedal-powered sewing machines. Amish harness-makers hand-make the company's leather products, and the firm employs a sales team who ride on horseback. Rebecca made these decisions to demonstrate her passion for animals as well as provide opportunities for local communities.

For many years, Rebecca Ray Designs relied upon word-of-mouth marketing and sales at dog and horse shows. Rebecca assumed the role of leader, marketing manager, and all the other managerial functions. In 2007 Rebecca Ray Designs won the category of *Country Living* magazine's Pitch Your Product competition. Sales began to increase, but Rebecca underestimated the human resources skills needed to expand. She decided she needed more assistance. With the help of sales representatives, the number of boutiques willing

Rebecca Yuhasz Smith, founder and manager of Rebecca Ray Designs, implements functions of management within her company.

Source: Courtesy of Rebecca Ray Designs, LLC. © Kevin Winter-Churchill.

to sell Rebecca Ray Designs went from 35 to about 50. The company also hired a producer to do promotional videos for the company website and signed a contract to co-brand products with *Country Living*.

Today Rebecca's luxury products include handbags, accessories, and home décor sold at 300 retailers as well as online. She continues working closely with the artisans to maintain the high artistic quality of the products. Due to her reputation for quality, the Kentucky Derby used gift bags designed by Rebecca Ray for its VIP guests. In her role as manager, Rebecca Yuhasz Smith developed important managerial skills and learned from mistakes. Her leadership turned Rebecca Ray Designs into a socially responsible, successful high-fashion business.[7]

Management Roles

Another aspect common to all managers is the role that management activities serve within organizations. By role, we mean a set of similar organized activities that serve a specific purpose for the organization. Henry Mintzberg, a noted management professor, has published several reports about what managers did for a number of days and took detailed notes about whom they met with, what they did, and the purpose of their activities.[8]

We have already grouped management activities into planning, organizing, leading, or controlling, all of which emphasize the work process for which managers are responsible. Mintzberg described ten specific roles that managers perform, which, in turn, can be grouped into three larger categories—interpersonal, informational, and decisional (Table 1.4). While Mintzberg's roles also categorize management activities, they describe

TABLE 1.4 Mintzberg's Ten Management Roles

General Role Category	Specific Role	Example Activity
Interpersonal	Figurehead	Attending award banquet
	Liaison	Coordinating production schedule with supply manager
	Leadership	Conducting performance appraisal for subordinates
Informational	Monitor	Contacting government regulatory agencies
	Disseminator	Conducting meetings with subordinates to pass along policy changes
	Spokesperson	Meeting with consumer group to discuss product safety
Decisional	Entrepreneur	Changing work process
	Disturbance handler	Deciding which unit moves into new facilities
	Resource allocator	Deciding who receives new computer equipment
	Negotiator	Settling union grievance

more specific categories of work, activities with individuals external to the organization, and activities that support work activities. As such, Mintzberg's roles provide additional information for understanding management. His ten categories, taken together, also underscore our previous point that gathering information, making decisions, and implementing decisions are the critical processes of management.

Interpersonal Roles

interpersonal roles: Activities that involve interacting with others who may be external or internal to the organization at a higher or lower level than the manager.

Interpersonal roles refer to activities that involve interacting with others who may be external or internal to the organization at a higher or lower level than the manager. These roles allow the manager to gather information for the decisions that must be made. The first of the interpersonal roles, figurehead, describes the formal activities in which the manager acts as a public official for the company. These activities may range from award banquets to ribbon-cutting ceremonies for the opening of new offices. In this role, managers often deal with people external to the organization, and the activities are not directly related to the work process. In the liaison role, the manager interacts with peers outside of the organization. This role is, therefore, composed of a network of relationships. Online social networking sites, such as Facebook, LinkedIn, and Twitter, provide the opportunity to reach almost anyone interested in the organization. Southwest Airlines has an entire team monitor its Twitter feed to answer customer concerns.[9]

As we have already mentioned, the leadership role requires actions that define and direct the work activities of employees. This role naturally requires the manager to obtain information concerning the status of the work activities of members of the organization.

Informational Roles

informational roles: Activities—including reporting, preparing data analyses, briefings, delivering mail, emailing, websites, and making telephone calls—that focus on data important for the decisions the manager needs to make.

The second category of roles includes activities that Mintzberg regarded as focused almost exclusively on the transmission of information. **Informational roles** are activities—including reporting, preparing data analyses, briefings, delivering mail, emailing, websites, and making telephone calls—that focus on data important for the decisions the manager needs to make. In describing these roles, Mintzberg referred to the manager as being the "nerve center" and the "focal point" of information for the organization. For example, a manager of a securities investment group receives information from the company's research division and outside consultants regarding both securities that are expected to do well in the future and those that are not, and passes this information to the brokers in the group. The brokers, in turn, gather information about clients' attitudes concerning investing. They then give this information back to the manager.

As monitor, a manager seeks information to detect problems or opportunities, obtain general knowledge about the work situation, and make necessary changes. While much of this information comes from formal mechanisms such as websites, reports, news media, and public forecasts, more comes from informal conversations with both organization members and those external to the organization. Managers use this information in two ways: (a) to review performance and plans for changes in the work process and (b) partly to pass on to others in the manager's informational roles of disseminator and spokesperson.

A spokesperson provides information to those external to the organization.

As *disseminator*, the manager sends information from external sources to various parts of the work group and information from internal sources to those both internal and external to the organization. This information is of two types: facts and value information. Factual data are of observable events that can be checked for accuracy, such as production figures, contract specifications, and so on. A United Way manager, for example, will tell the volunteer fund raiser how close to the goal is the total amount raised. Value information is about preferences—that is, the opinions and attitudes of others about "what ought to be" or the present condition of the work or products. Customer judgments of product safety are one example.

In the *spokesperson* role, the manager provides information about the work group to those outside of the group. Two parties are of special concern. One is the manager's own immediate superior, because the manager's boss is also involved in planning, coordinating, leading, and controlling and must have as much information as possible to perform those functions. For example, a regional sales manager needs to know the correct sales performance of all the groups in the region before planning an upcoming sales campaign. The second is the organization's "public," which includes customers, suppliers, trade organizations, government agencies, consumer groups, and the press. Because of the manager's position in the work unit, he or she becomes the expert and the logical contact person for all information about the unit.

Decisional Roles

Mintzberg describes decisional roles as the most crucial part of the manager's work. **Decisional roles** are activities that deal primarily with the allocation of resources in order to reach organizational objectives. Managers use the information gathered in the interpersonal and informational roles to make judgments that affect both the short- and long-term well-being of the firm. In the role of entrepreneur, the manager acts as the initiator and designer of changes within the work group. These changes may be in employee skills, work redesign, information reports, and goods or services provided. The decisions require as much factual data as possible. For example, productivity reports, customer satisfaction surveys, consumer buying patterns, trends in the cost of raw materials, and educational and training statistics are some of the data that can be used.

decisional roles: Activities that deal primarily with the allocation of resources in order to reach organizational objectives.

Decisional roles deal with allocating resources.

While the entrepreneur role deals with voluntary change by the manager, the role of disturbance handler deals with change forced on the manager by other factors. The manager acts because it is a necessity—a disturbance occurs and a solution must be found. There are three types of disturbances: conflicts among individuals, interaction difficulties between one unit and another, and conflicts over the resources of conditions that may cause such disturbances as departure damage to the physical facility, the loss of an important customer, a sudden rise in the price of labor or raw materials, or a disagreement between subordinates. An economic or financial crisis can change purchasing patterns and the business environment. For the most part, these disturbances require quick action and solutions to the problem. More long-term adaptations are subsequently developed.

Another decisional role is that of resource allocator, who both protects and uses the unit's assets—money, time, material and equipment, human resources, data, and reputation. Control systems are used to protect resources such as the cost of travel, materials, and training. Such control systems are the result of decisions to conserve resources. For example, Johnson Controls Inc. provides technology products to optimize energy and operational efficiencies in buildings.

The final role is that of negotiator, which focuses on reaching agreements with others outside the work group on work-related issues or materials, such as labor unions and leasing agreements concerning machinery and vehicles. This role includes agreements with other units within the organization regarding the arrival and quantity of necessary goods, use of common equipment, and the exchange of rare personal skills. It can also include reforming and restructuring companies. This role requires planning a communication strategy for negotiation, thinking about alternatives, and analyzing the relationships in the negotiation.

Mintzberg's description of roles provides important information about the specific activities that managers perform in carrying out the planning, organizing, and leading functions. In addition, it also provides more detail about activities involved in the management process of collecting information, making decisions, and implementing them. All of this information is intended to present the clear idea that management is not "the ability to work with others" or a function of the "personality" of the manager. Rather, management is a complex set of activities that use extensive skills, knowledge, and abilities to perform—many of which can be learned.

Management Skills

In a general discussion of management such as this, it is useful to describe what skills are necessary to operate successfully as a manager. Given the complexity of management, it is not possible to list all of the necessary skills; instead, we will discuss a representative sample of the general and specific skills that managers need.

General Skills

One way to categorize skills that managers need is by classifying them as interpersonal, technical, or conceptual.[10]

Interpersonal Skills

Many of the ten management roles described by Mintzberg involved interacting with others inside and outside of the organization. The success of these depends directly on a manager's **interpersonal skills**, such as communication, listening, conflict resolution, and leading that are necessary to work with others.

Interactions with others take many forms. Within a work unit, for example, a manager might select and set up new computer systems, review an employee's work performance, or try to determine if an employee's poor performance is a result of drug or alcohol addiction. Activities outside the work unit are equally varied, and may include responding to

interpersonal skills: Skills such as communication, listening, conflict resolution, and leading that are necessary to work with others.

Interpersonal communication includes clear statements, listening, and reaching mutually acceptable agreements.

hostile consumer or environmental groups concerning the firm's sustainability; joining a trade association to learn more about ethics and compliance programs; or donating time to a community service organization. In each of these instances, the manager's interpersonal skills in clearly communicating, listening to others, and arriving at a mutually acceptable agreement become essential to the organization's well-being. Many job applications request applicants with interpersonal skills.

Technical Skills

Most managers work within a specific department or administrative unit of an organization, and, in most cases, such departments handle a specialized portion of the firm's work. Therefore, there are accounting managers, research and development managers, sales managers, scheduling managers, and so on. These managers use their departments' resources to plan, organize, lead, and control the work of the organization.

To manage their departments' work, managers must have **technical skills**, or the knowledge and ability to accomplish the specialized activities of the work group. For example, the accounting manager must know current tax reporting regulations, how to apply accounting systems to new products, and how to compile financial reporting data. If the manager lacks these skills, he or she will not be able to make correct decisions or answer employees' questions about job tasks. Obviously, the more complex and advanced the work of the department becomes, the more technical skill the manager requires.

technical skills: The knowledge and ability to accomplish the specialized activities of the work group.

For example, financial managers in investment banks frequently are concerned with only one investment area such as bonds, derivatives, or hedge funds. Therefore, these managers must be extremely knowledgeable about the particular investment area they are managing. In many organizations, a manager's career track is within one technical area until he or she reaches the very highest levels of management.

Conceptual Skills

Earlier, we said that a key part of management is gathering information and making and implementing decisions. **Conceptual skills**, the intellectual abilities to process information and make accurate decisions about the work group and the job tasks, are essential to this process. First, a manager must be able to understand and retain a large amount of

conceptual skills: The intellectual abilities to process information and make accurate decisions about the work group and the job tasks.

data, obtained while carrying out his or her informational role. Second, he or she must analyze this data in various ways in order to understand their meaning.

Some analyses are statistical, such as forecasts of consumer demand based on past buying patterns. Other analyses are essentially judgmental, such as estimating consumer demand by taking into account expected changes in the local economy. Third, the manager must use an analysis to select a course of action among several options. If the economy is expected to expand over the next six months, for example, should the firm increase production and marketing activities? These decisions require the conceptual skills of reasoning, information processing, and evaluation.

Specific Skills

For many years, organizations have been trying to identify the specific skills that are related to managerial job performance. The following are a few skills that researchers have identified across several different organizations:

- *Job knowledge:* Knowing the facts about equipment, materials, and the work process, as well as the relationships among all parts of the work organization. Example: Knowing about personal computers' antivirus programs.

- *Oral communication:* Verbally presenting information to others in such a manner that the information means the same to everyone. Example: Communicating work objectives to all members of a work team.

- *Persuasiveness:* Influencing others who have different viewpoints to reach agreement on an acceptable plan of action. Example: A committee member explaining a possible solution that would impact future group actions.

- *Problem analysis:* Determining why a situation does not conform to standards and deciding what to do about it. Example: Determining why a group of products has failed final inspection.

- *Cooperativeness:* Working easily and well with others in group projects. Example: The interaction of members of a strategic planning committee.

- *Tolerance of stress:* Continuing work performance in adverse or hostile circumstances. Example: Multiple projects coming to completion at approximately the same time.

- *Negotiation:* Arriving at mutually acceptable joint decisions. Example: Agreeing with a supplier as to a mutually acceptable price for raw materials.

- *Assertiveness:* Clearly and consistently expressing a point of view on a topic being discussed. Example: Individual performance review with a subordinate who has a deficiency in work activities.

- *Initiative:* Determining what work activities must be pursued and starting them. Example: Determining what must be done to successfully operate new production equipment.

These are only a few of the skills research has identified as necessary for successful managerial work. Hopefully, the relationship between these specific skills and the general categories of technical, interpersonal, and conceptual skills is obvious: These specific skills are subparts of the general categories. They all involve interacting with others, evaluating the work process, or making decisions.

Social networking has advanced through email, text messaging, blogging, social networks, mobile applications, and various computer software applications. It has become so common in organizations that managers may need to develop specific skills for these electronic environments. For example, email is not always a substitute for oral communication to negotiate on initiatives. Many firms are trying to find the best way to use Twitter, Facebook, blogs, and other digital media to enhance management skills and business activities.

You're the Manager . . . What Would You Do?

THE COMPANY: Mrs. Acres Homemade Pies
YOUR POSITION: Owner
THE PLACE: Ames, Iowa

As a child growing up in the Midwest, Shelly Acres learned how to make pies from her mother and grandmother—rhubarb, boysenberry, apple, almost any variety you can imagine. The pies were always praised and never lasted long enough to cool off. When Acres graduated from Iowa State University with a business administration degree, she decided to take some big risks and enter the world of business by making and marketing specialty pies. She had to plan, organize, and control the business with limited experience.

Acres and a supportive friend bought a commercial oven from a bakery that had gone out of business and purchased used food processors to knead the pie crusts. She converted one of the machine sheds on her family's farm into a small pie factory. To support the business and convert the shed, Acres borrowed $25,000 from a local bank. As she was unable to get the loan on her own financial merit, her parents had to cosign the note and put up their home as collateral. They cosigned because they believed in their daughter's skills and vision in organizing the venture.

Acres' conservative business plan for Mrs. Acres Homemade Pies was to sell them initially through local supermarkets and select family restaurants. This required communicating with customers about the quality of the product. The company name sprang from the notion that the image for the pies should be that of a grandmother, not a 23-year-old college graduate. The image was further extended to incorporate the use of all-natural ingredients, the fact that the pies were homemade, and the unique variety of flavors available.

In the first six months, Acres and a few part-time employees made 100 pies per day at a gross profit margin of $1.70 for each pie. The reception to the pies was extraordinary: restaurants began to produce table promotional pieces featuring the local pies, and production could not keep up with demand. Acres made a profit of nearly $3,500 per month of the first half year. Local magazines and newspapers approached her for interviews and recipes for these "hot" pies. She seemed to have the ability to control daily operations and continue expansion.

Acres began expanding operations, borrowing an additional $10,000. The staff increased from three part-time to four full-time employees, and sales increased from 100 to 400 pies per day. All the employees were loyal friends whom she knew growing up in Iowa. Profits soared to $18,000 per month. The key to success for Mrs. Acres Pies was Acres' close supervision, the strong support and motivation of her employees, a profit-sharing plan that spurred productivity and innovation for new recipes/flavors of pies, and a keen business sense. Her employees began to feel they were part owners of the business.

Currently, demand has again accelerated beyond supply and Acres is faced with several options. She can expand present facilities and add more staff possibly beyond her inner circle of friends. She can lease or purchase new facilities—with higher production and lower distribution costs, the gross profit margin could be increased. A national frozen pie company has suggested a joint alliance to make pies for national supermarket chains under her name, recipes, and guidance, and she would not have to continue to manage production. A breakfast chain has also proposed a joint venture for production and marketing of her pies under a licensing arrangement that would give her a percentage of each pie sold with minimal involvement on her part.

QUESTIONS

1. What management skills has Acres used to make Mrs. Acres Homemade Pies successful?

2. What challenges does she face as she evaluates these options?

3. What is your recommendation for the future of Acres' business?

Mrs. Acres Homemade Pie

Source: pilipphoto/Shutterstock

Situational Differences in Management Activities

The main emphasis of this chapter so far has been on the similarities of management activities across organizations. However, if you were to observe the activities of several managers, you would probably be impressed with how different their specific tasks are, even though these tasks address the same management process and functions. In this section we will explore some of the characteristics of organizations that cause these differences in management activities: level of management, area of management, organizational size, organizational culture, industry, and whether the organization is for-profit or nonprofit.

Level of Management

upper managers: Managers who spend most of their time planning and leading because they make decisions about the overall performance and direction of the organization.

middle managers: Managers who receive broad statements of strategy and policy from upper-level managers and develop specific objectives and plans.

lower or first-line managers: Managers concerned with the direct production of items or delivery of service.

Managers may be classified according to their level or position within the organization. We commonly categorize managers as being in lower, middle, or upper levels of management; however, these terms generally apply only in organizations large enough to have specialization. **Upper managers** spend most of their time planning and leading because they make decisions about the overall performance and direction of the organization. Therefore, they are usually involved in the development of goals and strategies to achieve those goals. Conceptual and interpersonal skills are especially important. Chief executive officer (CEO), chief financial officer (CFO), chairman, president, and executive vice president are common titles at this level. **Middle managers** are those managers who receive broad statements of strategy and policy from upper-level managers and develop specific objectives and plans. They spend a large portion of their time in planning and organizing activities. Conceptual and technical skills underlie these activities. Examples of the titles of middle managers are product manager, department head, plant manager, and quality control manager. **Lower or first-line managers** are those concerned with the direct production of items or delivery of service. These actions require leading and controlling. Because first-line managers train and monitor the performance of their subordinates, technical skills are especially important. Common titles are supervisor, sales manager, loan officer, and store manager. Middle- and upper-level managers coordinate the activities of specialized lower-level managers.

Source: baranq/Shutterstock

First-line managers are concerned with operations and services.

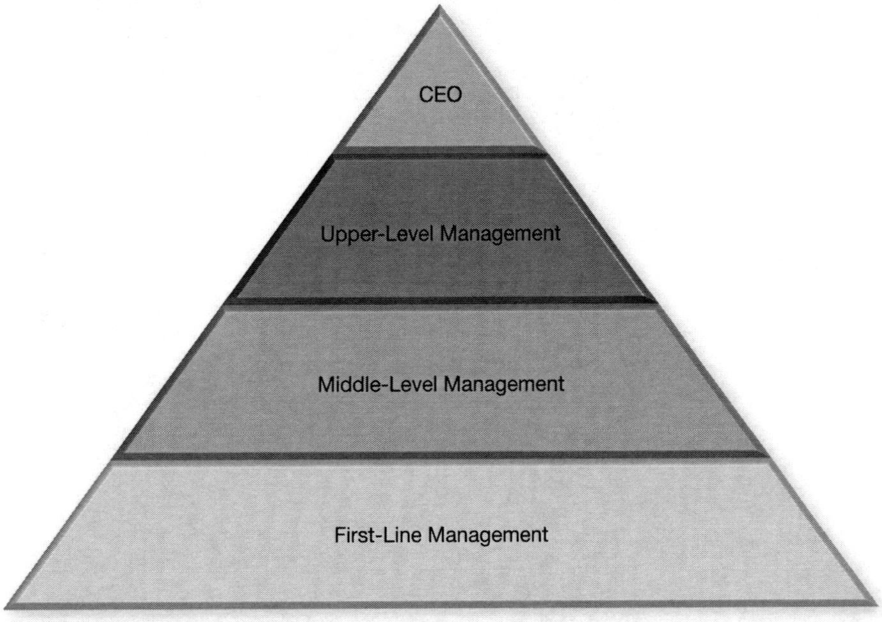

FIGURE 1.2
**Different Levels
of Management**

In terms of differences in activities necessary for performance, upper-level managers have numerous contacts with people external to the organization, such as when they negotiate agreements or provide information about organizational activities. Middle-level managers often associate with other managers of the organization to collect information and plan how to implement programs. Lower-level managers generally work with non-managerial employees on technical tasks. Figure 1.2 shows the different levels of management.

Area of Management

We will discuss functional units, or areas of organization, in more detail later on. For now we will refer to these functional areas in terms of jobs with similar technical content. Human resources management, marketing, and production could all be functional areas of one organization, and managers in each of these areas must gather information, make decisions, and implement programs that are appropriate for their area. For example, **human resources managers** are concerned with developing and carrying out systems that are used to make decisions about employees such as selection, training, and compensation.

Marketing managers develop marketing strategies and make decisions about how to implement those strategies. Marketing managers are responsible for selecting target markets and planning, pricing, promoting, and distributing products. **Finance managers** focus on obtaining the money needed for the successful operation of the organization and using that money in accordance with organizational goals. Financial managers project income and expenses, determine short- and long-term financing needs, and monitor and protect the financial resources of the organization. Accountants maintain and monitor a firm's financial records. For public corporations they develop financial statements including the balance sheet, statement of cash flows, and income statement. **Production and operations managers** schedule and monitor the work process that turns out the goods or services of the organization. They help to convert resources into final products. **Information technology (IT) managers** implement, maintain, and control technology applications. For instance, an IT manager might develop and maintain the company's computer network. Other managers manage areas such as ethics and compliance, public relations, and administrative functions.

Although each of these managers engages in planning, organizing, leading, and controlling, these functions take different forms due to the different technical information among them. The human resources manager may plan an instructional program on sexual

human resources managers: Managers concerned with developing and carrying out systems that are used to make decisions about employees such as selection, training, and compensation.

marketing managers: Managers who develop marketing strategies and make decisions about how to implement those strategies.

finance managers: Managers who focus on obtaining the money needed for the successful operation of the organization and using that money in accordance with organizational goals.

production and operations managers: Managers who schedule and monitor the work process that turns out the goods or services of the organization.

information technology (IT) managers: Managers who implement, maintain, and control technology applications.

Source: Alpha Prod/Shutterstock

Production and operations managers are responsible for goods and services.

harassment, while a marketing manager may plan a national television sales campaign. Both programs are developed to provide information to others. However, how the two proceed and the activities that they perform are quite different.

Organizational Size

Generally, the larger a firm is, the more specialized will be its managers' activities. For example, the owner of a small business often functions as the chief executive officer, chief financial officer, marketing director, and production manager. On the other hand, large firms tend to employ managers who have the specialized training and experience required to work in a narrow range of activities.

Large organizations are also characterized by more formalized rules, procedures, and policies, essential to coordinating the work activities of a large number of employees. Formalization affects a manager's activities in many ways, including the requirement of much more paperwork and reporting forms—such as work schedules, selection procedures for hiring new employees, and production or quality reports. Many interactions between manager and subordinates are also formalized, such as grievance and discipline meetings, performance evaluation sessions, and salary adjustment discussions. Small firms frequently have much less formalization, and coordination of employees is achieved through daily interaction. Often the only reports or forms a small business manager must complete are those necessary for legal compliance or financial reporting.

Organizational Culture

organizational culture: The values, norms, and artifacts shared by members of an organization.

Organizational culture refers to the values, norms, and artifacts shared by members of an organization. This results in the beliefs, traditions, philosophies, rules, and heroes that are shared by organizational members. The culture of an organization distinguishes it from others and shapes the actions of its members. For example, by pending necessary time and resources, 3M encourages individuals to experiment with the development of products. Much latitude is given to an individual at 3M to pursue projects that initially do not look promising. As an example, Post-it brand notes were developed from glue that failed in its initial purpose. The glue was not able to bond items together very well. How-

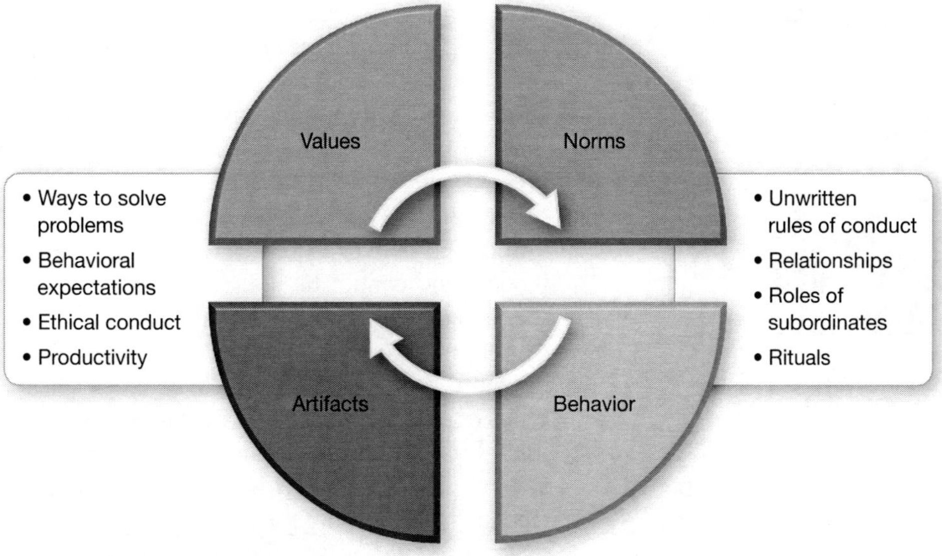

FIGURE 1.3
**Elements of an
Organizational Culture**

- Ways to solve problems
- Behavioral expectations
- Ethical conduct
- Productivity

Values

Norms

- Unwritten rules of conduct
- Relationships
- Roles of subordinates
- Rituals

Artifacts

Behavior

ever, over time, this inadequate glue became the critical feature of a multimillion-dollar product. Other organizations have cultures that use financial data as the primary basis of decision making. A manager at 3M might engage in actions that encourage an employee to develop a potential product, but at another company, the manager may order the employee to cease all activities because of the cost. Google is another firm that encourages employees to take work time to work on their own projects.

There are four main components of culture. *Values* are the basic beliefs that define the success of employees in the organization. They are viewed as long-term, enduring beliefs about decisions. Ritz-Carlton holds quality customer service as a major value and allows employees to spend a certain amount of money to display exemplary customer service. Individuals use the norms of the organization in their decisions. *Norms* are expectations that dictate and clarify appropriate behaviors. For example, an airline pilot is expected to wear a uniform to work every day. Often norms are so rigidly enforced that they become rules that state explicit requirements for the job. The third component, *artifacts*, includes rites, rituals, routines or ceremonies, and websites the company uses to show employees more tangible examples of expectations. For example, the Colorado-based sustainable brewery New Belgium gave employees ownership in the company and will send employees that have been with the company for five years on an all-expenses-paid trip to Belgium to learn about beer culture. *Behavior* results in actions, activities, and relationships in carrying out tasks. Values, norms, and artifacts are the basis for most behavior in organizations. All organizations have a culture, even if a manager does not actively work to develop one. Figure 1.3 shows the four different elements of culture.

Industry

The industry that an organization operates in determines the knowledge and skills its managers must possess. A manager in an oil-refining company needs knowledge of manufacturing, chemistry, and environmental laws, whereas a banking manager needs knowledge of investments, risk management, currency exchange rates, and titles laws. There are major differences in the activities of managers with the same titles but who operate in different industries. For example, a regional marketing manager for a consumer packaged goods company may deal extensively with planning, advertising, and sales promotions. On the other hand, a regional marketing manager for an industrial equipment manufacturing company may spend little time with such activities, and instead communicate directly with current and potential clients to determine specifications and the uses of equipment for the future. A manager in a health care organization may spend a great deal of time managing government regulations, and ethics and compliance requirements.

Nonprofit organizations do not have typical business goals, but effective management remains important to their success.

for-profit companies: Organizations owned either privately by one or more individuals or publicly by stockholders.

nonprofit organizations: Institutions such as governments, social cause organizations, and religious groups that cannot retain earnings over expenses, do not have equity interests, and cannot be bought or sold.

For-profit companies are owned either privately by one or more individuals or publicly by stockholders. These organizations must pay taxes on profits and may be bought and sold. **Nonprofit organizations** are institutions such as governments, social cause organizations, and religious groups that cannot retain earnings over expenses, do not have equity interests, and cannot be bought or sold. Greenpeace, the Special Olympics, and United Way are examples of nonprofits.

There are two differences between these two types of organizations that affect management activities. First, nonprofit organizations frequently have several groups of individuals who have a major influence in setting the goals of the organization. For example, state universities are influenced by legislators, university administrators, faculty, staff, students, and state taxpayers in determining their goals and operations. Often, these groups have conflicting opinions as to what is desirable. For example, faculty may wish for fewer classes and more time allocated for research. State legislators often ask for more classes and less time for research. In contrast, for-profit organizations, such as Microsoft or Apple Inc., ordinarily have closer agreement as to their goals and activities.

The second difference is in how funds are generated and what may be done with them. Nonprofit organizations generally raise part of their necessary funds from the sale of goods or services; often the remainder is from government support or charitable contributions. For-profit organizations exist primarily on the sale of goods and services and, secondarily, on investments of corporate assets. These differences affect, among other things, the planning and organizing activities of managers in the two types of organizations.

Emerging Trends in Management

Management remains a very dynamic area requiring an understanding of emerging trends. Changes in technology, transportation, and social concerns all influence the nature of management. While a number of these trends will be addressed and integrated in the content of this book, we introduce three important trends that are impacting businesses today: e-business, global organizations, and ethics and social responsibility.

E-Business

Electronic business (e-business) involves achieving management goals through the use of the Internet. Digital media are electronic media that allow all types of communication through computers, smartphones, and other digital devices. The Internet has changed the face of management, allowing businesses to connect with customers, develop collaborative relationships with suppliers and employees, and make the company's products more accessible globally. The Internet enables more efficient transactions in working with suppliers as well as those firms to which they outsource activities. The telecommunication opportunities created by the Internet do not change the basic management functions and responsibilities but has drastically changed how activities are carried out and the implementation of strategies. For instance, the Internet has facilitated new business models such as Amazon.com, eBay, and Google that do not have physical retail locations but take place entirely on the Internet. Other traditional businesses, including Home Depot, Barnes & Noble, and Best Buy, have had to respond by developing an online presence in addition to their physical stores. Finally, some traditional retail businesses, such as supermarkets, have literally merged with Internet companies to create new mixed business

E-business models are growing rapidly.

models. The recent merger of Whole Foods Supermarkets with Amazon.com is a good example of this phenomenon. Most companies that have a strong Internet presence have had to make sure that managers are competent with information technology advances necessary to stay competitive.

On the other hand, while the Internet can make management more effective and efficient, it has also created challenges. Privacy, online fraud, intellectual property theft, and employee distractions and time theft have increased as a result. Companies can increase their ability to connect with users by tracking their Internet activities. Many websites install cookies, or strings of text that can be used to identify people, on users' computers when they visit the site. Cookies help companies to engage in better marketing. Amazon.com, for instance, uses cookies to track users' activities on its sites and make recommendations based upon their purchases. Yet many users do not feel comfortable having their online activity traced. User information can also be stored and sold to other companies. Google keeps track of search engine search terms that people input, although it claims that this information is anonymized after a certain time period.

Online fraud occurs when hackers break into computer systems and steal personal information such as credit card numbers, passwords, and other sensitive information. Fraudsters have also used the Internet to trick users into sending them money or giving up their personal information. While the Internet makes information much more accessible to both companies and consumers, it also makes it easier to upload and/or download copyrighted materials. The movie and music industries have been hard hit by illegal downloads, losing millions in revenue. Finally, the Internet can be a distraction for employees when used for non-work purposes. Employees of today's generation expect to be able to access sites such as Facebook and YouTube. However, this also enables employees to misuse these sites by spending large amounts of time on Facebook, Twitter, YouTube, and other digital media. Many employees waste work time each day on social media sites engaging in non-work activities. While they might not consider it to be a serious issue, such time theft can cost a company greatly.

Global Organizations

International business refers to expanding business activities beyond national boundaries. Technology advances such as the Internet as well as changing economic and political

Management provides global opportunities.

conditions are making it easier for companies to expand globally. Expanding beyond national boundaries can provide opportunities for company growth. For example, companies including Caterpillar, Yum! Brands, Nike, McDonald's, General Motors, and Procter & Gamble earn at least half of their revenue outside of the United States. Walmart operates in well over two dozen countries outside of the United States, and Starbucks has thousands of shops in more than 70 countries. Even small businesses encounter global marketing opportunities and sell products outside of their own countries. Many small businesses can export their products through eBay, Amazon.com, and their own websites. In addition, a number of businesses need employees with specific skills and recruit from countries where they can find the best talent. This has created diversity in organizations that has helped foster creativity and innovation.

Businesses have also benefited from the practice of outsourcing. Outsourcing occurs when an organization transfers manufacturing, services, and other functions to countries where labor and supplies are less expensive. Nike's footwear is produced by factories in countries such as Vietnam. Apple Inc. uses Chinese manufacturers to assemble components for its iPads and iPhones. Outsourcing is able to save companies labor costs, which can translate into less expensive prices for consumers. However, outsourcing has also been highly criticized in the United States for taking away American jobs. The welfare of employees working at factories in less developed parts of the world has also been a concern. Apple was highly criticized after dangerous working conditions and suicides were discovered at its Chinese contractor Foxconn. Businesses have the responsibility to monitor the companies they outsource from to ensure they are adhering to appropriate standards.

Ethics and Social Responsibility

Leadership in promoting ethical and socially responsible business decisions has become a significant managerial responsibility. Today, top managers and the board of directors are responsible for creating an ethical organizational culture that responds to the desires of stakeholders. Many companies have suffered reputational damage and fines for business misconduct. The *Wall Street Journal* reports on a regular basis how a number of companies took excessive risks and violated basic ethical conduct. On the other hand, ethical and socially responsible companies create an environment where there are more loyal employees and satisfied consumers. Shareholders should support ethical conduct because an *Ethisphere* magazine survey has found that the world's most ethical companies have better stock growth than some of the widely used indexes, including the Standard & Poor's 500 index.[11]

Ethics can relate to all managerial decisions.

While ethics in an organization can relate to all managerial decisions, social responsibility refers to an organization's obligation to maximize its positive impact and minimize its negative impact on society. This results in understanding stakeholders and social responsibility issues that are important to them. Some of the more important areas today include concerns about sustainability, community relations, product safety, and social issues including employee well-being. Although all of these issues are important, many businesses are focusing on sustainability to protect the long-term well-being of the natural environment as it relates to individuals, organizations, and business strategies. Many companies try to have their products certified as "green" and engage in activities such as recycling and energy use reduction to help protect the environment.

Can You Learn Management in Class?

The answer to this, not surprisingly, is "Sure!" If the answer were no, what would we do with the rest of the book? You can certainly learn valuable aspects of management in a college or university class. As evidence, many organizations develop or require formal training in management that is very similar to the topics of this text and the format of your class.[12] We have discussed that management is a process of collecting information, making decisions, and implementing decisions about how to use the organization's resources to reach its objectives. Formal classes like this one are valuable for learning what data sources and types of information are useful for making specific decisions. Classes can also point out the relationships among variables used in decision making. For example, you will learn about the relationship of organizational rewards to the employee's job performance in a later chapter. Knowing this relationship will be useful in deciding how to use rewards within the organization.

In addition to presenting factual data and relationships among data, formal classes can help you develop conceptual and analytical skills, which are needed by all managers. The vignettes, cases, and boxes in the chapters of this text describe work situations that can be valuable in helping you develop these skills. Finally, the discussion of organization and human behavior principles should serve as an important basis for the managerial activities associated with leading.

However, there are two aspects of management that cannot be taught fully in an introductory management textbook or class. The first is the job knowledge necessary to be successful as a manager in a specific functional area of an organization; you must acquire this knowledge from your other courses and job experience. If you are interested in being a financial manager, for example, you must acquire the basic knowledge from your finance courses and perhaps from internships or other employment in the finance industry; if your interest is in marketing management, this job knowledge must come from your marketing courses as well as from experience as a consumer and employee.

The second aspect that cannot be taught fully is implementation of decision making. We will discuss how managers go about getting their plans and decisions carried out within organizations. Simulations, role plays, and exercises can help you reproduce and develop these skills. However, these teaching techniques frequently lack the long-term, repetitive interaction that characterizes management. Some form of on-the-job training is a more appropriate vehicle for teaching this skill.

Summary and Review

- *Define management and describe its purpose in organizations.* Management is concerned with using the resources of the organization to reach the organization's objectives. Its purpose is to use these resources effectively and efficiently so that the objectives of the organization are achieved with a minimum of cost.

- *Determine the effect that management actions have on the manager and others in the organization.* Because management is essentially a decision-making process, it affects others. The consequences of a manager's decisions may have either a positive or negative effect on the manager, the manager's subordinates, and the organization, as well as other groups.

- *List the major functions of managers.* The four management functions are planning (determining what the organization will specifically accomplish and deciding how to accomplish these goals); organizing (designing jobs for employees, grouping these jobs together into departments, and developing working relationships between organizational departments and employees to carry out the plans); leading (influencing others' activities to achieve set goals); and controlling (ensuring that an organization's actions lead to achievement of its objectives).

- *Explain the importance of decision making in management activities.* Because managers must use resources to reach the organization's objectives, they insist on continuously making decisions about how to best use these resources. The manager must gather important data to be considered and, based on the data, make and then implement the decision required. A correct decision can be useless if it is not implemented appropriately.

- *Describe the many roles managers play in an organization.* Henry Mintzberg described ten specific roles that can be placed into three broad categories. Interpersonal roles involve interaction with others who are external or internal to the organization, at the same level as the manager or at higher or lower levels. Informational roles focus on obtaining data that are important for the decisions made by the manager. Decisional roles deal primarily with the allocation of resources in order to reach organizational objectives. Mintzberg's detailed description of each of the specific roles provides valuable descriptions of management tasks.

- *Specify why different managers perform different job activities.* Management is similar across all organizations in that managers are all involved with planning, organizing, leading, controlling, and decision making; their activities may also be described in terms of common roles they play within their organizations. However, the specific job activities of managers differ greatly both among and within organizations because of differences in the level of management, functional area, organizational size and culture, and industry.

- *Identify some emerging trends in management.* There are three major trends that are impacting businesses today: e-business, global organizations, and ethics and social responsibility. Electronic business (e-business) involves achieving management goals through the use of the Internet. The Internet has changed the face of management, allowing businesses to connect with customers, develop collaborative relationships with suppliers and employees, and make the company's products more accessible globally. International business refers to expanding business activities beyond national boundaries. Technology advances such as the Internet as well as changing economic and political conditions are making it easier for companies to expand globally. Expanding beyond national boundaries can provide opportunities for company growth. Leadership in promoting ethical and socially responsible business decisions has become a significant managerial responsibility. Many companies have suffered reputational damage and fines for business misconduct.

- *Review what you can reasonably learn from a textbook about how to perform management activities.* Some aspects of management can be learned in formal classroom situations. Most organizations teach management to their employees through training programs that are similar in format to college classrooms. Learning management in this format can help you understand sources of information and relationships among variables, basic principles to use in decision making, and the fundamentals of how to implement decisions. However, job knowledge relevant for specific functional areas of an organization and the requisite interpersonal skills can most effectively be learned in one's unique working environment.

■ *Evaluate a small business owner's management skills and propose a future course of action for the firm.* The "Business Dilemma" box presents questions for the owner of the firm. Should the owner continue to expand or form a joint venture with large companies for expansion? Your assessment of the owner's skills and ability to manage rapid expansion will determine your answer.

Key Terms and Concepts

conceptual skills 13

controlling 8

decisional roles 11

effectively 3

efficiently 3

finance managers 17

for-profit companies 20

human resources managers 17

information technology (IT) managers 17

informational roles 10

interpersonal roles 10

interpersonal skills 12

leading 7

lower or first-line managers 16

management 3

managers 3

marketing managers 17

middle managers 16

nonprofit organizations 20

organizational culture 18

organizations 3

organizing 6

planning 6

production and operations managers 17

resources 3

stakeholder 5

technical skills 13

upper managers 16

Ready Recall

1. Define management and indicate what its principal purposes are and why managers are essential to organizations.
2. What are the resources of the organization? How are these used in management decision making?
3. What are the four functions of management? How are they related to the work process?
4. Describe the steps in management decision making. What are the difficulties in making management decisions?
5. Discuss the three general roles of management. What are the purposes of these roles? What specific roles fall under each general role?
6. Discuss the general skills necessary to be successful in management. How do these relate to both the management roles and management decision making?
7. How do management activities differ across organizations? Describe the specific effects of organization size, industry type, organizational culture, and profit vs. nonprofit organizations on these differences.
8. How do management activities differ within an organization? Describe the specific effects of level of management and functional specialty on these differences.
9. Discuss the impact that management decisions have on others.
10. Discuss how management may be learned in a class setting.

Expand Your Experience

1. Interview a small sample of managers. Discuss the specific, major tasks that these managers perform. Relate these tasks to the management functions of planning, organizing, leading, and controlling.
2. Obtain descriptions of recent decisions made by managers in specific organizations as reported in sources such as *The Wall Street Journal*. Discuss what information would be useful to know before making the decisions. Also discuss how accessible and accurate such information may be.
3. Obtain job descriptions of various management positions. Discuss the specific skills that are necessary to perform the tasks of these job descriptions.

Management Skills

For each statement, check the column that best describes you. When you are finished, calculate your score.

Management Skills Self-Assessment

		Always	Almost Always	Sometimes	Almost Never	Never
1	I try to solve problems myself before asking anyone for help.					
2	I delegate work to those who have the most free time.					
3	I follow up with team members when their behavior creates a negative impact.					
4	I make decisions based on analysis, rather than instinct.					
5	I let my team members figure out how to work together without my input.					
6	I give team members a chance to correct their mistakes before reprimanding them.					
7	I believe that technical skills are the most important skills needed to be an effective manager.					
8	I talk with my team about successes and areas for improvement.					
9	I assist team members in gaining a better understanding of issues and forge agreements.					
10	I try to resolve inefficiencies in my department's processes.					
11	When constructing a team, I ensure that each person has a set of different but complementary skills.					
12	I try to avoid conflict when interacting with team members.					
13	I approach motivating team members based on their individual characteristics.					
14	When a significant mistake is made, I notify my superior, and learn from the mishap.					
15	I accept conflict in a newly formed team as an inevitable stage in the team development process.					
16	I try to relate team members' individual goals to those of the organization.					
17	When constructing a team, I avoid choosing individuals with similar skills and characteristics.					
18	I trust team members to do a good job.					
19	I maintain open communication with each team member individually so that they feel like they are an active participant of the group.					
20	I keep team members up-to-date on recent changes in the organization.					

Scoring Your Assessment
Never = 1
Almost Never = 2
Sometimes = 3
Almost Always = 4
Always = 5

Add your score according to the above rubric, and then find the category that corresponds to your score in the text that follows.

20–45 If your score falls in this range, your management skills need improvement. This textbook will help you become aware of behaviors and characteristics that make a good manager. Organization, communication, and leadership are just a few examples of these types of skills.

46–75 If your score falls in this range, you are exhibiting good managerial skills. Take note of your strengths and begin practicing behaviors in areas that need improvement. This textbook will give you direction in the areas where your scores are low, so be alert for concepts and exercises that will help you improve your managerial skills.

76–100 If your score falls in this range, you are probably an excellent manager. Beware of becoming complacent and strive to strengthen your skills further. Take note of the areas wherein your scores were low and work to develop them. This textbook will keep you focused on managerial skills and will give you some examples that you can follow.

Case 1: The Management Process at New Belgium Brewing

Through the implementation of efficient and effective management, New Belgium Brewing (NBB) has grown from operating out of the founder's basement to having two state-of-the-art facilities and over 800 employees. New Belgium was founded after co-founder Jeff Lebesch took a trip to Belgium and was inspired to produce a high-quality beer in his hometown of Colorado. After consistently experimenting in his basement with a special strain of yeast used in Belgian-style ales, Lebesch began the entrepreneurial endeavor of marketing his product. Lebesch enlisted his wife at the time, Kim Jordan, to help market the beer and deliver it to local store shelves.

The first brew was named Fat Tire Amber Ale. Retailers were initially reluctant to place the beer on store shelves; however, NBB eventually developed a strong customer base that propelled the brand to become a household name. Today NBB is the fourth-largest craft brewery in the United States and eighth-largest overall. Craft brewers such as New Belgium Brewing maintain a high level of integrity.

Since the beginning, the founders and employees have operated with a set of core values and beliefs. Jeff and Kim pledged to create a high-involvement organizational culture toward which all employees are expected to equally and ethically contribute toward. From planning goals and ways to attain objectives to organizing and assigning responsibilities, the two entrepreneurs assumed a leadership role. They led employees to accomplish tasks that helped them develop conceptual skills when facing any type of issue at hand. Controlling and monitoring activities and correcting for mistakes enabled them to operate in a profitable manner while providing a product that is environmentally and socially responsible. The founders did not stray from their initial vision, and through positive leadership, the entrepreneurs prompted employees to set and achieve goals

Source: Nitr/Shutterstock

through proper planning and organization in all aspects of the business.

With leadership being the crucial aspect of any business, it is important that all levels of management are involved in developing goals and strategies for the company's strategic vision. Bryan Simpson—New Belgium's public relations (PR) director—describes New Belgium Brewing's culture in the following way:

> Progressive business practices like employee ownership and open book management enable our co-workers to share in the company's success and in our challenges, pulling us together as a team and a family. It's especially rewarding to see that the values that have driven us for the last 25 years continue to resonate with our co-workers and show results in the marketplace. As a member of the B Corp community, we believe business can be a powerful force for good in this world.

This leadership style has proven to be successful and informational for employees. Employees are encouraged to take an active role in the organization and are provided with a number of incentives to contribute toward a socially responsible culture. To celebrate employees' birthdays, a catered lunch is provided along with a free massage once a year. They get a free beer every day and a 12-pack once a week. Employees are also allowed to bring children and dogs to work to help alleviate the strain on finding places for them during the workday. On the anniversary of employees' first year working for the company, they are given a cruiser bicycle; on the fifth anniversary, they receive a free flight to Belgium to allow for growth and development within the beer culture. Employees who have been with the company for ten years are eligible for a four-week paid sabbatical. Employees are also encouraged to volunteer with various organizations and causes. By doing this, they are able to receive one hour of reimbursement for every two hours of volunteer work performed.

In 2012 Kim Jordan, who had become CEO, made the decision to allow employees at New Belgium to purchase her remaining controlling shares. This led New Belgium to become a 100 percent employee-owned company. From 2000 to 2012, New Belgium was 41 percent employee-owned. Today it is now fully operated through an employee stock ownership plan. During her tenure as CEO, Kim continued to emphasize a high-involvement organizational culture, a practice likely to continue under new CEO Steve Fechheimer. For instance, NBB allows employees to see the financial costs and current performance summaries of the company and provides financial training so that employees are able to understand the books and ask questions about any concerns. With this "open-book" management style, employees are able to take control of their future and see what effect they are having within the industry.

The company operates in a socially aware manner and encourages employees to do the same. New Belgium offers an onsite recycling center and encourages employees to ride fat-tired cruiser bikes that the company provides for them after one year of employment. New Belgium strives to produce a cost- and energy-efficient product that reduces NBB's impact on the environment. For example, NBB is the first fully wind-powered brewery in the United States, after employees and owners unanimously agreed to invest in a wind turbine. The company also installed a photovoltaic system that produces 3 percent of the company's electricity and uses sun tubes to provide natural lighting all year long.

All of these management decisions have put New Belgium in an enviable position not just among breweries but the business world as whole. NBB's commitment to social responsibility has earned the company the coveted distinction of being a Certified B Corp—a title bestowed by the nonprofit B Lab that reflects NBB's adherence to the highest standards of business practices. As of 2017, NBB's B Score was in the top 10 percent of all certified B Corporations, and it had been awarded "Best for the World" by the same organization. The company's employee-focused organizational structure has garnered attention as well. In 2016, NBB appeared on *Outside Magazine*'s list of "best companies to work for" for the eighth year in a row.

With a consistent and positive company culture, New Belgium has provided exceptional leadership for employees to continue the vision, direction, and values the company initially developed.[13]

1. How did Kim and Jeff carry out the management function at NBB?
2. Describe ways in which the founders assumed decisional roles in their work.
3. How would you describe New Belgium Brewing's organizational culture?

Notes

1. Kate Taylor, "The Incredible Story of How Chick-fil-A Took over Fast Food," *Business Insider*, January 25, 2016, http://www.businessinsider.com/chick-fil-a-history-and-facts-2016-1/#chick-fil-a-has-its-roots-in-a-restaurant-called-the-dwarf-grill-opened-by-founder-truett-cathy-in-1946-1 (accessed November 2, 2017); "Who We Are," Chick-fil-A, https://www.chick-fil-a.com/About/Who-We-Are (accessed November 2, 2017); Hayley Peterson, "Why Chick-fil-A's Restaurants Sell 4 Times as Much as KFC's," *Business Insider*, August 1, 2017, http://www.businessinsider.com/why-chick-fil-a-is-so-successful-2017-8 (accessed November 2, 2017).

2. Vida G. Scarpello and Robert J. Vandenberg, "The Satisfaction with My Supervisor Scale: Its Utility for Research and Practical Applications," *Journal of Management* 13 (Fall 1987), 447–466.

3. CBS Interactive Inc., "FDA: Chobani Products May Have Sickened More Than 89 People," *CBS News*, September 10, 2013, http://www.cbsnews.com/8301-204_162-57602200/fda-chobani-products-may-have-sickened-more-than-89-people/ (accessed September 12, 2013).

4. The Associated Press, "A Timeline of Southwest Airlines at a Glance," *Seattle Times*, June 25, 2009, http://seattletimes.com/html/nationworld/2009383963_apussouthwesttimeline.html (accessed July 23, 2013); Chuck Lucier, "Herb Kelleher: The Thought Leader Interview," *Strategy + Business*, June 1, 2004, http://www.strategy-business.com/article/04212?pg=0 (accessed July 23, 2013).

5. Mary Schlangenstein and John Hughes, "Southwest CEO Risks Keep-It-Simple Strategy to Reignite Growth," *Bloomberg*, September 28, 2010, http://www.bloomberg.com/

news/2010-09-27/southwest-airlines-agrees-to-buy-airtran-for
-1-4-billion-in-cash-shares.html (accessed July 23, 2013).

6. Raymond A. Katzell and Richard A. Guzzo, "Psychological
Approaches to Productivity Improvement," *American Psychologist 38* (April 1983), 468–472.

7. Kathyrn Kroll, "Rebecca Ray Designs Grew After Owner
Let Others into Business," Cleveland.com, June 21, 2009,
http://www.cleveland.com/business/index.ssf/2009/06/
rebecca_ray_designs_grew_after.html (accessed November 11,
2017); "About Us," Rebecca Ray Designs, http://rebecca-ray
-designs.myshopify.com/pages/about-us (accessed July 22,
2013); Karen Ammond, "Rebecca Ray Designs," December 13,
2012, http://eliteprofessionals.org/2014/10/05/rebecca-ray
-designs/ (accessed November 11, 2017); Holly Phillips,
"Horse Love: Rebecca Ray Designs," *The English Room*,
September 1, 2015, http://www.theenglishroom.biz/2015/09/
01/horse-love-rebecca-ray-designs/ (accessed November 11,
2017).

8. Henry Mintzberg, *The Nature of Managerial Work* (Englewood Cliffs, NJ: Prentice-Hall, Inc., 1973).

9. Elizabeth Holmes, "Tweeting Without Fear," *The Wall Street
Journal*, December 9, 2011, B1.

10. Robert A. Katz, "The Skills of an Effective Administrator,"
Harvard Business Review 52 (September/October 1974),
90–102.

11. Apparently, good ethics is good business. Although all managers are responsible for the ethical conduct of their subordinates, there are also important managerial positions for those
who oversee ethical programs and training in organizations.

12. Brian O'Reilly, "How Execs Learn," *Fortune*, April 5,
1993, 52–58.

13. "Corporate Sustainability Report," New Belgium Brewing,
http://www.newbelgium.com/docs/default-source/
sustainability/2017sustainabilitybrochure.pdf?pdf
=sustainabilityreport (accessed September 18, 2017); Kelly K.
Spors, "Top Small Workplaces 2008," *The Wall Street Journal*,
February 22, 2009, http://online.wsj.com/article/
SB122347733961315417.html (accessed April 16, 2013);
"We Are 100% Owned," New Belgium Brewing, http://www
.newbelgium.com/community/Blog/13-01-16/We-are-100
-Employee-Owned.aspx (accessed July 23, 2013); the facts of
this case are from Peter Asmus, "Goodbye Coal, Hello Wind,"
Business Ethics 13 (July/August 1999), 10-11; Darren Dahl,
"New Belgium Brewing's Ownership Culture Wins Again,"
Forbes, November 19, 2016, https://www.forbes.com/sites/
darrendahl/2016/11/19/new-belgium-brewings-ownership
-culture-wins-again/#7c19ef382b6a (accessed September 18,
2017); Susan Adams, "New Belgium Brewing Hires a New
CEO from the Liquor Industry," *Forbes*, July 17, 2017, https://
www.forbes.com/sites/susanadams/2017/07/17/new-belgium
-brewing-hires-a-new-ceo-from-the-liquor-industry/
#4414498e5e7a (accessed November 12, 2017).

History of Management Thought

Chapter Outline

Source: Andrey Armyagov/Shutterstock

After reading this chapter, you will be able to:

- Specify the major cultural changes that preceded the development of modern management practice and thought.
- Explain the major theories within the classical approach to management.
- Examine some of the major contributions to the development of the behavioral approach to management.
- Describe the systems approach to management theory and identify the early contributors to this perspective.
- Relate the significance of the contingency approach within the study and practice of management.
- Summarize more current management knowledge and practices that have become popular in the twenty-first century.
- Apply the management theories discussed in this chapter to a manager's efforts to revitalize a small business.

Business Maxims, Circa 1890

The following maxims are typical of the simple and straightforward advice for the practice of good management that prevailed in the late-nineteenth century.

1. Your first ambition should be the acquisition of knowledge pertaining to your business.

2. Above all things acquire a good, correct epistolary style, for you are judged by the business world according to the character, expression, and style of your letters.

3. During business hours attend to nothing but business, be prompt in responding to all communications, and never suffer a letter to remain without an answer.

4. Never fail to meet a business engagement, however irksome it may be at that moment.

5. Lead a regular life, avoid display, and choose your associates discreetly, and prefer the society of men of your own type.

6. Avoid litigation as much as possible, study for yourself the theory of commercial law, and be your own lawyer.

7. Never run down a neighbor's property or goods or praise up your own. It is a mark of low breeding and will gain you nothing.

8. Never misrepresent, falsify, or deceive; have one rule of moral life, never swerve from it, whatever may be the acts or opinions of other men.

9. Watch the course of politics in national affairs, read the papers, but decline the acceptance of political positions if you wish to succeed in a certain line of business. Never be an office seeker.

Maxims for business served early managers with some basic principles for decision making.

10. Be affable, polite, and obliging to everybody. Avoid discussions, anger, and pettishness. Interfere with no disputes that are the creation of others.

11. Never form the habit of talking about your neighbors, or repeating things that you hear others say. You will avoid much unpleasantness, and sometimes serious difficulties.

12. Never sign a paper for a stranger. Never sign a paper without first reading it carefully.

13. Goods well bought are half sold, and goods in a store are better than bad debts.

14. Write in a good, plain, legible hand.

15. Never gamble or take chances on the Board of Trade.

16. Keep your word as good as a bank.[1]

Introduction

Hundreds of thousands of students will complete some sort of formal undergraduate or graduate course in management this year, and next year, and probably the next. Every day, millions of people go to work and perform a managerial-oriented job. However, the large-scale study and practice of management, as we know it today, has not always been the case. There was a time in history when not only was management not commonly practiced and studied, but those people who engaged in commerce and trading were considered lower class and were denied the right to vote.[2] The topic of this chapter will focus on the development of "management" as a widely accepted body of knowledge. It may be interesting for you to learn why you are taking a principles of management class when your grandparents or great-grandparents probably did not have the opportunity.

In this chapter, we will consider two major aspects of the history of management thought. One involves the major developments within the history of Western civilization that stimulated the evolution of the practice and study of management. The other is the development of major perspectives of management thought and some of the important contributors to the various perspectives.

Historical Background

To understand the evolution of the study and teaching of management principles and concepts, we need to establish a general cultural framework of the social, economic, and political forces that have influenced our ideas about management. **Social forces** refer to the relationship of people to each other within a particular culture. **Economic forces** refer to the relationship of people to resources, and **political forces** refer to the relationship of individuals, their rights, and their property to the state.[3] Four major developments in Western culture set the stage for the systematic study and teaching of management that began during the late 1800s and early 1900s: (1) the Protestant ethics, (2) capitalism and the division of labor, (3) the Industrial Revolution, and (4) the productivity problem.

The Protestant Ethic

Between the fall of the Roman Empire and the Renaissance, from about A.D. 600 to A.D. 1500, was a period of time known as the Middle Ages. Frequently described by historians as the "Dark Ages," this was a time of almost complete stagnation of education and scientific and literary progress. Poverty and ignorance were the principal characteristics of the masses of society, and the primary concern of individuals was to protect themselves against murder, robbery, and violence.[4] During this period, the church's promise of an afterlife was virtually the only consolation for those bearing the hardships and bleakness of life on earth. This promise required that people think only of salvation from this life and moving on to the next world, and little thought was given to how life on earth might be improved.

A challenge to this philosophy of life was led by Martin Luther and John Calvin, who believed that each person should consider himself or herself part of the "elect," those who would be treated well in the afterlife. As a member of this elect, each individual was urged to fulfill the obligations of his or her earthly calling. This notion of everyone being worthy and having a calling on earth, as opposed to the Dark Ages belief in the calling of only a royal few, led to a new interpretation of the purpose of life—referred to as the Protestant ethic. The **Protestant ethic**, or work ethic, held that instead of merely waiting on earth for release into the next world, people should pursue an occupation and engage in high levels of worldly activity so that they could fulfill their calling.[5] Society interpreted the Protestant ethic as a mandate for people to work hard, to use their wealth wisely, and to live self-denying lives. This created a new age of self-determination, self-control, and individualism.[6]

Capitalism and the Division of Labor

Another major societal change that occurred following the Middle Ages was the move from feudalism to capitalism and the division of labor. After the fall of the Roman Empire, slavery in Europe became uneconomical. Feudalism prevailed in place of slavery as serfs tilled plots of land owned by lords in exchange for military protection. Feudalism resulted in a society of rigid class distinctions in which all rights of ownership, wealth, and control of all markets were assigned to the government, the church, and a small privileged class of people. The masses had no such rights.

In the 1700s, this rigid system of allocation of resources was challenged by the ideas set forth in the economic theory of **capitalism**. As described in economist Adam Smith's *The Wealth of Nations*, the basic tenets of capitalism are the following:

1. Natural laws of supply and demand and free competition within the marketplace will efficiently regulate the flow of resources within a society.
2. All individuals should have the right to accumulate wealth.
3. All individuals should have the right to private ownership of property.
4. Division of labor would lead to great gains in productivity.[7]

social forces: The relationship of people to each other within a particular culture.

economic forces: The relationship of people to resources.

political forces: The relationship of individuals, their rights, and their property to the state.

Calvin.

Source: Renata Sedmakova/Shutterstock

Calvin supported the Protestant ethic, or work ethic.

Protestant ethic: An interpretation of the purpose of life, stating that, instead of merely waiting on earth for release into the next world, people should pursue an occupation and engage in high levels of worldly activity so that they can fulfill their calling.

capitalism: An economic system wherein the natural laws of supply and demand and free competition within the marketplace will efficiently regulate the flow of resources within a society.

Adam Smith's *The Wealth of Nations* describes the basic philosophy of capitalism.

division of labor: The idea of breaking an entire job into its component parts and assigning each specific task to an individual worker; also called specialization.

Division of labor, also called specialization, is the simple idea of breaking an entire job into its component parts and assigning each specific task to an individual worker. This contrasts with the traditional craft approach to production in which one craftsman performs all the component tasks required to produce an entire product from beginning to end. Smith described in detail the outcome and advantages of division of labor in the first three chapters of *The Wealth of Nations*.[8] Increased output would result due to increased expertise by each worker (because each is concentrating on a smaller component of the task), time saved from not repeatedly switching from one task to another, and the invention of specialized machines for each component of the overall job. Smith also acknowledged that the dysfunctional aspect of division of labor was that a lifetime spent doing a very specialized, narrow job could result in boredom, and lack of intellectual and/or social development.[9] Henry Ford would use the concept of job specialization to popularize the assembly line model, where workers on an assembly line would add different parts in sequential order to quickly create the finished product.

The Industrial Revolution

The final development needed to launch the world toward large-scale business and industrialization was the refinement of the use of the steam engine and the ensuing Industrial Revolution in England and America. In 1765, James Watt developed the first workable steam engine and 12 years later began the manufacture of the engines for industrial use.[10] Power-driven machinery gave rise to the factory system where people came together under one roof to manufacture products rather than working in their homes. This was necessary because even though power-driven machinery lowered production costs, capital requirements were increased to the point where few individuals could afford to buy and install machinery at home. Instead, workers had to travel to work—to the factory.[11]

Techniques for mass-production of standardized products, made from interchangeable parts in a factory system using steam-powered machines, were the hallmarks of the American manufacturing system in the late 1800s.[12] By the turn of the twentieth century, the possibilities of manufacturing seemed endless. Lower production costs led to lower prices and expanded markets. Innovation led to countless new inventions. Inventions and expanded markets led to large-scale production that resulted in an abundance of material goods such as the world had never seen.

These major developments in Western culture led to an age of great technological advancement and creation of individual wealth, but these gains did not come about easily. Instead of steady progress, a certain degree of chaos existed in industry at the dawn of the twentieth century due to changes in philosophies of life, economic structures, and manufacturing systems. Businessmen and politicians perceived the chaos in terms of a national "productivity problem." Frustration with the inefficiencies of manufacturing practices of the day and concern over the "question of national efficiency"—waste of natural resources and human effort—was widely expressed.[13] Three issues formed the basis of the productivity problem.

First, there was the technical and behavioral problem of meshing workers and machines. With so many new machines available, there was confusion as to how best to use them in the workplace. Moreover, widespread fear of machines existed among factory workers. People feared that

Power-driven machinery gave rise to the factory system.

substituting machine power for human energy would result in the elimination of their jobs, and they were often physically afraid of large, dirty, noisy, and dangerous factory machines.

A second obstacle to the improvement of efficiency was general inexperience in the operation of organizations and factories of the size needed to achieve the economies of scale inherent in mass production and distribution (that is, making large volumes of a product to lower the cost per item). With the exception of religious and military enterprises, large organizations did not exist. Few owners and employees were accustomed to working in groups much larger than an extended family. Size brought with it a need for different authority structures, standardized operating procedures, and overall depersonalization of the workplace. These phenomena were new to most people and not welcomed by many.

Finally, the third and most critical issue was the widespread lack of both management and trained managers. Slowly the realization occurred that further progress in industry depended on systematic management rather than on the charismatic talents of a few extraordinary men—the so-called "captains of industry." With this realization came

The development of machines helped increase productivity.

FIGURE 2.1
**Major Management
Theories**

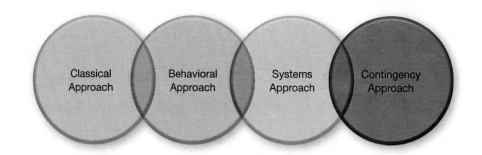

the need to define the role of management and managers as a unique and necessary factor of production. Bringing the first three factors of production—raw materials, capital, and labor—together on a large scale with power-driven machines could no longer be accomplished without the presence of management. Management was the missing link to future productivity gains, and it was now time to begin its formal systematic study and teaching.

The Development of Management Theories

management theory: A systematic statement, based on observations, of how the management process might best occur, given stated underlying principles.

A **management theory** is a systematic statement, based on observations, of how the management process might best occur, given stated underlying principles. However, there is no single universally accepted and practiced management theory—instead, there are many. Although the practice of management has existed in its most basic forms since ancient times, the systematic study and teaching of management has, as noted above, existed on a widespread basis for only the past roughly 100 years. Relative to other areas of study such as mathematics and literature, this makes management a young discipline.

The commonly accepted system of grouping management theories that we will follow in this chapter categorizes the major perspectives from which to study management as the (1) classical approach, (2) behavioral approach, (3) systems approach, and (4) contingency approach (see Figure 2.1). The thrust of this chapter is to establish the major categories of management theories and how they came to exist in the development of management thought.

The Classical Approach

classical approach: An approach to management that stresses the manager's role in a formal hierarchy of authority and focuses on the task, machines, and systems needed to accomplish the task efficiently.

The **classical approach** to management stresses the manager's role in a formal hierarchy of authority and focuses on the task, machines, and systems needed to accomplish the task efficiently. This approach to management thought has two components: scientific management and administrative management. The theories included in the classical approach—the first well-developed frameworks of management—emerged in the late 1800s and early 1900s. Table 2.1 summarizes the major thinkers who contributed to the classical approach.

Scientific Management

scientific management: A theory within the classical approach that focuses on the improvement of operational efficiencies through the systematic and scientific study of work methods, tools, and performance standards.

Scientific management is a theory within the classical approach that focuses on the improvement of operational efficiencies through the systematic and scientific study of work methods, tools, and performance standards. The development of scientific management began as a movement to define management as a separate and systematic factor of production.

In 1886, Henry Towne (1844–1924) presented a paper to the American Society of Mechanical Engineers (ASME) in which he stated that the time had come to blend the study and functions of engineering with those of business economics into one field and function. He labeled this function the "management of works" or "shop management" and argued that it was such an important industrial function that ASME should form a sepa-

TABLE 2.1 Contributors to the Classical Approach to Management

Scientific Management Thinkers	Contributions
Frederick Taylor	Developed the theory of scientific management. Stated that managers have the responsibility to discover the "best way" to complete the work task, select and train workers, cooperate with and provide incentives to workers, and divide work and responsibility evenly between managers and workers.
The Gilbreths	Discovered ways to increase efficiency through motion and recommended methods of reducing fatigue among workers.
Henry Gantt	Developed the Gantt chart and pioneered humanitarian management and business morality.
Morris L. Cooke	In an attempt to reduce inefficiencies, applied principles of scientific management to higher education, government agencies, and the management of World War I.
Administrative Management Thinkers	**Contributions**
Henri Fayol	Developed the functional definition of management, emphasized the necessity of teaching management, and developed general principles of management, including centralization and division of work.
Max Weber	Emphasized bureaucracy as a theory of management by office or position based on rationality. Advocated for impersonal and logical rules, including clear division of labor and selection based on technical qualifications.

rate division for the recording and sharing of experiences related to shop management.[14] It is important to note that, like Towne, most of the first management writers were engineers by training, which explains much of the overall emphasis of early management theories on machines, tools, work methods, and costs of production.

The notion of shop management developed into an entirely new science mostly due to the efforts of Frederick W. Taylor, who is often called the "father of scientific management." As a result of time spent in the steel mills of Philadelphia, first as a laborer and later as an engineer, Taylor concluded that the productivity problem of the day was due to lack of attention given to the management of men and their work. This was contrary to the beliefs of many businessmen of the day, who chose to blame the productivity problem on the pure laziness of common laborers. Taylor's drive to develop principles and methods of management based on logic, reason, and the scientific method of experimentation and observation was based mainly on his observations of "soldiering" among steel mill laborers.

Scientific management began as a movement to define management as a separate and systematic factor of production.

Source: Aaron Amat/Shutterstock

Beyond the natural tendency of humans to "take it easy and work at a slow, easy gait," **soldiering** is the systematic slowdown in work by laborers with the deliberate purpose of keeping their employers ignorant of how fast the work can be done.[15] Taylor said that soldiering existed in factories because employers did not know how much work could be done; laborers believed that if they worked too fast, they would work themselves and others out of jobs, and workers did not know how to do their jobs efficiently. Consequently, Taylor argued that the lack of productivity was management's fault, not laborers'.[16]

soldiering: The systematic slowdown in work by laborers with the deliberate purpose of keeping their employers ignorant of how fast the work can be done.

Source: Dariush M/Shutterstock

Soldiering is the systematic slowdown in work by laborers with the deliberate purpose of keeping their employers ignorant of how fast the work can be done.

Principles of Scientific Management

After almost 26 years of investigating the problems of low productivity, Taylor devised the principles of scientific management. According to these scientifically derived principles, the role of management is to perform the following:

1. Develop the "one best way" to perform any task.
2. Scientifically select, train, teach, and develop each worker.
3. Cooperate with workers and provide an incentive to ensure that the work is done according to the "one best way."
4. Divide the work and the responsibility equally between management and the workers.

The first principle refers to the idea that, for every task, there exists one way to do the job that will result in the highest rates of output and the highest rates of earnings for the laborer, and will not totally physically drain the laborer. The manager will develop the one best way based on reason, logic, and scientific observation and experimentation. It will include the movements and motions of the laborer as well as the correct tools and placement of machines within the work area.

The second principle states that it should not be up to the worker to pick the job he or she wants to do and then learn it through trial and error. Rather, it is the manager's job to select people for jobs based on their mental and physical traits and abilities and to place only those individuals best suited for a particular task in the job. Then it is the manager's job to continue to train and develop the selected employee until he or she is successful at the task.

Principle three implies that it is the manager's job to devise methods and rates of pay that will make it in the workers' best interests to perform their jobs according to the one best way they have been taught to do the job for which they were selected. Overall, this principle also means that it is the manager's job to look after the best interests of his or her employees as well as the best interests of the firm.

The final principle states that managers must take over all the work for which they are better prepared than the worker is (i.e., the planning or primarily mental aspects of work). In the past, almost all work—physical and mental—and the greater part of the responsibility for getting the work done was thrown on the workers. In other words, Taylor was conveying that workers will not be able to, and should not be expected to, perform to the fullest extent unless management has already determined the best way to do the job, selected and trained the best people for each job, provided adequate rewards for work done well, and taken over the work for which management was better prepared.

Assumptions of Scientific Management

The assumptions of Taylor's scientific management, for which he was later criticized, related to his view of the nature of people. The first assumption was that employers and employees had mutual interests associated with economic gain. Taylor believed that it was possible for employees to get what they wanted—high wages—at the same time that employers got what they wanted—low costs. He philosophized that a "mental revolution" had to occur among employees and employers whereby both groups would come to believe that mutual interests did exist and could be achieved through mutual cooperation—that a so-called "win-win" situation could be created.

A second assumption was that man is a rational being and economically motivated. Taylor assumed that people would follow any work methods and system based on reason and logic if it would allow them to fulfill their economic needs. The last assumption Taylor made was that, for every man willing to work hard, there was a job for which he was ideally suited according to his mental and physical traits and abilities. If placed in this job, he could be a "first-class-man," one who performed better than most at his job and earned higher than average wages for his work at that job.

Taylor believed it is the manager's job to select people for jobs based on their mental and physical traits and abilities.

Criticisms and Contributions of Taylor

Frederick Taylor and scientific management became quite well known throughout the country in 1910, when newspapers reported expert testimony before the Interstate Commerce Commission that railroads should not be allowed to raise their rates, but should instead reduce their costs through the use of scientific management. Scientific management achieved even more notoriety in 1911–1912, when a congressional investigation was held to determine if scientific management was abusive to workers. This was in response to strikes that had occurred over the use of Taylor's methods. The investigation found no concrete evidence of abuse, but the negative publicity was devastating to Taylor. He was quite impatient with critics, who were often not well informed, and who argued that the use of scientific management's efficiency methods led to the exploitation of workers by getting them to produce more and causing large reductions in the workforces of companies using scientific management. Years after his death, Taylor's critics have said that he failed to give credit to others for the work they did and that perhaps some of the data reported in his studies of various jobs may have been fabricated to some extent.[17]

Despite the criticisms, there is much evidence that Taylor's ideas about management and methods of studying work remain generally in use today. His strong support of the use of science and precise measurement methods prevails currently in the areas of management study and practice known as the quantitative approach, management science, and production/operations management. The **quantitative approach** emerged several decades later, during World War II, as a viewpoint of management that emphasizes the application of mathematical models, statistics, and structured information systems to support rational management decision making. **Management science** has developed into the field of management that includes the study and use of mathematical models and statistical methods to improve the effectiveness of managerial decision making. Production/operations management is a somewhat narrower branch of the quantitative approach that

quantitative approach: A viewpoint of management that emphasizes the application of mathematical models, statistics, and structured information systems to support rational management decision making.

management science: The field of management that includes the study and use of mathematical models and statistical methods to improve the effectiveness of managerial decision making.

Scientific management uses mathematical models and statistical methods to improve the effectiveness of managerial decision making.

focuses on managing the process of transforming materials, labor, and capital into useful goods and/or services.[18]

The Gilbreths

Frank Bunker Gilbreth (1868–1924) and Lillian Moller Gilbreth (1878–1972) were perhaps the first "dual-career couple" and are known for their contributions to the scientific management movement. Through his careful study of bricklaying, Frank was able to reduce the number of motions necessary to lay bricks by 89 percent and increased the number of bricks laid from 120 to 350 per hour. His methods are still used by modem bricklayers.

Frank Gilbreth met and married Lillian Moller in 1904. She pursued formal studies in psychology in the belief that it would help in her husband's work. Her thesis was published as a book, *The Psychology of Management*, that stands in management literature as one of the first contributions to understanding the human implications of scientific management.[19]

Through studying motion, Frank Gilbreth developed efficient methods of bricklaying that are still used today.

Another of Frank Gilbreth's innovations was the use of motion picture technology to analyze the motions used in a job. Gilbreth attached small lights to an employee's hand, while he was filmed performing a manual task, to trace the movements of the lights through time exposure (called a cyclegraph). The findings of these studies resulted in a classification of 16 basic work motions the Gilbreths called "therbligs" (which is Gilbreth spelled backward).[20]

Based upon their time and motion studies, the Gilbreths made many specific recommendations for means of reducing fatigue. Examples of these include improved footrests and chairs, comfortable shoes and clothing, rest periods and comfortable restrooms, elimination of unnecessary bending and twisting of the body, and proper heating and cooling of the work area.[21]

Henry Gantt

If not for Henry L. Gantt (1861–1919), scientific management might have been lost in a storm of criticism. He spent many years as a mechanical engineer and consultant making it plain that scientific management was more than just an inhuman attempt to speed up labor. Though he is best known for creating the Gantt chart—a simple graph method of scheduling work according to the amount of time required instead of the quantity of work to be performed—his real claim to fame lies in his role as a passionate advocate of workplace democracy and humanitarian management.

Gantt took every opportunity to humanize scientific management, such as inventing a task and bonus system that offered foremen a bonus for every worker who succeeded, and that motivated foremen to show interest in their employees and help them achieve as much as they could. Gantt's concern for devotion to service in the business system, and his call for "morality in the habits of industry," made him a pioneer in the area of business ethics and corporate social responsibility as they are studied in management today.[22]

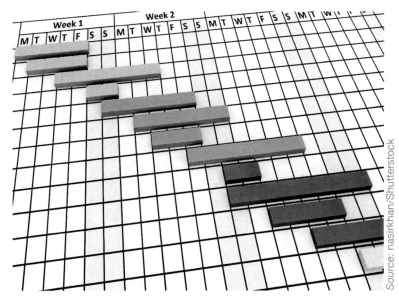

Along with creating the Gantt chart, Henry Gantt was also a passionate advocate of workplace democracy and humanitarian management.

Morris L. Cooke

Morris Llewellyn Cooke (1872–1960) was one of the four men originally authorized to teach Taylor's management methods. He is remembered as a true "radical" of his time for his role as a militant proponent of conservation, public power, and regional planning. Cooke's unique contribution to scientific management lies in his relentless attempts to apply the gospel of efficiency in higher education, government agencies, and the management of World War I. As the appointed management expert to the Carnegie Foundation for the Advancement of Teaching, Cooke compiled a report on the efficiency of university management practices that was considered a "bombshell." The gist of the report was that universities did not follow a single principle of scientific management and that there was an alarming lack of cooperation among professors, which resulted in intolerable levels of inefficiency. Cooke went so far as to suggest that college professors be paid based on their efficiency and that the system of life-long tenure should be eliminated.[23]

Administrative Management

Another component of the classical approach to management theory is **administrative management**, which emphasizes the universality of management as a function that can be applied to all organizations—large, small, for-profit, not-for-profit, political, religious, or any other. This contrasts with scientific management's emphasis on the role of a manager in the efficient use of resources primarily in industrial organizations. Administrative management theories focus on the need to organize and coordinate the workings of the entire organization instead of dwelling on organizing the work of individual workers, as in scientific management. Two important contributors to administrative management are Henri Fayol and Max Weber.

administrative management: The universality of management as a function that can be applied to all organizations.

Henri Fayol

Henri Fayol (1841–1925) was well educated and had a long and distinguished career as an engineer and manager in a large mining company in his native France. Fayol's work as a philosopher of administration, done mostly during the last ten years of his life, earned him a place of respect and importance in French history similar to that held by Frederick Taylor in the United States. His theories were originally published in a monograph, *General and Industrial Management*, in 1916. Although Taylor and Fayol were contemporaries, writing at about the same time, Fayol's work did not become well-known in the United States until the 1950s because translation of his work into English was slow and did not begin until 1930.

FIGURE 2.2
The Functional Definition of Management

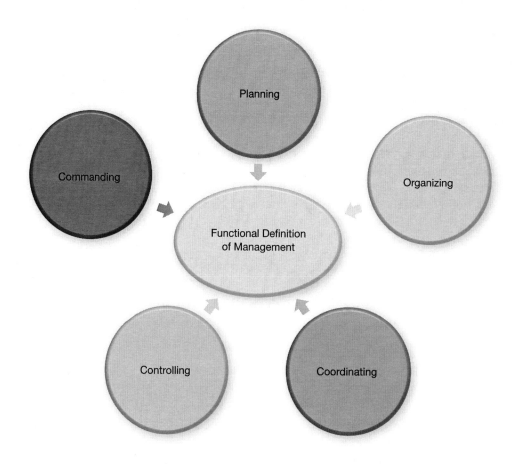

Fayol believed that managers needed to know more about how to read and write than about mathematics.

One of Fayol's main contributions to management thought is that he devised what has become known as the functional definition of management (Figure 2.2), which states that management is "to forecast and plan, to organize, to command, to coordinate and to control. . . ."[24] You will recognize that this definition of management is similar to our own and forms the basis of the organization for this text—and almost all principles of management books—with major sections about planning, organizing, leading (commanding and coordinating), and controlling.

Another of Fayol's major contributions to the development of management thought is his ideas about the possibility and necessity of teaching management. He believed that the education available for future managers in his day was much too oriented toward mathematics and engineering, and that managers needed to know much more about how to read and write than about mathematics. Further, Fayol strongly advocated experience—in the shop and at home through the management of family affairs—as an important component of management education.[25] In Table 2.2 we share some interesting facts about Fayol, Taylor, the Gilbreths, and others discussed throughout this chapter.

Finally, Fayol developed a comprehensive list of general principles of management. Fayol referred to this list as an indispensable code needed for the management of busi-

TABLE 2.2 **Did You Know?. . .**

- Frank and Lillian Gilbreth had 12 children, and a book and movie, *Cheaper by the Dozen*, depicts their life and attempts to apply their ideas about the elimination of wasted motion to everyday family life?
- Frederick Taylor and a partner won the U.S. Doubles Tennis Championship in 1881?
- Chester Barnard failed to receive an undergraduate degree from Harvard University because he completed all requirements except for the lab portion of a science course, which he was "too busy" to take?
- One of Edwards Deming's first jobs in the 1920s was at Western Electric's Hawthorne Plant in Chicago, where the famous Hawthorne Experiments took place?
- Lillian Gilbreth's doctoral dissertation was published under the name L. Gilbreth, as a means of disguising the fact that it was written by a woman?
- Frederick Taylor never accepted a penny of pay or traveling expense reimbursement for any of his lectures at Harvard or other places?
- Henri Fayol had intended to write two more parts to his book, *General and Industrial Management*, but died before they could be completed?

ness, industry, politics, religion, war, or philanthropy, in addition to religious and moral codes already in existence. The following describes Fayol's list of general principles:

- *Division of Work:* Dividing the work among employees decreases the amount of things employees must consider and produces better work.
- *Authority and Responsibility:* Managers must have the ability to assign work if they are to take responsibility for achieving work tasks.
- *Discipline:* There must be a respect for agreements between the organization and its employees. This means that agreements should be clear and fair, and disobedience should be penalized.
- *Unity of Command:* An employee should receive orders from only one superior.
- *Unity of Direction:* Tasks that have the same purpose should have only one person in charge with one plan.
- *Remuneration of Personnel:* Pay should be fair and meet employee needs. Employees should be rewarded for good performance.
- *Centralization:* The degree of centralization of an organization will vary depending upon each individual case, but the amount of centralization should optimize the talents of its employees.
- *Scalar Chain:* Communication should flow from top to bottom, except in cases where quick decisions are needed.
- *Order:* Each employee should be placed in the position that he or she best fits.
- *Equity:* Employees should be treated with justice and kindness.
- *Stability of Tenure of Personnel:* Employees must be provided with enough time to learn their jobs well.
- *Initiative:* Managers should encourage all employees to take initiative in decision making and the development of plans. This will empower employees and lead to a more productive organization.
- *Esprit de Corps:* Managers should create unity and teamwork among employees. Some ways of doing this is by encouraging oral communication and discouraging jealousy among employees.[26]

Max Weber

German philosopher Max Weber (1864–1920) spent most of his life as a student and scholar in a broad range of areas such as sociology, religion, economics, and political science. He focused all of his education with his observations of industry in both Germany and the United States to form a theory of how large organizations might operate more efficiently. Weber saw the issue of size as the impediment to the progress of industry. He felt that the only means of operating large organizations efficiently was to design and operate them as rationally as possible. Toward that end, he devised a pure form of organization based on rationality called bureaucracy (from the German word *Büro*, meaning "office").

bureaucracy: A theory of management by office or position, rather than by person, based on rational authority.

According to Weber, **bureaucracy** is a theory of management by office or position, rather than by person, based on rational authority. In bureaucracy, it matters not who (from what family or class) you are, but instead it matters what (job or position within the organization) you are, where matters of authority and value are concerned. Due probably to his academic rather than practitioner background, Weber never intended for his very theoretical ideas of the ideal—but probably not attainable—form of organizations to be used as guidelines for practicing managers; rather, he intended them as food for thought as to a new basis for authority.

Weber envisioned an organization developed around a set of impersonal and logical rules, routines, clear divisions of labor, selection based on technical qualifications, and strict adherence to a clear chain of command. He felt that observance of these disciplines would allow for orderly and systematic management of large groups of people that was not possible when personal preferences, which were likely to be illogical, and loyalty to individuals were the basis for operations.[27]

Indeed, many of us cringe at the word bureaucracy, as it brings to mind frustration, waste, and red tape. It is interesting to note that this would not have surprised Weber. He expressed his own doubts about the overuse of his model when he said, "It is horrible to think that the world could one day be filled with nothing but those little cogs, little men clinging to little jobs and striving towards bigger ones. . . . A passion for bureaucracy . . . is enough to drive one to despair."[28]

Source: Jorgen mcleman/Shutterstock

The word *bureaucracy* brings to mind frustration, waste, and red tape.

Contributions of the Classical Approach to Management Theory

As indicated by the label "classical," the theories we have explored in this section are those that have formed the main roots of the study and practice of management as we know it today. Within the classical approach we find the very definition of management as it had to be initially carved out as a separate and distinct function from economics, sociology, and engineering in the late nineteenth and early twentieth centuries. Often the main criticism of the classical theories is that they focused too narrowly on work, machines, authority structures, and efficiency, and that they ignored the human aspect of work. However, while these theories certainly emphasized work and getting it done efficiently, you should not forget the basic purpose behind each theory: to improve the standard of living and quality of life for all members of the organization and society in general.

The Behavioral Approach

Classical management theories are broadly based on the assumption that work is a rational endeavor pursued for almost purely economic reasons, and, consequently, that the behavior of people at work will be fairly predictable and easy to understand. However, when you realize that this assumption often does not hold true—that often work is not a rational, logical, or reasonable process and that, to many people, work is more than just a means of satisfying economic needs—the need to study and understand human behavior becomes very important. The theories of management beginning to develop during the early 1900s that looked at the role of management in this light, as well as the effects of machines, authority, and systematic management on human behavior, are referred to as the behavioral approach to management theory. The **behavioral approach** is a view of management that emphasizes understanding the importance of human behavior, needs, and attitudes within formal organizations. In our study of this approach we will discuss the ideas of Mary Parker Follett, the conclusions of the Hawthorne Experiments, and the contributions of Abraham Maslow, Douglas McGregor, Sigmund Freud, and Carl Jung. Table 2.3 summarizes the contributions of these important thinkers.

behavioral approach: A view of management that emphasizes understanding the importance of human behavior, needs, and attitudes within formal organizations.

Mary Parker Follett

Mary Parker Follett (1868–1933) was not an engineer, psychologist, or manager of any sort, yet she has been credited with making contributions to the development of management thought that are as important as those made by Taylor and Fayol.[29] Follett was one of the earliest management thinkers to advocate a break from the classical management school and to view effective management as based on the self-control of groups of workers and cooperation.

Follett's strong views on the importance of society "learning to live together" and group efforts as solutions to problems of both business and society grew out of her political science education and her experiences in social work.[30] In addition to many published papers and lectures given during the early 1930s, Follett's best-known works were two

TABLE 2.3 Contributors to the Behavioral Approach to Management

Behavioral Management Thinkers	Contributions
Mary Parker Follett	Underscored the importance of work groups, arguing that work groups are one of the primary sources of influence on worker behavior. Advocated for shared self-control in groups, a precursor to the later concept of self-directed work teams.
Elton Mayo	From the Hawthorne Experiments he discovered that social relationships and trust helped motivate employees to increase output. Essential for later theories of motivation and the human-relations movement.
Abraham H. Maslow	Proposed that managers could motivate workers by meeting their needs. He proposed five needs that all humans have. Meeting these five needs can help employees achieve fulfillment in their work.
Douglas McGregor	Developed Theory X and Theory Y to categorize managers and their views toward employees.
Sigmund Freud	Claimed that individuals, generally unconsciously, "transfer" relationships with important people from their childhood or their past onto relationships in the future—including work relationships.
Carl Jung	Proposed that people have individual differences and that such personality differences play a major role in how they work, deal with other people, handle conflict, and so on.
Katharine Cook Briggs and Isabel Briggs Myers	Based on Carl Jung's ideas, developed the Myers-Briggs Type Indicator to classify personalities. Has been helpful in deciding what careers may be suitable for individuals based upon their personality.

Mary Parker Follett believed that work groups are a primary source of influence on worker behavior—more so even than management's control and reward systems.

books she wrote: *The New State*, published in 1918, and *Creative Experience*, first published in 1924.

Among Follett's contributions to the behavioral approach to management were her ideas about the importance of groups in managing work situations. She argued that work groups are one of the primary sources of influence on worker behavior—more so even than management's control and reward systems. In fact, she believed that groups of workers had the ability to control themselves, and she advocated a group-oriented process of shared self-control based on group members' power with each other rather than power over each other.[31] This idea is currently considered as "innovative" relative to the use of self-regulating or self-managing groups.

Follett's ideas of shared power and human cooperation earned her an international reputation as a political and business philosopher. She viewed business leaders, rather than political leaders, as the hope for the future.[32]

The Hawthorne Studies

Hawthorne studies: A group of studies that provided the stimulus for the human-relations movement within management theory and practice.

One of the most often told—some would say "mistold"—stories' concerning management history is that of the **Hawthorne studies**. The Hawthorne studies provided the stimulus for the human-relations movement within management theory and practice. The story began at Western Electric Company's Hawthorne plant in Cicero, Illinois, in 1924. It was there that a series of experiments were begun to try to answer scientifically a fairly simple question: What is the effect of workplace lighting on workers' output?

To answer this seemingly simple question, researchers from MIT came to the Western Electric plant and began a series of experiments with several different groups of factory operators. After three years of experimentation, careful observation, and record keeping, the researchers concluded that productivity rose regardless of whether the level of lighting was increased or decreased. Something other than lighting was affecting worker output to a great degree.[33]

George Pennock, the assistant works manager, had been following the studies and was very interested in the notion that something other than the lighting changes had caused worker output to increase. So, beginning in April 1927 and continuing until May 1933,

The History of Haney's Appledale Farm

The aroma of fresh-baked apple pies with a hint of cinnamon fills the doorway to Haney's Appledale Farm and Market. This small Kentucky family-owned business is a tourist attraction; folks come from near and far to buy apples, peaches, pies, and many other fresh-fruit culinary treats. Located in Nancy, Kentucky, this family-farm business has been in operation since 1870. Currently, Haney's is run by brothers Don and Mark. They are the fifth generation of the Haney family to operate the business.

In 1870, Haney's Appledale Farm was established as Cloverdale Farm; at that time, it was only a small roadside fruit stand. Early on, its name was changed to Appledale to better reflect its emphasis on apple growing. Today, it is a sustainable 450-acre family farm that devotes 350 acres to trees. The farm grows 35 varieties of apples and 15 varieties of peaches. The trees are cultivated to provide a staggered and longer growing season. Tree management is a key to the company's success and the longevity of the business. The dwarf trees are pruned to bend toward the ground, making it easy to harvest the fruit. With 150 years in the business, Haney's has updated its technology and embraced changes in management thought.

The Haneys pride themselves on employing conservation and sustainable practices in their farm operations. They employ integrated pest management (IPM), which includes special traps so that they can identify pests, take immediate action to eliminate the invasive intruders, and minimize risks to human health and the environment. The company's expertise and reputation have been a boon for Kentucky's Department of Agriculture, which has been trying to expand and improve agribusiness and agri-tourism in the state. With a loyal customer base and a willingness to share its expertise on fruit-tree management with local farmers, Haney's greatly enhances both initiatives.

In season, customers can pick their own apples or peaches on the farm's orchards. The farm's retail market sells apple-related items such as cookies, cakes, jams, jellies, preserves, apple cider, caramel apples, and Haney's Apple Slush, a drink guaranteed to quench thirst on the hottest of days. The bakery has created a signature Fried Apple Pie made from scratch every day. Although the Haneys have had offers to go national with this product, they have declined the opportunity so that product integrity can be maintained. They also sell locally grown nectarines, pears, and pumpkins; local growers provide summer vegetables and fresh beef. As a retail market, Haney's enables the farmers to keep 100 percent of the profit.

Source: Africa Studio/Shutterstock

In addition to his role running Haney's farms, Mark Haney is the president of the Kentucky Farm Bureau, an organization that represents the interests of agricultural producers and rural communities. The Kentucky Farm Bureau provides services that include public affairs, insurance, women's leadership activities, commodity market information, and scholarships. It certifies roadside markets and supports agribusiness and agri-tourism efforts. Member benefits include collective advertising, promotional items, educational and tour opportunities, and other marketing support. It also promotes a "local foods" movement that has grown in its 20-year history to 99 markets throughout the state.

Although the demands of being the president of the Kentucky Farm Bureau keep Mark Haney busy traveling, he tries to return to the farm on Thursdays and work through the weekends. Each of the Haney brothers has three children who help with the business, but they all pursue professional careers away from the farm. The children have expressed a desire to see the farm continue, but at this time, none of them has stepped forward to assume the operation full-time.

Now in their sixties, the Haney brothers live in harmony with the earth as generations before them. There is no company mission, vision statement, or organizational chart. They live simply; their mantra is "Be honest and give more than you take." The Haneys take pride that all their fruit is handpicked. Little advertising is done, as they use word-of-mouth referrals from satisfied, happy customers. One of their most effective tools is Facebook and a website to let customers know when the harvest is ready. The 150-year history of the Haney family farm illustrates how businesses that embrace change in management thought and practice can prosper through many generations.[34]

Western Electric conducted more experiments, involving a group of six female telephone relay assemblers. Every few weeks, the company made some change related to hours worked, rest periods, incentive pay, hot lunches, etc.[35]

According to published reports, output bounced up and down throughout the manipulations with an overall trend toward greater output than before the experiments began. No clear relationships between any of the varied factors and worker output could be detected. It became clear that something unusual was occurring. Pennock sought professional advice from two professors, Claire Turner of MIT and Elton Mayo of Harvard University.[36]

Upon joining the research team, Mayo conducted a phase of the Hawthorne Experiments known as the interviewing program. During interviews with members of the research team, employees were given an opportunity to talk freely in complete confidence about anything, personal or work-related, of concern or interest to them. Mayo observed that the employees seemed to lose their shyness and fear. In short, the employees mentioned that they had come to trust and feel valued by their coworkers, supervisors, and the company.[37] After studying all the data and conducting even more experiments, Turner and Mayo both concluded separately that the rise in output was due to workplace factors related to the social relationships among the workers themselves and between the workers and their supervisors.

Contribution of the Hawthorne Experiments

The general conclusion drawn from the Hawthorne studies was that human relations and the social needs of workers are a crucial aspect of business management. Feeling "valued" at work and having trust in the organization are important. This gave factory management a social dimension as well as an economic dimension. From this point on, employees would be viewed as members of informal groups of their own, with their own leadership and codes of behavior, instead of as just unrelated individual workers assigned to perform individual tasks. This change in the direction of management theory and practice is often referred to as the **human-relations movement**.

human-relations movement: A practice whereby employees came to be viewed as informal groups of their own, with their own leadership and codes of behavior, instead of as just unrelated individual workers assigned to perform individual tasks.

Nothing as well known as the Hawthorne studies could go without criticism. Scholars have criticized the studies as having too many uncontrolled variables to permit valid conclusions.[38] Others have (1) criticized the interpretation of the data as having been biased toward pushing for support of the importance of the social and human relations aspects of work, (2) said that the results have been overstated, and (3) said that re-analysis of the data does not support the conclusions that physical and economic factors did not affect workers' output.[39]

Regardless of the actual experimental results, the fact remains that the Hawthorne Experiments were the first set of lengthy tests conducted in the workplace to study actual worker behavior. Many, including Mayo, see their main contribution as stimulating thinking and research about the nature and significance of human behavior, feelings, and attitudes at work, and the role of the informal group in formal organizations.

Abraham H. Maslow

Psychologist Abraham H. Maslow (1908–1970), an early humanist psychologist, developed one of the most widely recognized needs-based theories of human motivation. He is best known for his hierarchy of human needs theory, published in 1943, in which he proposed that humans have five needs: physiological, safety, social, self-esteem, and self-actualization needs.

Maslow advocated a humanistic approach to management, which did not mean simply being nice and maintaining good human relations. Instead, it required taking the basic innate nature and needs of human beings into account in management theories and practices. Maslow proposed that people's behavior at work could be explained by a need for something beyond the money essential for their basic existence. This differed from classical management theories, which emphasized the role of pay as the sole source of employee motivation. Maslow also stated that after an employee's basic survival and

Abraham Maslow believed that after an employee's basic survival and security needs were fulfilled by money, other needs would become important as a source of continued motivation to work.

security needs were fulfilled by money, other needs would become important as a source of continued motivation to work. The top rung and ultimate need of all humans was self-actualization, the need to fulfill one's full potential. Work could be a major source of fulfillment of this need. Work could be designed in such a way that people could fulfill their full potential at work.

Douglas McGregor

Douglas McGregor (1906–1964) spent most of his career teaching and conducting research at MIT. As president of Antioch College he came to realize, as a practicing manager, that effective management required a thorough understanding and consideration of human nature and human behavior. Like Maslow, McGregor advocated a humanistic approach to management.

McGregor is best known for Theory X and Theory Y, as presented in his book, *The Human Side of Enterprise* (1960). He felt that managers' individual assumptions about human nature and behavior determined how they managed their employees. How managers treated employees then led to how employees behaved. **Theory X** is the assumption that people are naturally lazy, must be threatened and forced to work, have little ambition or initiative, and do not try to fulfill any need higher than security needs at work. Theory X assumptions represented traditional management views of direction and control. Foxconn, a Taiwanese electronics contract manufacturing company, adopted more of a Theory X view. The company became embroiled in controversy after several workers from its factories committed suicide. Subsequent investigations found that the employees worked long hours in poor working conditions under a militaristic corporate culture.[40]

Theory Y is the assumption that people naturally want to work, are capable of self-control, seek responsibility, are creative, and try to fulfill higher-order needs at work. Theory Y assumptions represented a new view of the integration of human and organizational needs and goals. Ultimate Software has adopted Theory Y in the way it treats employees. Employees receive 100 percent healthcare premiums and a free vacation every two years.[41] Theory X and Y are intuitively simple and easy-to-understand concepts that are still widely applied today.

Theory X: The assumption that people are naturally lazy, must be threatened and forced to work, have little ambition or initiative, and do not try to fulfill any need higher than security needs at work.

Theory Y: The assumption that people naturally want to work, are capable of self-control, seek responsibility, are creative, and try to fulfill higher-order needs at work.

Theory Y managers assume that employees want to work, are capable of self-control, seek responsibility, are creative, and try to fulfill higher-order needs at work.

Sigmund Freud

Sigmund Freud (1856–1939), perhaps history's leading psychologist/psychiatrist, may not typically be thought of as a leader in management thought. Freud's writings covered many topics, which are related to the field of "management" viewed broadly, but his work on "transference" alone probably qualifies him as having a major impact in the area. Freud believed that individuals, generally unconsciously, "transferred" relationships with important people from their childhood or their past onto relationships in the future. For example, a person that had a troubled or difficult relationship with his or her father might "transfer" such a relationship in the future onto a male supervisor (i.e., have a troubled or difficult relationship with the supervisor). Being aware of the possibility of such Freudian transferences is thus a very important skill with respect to effective management leadership. Moreover, it is important for employees to understand that how they relate to authority figures and others in the workplace relates, at least in part, to how they related to authority figures and others in the past.[42]

Carl Jung and Myers Briggs

Perhaps the biggest challenger to Freudian thought was psychiatrist Carl Jung (1875–1961). Once a follower of Freud, Jung eventually diverged from his mentor and began to research the influence of archetypes and personality traits on individuals. In his 1921 text, Jung proposed that people have individual differences and that such personality differences play a major role in how they work, deal with other people, handle conflict, and so on. For example, some people are extraverted while others are introverted. Moreover, some people evaluate information and make decisions in a rational and logical manner, while others go more with their intuition.[43]

Jung's ideas would eventually be adapted to form the Myers-Briggs Type Indicator (MBTI). The MBTI was developed by Katharine Cook Briggs and her daughter Isabel Briggs Myers. Katharine had noted that when Isabel Briggs brought her boyfriend, Clarence Myers, home to meet her parents, his personality type was different from her daughter's (more intuitive). In response to this experience and with a desire to make Jung's academic work more understandable and usable to the general public, they developed the MBTI.[44] From a business perspective, it has been found to be helpful in deciding what

Jung proposed that people have individual differences and that such personality differences play a major role in how they work, deal with other people, and handle conflict.

careers may be most suitable for individuals based upon their personality. Today, the MBTI is a widely used personality test administered by a variety of businesses and organizations. The MBTI groups individuals according to extroversion versus introversion, sensing versus intuition, thinking versus feeling, and judging versus perception.

The Systems Approach

The **systems approach** to management theory views organizations and the environments within which they operate as sets of interrelated parts to be managed as a whole in order to achieve a common goal.[45]

A **system** is an arrangement of related or connected parts that form a whole unit. As systems, organizations consist of inputs, transformation processes, outputs, and feedback. Contemporary system theorists find it helpful to analyze the effectiveness of organizations according to the degree to which they are open or closed. A **closed system** interacts little with its external environment and therefore receives little feedback from or information about its surroundings. An **open system**, on the other hand, continually interacts with its environment and therefore is well informed about changes within its surroundings and its position relative to these changes. Most successful organizations adopt an open system because of the need to carefully monitor surroundings and adapt to changing trends. Facebook, for instance, must constantly be on the lookout for competitors, observe how consumer Internet habits are changing, and look for opportunities to break into other industries.

A **subsystem** is any system that is part of a larger one. **Entropy** is the tendency of systems to deteriorate or break down over time. **Synergy** is the ability of the whole system to equal more than the sum of its parts.[46] In other words, when we view organizations as systems, we must understand that there is a natural tendency for the organization to become less effective over time unless feedback and information from the environment are integrated into the system. The ultimate advantage of forming an organization is that it allows us to achieve more together than all of us as individuals could achieve separately. Management is indeed just one component of an organization that must be carefully attuned to the other components. In this section we will consider two systems theorists, Chester Barnard and W. Edwards Deming.

Chester Barnard

Chester Barnard (1886–1961) rose through the ranks to become president of New Jersey Bell, then a division of American Telephone and Telegraph (AT&T). Barnard was a self-made scholar whose ideas have influenced the development of the systems approach, the

systems approach: An approach to management theory that views organizations and the environments within which they operate as sets of interrelated parts to be managed as a whole in order to achieve a common goal.

system: An arrangement of related or connected parts that form a whole unit.

closed system: An organization that interacts little with its external environment and therefore receives little feedback from or information about its surroundings.

open system: An organization that continually interacts with its environment and therefore is well informed about changes within its surroundings and its position relative to these changes.

subsystem: Any system that is part of a larger one.

entropy: The tendency of systems to deteriorate or break down over time.

synergy: The ability of the whole system to equal more than the sum of its parts.

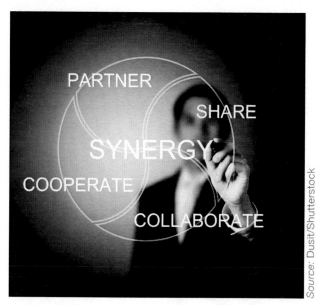

Forming an organization allows us to achieve more together than all of us as individuals could achieve separately.

behavioral approach, and the field of organization or administrative theory that is an aspect of the classical approach to management theory.[47]

Cooperative Systems

In the early pages of his book, *The Functions of the Executive*, Barnard expressed the need for a universal theory of management that would guide managers in effectively adjusting the workings of the organization to a constantly changing external environment.[48] Toward this end, he devised a theory of managing organizations as cooperative systems. Barnard's basic premise is that formal organizations—within which we all work and by which we are all educated and governed—are necessary so that individuals can accomplish tasks that they could not accomplish working on their own.

An important factor in cooperation is the recognition of each individual's special abilities. Barnard cautions that cooperation requires the acceptance and adoption of a group, not a personal purpose. He wrote that members of an organization are more willing to cooperate when they believe in the organization's purpose or goal. Getting them to believe is a major function of a manager.[49]

Acceptance Theory of Authority

acceptance theory of authority: The theory that, in formal organizations, authority flows up, because the decision as to whether an order, or communication, has authority lies with the person who receives the communication.

Barnard stated that the major means of ensuring the cooperation of individuals was through communication. He even defined authority relative to communication: Authority is the degree to which an organizational member accepts communication directed at him or her as something that should govern his or her actions. The **acceptance theory of authority** states that in formal organizations, authority flows up, because the decision as to whether an order, or communication, has authority lies with the person who receives the communication. Organization members will accept communications (orders) as authoritative if four conditions are met: (1) they could and did understand the com-

An important factor in cooperation is the recognition of each individual's special abilities.

municated order; (2) they believed that the order was consistent with the organization's purpose at the time of their decision; (3) they believed that the order was compatible with their personal interests as a whole; and (4) they were mentally and physically able to comply with the order.[50]

W. Edwards Deming

W. Edwards Deming (1900–1993) has been credited with transforming Japan's postwar economy more than 50 years ago. During his lifetime, Deming was desperate to get his dual message of continuous improvement of the system and zero defects through to American managers, workers, government officials, and educators.[51] It is important for you to learn that Deming's work is appropriately classified as a systems theory of management.

One of Deming's major contributions was to integrate various aspects of workplace dynamics into an overall approach in which all dimensions of the formal organization and its environment are considered as part of one system. Some have referred to Deming as a "capitalistic revolutionary" who transformed our notions of quality into a driver of profits instead of a cost of doing business.[52]

The Contingency Approach

During the 1960s a new phrase, "it depends," began to appear regularly in management literature. This signaled a move by theorists to yet another perspective of management that was noticeably different from the "one best way" approach followed by previous management theorists. The phrase "it depends" characterized the **contingency approach** to management theories, which emphasizes identifying the key variables in each management situation, understanding the relationships among these variables, and recognizing the complex system of cause and effects that exists in each and every managerial situation.[53] For example, an organization with a highly unstable operating environment should be structured and organized quite differently than one operating in a very stable environment. This is in contrast to Weber's idea of a pure bureaucracy as the one best way of organizing. Further, managers should use a different degree of supervision and control on employees who are very willing and able to do a job than on those who are not willing or able to perform their jobs.

contingency approach: An approach to management theories that emphasizes identifying the key variables in each management situation, understanding the relationships among these variables, and recognizing the complex system of cause and effects that exists in each and every managerial situation.

The contingency approach is especially common in areas of management such as strategic planning, leadership styles, use of technology, design of reward systems, and organizational design. Generally, it is considered to be an outgrowth of the systems approach. While criticized as being inadequate as a true theoretical basis, the contingency approach has inspired research and understanding relative to how the gap between theory and practice may be bridged.

Twenty-First-Century Management

As management moved into the twenty-first century, a number of scandals began to impact how businesses operate. The fraud of Enron, Worldcom, and Tyco, as well as the downfall of established organizations such as Bear Stearns and Lehman Brothers, highlighted the need for additional oversight and controls to ensure ethical conduct. Additionally, with the increasing globalization of the world, companies are finding the need to adapt quickly and make better use of their workers' talents and insights to secure a competitive advantage. Two thinkers that have been influential in the way business has been evolving in the past decade are Peter Drucker and Peter Senge.

Peter Drucker

Although his writings spanned from the 1930s, Peter Drucker (1909–2005) has been called "the founder of 21st century management."[54] His prolific writings, which spanned

You're the Manager . . . What Would You Do?

THE COMPANY: EMS Corporation
YOUR POSITION: Owner
THE PLACE: Tampa, Florida

When Jim Keller took over EMS Corporation, a linen and bedding manufacturer, the company was near bankruptcy and employee morale was at an all-time low. EMS was losing $2 million a year and was plagued with high absenteeism, employee turnover, and accidents. At his first meeting with employees, Jim saw a level of apathy and abandonment that spurred his determination to revitalize the plant and its employees. He realized that the only way to save the company was to rekindle the employees' interest in its survival.

Jim, along with key employees, developed the "Initiative," a program he designed to get employees interested in the plant and to raise productivity. He set simple goals for product quality, safety, cleanliness of workspaces, and productivity. When the employees attained 100,000 hours with no recordable accidents, Jim closed the plant for a day and everyone celebrated with a "Barbecue Bash." When Jim had the departments compete against one another for a trophy, production increased dramatically. As a result of the company's setting measurable performance goals and offering rewards, employees began to care about the company's fate. After just four months, EMS showed a profit for the first time in years.

Keller improved the "Initiative" by offering all employees a full range of business courses—accounting, plant auditing, purchasing, etc.—to help them understand EMS's production reports and financial status. The goal was to get employees to understand the huge amounts of data required to monitor the firm's performance. Keller wanted employees to be able to gauge the impact of their activities on the plant and set their own performance standards to help improve the company.

Employees were given constant reminders of how they were doing. An electronic message board running continuous production reports was installed in the cafeteria. Employees who exceeded their production quotas were given a bonus under a plan known as "Output is sunny . . . now give us some money." Employees also received bonuses for ideas that improved the company's operations.

The employees were motivated to make EMS succeed because they understood not only the physical aspects of their jobs, but also how the company was doing and what needed to be done for success. When the company did well, so did they. Jim Keller's efforts and plans were enormously successful.

QUESTIONS

1. What schools of management thought is Jim Keller applying in revitalizing EMS?

2. What other management theories could you apply in the revitalization effort?

3. Contrast these actions against those that a factory manager of the early 1900s might have taken.

---

almost 70 years, contributed insights that would mold modern-day business. He had a profound influence on management thought during the latter part of the twentieth century and the beginning of the twenty-first century. For instance, he coined the term *management by objectives* in his 1954 work *Practice of Management* to emphasize the need to define and adhere to clear objectives that both managers and employees agree upon and understand.[55] This concept would be further developed by Drucker's student and adopted by Hewlett-Packard as part of the HP Way.[56] Drucker believed management was something of a "liberal art," and his management theories were highly interdisciplinary in nature drawing from history, religion, culture, sociology, and so on.[57] The business school at Claremont Graduate University in California is named after him and takes such a broad, interdisciplinary approach toward management education.

knowledge worker: A person who works primarily with information or one who develops and uses knowledge in the workplace.

His book, *The Landmarks of Tomorrow*, developed the concept of the **knowledge worker** and supported the movement of modern management away from physical capital (e.g., machines and steel mills) to so-called "human capital" (e.g., workers with portable knowledge creating products such as computer programs and other knowledge-based products).[58] Drucker predicted that knowledge workers would become increasingly important in the future, a prediction that became reality in the twenty-first century. Today, managers recognize that even traditional manual laborers can be knowledge workers and contribute important insights to the company. In recognition of this, Dow Chemical shares sales and day number information with everyone in the firm, including workers doing the "heavy lifting."[59] With the onset of the Internet and social media, knowledge workers are able to collaborate like never before. This environment of collaboration and teamwork is changing the dynamic of the workplace, contributing to greater collective intelligence among organizations.[60]

Drucker also strongly emphasized the role of government and the nonprofit sector in the field of management in the modern era. In particular, he felt that non-governmental organizations need to play an increasingly important role in countries around the world. Drucker felt strongly that business and management was an important part of global society.

Another of Drucker's insights has taken on renewed importance after the accounting and financial scandals of the early twenty-first century. For years Drucker emphasized a balance between achieving short-term goals and the long-term sustainability of the organization. Drucker also emphasized the importance of corporate social responsibility, in which managers not only work toward the success of their organizations but also contribute toward bettering society.[61] These concepts have come to the forefront in recent years. The failure of many large institutions such as Lehman Brothers from large-scale risk-taking demonstrated a short-term focus on quick profits rather long-term success. These scandals have called for a renewed emphasis on long-term sustainability and a concern for stakeholders. No longer is it acceptable for organizations simply to pursue profitability. Instead, there is an expectation that businesses adopt a stakeholder orientation that can improve the lives of the community at large. Drucker was remarkably perceptive in predicting future management trends and changing views of business.

The Learning Organization

One of the most recent highly influential individuals in the field of management thought has been Peter Senge (1947–). Dr. Senge, who works at the MIT Sloan School of Management, has emerged as a major influence in the field of "organizational development" with his conceptualization of businesses as **learning organizations**. As developed initially in his book, *The Fifth Discipline: The Art and Practice of the Learning Organization,*[62] Senge maintains that modern organizations must be in a state of constant learning through continuous improvement and adaptation. Senge notes that while organizations need to be constantly learning and open to change, they will face various challenges, including a reluctance to change the firm's corporate culture.[63]

learning organizations: Refers to companies that facilitate the learning of their members and continuously transform themselves.

Somewhat similar to Peter Drucker's emphasis on the role of "knowledge workers," Senge points out the importance of individual learning, or personal mastery, in organizations. Organizations with employees that can learn quickly and develop personal masteries will likely have a competitive advantage over organizations whose workforces are not as adept at continual learning. In addition to personal mastery, learning organizations also stress systems thinking, or the recognition that organizations consist of interrelated relationships; mental models, or generalizations about how the company views the world; building a shared vision; and team learning.[64]

Management Theory: Past, Present, and Future

This chapter has been about beginnings, the individuals who pioneered these beginnings, and the times in which the beginnings occurred. Within the ideas of those before us lie our directions for the future. If we include the beginnings of management history, theory, and practice in our ideas and behaviors, then our journey through organizations may be a little smoother and more meaningful. We can learn from history. Each major approach to management theory that we have examined has added significantly to our current knowledge about management. The ideas embedded in each approach have also changed, in some respects, the way managers think and act. Contemporary managers and managers of the future benefit most from understanding and applying selected aspects of each approach.

The classical approach is still very evident today in our continued emphasis on the importance of efficient methods of operations and the use of quantitative methods in basic administrative principles of authority and division of labor, as well as in the prevalence of bureaucracy in our formal organizations. The behavioral approach is evident in the importance placed on people as the most valuable assets of organizations and in the increasing attention paid to creating a working environment and work teams in which our human needs are addressed. Evidence of the systems approach to management theory is quite apparent in attempts to manage organizations so that they meet the needs and challenges of the external environment and in the strong interest in total quality management methods. Finally, evidence of the influence of contingency approaches to management is found in the unique and varied success stories we hear every day from managers in many different and complex managerial situations.

Contemporary views of management that are in the process of being tested and evaluated today are fundamentally based on some aspect of theories we have considered in this chapter. For example, Peter Senge's work on learning organizations directly relates to the earlier works of Drucker, Maslow, and even Carl Jung.

Nothing stays the same. Remember we said that what we have studied in this chapter, although it spans a time period of around a hundred years (Figure 2.3), is only the beginning. Management theories and the study of management will continue to change today and tomorrow. While the changes are bound to be many and varied, they are likely to revolve around our efforts to compete in a global economy and our need to simultaneously increase productivity (benefits to the firm) and quality of work-life (benefits to the individual). These are important challenges for which we will be well prepared if we follow the ideas of the past, present, and future.

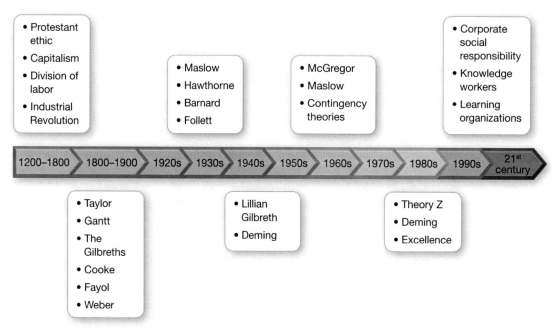

FIGURE 2.3 A Timeline of the Development of Management Theory

- *Specify the major cultural changes that preceded the development of modern management practice and thought.* Major cultural changes that preceded the evolution of modern management practice and thought were the development of capitalism and the Industrial Revolution. These changes culminated in a period of industrial chaos and low productivity that gave rise to the definition and development of management as a critical factor of production.

- *Explain the major theories within the classical approach to management.* The classical approach to management stresses the manager's role in a formal hierarchy of authority and focuses on the task, machines, and systems needed to accomplish the task efficiently. The major theories that developed within this approach were Taylor's scientific management, Fayol's administrative theory, and Weber's theory of bureaucracy.

  Scientific management's overall emphasis was the systematic study of and experimentation with workers' tasks, methods, and tools as a means of improving worker efficiency. It had many contributors in addition to Taylor, including Frank and Lillian Gilbreth, Henry Gantt, and Morris L. Cooke. Fayol's theory was broader than scientific management and was directed at defining management as a universal process composed of four functions, and at developing principles needed to coordinate all the activities of the entire organization. Weber's ideas about bureaucracy added the concept of rational authority and management by position to classical management theory.

- *Examine some of the major contributions to the development of the behavioral approach to management.* The behavioral approach to management thought emphasizes the importance of human behavior, needs, and attitudes within organizations. Some management theorists and researchers who made major contributions to the development of the behavioral approach were Mary Parker Follett, those associated with the Hawthorne studies, Abraham Maslow, and Douglas McGregor. Follett had strong views on the importance of integrative unity, shared power, and human cooperation. She looked to managers as the means for improving society. The Hawthorne studies, through a long series of different experiments, brought to managers' attention the critical nature of the social needs of workers and led to the development of the human-relations movement. This signaled the beginning

of the joining of management with psychology. Maslow proposed that people's behavior at work could be explained by human needs for something beyond the money earned for basic existence. Self-actualization was the highest-order need identified by Maslow, and management practices directed toward satisfying this need pointed to a new direction for management theory and practice. McGregor labeled and explained a nontraditional approach known as Theory Y, in contrast to the traditional approach of Theory X. Freud's work on "transference" is an important skill with respect to effective management leadership, and Jung's work on personality types helped lead to the development of the Myers-Briggs Type Indicator.

- *Describe the systems approach to management theory and identify the early contributors to this perspective.* The systems approach to management theory views organizations and the environment within which they operate as sets of interrelated parts to be managed as a whole in order to achieve a common goal. Cooperative systems and the acceptance theory of authority were two aspects of Barnard's view of how organizations must be managed so that they can adjust effectively to a constantly changing external environment. Deming was a contemporary contributor to the systems approach whose work began in the 1940s.

- *Relate the significance of the contingency approach within the study and practice of management.* The contingency approach is significant because it has helped bridge the gap between theory and practice. It emphasizes identification of key variables in each management situation and as such maintains that there is no one best way to manage. The contingency approach is widely followed in areas of management such as strategic planning, leadership, and organization design.

- *Summarize more current management knowledge and practices that have become popular in the twenty-first century.* Peter Drucker is often called the "father of modern management" because of his influence on modern management practices. His predictions about the importance of knowledge workers, long-term sustainability, and corporate social responsibility have become important parts of management in the twenty-first century. Peter Senge's theory of learning organizations states that modern organizations must be in a state of constant learning through continuous improvement and adaptation.

■ *Apply the management theories discussed in this chapter to a manager's efforts to revitalize a small business.* The "Business Dilemma" box describes the steps a manager took to revitalize a failing small business. You should be able to assess and apply the schools of management thought that Mr. Jim Keller applied to the situation and understand why he chose those theories over others.

Key Terms and Concepts

acceptance theory of authority 52

administrative management 41

behavioral approach 45

bureaucracy 44

capitalism 33

classical approach 36

closed system 51

contingency approach 53

division of labor 34

economic forces 33

entropy 51

Hawthorne studies 46

human-relations movement 48

knowledge worker 54

learning organizations 55

management science 39

management theory 36

open system 51

political forces 33

Protestant ethic 33

quantitative approach 39

scientific management 36

social forces 33

soldiering 37

subsystem 51

synergy 51

system 51

systems approach 51

Theory X 49

Theory Y 49

Ready Recall

1. What cultural changes led to the emergence of management as the fourth factor of production? What are the other three factors of production?
2. Compare and contrast the various approaches to management theory.
3. What are the principles and assumptions of scientific management?
4. What contributions to scientific management were made by people other than Taylor?
5. On what type of authority is bureaucracy based?
6. What four things should managers do to ensure that their authority will be accepted by subordinates?
7. What were the unexpected results of the Hawthorne studies and what conclusions were drawn from these results?
8. What issues formed the basis of the productivity problem at the turn of the twentieth century?
9. What were Fayol's main contributions to management thought?
10. What are the various characteristics of systems?
11. Describe the term *knowledge worker* and why it is important to management today.
12. What are some of the characteristics of a learning organization?

Expand Your Experience

1. Do you think too much or too little emphasis is placed on human relations within the work environment? What direction do you think should be taken in the future relative to an emphasis on human relations? Why?
2. What events and trends in society, technology, and economics do you think will shape management theory in the future?
3. View the movie or buy the book *Cheaper by the Dozen* and report on how the Gilbreths tried to incorporate their passion for efficiency into their family life.

Strengthen Your Skills

Application of the Four Management Theories

As you read the scenario below, keep the four main management theories in mind. When you are finished, answer the questions following the scenario.

Scenario

Cool Steel Company (CSC) is a player in the very traditional, highly competitive, cyclical steel business. CSC's competitive advantage lies in their stellar performance, with strong earnings growth and high return on equity in an industry that has been producing staggering losses in both jobs and dollars during the past decade.

Company founder and Chairman Jim Quintero and his managers run the business like entrepreneurs rather than bureaucrats. The philosophy of the 40-year-old company is centered on employees. Employees are paid well, treated well, and given ownership of the company. When he began the company, Quintero was determined to establish a climate in which workers would find it in their own best interests to be productive. He also was determined to treat his workers with respect and to demonstrate that he trusted them to do their best work for the good of the company and themselves. To this end, he removed all time clocks from the plant, as well as first-level supervisors. CSC does not give its workers coffee breaks. However, it does provide free coffee to be enjoyed when an individual feels it is appropriate. Also, using their own judgment, workers may refuse to ship a product if they feel its quality is below standard. Employees are able to make these kinds of decisions because they are given the responsibility and the internal and external knowledge to do so.

CSC pays all employees a salary. Basic pay is relatively low, but bonuses and profit sharing bring CSC wages up to union levels. When the company suffers, so do the employees, because so much of their pay is tied to performance. This means that workers automatically take pay cuts when orders drop, but because they own a large chunk of the business, the workers are less resentful because they know the decline in their pay is helping protect their long-term investment in the company.

QUESTIONS

1. Identify aspects of Jim Quintero's management style according to the four main management theories (Classical, Behavioral, Systems, and Contingency).
2. Explain each aspect in detail and take note of any advantages and/or disadvantages to each approach.
3. How would you approach management with respect to the four main management theories?

Case 2: How Business Schools Began

Oh, but for the good old days when everything you needed to know to be a successful business manager could be contained in one book! Such was the case when J. L. Nichols, principal of the North-Western Business College in Naperville, Illinois, published *The Business Guide; or Safe Methods of Business*. He recommended his book as a "cheap form of full information as to methods of doing business." Or perhaps, instead of a minimum of four years of college education, you could have educated yourself completely by studying *How To Do Business*. Published in the late 1890s, this comprehensive text contained in one volume every topic of business considered important from banking, letter writing, grammar, and mechanic's arithmetic to business geography (see the opening vignette).

The notion of the formal study of business as a separate, fully developed curriculum of undergraduate education began to take shape in 1881 with the formation of the Wharton School of Finance and Economy at the University of Pennsylvania in Philadelphia. It was the desire of Joseph Wharton, a successful financier and iron manufacturer, that with his initial $100,000 endowment the University of Pennsylvania develop a program of college education that would "fit for the actual duties of life . . . men other than lawyers, doctors and clergymen." Wharton's plan was that the $6,000 in interest earned by the $100,000 endowment plus $150 a year in tuition fees from each of 40 students would provide funds to pay the $3,000 salary of the dean of the business school and a $1,500 salary for each of the five professors, with $1,500 left over to buy books and provide student research grants.

The school opened with 13 students enrolled in a three-year program taught by one full-time and one part-time professor. Enrollment rose to 113 by 1894, and the curriculum was expanded to four years. By 1911, all U.S. universities

Source: Morphart Creation/Shutterstock

Early business schools had only a few students, today business is the most popular degree to pursue.

housed a total of 30 undergraduate business programs, and by 1925 there were 164 colleges of business. By 1960 the count was 860, with an estimated student population of 600,000 in 1970.

When the Wharton School was founded in 1881, the U.S. labor force included 17 million workers, and over half of them had agriculture-related jobs. Employers of that time expressed the need for employees with a little knowledge of bookkeeping, some commercial geography, mathematics, and the ability to write clearly.

World War I was a turning point for business degrees. The war created more work as well as demand for greater business acumen. The economy shifted from an agricultural base to a manufacturing one. An example of this shift is the automobile industry. Automobile production became a big industry in urban areas and caused people to leave farms for the higher-paying manufacturing jobs. Consequently, to handle these more complex jobs, education became more important.

After WWI, emphasis shifted from basic, bottom-line ideas to overall business environment issues. Personnel practices, marketing, and the further development of accounting beyond just crunching numbers became important issues for effective managers. Schools were then forced to adjust to this shift in focus, as well as to the increase in the number of students interested in business. By 1940, there were 18,549 undergraduate, 1,139 master's, and 37 doctoral degrees awarded in business.

The makeup of students also affected what was taught in business schools. In the 1940s and 1950s, because of WWII veterans returning to the classrooms, students were older and more interested in courses that covered more complex issues. Schools responded by hiring professors with diverse backgrounds. Business schools, striving for prestige, became more broad in nature, teaching a variety of topics, to attract even more students.

The 1970s brought a reversal of this trend, back to more specific courses. Statistics, production management, and decision making were now specific tracks within the business discipline. Enrollment among the 18- to 24-year-old group increased during this time, leading schools to develop programs that covered the full range of business subjects, from the basics in economics and business law to the more advanced issues such as specific courses of action for different industries.

In the 1980s and 1990s, business became the most popular degree to pursue. Forty percent of all degrees awarded were business related; MBAs were turned out by the tens of thousands every year. Today, employers are once again changing their definitions of what a business degree should entail. Current issues such as sustainability, global business, social entrepreneurship, and intellectual technology are forcing schools and students to rethink their approach to business once again. This dynamic nature of business will cause the content of business degrees to change constantly. The challenge will be for industry and academic institutions to work together and be flexible so that students will know what they need to know and be able to adjust quickly once they earn that all-important degree.[65]

1. What do you think about going back to the "good old days" when business education was less formal and more general?
2. What changes do you think will occur within business schools in the next 10 to 20 years? What will be the basis for these changes?
3. How are business school students of today different from those in the past? What difference does this make?

Notes

1. J. L. Nichols, *The Business Guide; or Safe Methods of Business*, 18th ed. (Cleveland: Lauer & Mattill, 1890).

2. Daniel A. Wren, *The Evolution of Management Thought*, 3rd ed. (New York: John Wiley and Sons, 1987): 17.

3. Wren, *The Evolution of Management Thought*, 6–7.

4. Wren, 20; and Claude S. George, Jr., *The History of Management Thought* (Englewood Cliffs, NJ: Prentice-Hall, Inc., 1968), 27.

5. Wren, 22–25.

6. Max Weber, *The Protestant Ethic and the Spirit of Capitalism* (New York: Charles Scribner's Sons, 1958; originally published in 1776).

7. Adam Smith, *An Inquiry into the Nature and Causes of the Wealth of Nations* (New York: Modern Library, 1937; originally published in 1776).

8. Smith, *The Wealth of Nations*.

9. Smith, 340.

10. Wren.

11. Claude S. George, Jr., *The History of Management Thought* (Englewood Cliffs, NJ: Prentice-Hall, Inc. 1968), 49.

12. Wren.

13. Frederick W. Taylor, *Scientific Management* (New York: Harper & Row, 1947; originally published in 1911).

14. Wren, 87.

15. Taylor, *Scientific Management*, 21.

16. Taylor.

17. See, for example, Charles D. Wrege and Amedeo G. Perroni, "Taylor's Pig-Tale: A Historical Analysis of Frederick W. Taylor's Pig Iron Experiment," *Academy of Management Journal* 17 (March 1974): 6–27; and Charles D. Wrege and Anne Marie Stotka, "Cooke Creates a Classic: The Story Behind F.W. Taylor's Principles of Scientific Management,' *Academy of Management Review* 3 (October 1978): 736–749.

18. The definitions in this section are based on material presented in William A. Ruch, Harold E. Fearon, and David C. Wieters, *Fundamentals of Production/Operations Management*, 5th ed. (St. Paul: West Publishing, 1992).

19. Daniel A. Wren, "In Memoriam: Lillian Moller Gilbreth (1878–1972)," *Academy of Management Journal* 15 (March 1972): 7–8.

20. W. R. Spriegel and C. F. Meyers, eds., *The Writings of the Gilbreths* (Homewood, IL: Irwin, 1953), 284.

21. Spriegel and Meyers, *The Writings of the Gilbreths*, 152–153.

22. The material on Henry Gantt is from unpublished notes prepared by Dr. Richard Lutz, Management Department, College of Business, University of Akron; and "Famous Firsts: Charting a Way to 'Democracy'," *Business Week*, January 11, 1964, 44–46.

23. The material on Morris Cooke is from unpublished notes prepared by Richard Lutz; and "Famous Firsts: Extending the Scientific Gospel, *Business Week*, April 18, 1964, 132–136.

24. Henri Fayol, *General and Industrial Management* (London: Sir Isaac Pitman & Sons, Ltd., 1949).

25. The material on Henri Fayol is from the preface and body of Henri Fayol, *General and Industrial Management*, with a foreword by L. Urwick (London: Sir Isaac Pitman & Sons Ltd., 1949).

26. Henri Fayol, *General and Industrial Management* (London: Sir Isaac Pitman & Sons, Ltd., 1949).

27. Based on Wren; and Richard Weiss, "Weber on Bureaucracy: Management Consultant or Political Theorist?" *Academy of Management Review* 8 (April 1983): 242–248.

28. Quoted in Reinhard Bendix, *Max Weber: An Intellectual Portrait* (Garden City, NY: Doubleday Co., 1960), 464.

29. Lee D. Parker, "Control in Organizational Life: The Contribution of Mary Parker Follett," *Academy of Management Review* 9 (October 1984): 736–745.

30. "Famous Firsts: Sibyl of a Modern Science," *Business Week*, November 21, 1964, 196ff.

31. Parker, "Control in Organizational Life."

32. Mary Parker Follett, *Creative Experience* (New York: Peter Smith, 1924).

33. Richard H. Franke, "The Hawthorne Experiments: Empirical Findings and Implications for Management," Paper presented at the *Academy of Management* meeting, August 1987, New Orleans.

34. Haney's Appledale Farm, http://www.haneysappledalefarm.com/ (accessed December 8, 2017); Mark Haney, "Agriculture Takes Center Stage as Consumers Drive Local Food Movement," Kentucky Farm Bureau Newsroom, July 7, 2015, http://kyfbnewsroom.com/agriculture-takes-center-stage-as-consumers-drive-local-food-movement/ (accessed December 8, 2017); Mark Haney, "President's Column," *Kentucky Farm Bureau Magazine* 16, No. 8 (October 2017), p. 3, https://www.kyfb.com/federation/newsroom/kentucky-farm-bureau-news/kfbn-2017/october-2017/ (accessed December 8, 2017); Leticia Hendrikson, "Haney's Appledale Farm," Kentucky Heir Blog, October 22, 2010, https://kentuckyheir.com/2010/10/22/haneys-appledale-farm-nancy-kentucky/ (accessed December 8, 2017); Kentucky Department of Agriculture, "Power of the Neighborhood Market," https://www.kyagr.com/marketing/documents/EDU_Power-of-the-Neighborhood-Market.pdf (accessed December 8, 2017); Kentucky Farm Bureau, "Voice of Kentucky Agriculture," July 31, 2017, https://www.kyfb.com/federation/newsroom/kentucky-farm-bureau-the-voice-of-kentucky-agriculture/ (accessed December 8, 2017); Kentucky Farm Bureau, "KFB President Mark Haney Announces Formation of Water Management Working Group," *Kentucky Farm Bureau Magazine* (December 9, 2014), https://www.kyfb.com/federation/newsroom/haney-announces-water-management-working-group/ (accessed December 8, 2017); Kentucky Farm Bureau, "KFB President Mark Haney Emphasizes KFB Loves KY During Annual Address," Kentucky Farm Bureau Newsroom, December, 2, 2016, https://www.kyfb.com/federation/newsroom/kfb-president-mark-haney-emphasizes-kfb-loves-ky-during-annual-address/ (accessed December 8, 2017); "Down on the Farm," Kentucky Living, April 1, 2003, https://www.kentuckyliving.com/archives/down-on-the-farm (accessed December 8, 2017); Kentucky Department of Travel, "Haney's Appledale Farm," 2017, https://www.kentuckytourism.com/haneys-appledale-farm/2267/ (accessed December 8, 2017); Dianne Kroncke, "Give More Than You're Taking—Appledale Farm Interview with Don Haney," Phone Interview, Auburn University, Alabama, November 13, 2017; Diane Kroncke, "Personal Interview, Be the Best," Appledale Farm Interview with Mark Haney, Phone Interview, Auburn University, Alabama, November 29, 2017; Dianne Kroncke, "Personal Interview with Kaycee Rader of Nancy, Kentucky," Grand Floridian, Orlando, Florida, November 20, 2017; Lake Cumberland, Somerset Polaski County Tourism, "Agritourism," 2015, http://www.lakecumberlandtourism.com/explore/agritourism (accessed December 8, 2017); Tricia Neal, "The Nancy Connection," *Commonwealth Journal*, December 9, 2010, http://www.somerset-kentucky.com/news/local_news/the-nancy-connection/article_fb7e5f3a-7366-5f36-bfe0-debdf1bb7960.html (accessed November 12, 2017); Mark Haney, "Mark Haney Association Plans Should Be Part of Health Care Reform; Would Provide Bargaining Power," *Northern Kentucky Tribune*, September 26, 2017, http://www.nkytribune.com/2017/09/mark-haney-association-plans-should-be-part-of-health-care-reform-would-provide-bargaining-power/ (accessed December 8, 2017); University of Kentucky, Agriculture, Integrated Pest Management Programs, College of Agriculture, Food and Environment, "Historical Data on Integrated Pest Management Programs," https://ipm.ca.uky.edu/trapdata (accessed November 27, 2017); "Integrated Pest Management," *Wikipedia*, November 22, 2017, https://en.wikipedia.org/wiki/Integrated_pest_management (accessed December 8, 2017); "Haney's Appledale Farm," Words to Live By, 2017, https://www.wordstoliveby.com/blogs/words-we-live-by/haneys-appledale-farm (accessed December 8, 2017).

35. Richard H. Franke, "The Hawthorne Experiments: Empirical Findings and Implications for Management," paper presented at the *Academy of Management* meeting, August 1987, New Orleans.

36. Franke.

37. Wren, 238.

38. This material is based on information in unpublished notes and materials pertaining to the Hawthorne experiments prepared by Dr. Richard Lutz, University of Akron.

39. John G. Adair, "The Hawthorne Effect: A Reconsideration of the Methodological Artifact," *Journal of Applied Psychology*, 1984, 334–345; Alex Carey, "The Hawthorne Studies: A Radical Criticism," *American Sociological Review*, June 1967, 403–416.

40. Stan Grant, "Inside story of Foxconn shrouded in secrecy," *CNN*, February 6, 2012, http://www.cnn.com/2012/02/06/world/asia/foxconn-worker-difficulties/index.html (accessed September 20, 2013).

41. Fortune, "100 Best Companies to Work For: Ultimate Software," *CNN Money*, 2013, http://money.cnn.com/magazines/fortune/best-companies/2013/snapshots/9.html?iid=bc_sp_list (accessed December 29, 2017).

42. Franke.

43. Carl G. Jung, *Psychological Types* (Princeton, NJ: Princeton University Press, 1921).

44. "70 Years of the MBTI® Assessment," OPP website, https://www.opp.com/en/tools/MBTI/Myers-Briggs-history (accessed December 29, 2017).

45. Fremont E. Kast and James E. Rosenzweig, "General Systems Theory: Applications for Organization and Management," *Academy of Management Journal* 15 (December 1972): 447–465.

46. Kast and Rosenzweig.

47. Wren.

48. Chester I. Barnard, *The Functions of the Executive* (Cambridge, MA: Harvard University Press, 1938), viii, 6.

49. This material on Chester Barnard is based on unpublished notes prepared by Richard Lutz, University of Akron.

50. Wren, 269.

51. Jeremy Main, "The Curmudgeon Who Talks Tough on Quality," *Fortune*, June 25, 1984, 118–122.

52. Lloyd Dobyns Clare Crawford-Mason, *Quality or Else* (Boston: Houghton-Mifflin Company, 1991); John Loring, "Dr. Deming's Traveling Quality Show," *Canadian Business*, September 1990, 38–42.

53. Wren, 358–359.

54. Steven Denning, "The Founder of 21st Century Management: Peter Drucker," *Forbes*, March 1, 2013, https://www.forbes.com/sites/stevedenning/2013/03/01/the-founder-of-21st-century-management-peter-drucker/#52eee1744988 (accessed December 29, 2017).

55. Peter Drucker, *The Practice of Management* (New York: Harper & Row, 1954).

56. Economist staff, "Management by objectives," *The Economist*, October 1, 2009, http://www.economist.com/node/14299761 (accessed December 29, 2017).

57. Rick Wartzman, "Management as a Liberal Art," *Bloomberg Businessweek*, August 7, 2009, https://www.bloomberg.com/news/articles/2009-08-07/management-as-a-liberal-art (accessed December 29, 2017).

58. Peter Drucker, *The Landmarks of Tomorrow* (New York, Harper, 1959).

59. Evan Rosen, "Every Worker Is a Knowledge Worker," *Bloomberg Businessweek*, January 11, 2011, https://www.bloomberg.com/news/articles/2011-01-11/every-worker-is-a-knowledge-worker (accessed December 29, 2017).

60. Jaroslava Kubátová, "Growth of Collective Intelligence by Linking Knowledge Workers through Social Media," *Challenges of the Knowledge Society*, 6th ed. (2012): 1385–1395.

61. Francis Hesselbein, "How Did Peter Drucker See Corporate Responsibility?" *Harvard Business Review*, June 9, 2010, http://blogs.hbr.org/2010/06/how-did-peter-drucker-see-corp/ (accessed December 29, 2017); "Peter Drucker's Life and Legacy," The Drucker Institute, http://www.druckerinstitute.com/link/about-peter-drucker/ (accessed December 29, 2017).

62. Peter Senge, *The Fifth Discipline: The Art and Practice of the Learning Organization* (New York, Doubleday, 2006).

63. Peter Senge, *The Dance of Change: The Challenges of Sustaining Momentum in a Learning Organization* (New York: Crown Business, 1999).

64. Peter Senge, *The Fifth Discipline: The Art and Practice of the Learning Organization* (New York, Doubleday, 2006); David Crookes, "Systems Thinking in Learning Organizations," *Society of Petroleum Engineers*, 22–24.

65. Paul S. Hugstad, *The Business School in the 1980s: Liberalism versus Vocationalism* (New York: Praeger Publishers, 1983); *The Association of Collegiate Schools of Business: 1916–1966* (Homewood, Ill: Richard D. Irwin, Inc., 1966); "Famous Firsts: How Business Schools Began," *Businessweek*, October 12, 1963, 114–116.

The Environment of Management

CHAPTER **3**

Source: Rawpixel.com/Shutterstock

Chapter Outline

After reading this chapter, you will be able to:

- Define the term *environment*.
- Formulate the components of the general environment, task environment, and internal environment.
- Examine the major factors in the general environment.
- Analyze the major factors in the task environment.
- Specify the major factors in the internal environment.
- Explain the stakeholder approach to viewing the environment.
- Distinguish the major ways that an organization can attempt to manage its environment.
- Specify why the external environment is important for organizations.
- Assess the environmental forces affecting business.

Dollar General Invests in Strategic Segmentation

Dollar General's operations are based on understanding its task environment, which includes suppliers, customers, and competitors. In particular, Dollar General has a strong understanding of the economic environment that impacts its customers. The company has overtaken the competition by recognizing that the large income gap in the United States leaves a significant market of locations untouched by rival stores. As such, Dollar General's business model focuses on selling small-ticket items to a target market of low-income consumers on tight budgets. In places like Decatur, Arkansas, a high poverty rate (at 32 percent) and a median household income under $35,000 make the area an unattractive location for larger stores. Many stores are not able to justify entering into a low-income market with a customer base that largely relies on government assistance to buy necessities. However, understanding this market is where Dollar General found its niche.

Larger chain stores—such as Walmart or Whole Foods—along with smaller local stores find it difficult to sustain operations in these markets. Even low-cost retailer Walmart faces a startup cost of $15 million when creating a new Supercenter, in contrast with the $250,000 that Dollar General spends on a new store. Dollar General makes good use of its shelving space, fitting a variety of different products within a space one-tenth the size of a Walmart store. This large assortment of products helps offset the setbacks in customer service some Dollar General stores experience as the company keeps costs low by hiring fewer workers.

Although Dollar General's sales per square foot are about half of Walmart's and far below the industry average, its gross profit margins were 30.9 percent during the years 2012–2017, compared with Walmart's 25.1 percent. In addition to the low startup costs and higher margins, Dollar General does not carry large-ticket purchases like bikes and appliances; instead, it focuses on the basics, such as toilet paper and laundry detergent. Understanding that its leading target market shops paycheck-to-paycheck, the store avoids selling items in bulk like many competitors in the industry.

In 2016, Dollar General's chief executive officer (CEO) Todd Vasos discussed the company's vision to target all of the opportunities in the United States and add to the chain's existing 12,483 stores. The idea was to seek out small and very small towns consisting of low-income households and individuals who rely on government assistance. These are areas that are not looking to thrive economically but primarily to survive in a growing economy. Dollar General announced the intention to add around 1,000 new stores in 2017 as part of its $22 billion expansion plan.

Source: Jonathan Weiss/Shutterstock

Dollar General is not the only company with intentions to expand, however. It faces intense competition from many facets of the industry, ranging from current competitors to new entrants. Historically, its most direct competitor has been Dollar Tree Inc., which also owns Family Dollar and has a business model similar to Dollar General's. According to Dollar Tree Inc., it expects that the U.S. economy can sustain an additional 10,000 Dollar Trees and 15,000 Family Dollars on top of the company's current 14,500 stores.

Despite its higher costs of operations, Walmart could also become a formidable competitor to Dollar General. Walmart is working toward reducing prices, prompting Dollar General to cut prices on hundreds of items. Dollar General must keep prices low, so it has to be aware of products that could be substitutes for the products it sells. Dollar General also knows that as its footprint expands, its costs will likely increase, and it will have to find different ways to compete. After Walmart announced a $2.7 million investment into better employee training and benefits, Dollar General began to boost compensation for managers at some of its stores. This has begun to reduce turnover costs.

Dollar General could face even more change in its external environment. The U.S. Food and Drug Administration is piloting a program allowing those with food assistance cards to order their groceries online. This program could potentially allow larger chains to penetrate low-income areas by bypassing many of the previous barriers. Ten companies have signed on, including Walmart and Amazon.com Inc. Recently, Amazon.com Inc. has made inroads in the grocery market with its acquisition of Whole Foods Market Inc. Despite the fact that these big players may not find immediate success in the rural market, Dollar General has many current and future environmental factors to consider.

Although it may not be providing numerous high-salary jobs or offering top-notch health products, Dollar General offers an option for those who would not otherwise have one. It is committed to continuing its strategy of recognizing and catering to "Anytown, USA."[1]

Introduction

The success of Dollar General comes in large part from the managerial ability to recognize changing trends and understand the competition. Knowledge of the environment in which a business operates is essential. In this chapter, we discuss the interaction between an organization and its environment, and we will answer the following questions: What does the organizational environment mean? Why is it important to an organization? Are certain areas of the environment more pertinent than others? How do managers interact with the environment?

The Nature of the Environment

Managers must constantly be aware of factors both internal and external that affect their decisions and actions. For example, the Dodd-Frank Wall Street Reform and Consumer Protection Act passed in 2010 is likely to have a major impact on financial institutions. The Dodd-Frank Act is intended to reform the financial system by monitoring or reducing the risky financial practices that helped lead to the last recession. Among the provisions of the Dodd-Frank Act was the creation of a somewhat controversial Consumer Financial Protection Bureau to protect consumers from complex financial instruments. Banks, financial institutions, and retailers have to adjust to this change in the external environment.

Another example of changing environmental trends involves the restaurant industry. Various consumer groups' protests about the health risks associated with obesity are leading to many changes in the menus of fast-food restaurants and a more explicit presentation of ingredients on food packages. In 2010, a law was proposed that would require fast-food chains with over 20 locations to place all nutrition facts on menus and vending machines. This law was an attempt to make consumers more aware of the choices they make when eating out. Menu labeling has proven to be challenging and has been opposed by different businesses. Pizza chains across the United States have been resistant, claiming that these regulations would affect growth and hurt the profitability of their franchisees.[2]

We consistently hear how organizations have succeeded or failed due to their adaptation, or lack thereof, to their environment. A major argument for why Eastman Kodak declared bankruptcy is due to its reluctance to invest in digital cameras out of fear that doing so would cannibalize its film business. Managers must be able to determine what factors of the organization's world affect its operation and how these factors may be successfully addressed.

Source: ollyy/Shutterstock

Success is determined by the ability to adapt to the environment, something that Eastman Kodak did not do well in overlooking the impact of digital cameras on the film business.

The **environment** refers to all those factors that affect the operation of the organization. It is inherently complex, with many individuals and groups affecting the firm. Many of these are constantly changing and difficult to control; however, this does not allow managers to ignore them. Managers must learn to perceive the environment accurately in order to deal effectively with these factors. Companies planning to open high-end restaurants during a recession may not be as successful as those offering more lower-priced menu options. Although these restaurants cannot control for economic conditions, they might choose to add discounted items or offer special deals to attract price-conscious consumers.

environment: All of those factors that affect the operation of the organization.

Figure 3.1 presents the components of the environment within which a manager must operate. As you can probably guess, the **external environment** refers to all the factors outside the organization that may affect the managers' actions. While such a definition is

external environment: All of the factors outside the organization that may affect the managers' actions.

FIGURE 3.1
The Organizational Environment

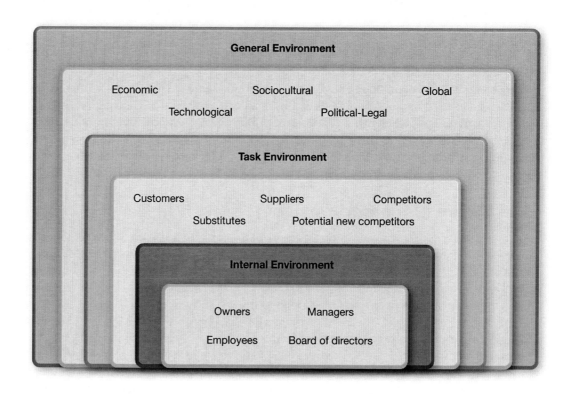

General Environment

Economic   Sociocultural   Global

Technological   Political-Legal

Task Environment

Customers   Suppliers   Competitors

Substitutes   Potential new competitors

Internal Environment

Owners   Managers

Employees   Board of directors

general environment: The broad, complex factors that affect all organizations.

task environment: Those factors that have a direct effect on a specific organization and its managers, including customers, suppliers, competitors, substitutes, and potential new entrants to the industry.

internal environment: All factors that make up the organization, such as the owners, managers, employees, and board of directors.

accurate, it is not very specific. Therefore, we divide the external environment into two parts. The first is the **general environment**, which refers to the broad, complex factors that affect all organizations. These factors include sociocultural, political-legal, technological, economic, and global influences. General Motors and Ford have been significantly impacted by fluctuating oil prices and consumers' growing demand for more energy-efficient vehicles. Both companies have shifted production away from trucks and SUVs to compact fuel-efficient models. However, as the economy began to recover after the most recent recession, sales of SUVs began making a comeback. This demonstrates how quickly the business environment can shift. The makeup and trends in each of these factors are the same for many companies. However, they affect organizations in different ways.

The second part of the external environment is the **task environment**, which is composed of those factors that have a direct effect on a specific organization and its managers, including customers, suppliers, competitors, substitutes, and potential new entrants to the industry. These factors usually vary in importance among organizations. Customer desires, promotions, and product improvements made by competitors greatly impact the cell phone market. However, there can be some factors that are common to several organizations, particularly those that are in the same industry. Within the organization itself is a third element, the **internal environment**, that includes all factors that make up the organization, such as the owners, managers, employees, and board of directors. These factors, of course, directly affect actions that a manager may take. At The Galleon Group, for instance, there was an internal environment that was supportive of using insider trading to make profits. The founder of The Galleon Group, Raj Rajaratnam, allegedly encouraged these illegal tactics and was later convicted of insider trading. On the other hand, the managers at Twitter, Inc.—with over three dozen offices throughout the world—lead their company to success as one of the top 10 most visited websites on the Internet.

The General Environment

The general environment refers to broad factors such as legal systems, population trends, economic conditions, and workers' educational levels. These forces influence all organizations, but they affect different organizations to different degrees. For example, the aging of the U.S. population may result in a potential decrease in consumption for soft drink bottlers but a potential increase for wineries. For the first time, singles outnumber couples in the United States, opening new opportunities for ready-to-eat meals, smaller package sizes, vacations, dating services, and more. As previously stated, we can categorize general environment forces into five groups: sociocultural, political-legal, technological, economic, and global dimensions of the environment.

The Sociocultural Dimension

The **sociocultural dimension** of the general environment includes the demographics, attitudes, and the values of the society within which an organization operates. Influences such as reference groups, social class, opinion leaders, and subcultures are part of the sociocultural dimension. This dimension is especially important because it determines the goods, services, and standards that society values.

sociocultural dimension: The aspect of the general environment that includes the demographics, attitudes, and the values of the society within which an organization operates.

Demographics are measures of various characteristics of the people and social groups who make up a society. Age, gender, and income are examples of commonly used demographic characteristics—often major determinants of consumer demand. For instance, Preference hair color targets women, Axe body spray is targeted toward young males, and Gymboree appeals to parents of young children.

Values refer to certain beliefs that affect different evaluations and behavior related to firms and products. Changes in how a society values an item or behavior can greatly affect a business. For instance, changes in how society views what is "healthy" have had

Source: Warren Goldswain/Shutterstock

Age and gender are common demographic measures.

a tremendous impact on the fast-food industry, with the elimination of trans-fats in many foods. The city of New York has gone so far as to make trans-fats illegal. In an attempt to further this ban, former mayor Michael Bloomberg tried to ban sugary soft drinks exceeding 16 ounces. His plan was to limit those being sold in restaurants, stadiums, and movie theaters, among other places. Many groups opposed such a ban, and it was revoked after a state judge blocked it.[3] Boston Market has also responded to health concerns by lowering the sodium in three of its signature items and removing salt shakers for in-restaurant dining tables.[4] Our values concerning the meaning of the word "healthy" continue to evolve, with consumers demanding food that is both tasty and more nutritious.

The Political-Legal Dimension

political-legal dimension: Within the general environment, the nature of the relationship between various areas of government and the organization.

The **political-legal dimension** of the general environment refers to the nature of the relationship between various areas of government and the organization. This dimension, composed of the political, legal, and regulatory elements, is important to organizations for several reasons:

1. It can constrain how a business operates. For instance, the Clayton Antitrust Act prevents anticompetitive activity by prohibiting certain types of conduct. Price discrimination, exclusive dealing, being a director of two or more competing corporations, and rules relating to mergers and acquisitions require compliance with the legal environment. Both Microsoft and Intel have been fined by the European Union for antitrust activities. In addition, regulations in other countries also impact the general environment. Table 3.1 lists some of the most important laws impacting business in the United States.

2. Manipulation of the political-legal processes can provide major competitive advantages to organizations. For example, the U.S. healthcare industry has lobbied against healthcare reform and government-sponsored healthcare for many years out of fear that it would cut into private companies' profits. Table 3.2 provides examples of organizations that spend money on lobbying. Note the prevalence of the medical, defense, telecommunications, and technology companies. These industries are often heavily regulated, and new legislation could have a profound impact on the operations of these firms.

3. The political-legal dimension provides stability within which organizations can effectively plan and operate. The basis of most business relationships is the legal contract that spells out the obligations and duties of the respective parties. Failure to abide by such a legal document may result in a lawsuit that requires the offending party to pay damages to "make the other party whole." Most ethical disputes between companies and/or consumers are addressed through lawsuits.

TABLE 3.1 Major Federal Laws That Affect Business Decisions

Name and Date Enacted	Purpose
Sherman Antitrust Act (1890)	Prohibits contracts, combinations, or conspiracies to restrain trade; establishes as a misdemeanor monopolizing or attempting to monopolize.
Clayton Act (1914)	Prohibits specific practices such as price discrimination, exclusive-dealer arrangements, and stock acquisitions whose effect may noticeably lessen competition or tend to create a monopoly.
Federal Trade Commission Act (1914)	Created the Federal Trade Commission; also gives the FTC investigatory powers to be used in preventing unfair methods of competition.
Robinson-Patman Act (1936)	Prohibits price discrimination that lessens competition among wholesalers or retailers; prohibits producers from giving disproportionate services or facilities to large buyers.

TABLE 3.1 Major Federal Laws That Affect Business Decisions *(Continued)*

Name and Date Enacted	Purpose
Wheeler-Lea Act (1938)	Prohibits unfair and deceptive acts and practices regardless of whether competition is injured; places advertising of foods and drugs under the jurisdiction of the FTC.
Lanham Act (1946)	Provides protections for and regulation of brand names, brand marks, trade names, and trademarks.
Celler-Kefauver Act (1950)	Prohibits any corporation engaged in commerce from acquiring the whole or any part of the stock or other share of the capital assets of another corporation when the effect would substantially lessen competition or tend to create a monopoly.
Fair Packaging and Labeling Act (1966)	Prohibits unfair or deceptive packaging or labeling of consumer products.
Magnuson-Moss Warranty (FTC) Act (1975)	Provides for minimum disclosure standards for written consumer product warranties; defines minimum consent standards for written warranties; allows the FTC to prescribe interpretive rules in policy statements regarding unfair or deceptive practices.
Consumer Goods Pricing Act (1975)	Prohibits the use of price maintenance agreements among manufacturers and resellers in interstate commerce.
Trademark Counterfeiting Act (1984)	Imposes civil and criminal penalties against those who deal in counterfeit consumer goods or any counterfeit goods that can threaten health or safety.
Trademark Law Revision Act (1988)	Amends the Lanham Act to allow brands not yet introduced to be protected through registration with the Patent and Trademark Office.
Nutrition Labeling and Education Act (1990)	Prohibits exaggerated health claims; requires all processed foods to contain labels with nutritional information.
Telephone Consumer Protection Act (1991)	Establishes procedures to avoid unwanted telephone solicitations; prohibits marketers from using an automated telephone dialing system or an artificial or prerecorded voice to certain telephone lines.
Federal Trademark Dilution Act (1995)	Grants trademark owners the right to protect trademarks and requires relinquishment of names that match or parallel existing trademarks.
Digital Millennium Copyright Act (1996)	Refined copyright laws to protect digital versions of copyrighted materials, including music and movies.
Children's Online Privacy Protection Act (1998)	Regulates the collection of personally identifiable information (name, address, e-mail address, hobbies, interests, or information collected through cookies) online from children under age 13.
Do-Not-Call Implementation Act (2003)	Directs the FCC and FTC to coordinate so that their rules are consistent regarding telemarketing call practices including the Do Not Call Registry and other lists, as well as call abandonment; in 2008, the FTC amended its rules and banned prerecorded sales pitches for all but a few cases.
Credit CARD Act (2009)	Implements strict rules on credit card companies regarding topics such as issuing credit to youths, terms disclosure, interest rates, and fees.
Dodd-Frank Wall Street Reform and Consumer Protection Act (2010)	Promotes financial reform to increase accountability and transparency in the financial industry, protects consumers from deceptive financial practices, and establishes the Bureau of Consumer Financial Protection.

TABLE 3.2 Organizations That Engage in Lobbying

AT&T	AFL-CIO (union)
Google	American Federation of Teachers
Blue Cross/Blue Shield	Chevron
U.S. Chamber of Commerce	Direct Selling Association

The *political element* of the political-legal dimension refers to businesses' involvement in forming public policy. Businesses' use of political action committees (PACs) and other groups trying to modify key pieces of legislation on both the national and local level has become incredibly widespread. In addition, businesses have increasingly had to contend with various interest groups, such as groups opposed to high-fructose corn syrup or artificial sweeteners in foods.

The legal element is the use of the judicial branches of government to resolve disputes between parties. The traditional basis for litigation constituted contracts and torts (legal wrongs), such as negligence. However, recent developments in such areas as strict product liability and class-action lawsuits have expanded the potential liability for a firm. Unsuccessfully pursuing a case in court may have unpleasant public relation effects as well as financial losses.

The third part of the political-legal dimension is the regulatory element. Table 3.3 lists some of the more prominent regulatory agencies applying federal regulations and laws that can greatly affect organizational operations. The Federal Trade Commission, for example, regulates trade practices and is empowered to investigate illegal activities.

Source: Mark Poprocki/Shutterstock

Political action committees are used by businesses to influence pending legislation and regulations.

Business organizations commonly view government regulation negatively because complying with regulations increases the cost of doing business. Managers often think that regulation limits businesses' decision options. For example, the Sarbanes-Oxley legislation requires large public firms to spend millions of dollars annually to document their compliance with legal, regulatory, and corporate governance related to financial activities.

technological dimension: Within the general environment, the knowledge and process of changing inputs (resources, labor, and money) to outputs (goods and services).

The Technological Dimension

The **technological dimension** of the general environment refers to the knowledge and process of changing inputs (resources, labor, and money) to outputs (goods and services). An understanding of a business's technology component can have an important impact on its profitability and growth. Understanding the technological infrastructure in international transactions is of special importance to organizations.

TABLE 3.3 U.S. Regulatory Bodies Affecting American Business

Consumer Product Safety Commission	Occupational Safety and Health Review Commission
Environmental Protection Agency	Federal Communications Commission
Department of Justice	National Labor Relations Board
Equal Employment Opportunity Commission	Federal Reserve Board
Food and Drug Administration	Surface Transportation Board
Federal Trade Commission	Nuclear Regulatory Commission
National Transportation Safety Board	Federal Energy Regulatory Commission
Securities & Exchange Commission	Federal Deposit Insurance Corporation
Consumer Financial Protection Bureau	

Many of the habits and behaviors of consumers are influenced by technology. Because of the technological innovations in communications marketers can now reach vast numbers of people cheaply and efficiently through a variety of media. Text messaging, mobile advertisements, and social networking help marketers interact with customers, make appointments, and handle last-minute orders or cancellations. Because of the popularity and convenience of text messaging, marketers are responding to the change in consumer behavior. Restaurants, for example, can send their lunch specials to subscribers' cell phones, along with coupons and other discounts.

The vast majority of U.S. homes have Internet access. The Internet is a major tool for communicating, researching, shopping, and even entertaining. The use of video online, especially through YouTube, exploded in the first decade of the twenty-first century. Smartphones allow consumers to access the Internet on the move. Streaming over Netflix has supplanted video rental shops. However, while the Internet has made lives easier in some respects, we are increasingly concerned about protecting our privacy and intellectual property. Websites and online firms such as Megaupload and Pirate Bay have enabled illegal downloading of copyrighted content.

It is important for firms to identify technologies that have the potential to change an industry. For example, wireless devices in use today include radios, smartphones, tablet computers, TVs, and car keys. Companies must keep up with trends and adapt to technological advances to remain competitive. The degree to which a business is technologically based also influences its managers' response to technology.

The effect of technology on society relates to the process of change, the spread of the technology, and the resilient nature of the technology. The process of change refers to the extent that change affects societal structures and institutions, including social relationships, regulations, and the education system. The advent of online streaming, for instance, is changing the way people watch and purchase movies. Consumers can now pay a flat fee every month on sites such as Netflix and Hulu for unlimited access to a variety of TV shows and movies, which is taking market share away from more traditional video stores and movie theaters. Spread refers to the extent of the technology's impact across society. For instance, MP3 players have changed the way that most Americans listen to music, allowing them to customize the songs they listen to for less expensive prices than traditional CDs. Finally, the resilient nature of technology refers to the way that it strongly facilitates faster development of technological advances and other innovations. Whereas

Source: JMiks/Shutterstock

QR codes allow consumers to scan ads, signs, and billboards to learn more about a company's products.

it once took years to develop new products, technology has enabled companies to introduce new products quicker—in some cases, a matter of months. One need only look at the technological industry itself to note the continual obsolescence of products and the introduction of upgraded versions.

The Economic Dimension

economic dimension: The overall condition of the complex interactions of economies throughout the world.

The **economic dimension** reflects the overall condition of the complex interactions of economies throughout the world. Certain economic conditions of special concern to organizations include interest rates, inflation, unemployment rates, gross national product, and the value of the U.S. dollar against other currencies. For example, the value of the Japanese yen or the European Union's euro versus the U.S. dollar affects the relative prices of exports and imports from these countries. Changing economic conditions can greatly affect how organizations react. For instance, during times of high interest rates, the cost of borrowing money increases, making it more difficult for the firm to expand. More recently, interest rates have been low, but the availability of money has been tight. Businesses, as well as consumers, have had difficulty qualifying for loans. Conversely, high unemployment rates mean that labor is more available at a lower price.

The general economic climate greatly affects the organization's prosperity and survival. During "boom" or growth periods, consumers are more likely to purchase the firm's products and capital is easier to acquire, facilitating expansion and increased production. When growth slows, as in a recession, customers stop buying, unemployment rises, profit margins drop, and production declines. Some businesses do well in a recession. For example, Costco's sales increase as customers search for deals and make more prudent buying decisions. Companies like McDonald's also fare well as families trade down from more expensive restaurants.

One of the key economic issues in the U.S. economy is arguably the budget deficit. For many years, the government has spent more than it received in tax revenues, so it has borrowed money to cover the difference. Many economists have argued that this practice acts as a drag on the domestic economy. Others, however, have argued just the opposite. The major U.S. tax reform legislation of 2017, for example, will increase the U.S. gov-

Source: MaxxiGo/Shutterstock

Global economic indicators include stock market performance, interest rates, and employment levels.

ernment deficit by a massive $1.5 trillion over a period of ten years. The idea is that by significantly cutting taxes, particularly taxes on corporate income, much greater U.S. economic growth and investment will occur. Stay tuned!

The **global dimension** of the general environment refers to those factors in other countries that affect the organization. There is no doubt that the global dimension is becoming increasingly important to almost all aspects of business. U.S. firms engage in a variety of international trading relations. They may export or import products, license their trademarks or products to overseas companies, engage in joint ventures with foreign partners, or go international in the building of facilities. Some firms like Google and Amazon were born global, treating the entire world as their market.

International business is a two-way relationship. American firms such as Boeing, Microsoft, and AT&T have long-established international presences. Firms such as Subway are rapidly growing their international presence through franchising. Subway has surpassed McDonald's as the world's largest chain of restaurants.[5]

When U.S. businesses venture abroad, they need to thoroughly understand the elements of the environment in which they will operate. Consumer buying habits abroad may be completely different from those in the United States. Governmental expectations toward business will differ significantly. For example, the business environments of China and the United States create the need for major adaptations in business operations. In India, large foreign retailers such as Walmart had to enter into joint ventures with local companies if they wanted to open stores in the country. Expectations about cost and service may also be quite different.

global dimension: Pertaining to the general environment, those factors in other countries that affect the organization.

The Task Environment

The task environment includes a firm's competitors in industry as well as those parties that have a direct influence on the industry and firm. These include suppliers, customers, organizations that produce substitute goods or services, and current and potential new competitors. It is the overall impact of these five different factors that has a major effect on the overall profitability and competitive position of the firm within its industry.

Suppliers are organizations and individuals who provide resources to other organizations. They supply inputs such as products, raw materials, capital, labor, and information. Their power lies in their ability to control the flow of these inputs and set prices. Suppliers in China have a significant advantage over U.S. firms with lower wages and production costs. Thus, the power of a supplier is related to the prices of its products. A business is at an advantage if it has many suppliers for a particular resource and at a disadvantage if it has only a few. A supplier may also be in a strong position if the cost of switching suppliers is high. In retailing, we have seen a dramatic shift in power from big suppliers such as Johnson & Johnson and Proctor & Gamble to big-box retailers and discounters such as Walmart. However, the actions of suppliers can still have a profound effect on retailing. For example, Lululemon recently could not supply stores with enough inventory when suppliers did not provide fabric in a timely manner.

As another example, airlines have a limited number of manufacturers from which to buy aircraft. These manufacturers can essentially determine the delivery time of most orders and limit the number of optional features that can be provided. When the airline industry was stronger economically and its members were enjoying high demand, the airplane manufacturers' ability to deliver new planes was a major factor in the strategic planning of carriers such as Delta and American Airlines. Moreover, the availability of planes limited future planning. On the other hand, for fast-food restaurants such as McDonald's, Wendy's, and Burger King, suppliers for potatoes are plentiful and relatively easy to

suppliers: Organizations and individuals who provide resources to other organizations.

change. They have very little control or power over restaurants and do not ordinarily limit the restaurants' planning or operation.

Customers

customers: Those who purchase an organization's goods and/or services.

Customers, of course, are those who purchase an organization's goods and/or services. They may be individuals or other organizations. A customer may be the final recipient (user) of the good or service or serve as an intermediary. Clothing stores, for example, are the customers of either manufacturers or distributors. These stores, in turn, sell the garments to their individual customers. Because of a need for products, we typically think of the customer as being dependent on the business. However, the customer is also a powerful force in an organization's operation.

The power of the customer increases in the following situations:

1. The firm's product is not significantly different from that of its competitors. Many financial institutions, for example, offer MasterCard or Visa credit cards. The customer can easily change among these institutions. Consequently, companies that issue these cards continually gather information about customer attitudes and needs for additional services. For example, rewards for purchases may vary a great deal. Customer influence in the organization's operations is very evident.

2. The cost of the product is a significant expense for the customer. Consumers usually have more stringent standards of product features for automobiles, boats, and retirement investments than for magazines, shoes, and video games. They will more seriously attempt to negotiate a reduced price or special features for expensive items. Expensive items often involve shopping, while inexpensive items are usually purchased as convenience items.

3. The customer is a major buyer of the firm's total goods or services. Because of this, the firm actually depends on the buyer. Many businesses are in this situation because they become suppliers to firms like Best Buy, Walmart, and Costco. One substantial order automatically makes that customer an important factor in the organization's operations. The customer can exert great control on the supplier because of the dependency of the supplier.

Source: Kinga/Shutterstock

Customers are the purchasers of products for personal use or act as an intermediary in an organizational purchase.

Substitutes

Substitutes are goods or services that may be used in place of those furnished by a given business. Substitutes for a company's goods or services can limit how much it may charge. For example, if its price is low enough, plastic may be an attractive substitute for rubber—assuming it can be used for the same purpose. Often substitutes come as a result of technological innovation.

substitutes: Goods or services that may be used in place of those furnished by a given business.

Substitutes can have a very serious effect on a business by diminishing or eliminating consumers' demand for its products. Red Bull is sometimes substituted for Pepsi and Coca-Cola, cutting into market share. Depending on the cost of the substitute, its effect can be quite rapid.

Competitors

Competitors are other organizations that produce similar, or in some cases identical, goods or services. Many jewelry stores order their rings, pins, and earrings from the same limited number of suppliers. The only differences among jewelers may be in the (usually) small number of crafted items. Similarly, automobile dealers compete not only with other dealers who have the same vehicles but also with those who sell rival makes and models. Through websites such as cars.com, customers can shop for availability at the lowest price.

competitors: Other organizations that produce similar, or in some cases identical, goods or services.

Competitors are often the most powerful force in a firm's operations. Prices, services, and after-sales support are all directly compared with those of competitors. Home Depot and Lowe's are in direct competition in the home improvement market. They often locate across the street from one another's stores. All companies attempt to gain an advantage on competitors in some part of the business operation, and they hope this advantage will result in increased sales. Lowe's claims to have a more comfortable atmosphere that women prefer. Companies are constantly monitoring others in the same field and trying to anticipate what they might do in the future. Sometimes, responses to competitors may actually be costly to the organization.

Some competitors are very large and dominate the industry, whereas others are very small and not dominant players in the marketplace.

On the other hand, sometimes it is not apparent who a company's competitors are. For example, who are the competitors of Dunkin' Donuts? We can look first at other large national competitors. Tim Horton's started in Canada but recently merged with U.S.-based Burger King, and it is expanding considerably in the United States. Starbucks offers coffee drinks and other breakfast items to compete with Dunkin' Donuts offerings. There may also be regional and local rivals, such as bakeries, and other businesses, such as supermarkets, that make donuts as part of their larger marketing efforts. In addition, Dunkin' Donuts now has to contend with microwave donuts and prepackaged donuts from companies like Dolly Madison.

Potential New Competitors

If an industry is profitable, it will attract the attention of other businesses seeking expansion opportunities and pose a threat to those already in the industry. **Potential new competitors**, then, are companies not currently operating in a business's industry but which have a high potential for entering the industry. Businesses must collect information concerning the probability of entry of these interested organizations. They must also ensure that their own operations are as efficient as possible and that their goods and services do not have any major weaknesses of which these potential new entrants could take

potential new competitors: Companies not currently operating in a business's industry but which have a high potential for entering the industry.

advantage. The decision to enter an industry will depend, in part, on the barriers—the costs and difficulties—to entry. High barriers include the following:

- *High entrance costs:* These costs could be because of expensive equipment, location, or lack of availability of skilled employees. The automobile industry requires high entrance costs to break into it, which is one major reason why there are only a few automobile companies today. It would be impossible to build a new railroad and compete with Burlington Northern.

- *Economies of scale:* These represent the reduction in production costs that is the result of making and selling goods in large quantities. More specifically, it means that the cost per unit goes down as the organization produces more units. Existing organizations are probably already operating at a high volume; any new entrant must have a large number of customers from the outset to be competitive with those companies already in the industry. The steel industry is incredibly difficult to enter because of the large sunk costs of setting up factories for production and because any new competitors must be able to sell goods as cheaply as established firms.

- *Lack of access to distribution channels:* If an organization cannot get its products into the hands of customers, it may not succeed. For new competitors, it is hard to get products into highly established markets, including retailers such as Target and Walmart. However, websites and online retailers such as Amazon have increased the ability to gain access to distribution.

- *Lack of technical expertise:* Each industry has a specific set of knowledge and skills necessary to deliver goods or services. Many industries, such as pharmaceuticals, engineering, and technology require high levels of technical expertise and research and development resources to be competitive. Sometimes unique skills and technical expertise can put one company at an advantage over the other. For instance, many electronics and computer firms have tried to copy Apple's business strategies but have not been able to definitively figure out how to replicate them.

The Internal Environment

The makeup of a firm's internal environment can vary greatly. We will discuss characteristics of this environment, such as job design, organizational structure, work teams, employee motivation, and human resources management programs, in later chapters. Consequently, we will address only briefly some of the broad factors of the internal environment here. Regardless of organizational form, size, or scope, all firms have owners, managers, and employees. Additionally, state laws require all corporations to have boards of directors. Frequently, public institutions and unincorporated businesses will have an equivalent group in the form of a board of trustees.

Owners

Owners can have various degrees of influence and power within an organization. Small entrepreneurial firms normally have a very "hands-on" owner (or owners) who seek to have control over all aspects of the firm. In corporations, shareholders collectively hold ownership. However, many shareholders see their possession of stock not as a form of ownership, but rather as a form of investment, and consequently they do not seek to exert control over management. This has led to a separation of ownership and control in many corporations.

A current trend involves large institutional investors, mostly mutual funds and pension funds, exerting increasing control over corporate management. These institutional investors are demanding greater upper management accountability. For instance, shareholders are demanding better alignment between executive compensation and business

Apple Puts a Shine on Its Retail Experience

Apple recognizes that many internal and external decisions and actions that affect the operation of the organization must be understood. Apple's success is based on the ability to deal effectively with a changing environment. Over the past five years, Apple has competed against Google for the title of the most valuable brand in the world. Much of Apple's success can be attributed to its innovative products, such as the iPad, iPod, and iPhone. Apple is an expert at the technological dimension of the general environment. The company has garnered a reputation for discovering consumers' technological needs before the consumers themselves know they have them. However, Apple has also made a profound mark in the world of retailing. Its stores, which were first opened in 2001, are the fastest-growing retail stores in history. An obvious draw is store design—modern and spacious, creating a relaxed, low-pressure atmosphere. The stores are like showrooms that allow customers to test products and take educational classes.

To truly understand Apple's retail success, it is important to look beneath the surface. According to *Forbes* contributor Steve Denning, two keys to Apple's success are *delight the customer* and *avoid selling*. At Apple retail stores, the customer comes first. Apple focuses extensively on meeting customer needs and wants. This focus significantly alters employee behavior and complements the *avoid selling* mantra. Rather than pushing products on consumers, Apple store employees are asked to listen and assist. Employees go through extensive training to prepare for any situation that may arise. They are trained to speak with customers within two minutes of them entering the store and focus on nonverbal cues to determine how customers are feeling. The company displays products throughout the store to showcase what the company has to offer and encourage customers to engage with Apple employees. Apple also installed iPad stations equipped with a customer service app designed to answer customer questions. If the customer requires additional assistance, he or she can press a help button on the app, and an Apple employee will promptly address the customer's question.

Apple has been so successful in the retail arena that other stores are looking to adopt its retail strategies. At one point, Apple measured its retail profitability and found that annual retail sales per square foot totaled $4,406. This excludes online sales, which, taken together, make Apple more profitable per square foot than many luxury retailers. With nearly 500 stores lo-

Apple products continue to be successful and in high demand.

cated in 17 different countries, Apple is hands-down one of the most profitable and valuable retail spaces in the world.

Despite its success, however, Apple is always looking for ways to improve the customer experience. The company is determined to keep its retail stores relevant and exciting for customers. Apple's retail chief announced the firm's intention to expand from being a place that sells gadgets to assuming a more "town square" feel that incorporates the entire community. For instance, stores are adding what Apple calls "boardrooms" dedicated specifically to business customers. Apple wants to expand what it calls its "genius bar," which offers tech support for Apple software and hardware, to a "genius grove" with employees who specialize in more specific areas of customer support. Apple even plans to expand some of its more lucrative stores by adding public plazas that will offer free Wi-Fi and host events. Apple desires to make its stores less of a "shopping" destination and more of a place for "hanging out."

In an attempt to compete, Microsoft and Sony have opened some of their own stores. Other industries are using Apple products to enhance their businesses. It is likely that if Apple's new concept of a community store takes hold, competitors will follow suit with similar store redesigns. Yet the success and popularity of Apple stores create significant barriers for new competitors wishing to enter the market. Apple's blend of exceptional products, appealing stores, and knowledgeable and dedicated employees creates a top-notch customer experience and is having enormous repercussions for the retail industry as a whole.[6]

performance. For example, shareholders at Citigroup initially rejected the bank's proposed executive compensation plan because they felt the firm was not doing well enough to warrant high executive compensation. However, shareholders later ultimately approved a plan for enhanced executive pay after firm performance clearly improved.[7]

Managers

In the smallest companies, the owner is the sole manager of the firm and fulfills all typical management tasks. As the organization expands and becomes more complex, however, the owner will normally bring in additional persons to act as managers.

For the purpose of interacting with the external environment, we can identify three types of managers: strategic or institutional, technical, and operational. Strategic managers normally are involved with setting the overall direction of the organization. James Quincy, CEO of Coca-Cola, is a strategic manager who helps set the direction for the company. Usually from top management, they are concerned primarily with macroeconomic factors. Technical managers serve under the strategic managers and act to coordinate the various levels—that is, to serve as the middle managers. Operations managers are the ones who in some manner transform the organizational inputs into finished outputs; they are typically lower-level line managers or supervisors.

Recent trends in American business indicate that many organizations are "flattening" the organizational hierarchy and eliminating many of the technical managers. This has brought the strategic and operational levels into more immediate contact and is intended to improve communication and bring the strategic managers "closer" to the customer.[8] This also increases the draw of empowerment for the managers.

Employees

One important way of classifying employees is as unionized and non-unionized. The difference between these two groups is important in terms of their effect on the internal environment. Unionized employees are represented by labor unions, which, in essence, attempt to exert a strong influence on wages, working conditions, and job duties through a negotiation process with management called collective bargaining. Thus, the relationship between managers and unionized employees is quite different from that between managers and non-unionized employees. The former relationship is more formalized and dictated by the negotiated contract between the union and the organization. The desire to compete more effectively globally has resulted in unions in the auto industry making concessions to facilitate more price competitiveness with global firms. The number of unionized employees has been decreasing in recent years.

Two general environmental factors, sociocultural and technological, are affecting the demands of management on employees. Changing demographics is creating an older and more culturally diverse workforce, and technological change is forcing employees to acquire more complex skills. When these factors are coupled with an increase in the use of relatively low-paid, skilled foreign workers in countries such as those in China and India, tremendous challenges are created for the American worker. Many organizations are trying to meet these challenges by increasing employees' skills through training and then turning to employee involvement programs to take advantage of these skills. Ford has used simulated factories to train its factory workers before they begin work in the plant.[9]

Corporate Governance

corporate governance: The formal system of oversight, accountability, and control for organizational decisions and resources.

Corporate governance is the formal system of oversight, accountability, and control for organizational decisions and resources. Most corporations have some form of oversight that involves a system of checks and balances that limit the chance that employees and managers will deviate from corporate policies. Another key idea when discussing governance is accountability, which relates to how well the workplace decisions are aligned with a firm's strategic direction. Firms also need control, which involves the process of

You're the Manager . . . What Would You Do?

THE COMPANY: Travera Motors
YOUR POSITION: Strategy Consultant
THE PLACE: Silicon Valley, California

Travera Motors is an electric car company founded in 2000 with the purpose of addressing a growing change in the general automobile environment: carbon emissions. Because of the increasing attention that the effects of global warming have received, many people are changing their behaviors to reduce their carbon footprint. Travera Motors saw an opportunity in this shift of the sociocultural dimension of the environment. It decided to design an electric vehicle that produced zero carbon emissions. The end goal of the company is to reach the mass market in a matter of 10 years with an affordable and convenient alternative to gas guzzling vehicles.

One major challenge the company has faced is the lack of widespread electric charging stations. This has made purchasing these vehicles impractical for some consumers. On the other hand, the company is encouraged by changes in the political-legal dimension of the general environment. Because the government wants to promote reduction in emissions, it is offering subsidies and tax breaks for those who purchase a Travera Motors vehicle.

Founder and millionaire Martin Ross knows that in order to achieve his goal of reducing emissions, he not only has to create a completely electric vehicle but also has to invest in the infrastructure that supports these vehicles. Ross began by creating a high-end luxury sports car that targeted an affluent customer base. He believed this would serve to build profits to reinvest in the technology, which, in turn would eventually drive down costs so those in the mass market could afford to purchase the vehicles. Travera Motors did not want to compromise its sustainability initiative by making a hybrid vehicle (electric and gas capabilities). The goal is to be as sustainable as possible. Ross knows that another aspect of being true to his goal requires that he structure his operations to rely on renewable energy sources.

Through increasing progress in the technological dimension of the environment, Travera released its sports car model, the Travera 2000, for $100,000 in 2003. The hype over the vehicle and its technology was widespread, and over the next four years, the company sold over 2,500 units. While this was not a lot of sales, it was enough to continue investing in the infrastructure, in renewable energy sources to support Travera's operations, and in building a more affordable family-style

Source: GLYPHstock/Shutterstock

Travera Motors manufactures environmentally friendly automobiles.

vehicle. In 2008 a lower-cost family-style model made its debut as the Travera 3000, priced at $71,000. This vehicle also received recognitions, such as safest car on the road and Car of the Year.

Despite the company's progress, it is clear that it will not be able to meet its 10-year goal due to economic dimensions, such as consumer purchasing power. While the Travera 3000 is less expensive than the Travera 2000, it is still in a higher price range than most people can afford. Additionally, while the electric charging infrastructure has improved, it is still not convenient for many consumers. Martin Ross has tasked you with devising a plan for the company.

QUESTIONS

1. Discuss in detail the various elements of the general environment that Travera is dealing with (sociocultural, political-legal, technological, and economic dimensions). How are they affecting the company, and how might the company control these dimensions?

2. Martin Ross may be stretching himself and his resources too thin by trying to build the vehicles, create a widespread charging infrastructure, and use only renewable energy sources. While this is an admirable plan, is it sustainable for the business? What are some ways he could lift some of the burden off his shoulders and still achieve his goals? (Think about licensing his technology to larger automakers who have more resources as well as other alternatives.)

3. Is reaching the 10-year goal important? Why not just add five more years to the plan? What would the consequences be?

auditing and improving organizational decisions and actions. The firm's board's philosophy regarding oversight, accountability, and control directly affects how effective corporate governance is.

In corporations, the board of directors has the important task of representing the stockholders in their capacity as owners. Elected by the stockholders, the board is charged with ensuring that the corporation is being managed so as to increase stockholder wealth. The board is normally called on to approve major strategic decisions and to hire key personnel, most notably the chief executive officer (CEO).

In many corporations, however, the board seldom plays a major role. The CEO often controls the board through his or her nomination of board members, and the CEO often influences the board through company perks and lucrative consulting contracts. As a result, critics argue that boards of directors do not exert the control they are legally obligated to provide.

Corporate governance has become an increasingly salient topic in the twenty-first century, as a series of high-profile governance failures have put a spotlight on the issue. The Sarbanes-Oxley Act provided the most significant piece of corporate governance reform since the 1930s. Now both CEOs and CFOs are required to verify and certify that their quarterly and annual financial reports are accurate and honest reflections of firm's performance. The act required more independence of boards of directors, protected whistle-blowers, and established a Public Company Accounting Oversight Board. Even this legislation was not comprehensive enough to stop a major corporate governance meltdown in the financial industry in the latter part of the decade, however. The failure of firms such as AIG, Bear Stearns, and Countrywide again made people question the ethics of these corporations and made many clamor for even stronger reforms and legislation to support better corporate governance and oversight. This led to the passage of the Dodd-Frank Act in 2010. Among its provisions, the Dodd-Frank Act created a whistleblower bounty program to encourage whistle-blowers to report misconduct. Whistleblower reports that result in convictions of more than $1 million can receive 10 to 30 percent of the sanction.[10]

primary stakeholders: Those who have a formal and/or contractual relationship with the firm, such as customers, suppliers, employees, regulators, investors, and communities.

secondary stakeholders: Groups that have a less formal connection to the organization, such as environmentalists, special interest groups, and the media.

stakeholder orientation: The degree to which a firm understands and addresses stakeholder demands.

Stakeholder View of the Environment

One way managers evaluate the environment is through the *stakeholder view*. A stakeholder is a person or a group that can affect, or is affected by, an organization's goals or the means to achieve those goals.[11] Stakeholders for a particular firm may include **primary stakeholders**, or those who have a formal and/or contractual relationship with the firm, such as customers, suppliers, employees, regulators, investors, and communities. **Secondary stakeholders** are groups that have a less formal connection to the organization, such as environmentalists, special interest groups, and the media. The degree to which a firm understands and addresses stakeholder demands is called a firm's **stakeholder orientation**. This orientation comprises three sets of activities: (1) the organization-wide generation of data about stakeholder groups and assessment of the firm's effects on these groups, (2) the distribution of this information throughout the firm, and (3) the organization's responsiveness as a whole to this intelligence.

In the stakeholder view, the firms and agents in the external environment are interrelated. Also, external stakeholders may be related themselves—for example, consumer groups and broadcast media.

Source: arka38/Shutterstock

These six groups are primary stakeholders of the organization.

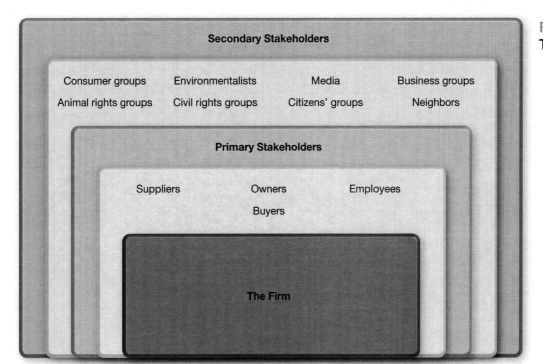

FIGURE 3.2
The Stakeholder View

Key to this view is that there is a two-way interaction between the stakeholder and the firm. The firm is at the center of a network of actors that the organization can hopefully identify and then manage. As stakeholders become more informed and vocal, a stakeholder orientation has become increasingly important for firms. Figure 3.2 illustrates the stakeholder view of the environment.

Identifying Stakeholders

The first step of interacting with the environment is to identify the specific individuals and groups that affect the organization. Stakeholders are in a position of power relative to the firm because they are in a position to withhold organizational resources through mechanisms like boycotts and negative publicity. The manager is concerned with creating a **stakeholder map,** a representation of the organization's stakeholders and their stakes. A stake can be of three basic types: an equity interest, such as a stockholder or lender may have; a market interest, which might be shared by buyers or suppliers; or an influencing interest, which may be represented by the government or an interest group.[12] The ability to visualize this universe through a stakeholder map is necessary for deciding how to manage the environment properly. For instance, a small coffee shop near a college campus might identify its primary customers as college students. Employees tend to be students working part-time to pay for school. Regulators would include the local government. Since the coffee shop also has to obey federal laws and pay taxes, the federal and state governments are also important considerations. Figure 3.3 shows a simplified hypothetical stakeholder map for a toymaker.

stakeholder map: A representation of the organization's stakeholders and their stakes.

Gathering Information about Stakeholders in the Environment

Once the stakeholder map has been determined, the next step is to set up organizational processes for collecting information about the stakeholders. Such information allows the organization to anticipate changes in its environment and develop plans to respond to these changes. This collection of information can be done informally, in a haphazard manner. However, there are a number of techniques that most organizations use to collect information more systematically and accurately.

FIGURE 3.3
Stakeholder Map of Toy Maker

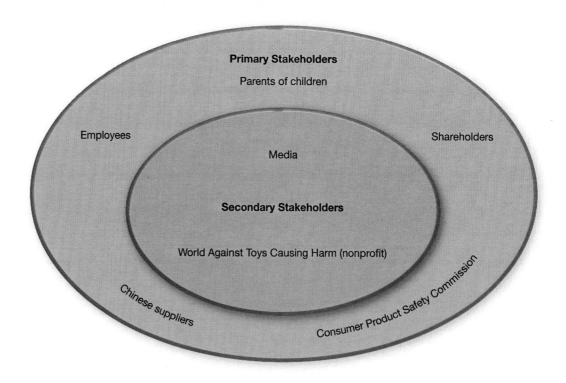

Primary Stakeholders

Parents of children

Employees

Shareholders

Media

Secondary Stakeholders

World Against Toys Causing Harm (nonprofit)

Chinese suppliers

Consumer Product Safety Commission

Customer Surveys

Customer surveys normally involve the use of interviews, written questionnaires, or online surveys to determine the opinions and attitudes of current and potential customers. After placing an order online, some retailers ask if you can share your thoughts on the experience in an effort to help them improve your shopping on a future visit.

Source: garagestock/Shutterstock

Increasingly, customer surveys are conducted online.

Economic Forecasting

Economic forecasting creates a framework for predicting future movements in the economy by looking at past economic indicators. At the national level, forecasters use such data as the gross national product (GNP), disposable income, and the unemployment rate. Retailers that anticipate an economic downturn might want to consider product discounts and changes to their marketing strategies indicating the quality and durability of their products.

Trend Analysis

Trend analysis develops models based on current trends and projects into the future. Many firms are keeping a close eye on technological trends including social media, cloud computing, and mobile payments.[13] Companies that are able to anticipate and prepare for emerging trends gain a significant competitive advantage.

Techniques for Interacting with the Environment

After the manager has identified the relevant stakeholders and collected information about future trends involving these stakeholders, he or she must develop some means of interacting effectively with the environment. Through these interactions, the manager is trying to maximize well-being by gaining a competitive advantage or by blunting the negative effects that these stakeholders can have on operations.

Although there are numerous actions that the organization may take, some of the most common are the following:

- *Public Relations:* Information that explains the firm's activities in a favorable manner that is regularly transmitted to the public. Colorado-based Crimson Renewable Energy may develop press releases or other printed media discussing the benefits of biofuels. Although the manager may release such information to the external environment, groups in the internal environment also regularly use the information.

- *Boundary Spanning:* Representatives of the organization regularly meet with stakeholders, such as sales agents with customers or purchasing agents with suppliers, to present the current and future status of the organization and try to influence the stakeholders' immediate and future actions toward the company. At the very least, the representative attempts to gain information about the stakeholders' beliefs and attitudes about the organization. The media is an important stakeholder to interact with during crises such as product recalls or environmental disasters. Consumers often turn to the media for information during times of crises or disasters.

- *Lobbying:* Members of the organization meet with government officials in an attempt to influence their votes on some policy that will affect the organization. Physicians and educators have two of the most active lobby groups at both the federal and state levels.

- *Negotiation:* The organization arrives at a formal, legal agreement with stakeholders through a discussion that may include cost, time, and method of transportation. This technique is commonly used with both internal and external environmental forces. Labor contracts, sales agreements, and facility leases are examples of negotiation. It is desirable for the organization to formalize the impact of the stakeholder so that it can predict with certainty what the stakeholder will do in the future, which makes planning much easier and more accurate. This is the reason sports teams agree to long-term contracts with their superior players.

Source: mdgn/Shutterstock

Many lobbyists attempt to influence voting in Congress.

- *Alliances:* The organization joins with other organizations, frequently competitors, to engage in an activity that promises great benefit. Other forms of alliances are takeovers, mergers, and acquisitions. In takeovers and acquisitions, one organization buys a competitor, supplier, or customer. (Often the organization is acquired against the wishes of its managers.) This happens through a direct offering to the company's stockholders, who make a profit on the sale of their stock. Southwest Airlines paid $1.4 billion to acquire AirTran.[14] Mergers are the joining of two organizations to form a larger, combined firm. Many well-known organizations have undergone mergers and acquisitions sometime in their history. GlaxoSmithKline resulted from the merger of Glaxo Wellcome and SmithKline Beecham.

- *Organizational Restructuring:* This involves changes in the organization's structure and the working arrangement among its internal parts. Frequently, these changes include laying off employees in an attempt to reduce the costs of doing business and to make the organization competitive against other organizations. In recent years, many individuals affected by layoffs have been middle-level managers. The ESPN cable network announced it was laying off about 400 employees to try and improve profitability.[15]

The Importance of the External Environment

Our basic premise is that the external and internal environments must be compatible and appropriately linked to the organization's goals and objectives if the organization is to be successful. Both the external and internal environments present threats and opportunities to the organization—that is, factors that can either hinder or help future performance. Managers must perceive these threats and opportunities and react accordingly. The remainder of this chapter will focus on the importance of the external environment to the organization and its managers.

Constraints on Viewing the Environment

How difficult is it to gain an accurate view of the external environment? As you might guess, the answer is "very difficult." There is simply a large amount of changing information of which to keep track. This problem is worsened by the added difficulty of how to collect and process the information. The following are common problems in receiving and using information about the external environment:

- *Limited Capability:* Although there is great variation among individuals, human beings are restricted in their cognitive ability to receive, process, and store information. When overloaded with information, we often use either just a small amount of the information or very basic decision rules when evaluating the information. Managers are increasingly using electronic means such as executive information systems to deal with these limitations. However, even these systems have limitations regarding how to collect and input data, how to determine models to be used for analysis, and how to test various scenarios that represent future alternatives of the organization and the environment.

- *Lack of Information:* As you can guess, it is often difficult to obtain the information necessary to make thoughtful decisions. Either the information is simply inaccessible or the company lacks the structure and/or the systems to collect the data. This is particularly true for small firms. A small retail clothing store may want data about local residents' participation in various social and recreational events. Unfortunately, such data are not part of common records such as the U.S. Census or various economic measures. Most small businesses have neither the expertise nor the funds to conduct their own consumer surveys.

- *Superfluous Information:* Sometimes the opposite may happen. The organization may receive too much information, especially in today's information-rich society.

Small businesses have an especially difficult time collecting information to help them more effectively manage their businesses.

All types of print and visual media, as well as specialized databases, overwhelm managers. Such databases may not be relevant to the problem at hand, however. For example, regional and national economic forecasts frequently assume that future patterns among economic variables will be the same as those of the past. In a changing economy, the data from these models may not be relevant for the organization's planning.

- *Current Organizational Constraints:* The organization's current situation may prevent it from properly evaluating the environment. The firm's present view may bias its ability to perceive the environment as it is changing. The firm may have already spent resources that may be lost if new actions must be taken to conform to the changing view.

Viewing the environment in order to anticipate change and respond accordingly is a skill that executives attempt to develop. Certain organizations pride themselves on their ability to develop such skills in their managers and actively work to remove any impediments to doing this. 3M, for instance, has had enormous success. It developed a glue that had an apparent flaw—it did not adhere very well. Given the environment in which glue is sold, such a discovery would normally wind up in a landfill. But one of 3M's employees saw a use for such a product: It could be applied to a small piece of paper that could be used as a marker on other documents. Out of such a sticky situation came 3M's hugely successful Post-it brand notes.[16]

Dimensions of the External Environment

The ability to assess the external environment and match a firm's capabilities with perceived needs is the key to its ability to survive and prosper. Not doing this can mean the failure of the organization, not to mention an increase in fees paid to bankruptcy attorneys. Perceiving the external environment accurately and responding appropriately may result in a competitive advantage and success.

The external environment may be thought of as differing among organizations in two dimensions, homogeneity and change. The degree of homogeneity is the extent that the external environment varies from being relatively simple (having few elements that affect the organization) to relatively complex (having many elements that affect the

FIGURE 3.4
Types of External Environments

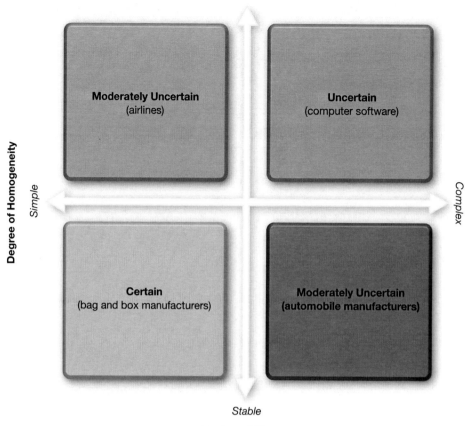

organization). A domestic firm that goes global will encounter a number of complexities as it tries to adapt to different laws and cultures. The degree of change refers to the extent that the external environment is relatively stable (change occurs slowly and/or predictably) or relatively dynamic (change occurs rapidly and/or unpredictably). The interaction of these two dimensions determines the extent of uncertainty that a business faces in its external environment (Figure 3.4).

While all environments have some uncertainty, the least amount occurs in simple, stable environments. Few factors affect the organization, and these factors change in a relatively slow or consistent manner. Cardboard box manufacturers operate in such an environment; there are few competitors, and consumers' tastes in cardboard boxes do not change dramatically over time. When the environment is high on one dimension and low on the other, a moderately uncertain environment exists for the organization. Airlines operate in a simple but dynamic environment; factors such as competitors, markets, and technology remain relatively constant for all, but fare prices are extremely changeable and unpredictable. Dynamic and complex environments are the most uncertain. Such an environment characterizes the technology industry. New competitors are common, and customer needs change rapidly.

As we will point out in several subsequent chapters, the degree of uncertainty in the external environment affects many features of the internal environment, including the characteristics of structure, the degree of centralization of decision making, and the extent of formal policy and procedures. As you may be able to guess, increased uncertainty usually corresponds to fewer levels of management, more employees involved in decision making, and fewer policies and procedures. Another way of thinking about this is that an increased level of uncertainty requires a firm to gather and quickly process increased levels of information about the environment. This is necessary in order to read external factors accurately. The firm must be appropriately designed to collect and evaluate this necessary information.

Summary and Review

- *Define the term* environment. The organizational environment includes all those factors that affect the operation of the organization. Its three main components are the general environment, the task environment, and the internal environment.

- *Formulate the components of the general environment, task environment, and internal environment.* The general environment refers to the external factors that affect all organizations, including economic, technological, sociocultural, political-legal, and global dimensions. The task environment includes the external factors that are specific to an organization, such as customers, suppliers, competitors, substitutes, and potential new entrants to the industry. The internal environment includes all the factors that make up the organization, such as the owners, managers, employees, and board of directors.

- *Examine the major factors in the general environment.* The sociocultural dimension of the general environment includes the demographics and the values of the society within which the firm operates. The political-legal dimension refers to the nature of the relationship between various areas of government and the organization. The technological dimension of the general environment refers to the knowledge and process of changing inputs (resources, labor, money) to outputs (goods and services). The economic dimension reflects the overall condition of the complex interactions of economies the world over. The global dimension of the general environment refers to those factors in other countries that affect the organization.

- *Analyze the major factors in the task environment.* Suppliers are organizations and individuals that provide resources to other organizations. Customers buy an organization's goods and/or services. Substitutes are goods or services that may be used in place of those of the business. Competitors are other organizations that produce similar, or in some cases, identical goods or services. Potential new competitors are companies not currently operating in a business's industry but which have a high potential for entering the industry.

- *Specify the major factors in the internal environment.* Owners can have various degrees of influence and power within an organization. In the smallest organizations, the owner is the sole manager of the firm and fulfills all typical management tasks, but as organizations expand and become more complex, more managers will be brought in. Managers may be divided into three types: strategic or institutional, technical, and operational.

The relationship between managers and unionized employees is dictated by the negotiated contract between the union and the firm and is more formalized than is the relationship between managers and non-unionized employees. Changing demographics and technology are creating changes in the workforce. In corporations, the board of directors has the important task of representing the stockholders in their capacity as owners.

- *Explain the stakeholder approach to viewing the environment.* The stakeholder view of the environment is concerned with those individuals or organizations that could affect the organization. Primary stakeholders have ongoing relationships with the organization through formal contracts, ownership, or monitoring of a legal obligation of the organization. Secondary stakeholders do not have a formal connection to the firm but may affect it through public opinion. Some secondary stakeholders are environmental groups, community activists, and civil rights groups. The stakeholder view of the environment realizes that stakeholders, though external to the organization, constantly influence the organization. The nature of the relationship between the stakeholders and the organization is dynamic, meaning that change is continual. Factors such as government regulation may be an advantage in some cases and a disadvantage in other cases.

- *Distinguish the major ways that an organization can attempt to manage its environment.* There are a number of ways in which the organization can interact with and manage its external environment. All involve attempts by the organization to lessen the threats and take advantage of the opportunities. By managing the environment, the organization reduces the uncertainty of the environment and makes it more predictable and controlled. Some common techniques are public relations, boundary spanning, lobbying, negotiation, forming alliances, and organizational restructuring.

- *Specify why the external environment is important for organizations.* The external environment presents threats and opportunities for the organization that must be addressed. Managers must perceive these threats and opportunities and react accordingly.

- *Assess the environmental forces affecting business.* The "Business Dilemma" box presents an opportunity for you to analyze the environmental forces affecting a business. An analysis of all the environmental factors affecting Travera Motors should enable you to make some recommendations about future directions for the company.

Key Terms and Concepts

competitors 75

corporate governance 78

customers 74

economic dimension 72

environment 65

external environment 65

general environment 66

global dimension 73

internal environment 66

political-legal dimension 68

potential new competitors 75

primary stakeholders 80

secondary stakeholders 80

sociocultural dimension 67

stakeholder map 81

stakeholder orientation 80

substitutes 75

suppliers 73

task environment 66

technological dimension 70

Ready Recall

1. What is the external environment? How does it affect an organization?
2. Define and give examples of the sociocultural dimension of the external environment.
3. Why is the political-legal dimension of the external environment important for an organization?
4. What are some of the elements of the economic dimension of the external environment?
5. What are stakeholders? How are they related to an organization?
6. What are the elements of the task environment? Which of these are the most important to an organization?
7. Discuss briefly how suppliers and customers may have power over an organization.
8. Briefly describe some techniques that are used by organizations to interact with their environments.
9. What is meant by uncertainty in the external environment?
10. What do organizations try to accomplish when they attempt to manage their external environment?

Expand Your Experience

1. Interview managers from both a for-profit and a non-profit organization about the organizations' stakeholders. Draw a stakeholder map for each organization and compare the stakeholders of each map.
2. Interview managers from both a private and a public organization about the techniques each uses to gather information about the external environment and the techniques that are used to attempt to manage the environment. Compare the techniques used by the two different organizations.
3. Analyze the environmental factors affecting either your college or university or your place of employment. How does the organization gather information about these forces? Is it aware that some of these forces are changing? How is it responding to changes in its environment?

Strengthen Your Skills

Understanding the General Environment

You now know that the general environment consists of five influences: sociocultural, political-legal, technological, economic, and global. Businesses must take these influences into account when monitoring the environment and making important decisions. Often a decision will be impacted by more than one of these influences. Read the following ten business situations. Using the matrix, check off which influences apply to that scenario.

Scenario 1: Starbucks is encountering problems with one of its locations in China. Many Chinese consumers are unhappy that Starbucks built a retailer in the Forbidden City. They feel like the American firm is encroaching on an important part of Chinese heritage.

Scenario 2: Kodak gets much of its revenues from film. When digital cameras start becoming popular, Kodak is hesitant to invest in digital technology because it could cannibalize its film business. This decision costs Kodak dearly.

Scenario 3: Walmart wants to enter India. However, Indian regulations impose certain restrictions for foreign firms. For this reason, Walmart partnered with a domestic firm in a joint venture so it could enter the market.

Scenario 4: Some discount retailers actually profited during the most recent recession. Cash-strapped consumers often chose to forgo their preferred stores to shop at discount retailers like T.J. Maxx.

Scenario 5: Electric vehicles are becoming more popular with a growing consumer interest in sustainability. However, many consumers still find electric vehicles too expensive to afford. Automakers are looking for new ways to decrease costs and reduce the price of these vehicles.

Scenario 6: Recognizing that the Internet was changing the world as we know it, an entrepreneur named Jeff Bezos conceived of an online company called Amazon.com. This online store would allow sellers to sell books at different price points, giving consumers more choices about how much to pay for certain items. Amazon.com began to overtake traditional bookstores because the products sold on the site were often less expensive and more convenient for consumers.

Scenario 7: Pfizer has hired lobbyists to try and influence a new law that would impact how pharmaceutical firms market certain medications.

Scenario 8: Coca-Cola faces many challenges in its quest to expand in Africa. It must sell its products at prices low enough for the population to afford, but if it sells its products too low, then it could impact profits.

Scenario 9: In an attempt to market its beers to the growing Hispanic population in America, Anheuser-Busch is developing Spanish advertising messages and is hiring Hispanic celebrities in its marketing campaigns.

Scenario 10: While its success largely depends on gathering data from its users, Facebook has faced governmental scrutiny regarding its data sharing and collection practices. The government is monitoring Facebook to make sure that it does not violate user privacy laws. Facebook must strike a balance between profit and user privacy.

	Sociocultural	Political-Legal	Technological	Economic	Global
Scenario 1					
Scenario 2					
Scenario 3					
Scenario 4					
Scenario 5					
Scenario 6					
Scenario 7					
Scenario 8					
Scenario 9					
Scenario 10					

Case 3: Chips and Dips—Chipotle Recovers from Environmental Challenges

Chipotle Mexican Grill has always done things a bit differently from other restaurant chains. Steve Ells, founder and co-CEO, established the first Chipotle restaurant in 1993 as a high-end fast-casual restaurant chain after finishing his education at the Culinary Institute of America. Fast-casual chains do not provide table service but offer higher-quality items than fast-food restaurants.

When starting his own restaurant, Ells knew he wanted to make management decisions based on whether he feels the decision is beneficial for the chain to implement, even if it costs more money. He wanted to set himself apart in his competitive environment by creating a customer-service-oriented atmosphere different from others in the industry, where customers could see their food being prepared with

Source: Studio Barcelona/Shutterstock

fresh ingredients. He also changed the design of the waiting line to make it more intuitive and less restrictive to customers and visited the factory farms that were his suppliers. Uncomfortable with how the animals were being raised, he decided to source his meat from smaller, local farms. Having a working knowledge of his task environment—which includes suppliers, competitors, and customers—allowed Chipotle to efficiently reach objectives with adequate resources.

Furthermore, Chipotle's "food with integrity" offerings use fresh food with ingredients grown naturally and sustainably by local farmers whenever possible. About 40 percent of the beans used in its food offerings are organic, and Chipotle purchases about 10 million pounds of vegetables from local farms every year. Ells's leadership as an upper-level manager permits him to position Chipotle as a high-quality, socially responsible fast-casual restaurant. Chipotle attempts to create high customer satisfaction by ensuring that products are of the best quality, which means that it spends a great deal of time investigating ways to improve the taste and quality of its products. For instance, a team of engineers created a new machine that heats tortillas evenly because the distributor could not make one according to acceptable standards.

However, even the best managers face hardships. In the fall of 2015, Chipotle became a household name not because of its corporate structure, customer service, or even product offerings—it became a household name because of an outbreak of *Escherichia coli* that was traced to a small number of stores. Ells reacted quickly, closing 43 restaurants in two states in order to completely rid the stores of any possible contaminated products, completely clean and sanitize their entire kitchens, and retrain staff on proper food-handling procedures. The chain distributed free-burrito coupons to win back customers. Up until this point, Chipotle's internal environment was one focused on professional development and leadership training. Although this promoted a positive working culture, it lessened the emphasis on control measures and corporate governance. The outbreak led Ells to overhaul Chipotle's managerial focus from career development back to day-to-day activities. As Public Relations Director Chris Arnold describes the events, "Most incentives for restaurant managers were tied to their effectiveness in developing people

to go off to be restaurant managers. Now their incentives are driven entirely by five different metrics [concerning service and food safety]."

Competition has also been increasing, requiring Chipotle to constantly analyze its competitive environment. It is important for Chipotle to understand what customers might view as substitutes so that it can recognize its rivals and determine how to price its products competitively. One major type of competitor Chipotle faces is fast-food chains. When Chipotle first started gaining in popularity, some analysts predicted it would be the end of fast-food chains like McDonald's. This has not happened. Despite the unique options fast-casual restaurants like Chipotle offer, consumers still appreciate the low cost and familiarity of classic fast-food chains like McDonald's, Wendy's, and Burger King. These chains are also recognizing that consumers desire to eat healthier and are beginning to offer healthier menu options.

Chipotle also faces competition from fast-casual chains like Panera Bread. Much like Chipotle, Panera capitalizes on selling food made with fresh ingredients. It is estimated that 87 percent of Chipotle chains have a Panera restaurant located within 10 minutes by car. The fast-casual dining chain Qdoba is a direct competitor to Chipotle because it also operates in the Mexican food market. The *E. coli* outbreak at Chipotle may have driven some of Chipotle's customers to these fast-casual rivals.

Despite the unfortunate circumstances surrounding the outbreak in 2015, which led to a near-collapse of the chain and a crisis of confidence from investors, Ells used his strong understanding of the environment to weather the crisis. As a decisive manager with a strong understanding of his environment, he was able not only to maintain customers but to grow sales back to their original state by early 2017. One of the people affected by the *E. coli* outbreak even asked for free burritos as part of her settlement! Chipotle sent her dozens of free-burrito coupons.[17]

1. How does Chipotle manage its task environment?
2. How would you describe Chipotle's internal environment?
3. Evaluate the stakeholder reaction to Chipotle's *E. coli* problem.

Notes

1. Hayley Peterson, "Dollar General Is Defying the Retail Apocalypse and Opening 1,000 Stores," Aol.com, April 8, 2017, https://www.aol.com/article/finance/2017/04/08/dollar-general-is-defying-the-retail-apocalypse-and-opening-1-00/22031477/ (accessed November 22, 2017); Krystina Gustafson, "Dollar General Is Starting to Look a Lot Like Wal-Mart," CNBC, March 16, 2017, https://www.cnbc.com/2017/03/16/dollar-general-is-starting-to-look-a-lot-like-wal-mart.html (accessed November 22, 2017); "Dollar General (DG)," Yahoo! Finance, https://finance.yahoo.com/quote/DG/financials?p=DG (accessed November 22, 2017); Mya Frazier, "Dollar General Hits a Goldmine in America," *Bloomberg Businessweek*, October 11, 2017, https://www.bloomberg.com/news/features/2017-10-11/dollar-general-hits-a-gold-mine-in-rural-america (accessed November 22, 2017).

2. Mary Clare Jalonick, "FDA Head Says Calories Counts Are a 'Thorny' Issue as Supermarkets Lobby to Be Exempted," *Times Colonist*, March 12, 2013, http://www.timescolonist.com/business/fda-head-says-menu-calorie-labeling-thorny-issue-as-supermarkets-lobby-to-be-exempted-1.89481 (accessed December 29, 2017).

3. Chris Dolmetsch and Henry Goldman, "New York Soda Size Limit Statute Barred by State Judge," *Bloomberg*, March 11, 2013, https://www.bloomberg.com/news/articles/2013-03-11/new-york-city-soda-size-limitations-barred-by-state-court-judge (accessed December 29, 2017).

4. Bruce Horovitz, "Boston Market Shakes Salt Habit," *USA Today*, August 21, 2102, A1.

5. Julianne Pepitone, "Subway Beats McDonald's to Become Top Restaurant Chain," CNNMoney, March 8, 2011, http://money.cnn.com/2011/03/07/news/companies/subway_mcdonalds/index.htm (accessed December 29, 2017).

6. Scott Martin, "How Apple Rewrote the Rules of Retailing," *USA Today*, May 19, 2011, p. 1B; Steve Denning, "Apple's Retail Success Is More than Magic," *Forbes*, June 17, 2011, https://www.forbes.com/sites/stevedenning/2011/06/17/apples-retail-stores-more-than-magic/#658a26b228a2 (accessed November 25, 2017); Jefferson Graham, "At Apple Stores, iPads at Your Service," *USA Today*, May 23, 2011, p. 1B; Yukari Iwatani Kane and Ian Sherr, "Secrets from Apple's Genius Bar: Full Loyalty, No Negativity," *Wall Street Journal*, June 15, 2011, https://www.wsj.com/articles/SB10001424052702304563104576364071955678908 (accessed November 25, 2017); Don Reisinger, "Apple's Retail Stores Are Undergoing a Dramatic Makeover," *Fortune*, August 29, 2016, http://fortune.com/2016/08/29/apples-flagship-stores-retail-chief-angela-ahrendts-makeover/ (accessed November 25, 2017); Jeff Beer, "Apple, Google, and Microsoft Ranked Three Most Valuable Global Brands of 2017," *Fast Company,* September 25, 2017, https://www.fastcompany.com/40472610/apple-google-and-microsoft-ranked-three-most-valuable-global-brands-of-2017 (accessed November 25, 2017); Marco della Cava, Jessica Guynn, and Elizabeth Weise, "Apple Stores Get Major Makeover," *USA Today*, May 19, 2016, https://www.usatoday.com/story/tech/news/2016/05/19/apple-store-gets-major-makeover/84596138/ (accessed November 25, 2017); Sean O'Kane, "Apple Is Redesigning Its Biggest Stores for the First Time in 15 Years," The Verge, April 25, 2017, https://www.theverge.com/2017/4/25/15419398/apple-store-redesign-genius-bar-grove (accessed November 25, 2017); "Apple Stores," MacRumors, https://www.macrumors.com/roundup/apple-retail-stores/ (accessed November 25, 2017).

7. Donal Griffin, "Citigroup Wins Shareholder Support for Compensation Plan," *Bloomberg*, April 24, 2013, http://www.bloomberg.com/news/2013-04-24/citigroup-wins-shareholder-support-for-compensation-plan.html (accessed December 29, 2017).

8. John Huey and Andrew Erdman, "Managing in the Midst of Chaos," *Fortune*, April 5, 1993, 38.

9. Michael Wayland, "Ford Training New Employees with Simulated Factory," M Live, July 31, 2013, http://www.mlive.com/auto/index.ssf/2013/07/ford_training_new_employess_wi.html (accessed December 29, 2017).

10. Samuel Rubenfeld, "SEC Issues First Dodd-Frank Whistleblower Award," *Wall Street Journal*, August 21, 2012, http://blogs.wsj.com/corruption-currents/2012/08/21/sec-issues-first-dodd-frank-whistleblower-award/ (accessed December 29, 2017).

11. R. Edward Freeman, *Strategic Management: A Stakeholder Approach* (Boston: Pittman, 1984).

12. Freeman, *Strategic Management: A Stakeholder Approach*, 60–61.

13. Rhonda Abrams, "Strategies: 7 Small-Business Trends to Analyze," *USA Today*, May 17, 2013, http://www.usatoday.com/story/money/columnist/abrams/2013/05/17/small-business-trends-for-entrepreneurs/2192817/ (accessed December 29, 2017).

14. Aaron Smith, "Southwest to Acquire AirTran," *CNN Money*, September 27, 2010, http://money.cnn.com/2010/09/27/news/companies/southwest_airtran/index.htm?cnn=yes (accessed December 29, 2017).

15. Todd Spangler, "ESPN to Lay Off Hundreds of Employees," *Variety*, May 21, 2013, http://variety.com/2013/biz/news/espn-layoffs-disney-to-cut-hundreds-of-employees-1200484819/ (accessed December 29, 2017).

16. S. J. Diamond, "Clever, but Who Thought of It?" *Los Angeles Times*, December 6, 1991, D1.

17. U.S. Food and Drug Administration, "FDA Investigates Multistate Outbreak of *E. Coli* O26 Infections Linked to Chipotle Mexican Grill Restaurant," https://www.fda.gov/food/recallsoutbreaksemergencies/outbreaks/ucm470410.htm (accessed October 17, 2017); Diana Bradley, "Chris Arnold Guides Chipotle's Crisis Comeback," *PR Week*, https://www.prweek.com/article/1438230/chris-arnold-guides-chipotles-crisis-comeback#AB5RGAbJLBziCe3l.99 (accessed October 17, 2017); Erin Douglas, "Chipotle Shows Signs of Recovery with New Menu Items in Testing, but Is It Enough?" *Denver Post*, http://www.denverpost.com/2017/07/14/chipotle-new-menu-items-revenue-ecoli/ (accessed October 17, 2017); Jim Edwards, "How Chipotle's Business Model Depends on NEVER Running TV Ads," *Business Insider*, March 16, 2012, http://www.businessinsider.com/how-chipotles-business-model-relies-on-never-doing-tv-advertising-2012-3 (accessed November 22, 2017); "Chipotle Selects MicroStrategy as Its Enterprise Business Intelligence Solution," Market Watch, August 21, 2012, http://www.marketwatch.com/story/chipotle-selects-microstrategy-as-its-enterprise-business-intelligence-solution-2012-08-21 (accessed September 13, 2012); Jefferson Graham, "Chipotle Resists Tech Automation at Restaurants," *USA Today*, August 16, 2012, http://www.usatoday.com/tech/columnist/talkingtech/story/2012-08-15/talking-tech-chipotle-app/57079794/1 (accessed September 13, 2012); Joel Stein, "The Fast Food Ethicist," *Time*, July 23, 2012, pp. 39–44; "Investor Relations Press Release," Chipotle Grill, February 5, 2013, http://ir.chipotle.com/phoenix.zhtml?c=194775&p=irol-newsArticle&id=1781728 (accessed November 22, 2017); Duff McDonald, "Esquire's Most Inspiring CEO in America: Steve Ells, Founder and Co-CEO, Chipotle," *Esquire*, 2012, http://www.esquire.com/features/most-inspiring-ceo-1012-steve-ells#slide-12 (accessed June 24, 2013); "Chipotle's CEO Discusses Q1 2013 Results—Earnings Call Transcript,"

Seeking Alpha, April 18, 2013, http://seekingalpha.com/article/1353311-chipotle-s-ceo-discusses-q1-2013-results-earnings-call-transcript?part=single (accessed November 22, 2017); Caitlin Dewey, "Analysts Predicted Chipotle Would Be the Death of McDonald's. They Were Wrong," *Washington Post*, October 26, 2017, https://www.washingtonpost.com/news/wonk/wp/2017/10/26/why-mcdonalds-is-beating-out-the-fresh-healthy-competition/?utm_term=.82e8dfcaa5c3 (accessed November 22, 2017); Akin Oyedele, "Chipotle's Biggest Competitor Is a Soup-and-Sandwich Chain," *Business Insider*, March 29, 2017, http://www.businessinsider.com/chipotle-competition-panera-bread-2017-3 (accessed November 22, 2017); Hollis Johnson, "I Compared Chipotle's Food to Another Major Mexican-Food Competitor—and the Winner Shocked Me," *Business Insider*, October 14, 2015, http://www.businessinsider.com/chipotle-vs-qdoba-review-2015-10 (accessed November 22, 2017); Sarah Begley, "Chipotle Customer Who Got *E. Coli* Asks for Free Burritos in Settlement," *Time*, September 14, 2016, http://time.com/4490672/chipotle-ecoli-free-burritos-settlement/ (accessed November 22, 2017); Jen Wieczner, "Chipotle's 'Free Burrito' Coupons Are Making People Less Scared to Eat There," *Fortune*, May 4, 2016, http://fortune.com/2016/03/04/chipotle-coupons-ecoli/ (accessed November 22, 2017).

Ethics and Social Responsibility

CHAPTER 4

Source: Thanakorn.P/Shutterstock

Chapter Outline

After reading this chapter, you will be able to:

- Define business ethics and explain its importance to management.
- Detect some of the ethical issues that may arise in management.
- Specify how personal moral philosophies, organizational relationships, and opportunity influence decision making in management.
- Examine how managers can try to foster ethical behavior.
- Define social responsibility and discuss its relevance to management.
- Debate an organization's social responsibilities to owners, investors, employees, and consumers, as well as to the environment and the community.
- Determine the ethical issues confronting a hypothetical business.

Eaton Drives to Maintain a Successful Ethics Program

Eaton Corporation is a power management company based in Cleveland, Ohio. The company produces over 900,000 different industrial components, employs 95,000 people globally, and generates over $19.7 billion in annual sales. These large-scale operations require Eaton to have a strong ethics and compliance program. It has been recognized as one of *Ethisphere Magazine*'s World's Most Ethical Companies for eight consecutive years. Eaton prides itself on its values-based culture and believes that high performance is only achieved by "doing business right." Eaton is also committed to social responsibility, which involves maximizing its positive impact on society while minimizing its negative impact.

At the heart of Eaton's values-based culture is a detailed code of ethics. Eaton's code of ethics contains standards meant to reduce the opportunity for misconduct by prescribing acceptable and unacceptable behaviors within the organization. Not only must all Eaton employees comply with the code of ethics, but they have a responsibility to report any suspected violation of the code—also known as whistle-blowing. Eaton's code of ethics covers 12 areas, including obeying the law, delivering quality, and respecting diversity and fair employment practices.

To ensure that employees follow and value the code of ethics, Eaton supports its ethical culture at all levels of the company. This support is an important organizational factor in the ethical decision-making process because employees are likely to follow the example of managers who exemplify ethical behavior. Eaton's Global Ethics Office is charged with the daily administration of the company's code of ethics. The purpose of the Global Ethics Office is "to demonstrate that Eaton's ethical standards are both current and at the highest level and that our Code of Ethics is fully known and followed wherever we do business." The Global Ethics Office provides employees with the information, tools, guidance, training, and support they need to comply with the code of ethics.

Ethics programs are useless if they are not communicated effectively to employees. For this reason, all new employees, including those from acquired businesses, go through ethics training immediately after they join Eaton. The company also has tools to help employees to monitor their own behavior before an ethical issue develops. For example, Eaton employees can record entertainment and gifts online, which fosters transparency.

At Eaton, employees are encouraged to report "any ethical concern or any potential or actual legal or financial violation." Employees can get information or report misconduct to the Global Ethics Office via regular mail, email, or Eaton's 24-hour Ethics and Financial Integrity Help line. Non-English-speaking employees

Eaton's Golf Pride brand is the leading provider in golf club grips.

can write emails and letters to the Global Ethics Office in their native language, and Eaton will translate them. The company wants to ensure that violations do not go unchecked, domestically or internationally.

Concern for the environment is an important part of social responsibility. In 2016 Eaton modified its vision statement to focus on sustainability: "To improve the quality of life and the environment through the use of power management technologies and services." The company believes that sustainability is not only an ethical issue but also a way to make its business thrive. Eaton is undertaking three initiatives to increase its environmental impact: selling sustainable products, decreasing its environmental footprint, and reporting its progress toward its environmental goals.

Eaton incorporates sustainability into its consumer relations by supplying products that help customers reduce their energy consumption, such as monitoring software, power management systems, and high-efficiency transformers. These products help customers increase the energy efficiency of buildings, vehicles, and machinery; conserve natural resources; shrink their carbon footprints; and reduce their environmental impact.

Overall, Eaton Corporation has a company-wide commitment to ethical business. Eaton's code of ethics provides a stable foundation for the company's business decisions. Both the firm and its employees know what is expected from them and how to make difficult ethical decisions. The Global Ethics Office acts as a valuable guide when following the code of ethics, making legal and ethical behavior accessible to everyone connected with Eaton. Eaton backs up its business philosophy with ethical actions. It develops and sells products that help customers to reduce their environmental impact, and it strives to become a more sustainable business itself. Eaton's ethical culture is the key to its reputation and global success.[1]

Introduction

The Eaton focus on ethics programs and an ethical culture drives its approach to integrity in all management activities. Without acceptable conduct, a firm will lose the support of stakeholders and even face sanctions from regulatory authorities. This chapter addresses ethics and social responsibility, two of the most important areas in establishing management trust and respect. During the first few decades of the twenty-first century, scandals at corporations such as Volkswagen and Wells Fargo, as well as sports teams, were associated with ethics and social responsibility failures.

In the first half of this chapter we explore the role of ethics in management decision making. First, we define business ethics and explain why it is important to understand the role of ethics in management. Next, we explore a number of ethics issues to help you recognize such issues when they arise, and we discuss the process through which individuals make ethical decisions. Finally, we look at steps managers can take to improve ethical behavior in their organizations. The second half of the chapter focuses on social responsibility. First, we describe the nature of social responsibility and its evolution. Next, we explore some important social responsibility issues and the ways companies have responded to them. Finally, we discuss how organizations may manage their operations to fulfill their social responsibilities, including conducting social audits.

What Is Business Ethics?

Business ethics refers to principles, values, and codes of conduct that define acceptable behavior in business. Stakeholders, including employees, customers, government regulators, special interest groups, communities, competitors, and an individual's personal morals and values determine what acceptable behavior in business is. For example, we generally feel that ethical managers strive for success while being fair, just, transparent, and trustworthy.

business ethics: Principles, values, and codes of conduct that define acceptable behavior in business.

This chapter does not prescribe a particular philosophy or process as the best or most ethical; it does not tell you how to judge the ethics of others. It will help you detect ethical issues and see how decisions are made within individual work groups as well as within the organization as a whole. Understanding how people make ethical decisions should help you improve your own ethical performance. Although we do not tell you what you ought to do, others—your superiors, coworkers, and family—will make judgments about the ethics of your actions and decisions. Learning how to recognize and resolve ethical issues is an important step in evaluating ethical decisions in management.

Why Is Ethics Important in Management?

In Chapter 1, we said that making decisions is an important aspect of management. Ethical considerations exist in nearly all management decisions. The most basic ethical concerns have been codified as laws and regulations that encourage conformity to society's values and attitudes. At a minimum, managers are expected to obey these laws and regulations. Most legal issues arise as incorrect ethical choices that society deems unacceptable. However, all actions deemed unethical by society are not necessarily illegal, and both legal and ethical concerns change over time.

You have only to pick up *The Wall Street Journal* or *USA Today* to see how truly difficult it is to deal with legal and ethical issues. Scandals at HSBC related to anti–money laundering laws resulted in $1.9 billion in fines, Volkswagen paid billions in fines in the United States for attempts to cheat on emissions requirements, and Wells Fargo opened millions of accounts without customer knowledge—all of these are ethical issues and attest to the difficulty in detecting and determining whether an action has violated a legal or ethical standard. Additionally, there is often a fine line between ethics and laws, and just because something is technically legal does not necessarily mean that it is ethical.

It is important to recognize that business ethics goes beyond legal issues; ethical decisions foster trust among individuals and in business relationships. Unethical decisions

Business ethics is often referred to as maintaining and managing organizational integrity.

destroy trust and make the continuation of business difficult, if not impossible.[2] If you were to discover that a manager had misled you about company benefits when you were hired, for example, your trust and confidence in the company would probably diminish. If you learned that a colleague had lied to you about something, you would probably not trust or rely on that person in the future. From another perspective, mistakes may be unintended or events may alter a manager's intent or commitments. There may be miscommunication concerning promises in some cases. Therefore, business ethics involves many gray areas or borderline decisions about what is ethical or unethical. For example, there may be debate about what constitutes abusive behavior.

Well-publicized incidents of unethical activity strengthen the public's perception that ethical standards in business need to be raised. For example, the risky lending practices of companies that helped lead to the most recent financial crisis have prompted the U.S. government to establish widespread reform for the financial industry, including the passage of the Dodd-Frank Wall Street Reform and Consumer Protection Act. In another more generic example, a plant that closes in order to save costs may make sense from a business standpoint, but the workers will feel quite differently. Canadian workers at a Caterpillar factory faced this issue when the company decided to shut down a plant and relocate to an American city after a labor dispute resulted in strikes and lockouts.[3] Obviously, the workers will question the ethics of the plant closing decision and may even spark legal issues for the company. Often, questions that start as ethical conflicts turn into legal disputes when cooperative conflict resolution cannot be accomplished. On the other hand, companies sometimes take aggressive actions to enforce their own ethical standards. Such examples support the notion that most decisions can be judged right or wrong, ethical or unethical.

Although they are often not well publicized, there are many ethical firms. For example, Xerox, Whole Foods, Herman Miller, and Marriott get high marks for ethical conduct and social responsibility. *Ethisphere Magazine* has examined the profitability

Many companies believe that their ethical conduct contributes significantly to their overall profitability.

of the World's Most Ethical companies in comparison to the S&P 500. The World's Most Ethical companies have outperformed the S&P each year.

There is a genuine human concern that employees sense and appreciate. Indeed, most organizations and managers do try to make ethical decisions; however, it is the unethical decisions that are publicized and result in public outcries for change.

Recognizing Ethical Issues in Management

Learning to recognize ethical issues is the most important step in understanding ethics in management. An **ethical issue** is an identifiable problem, situation, or opportunity that requires a person or organization to choose among several actions that may be evaluated as ethical or unethical. The "line" between an issue and an ethical issue is the point at which accepted rules no longer serve, and the decision maker is faced with the responsibility for weighing moral rules and making a choice. In management, the decision often requires weighing monetary profit or personal interests against what the individual, work group, or organization considers honest and fair.

ethical issue: An identifiable problem, situation, or opportunity that requires a person or organization to choose among several actions that may be evaluated as ethical or unethical.

A good way to judge the ethics of a decision is to look at the situation from several viewpoints: Should a manager pressure employees into lowering product quality in ways the customer cannot detect in order to reduce costs? Should an engineer agree to divulge her former employer's trade secrets to ensure that she gets a better job with a competitor? Should a personnel manager omit facts about an employee's poor safety record to help the employee find a new job? What if a manager fails to use renewable energy, even if it stands to increase long-term profits for the company? Such questions require the decision maker to calculate the ethics of his or her choice.

Many business issues may seem straightforward and easy to resolve, but in reality, a person often needs several years of experience in business to understand what is acceptable or ethical. Many acceptable behaviors in your private life may not be acceptable in business. For example, when does offering a gift—such as season basketball tickets—to a business associate become a bribe rather than just public relations? Obviously, there are no easy answers to such a question. But the size of the transaction, the history of personal relationships within the particular company, as well as many other factors may determine whether others will judge an action as right or wrong. If you give your basketball tickets to a friend with whom there is no business relationship, the ethical issue vanishes.

Managers directly influence the ethical issues within an organization because they guide employees and direct the organization's activities. They should be especially concerned about ethical issues related to their organization's impact on the environment, the firm's ethical standards, plant closings and layoffs, employee discipline and benefits, discrimination, health and safety, privacy, drug and alcohol abuse in the workplace, and the achievement of organizational objectives in an efficient and ethical manner.

Ethics is also related to the culture in which a business operates. In the United States, for example, it would be inappropriate for a businessperson to bring an elaborately wrapped gift to a prospective client on their first meeting: The gift could be viewed as a bribe. In Japan, however, it is considered impolite not to bring a gift. In Mexico, a small payment called *la mordida* (the "bite") may be considered necessary for doing business. Experience with the culture in which a business operates is critical to understanding what is ethical or unethical. Understandably, there is considerable debate over whose ethics should apply in international business. U.S. managers need to respect

All businesses face ethical risks in their decision making.

Source: Freedomz/Shutterstock

An example of a conflict of interest is accepting or paying a bribe.

other cultures, establish standards, and avoid violating U.S. or foreign laws when doing business globally.

To help you understand ethical issues that perplex managers today, we will explore some ethical issues that may affect management decisions. Obviously, it is not possible to discuss every issue that may arise, but a discussion of a few can help you recognize the ethical decisions and issues that managers have to deal with daily.

Ethical Issues in Management

As stated earlier, a decision becomes an ethical issue when accepted rules no longer apply and the decision maker must use his or her own moral principles and standards to decide what is right or wrong. Managers have an obligation to ensure that their ethical decisions are consistent with company values, codes of ethics, and policies—as well as community and legal standards. The following represent some examples of ethical issues from different management areas.

Organizational Relationships

Relationships with subordinates, coworkers, and superiors may result in ethical issues such as maintaining confidentiality in personal relationships; meeting obligations, responsibilities, and mutual agreements; and avoiding undue pressure that may force others to behave unethically. Today abusive and intimidating behavior is considered one of the most reported ethical concerns in the workplace by the Ethics Resource Center. Ethical issues arise when employees are asked to lie to customers and other employees about the quality of a product, as when a supermarket employee is told to tell customers that the seafood is fresh when, in fact, it was previously frozen. A manager may ask employees to do things that are in conflict with their personal ethics, or the organization may provide only vague or lax supervision on ethical issues, providing the opportunity for unethical behavior. Managers who offer no ethical direction to employees create many opportunities for manipulation, dishonesty, and conflicts of interest.

Operations and Communications

Many opportunities for unethical activity exist in the area of operations and communications. At first, it could be just an ethical issue, but when employees cover up and destroy records, it may turn into an illegal activity. The now-defunct accounting firm Arthur Andersen faced this problem when it was accused of destroying documents related to its involvement with Enron. Many companies have gotten into ethical trouble by covering up safety defects or by not being honest about the true quality of products. As mentioned earlier, Volkswagen did this by covering up the emissions released from its diesel-engine vehicles. An ethical issue exists when a company is not truthful about important information related to product quality. A number of Chinese firms have been found guilty of safety, defects related to lead paint in toys, defective tires, and drywall as well as health issues associated with the production of milk and dog food.

Sexual harassment has emerged as a major ethical issue in the workplace and has become one of the top news stories. Some high-ranking executives have been accused of taking advantage of their positions of power to obtain sexual favors. Many women more recently have come forward with details of the alleged sexual abuse in the past. Although sexual harassment is more transparent today, it has also led to decisions by some firms to avoid placing women in positions with high risk. For example, the New England Patriots moved some women out of positions where they have private contact with players. Firms need to assess risk but continue to provide equal opportunity in the workplace.

Sexual harassment has also been alleged in the political and entertainment arenas. Some have levied complaints against the Department of Justice's handling of sexual harassment cases as well as many sealed cases regarding House members, senators, and staffers in Congress. The entertainment industry has many highly visible cases of actors, producers, and other members of the industry engaging in sexual misconduct.

Employee Relations

The area of human resources management is a minefield of ethical issues. The process of acquiring, developing, and compensating people to fill the organization's human resources needs generates many ethical issues. For example, testing procedures used in hiring personnel may violate an individual's rights. While it is not yet illegal, some states are cracking down on employers for forcing employees to give them access to employees' social media profiles. The disclosure of personnel records and personality tests represents an ethical issue when it violates workers' privacy. Performance appraisals are another ethical issue if appraisals are based on favoritism and political opportunism. Decisions regarding promotions, transfers, separations, and financial compensation that are not based on objective criteria will provide opportunities for conflicts. Many firms have been accused of discrimination in hiring and promotions. Firms such as Walmart, Home Depot, and Costco have all been accused in class-action lawsuits of gender discrimination in promotions and hiring.[4]

Ethical issues related to discrimination and prejudice affect business activities at many levels. Discrimination based on race, sex, age, or other identifiable characteristics is an ethical issue and can become a legal statistic—when managers or company policy fails to control or prevent discrimination. The clothing retailer Wet Seal found this out after a class-action lawsuit in Pennsylvania accused the company of denying African-American employees equal pay and promotion opportunities. The company paid $7.5 million to settle the lawsuit.[5]

Strategies that management uses to develop human relations programs can also create ethical concerns. Strategies for motivating employees, such as methods of reward and punishment, can lead to unethical behavior. For example, if managers reward employees for achieving results without concern for how those results were achieved, they may send the wrong message to employees about what activities are acceptable and even encourage unethical actions to achieve results. For example, Walmart executives in Mexico were alleged to have paid bribes to government officials. Companies must consider the long-term effects of punishment/reward systems before selecting a policy. For instance, top-performing salespersons are not punished as often as low-performing salespersons when found guilty of misconduct.

You're the Manager . . . What Would You Do?

THE COMPANY: Bingo's Pizza
YOUR POSITION: Co-owner
THE PLACE: Dallas, Texas

Bingo's Pizza began delivering pizzas in 1969 when, with his sister, Jon McClanahan decided that customers would respond to having the pizza delivered for a small fee. Originally operating out of the Fort Worth area, Bingo's tested its delivery system and found that consumer response was overwhelming. Publicity for the company came quickly and easily as people were delighted and supportive of the delivery service. The company grew from one small store in Fort Worth to five, with an additional nine in the Dallas area, four in Waco, and four in Austin, with negotiations beginning for units in Houston.

The success of the delivery concept brought on competition from the major pizza manufacturers who tried their hand at delivery. Jon's sister and partner Stephanie was a computer whiz, having majored in computer science at Texas A&M University. Stephanie thought that if they developed an information database, they could become more efficient and gain significant insights into consumer buying behavior and consumption patterns. Jon felt their current system and software could use improvement and instituted a test of a new ordering system.

After successfully testing this system, Jon and Stephanie put the new order network in place in all of their restaurants. After three months of success, they wanted to gain some publicity for this new system, just as they had when they first instituted delivery service. After several days of attempting to write press releases, Stephanie had an idea. "I know we've only been running this system for a few months," she said. "But let's give an award to the family that eats the most Bingo's pizza. McDonald's gave their best customer in Lubbock a card

Bingo's Pizza deals with ethical issues in the workplace.

good for free food and they received publicity across the country. We can use the giveaway as a springboard to talk about the computer system." Jon had not thought of that angle, and he liked the idea. He asked Stephanie to determine the "winner" and get back to him.

Stephanie found that the biggest consumer of Bingo's pizza worked outside Waco and had ordered a pizza every weekday for the past three months that the system had been in place. Stephanie put together a program to give him a nice prize—Bingo's gift certificates—and arranged for the newspaper to accompany her to make the award. You must decide how to proceed with this plan.

QUESTIONS

1. Critique Stephanie's plan.
2. What are the potential ethical issues associated with this plan?
3. How would you proceed?

Making Decisions about Ethical Issues

Recognizing specific ethical issues can be difficult in practice. Whether a decision maker recognizes an issue as an ethical one is often determined by characteristics of the issue itself. Table 4.1 provides some facts about organizational misconduct in the United States.

Managers tend to be more concerned about issues that affect those close to them, as well as issues that have immediate rather than long-term consequences. Thus, the perceived intensity of an ethical issue may vary substantially, with only a few issues receiving scrutiny and many issues receiving less attention.[6]

Table 4.2 lists some questions you may want to ask yourself and others when trying to determine whether an action is ethical. While open discussion of ethical issues does not eliminate ethical problems, it does promote both trust and learning in an organization.[7] When people feel that they cannot discuss what they are doing with their coworkers or superiors, an ethical issue may exist. Once a person has recognized an ethical issue and can openly discuss it with others, he or she has begun the ethical decision-making process.

TABLE 4.1 Organizational Misconduct in the United States

Misconduct Facts	Percentages
Observed misconduct	30%
Abusive behavior	22%
Lying to stakeholders	22%
Conflict of interest	19%
Pressure to compromise standards	22%
Report observed misconduct	76%
Experience retaliation for reporting	53%

Source: Ethics and Compliance Initiative, 2016 Global Business Ethics Survey™: Measuring Risk and Promoting Workplace Integrity (Arlington, VA: Ethics and Compliance Initiative, 2016), p. 43.

TABLE 4.2 Questions to Consider Whether an Action Is Ethical

- Does the conduct comply with your organization's code of ethics or policies?
- How do other people in the organization feel about the action? Would they approve of your doing it?
- Are there any industry trade groups that provide guidelines or codes of conduct that address this issue?
- Will your decision or action withstand open discussion with coworkers and managers and survive untarnished?
- How does the decision align with your personal beliefs and values?

The Ethical Decision-Making Process

It is difficult for some people to believe that an organization can exert a strong influence on ethical behavior. In our society, we want to believe that we, as individuals, control our own destiny. However, teams and work groups, not individuals, often make the ethical decisions within the organization. Most new employees in highly bureaucratic organizations have almost no input into how things will be done in terms of basic operating rules and procedures. Employees may be taught management tactics and the way to resolve problems. Although many personal ethics issues may seem straightforward and easy to resolve, most managers make ethical decisions within the context of their organizations. Employees often accept the recommendations of accountants, lawyers, and experienced managers if they are concerned about an ethical decision.

To better understand the significance of ethics in management decisions, it is helpful to examine the factors that influence how a person makes ethical decisions: an individual's personal values, organizational factors, and opportunity (Figure 4.1).

The Role of Individual Factors in Ethical Behavior

Individual values, also known as moral philosophies, are sets of principles that describe what a person believes are the right way to behave. People learn these principles by interacting with family members and social groups and in formal education. Individuals may be guided by different values, however. Each moral philosophy has its own concept of what is ethical and the proper rules for behavior. This, in turn, influences what a person

individual values: Also known as moral philosophies, are sets of principles that describe what a person believes are the right way to behave.

FIGURE 4.1
Factors Influencing
Behavior

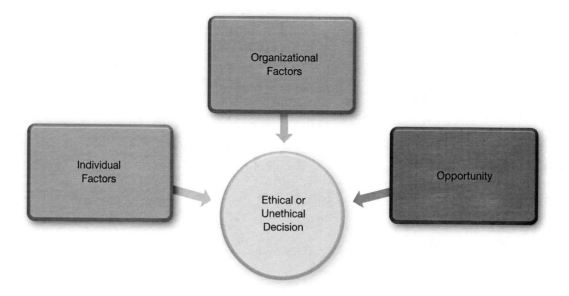

identifies as ethical and how strongly he or she feels about those issues. Moral philosophies can be broken into two categories: utilitarianism and deontology.

Believers in **utilitarianism** seek the greatest satisfaction for the largest number of individuals. Utilitarians evaluate the ethics of an action or decision on the basis of its consequences for all affected persons. When confronted with an ethical issue, the utilitarian manager weighs the costs and benefits of the consequences of all possible alternatives, and then chooses the one that benefits the most people. Employees may bend the rules if most stakeholders will benefit. For example, a CEO of a struggling company might consider making misleading statements that the firm is doing well. The CEO might honestly believe that reassuring investors and attracting new ones will help the company rebound, allowing employees to keep their jobs. On the other hand, a truly utilitarian philosophy would also evaluate the impact this misrepresentation would have on investors. If the company does go out of business, investors could lose millions. In addition, the CEO should also consider what might happen if caught by regulatory authorities. In such a case, the company would not only likely founder but the CEO could face serious legal penalties. A utilitarian CEO would take all these possibilities into account and choose the solution that he or she believes would benefit the most stakeholders.

In contrast, **deontology** focuses on human rights and values and on the intentions associated with a particular behavior. Deontologists judge an action by whether it infringes on individual rights or universal principles such as the Golden Rule, equality, or justice. In other words, utilitarians are more concerned with the end results, whereas deontologists are concerned with the means to get those results. In business, deontology is consistent with the idea that basic principles of acceptable conduct exist. A manager adopting this philosophy believes that he or she has a moral obligation to safeguard workers' health and safety and to make decisions that support individual rights without regard for the cost. A manager's decision to avoid discrimination in hiring is based on formalistic principles of equality. The manager's decision not to lie would be based on the principle that lying is wrong and not acceptable. Sometimes both deontology and utilitarianism influence the same decision.

Organizational Factors

Successful managers achieve their company's objectives in part by influencing their employees' behavior. If the pressure to produce a result—such as increasing profits—is especially great, the pressure to perform is also strong. How an employee achieves goals is shaped by the ethical climate of the organizational policies set by supervisors and the conduct of coworkers.

utilitarianism: A philosophy where believers seek the greatest satisfaction for the largest number of individuals.

deontology: Focuses on human rights and values and on the intentions associated with a particular behavior.

Managers have a significant impact on employees' conduct.

The greater a person's exposure to unethical behavior, the greater is the likelihood that he or she will act unethically. Moreover, employees' perceptions of the ethics of their coworkers and managers are often a stronger predictor of behavior than what employees personally believe to be right or wrong.[8] For example, an employee who sees her co-workers regularly take home company supplies for personal use may engage in the same behavior even if she personally believes it is wrong. Thus, the overall ethical climate in an organization sets the standards for employee conduct. Managers should keep this in mind.

The authority of an employee's superiors also affects ethical behavior. Powerful managers can affect employees' daily activities and directly influence behavior by implementing the company's ethical culture. If managers act unethically, employees may feel that such activities are acceptable within that organization; if a manager asks an employee to do something unethical, the employee may feel pressured to perform the activity even though he feels it is wrong. Accountant Betty Vinson of WorldCom was pressured by her superiors to manipulate the numbers to hide the financial difficulties the company was encountering. Although it was against her personal beliefs, Vinson was persuaded it was the only way of saving the company. Consequently, the role of management is extremely important in fostering ethical behavior in an organization.

Managers who do not view ethics as important may encourage employees to act contrary to their personal ethics. Some employees succumb to organizational pressures rather than following their own values, rationalizing their decisions by maintaining that they are simply "following orders." However, this rationalization has several weaknesses:

1. People who work in organizations can never fully abdicate their personal, ethical responsibility when making business decisions. Claiming to be an agent of the corporation is not accepted as a legal excuse and is even less defensible from an ethical perspective.
2. It is difficult to determine what is in the best interest of the organization. Short-term profits earned through unethical behavior may not be in the long-term interest of the company.
3. A person in a business has a responsibility to parties other than the organization, Stakeholders must be considered when making ethical decisions.[9]

For these reasons, this rationalization does not often hold up in a court of law.

Because employees' perceptions of the ethics of their coworkers influence their behavior, it should not be surprising that work groups within an organization have a strong impact on ethical behavior. In fact, work groups, or the perceived ethicalness of work groups, represent the most important factor affecting daily ethical decisions. The levels of conflict between employees may directly or indirectly influence the amount of unethical behavior within an organization.[10] The more conflict that exists within an organization, the lower the perceptions of the ethicalness of the work group. Because coworkers are so important in accomplishing daily business activities, it is important to support the ethics of the work group. If managers can provide direction and encourage ethical decision making, then the work group becomes a force to help the individuals make better ethical decisions. When managers allow greater participation with regard to the design and implementation of projects, conflict within the work groups is reduced and ethical behavior may improve.

The Role of Opportunity

Opportunity refers to conditions that limit unfavorable behavior and/or reward favorable behavior. These conditions could create the opportunity for an employee to act ethically or unethically. A person who is rewarded or is not punished for unethical behavior is likely to repeat the behavior; a person who receives no reward or is punished for behaving unethically probably will not repeat the action. For example, if a Texas Instruments Inc. employee is caught violating the company's ethical standards, as spelled out in its code of ethics, the employee may be reprimanded, placed on probation, suspended, or even fired. These disciplinary procedures send a message to Texas Instruments employees that unethical or illegal behavior will not be tolerated and make it less likely that an employee will repeat the action that resulted in punishment.

The greater the reward or the smaller the punishment for unethical behavior, the greater is the likelihood that unethical behavior will recur. Indeed, opportunity to engage in unethical behavior has been found to be a better predictor of unethical behavior than one's personal beliefs or the beliefs of peers.[11]

Companies can mitigate the negative effects of opportunity within an organization by adopting one of two control systems: values orientation or compliance orientation. A values orientation relies on shared values between the company and the employees. These values tend to be ideals and can bring cohesiveness to the organization if all members subscribe to the same values. While consequences to unethical behavior are present in this system, the opportunity for unethical behavior may exist to varying degrees as ideals can be interpreted differently among employees.

Source: sen khammoo/Shutterstock

Without the proper guidance and training, employees can engage in behaviors that personally benefit them and violate organizational legal and ethics guidance.

A compliance orientation requires that employees learn and pledge to a specific type of conduct. It uses language that that teaches employees the rules and consequences for noncompliance. Setting clear boundaries for acceptable and unacceptable behavior and assigning consequences to these behaviors, aids the employees in their decision making. When employees understand that their behaviors will be met with consequences, either good or bad, there is little room for ambiguous personal interpretation of how they should act within the company. Reducing the employees' need to interpret a situation eliminates the opportunity for unethical behavior and strengthens the opportunity for ethical behavior.

Both control systems serve the same purpose, to reduce the opportunity for unethical behavior, and the decision as to which one to adopt will depend on a firm's leadership, culture, and employees. However, a values orientation sharpens employees' abilities to reason ethically, making them more aware of ethical situations in the workplace, and make better decisions. The compliance orientation, while effective, focuses the employee's attention more on the consequences of not behaving ethically. This focus is not as likely to change an organization's ethical culture.[12]

Ethics and Compliance Programs

Ethics and compliance programs are designed to support ethical decision making and develop an ethical culture. An ethical culture depends on the values, norms, and behaviors that are instilled within the organization. Ethics programs normally focus on values that provide more abstract core ideals such as accountability and teamwork. Compliance identifies ethical issues and develops rules that require employees to adhere to mandatory conduct. For example, a company may have a rule that an employee cannot accept a gift or promotional item from a supplier with a value of more than $25. Understanding how people choose their standards of ethics and what prompts a person to engage in unethical behavior can help improve ethical behavior in organizations. Most organizations have adopted an ethics program to avoid misconduct and help employees reach a consensus on appropriate action. Leadership is important in developing an ethics program, with top executives and the board of directors providing a system to help the organization deal with ethical issues. Establishing and enforcing ethical standards and policies can help reduce unethical behavior by prescribing which activities are acceptable and which are not, and by removing the opportunity to act unethically. For instance, if top management does not support the program or ensure that employees are adhering to the company's ethical policies, then the program will fail to encourage ethical behavior.

Most organizations have accepted some standard components of an effective ethics program. These steps are based on best practices and the recommendation of the Federal Sentencing Guidelines for Organizations that use these requirements in assessing the due diligence of the company if there is misconduct. Table 4.3 highlights seven minimum requirements for a successful ethics and compliance program.

It is difficult for employees to determine what acceptable behavior is if a company does not have uniform policies and standards. These standards should be based on the assessment of risk and the identification of key ethical issues. Without such policies and standards, employees are likely to base decisions on how peers and superiors behave. Professional **codes of ethics** are formalized rules and standards that describe and delineate what the organization expects of its employees. For instance, Nike has formal ethics codes for both its employees and its suppliers that it expects them to follow. Establishing codes of ethics is the first step in developing an effective ethics and compliance program.

codes of ethics: Formalized rules and standards that describe and delineate what the organization expects of its employees.

TABLE 4.3 Seven Steps for Effective Ethics and Compliance Programs

1. Standards and procedures, such as codes of ethics, that are reasonably capable of detecting and preventing misconduct.
2. High-level personnel who are responsible for an ethics and compliance program.
3. No substantial discretionary authority given to individuals with a propensity for misconduct.
4. Standards and procedures communicated effectively via ethics training programs.
5. Systems to monitor, audit, and report misconduct.
6. Consistent enforcement of standards, codes, and punishment.
7. Continuous improvement of the ethics and compliance program.

Source: Adapted from U.S. Sentencing Commission, *Federal Sentencing Guidelines Manual*, effective November 1, 2004 (St. Paul, MN: West, 2008).

Many companies engage in ethics training with their employees to make them aware of the ethical issues and how the company would like for them to respond when facing uncertainty.

Codes of ethics and ethics-related corporate policy foster appropriate behavior by limiting the opportunity to behave unethically through the use of punishments for violations of the rules and standards. The enforcement of such codes and policies through rewards and punishments increase the acceptance of ethical standards by employees.

In order for codes of ethics to be effective, top managers including the board of directors, CEO, and chief ethics officer should proactively support the ethics and compliance program. Because employees look to management for direction, they have the opportunity to model acceptable standards and practices for employees. An *ethics officer* is responsible for managing the organization's ethics and compliance program. Among his or her duties, the ethics officer is responsible for overseeing ethics training, assessing ethical risks within the organization, monitoring the firm's ethical conduct, establishing confidential reporting mechanisms that employees can use to report concerns, ensuring compliance with all laws and regulations, disciplining those caught violating ethical rules and policies, and updating the code or revising the program whenever needed. It is imperative that managers in the organization work together to monitor and enforce ethical decision making.

Top managers and the board of directors must also make sure that those put in charge of the ethics program do not have a propensity for misconduct. You would not expect the captain of a large ocean liner to have a previous record of alcohol abuse while on duty. Instead, you expect him or her to obey appropriate policies and regulations, avoid misconduct, and have the knowledge needed to perform his or her duties effectively. The same applies to those in charge of ethics programs. It is important to avoid putting someone in authority of an ethics and compliance program who has had problems with misconduct in the past. Best practices as well as recommendations from government agencies claim that the ethics officer should be able to report directly to the board of directors.

Communication of codes, standards, and requirements through training programs is essential. While codes of ethics are important in communicating the firm's ethical standards, they are not sufficient on their own. Too often companies believe an ethics code will be enough to familiarize employees with ethical decision making. However, as with anything in life, ethics should be practiced to be learned. Ethics training programs are necessary to familiarize employees with the types of situations they may encounter on their jobs. A strong training program also alerts employees to the company's commitment toward ethical conduct and allows them to ask more detailed questions about ethical procedures. Training programs can involve a wide range of teaching methods, including case studies, behavioral simulations, instructional videos, computer-based instruction, ethics games, and more.

Systems are needed to monitor the program's effectiveness as well as report misconduct. Organizations must also continually review and monitor the firm's ethical culture. One effective way of monitoring the effectiveness of a firm's ethics and compliance program is by conducting an ethics audit. An **ethics audit** is a comprehensive evaluation of a firm's ethics and compliance program and its ethical decisions used to determine whether the program is effective. Ethics audits can help managers uncover hidden ethical risks as well as identify areas for improvement. Managers might also want to provide questionnaires to understand employee perceptions of the firm's ethical culture. Often employees have a better idea of the inner workings of the organization, so getting them involved in the ethics program is imperative.

> **ethics audit:** A comprehensive evaluation of a firm's ethics and compliance program and its ethical decisions used to determine whether the program is effective.

Employees are also more likely to witness misconduct at different levels of the organization. In order to discover and address ethical issues, managers should provide mechanisms that employees can use to report misconduct or concerns. **Whistle-blowing** occurs when employees expose an employer's wrongdoing. This might occur internally or externally. Internal reporting is when an employee reports questionable behavior to a manager or through a hotline. Research suggests that the more ethical the company's culture, the more likely employees are to report concerns internally to managers or to use a hotline.[13] Companies must develop open communication and trust in order to nurture ethical decisions.

> **whistle-blowing:** Occurs when employees expose an employer's wrongdoing. This might occur internally or externally.

It is difficult without ethics training, clear channels of communication, and ethics advocates within the company to provide support throughout the organization. Since some employees fear repercussions for reporting unethical behavior, many firms have set up ethics hotlines that employees can call in order to discuss ethics issues anonymously. In fact, Sarbanes-Oxley has made it mandatory for public companies to have a whistleblower system in place.[14] There is no substitute for individuals thinking through ethical dilemmas and feeling comfortable with their choices.

External reporting occurs when whistleblowers report wrongdoing to outsiders, such as the media or government regulatory agencies. The resulting negative publicity could be seriously damaging to the company. However, it can also be extremely important in discovering misconduct. Whistle-blowers involved with Enron, Lehman Brothers, and Bernard L. Madoff Investment Securities attempted to warn authorities that misconduct was occurring at the company. Failure to listen to whistle-blowers can result in serious misconduct that can damage many stakeholders. Recognizing that whistle-blowers are important in stopping misconduct, the government created a bounty program for whistle-blowers whose allegations result in a conviction of more than $1 million. Under this program, whistle-blowers can receive between 10 and 30 percent of the money.[15]

If a company is to maintain ethical behavior, its policies, rules, and standards must encourage ethical decision making and be enforced through a system of rewards for proper behavior and punishments for unacceptable behavior. Reducing unethical behavior is a goal no different from increasing profits or cutting costs. The manager sets a goal—achieving greater ethical behavior among company employees—and measures

Source: Lisa S./Shutterstock

Ethics hotlines often serve to allow employees to report potential organizational misconduct and receive guidance on the most appropriate conduct.

the outcome. If the number of employees making ethical decisions regularly is not increasing, the manager needs to determine why and take corrective action through stronger enforcement of current standards and policies or by strengthening the standards and policies themselves.

Additionally, there must be continuous improvement of ethics and compliance programs. Ethics programs are never static but always have room for improvement, particularly as new issues constantly arise. The implementation of an ethics program provides a plan for action in operational terms and establishes the means of which the organization's ethical performance will be monitored, controlled, and improved. As the program is implemented, the standards, structures, and resources can be continuously improved to align the company's values and codes of ethics with its employees.

The Nature of Social Responsibility

social responsibility: The obligation a business assumes to maximize its positive impact and minimize its negative impact on society.

Many consumers and social advocates believe that businesses should not only make a profit but also consider the social implications of their activities. **Social responsibility** is the obligation a business assumes to maximize its positive impact and minimize its negative impact on society. While many people use the terms *social responsibility* and *ethics* interchangeably, they do not mean the same thing. Ethics relates to an *individual's* or *business's* values, principles, and standards and the resulting decisions he or she makes, whereas social responsibility is a broader concept that concerns the impact of an *organization's* activities on stakeholders. In other words, ethics has more of a micro focus related to individual and group decisions, whereas social responsibility has more of a macro focus related to how decisions affect stakeholders. From an ethical perspective, we may be concerned about managers' conflict of interest concerning hiring friends or relative for positions in their firms; from a social responsibility perspective, we might be concerned about the impact that this may have on the community's well-being. Thus ethics relates to social responsibility because having a positive impact on society involves making ethical decisions about issues that impact stakeholders.

There are four stages of social responsibility: financial viability; compliance with legal and regulatory requirements; ethics, principles, and values; and corporate citizenship (Table 4.4).[16] A business whose *sole* objective is to maximize profits is not likely to consider its social responsibility, although its activities will probably be legal. Profits are an essential first step, and legal and regulatory responsibilities are the next step. A business that makes no profit or that commits illegal conduct probably will not be around long enough to get to the higher levels of social responsibility. We have discussed ethical conduct, and corporate citizenship involves additional activities that may not be required but which promote human welfare or goodwill. Corporate citizenship requires voluntary activities to strategically align the organization with social issues and contributions to philanthropic causes. While the first two stages have long been acknowledged, ethical issues and corporate citizenship are more recent concerns.

A business that is concerned about society as well as earning profits is likely to invest voluntarily in socially responsible activities. Outdoor clothing and gear company Patagonia, for instance, donates 1 percent of its profits toward environmental causes. Such businesses win the trust and respect of their employees, customers, and society by implementing socially responsible programs, and, in the long run, increase profits. Companies that fail to act responsibly risk losing consumers and may encourage the public and gov-

TABLE 4.4 **Social Responsibility Requirements**

Stage 1: Financial Viability
Stage 2: Compliance with Legal and Regulatory Requirements
Stage 3: Ethics, Principles, and Values
Stage 4: Corporate Citizenship

Source: nasirkhan/Shutterstock

Corporate social responsibility deals with economic, legal, ethical, and philanthropic interests of stakeholders.

ernment to take action to restrict their activities. Most companies today consider being socially responsible a necessary cost of doing business.

Arguments for and Against Social Responsibility

Although the concept of social responsibility is receiving more and more attention, it is still not universally accepted. Among the arguments against social responsibility are the following:

1. It sidetracks managers from the primary objective of business—earning profits. Every dollar donated to social causes or otherwise spent on society's problems is a dollar less for owners and investors.
2. Participation in social programs gives businesses greater power, perhaps at the expense of particular segments of society.
3. Some people also question whether business has the expertise needed to assess and make decisions about social problems.
4. Many people believe that social problems are the responsibility of government agencies and officials, who can be held accountable by voters.

There are equally strong arguments for asking business to take responsibility for social issues, including the following:

1. Business helped to create many of the social problems that exist today, so it should play a significant role in solving them, especially in the areas of pollution reduction and toxic waste cleanup.

2. Businesses should be more responsible because they have the financial and technical resources to help solve social problems.
3. As members of society, businesses should do their fair share to help others.
4. Socially responsible decision making by business organizations can prevent increased government regulation.
5. Social responsibility is necessary to ensure economic survival: If businesses desire educated and healthy employees, customers with money to spend, and suppliers with quality goods and services in years to come, they must take steps to help solve the social and environmental problems that exist today.

Evolution of Social Responsibility

Before the twentieth century, businesses were largely responsible for defining how they would interact with society; their sole motivation was profit. Consumers could sue businesses that engaged in unscrupulous activities, but such action was expensive and the chances of winning slim. There were no consumer advocates or government agencies to protect consumers and society against deceptive advertising, defective products, or practices that harmed people and the environment. The rule for consumers was *caveat emptor*—"let the buyer beware." Generally, consumers were so anxious for new products that they did not want government intervention. As more and more businesses entered the marketplace, however, competition grew fierce and abuses continued until it was inevitable that the government would have to intervene to protect consumers and workers.

Congress passed laws to reduce the monopolistic tendencies of big business and force companies to provide safer products and work environments. Federal agencies such as the Federal Trade Commission and the Securities and Exchange Commission were set up to protect consumers and police industry. Businesses gradually began to develop a sense of social responsibility when they realized that promotion, sales, and efficient production alone would not increase profits. By the 1950s, after finding that the key to increasing sales is to produce things that people want and need, businesses began to ask customers what they needed and to develop products to meet those needs. At the same time, employees were demanding better working conditions, and management and owners began to listen to them. Companies also began to seriously address the public outcry for product safety and reliability.

The 1960s represented a decade of change on nearly every front. Civil rights abuses, deterioration of the environment, concerns about product safety, and the Vietnam War led Americans to reexamine their values and priorities. People began to recognize that manufacturing processes and waste-disposal methods were harming the environment, and that women and minorities had been denied their full rights in the workplace. The public began to demand that everyone—individuals, government, and businesses—take greater responsibility for their actions. IBM and other companies saw that the way to build a positive image with the public and to ensure future sales was to act in a socially responsible manner.

Scandals during the past 20 years, including the financial crisis brought on by subprime mortgages and risky financial products, have reiterated the need for ethics and social responsibility. Businesses today are expected not only to earn profits

The legal and regulatory environment has had significant impact upon organizational awareness of stakeholder needs.

for shareholders but to take into account additional stakeholders, including communities and the environment. This trend has resulted in green product offerings and supply chain practices, community service, volunteerism, and other socially responsible initiatives. More and more businesses view the adoption of socially responsible management techniques, manufacturing processes, charitable donation policies, and more as necessary for meeting the demands of society. In addition, this greater societal demand for socially responsible business activities has led firms such as Whole Foods, Starbucks, Waste Management, and The Container Store to view socially responsible activities as a way to gain competitive advantages.

Social Responsibility Issues

As with ethics, managers consider social responsibility on a daily basis as they deal with real issues. Among the many social responsibility issues they must consider are their organizations' relations with owners/investors, employees, customers, the environment, and the community. These key stakeholder groups are associated with the impact of corporate decisions on their well-being. Table 4.5 provides some examples of stakeholder issues. Social responsibility is a dynamic area with issues changing constantly in response to society's desires.

It is often assumed that ethics and social responsibility mean the same thing. As we have already mentioned, they are not synonymous. Ethical decision making occurs when decisions about issues are judged as right or wrong, ethical or unethical. Social responsibility is a broader concept and includes how decisions impact all stakeholders and society.[17] Ethics is embedded in every managerial decision as it relates to questions about right or wrong. Many of these decisions impact the internal environment, including work relationships and the integrity of the work environment. We agree that the impact of managerial decisions on stakeholders does have social responsibility implications. But many

TABLE 4.5 Examples of Stakeholder Issues

Stakeholder Group	Stakeholder Issues
Employees	1. Compensation and benefits 2. Diversity 3. Occupational health and safety 4. Communications
Customers	1. Product safety and quality 2. Customer complaints and concerns 3. Disadvantaged or challenged consumers 4. Truthfulness of communications
Investors	1. Transparency of financial information 2. Shareholder rights 3. Corporate governance 4. Return on investment
Community	1. Public health and safety 2. Sustainability 3. Corporate citizenship 4. Economic contributions
Environmental Groups	1. Minimizing energy use 2. Minimizing emissions and waste 3. Enhancing the viability of animal and plant life 4. Minimizing adverse environmental effects of products

Many organizational social responsibility initiatives deal with stakeholder concerns and environmental issues.

people only look at ethics as decisions that can affect the environment, enhance sustainability, improve communities, avoid harm to vulnerable stakeholders including children and other disadvantaged groups, etc. Social responsibility issues relate to social issues, consumer protection, corporate governance, legal responsibilities, employee well-being, and sustainability.

While ethical decisions have significant social responsibility ramifications, the managerial decisions made on a daily basis impact the firm's ethical culture as well as its profitability and success. This section highlights a few of the many social responsibility issues that managers face; as managers become aware of and work toward the solution of current social problems, new ones will certainly emerge.

Relations with Owners and Investors

Businesses must be responsible to their owners or shareholders, who are primarily concerned with earning a profit or a return on their investment in a company. In a small business, this responsibility is fairly easy to fulfill because the owner(s) personally manages the business or knows the managers well. In larger businesses, particularly corporations owned by thousands of stockholders, assuring responsibility to the owners becomes a more difficult task.

A business's responsibilities to its owners and shareholders, as well as to the financial community at large, include maintaining proper accounting procedures, providing all relevant information to investors about the current and projected performance of the firm, and protecting the owners' rights and investments. Good corporate governance and compliance with regulations such as the Sarbanes-Oxley Act and the Dodd-Frank Wall Street Reform and Consumer Protection Act create transparency and confidence. In short, a business must maximize the owners' investment in the firm in a socially responsible manner.

Employee Relations

Another issue of importance to business is its responsibilities to employees, for without employees a business cannot carry out its goals. Employees expect businesses to provide them a safe workplace, to pay them adequately for their work, and to tell them what is happening within their company. They want employers to listen to their grievances and treat them fairly.

Congress has passed several laws regulating safety in the workplace, many of which are enforced by the Occupational Safety and Health Administration (OSHA). Labor unions have also made significant contributions to achieving safety in the workplace and improving wages and benefits. Most organizations now recognize that the safety and satisfaction of their employees is a critical ingredient in their success, and many strive to go beyond what is expected of them by the law. Zappos and The Container Store, for instance, focus extensively on employee happiness. While Zappos tries to create a fun, participative environment for employees, The Container Store provides extensive employee training, better pay than comparable retailers, and even a "We Love Our Employees" Day on Valentine's Day. These organizations have discovered the fact that healthy, satisfied employees supply more than just labor to their employers. Employers are beginning to realize the importance of obtaining input from even the lowest-level employees to help the company reach its objectives.

Employee recognition programs have a significant impact on employee loyalty and satisfaction.

A major social responsibility for business is providing equal opportunities for all employees regardless of their gender, age, race, religion, sexual orientation, or nationality. Women and minorities have been slighted in the past in terms of education, employment, and advancement opportunities; additionally, many of their needs have not been addressed by business. For example, women—who continue to bear most childrearing responsibilities—often experience conflict between those responsibilities and their duties as employees. In the workplace, women continue to be paid less than men for equal work. Today, many Americans believe business has a social obligation to provide special opportunities for women and minorities to improve their standing in society.

Consumer Relations

A critical issue today is business's responsibility to consumers. Consumers look to business to provide them with satisfying, safe products and to respect their rights as consumers. The activities undertaken by independent individuals, groups, and organizations to protect their rights as consumers are known as **consumerism**. To achieve their objectives, consumers and their advocates write letters to companies, lobby government agencies, make public service announcements, and boycott companies whose activities they deem irresponsible.

consumerism: The activities undertaken by independent individuals, groups, and organizations to protect their rights as consumers.

Many of the desires of those involved in the consumer movement have a foundation in John F. Kennedy's 1962 consumer bill of rights, which highlighted four rights. The *right to safety* means that business must not knowingly sell anything that could result in personal injury or harm to consumers. Defective or dangerous products erode public confidence in the ability of business to serve society. They also result in expensive litigation that ultimately increases the cost of products for consumers. This is why many firms will institute product recalls even when there is a slim possibility of defects or contamination. Grocery stores, including Piggly Wiggly and Lowes, issued a voluntary recall of frozen biscuits in 12 states due to fears of *Listeria* contamination. *Listeria* is a type of bacteria that can cause serious and sometimes fatal infections if consumed. Although no one was reported sick at the time of the recall, the stores issued the recall as a precautionary measure.[18] The *right to be informed* gives consumers the freedom to review complete information about a product before they buy. This means that detailed information about ingredients, risks, and instructions for use is to be printed on labels and packages. The *right to choose* ensures that consumers have access to a variety of goods and services at competitive prices. The assurance of both satisfactory quality and service at a fair price is also a part of the consumer's right to choose. The *right to be heard* assures consumers that their interests will receive full and sympathetic consideration when the government formulates policy. It also assures the fair treatment of consumers who voice complaints about a purchased product.

Consumers want not only a multitude of products that improve the quality of life but also a healthy environment so that they can maintain a high standard of living over their lifetimes. Sustainability has become a leading issue in the twenty-first century as both business and the public acknowledge the damage done to the environment by past generations. Today's consumers are increasingly demanding that businesses take a greater responsibility for their actions and impact on the environment. For example, pollution has emerged as one of the major sustainability issues.

Pollution

A major issue in the area of environmental responsibility is that of pollution. Water pollution results from the dumping of toxic chemicals and raw sewage into rivers and oceans, from oil spills, and from the burial of industrial waste in the ground where it may filter into underground water supplies. Fertilizers and insecticides used in farming and grounds maintenance also drain into water supplies with each rainfall. Water pollution problems are especially notable in heavily industrialized areas. A growing concern is the discovery of trace amounts of pharmaceuticals in certain supplies of water. Large oil spills such as the BP *Deepwater Horizon* disaster kill many marine animals and damage the livelihoods of local fishermen. Due to the illnesses that contaminated water can cause, society is demanding that water supplies be clean and healthful to reduce the potential danger from polluting substances.

Air pollution is usually the result of smoke and other wastes emitted by manufacturing facilities, as well as carbon monoxide and hydrocarbons emitted by motor vehicles. In addition to the health risks posed by air pollution, when nitrous oxides and sulfur dioxides from the emissions of manufacturing facilities react with air and rain, acid rain results. Acid rain has contributed to the deaths of many valuable forests and lakes in North America as well as in Europe.

Air pollution may also contribute to the greenhouse effect, in which carbon dioxide collects in the Earth's atmosphere, trapping the sun's heat and preventing the Earth's surface from cooling. This phenomenon is called global warming. Chlorofluorocarbons

Source: Ekton/Shutterstock

Air pollution is a significant global environmental issue.

also harm the Earth's ozone layer, which filters out the sun's harmful ultraviolet light; this too may be a cause of the greenhouse effect. Global warming is controversial, however, and some scientists doubt its existence. Yet a major concern for society is the melting of the Earth's polar ice caps. Melting has appeared to have increased in the last few decades. This melting is believed to be a result of global warming. Extensive melting could lead to the flooding of coastal cities. Species that live along the ice caps, such as polar bears, are at risk of extinction if the rate of melting continues to increase.

Land pollution results from the dumping of residential and industrial waste, strip mining, forest fires, and poor forest conservation. Land pollution is tied directly to water pollution because many of the chemicals and toxic wastes that are dumped on the land eventually work their way into the water supply. Dumping of toxic wastes in Love Canal (near Niagara Falls, New York) caused later residents to experience high rates of birth defects and cancer before they were forced to abandon their homes by the U.S. government in the late 1970s and early 1980s. In Ecuador Chevron has been in a battle against the government amidst allegations that Texaco, which Chevron later acquired, polluted rainforest land.[20] In Brazil and other South American countries, rain forests are being destroyed to make way for farms and ranches, at a cost of the extinction of the many animals and plants (some endangered species) that call the rain forest home. Large-scale deforestation also depletes the oxygen supply available to humans and other animals.

Related to the problem of land pollution is the larger issue of how to dispose of waste in an environmentally responsible manner. Also compounding the waste disposal problem is the fact that more than 50 percent of all solid waste is comprised of plastic goods, which does not decompose. Many communities passed laws that prohibit the use of Styrofoam for this reason.

Response to Environmental Issues

Partly in response to federal legislation such as the National Environmental Policy Act of 1969 and partly due to consumer concerns, businesses are responding to environmental issues. Many small and large companies—from Walt Disney Co. and Chevron—have created a new executive position, a vice president of environmental affairs, to help them achieve their business goals in an environmentally responsible manner. ExxonMobil is publishing estimates on the effects of its business on climate change and policies to deal with climate change.

Many firms are trying to eliminate wasteful practices, the emission of pollutants, and the use of harmful chemicals from their manufacturing processes. Other companies are seeking ways to improve their products. Automakers from all over the world are trying to develop automobiles that run on alternative fuels—electricity, solar power, natural gas, and methanol. Walmart highlights products it deems environmentally responsible so consumers can readily identify them; it also sponsors recycling centers in the parking lots of some stores. Many businesses have turned to recycling, the reprocessing of previously used materials—aluminum, paper, glass, and some plastic—for new purposes. Kellogg's, for example, uses recycled paper in the packaging of its cereal products. Some coffee shops have started using cups made from corn plastic rather than from regular plastic or Styrofoam. Best Buy encourages consumers to recycle their old electronics (e-waste) at their stores. Such efforts to make products, packaging, and processes more environmentally friendly have been labeled "green" business.

It is important to recognize that, with current technology, environmental responsibility requires trade-offs. Society must weigh the huge costs of limiting or eliminating pollution

Source: carmen2011/Shutterstock

Logos such as this represent recycling priorities: reduce, reuse, and recycle.

Sseko Takes Steps in Social Entrepreneurship

Liz Forkin Bohannon, founder and CEO of Sseko Designs, a socially minded fashion and design company from Portland, Oregon, uses the company as a platform to empower women in Uganda and East Africa. Social entrepreneurship involves creating social value or solving social problems using a business model. In 2008, after traveling to Uganda, Liz was appalled to see the extreme poverty of the people. She discovered that the top 2 percent of high school girls who were eligible to go to a university had to return to their villages and work for nine months to save money for tuition. Most of these girls did not continue their education because their families needed the money for their subsistence. She also learned that these women preferred to work rather than receive a handout. Employee relations is a large part of why Liz chose to start her business in Uganda.

Her first attempt at a socially conscious for-profit business was a short-lived chicken farm. It was then she recalled her college days when she made sandals that used ribbons to avoid the noise made by flip-flops. She redesigned the product by purchasing rubber flip-flop bottoms tied with ribbon. For two weeks, she looked for suppliers while gaining skills in sandal making through tutorial videos on YouTube. She developed a work-study model for Ugandan women who showed college potential. Sseko offers women employment during the nine-month period they have to earn revenues for college. The women make sandals and other products to sell to U.S. consumers. In the process, they learn skills and have the chance to earn wages for college. The sandals became an immediate success when Martha Stewart recommended them in her gift ideas. Sseko's inventory was soon depleted.

To continue the company's growth, Liz and her husband sought funding via the popular ABC reality show *Shark Tank*. Entrepreneurs Mark Cuban, Barbara Corcoran, Kevin O'Leary, Lori Grainer, and Robert Herjavec were offered a 10 percent stake in Sseko for a $300,000 investment. However, Sseko had suffered a $90,000 loss the year earlier and anticipated it would lose money that year as well. The Bohannons explained that the reason for the loss was that they were putting more money into development and hiring more salespeople. They expressed their belief that as more Americans learned about Sseko and its social mission, sales would increase. Debt, managed correctly, can help a firm because it allows it to take on opportunities it would not normally have with limited funds. However, a negative cash flow often turns off investors. Of greatest concern to the sharks was the belief that the Bohannons overvalued their business.

Source: Dirima/Shutterstock

Seeko employs young Uganda women to make sandals and other products for the U.S. market.

The sharks maintained that the company was too focused on its social mission and philanthropy and not enough on profitability. The Bohannons countered that many of today's retailers and customers value companies with a social mission. They maintained that if a company supports a cause the consumer cares about, its brand will be viewed more favorably. They told the sharks that the key to increasing Sseko's profits was to continue social responsibility. Although the sharks declined the opportunity to invest, Sseko's exposure on the show resulted in a 500-fold increase in website traffic and a 1,000 percent increase in sales for that month.

Sseko Designs has already had a major impact on Uganda. Not only is it the largest footwear manufacturer—resulting in more jobs for Uganda and for the Ethiopian and Kenyan artisans who create crafted products for Sseko to sell—it also serves to empower women. Each employee is encouraged to save 50 percent of her salary, which goes into her personal Sseko savings accounts for nine months, after which the account receives a 200 percent match from the company. Additional funding for these scholarships comes from the Sseko Fellows program. This program began two years ago and has 300 fellows. Sseko fel-

Sseko Takes Steps in Social Entrepreneurship *(continued)*

lows are U.S. social entrepreneurs who sell the company's products directly. Every Sseko fellow is matched with a Sole Sister in Uganda, and every dollar of Sseko product sold in the United States by one of these fellows provides income for the fellow and generates funding to help send a Sole Sister to college. To date, 87 female employees have been able to get a university education thanks to Sseko Designs.

Sseko has developed its reputation through social entrepreneurship by making a profit and maximizing its positive impact on society. By being socially responsible, Sseko shows that there is no conflict between being concerned for the well-being of others and operating a business. In addition, Sseko has established ethical values that serve many stakeholders. In a way, Sseko's social entrepreneurship provides it with its competitive advantage.[19]

against the health threat posed by the pollution. Environmental responsibility imposes costs on both business and the public. Although people certainly do not want oil fouling beautiful waterways and killing wildlife, they insist on low-cost, readily available gasoline, heating oil, and goods. People do not want to contribute to the growing garbage disposal problem, but sometimes do not want to pay more for "green" products packaged in an environmentally friendly manner, to recycle as much of their own waste as possible, and to permit the building of additional waste disposal facilities. Thus, managers must coordinate environmental goals with other social and economic ones.

Alternative and Renewable Energy

With ongoing plans to reduce global carbon emissions, countries and companies alike are looking toward non-carbon-based alternative energy sources. Traditional fossil fuels are problematic because of their emissions, but also because stores have been greatly depleted. Foreign fossil fuels are often imported from politically and economically unstable regions, often making it unsafe to conduct business there. With global warming concerns and fluctuating gas prices, the global governments have begun to recognize the need to look toward alternative forms of energy as a source of fuel and electricity. There have been many different ideas as to which form of alternative energy would best suit the United States' energy needs. These sources include wind power, geothermal energy, solar power, nuclear power, biofuels, and hydropower.

Wind Power

The Great Plains of the United States is one of the greatest sources of wind energy in the world, and many people believe that harnessing this energy will go a long way toward providing for the United States' energy needs in the future, possibly up to 20 percent of total energy needs. However, a number of roadblocks remain between taking abundant wind and turning it into affordable energy. Restructuring the nation's power grids to efficiently transmit wind, solar, and other forms of renewable energy will take significant investments. Widespread adoption of wind power has been slowed in the United States by the high cost of the turbines as well as limitations on an outdated national power grid. The technology is more expensive and less efficient than fossil fuels currently, but advances are being made. Many people believe that the United States will be a wind power hot spot in the future. Many organizations also strongly support the use of wind power. New Belgium Brewing, through the purchase of wind power credits, became the first wind-powered brewery in the country.

Geothermal Power

Another form of renewable energy is geothermal power. Geothermal energy comes from the natural heat inside the earth, which is extracted by drilling into steam beds. Though

Here is a geothermal plant in New Zealand.

startup costs are high to build geothermal plants, geothermal energy is a relatively clean energy source. The drilling is not pollution free, but its carbon dioxide emissions are one-sixth those produced by efficient natural gas power plants. Geothermal plants also use a lot less water than coal power plants, and unlike wind or solar energy, geothermal power can provide a steady flow of electricity every day of the year. Some IKEA stores use geothermal power to help meet their energy needs.

Despite these advantages, geothermal energy extraction is expensive and supplies less than half of 1 percent of the world's global energy production. It provides one-third of 1 percent of the energy used in the United States. Part of the problem may be that geothermal drilling sites are not readily available everywhere; certain factors, like the permeability of rock, must be taken into account. However, when organizations do tap into geothermal power, the costs savings can be significant. Lipscomb University in Nashville, Tennessee, uses a geothermal heating and cooling system in its Ezell Center that saves the university $70,000 annually on heating and cooling.

Solar is a growing renewable energy source.

Solar Power

Solar power uses the energy from the sun to generate electricity and hot water. This 100 percent renewable, passive energy source can be converted into electricity through the use of either photovoltaic cells (solar cells) on homes and other structures or solar power plants. The major disadvantages of solar power are that the technology remains expensive and inefficient compared to traditional fossil fuel–generated energy, and that the infrastructure for mass production of solar panels is not in place in many locations. Given the strong sunshine in places like the U.S. Southwest and California, solar power has gained a lot of support in the United States. A report from the U.S. Department of Energy states that solar energy usage is at a new high. Solar energy is becoming an increasingly viable alternative for businesses to cut their pollution and emissions. For instance, many California Walmart facilities, with their huge flat roofs perfect for solar panels, now use solar power to generate electricity. Everywhere you look, the move to harvest the sun's power is growing. The demand for solar power is growing, particularly in the United States, Germany, and China.[21]

Nuclear Power

Countries throughout Europe have managed to greatly reduce their emissions through the implementation of nuclear power plants, yet this form of power remains controversial. Because of the danger associated with nuclear meltdowns and radioactive waste disposal, nuclear power has earned a bad reputation in the United States. On the one hand, nuclear power is pollution-free and cost-competitive. On the other hand, critics are concerned with the safety of nuclear power plants and the disposal of waste. As the production of nuclear power gives off radiation, the safety of workers and the transport of nuclear waste are prime concerns. The Chernobyl accident in the Ukraine in 1986 is the most infamous disaster. The nuclear reactor malfunctioned, resulting in the deaths of 30 people from radiation, and possibly thousands more have experienced negative health effects to this day. Since then, nuclear reactor safety has been improved, yet the potential dangers of nuclear power remain major issues. The dangers of nuclear power were demonstrated after an earthquake and resulting tsunami damaged nuclear reactors in Japan, resulting in a nuclear emergency for the nation. Some are also concerned that nuclear power plants could be targets for terrorist attacks.

Biofuels

Biofuels are fuels derived from organic materials like corn, sugarcane, vegetable oil, and even trash. While ethanol made from sugarcane has been widely used in Brazil for decades, the idea of biofuels is relatively new in the United States. This idea has become especially popular with those who want to reduce their car's carbon output or who are concerned with the nation's addiction to foreign oil. Automobile makers have begun to create flex-fuel and hybrid vehicles that can run on biofuels or gasoline. General Motor's Chevrolet Volt is an electric car with a backup motor for distances over 40 miles. When it uses gasoline, the Volt is designed to run on E85, a blend of 85 percent ethanol (a type of alcohol that can be used as a biofuel) and 15 percent gasoline.

Legal mandates to incorporate biofuels have been passed in some countries. In 1976, for example, the Brazilian government made it a requirement to blend gasoline with ethanol. As a result, Brazil currently is the largest exporter of bioethanol. Part of the reason why biofuels have not been as popular in the United States has to do with the source of the fuel. While Brazil uses sugarcane, which is convertible to fuel because of its high sugar content, the United States relies on corn, which is not as easily converted to fuel. Biofuels are also controversial because they currently use food crops—widespread adoption of biofuels could lead to food shortages. The biofuel infrastructure in the United States also lags behind that in Brazil. Biofuel production in other countries like the Philippines has been criticized because it has contributed to rapid deforestation of ecologically sensitive areas—companies in a rush to create profits from the popularity of biofuels have installed plantations on former jungle land, for example.

Researchers have been hard at work developing new technologies that could produce biofuels without deforestation of land or food

Ethanol can be produced from corn as well as other plants.

Hydropower has been a renewable source of energy for hundreds of years.

Source: Constantine Androsoff/Shutterstock

supplies. Cellulosic ethanol would be made from nonedible plants like grasses, sugarcane waste, and wood waste. Algenol, or biofuels made from algae, is also being investigated.

Hydropower

Throughout history, people have used water as a power source and a means of transportation. From the water-powered mills of centuries past to modern hydroelectric dams, water is a powerful renewable energy source. Although in the United States hydroelectric power only provides 7 percent of total output, hydroelectric provides 19 percent of total electricity production worldwide, making it the largest form of renewable energy.

As with all other forms of energy production, hydropower has benefits and downsides. One of the major downsides is the destruction of wildlife habitats, and sometimes even human habitations, when valleys are flooded using dams. Hydroelectricity also disrupts the lifecycles of aquatic life. Damming the Columbia River between Washington and Oregon decimated the region's salmon industry, for example. Benefits of hydroelectric energy include little pollution and inexpensive maintenance costs, once the infrastructure is in place.

Community Relations

A final issue for businesses concerns responsibilities to the general welfare of the communities and societies in which they operate. Many businesses simply want to make their communities better places in which everyone can live and work. Although such efforts cover many diverse areas, some other actions are especially noteworthy. The most frequent way that businesses exercise their community responsibility is through donations to local and national charitable organizations. After realizing that the current pool of prospective employees lacks many basic skills necessary to work, many companies have become concerned about the quality of education in the United States. Although some members of the public fear business involvement in education, others believe that if business wants educated employees and customers in the future, it must help to educate them.

Business is also beginning to take more responsibility for the hard-core unemployed— some mentally or physically handicapped and some homeless organizations such as the National Alliance of Businessmen fund programs to train the hard-core unemployed so that they can find jobs and support themselves. In addition to fostering self-support, such opportunities enhance self-esteem and help people become productive members of society.

Source: Andrei_R/Shutterstock

Social audits inform management about ethical and social performance.

Social Audits

To determine whether it is adequately meeting the demands of society as well as its own social responsibility objectives, an organization can measure its performance through a voluntary social audit. (The term *audit* comes from *audio*, the Latin verb for "to listen.") The **social audit** is a systematic examination of the objectives, strategies, organization, and performance of the social responsibility function. In a social audit, managers evaluate a company's long- and short-term contributions to society to determine whether the firm's social responsibility approach is working. The social audit can also enhance a company's social responsibility efforts by helping management evaluate the effectiveness of current programs and recommend activities for the future.

Managers should conduct a social responsibility audit on a regular basis—perhaps annually—to develop a good benchmark of where the company has been and where it is going. Conducting the audit involves five fundamental activities:

1. Identifying ongoing and new programs that support socially responsible actions and programs,
2. Determining the resources and the cost of resources that are required to support the programs and the benefits that have been achieved to date,
3. Identifying organizational objectives and making certain that social responsibility activities support those objectives,
4. Defining the reasons for undertaking particular social responsibility programs or supporting certain causes, and
5. Evaluating the success of each social responsibility program undertaken and identifying benchmark goals for future involvement.

The concept of auditing implies an official examination of social responsibility activities; however, these audits are often designed to occur informally. Most of the problems that arise in an audit can be attributed to the fact that there are few standards for evaluating social responsibility. The resulting information from the audit should be as quantitative and accurate as possible, depicting both the positive and negative findings.

A social audit can indicate to a firm whether it is living up to the expectations of society. It can pinpoint areas where the firm can take additional steps to maximize the positive effect of its activities as well as to minimize their negative impact. Used effectively, the social audit provides a tool for managers to help their firms become better citizens by contributing positively to society.

social audit: A systematic examination of the objectives, strategies, organization, and performance of the social responsibility function.

■ *Define business ethics and explain its importance to management.* Business ethics refers to moral principles and standards that define acceptable behavior in the world of business. Ethical considerations exist in nearly all management decisions. Ethical decisions foster trust among individuals and in business relationships; unethical ones destroy trust and make the continuation of business difficult, if not impossible.

■ *Detect some of the ethical issues that may arise in management.* An ethical issue is an identifiable problem, situation, or opportunity requiring a person or organization to choose from among several actions that must be evaluated as ethical or unethical. Managers should be concerned about ethical issues related to their organization's impact on the environment, the firm's ethical standards, plant closings and layoffs, employee discipline and benefits, discrimination, health and safety, privacy, and drug and alcohol abuse in the workplace, as well as the achievement of organizational objectives in an efficient and ethical manner.

■ *Specify how personal moral philosophies, organizational relationships, and opportunity influence decision making in management.* People are guided by different moral philosophies (a set of principles setting forth what is believed to be the right way to behave), each having its own concept of rightness or ethicalness and rules for behavior. Two categories of moral philosophies are utilitarian and deontology. Organizational relationships—including the influence of managers, coworkers, and the work group—are important factors in ethical decision making. The greater a person's exposure to unethical behavior by managers and coworkers, the greater is the likelihood that the person will behave unethically. Opportunity is a set of conditions that punish unfavorable behavior or reward favorable behavior. A person who is not rewarded or is punished for unethical behavior is not likely to repeat the behavior.

■ *Examine how managers can try to foster ethical behavior.* Managers can change the organizational environment to promote ethical behavior among employees by limiting opportunity. One important way to do this is through the development of effective ethics and compliance programs. Adopting formal codes of ethics and policies is important because they reduce the incidence of unethical behavior by informing employees of what is expected of them and providing punishments for those who fail to comply. Support from top management is needed for the program to be effective. Often an ethics officer is assigned to manage the organization's ethics and compliance program. Top managers and the board of directors must make sure that those put in charge of the ethics program do not have a propensity for misconduct. Ethics training helps to familiarize employees with the ethical situations they might come across in the workplace. Monitoring the progress of the ethics program is crucial, and managers can use ethics audits to evaluate the effectiveness of an ethics and compliance program and identify weaknesses to be corrected. Managers should also encourage employees to report ethical concerns or observed misconduct. Additionally, if a company is to maintain ethical behavior, managers must enforce its policies, rules, and standards to encourage ethical decisions through a system of rewards for proper behavior and punishments for unacceptable behavior. Finally, managers should continuously seek to improve the company's ethics and compliance program.

■ *Define social responsibility and discuss its relevance to management.* Social responsibility is the obligation an organization assumes in order to maximize its positive impact and minimize its negative impact on society. Socially responsible businesses may win the trust and respect of their employees, customers, and society, and in the long run increase profits. There are strong arguments both for and against social responsibility by businesses.

■ *Debate an organization's social responsibilities to owners, investors, employees, and consumers, as well as to the environment and the community.* Organizations must be responsible to their owners and investors, who expect to earn a profit or a return on their investment in the company. Businesses must maintain proper accounting procedures, provide all relevant information to investors about the current and projected performance of the firm, and protect the owners' rights and investments. In relations with employees, businesses are expected to provide a safe workplace, pay employees adequately for their work, and treat employees fairly. Consumerism refers to the activities undertaken by independent individuals, groups, and organizations to protect their rights as consumers. Consumers' basic rights are spelled out in John F. Kennedy's 1962 consumer bill of rights: the right to safety, the right to be informed, the right to choose, and the right to be heard. Increasingly, society expects business to take greater responsibility for the environment. Among the issues of environmental responsibility are water, air, land, and noise pollution. Many businesses engage in activities to make the communities in which they operate a better place in which everyone can live and work.

■ *Determine the ethical issues confronting a hypothetical business.* The "Business Dilemma" box presents an opportunity for you to study an ethical dilemma at Bingo's Pizza. Using the material presented in the chapter, you should be able to analyze the ethical issues present in the dilemma, evaluate the McClanahan's plan, and develop a course of action for the firm.

Key Terms and Concepts

business ethics 95

codes of ethics 105

consumerism 113

deontology 102

ethical issue 97

ethics audit 107

individual values 101

social audit 121

social responsibility 108

utilitarianism 102

whistle-blowing 107

Ready Recall

1. Define business ethics. What groups determine whether a business activity is ethical?
2. What is an ethical issue?
3. Distinguish between the utilitarian philosophy and deontology. Supply an example of a business that has used each to make a decision.
4. How does opportunity contribute to unethical decisions in business?
5. What is a code of ethics? How can managers reduce unethical behavior in business?
6. Distinguish between ethics and social responsibility.
7. List and discuss the arguments for and against social responsibility by business. Can you think of any addi-

tional argument (for or against)? Can you take a position (for or against) and defend it?
8. What responsibilities does a business have toward its employees?
9. What responsibilities does business have with regard to the environment? What steps have been taken by some responsible businesses to minimize the negative impact of their activities on the environment?
10. What is a social audit? How can a social audit help a business improve its social responsibility activities?

Expand Your Experience

1. Discuss some recent examples of businesses engaging in unethical practices. Why do you think the business chose to behave unethically? What action might the business have taken?
2. Discuss with your class some possible methods of increasing ethical standards in business. Do you think that business should regulate its own activities or should the federal government establish and enforce

ethical standards? How do you think businesspeople feel?
3. Find some examples of socially responsible businesses in newspapers or business journals. Explain why you believe their actions are socially responsible. Why do you think a given company chose to act as it did?

Strengthen Your Skills

Making Decisions about Ethical Issues

Below are three debate issues. Form three groups of four to six people and choose one of the debate issues. Each of the three groups will then be divided evenly, such that one group argues for one side of the issue while the other group argues the opposing side. This exercise will help you understand the nuances of ethical decision making

through practice. Each team will be given five to ten minutes to debate their side of the issue.

Debate Issue 1: *Is Google Violating Users' Privacy?*

With two billion Google searches a day, Google is the preferred search engine for many consumers. Much of its popularity is due to the superior services it offers. Although

Google does not charge for its services, critics point out that Google's services may actually be costing users their right to privacy. Google keeps all of its users' search queries forever, although after 18 months these queries become "anonymized." In other words, they cannot be tracked back to the user. Google maintains that it uses these searches responsibly to refine its search engine. It also has privacy disclosures fully visible on its main page. On the other hand, the Third Party Doctrine and the Patriot Act allow the government to access users' Internet information without a judge's oversight for national security purposes. Google has been subpoenaed in the past by investigators for user information. Even anonymized data have been used to track a specific person or computer.[22]

1. Google's storage of user data is legitimate and does not constitute a violation of user privacy.
2. Google should not store users' data as this data can be misused or accessed by the government.

Debate Issue 2: *Is Health Care a Right or a Privilege?*

The Universal Declaration of Human Rights, adopted by the United Nations in 1948, proclaims that "everyone has the right to a standard of living adequate for the health and well-being of oneself and one's family, including food, clothing, housing, and medical care." Hard work and healthy living does not assure being healthy. With the high costs of health care, many consumers cannot afford health insurance. The U.S. government has followed other industrialized nations in adopting universal health care.

However, critics argue that it is the individual's responsibility, not the government's, to ensure personal health. Many health problems, such as obesity and diabetes, can often be prevented by individuals choosing to live healthier lifestyles. Another concern involves the cost of health care. Critics believe universal health insurance will increase costs because more people will depend upon the government for health care. This in turn might cause costs

to be passed onto the consumers and prompt the government to limit certain types of care. Guaranteeing health care for all may lead people to make riskier decisions because they know that if they get hurt, they are guaranteed health care coverage.

1. Because health care protects life, it is a fundamental right and should therefore be ensured by the federal government.
2. Health care is a privilege and should not be provided by the government because of the high costs involved.

Debate Issue 3: *Examining Warren Buffett as an Effective Leader*

Warren Buffet has been the leader of Berkshire Hathaway, Inc., for more than 40 years. Buffet has been viewed as an ethical leader who emphasizes integrity in his manager choices. His conglomerate is one of the largest companies in the United States. Buffet relies on the character of the CEOs of the various companies in his conglomerate, and in many cases, he may only have a few conversations with the CEO over the course of the year. His trust in his associates was undermined when David Sokol, the leading contender to succeed him, resigned after revelations that he had purchased $10 million in shares of a chemical maker a week before recommending the purchase of the company to Buffett. This broke the company's insider trading rules and duty of candor. While Sokol's trading may fall in a gray area of the law, there are certainly questions about Sokol's disclosures.[23]

1. Warren Buffett is correct in trusting those around him to have high integrity and the ability to make ethical decisions based on their character.
2. Warren Buffett needs to focus more on organizational ethical codes and compliance and less on the character of the manager that he puts in charge of the company.

Case 4: Bank on It: Wells Fargo's Ethical Culture Challenged

Until recently, Wells Fargo was the world's largest bank. Its victory was short-lived, however, when J.P. Morgan overtook Wells Fargo in 2016. The loss of its place as the world's biggest bank came in the wake of a large-scale cross-selling scandal in which it was revealed that Wells Fargo employees had faked 3.5 million customer accounts to meet short-term sales goals. Approximately 5,300 employees were fired, and the firm was slapped with a $185 million fine by the Consumer Financial Protection Bureau (CFPB).

September 2016 marked the unfolding of Wells Fargo's entanglement in a widespread scandal that would implicate several high-level executives and thousands of employees. On September 8, the CFPB, the Los Angeles City Attorney, and the Office of the Comptroller of Currency

levied a massive $185 million fine against Wells Fargo, claiming the firm had opened up and/or applied for 2.1 million customer bank or credit card accounts without permission from customers. Furthermore, a bank official acknowledged that the company had terminated over 5,300 employees in relation to the allegations.

Investigations revealed that controversial sales goals most likely encouraged employees to open accounts without customers' permission and knowledge. Employees had continually engaged in fraudulent activities such as opening up fake bank accounts and falsifying signatures to satisfy sales goals and earn financial rewards under the bank's incentive-compensation program. Evidence shows that Wells Fargo had unrealistic sales goals and did not

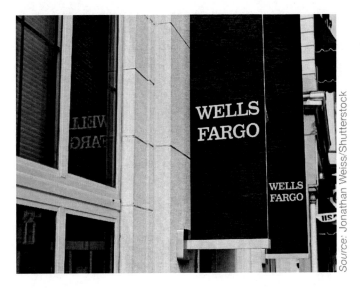

have systems in place to ensure employees were actually engaging in selling.

Although the accusations claimed Wells Fargo employees had opened fake customer accounts since 2011, managers at Wells Fargo claim these same practices had been occurring long before. Susan Fischer, a former Wells Fargo branch manager, confirmed that these shocking sales tactics that encouraged employees to open unauthorized accounts had been around much longer than bank executives have acknowledged. A letter to the CEO from 2007 was recovered that described how employees were opening up fake accounts and forging customer signatures. CEO Stumpf claims he never received this letter or similar letters. However, several employees are coming forward to claim that they reported the misconduct and had their employment terminated as a result. If true, this would directly violate laws that protect whistle-blowers from retaliation.

To reach its lofty sales goals, Wells Fargo also set up incentives to engage employees, which increased commissions around the product being emphasized. These products were cross-sold to customers with an aggressive sales incentive program tied to employee compensation. This incentive program suggests that Wells Fargo executives, managers, and employees forgot that a bank's reputation is built on a basic cultural value of trust. Rather, it falsely became a leader in the banking industry through the utilization of unrealistic sales goals. Managers at many branches played a large role in the establishment of unauthorized accounts.

Yet the responsibility for the misconduct stemmed even further up the organization. After all, if the managers'

branches did not meet these new goals, not only could employees be terminated but the managers as well. Although employees opened the accounts and managers implemented procedures to ensure goals were met, the high-level executives who initially set the goals are the most relevant decision makers in this ethical dilemma. These executives were faced with the challenge of finding new ways to distinguish the bank as the leader in the banking industry. To do so, Wells Fargo executives made the decision to establish the sales of simple-to-understand, simple-to-use products such as credit and debit cards, coupled with traditional banking services such as car and home loans. These products were then cross-sold to customers with an aggressive sales incentive program. Once Wells Fargo branch employees realized they could not reach the high set goals, many began opening unauthorized accounts so it would look like they were meeting the goals.

As a result of the scandal, bank customers felt deceived. The bank reported that checking-account openings had fallen 43 percent and credit card applications 55 percent from the year before. The situation worsened in 2017 when the bank discovered 1.4 million more fake accounts, bringing the total number of fake accounts to 3.5 million. Today the bank finds its reputation in ruins thanks to unrealistic sales quotas and a coercive corporate environment.

Wells Fargo chose to adopt a short-term perspective for the temporary gains that came with committing fraud. If Wells Fargo executives and managers had prioritized *how* employees were making their sales goals, then they would have detected the fraud sooner and taken steps to correct it. Wells Fargo has replaced leadership at the top, is becoming more transparent about its past misconduct, and plans to improve ethics and compliance in the future. Often, firms that deal with highly visible misconduct develop some of the strongest ethical cultures in their industry going forward. Only time will tell in the case of Wells Fargo.[24]

1. How did Wells Fargo's focus on short-term gains violate the duties owed to consumers, regulators, and employees?
2. Describe how the Wells Fargo scandal demonstrates that organizational leaders must not only establish goals but also ensure that those goals are being acted upon appropriately.
3. Why are ethical values useless unless they are continually reinforced within the company?

Notes

1. Matthew Boyle, "Can Eaton Outrun the Recession?" *Bloomberg BusinessWeek*, January 6, 2009, http://www.businessweek.com/bwdaily/dnflash/content/jan2009/db2009015_224435.htm (accessed June 1, 2011); *CR Magazine*, "CR's 100 Best Corporate Citizens," 2017, http://www.thecro.com/wp-content/uploads/2017/05/CR_100Bestpages_digitalR.pdf (accessed September 22, 2017); "Eaton CEO Emphasizes Ethics," Carnegie Mellon Tepper School of

Business, http://tepper.cmu.edu/news- multimedia/tepper -stories/eaton-ceo-emphasizes-ethics/index.aspx (accessed June 1, 2011); Eaton Corporation, "2010 Annual Report," http://www.eaton.com/ecm/groups/public/@pub/@eaton/@ corp/documents/content/pct_260900.pdf (accessed September 22, 2017); Eaton Corporation, *2016 Sustainability Metrics* (Cleveland: Eaton Corporation, 2017), http://www.eaton.com/ ecm/groups/public/@pub/@sustainability/documents/content/ pct_3099477.pdf (accessed September 22, 2017); Eaton Corporation, "About Us—Fast Facts," http://www.eaton.com/ Eaton/OurCompany/AboutUs/CorporateInformation/FastFacts/ index.htm (accessed September 22, 2017); Eaton Corporation, "Accountability & Transparency," http://www.eaton.in/ EatonIN/OurCompany/Sustainability/Accountability Transparency/index.htm (accessed September 22, 2017); Eaton Corporation, *Code of Ethics*, 2015, http://www.eaton.com/ecm/ groups/public/@pub/@eaton/@corp/documents/content/pct_ 1223598.pdf (accessed September 22, 2017); Eaton Corpora- tion, "Community Involvement," http://www.eaton.com/flash/ eaton/materiality/localCommunityInvolvement.html (accessed September 22, 2017); Eaton Corporation, *Ethics: The Power of Doing Business Right* (Cleveland: Eaton Corporation, 2011), p. 6. Web version; Eaton Corporation, "Global Ethics and Compliance," http://www.eaton.com/Eaton/OurCompany/ GlobalEthics/index.htm (accessed September 22, 2017); Eaton Corporation, *Global Ethics—Ethics Guide* (Cleveland: Eaton Corporation, 2011); Eaton Corporation, "Governance," http:// www.eaton.com/Sustainability/governance/index.htm (accessed September 22, 2017); Eaton Corporation, "Message from the Chairman," http://www.eaton.com/flash/eaton/materiality/ chairman.html (accessed September 22, 2017); Eaton Corpora- tion, "Sustainability," http://www.eaton.com/Sustainability/ index.htm (accessed September 22, 2017); Eaton Corporation, "Wallet Guide," 2003[1]; Eaton Corporation, "Worldwide Gift and Entertainment Policy," http://www.eaton.com/ecm/groups/ public/@pub/@eaton/@corp/documents/content/ct_251820.pdf (accessed September 22, 2017); Ethisphere Institute, "World's Most Ethical Companies," Ethisphere, 2011, http://worlds mostethicalcompanies.ethisphere.com/honorees/ (accessed September 22, 2017); Wayne Heilmen, "UCCS Speaker: Ethics Policies Must Be Enforced Consistently," *Colorado Springs Gazette*, March 15, 2011, http://gazette.com/uccs-speaker -ethics-policies-must-be-enforced-consistently/article/114612 (accessed September 22, 2017).

2. Vernon R. Loucks, Jr., "A CEO Looks at Ethics," *Business Horizons* 30 (March–April 1987), 4.

3. James R. Hagerty, "Caterpillar Closes Plant in Canada After Lockout," *The Wall Street Journal*, February 4, 2012, https:// www.wsj.com/articles/SB1000142405297020388990457720009 53014575964 (accessed January 2, 2018).

4. Karen Gullo, "Costco Workers Win Class Certification for Bias Case," *Bloomberg*, Sept. 25, 2012, http://www.bloomberg .com/news/2012-09-25/judge-certifies-costco-sex-discrimina tion-case-as-class-action.html (accessed June 25, 2013).

5. John Kopp, "Wet Seal to pay $7.5m in discrimination lawsuit," *Denver Post*, May 10, 2013, http://www.denverpost .com/nationworld/ci_23215986/wet-seal-pay-7-5m -discrimination-lawsuit (accessed January 2, 2018).

6. Thomas M. Jones, "Ethical Decision Making by Individuals in Organizations: An Issue-Contingent Model," *Academy of Management Review* 2 (April 1991): 371–373.

7. Sir Adrian Cadbury, "Ethical Managers Make Their Own Rules," *Harvard Business Review* 65 (September–October 1987), 72.

8. O. C. Ferrell and Larry Gresham, "A Contingency Frame- work for Ethical Decision Making in Marketing," *Journal of Marketing* 49 (Summer 1985): 87–96.

9. Gene R. Laczniak and Patrick E. Murphy, *Ethical Marketing Decisions: The Higher Road* (Boston: Allyn & Bacon, 1993), 14.

10. Margaret Cunningham, "Walking the Thin White Line: A Role Conflict Model of Ethical Decision Making Behavior in the Marketing Research Process," Ph.D. Dissertation, Texas A&M University, 1991.

11. Ferrell and Gresham, "A Contingency Framework."

12. O. C. Ferrell, John Fraedrich, and Linda Ferrell, *Business Ethics Ethical Decision Making and Cases*, 9th ed. (Mason: South-Western Cengage Learning, 2013), p. 222.

13. Muel Kaptein, "From Inaction to External Whistleblowing: The Influence of the Ethical Culture of Organizations on Employee Responses to Observed Wrongdoing," *Journal of Business Ethics* 98(3), February 2011, 513–530.

14. "Ethics Hotline: Why Would an Employer Want to Estab- lish a Whistleblower or Ethics Hotline?" *Society for Human Resource Management*, November 7, 2017, https://www.shrm .org/resourcesandtools/tools-and-samples/hr-qa/pages/ whywouldanemployerwanttohaveawhistleblowerorethics hotline.aspx (accessed January 2, 2018).

15. Samuel Rubenfeld, "SEC Issues First Dodd-Frank Whistle- blower Award," *The Wall Street Journal*, August 21, 2012, http://blogs.wsj.com/corruption-currents/2012/08/21/sec-issues -first-dodd-frank-whistleblower-award/ (accessed January 2, 2018).

16. Archie B. Carroll, ''The Pyramid of Corporate Social Responsibility: Toward the Moral Management of Organiza- tional Stakeholders," *Business Horizons* 34 (July/August 1991), 42.

17. O. C. Ferrell, V. L. Crittenden, L. Ferrell, and W. F. Crittenden, "Theoretical Development in Ethical Decision Making," *AMS Review*, Vol. 3, No. 2 (June 2013), p. 57.

18. David Carrig, "Biscuit Recall Hits Food Lion, Other Grocery Stores in 12 States over *Listeria* Fears," *USA Today*, January 2, 2018, https://www.usatoday.com/story/money/business/2018/01/ 02/biscuit-recall-hits-food-lion-other-grocery-stores-12-states -over-listeria-fears/995438001/ (accessed January 2, 2018).

19. University of New Mexico Daniels Fund Ethics Initiative, "Sseko Designs: Empowering Ugandan Women," https:// danielsethics.mgt.unm.edu/pdf/Sseko.pdf (accessed November 24, 2017); Dianne Kroncke, "Sseko Designs Company Growth," phone interview with Kayla Joy Asbury, Portland, Oregon, October 13, 2017; Eugene Rowe, "Sseko Designs— Brianna Leever, Community Manager and Sseko Fellows Program," radio interview, http://www.hombabiz.com/sseko -designs-brianna-leever/ (accessed on October 12, 2017); Malia Spencer, "Life After 'Shark Tank' Is Pretty Good for One

Portland Startup," *Portland Biz Journals*, February 17, 2015, https://www.bizjournals.com/portland/blog/techflash/2015/02/life-after-shark-tank-is-pretty-good-for-one.html (accessed on October 12, 2017); Sseko Designs website, https://ssekodesigns.com/ (accessed on October 12, 2017); U.S. Mission Uganda, "Like Sseko Designs, You Too Can Take Advantage of the African Growth and Opportunity Act," United States Embassy in Uganda, June 27, 2016, https://ug.usembassy.gov/learn-ugandans-taking-advantage-african-growth-opportunity-act/ (accessed October 12, 2017); United States AID, "Sseko Designs, Uganda: An AGOA Success Story," https://www.usaid.gov/news-information/videos/node/218021 (accessed October 12, 2017); Pete Williams, "Liz Forkin Bohannon from Sseko and the Future of Retail," YouTube, https://www.youtube.com/watch?v=X11t0vy6wiY (accessed October 12, 2017).

20. Paul M. Barrett, "'Down the Rabbit Hole' in the Chevron Pollution Case," *Bloomberg Businessweek*, June 20, 2013, https://www.bloomberg.com/news/articles/2013-06-20/down-the-rabbit-hole-in-the-chevron-pollution-case (accessed January 2, 2018).

21. Brian Dumaine, "Brighter Days for First Solar," *Fortune*, May 20, 2013, pp. 37-38.

22. Morgan Downs (Producer), *Inside the Mind of Google* [DVD], United States: CNBC Originals, 2010.

23. Serena Ng and Erik Holm, "Buffett Jolted as Aide Quits," *The Wall Street Journal*, March 31, 2011, A1-A2; Gina Chon and Serena Ng, "Mixed Signals marked Sokol Meeting," *The Wall Street Journal*, April 2-3, 2011, B1-B2.

24. Paul Blake, "Timeline of the Wells Fargo Accounts Scandal," *ABC News*, November 3, 2016, http://abcnews.go.com/Business/timeline-wells-fargo-accounts-scandal/story?id=42231128 (accessed April 14, 2017); Matt Egan, "I Called the Wells Fargo Ethics Line and Was Fired," *CNN Money*, September 21, 2016, http://money.cnn.com/2016/09/21/investing/wells-fargo-fired-workers-retaliation-fake-accounts/ (accessed April 14, 2017); Emily Glazer, "Wells Fargo to Eliminate Product Sales Goals, Aiming to Rebuild Trust," *The Wall Street Journal*, September 13, 2016, https://www.wsj.com/articles/wells-fargo-cuts-all-sales-goals-as-it-seeks-to-rebuild-trust-1473766077 (accessed April 14, 2017); Emily Glazer and Christina Rexrode, "Wells Fargo CEO Testifies Before Senate Banking Committee," *The Wall Street Journal*, September 20, 2016, https://www.wsj.com/articles/wells-fargo-ceo-testifies-before-senate-banking-committee-1474390303 (accessed April 14, 2017); Matt Egan, "Wells Fargo Workers: Fake Accounts Began Years Ago," *CNN Money*, September 26, 2016, http://money.cnn.com/2016/09/26/investing/wells-fargo-fake-accounts-before-2011/ (accessed April 14, 2017); James Venable, "Wells Fargo: Where Did They Go Wrong?" Working Paper, Harvard University, February 9, 2017, http://scholar.harvard.edu/files/jtv/files/wells_fargo_where_did_they_go_wrong_by_james_venable_pdf_02.pdf (accessed April 14, 2017); Curtis C. Verschoor, "Lessons from the Wells Fargo Scandal," *Strategic Finance*, November 1, 2016. http://sfmagazine.com/post-entry/november-2016-lessons-from-the-wells-fargo-scandal/ (accessed April 14, 2017); Lisa Cook, "The Wells Fargo Scandal: Is the Profit Model to Blame?"

Knowledge @ Warton, University of Pennsylvania, September 13, 2016, http://knowledge.wharton.upenn.edu/article/how-the-wells-fargo-scandal-will-reverberate/ (accessed April 14, 2017); Geoff Colvin, "The Wells Fargo Scandal Is Now Reaching VW Proportions," *Fortune*, January 26, 2017, http://fortune.com/2017/01/25/the-wells-fargo-scandal-is-now-reaching-vw-proportions/ (accessed April 14, 2017); Brian Tayan, "The Wells Fargo Cross-Selling Scandal," *Harvard Law School Forum on Corporate Governance and Financial Regulations*, December 19, 2016, https://corpgov.law.harvard.edu/2016/12/19/the-wells-fargo-cross-selling-scandal/ (accessed April 14, 2017); Michael Corkery, "Wells Fargo Struggling in the aftermath of Fraud Scandal," *The New York Times*, January 13, 2017, https://www.nytimes.com/2017/01/13/business/dealbook/wells-fargo-earnings-report.html (accessed April 14, 2017); Lucinda Shen, "Wells Fargo Sales Scandal Could Hurt Growth Permanently," *Fortune*, April 13, 2017, http://fortune.com/2017/04/13/wells-fargo-report-earnings/ (accessed April 14, 2017);; Matt Egan, "5,300 Wells Fargo Employees Fired Over 2 Million Phony Accounts," *CNN*, September 9, 2016, http://money.cnn.com/2016/09/08/investing/wells-fargo-created-phony-accounts-bank-fees/ (accessed April 14, 2017); Laura J. Keller and Katherine Chiglinsky, "Wells Fargo Eclipsed by JPMorgan as World's Most Valuable Bank," *Bloomberg*, September 13, 2016, https://www.bloomberg.com/news/articles/2016-09-13/wells-fargo-eclipsed-by-jpmorgan-as-world-s-most-valuable-bank (accessed April 14, 2017); Laura Lorenzetti, "This Is the Most Valuable Bank in the World," *Fortune*, July 23, 2015, http://fortune.com/2015/07/23/wells-fargo-worlds-most-valuable-bank/ (accessed April 14, 2017); Matt Egan, "Letter warned Wells Fargo of 'widespread' fraud in 2007 – exclusive," *CNN Money*, October 18, 2016, http://money.cnn.com/2016/10/18/investing/wells-fargo-warned-fake-accounts-2007/ (accessed January 6, 2017); Stacy Cowley, "At Wells Fargo, Complaints about Fraudulent Accounts since 2005," *The New York Times*, October 11, 2016, http://www.nytimes.com/2016/10/12/business/dealbook/at-wells-fargo-complaints-about-fraudulent-accounts-since-2005.html (accessed January 6, 2017); Mark Snider, "Ex-Wells Fargo Bankers Sue over Firing amid Fraud," *USA Today*, September 25, 2016, http://www.usatoday.com/story/money/2016/09/25/ex-wells-fargo-employees-sue-over-scam/91079158/ (accessed January 6, 2017); Winston Craver, "Wells Fargo Draws Senators' Ire on Fraud Accounts Response," *Winston-Salem Journal*, December 23, 2016, http://www.journalnow.com/news/local/wells-fargo-draws-senators-ire-on-fraud-accounts-response/article_b2c44587-e2cf-5cb1-966e-6e20c89fa9d8.html (accessed January 6, 2017); Ian Mount, "Wells Fargo's Fake Accounts May Go Back More than 10 Years," *Fortune*, October 12, 2016, http://fortune.com/2016/10/12/wells-fargo-fake-accounts-scandal/ (accessed April 14, 2017); Stacy Cowley and Jennifer A. Kingson, "Wells Fargo to Claw Back $75 Million from 2 Former Executives," *The New York Times*, April 10, 2017, https://www.nytimes.com/2017/04/10/business/wells-fargo-pay-executives-accounts-scandal.html (accessed April 14, 2017); Matt Egan, "Wells Fargo Uncovers Up to 1.4 Million More Fake Accounts," *CNN Money*, August 31, 2017, http://money.cnn.com/2017/08/31/investing/wells-fargo-fake-accounts/index.html (accessed December 28, 2017).

Managing in a Global World

CHAPTER 5

Source: jannoon028/Shutterstock

Chapter Outline

Introduction

The Global Business Environment

Levels of Organizational
    Involvement in Global Business

Regional Trade Alliances
    and Agreements

Managing Global Business

After reading this chapter, you will be able to:

- Analyze the factors within the global trade environment that influence business.

- Specify the different levels of organizational involvement in international trade.

- Summarize the various trade agreements and alliances that have developed worldwide and how they influence business activities.

- Determine how global business affects management.

- Assess the opportunities and problems facing a small business considering expanding into international markets.

It's Not Folklore: Alibaba Has Global Online Reach

When Jack Ma founded Alibaba as an e-commerce business in 1999, he had never run a company and had no technology experience. Born and raised in Hangzhou, China, Ma learned English by conversing with tourists. Through these conversations, he gained a global perspective that complemented his entrepreneurial drive. After working as an English teacher, Ma took a trip to California's Silicon Valley and saw firsthand how the Internet was transforming the business world. He quickly realized the commercial potential of pioneering an online marketing channel in China so that small businesses could connect with local and international buyers of business goods and services.

Ma gathered a group of like-minded friends, who pooled $80,000 and their expertise to create an Internet marketplace he named "Alibaba" because of the association with opening doors and finding treasure. The initial business-to-business website did so well that Alibaba opened a second online marketplace for selling to consumers called Taobao, followed by an e-commerce mall for multinational retailers targeting Chinese consumers. In 2005, Ma formed a strategic alliance with Yahoo! Inc. cofounder Jerry Yang when he recognized the need for a search engine partner. The deal resulted in Yahoo purchasing a 40 percent stake in Alibaba for $1 billion.

Ma's launch of a Chinese e-commerce business was not without significant risk. Not many consumers engaged in e-commerce when Alibaba was founded. Obstacles existed in the economic and technological environments. Disposable incomes were still relatively low in China, and Internet connections were slow and expensive. The only ones able to access e-commerce easily were businesses, which is likely why Alibaba started as a business-to-business e-commerce retailer. However, as technology improved and disposable incomes increased, more Chinese consumers became interested in e-commerce. This led Alibaba to launch Taobao in 2003.

Changing technology and economic trends were not the only hurdles Alibaba had to overcome. China has a high level of uncertainty avoidance, meaning that Chinese consumers tend to avoid risk if possible. This makes establishing trust highly important. Entrepreneurs like Ma needed to find ways to establish trust between buyer and seller in order for e-commerce channels to work. Rating systems help to overcome this barrier, as well as real-time chat that allows buyers and sellers to learn about one another before they engage in transactions. These technologies help to alleviate the trust issues that come with e-commerce.

Source: Evan Lorne/Shutterstock

Today the company's many marketplaces and supporting businesses, such as electronic payment systems, serve more than 600 million customers in 240 nations. When it went public on the New York Stock Exchange in 2014, Alibaba raised $25 billion to fuel Ma's latest idea: working with Hollywood studios to forge new channels for distributing movies and programs in China and beyond. Ma's vision for expanding international business doesn't stop there. He set a goal to increase Alibaba's revenue outside China from 10 percent of total revenues to 50 percent.

Alibaba also has competitive advantages. It has held tightly to its top spot in China, where non-Chinese e-commerce sites have struggled. eBay's move into the market lasted only two years and ultimately concluded in the closure of its China Web unit. Similarly, Amazon has found little success in China, even with the launch of its Prime membership. Alibaba, with a 47 percent market share in China's online retail market, has made it more difficult for Amazon to compete on price, preventing the U.S. online retail giant from gaining traction. China, with approximately 890 million online shoppers, is overtaking the United States as the largest e-commerce market, and the opportunities are too good for many investors to pass up.

However, with growth comes ethical issues, and Alibaba is no exception. The company has faced bribery allegations and charges related to counterfeit goods in China as well as a probe into its accounting practices from the U.S. Securities and Exchange Commission. As the company expands, it has begun removing products that have been flagged as counterfeit. The enormous amount of counterfeit products available worldwide makes the pursuit of counterfeiters challenging. Despite concerns of political risk and the sale of counterfeit goods, investors have not been de-

It's Not Folklore: Alibaba Has Global Online Reach (continued)

terred. Today, Alibaba is one of the top 10 companies in the world based on market value, and Ma, with a net worth of $47 billion, is the richest man in China. Alibaba's success comes from understanding the global business environment. Managing with an understanding of the economic, legal, sociocultural, and political forces in the environment was necessary to gain a global competitive advantage.[1]

Introduction

Global business (globalization) is a strategy in which organizations treat the entire world or major regions of it as the domain for conducting business. It includes management decisions about business activities for the whole world, including the United States, rather than focusing on trade between countries. **International business** is a narrower concept defined as the buying, selling, and trading of goods and services across national boundaries. Falling political barriers and advancing communications and transportation technology are enabling many companies to sell their products overseas as well as in their own countries. And, as cultural and other differences among nations narrow, the trend toward the globalization of business is becoming increasingly important.

Already, consumers around the world can drink Coca-Cola and Dr Pepper; eat at McDonald's and Pizza Hut; see movies from Mexico, France, Australia, Japan, and China; and watch CNN and MTV on Toshiba and Sony televisions. The products you consume today are just as likely to have been made in South Korea or Germany as in the United States. Similarly, consumers in other countries buy Western electrical equipment, clothing, rock music, cosmetics, and toiletries, as well as computers, robots, and earth-moving equipment. Brands such as Coca-Cola, Sony, and Levi Strauss seem to make year-to-year gains in the global market.

In this chapter we explore management in this global market. First, we examine the sociocultural, political-legal, and economic environment of global business, which managers must understand to carry out their functions. Next, we discuss the levels of organizational involvement in international business. Then we look at some important regional trade alliances and agreements and the impact of foreign investment in the United States. Finally, we briefly discuss how global business affects management decisions on planning, organizing, leading, and controlling.

global business (globalization): A strategy in which organizations treat the entire world or major regions of it as the domain for conducting business.

international business: The buying, selling, and trading of goods and services across national boundaries.

The Global Business Environment

Managers considering international business must research a country's social, cultural, political, and legal background and obtain information about how to deal with its tariffs, quotas, and currency. Such research will help the company choose an appropriate level of involvement and operating strategies. Figure 5.1 illustrates the different environments that constitute the global management environment.

The Sociocultural Environment

Most businesspeople engaged in international trade underestimate the importance of social and cultural differences, but these differences can create nightmares for managers. Culture can be defined as a sort of blueprint of acceptable behavior in a society that

Many larger companies view most countries as markets for their products.

Source: Markus Pfaff/Shutterstock

FIGURE 5.1
Global Management
Environment

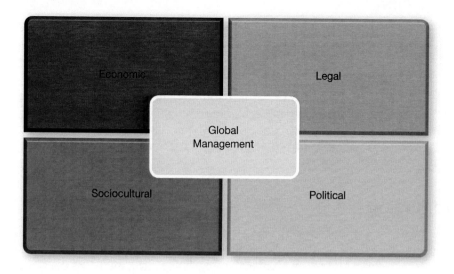

is passed from one generation to the next. Unfortunately, cultural norms are rarely written down, and what is written down may well be inaccurate.

Although it is possible to translate words from one language to another, the true meaning is sometimes misinterpreted or lost. For example, General Motors successfully marketed the Chevrolet Nova in the United States for many years, but GM had some problems selling the car abroad. In English, *nova* means "bright star," an acceptable name for a car. In Spanish, however, *nova (no va)* means "it does not go," which certainly does not convey a positive image for the car! Similarly, *Esso* in Japanese translates to "stalled car," so not surprisingly the Japanese were reluctant to fuel up with Esso gasoline. Americans found a German chocolate confection particularly unappetizing: It was marketed under the name Zit.[2] While such examples are humorous, they also illustrate the difficulties of conducting business in other languages and cultures.

Differences in body language and personal space are another aspect of culture that may affect international trade. Body language is nonverbal, usually unconscious communication through gestures, posture, and facial expression. Personal space is the distance at which one person feels comfortable talking to another. Americans tend to stand a moderate distance away from the person with whom they are speaking. Arab businessmen tend to stand face to face with the object of their conversation. Additionally, gestures vary from culture to culture, and gestures considered acceptable in American society—such as pointing—may be considered rude in others. Such cultural differences may generate uncomfortable feelings or misunderstandings when businesspeople of different countries interact.

The people of other nations quite often have a different perception of time as well. Americans and Germans value promptness: A business meeting scheduled for a specific time seldom starts more than a few minutes late. In Mexico and Spain, however, it is not unusual for a meeting to be delayed half an hour or more. Such a late start might produce resentment in an American negotiating in Spain for the first time.

Companies engaged in foreign trade must observe the national and religious holidays and local customs of the host country. In many Islamic countries, for example, workers expect to take a break at certain times of the day to observe religious rites. In Thailand and many other countries, public displays of affection between the sexes are unacceptable in advertising messages; in many Middle Eastern nations, showing the soles of your feet is considered an insult. Because India's Hindu population considers it taboo to eat beef, McDonald's markets hamburgers without beef; it instead offers lamb or vegetarian burgers.[3] Table 5.1 lists additional cultural variations that may affect business discussions.

Different countries may have different customs regarding respect for authority, as well. In Scandinavia, Great Britain, and the Netherlands, managers tend not to be too intim-

TABLE 5.1 Cultural Variations among Countries

■ Shaking the head in a horizontal direction in most countries means "no," while in India it means "yes." In the Hindi language the voice lowers in pitch at the end of a question.	■ Laughing is connoted in most countries with happiness. In Japan it is often a sign of confusion, insecurity, and embarrassment.
■ In Mediterranean European countries, Latin America, and Sub-Saharan Africa, it is normal, or at least widely tolerated, to arrive half an hour late for a dinner invitation, whereas in Germany and Switzerland this would be extremely rude.	■ In the UK, Ireland, and Commonwealth countries, the word "compromise" has a positive meaning (as consent, an agreement where both parties win something); in the USA it may have negative connotations (as both parties lose something).

idated by their superiors, which enables companies such as Shell Oil Company to encourage managers to provide feedback on their own superiors' performance. However, in countries such as Turkey, Greece, and France, there is a strong tradition of deference toward superiors, so managers in those countries may feel uncomfortable commenting on their superiors' actions.[4]

This lack of uniformity creates problems for both buyers and sellers in the international marketplace. American sellers, for instance, must package goods destined for foreign markets in liters or meters, and Japanese sellers must convert to the English system when they plan to sell a product in the United States. Tools also must be in the correct system if they are to function correctly. Hyundai and Honda service technicians need metric tools to make repairs on those cars.

The literature dealing with international business is filled with accounts of sometimes humorous but often costly mistakes that occurred because of a lack of understanding of the social and cultural differences between buyers and sellers. Such problems cannot always be avoided, but they can be minimized through research on the cultural and social differences of the host country. IBM, Motorola, and many other large companies now employ consultants to help train managers being transferred to other countries to understand cultural differences and how to solve problems related to these differences.[5]

Hofstede's Cultural Dimensions Theory

Management experts have attempted to develop frameworks to understand cultural and regional behavior patterns to help managers in conducting global business. One of the most prominent academic researchers in the area of national culture is Professor Geert Hofstede. After conducting a study on 100,000 IBM employees in 64 countries, Hofstede outlined five major cultural dimensions that profoundly impact the global business environment: individualism vs. collectivism, power distance, masculinity vs. femininity, uncertainty avoidance, and time orientation.[6] Table 5.2 provides examples of countries that exemplify these different characteristics.

The individualism/collectivism dimension relates to whether an employee tends to approach a situation more from an individual level or as a team. Individualists tend to be self-reliant and place a high level of importance on freedom and ambition. Collectivists place more value on the team than the individual. Employees from collectivist cultures value group harmony and the achievement of group goals. The United States tends to value more of an individualist approach, while China and Thailand have a collectivist approach.

Power distance refers to how much perceived power there is between managers and subordinates. In cultures with higher power distances, it would be less acceptable for a subordinate to question a manager's decision. For instance, in some countries like Australia—which are "low" on this dimension—it may be perfectly acceptable to address

TABLE 5.2 Five Major Cultural Dimensions

Cultural Dimension		Country
Individualism/Collectivism	Individualism	Australia
	Collectivism	Pakistan
Power Distance	High	Guatemala
	Low	Austria
Masculinity/Femininity	Masculinity	Venezuela
	Femininity	Sweden
Uncertainty Avoidance	High	Japan
	Low	Denmark
Long-Term Orientation	High	China
	Low	Nigeria

one's supervisor or boss by his or her first name. Despite the differences in roles, subordinates in these cultures see themselves on a more equal footing. However, in high power distance countries like Russia or Venezuela, this may be totally inappropriate because it would be viewed as a sign of disrespect.

The masculinity/femininity dimension involves the emotional characteristics valued within a culture. For instance, some cultures value characteristics such as assertiveness, competitiveness, and materialism—traditionally associated as masculine traits. In Japan and Hungary, competitiveness and assertiveness are high. Other cultures value more nurturing behaviors with an emphasis on relationships—generally associated with feminine behaviors. Norway tends to have a more feminine culture. For instance, in Nordic countries, men as well as women can take time off for work for parental leave (in the case of fathers, paternity leave).[7]

Uncertainty avoidance refers to how a culture handles uncertain situations. Cultures with high uncertainty avoidance tend to avoid risk and ambiguous situations. Uruguay, for instance, scores higher on uncertainty avoidance. In other countries, such as the United States and Canada, risk-taking in business is seen as an often necessary step for success and innovativeness.[8]

Finally, cultures tend to differ on how they perceive time. Some national cultures have a very long time horizon or orientation, while others want things to happen quickly. In Japan, for instance, a company might be willing to wait a decade until a new corporate division

Source: Scanrail1/Shutterstock

Uncertainty avoidance tends to be low in a country such as Denmark, which also ranks high in the happiness of its citizens.

starts making money. They are more willing to take a long-term view of the situation. A U.S. company may be willing to wait a year—at most! Consider the pressure on CEOs in the United States to make the numbers on the firm's quarterly reports.

GLOBE Project

More recently, a project was conducted to build on Hofstede's study of culture. The Global Leadership and Organizational Behavior Effectiveness (GLOBE) project was begun in 1993 and intended to identify different cultural dimensions in its study of leadership. The project surveyed thousands of business executives from 62 countries about nine different cultural variables/dimensions.[9] In addition to Hofstede's dimensions, the GLOBE Project studied humane orientation, assertiveness, performance orientation, gender egalitarianism, and future orientation. They also separated collectivism into in-group collectivism and institutional collectivism.

Humane orientation for example, examines the extent to which groups encourage and reward people for being generous, fair, caring, and altruistic. Southern Asian countries like India and Indonesia rank highly on this dimension, while some European countries like Germany and Australia rank relatively poorly. Germany and the United States score higher on the assertiveness dimension because they place high value on competition, while Nordic countries score lower. On the other hand, in terms of gender equality, Nordic countries scored high. Whereas New Zealand and the United States scored higher on the performance orientation, countries like Venezuela and Argentina tended to score lower as these cultures tend to place more emphasis on family. Finally, Singapore and Nordic countries tend to score high on a future orientation—meaning that they tend to score higher on planning and investing—while Russia and Kuwait tended to score lower.[10]

The Political-Legal Environment

The Political Environment

Like social and cultural customs, political considerations are very important and often change rapidly. For example, there has recently been considerable controversy in Germany regarding its role in the European Union (EU) and its continued usage of the euro as its currency. Germany's economy has been very strong, in contrast to many other struggling EU nations. Some argue that Germany should abandon the euro and return to its own national currency, the mark. Having the mark as its own currency, it is asserted, would give Germany more economic influence around the world. On the other hand, Germany's departure from the euro would have tremendous political effects as well as other reverberations. While these are major events, political considerations affect international business daily as governments enact tariffs, embargoes, or other types of trade restrictions in response to political events.

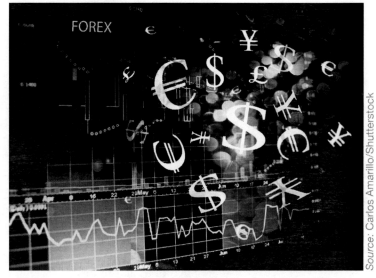

Evolving political influences have significant impact on decisions as to the form of currency adopted by a particular country.

Source: Carlos Amarillo/Shutterstock

Managers engaged in international trade must consider the relative stability of the countries in which they wish to do business. While countries such as Canada, Great Britain, and Japan are relatively stable, political unrest in other countries may create a hostile or even dangerous environment for foreign businesses. Civil war, terrorism, and frequent changes of government make it difficult for managers to plan for the future and may even expose a firm's employees to danger. The September 11, 2001, terrorist attacks at the World Trade Center and Pentagon in the United States showed that even relatively stable countries like the United States are subject to upheaval in today's inter-connected world. Countries like Somalia with its ongoing piracy and general unrest present ongoing issues to businesses operating in that region of the world.

Political concerns may lead a group of nations to form a cartel to generate a competitive advantage in world markets. A **cartel** is a group of firms or nations that agree to act

cartel: A group of firms or nations that agree to act as a monopoly and not compete with each other.

By maintaining control over production, OPEC attempts to maximize the revenue of member countries.

as a monopoly and not compete with each other. One successful cartel is the De Beers Central Marketing Organization, which markets industrial and gem-quality diamonds for South Africa, Russia, Zaire, and Botswana. Probably the most famous cartel is OPEC, the Organization of Petroleum Exporting Countries, founded in the 1960s to increase the price of petroleum throughout the world and to maintain high prices. By working to ensure stable oil prices, OPEC hopes to enhance the economies of its member nations.

The Legal Environment

Unlike social, cultural, and political barriers, laws are written down and usually are quite explicit. A firm that decides to enter the international marketplace must contend with the laws of its own nation, international laws, and the laws of the nation with which it will be trading.

The United States has a number of laws that affect domestic firms engaged in international trade. The **Webb-Pomerene Export Trade Act**, passed in 1918, for example, allows selected American firms desiring international trade to form monopolies in order to compete with foreign cartels. However, these firms are not allowed to limit free trade and competition within the United States or to use unfair methods of competition in international trade. The **Foreign Corrupt Practices Act (FCPA)**, passed in 1978, outlaws direct payoffs to and bribes of foreign governments or business officials by American companies. An American company is allowed to make small gifts where they are customary but may not make large payments or offer bribes to influence the policy decisions of foreign governments. This act specifies penalties for both the company and the individuals involved. The United States also has a variety of friendship, commerce, and navigation treaties with other nations. These treaties allow business to be transacted between citizens of the specified countries.

A more encompassing anti-bribery law is the **U.K. Bribery Act** passed in 2010. Under the Bribery Act, all organizations with business operations in the United Kingdom can be held liable for bribery, even if the bribery did not occur within the United Kingdom.[11] Additionally, while the FCPA is limited to bribing foreign officials, the U.K. Bribery Act covers any type of bribery. In fact, the first cases prosecuted under the law dealt with bribes between private businesspeople, including offering bribes to pass a taxi driver test and attempting to bribe a professor.[12] At first, the U.K. Bribery Act did not allow for facilitation payments like the FCPA, although this part of the law is being reconsidered.[13] Businesses can also be held responsible if their joint-venture partners or subsidiaries are caught in the act of bribery.[14] However, the U.K. Serious Fraud Office may provide leniency for those

Webb-Pomerene Export Trade Act: Allows selected American firms desiring international trade to form monopolies in order to compete with foreign cartels.

Foreign Corrupt Practices Act (FCPA): Outlaws direct payoffs to and bribes of foreign governments or business officials by American companies.

U.K. Bribery Act: All organizations with business operations in the United Kingdom can be held liable for bribery, even if the bribery did not occur within the United Kingdom.

TABLE 5.3 Corporate Tax Rates among Different Countries

Australia	30%
Denmark	22%
United Kingdom	20%
Israel	25%
Ireland	12.5%
United States	21%
Average Corporate Tax Rate	23.83%

Source: OECD, Taxation of Corporate and Capital Income, 2016 and 2018.

companies that have strong ethical controls, compliance programs, and oversight systems in place.[15]

The laws of other nations are often different from those of the United States. Many of the legal rights that Americans take for granted do not exist in other countries, and a firm doing business abroad must understand and obey the laws of the host country. Many nations forbid foreign nationals from owning real property outright; others have copyright and patent laws that are less strict than those of the United States. They may also have strict laws limiting the amount of local currency that can be taken out of the country and the amount of foreign currency that can be brought in. Table 5.3 lists the differentiation in corporate tax rates among countries. If a business wishes to succeed in another country, its managers must pay careful attention to their activities to ensure that it remains within that country's laws.

Source: wavebreakmedia/Shutterstock

Bribery is one of the most prosecuted global offenses.

Tariffs and Trade Restrictions

Tariffs and other trade restrictions are part of a country's legal structure but may be established or removed for many political reasons. An **import tariff** is a tax levied by a nation on goods bought outside its borders and imported into the country. A *fixed tariff* is a specific amount of money levied on each unit of a product brought into the country, while an *ad valorem tariff* is based on the value of the item. Most countries allow citizens traveling abroad to bring home a certain amount of merchandise without paying an import tariff. A U.S. citizen may bring $800 worth of merchandise into the United States duty-free. After that, U.S. citizens must pay an ad valorem tariff based on the cost of the item and the country of origin.[16] Thus, identical items purchased in different countries might have different tariffs.

The use of protective tariffs, which raise the price of foreign goods, has become a controversial topic, as Americans become increasingly concerned over the U.S. trade deficit. Protective tariffs allow more expensive domestic goods to compete with foreign ones. Many advocate the imposition of tariffs on products for certain items. They say protective tariffs insulate domestic industries, particularly new ones, against well-established and perhaps even subsidized foreign competitors. Tariffs also help when, because of low labor costs and other advantages, foreign competitors can afford to sell their products at prices lower than those charged by domestic companies. Some Americans argue that tariffs should be used to keep domestic wages high and unemployment low. However, critics of protective tariffs argue that their use inhibits free trade and competition.

import tariff: A tax levied by a nation on goods bought outside its borders and imported into the country.

Source: Iam_Anupong/Shutterstock

The United States currently has a trade-weighted average import tariff rate of 2.0 percent on industrial goods (representing 96% of industrial, non-agriculture goods).

exchange controls: Restrictions on the amount of a particular currency that may be bought or sold.

Exchange controls are restrictions on the amount of a particular currency that may be bought or sold. Some countries control their foreign trade by forcing businesspeople to buy and sell foreign products through a central bank. If Deere & Company, for example, receives payments for its tractors in a foreign currency, it may be required to sell the currency to that nation's central bank. When foreign currency is in short supply, as it is in many Third World and Eastern European countries, the government uses foreign currency to purchase necessities and capital goods and produces other products locally, thus limiting its need for foreign imports.

quota: The maximum number of units of a particular product that may be imported into a country.

A **quota** is the maximum number of units of a particular product that may be imported into a country. A quota may be established by voluntary agreement or by government decree. The United States imposes quotas on certain goods, including garments from China and Vietnam.

embargo: The suspension of trade in a particular product by the government.

An **embargo** is the suspension of trade in a particular product by the government. Embargoes are generally directed at specific goods or countries and may be established for political, health, or religious reasons. For example, the United States forbids the importing of cigars from Cuba for political reasons. Health embargoes prevent the importing of various pharmaceuticals, animals, plants, and agricultural products. Muslim nations forbid the importing of alcoholic beverages.

dumping: Occurs when a country or business firm sells products at less than what it costs to produce them.

One common reason for setting quotas is to prohibit dumping. **Dumping** occurs when a country or business sells products at less than what it costs to produce them. The United States set a tariff on Chinese solar panels after an investigation claimed that Chinese companies were dumping solar panels with extremely low prices.[17]

A company may dump its products for several reasons. Dumping permits quick entry into a market; it sometimes occurs when the domestic market for a firm's product is too small to support an efficient level of production. In other cases, technologically obsolete products that are no longer salable in the country of origin are dumped overseas. Dumping is relatively difficult to prove, but even the suspicion of it can lead to the imposition of quotas.

The Economic Environment

When considering doing business in another country, managers must look at its level of economic development as well as exchange rates.

TABLE 5.4 Percentage of Household Spending on Food

United States	6.4%
United Kingdom	8.2%
Australia	9.8%
Guatemala	40.6%
Philippines	41.9%
Kenya	46.7%
Nigeria	56.4%

Source: World Economic Forum, December 6, 2016, http://www.weforum.org.

Economic Development

The degree of economic development varies from country to country, and American businesspeople must recognize that they cannot take for granted that other countries offer the same things as the United States. Many countries in Africa, Asia, and South America, for example, are, in general, poorer and less economically advanced than those in North America and Europe. These countries are often called *less-developed countries (LDCs)*, characterized by low per capita income (income generated by the nation's production of goods and services divided by the population). LDCs represent a potentially huge and profitable market for many businesses. More economically advanced countries, such as the United States, Japan, Great Britain, and Canada, are often referred to as *industrialized nations*. Table 5.4 illustrates one measure of economic development among countries, the percentage of household spending on food.

One of the most common ways to measure a country's economic development is through **gross domestic product (GDP)**. Gross domestic product is the market value of a nation's total output of goods and services for a given period. The United States has the largest GDP of any country, at more than $18 trillion.[18] *GDP per capita* is GDP in relation to population. Although the GDP per capita of the United States is high at more than $50,000, other countries have higher GDP per capita. For instance, Qatar is considered to

gross domestic product (GDP): The market value of a nation's total output of goods and services for a given period.

Source: Susan Schmitz/Shutterstock

Kenya has some of the highest global expenditures on food because their food prices are so high.

TABLE 5.5 Comparative Analysis of Selected Countries

Country	Population (in millions)	GDP (in billions)	Exports (in billions)	Imports (in billions)	Internet Users (in millions)	Cell Phone Users (in millions)
Australia	23.23	$1,187	$191.7	$198.5	20.2	31
Brazil	207.35	$3,141	$184.5	$139.4	108.2	280.7
Canada	35.62	$1,682	$393.5	$413.4	32.4	29.5
China	1,379.30	$11,199	$1,990	$1,495	626.6	1,300
Costa Rica	4.93	$80.7	$10.15	$14.66	2.4	7.1
Germany	80.59	$3,980	**$1,322**	$1,022	70.3	99.5
India	1,281.94	**$8,662**	$268.6	$376.1	237.3	944
Japan	126.45	**$5,238**	$634.9	$583.5	109.3	152.7
Mexico	124.57	**$2,316**	$374.3	$387.4	49.5	102.2
Russia	142.26	**$3,751**	$281.9	$191.6	84.4	221
South Africa	54.84	$739.4	$75.16	$74.17	24.8	79.5
Thailand	68.41	$1,165	$214.3	$177.7	19.5	97.1
Turkey	80.85	$1,988	$150.2	$191	36.6	71.9
United States	326.63	**$18,570**	**$1,456**	$2,208	276.6	317.4
Venezuela	31.30	$427	$27.2	$20.19	13.6	30.5

Sources: Central Intelligence Agency, "REFERENCES :: GUIDE TO COUNTRY COMPARISONS," The World Factbook, https://www.cia.gov/library/publications/the-world-factbook/rankorder/rankorderguide.html (accessed January 6, 2018); World Bank, https://data.worldbank.org/indicator/NY.GDP.MKTP.CD (accessed January 6, 2018).

have the highest in the world at over $129,000.[19] Table 5.5 provides a comparative analysis of selected countries.

A *country's* level of development is determined largely by its **infrastructure**, the physical facilities that support its economic activities, such as railroads, highways, ports, air fields, utilities and power plants, schools, hospitals, communication systems, and commercial distribution systems. When doing business in LDCs, for example, a business may need to compensate for confusing distribution and communications problems, or even a lack of technology, in order to achieve its goals.

infrastructure: The physical facilities that support its economic activities, such as railroads, highways, ports, airfields, utilities and power plants, schools, hospitals, communication systems, and commercial distribution systems.

Exchange Rates

exchange rate: The ratio at which one nation's currency can be exchanged for another nation's currency or for gold.

The ratio at which one nation's currency can be exchanged for another nation's currency or for gold is the **exchange rate**. One British pound can be exchanged for about $1.62, and one Japanese yen for around one American cent, but this rate changes almost every day. Familiarity with exchange rates is important in international trade because a business seeking to import goods from another *country* often must obtain the other *country's* currency to complete the trade. A Kuwaiti company that wants to buy oil-field equipment from a U.S. company, for example, will have to exchange its dinars for American dollars—at the current exchange rate—to complete the purchase.

International Trade Facilitators

Although the sociocultural, political-legal, and economic environments may seem like daunting barriers to international trade, facilitators of international trade help managers get involved and succeed in global markets. These include the World Trade Organization, the World Bank, the International Monetary Fund, and the Organization for Economic Cooperation and Development (OECD). Additionally, individual countries may offer incentives to promote import and export trade, such as loans and free trade zones.

World Trade Organization (WTO)

The **World Trade Organization (WTO)** is a global association of member countries that promotes free trade. It has its origins in the General Agreement on Tariffs and Trade (GATT) developed in 1947. During the Great Depression of the 1930s, nations enacted so many protective tariffs covering so many products that international trade became virtually impossible. By the end of World War II, there was considerable international momentum to liberalize trade and minimize the effects of tariffs. GATT, signed by 23 nations, provided a forum for tariff negotiations.

World Trade Organization (WTO): A global association of member countries that promotes free trade.

Between 1948 when GATT was formally established and 1995, eight series of trade negotiations, or "rounds," were held under GATT, with each "round" leading to progressive reductions in trade barriers around the world. The final "round" of GATT, known as The Uruguay Round, led to the replacement of GATT by the World Trade Organization based in Geneva, Switzerland.

While GATT dealt primarily in merchandise trade, the WTO—and numerous agreements negotiated under it since 1995—are broader in nature. It covers topics as diverse as agriculture, services, and intellectual property. Today, more than 150 countries are members of the WTO and they account, on an aggregate basis, for more than 97 percent of global trade in goods and services. The WTO essentially establishes the rules of the game for trade among these numerous nations. Additionally, the WTO helps to resolve disputes, such as dumping conflicts between two countries.[20]

The World Trade Organization and World Bank support free trade and financial support to underdeveloped and developing countries.

World Bank

The **World Bank,** formally known as the International Bank for Reconstruction and Development, was established and supported by the industrialized nations in 1946 to loan money to underdeveloped and developing countries. Its first loan was in 1947 to the country of France for post–World War II reconstruction. Today, it continues to loan money to countries throughout the world for reconstruction and development. It also makes loans to poorer countries for infrastructure and social services purposes, with a strong emphasis in recent years on trying to reduce the prevalence of communicable diseases in many less wealthy/developed parts of the world. Finally, the International Development Association and the International Finance Corporation are associated with the World Bank and provide loans to private businesses as well as individual countries.

World Bank: Formally known as the International Bank for Reconstruction and Development, it was established and supported by the industrialized nations in 1946 to loan money to underdeveloped and developing countries.

International Monetary Fund

The **International Monetary Fund (IMF)** was established after the end of World War II in December 1945. Initially, only 29 countries signed its Articles of Agreement. Today, virtually every country in the world, over 180 in total, is part of the organization. The

International Monetary Fund (IMF): Basic mission is to oversee the international monetary system and help ensure stable currencies and exchange rates throughout the world.

IMF's basic mission is to oversee the international monetary system and help ensure stable currencies and exchange rates throughout the world. One major shift in this regard in the United States came in 1974 when the country relinquished the so-called "gold standard." Prior to that, the U.S. dollar had been pegged to a set or fixed rate of exchange to the commodity gold, in part as an historic attempt to control inflation. Today, absent the gold standard, other governmental initiatives are used to try and control inflation.

Organization of Economic Cooperation and Development

Organization of Economic Cooperation and Development (OECD): An international economic organization comprised of 30 countries that accept the basic principles of free-market economies and representative democracy; recommends and promotes policies to improve the well-being of consumers and societies across the world.

The **Organization of Economic Cooperation and Development (OECD)**, based in Paris, France, is an international economic organization comprised of 30 countries that accept the basic principles of free-market economies and representative democracy. The OECD, which includes nations such as the United States, Japan, Germany, and Poland, conducts considerable global economic and social development analyses. The OECD recommends and promotes policies to improve the well-being of consumers and societies across the world.[21] For instance, recognizing that bribery can be a serious hindrance to fair business practices, the OECD established the Anti-Bribery Convention consisting of legally binding standards making it illegal to bribe foreign officials.[22]

Levels of Organizational Involvement in Global Business

Businesses engage in international trade at many levels—from a small Kenyan business that occasionally exports African crafts, to a huge multinational corporation such as Chevron that sells products around the globe. The degree of commitment of resources and effort required increases according to the level at which a business involves itself in global trade. In this section we examine exporting and importing, trading companies, licensing and franchising, contract manufacturing, joint ventures, direct investment, and multinational corporations. Table 5.6 shows the different levels of organizational involvement in global business.

Exporting and Importing

exporting: The sale of goods and services to foreign markets.

Many companies first get involved in international trade when called upon to supply a foreign business with a particular product. **Exporting**—the sale of goods and services to

TABLE 5.6 Levels of Organizational Involvement in Global Business

Level of Involvement	Example
Exporting/Importing	A small sports business begins to export its products to Canada and Mexico.
Trading Companies	Trading company WTSC connects millions of buyers and sellers throughout the world.
Licensing and Franchising	Subway gives permission for an entrepreneur to open up a franchise operation in France as long as the owner pays the fee and adheres to the conditions of the franchiser.
Contract Manufacturing	Many apparel stores are hiring factories in Vietnam to manufacture apparel for them due to lower labor costs.
Joint Venture or Strategic Alliance	General Motors entered into a joint venture with Shanghai Automotive Industry Corp. to gain a better foothold in the Chinese market.
Direct Investment	Starbucks opens its first retail operation in Costa Rica.

TABLE 5.7 Leading Purchasers of U.S. Exports

Canada—$270 billion in purchases
Mexico—$230 billion in purchases
China—$114 billion in purchases
Japan—$62 billion in purchases
United Kingdom—$56 billion in purchases

Source: U.S. Census Bureau, 2016.

foreign markets—enables organizations of all sizes to participate in global business. A small software company may boost sales by exporting a computer program to buyers in other countries, in addition to selling within the United States.

Importing is the purchase of goods and services from a foreign source. For example, a grocery store chain may import bananas from Honduras and coffee from Colombia. The United States imports a variety of raw materials and manufactured goods from foreign companies, including petroleum, platinum, industrial diamonds, chrome, and bauxite. Table 5.7 lists the leading purchasers of U.S. exports.

importing: The purchase of goods and services from a foreign source.

Exporting sometimes takes place through **countertrade agreements**, which involve bartering products for other products instead of for currency. Such arrangements are fairly common in international trade, especially between Western companies and Eastern European nations. China has used countertrade agreements to invest in Africa. For instance, China developed an agreement with the Congo to trade infrastructure for metals.[23]

countertrade agreements: Exporting that involves bartering products for other products instead of for currency.

A company may export its wares overseas directly or import goods directly from their manufacturer, or it may deal with an intermediary, commonly called an export agent. Export agents seldom produce goods themselves; instead, they usually handle international transactions for other firms. Export agents either purchase products outright or take them on consignment. If they purchase them outright, they generally mark up the price they pay and attempt to sell the product in the international marketplace. They are also responsible for storage and transportation.

An advantage of exporting through an agent is that the company does not have to deal with foreign currencies or the red tape (paying tariffs and handling paperwork) of international business. A major disadvantage is that because the export agent must make a profit, either the price of the product must be increased or the domestic company must provide a larger discount than it would in a domestic transaction.

The U.S. imports large quantities of automobiles from abroad.

Trading Companies

A **trading company** acquires goods in one country and sells them to buyers in another country. Trading companies handle all activities required to move products from one country to another, including purchasing the products outright. They offer consulting, marketing research, advertising, insurance, product research and design, warehousing, and foreign exchange services to companies interested in selling their products in foreign markets. WTSC is a trading company that offers 24-hour-per-day online world trade that connects 20 million companies in 245 countries.[24] Trading companies are similar to export agencies, but their role in international trade is larger. By linking sellers and buyers of goods in different countries, trading companies promote international trade.

trading company: Acquires goods in one country and sells them to buyers in another country.

Franchising provides many established business opportunities for entrepreneurs.

licensing: A trade arrangement in which one company—the licensor—allows another company—the licensee—to use its company name, products, patents, brands, trademarks, raw materials, and/or production processes in exchange for a fee, or royalty.

franchising: A form of licensing in which a company—the franchiser—agrees to provide a franchisee a name, logo, methods of operation, advertising, products, and other elements associated with the franchiser's business, in return for a financial commitment and the agreement to conduct business in accordance with the franchiser's standard of operations.

contract manufacturing: Occurs when a company hires a foreign company to produce a specified volume of the firm's product to specification; the final product carries the domestic firm's name.

joint venture: When a company that wants to do business in another country finds a local partner (occasionally, the host nation itself) to share the costs and operation of the business.

strategic alliance: A partnership formed to create competitive advantage on a worldwide basis.

Licensing and Franchising

Licensing is a trade arrangement in which one company—the licensor—allows another company—the licensee—to use its company name, products, patents, brands, trademarks, raw materials, and/or production processes in exchange for a fee, or royalty. In a royalty agreement, the licensee agrees to pay the licensor a fixed percentage of the profits on each unit manufactured or sold. Coca-Cola and PepsiCo frequently use licensing as a means to market their soft drinks in other countries. Licensing is a way for a company to enter the international marketplace without spending large sums of money abroad and hiring or transferring personnel to handle overseas affairs. It also minimizes problems associated with shipping costs, tariffs, and trade restrictions.

Another advantage of licensing is that it allows the firm to establish goodwill for its products in a foreign market. This goodwill will help the company if it decides to produce or market its products directly in the foreign country at some future date. There are potential disadvantages to licensing as well. If the licensee does not maintain high standards of quality, the product's image may be hurt; therefore, it is important for the licensor to monitor its products overseas and to enforce its quality standards.

Franchising is a form of licensing in which a company—the franchiser—agrees to provide a franchisee a name, logo, methods of operation, advertising, products, and other elements associated with the franchiser's business, in return for a financial commitment and the agreement to conduct business in accordance with the franchiser's standard of operations. Wendy's, KFC (to be discussed in the end-of-chapter case), McDonald's, and Holiday Inn are well-known franchisers with international visibility.

Contract Manufacturing

A firm that does not wish to get involved with licensing arrangements may try **contract manufacturing**, which occurs when a company hires a foreign company to produce a specified volume of the firm's product to specification; the final product carries the domestic firm's name. Spalding, for example, relies on contract manufacturing for its sports equipment; Reebok uses Korean contract firms for the manufacture of many of its athletic shoes. Apple Inc. uses contract manufacturers to manufacture its iPhone and other products in China and elsewhere. Marketing may be handled by the contract manufacturer or by the original company. Some consumers have raised issues regarding the pay and other working conditions at contract manufacturers making products for major companies like Reebok and Apple.

Joint Ventures and Strategic Alliances

Many countries, particularly the less-developed ones, do not permit direct investment by foreign companies or individuals. Or, a company may lack sufficient resources or expertise to operate in a particular country. In such cases, a company that wants to do business in another country may set up a **joint venture** by finding a local partner (occasionally, the host nation itself) to share the costs and operation of the business. For example, the independent oil and gas exploration and production firm Heritage Oil partnered with Nigeria's Bayelsa Oil Company to establish a Nigerian oil company called Petrobay Energy. This joint venture will allow Heritage Oil to gain more of a foothold in the Nigerian oil and gas industry.[25]

A **strategic alliance** is a partnership formed to create competitive advantage on a worldwide basis. In some industries, such as automobiles, mobile phones, and computers, strategic alliances are becoming the predominant means of competing. International competition is so fierce and the costs are so high that few firms have the individual resources to go it alone. Thus, individual firms that lack the resources essential for international success may seek to collaborate with other companies.[26] An example of such an alliance is the agreement between Japan's Sony Corporation and the Swedish telecommunication company Ericsson to make mobile phones. The alliance combines Sony's consumer electronics expertise with Ericsson's technological leadership in the telecommunications industry.

Direct Investment

Companies that want more control and are willing to invest considerable resources in international business may consider **direct investment**, the purchase of overseas production and marketing facilities. With direct investment, a company may control the facilities outright, or it may be the majority stockholder in the company that controls the facilities. Many firms have direct investments in production plants and companies around the globe. Ford Motor Company and 3M, for example, own subsidiaries and manufacturing facilities in many foreign countries. Japanese-owned Nissan owns a plant in Smyrna, Tennessee, as well as other facilities internationally.

direct investment: The purchase of overseas production and marketing facilities; a company may control the facilities outright, or it may be the majority stockholder in the company that controls the facilities.

Outsourcing, a form of direct investment, involves transferring manufacturing or other functions (such as data processing) to countries where labor and supplies are less expensive. Many American computer, apparel, and athletic-shoe makers, for example, have transferred production to Asian countries, where labor costs are lower than in the United States. Many companies have also transferred certain operations to Mexican plants under the *maquiladora* system, under which U.S. companies supply labor-intensive assembly plants, called *maquilas*, with components for assembly, processing, or repair. The Mexican plant returns the finished products to the United States for further processing or shipment to customers. The company pays a U.S. tariff only on the value added to the product in Mexico. U.S. businesses benefit from Mexico's close proximity, low labor rates, and relatively cheap peso, while Mexico benefits from the increased economic development and the creation of new jobs. *Maquilas* are not limited to those associated with U.S. firms; increasingly, firms from Japan and other countries are outsourcing to Mexico.

outsourcing: Involves transferring manufacturing or other functions (such as data processing) to countries where labor and supplies are less expensive.

Outsourcing allows many companies to focus on what they do the best and allow others to partner with them to deliver successful products globally.

Multinational Corporation

The most committed or highest level of international business involvement is the **multinational corporation (MNC)**, a corporation, such as IBM, Exxon-Mobil, and Nestlé, that operates on a worldwide scale, without significant ties to any one nation or region. MNCs are more than simple corporations.

Initially, most multinational corporations were American firms that had increasing international commitments. Now, a growing number of MNCs have their headquarters in some nation other than the United States. Nestlé, with headquarters in Switzerland, operates hundreds of plants around the world and receives revenues from Europe; North, Central, and South America; Africa; and Asia. The Royal Dutch/Shell Group, one of the world's major oil producers and another MNC, has its main offices in The Hague, Netherlands, and London. Other MNCs include BASF, British Petroleum, Mitsubishi, Siemens, Chevron, Toyota, and Unilever.

multinational corporation (MNC): A corporation, such as IBM, ExxonMobil, and Nestlé, that operates on a worldwide scale, without significant ties to any one nation or region.

Regional Trade Alliances and Agreements

Although managers are increasingly viewing the world as one huge marketplace, various regional trade alliances and specific markets have created both difficulties and opportunities for organizations engaging in global business. In this section we focus on the

You're the Manager . . . What Would You Do?

THE COMPANY: Audiotech Electronics
YOUR POSITION: Sales Manager
THE PLACE: Birmingham, Alabama

Audiotech Electronics was founded in 1959 by a father and son working out of their garage to manufacture television station control consoles. Today, Audiotech employs 75 people and currently operates a 35,000-square-foot factory in Birmingham, Alabama, with two wholly owned subsidiaries. The company now manufactures control consoles for television and radio stations and recording studios. The company's products are used by all the major broadcast and cable networks, including CNN.

When Audiotech began, its custom-made consoles for recording studios were not widely available. Within a few years, the company switched from custom manufacturing to larger production to reduce the costs of its consoles and expand into new markets more rapidly. The company is involved in every facet of production—designing the systems, installing the circuits in its computer boards, and even manufacturing and painting the metal cases housing the consoles. The success of the metal-working division led to it being spun off as a separate subsidiary that does complete metal stamping, finishing, and painting. The second subsidiary manufactures tape playback cartridge machines and accessories for radio stations.

Audiotech consoles have unique features designed to meet specific customer needs. The Xenon series television console, for example, was the first marketed specifically for television stations. High-tech consoles modified for use in television stations can cost $300,000 or more, but the Audiotech model costs around half that amount. The Xenon models incorporate features traditionally found in recording systems, producing more sophisticated sound quality. The firm's newest products allow television correspondents to simultaneously hear and communicate with their

Source: dotshock/Shutterstock

Audiotech provides high-quality televisions.

counterparts in different locations. Such specialized products are potentially useful in every country with radio and television stations and recording studios.

Sales of Audiotech consoles have historically been strong in the United States but recently have stabilized, and little growth is occurring. Key personnel in the company are investigating the possibility of expanding the market for their product internationally. Even though Audiotech is a small, privately owned firm, they believe they should evaluate and consider global expansion.

QUESTIONS

1. What are the key considerations you should evaluate as sales manager in determining global expansion?

2. Do you think that a joint venture should be considered? What about the use of a contract sales force from the country you are entering?

3. What are some of the unique problems that a small business might face in global expansion that larger firms would not?

North American Free Trade Agreement (NAFTA): Went into effect on January 1, 1994, and effectively merged Canada, the United States, and Mexico into one market of about 400 million consumers by eliminating most tariffs and trade restrictions on agricultural and manufactured products among the three countries.

North American Free Trade Agreement, the European Union, the Association of Southeast Asian Nations (ASEAN), and the Southern Common Market (MERCOSUR).

The North American Free Trade Agreement (NAFTA)

The **North American Free Trade Agreement (NAFTA)**, which went into effect on January 1, 1994, effectively merged Canada, the United States, and Mexico into one market of about 400 million consumers. NAFTA eliminated most tariffs and trade restrictions on agricultural and manufactured products among the three countries. It is estimated that output for the North America trade area is over $7 trillion.

NAFTA liberalizes U.S. investment in Mexico and Canada, providing for intellectual property rights (of special interest to high technology industries); expands trade and services by requiring equal treatment of U.S. firms in both countries; and simplifies country-of-origin rules, which hinders Japan's use of Mexico as a staging ground for further market penetration into U.S. markets. In sum, NAFTA represents a comprehensive free-trade agreement among Canada, the United States, and Mexico. Today, Canada is the United States' top trading partner, while Mexico is the United States' third top trading partner following, not surprisingly, China. It is possible, though, that in coming decades China may actually surpass Canada as the United States' leading trading partner even given the free-trade advantages of NAFTA.

NAFTA eliminated most tariffs and trade restrictions between the United States, Canada, and Mexico.

One of the most controversial areas of NAFTA has been labor and environmental concerns related to the three countries. While environmental and labor/worker protections are generally comparable in both the United States and Canada, the protections in both these areas in Mexico lag considerably behind. Thus, there has been considerable concern that the free trade among the countries engendered by the agreement could produce a so-called "race to the bottom," or movement of Canadian and American jobs and production to Mexico. To help deal with these concerns, special labor and environmental side agreements were reached in conjunction with NAFTA, and special NAFTA labor and environmental commissions were established. These agreements are designed to help promote better enforcement of current labor/environmental laws and regulations in all three countries, especially Mexico. The hope is that with better enforcement standards, companies will not move to a country simply to take advantage of poorly enforced environmental/labor laws and regulations.

The European Union

One of the oldest regional alliances, the **European Union (EU)**, was established in 1958 to promote the movement of resources and products among member nations. The first six members were Belgium, France, West Germany, Italy, Luxembourg, and the Netherlands. In 1991, East and West Germany merged into one nation, and by 1992 the United Kingdom, Spain, Denmark, Greece, Portugal, and Ireland had joined as well. Until 1992, each nation functioned as a separate market, but at that time, the 12 nations merged into one of the largest world markets—the European Union, with more than 500 million consumers. The population of the European Union makes up 7 percent of the world population.[27]

European Union (EU): An economic and political union of 28 member nations that are located primarily in Europe.

Since 1992 and the Maastricht Treaty that made the EU a full economic union, the EU has expanded considerably. In 1995, Sweden, Finland, and Austria joined, bringing EU

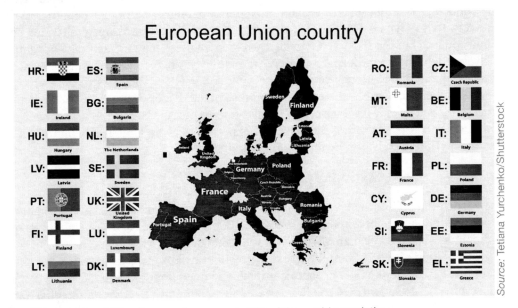

The EU consists of 28 nations and represents 7% of the world population.

TABLE 5.8 Countries of the European Union

Country	Currency	Country	Currency
Austria	Euro	Italy	Euro
Belgium	Euro	Latvia	Euro
Bulgaria	Lev	Lithuania	Euro
Croatia	Kuna	Luxembourg	Euro
Cyprus	Euro	Malta	Euro
Czech Republic	Koruna	Netherlands	Euro
Denmark	Danish krone	Poland	Zloty
Estonia	Euro	Portugal	Euro
Finland	Euro	Romania	Romanian leu
France	Euro	Slovakia	Euro
Germany	Euro	Slovenia	Euro
Greece	Euro	Spain	Euro
Hungary	Forint	Sweden	Swedish krona
Ireland	Euro	United Kingdom (pending Brexit)	Pound sterling

membership to 15. More recently, the trade bloc's expansion has been strongly eastward, with virtually all of the former Eastern European Soviet bloc countries (e.g., Poland, Hungary, Romania) now members of the 28-nation organization. Many of the countries in the EU adopted a common currency, the euro, which helps simplify transactions across borders.

Like NAFTA, however, the EU faces its own set of challenges. The EU has many arguable concerns regarding exchange and movement among the different countries. With relatively free movement of labor, for example, workers are moving to stronger economic countries in the EU like Germany, while businesses may try and take advantage of cheaper labor in countries like Greece. Germany's strong economy has also, as noted earlier, supported the strength of the euro. Table 5.8 lists the countries of the European Union and their standard of currency. It should be noted that on June 23, 2016, the United Kingdom voted to exit the European Union—referred to as "Brexit." While the precise timing of events is somewhat unclear, it is expected that the United Kingdom will be leaving the European Union by the summer of 2019.

Association of Southeast Asian Nations

Association of Southeast Asian Nations (ASEAN): Comprised of ten Southeast Asian countries with the goal to promote economic growth and overall progress in the area via trade and security.

The **Association of Southeast Asian Nations (ASEAN)** is headquartered in Jakarta, Indonesia and is comprised of ten Southeast Asian countries—Indonesia, Malaysia, Singapore, Philippines, Thailand, Vietnam, Brunei, Laos, Cambodia, and Myanmar. The region has a large population of over 600 million, and a growing GDP of more than $1.5 trillion. The goal of ASEAN is to promote economic growth and overall progress in the area via trade and security. In 1993 ASEAN countries passed the Common Effective Preferential Tariff Scheme to phase out and reduce tariffs between the countries over a ten-year period.[28] In terms of furthering its reach, ASEAN has in recent years signed free trade and/or economic partnership agreements with the countries of Japan, India, and Australia-New Zealand. The ASEAN-China Free Trade Agreement (ACFTA) went into full effect in 2015.

Southern Common Market (Mercosur)

The **Southern Common Market (Mercosur)** represents a political and economic agreement among the countries of Bolivia, Argentina, Brazil, Venezuela, Uruguay, and Paraguay. It was originally established in 1991 by the Treaty of Asunción. The South American Countries of Brazil, Argentina, and Venezuela are clearly the key economic powers in this important common market, which has about $100 billion in intra-Mercosur trade per year. There is also considerable political and educational integration and cooperation between and among the various Mercosur countries. Mercosur represents two-thirds of South America's population and is the fourth-largest trading bloc behind the EU, NAFTA, and ASEAN.[29]

Southern Common Market (Mercosur): A political and economic agreement among the countries of Bolivia, Argentina, Brazil, Venezuela, Uruguay, and Paraguay.

Managing Global Business

Competing in an increasingly global economy provides both challenges and opportunities for today's managers as they engage in the planning, organizing, leading, and controlling functions. Planning in a global economy requires managers to understand the sociocultural, political-legal, and economic environment of the countries in which they operate. Before moving outside their own borders, managers must conduct environmental analyses to evaluate the potential of and problems associated with various markets and to determine how best to penetrate those markets. Failure to do so may result in losses and even negative publicity.

Global adaptation to different business environments, however, often faces the key obstacle of the **self-reference criterion**, which involves an often unconscious referencing to the way things are done in one's own culture and experiences in making global business decisions. For example, if McDonald's had simply decided to apply American cultural values when it opened operations in India, it would have likely faced immediate disaster. Its traditional U.S. all-beef patty menu would not have sold well among India's Hindu consumers. Some companies rely on local managers to gain greater insights and faster response to changes within a country. Managers today need to "think globally, act locally"; that is, while constantly being aware of the whole picture, they must adapt their firms' strategies to accommodate local markets.

self-reference criterion: An unconscious referencing to the way things are done in one's own culture and experiences in making global business decisions.

Organizing a business operating in the global marketplace is also challenging. It is difficult enough to organize a domestic business to operate effectively and efficiently; the task is considerably more complex for a business with facilities and subsidiaries around the world. How much decision-making authority and responsibility will local managers have? What organizational structure is most appropriate for the firm? The answers to such questions depend on the firm's resources, the abilities of its managers, and the countries in which it does business.

Leading is an especially complex task for managers working outside their own country. Managers must learn to deal not only with different languages, but also with different customs, values, and work ethics. Moreover, what motivates an employee from the United States to work hard may not have value in another country with a different work ethic. How much supervision is acceptable in a certain country? How much participation should employees have? How should a manager discipline an employee for unacceptable behavior? Managers must learn to respect and accommodate the needs of their employees regardless of what country they are in.

Issues such as productivity, quality control, information systems, and more are just as important in overseas facilities as they are at home. Clearly, when a business fails to meet its goals in overseas markets, managers must determine why and take corrective action. Such action may involve altering strategies for a particular market or abandoning it altogether—both very costly alternatives.

Unilever Strategy: Make Developing Countries Lucrative

Unilever, a British-Dutch company, is a multinational corporation that operates 400 brands on a worldwide scale, without any ties to any certain region. Some of these brands are Dove and Lipton. Not so long ago, Unilever was hit by a weakened world economy. Less than a year later, however, the company rebounded by beating sales expectations. One factor in this rebound is Unilever's actions of raising prices in emerging economies. This decision required an understanding of the sociocultural and political-legal environment.

When first entering emerging markets, global companies like Unilever introduce simpler products at lower prices. As a large multinational corporation, Unilever must compete in an increasingly global competitive market. In raising prices, local competition must be considered. Now those prices are rising as the middle class has begun to desire more advanced products, but the challenge is to plan for products that are popular. As the middle classes increase in countries such as India and China, Unilever is seeing an opportunity to woo these consumers with more sophisticated packaging and upgraded products. It hopes that consumers have become so brand loyal to its products that they will be willing to pay the additional cost. Unilever's strategy is to make sustainable living commonplace. The company believes that this is the best long-term way to grow the business.

Unilever's predictions have so far come true. Many consumers in emerging markets are willing to pay more for their favorite brands, especially shampoos and deodorants. Unilever is also introducing products with improved features, such as a more concentrated version of its laundry detergent in Brazil. Understanding different cultures and customs often requires global firms such as Unilever to adapt certain products so that they will succeed in a particular market.

Despite the initial success, there is the risk that Unilever's price increases will cause it to alienate customers. Consumers in emerging markets tend to be highly price sensitive, with some markets—such as Hong Kong and South Korea—being more price sensitive than others. However, consumers in emerging economies also tend to pay more for products that they perceive as having more value. Therefore, Unilever's introduction of premium products perceived as

Source: Gil C/Shutterstock

having additional value is generating interest from consumers in these countries. This is important for Unilever because 60 percent of its revenues comes from emerging markets.

The potential opportunities in these countries are so important to Unilever that it uses brand-building teams to study the different markets. These teams are organized based on the country and local environments, allowing them to gain insights on consumer trends in that particular culture and determine which products will be most successful. Unilever will often relocate staff to different countries to immerse them in the culture and help the company gain more knowledge on the culture, income, and political environment. It also helps Unilever determine how it can use technology and innovative tools to reach consumers in far-off markets with less infrastructure—a challenge that many companies face as they expand into emerging economies.

The economic environment and the stability of a developing nation's economy can affect income from emerging markets. Unilever must be aware of changes in exchange rates and political trends as it develops strategies for new products at higher prices. Thus far the firm has proven that it is up to the challenge. The more insights Unilever has about specific markets, the more likely Unilever will succeed. In fact, in 2017 Unilever Indonesia was nominated as number 11 on *Forbes* magazine's list of World's Most Innovative Companies for its success within the region.[30]

As we've pointed out in this chapter, many past political barriers to trade have fallen or been minimized, opening and expanding new market opportunities. Managers who can meet the challenges of planning, organizing, leading, and controlling effectively and sensitively in the global marketplace can help lead their companies in meeting these opportunities. Multinational corporations such as General Electric and Ford, which derive a substantial portion of their revenues from international business, depend on savvy managers who can adapt to different cultures. Small businesses, too, can succeed in foreign markets when their managers have carefully studied those markets and prepared and implemented appropriate strategies. Being globally aware is therefore an important quality for today's managers and will become a critical attribute for managers in the twenty-first century.

Summary and Review

■ *Analyze the factors within the global trade environment that influence business.* The sociocultural environment includes culture, language, body language, local customs, time perception, religious considerations, and more. The Hofstede framework and the GLOBE project are two common frameworks for evaluating a country's culture. The political environment may relate to the stability of a country, while the legal environment establishes rules and regulations for conducting business in a certain country. Trade restrictions are part of the legal environment of a country, but their imposition may be politically motivated. The economic environment of a country affects how business may be conducted there and includes the level of economic development, what infrastructure exists, and exchange rates. Trade facilitators such as the World Trade Organization, the World Bank, the International Monetary Fund, and the Organisation for Economic Co-operation and Development foster global business by working to reduce trade restrictions and loaning money to developing nations.

■ *Specify the different levels of organizational involvement in international trade.* A company may be involved in international trade at several levels, each requiring a greater commitment of resources and effort. Exporting is the sale of goods and services to foreign markets; importing is the purchase of goods and services from a foreign source. Countertrade agreements involve bartering products for other products instead of currency. At the next level, a trading company links buyers and sellers in different countries to facilitate trade. In licensing, one company agrees to allow a foreign company the use of its company name, products, patents, brands, trademarks, raw materials, and production processes, in exchange for a flat fee or a royalty. Franchising is a form of licensing in which a franchiser agrees to provide a franchisee a name, logo, methods of operation, advertising, products, and other elements associated with the franchiser's business, in return for a financial commitment and the agreement to conduct business in accordance

with the franchiser's standard of operations. Contract manufacturing occurs when a company hires a foreign company to produce a specified volume of the firm's product to specification; the final product carries the domestic firm's name. A joint venture is a partnership in which companies from different countries agree to share the costs and operation of the business. The purchase of overseas production and marketing facilities is direct investment. Outsourcing, a form of direct investment, involves transferring manufacturing or other tasks to countries where labor and supplies are cheap. A multinational corporation is one that operates on a worldwide scale, without significant ties to any one nation or region.

■ *Summarize the various trade agreements and alliances that have developed worldwide and how they influence business activities.* There are many important regional trade alliances and agreements that create both difficulties and opportunities for business. These include NAFTA, the EU, ASEAN, and Mercosur.

■ *Determine how global business affects management.* Competing in an increasingly global economy provides both opportunities and challenges for today's managers and affects how they engage in planning, organizing, leading, and controlling. Global managers must guard against the self-reference criterion, which involves an often unconscious referencing to the way things are done in one's own culture and experiences in making global business decisions.

■ *Assess the opportunities and problems facing a small business considering expanding into international markets.* The "Business Dilemma" box presents a small business looking to expand into international markets. Using the material provided in the chapter, you should develop a plan for taking the business international; the planning process should include evaluating specific markets, anticipating problems, and analyzing methods of international involvement.

Key Terms and Concepts

Association of Southeast Asian Nations (ASEAN) 148

cartel 135

contract manufacturing 144

countertrade agreements 143

direct investment 145

dumping 138

embargo 138

European Union (EU) 147

exchange controls 138

exchange rate 140

exporting 142

Foreign Corrupt Practices Act (FCPA) 136

franchising 144

global business (globalization) 131

gross domestic product (GDP) 139

import tariff 137

importing 143

infrastructure 140

international business 131

International Monetary Fund (IMF) 141

joint venture 144

licensing 144

multinational corporation (MNC) 145

North American Free Trade Agreement (NAFTA) 146

Organization of Economic Cooperation and Development (OECD) 142

outsourcing 145

quota 138

self-reference criterion 149

Southern Common Market (Mercosur) 149

strategic alliance 144

trading company 143

U.K. Bribery Act 136

Webb-Pomerene Export Trade Act 136

World Bank 141

World Trade Organization (WTO) 141

Ready Recall

1. How do social and cultural differences create barriers to international trade? Can you think of any additional social or cultural barriers (other than those mentioned in your text) that might inhibit international business?
2. How do political issues affect global business?
3. What is an import tariff? A quota? Dumping? Why can dumping result in the imposition of tariffs and quotas?
4. What effect does a country's economic environment have on global business?
5. How does the World Trade Organization (WTO) facilitate trade?
6. At what levels might a firm get involved in global business? What level requires the least commitment of resources? What level requires the most?
7. Compare and contrast licensing, franchising, contract manufacturing, and outsourcing.
8. Discuss the opportunities that have arisen from the various regional trade alliances and agreements discussed in this chapter. Discuss the difficulties.
9. How can a manager become more globally aware? Why is being globally aware so important a quality in managers today?

Expand Your Experience

1. If the United States were to impose additional tariffs on automobiles imported from Japan, what would happen to the price of Japanese cars sold in the United States? What would happen to the price of American cars? What action might Japan take to continue to compete in the U.S. automobile market?
2. Study international trade issues from the perspective of the U.S. motion picture industry. What barriers does this industry face in entering foreign markets, and what are some ways it can address these barriers?
3. Identify a local company that is active in international trade. What is its level of international business involvement and why? Analyze the threats and opportunities it faces in foreign markets, as well as its strengths and weaknesses in meeting those challenges. Based on your analysis, make some recommendations for the business's future involvement in international trade. (Your instructor may ask you to share your report with the business.)

Strengthen Your Skills

Learning about Other Cultures

Break into groups of four. Read the scenario and character descriptions below, then choose a character role. After you act out your scenario, discuss the reflection questions at the end of the exercise.

Scenario: You and your team have been assigned to work on a project for your company. The assignment was made three months ago, and the final deliverable is three months from now. As is a normal custom for projects within the company, the manager of your department (not the team leader) has sent a progress evaluation form to each of you individually. You have all sent the completed evaluation forms back to your manager and are now in the conference room waiting to discuss your progress as a team with your manager. The manager walks in and, after greeting everyone, sits down and addresses some conflicting answers from the evaluation forms. The major areas of conflict include communication among members of the group and inefficient use of time. Each team member has a turn to discuss their viewpoint on these issues. Make sure to focus your discussion from the perspective of your character.

Surat (Male)/Areya (Female): You are from Thailand and have been living in the United States for two years. You hold Buddhist beliefs and value family relationships highly. You are courteous, polite, have self-control, and are respectful. You show your respect based on hierarchical relationships. Where people fall on the hierarchy determines on how you will treat that person. In order to get to know people, you ask personal questions, which can sometimes be unsettling to others. Sometimes, you deduce a person's status by the way they are dressed, the kind of car they drive, and so on. You place a great deal of emphasis on harmonious relationships and avoid conflict.

Your progress evaluation form comments: While I am the team leader, my ways of communicating goals do not seem to be resonating with some of the members of the team. For this reason, I set goals with a given time frame that are not being met by some of the others. Some of the work will be turned in correctly and on time, while other parts will reflect a perspective that was not agreed upon or it is not turned in at all. As the leader, I should be shown respect and not be confronted with arguments and conflict at every junction of the project.

John (Male)/Jane (Female): You are from the United States and have never been to another country. You value individualism and believe that everyone should be treated equal no matter what their position, title, or status. You tend to be highly confrontational and seem to lack patience with those who are not opinionated. When you are getting to know others, you make sure they know something about yourself. You like to take charge of situations, lead people, and make quick decisions. You are creative and want to leave a big mark on any project you undertake.

Your progress evaluation form comments: It seems that my suggestions are not being considered by the team leader. I often pitch ideas or suggestions that have the potential to create value for the project, but they are not being considered or discussed with other members of the team. I have a lot of contacts that are interested in becoming strategic partners, and I have offered to schedule meetings with them and our team. The leader says he/she will get back

with me, but definite decisions about this are not relayed back to me in a timely manner. My contacts are inquiring as to whether or not we will have this meeting, and I don't have a response for them. I feel like my reputation is being damaged by the leadership of this team.

Mikkel (Male)/Trude (Female): You are from Germany and have traveled to different countries, but haven't lived in another country for an extended period of time. The places and situations in which you tend to be most comfortable are those where rules and boundaries are clearly defined and there is little room for interpretation. You function best when uncertainty is minimal and avoid risk taking. You are very action-oriented and work to achieve your long-term plans without haste.

Your progress evaluation form comments: Despite the fact that I meet deadlines and turn in quality work, I am constantly being criticized for lack of creativity. I am in charge of long-term strategy for this project and have delineated a clear plan toward this purpose. However, because this plan is for the future, there is a lot of uncertainty. When I come up against potential issues in the face of this uncertainty, I do my best to come up with short-term action plans to mitigate against it. Some of my teammates feel that I am changing the plan too much and delaying the final long-term plan because of this. When I try to discuss it, there are too many opinions offered across the table. I become confused and don't know how to proceed effectively.

Soren (Male)/Ingrid (Female): You are from Sweden and have just moved to the United States. You value happiness and comfort so you are not preoccupied by working more hours than is required of you. When you are confronted with disagreements, you always try to compromise so that everyone leaves the situation partially satisfied. You like to talk through issues with everyone involved, and never try to dominate in situations. You are motivated by things that increase your quality of life such as free time and flexible work hours.

Your progress evaluation form comments: I feel like the team meetings and deadlines are too cumbersome. I am having to work too much overtime and am sacrificing my family time more frequently. When I try to discuss this with my teammates, I try to take everyone's opinions into account and come to a compromise. However, I am the only one on the team with a young family, so others are not sympathetic to my situation. My work is often turned in on time, but it takes me longer than it normally would because my thoughts are with my family.

QUESTIONS

1. What were the main issues you encountered in your scenario? Why were they issues? Talk about them in terms of the Hofstede framework.

2. If the scenario would have lasted for another five minutes, how do you think it would have escalated? Or do you think these issues would have been resolved? Explain your answers.

3. What could each of you have done differently in order to be more sensitive to the cultural differences without sacrificing your values or character?

Case 5: Uber Attempts to Make the Right Turn

Uber Technologies Inc. is a tech startup that provides ride-sharing services by connecting independent contractors (drivers) and riders with the use of an app. Uber has expanded its operations to 674 cities in 83 countries around the world. It has become a key player in the sharing economy, a new economic model in which independent contractors rent out their underutilized resources such as vehicles or lodging to other consumers. The company has experienced resounding success and is looking toward expansion both internationally and within the United States.

Due to its technology, Uber does not have as many constraints as taxi cabs do. A major reason Uber is so popular is because its app allows users to contact any drivers in the near vicinity. The Uber business model takes advantage of the smartphone technology of consumers and links them with independent drivers as their cabs. These drivers act as their own entrepreneurs. They pay Uber a commission but are free to run their businesses as they see fit. This provides a more potentially efficient and less expensive way for consumers to purchase transportation.

Uber has adopted the motto "Available locally, expanding globally" to describe the opportunities it sees in global expansion. As it expands into different countries, Uber is engaging in strategic partnerships with local companies. These alliances with local firms are especially important as Uber expands internationally because it allows the company to utilize the resources and knowledge of domestic firms familiar with the country's culture. Uber has partnered with Times Internet in India, Baidu in China, and AmericaMovil in Latin America. International expansion is a major part of Uber's marketing strategy, and it believes that consumers from other countries will appreciate its low cost, convenience, and freedom.

Despite its international success, many countries have regulatory hurdles that have caused trouble for Uber. Perhaps the biggest is the failure to obtain licenses even though Uber drivers offer many of the same services as a taxi. Governments have responded by banning Uber or Uber services due to the lack of professional licenses for drivers. For instance, in Spain, Uber shut down its ride-sharing service after a judge ruled that Uber drivers are not legally authorized to transport passengers and that it unfairly competes against licensed taxi drivers. Because the taxi industry is important to many cities, governments like Spain's are not looking favorably at what they view as an unfair competitive advantage that could potentially bankrupt the industry. Uber has since returned to Spain

Source: Worawee Meepian/Shutterstock

with UberX, which uses licensed drivers and places it more on par with licensed taxi drivers.

Uber faced similar problems in France. In 2011, Paris became the first city outside of the United States where Uber set up operations. However, local authorities attempted to ban one of its services because drivers did not need to be licensed. French police even raided Uber's Paris office. A French law was passed mandating that operating a service that connects passengers to non-licensed drivers is punishable with fines of over $300,000 and up to two years in prison. Hundreds of Uber drivers in France were issued fines for operating illegally.

Uber challenged that law, claiming that it is unconstitutional because it hinders free enterprise. A French court decided against banning Uber's service and sent the case to a higher court. This generated strong criticism from taxicab officials in France, as they claim that they have to license drivers, whereas Uber is currently free from this restriction. French courts later ruled against Uber, and the company no longer uses unlicensed drivers in the country.

India is Uber's second-largest market after the United States. In New Delhi, a woman's rape allegation led to a ban against app-based services without radio-taxi permits in the capital. In response to the alleged rape, Uber began adding "panic button" and tracking features to its app. Uber also began offering its service in New Delhi without charging booking or service fees.

Despite these changes, Uber continued to run afoul of Indian authorities. India asked Internet service providers to block Uber's websites because it continued to operate in the city despite being banned. However, it did not ban the apps themselves because doing so would require it to institute the ban across the entire country. Uber must tread carefully to seize opportunities in India without violating regulatory requirements. This is more difficult because Uber drivers are independent contractors who set their own schedules and make their own decisions about whether to work.

In 2015, a German court banned Uber services that use unlicensed drivers. Uber argued in court that the company itself is only an agent to connect driver and rider. Rules that apply to taxi services do not apply, and all services are deemed to be legal, according to Uber. The court ruled that Uber's business model clearly infringes the Personal Transportation Law because drivers transport riders without a personal transportation license. The injunction includes a fine of more than $260,000 per ride for non-compliance. If the injunction is breached, drivers could go to jail for up to half a year, in addition to the imposition of fines. The German Taxi Association (Taxi Deutschland) was pleased with the outcome and claimed that taxi services will remain in the hands of qualified people and keep everyone safer. Despite the ruling, an Uber spokesperson said that the company will not give up on Germany because other Uber services that use licensed drivers remain unaffected by the district court's verdict.

Uber faces many regulatory and legal issues outside of the United States. It has attempted to take a global approach to expansion by applying the same practices in other countries as it does in the United States. However, it is quickly realizing that it must take a more customized approach. Laws differ from country to country. Although Uber defines itself as an "agent" of its "individual contractors," many courts do not view its services in the same way. They are forcing Uber to comply with licensing laws or stop business in certain areas.

Despite Uber's challenges, the company has become widely popular among consumers and independent contractors. Supporters claim that Uber is revolutionizing the transportation service industry. Investors clearly believe Uber is going to be strong in the market in the long run.

One lesson that Uber will hopefully take to heart is the need to ensure that independent contractors using its app obey relevant country laws. Uber has to address these issues to uphold the trust of its customers and achieve long-term market success in different countries.[31]

1. What are some challenges Uber is facing as it expands globally?
2. Describe some of the barriers that Uber is encountering in different countries.
3. What type of management team is needed at Uber to address a very dynamic global environment?

Notes

1. Lulu Yilun Chen, "Online Giant Alibaba Aims Beyond China and E-Commerce: QuickTake," *The Washington Post*, November 13, 2017, https://www.washingtonpost.com/business/online-giant-alibaba-aims-beyond-china-and-e-commerce-quicktake/2017/11/13/9147da86-c846-11e7-b506-8a10ed11ecf5_story.html (accessed November 19, 2017); Katherine Rushton, "Alibaba Is Now the Biggest Retailer in the World," *Telegraph* (U.K.), October 28, 2014, http://www.telegraph.co.uk/finance/newsbysector/retailandconsumer/11193340/Alibaba-is-now-the-biggest-retailer-in-the-world.html (accessed November 25, 2017); Laura Lorenzetti, "Alibaba Heads to Hollywood with Its New Cash Stockpile," *Fortune*, October 28, 2014, http://fortune.com/2014/10/28/alibaba-heads-to-hollywood-with-its-new-cash-stockpile/ (accessed November 25, 2017); Bill George, "Jack Ma on Alibaba, Entrepreneurs, and the Role of Handstands," *The New York Times*, September 22, 2014, http://dealbook.nytimes.com/2014/09/22/jack-ma-on-alibaba-entrepreneurs-and-the-role-of-handstands/?_r=0 (accessed November 25, 2017); Frank Langfitt, "From a Chinese Apartment to Wall Street Darling: The Rise of Alibaba," *National Public Radio*, September 8, 2014, http://www.npr.org/blogs/parallels/2014/09/08/326930271/from-a-chinese-apartment-to-wall-street-darling-the-rise-of-alibaba (accessed November 25, 2017); Aaron Pressman and Adam Lashinsky, "Data Sheet—Alibaba's Vast and Growing Reach," *Fortune*, November 13, 2017, http://fortune.com/2017/11/13/data-sheet-alibaba-payments-shopping/ (accessed November 19, 2017); Daniel Keyes, "Amazon Is Struggling to Find Its Place China," *Business Insider*, August 30, 2017, http://www.businessinsider.com/amazon-is-struggling-to-find-its-place-china-2017-8 (accessed November 19, 2017); Kathy Chu, "Alibaba to Act Faster Against Counterfeits," *The Wall Street Journal*, May 15, 2014, B1; *Economist* staff, "E-Commerce with Chinese Characteristics," *Economist*, November 15, 2007, http://www.economist.com/node/10125658 (accessed November 25, 2017); Eric Markowitz, "From Start-up to Billion-Dollar Company," *Inc.*, April 6, 2012, https://www.inc.com/eric-markowitz/alibaba-film-dawn-of-the-chinese-internet-revolution.html (accessed November 25, 2017).

2. David A. Ricks, "How to Avoid Business Blunders Abroad," in *International Marketing*, ed. Subhash C. Jain and Lewis R. Tucker, Jr. (Boston: Kent Publishing Co., 1986), 109–111.

3. "Where's the Beef?" *Fortune*, January 24, 1994, 16.

4. Bob Hagerty, "Trainers Help Expatriate Employees Build Bridges to Different Cultures," *The Wall Street Journal*, June 14, 1993, B1, B6.

5. Hagerty, "Trainers Help Expatriate Employees."

6. G. Hofstede, B. Neuijen, D. D. Ohayv, and G. Sanders, "Measuring Organizational Cultures: A Qualitative and Quantitative Study across Twenty Cases," *Administrative Science Quarterly* 35(1990): 286–316; M. H. Hoppe, "Introduction: Geert Hofstede's Culture's Consequences:

International Differences in Work-Related Values," *Academy of Management Executive* 18(February 2004): 73–75; Geert Hofstede, "Cultural Constraints in Management Theory," *Academy of Management Executive* 7 (1993): 81–94; G. Hofstede and M. H. Bond, "The Confucian Connection: From Cultural Roots to Economic Growth," *Organizational Dynamics* 16 (1988): 4–21.

7. Avivah Wittenberg-Cox, "Where Both Parents Can 'Have It All'," *Harvard Business Review*, February 11, 2013, http://blogs.hbr.org/2013/02/where-both-parents-can-have-it/ (accessed December 29, 2017).

8. Philip R. Cateora, Mary C. Gilly, and John L. Graham, *International Marketing*, 15th ed. (New York: McGraw-Hill Irwin, 2011), 109–110.

9. GLOBE Project website, http://globeproject.com/ (accessed December 29, 2017).

10. Javidan Mansour and Robert J. House, "Cultural Acumen for the Global Manager: Lessons from Project GLOBE," *Organizational Dynamics* 29, no. 5(2001): 289–305.

11. Julius Melnitzer, "U.K. enacts 'far-reaching' antibribery act," *Law Times*, February 13, 2011, http://www.lawtimesnews.com/201102148245/Headline-News/UK-enacts-far-reaching-anti-bribery-act (accessed May 17, 2013).

12. Claire Hayhurst, "The UK Bribery Act and the US FCPA: The Key Differences," Association of Corporate Counsel, http://www.acc.com/legalresources/quickcounsel/ukbafcpa.cfm (accessed December 29, 2017); "Student jailed for £5,000 attempt to bribe professor over failed dissertation," *The Independent*, April 23, 2013, http://www.independent.co.uk/news/uk/crime/student-jailed-for-5000-attempt-to-bribe-professor-over-failed-dissertation-8584779.html (accessed December 29, 2017); Valerie Surgenor and David Flint, "The United Kingdom: The Bribery Act Strikes Again," Mondaq, December 13, 2012, http://www.mondaq.com/x/211498/White+Collar+Crime+Fraud/The+Bribery+Act+Strikes+Again (accessed December 29, 2017).

13. Samuel Rubenfeld, "The Morning Risk Report: Bribery Act Review Considers Facilitation Payment Exception," *The Wall Street Journal*, May 31, 2013, https://blogs.wsj.com/riskandcompliance/2013/05/31/the-morning-risk-report-bribery-act-review-considers-facilitation-payment-exception/ (accessed December 29, 2017).

14. Dionne Searcey, "U.K. Law on Bribes Has Firms in a Sweat," *The Wall Street Journal*, December 28, 2010, B1; Julius Melnitzer, "U.K. enacts 'far-reaching' antibribery act," *Law Times*, February 13, 2011, http://www.lawtimesnews.com/201102148245/Headline-News/UK-enacts-far-reaching-anti-bribery-act (accessed May 17, 2013).

15. Julius Melnitzer, "U.K. enacts 'far-reaching' antibribery act," *Law Times*, February 13, 2011, http://www.lawtimesnews.com/201102148245/Headline-News/UK-enacts-far-reaching-anti-bribery-act (accessed May 17, 2013).

16. U.S. Customs and Border Protection, *Know Before You Go: Regulations for International Travel by U.S. Residents* (Washington, D.C.: U.S. Department of Homeland Security, 2009).

17. Ryan Tracy, "Washington to Hit Beijing with Solar-Panel Tariffs," *The Wall Street Journal*, November 7, 2012, http://online.wsj.com/article/SB10001424127887323894704578105123838714546.html (accessed November 12, 2013).

18. World Bank, *Gross Domestic Product 2016*, http://databank.worldbank.org/data/download/GDP.pdf (accessed December 29, 2017).

19. Barbara Tesch, "RANKED: The 30 Richest Countries in the World," *Business Insider*, March 6, 2017, http://www.businessinsider.com/the-richest-countries-in-the-world-2017-3 (accessed December 29, 2017).

20. World Trade Organization, "What is the WTO?" http://www.wto.org/english/thewto_e/whatis_e/whatis_e.htm (accessed December 29, 2017).

21. OECD, "About the OECD," http://www.oecd.org/about/ (accessed December 29, 2017).

22. OECD, "OECD Convention on Combating Bribery of Foreign Public Officials in International Business Transactions," http://www.oecd.org/corruption/oecdantibribery convention.htm (accessed December 29, 2017).

23. Neha Gupta, "What is Countertrade?" Omitas Commerce Network Factsheet, http://www.complementarycurrency.org/ccLibrary/What%20Is%20Counter-Trade.pdf (accessed November 13, 2013).

24. WTSC website, http://www.wtsc.eu/ (accessed December 29, 2017).

25. Rigzone staff, Heritage Sets Up Southern Nigerian Joint Venture," Rigzone, November 13, 2013, http://www.rigzone.com/news/oil_gas/a/130108/Heritage_Sets_up_Southern_Nigerian_Joint_Venture (accessed December 29, 2017).

26.Thomas Gross and John Neuman, "Strategic Alliances Vital in Global Marketing," *Marketing News*, June 1989, 1–2.

27. Vienna Institute of Demography, "European Union Reaches 500 Million through Combination of Accessions, Migration and Natural Growth," http://www.oeaw.ac.at/vid/datasheet/EU_reaches_500_Mill.shtml (accessed November 13, 2013).

28. US-ASEAN Business Council, Inc., "Common Effective Preferential Tariff," 2013, http://www.usasean.org/regions/asean/afta/common-effective-preferential-tariff (accessed December 29, 2017).

29. Council on Foreign Relations, "Mercosur: South America's Fractious Trade Bloc," July 31, 2012, http://www.cfr.org/trade/mercosur-south-americas-fractious-trade-bloc/p12762 (accessed December 29, 2017).

30. Peter Evans, "World's Poor Open Wallets for Premium Products," *The Wall Street Journal*, January 1, 2015; Mehreen Khan, "Unilever Sales Beat Expectations as Prices Rise in Emerging Markets," *The Telegraph*, April 16, 2015, http://www.telegraph.co.uk/finance/newsbysector/epic/ulvr/11541020/Unilever-sales-beat-expectations-as-prices-rise-in-emerging-markets.html (accessed November 30, 2017); "Hindustan Unilever Hikes Prices of Select Brands," *Times of India*, September 13, 2013, http://timesofindia.indiatimes.com/business/india-business/Hindustan-Unilever-hikes-prices-of-select-brands/articleshow/22530667.cms (accessed on November 30, 2017); Unilever, https://www.unilever.com/about/who-we-are/our-vision/ (accessed December 5, 2017); Forbes, "The World's Most Innovative Companies," August

2017, https://www.forbes.com/companies/unilever-indonesia/ (accessed December 22, 2017); Parag Khanna, "The New World Order Is Ruled By Global Corporations and Megacities—Not Countries," *Fast Company*, April 20, 2016, https://www.fastcompany.com/3059005/the-new-world-order-is-ruled-by-global-corporations-and-megacities-not-countries (accessed December 22, 2017); Kate Magee, "Running the Global Show: Keith Weed, CMO of Unilever," Campaignlive .com, September 28, 2015, https://www.campaignlive.com/article/running-global-show-keith-weed-cmo-unilever/1365715 (accessed December 22, 2017).

31. Eric Auchard and Christoph Steitz, "German Court Bans Uber's Unlicensed Taxi Services," *Reuters*, March 18, 2015, http://www.reuters.com/article/2015/03/18/us-uber-germany -ban-idUSKBN0ME1L820150318 (accessed April 15, 2017); Nick Bilton, "Disruptions: Taxi Supply and Demand, Priced by the Mile," *The New York Times*, January 8, 2012, http://bits .blogs.nytimes.com/2012/01/08/disruptions-taxi-supply-and -demand-priced-by-the-mile/ (accessed April 15, 2017); Michael Carney, "Playing Favorites: Uber Adds New Security Features, but Only in Select Crisis-Riddled Markets," *Pando-Daily*, January 2, 2015, http://pando.com/2015/01/02/playing -favorites-uber-adds-new-security-features-but-only-in-select -crisis-riddled-markets/ (accessed April 15, 2017); Rob Davies, "Uber Suffers Legal Setbacks in France and Germany," *The Guardian*, June 9, 2016, https://www.theguardian.com/ technology/2016/jun/09/uber-suffers-legal-setbacks-in-france -and-germany (accessed April 15, 2017); *Economist* staff, "Uberworld," *The Economist*, September 3, 2016, p. 9; Matt Flegenheimer, "For Now, Taxi Office Says, Cab-Hailing Apps Aren't Allowed," *The New York Times*, September 6, 2012, http://www.nytimes.com/2012/09/07/nyregion/cab-hailing -apps-not-allowed-by-new-york-taxi-commission.html?_r=0 (accessed April 15, 2017); Anja Floetenmeyer, "Taxi Deutsch-land—Taxi Deutschland App Got Uber Banned throughout Germany," *Taxi Deutschland*, http://www.taxi-deutschland.net/ index.php/pressemitteilung/121-taxi-deutschland-app-got-uber -banned-throughout-germany (accessed May 21, 2015); Anna Gallegos, "The Four Biggest Legal Problems Facing Uber, Lyft and Other Ridesharing Services | LXBN," *LXBN*, June 4, 2014, http://www.lxbn.com/2014/06/04/top-legal-problems-facing -uber-lyft-ridesharing-services/ (accessed April 15, 2017); Jefferson Graham, "App Greases the Wheels," *USA Today*, May 27, 2015, p. 5B; Felicitas Hackmann, "uberPOP, Uber's Ride-Sharing Service, Pops up in More EU cities," *Venture-Beat*, April 15, 2014, http://venturebeat.com/2014/04/15/ uberpop-ubers-peer-to-peer-service-pops-up-in-more-eu-cities/ (accessed April 15, 2017); Karun, "Times Internet and Uber Enter into a Strategic Partnership, *Uber Blog*, March 22, 2015, http://blog.uber.com/times-internet (accessed April 15, 2017); R. Jai Krishna and Joanna Sugden, "India Asks Internet Service Providers to Block Uber Website in Delhi," *The Wall Street Journal*, May 14, 2015, http://www.wsj.com/articles/india-asks -internet-service-providers-to-block-uber-website-in-delhi -1431606032 (accessed April 15, 2017); Christopher Mims, "At Startups, People Are 'New Infrastructure,'" *The Wall Street Journal*, March 8, 2015, http://www.wsj.com/articles/at -startups-people-are-new-infrastructure-1425858978 (accessed April 15, 2017); Saritha Rai, "Uber Gets Serious About Passenger Safety in India, Introduces Panic Button," *Forbes*, February 12, 2015, http://www.forbes.com/sites/saritharai/ 2015/02/12/uber-gets-serious-about-passenger-safety-in-india -introduces-panic-button/ (accessed April 15, 2017); Sam Schechner and Tom Fairless, "Europe Steps Up Pressure on Tech Giants," *The Wall Street Journal*, April 2, 2015, http:// www.wsj.com/articles/europe-steps-up-pressure-on-technology -giants-1428020273 (accessed April 15, 2017); Joana Sugden and Aditi Malhotra, "Indian Officials Drafting National Rules for Uber, Other Taxi Apps," *The Wall Street Journal*, April 7, 2015, http://www.wsj.com/articles/indian-officials-drafting -national-rules-for-uber-other-taxi-apps-1428427528 (accessed April 15, 2017); Sam Schechner, "Uber Wins French Court Reprieve over Legality of Low-Cost Service," *The Wall Street Journal*, March 31, 2015, http://www.wsj.com/articles/uber -wins-french-court-reprieve-over-legality-of-low-cost-service -1427794312 (accessed April 15, 2017); Samantha Shankman, "Uber Gets into Ride-Sharing Game in Paris," Skift, February 4, 2014, http://skift.com/2014/02/04/uber-gets-into-the-ride -sharing-game-in-paris/ (accessed May 21, 2015); Aditi Shrivastava, "Uber Resumes Operations in Delhi Post 1.5 Months Ban," *The Economic Times*, January 23, 2015, http:// articles.economictimes.indiatimes.com/2015-01-23/news/ 58382689_1_indian-taxi-market-radio-taxi-scheme-uber -spokesman (accessed April 15, 2017); Spiegel, "Vermittlung Privater Fahrer: Gericht Verbietet Uber deutschlandweit," http://www.spiegel.de/wirtschaft/unternehmen/uber-urteil -gericht-verbietet-uber-deutschlandweit-a-1024214.html (accessed April 15, 2017); Taxi Deutschland, "Uber Legal Problems Worldwide," http://www.taxi-deutschland.net/ images/presse/Infografik_Uber-legal-issues_EN_v12_2015-02 -06_final.pdf (accessed May 21, 2015); Uber website, https:// www.uber.com/ (accessed April 15, 2017); UNM Daniels Fund Ethics Initiative, "Truth, Transparency, and Trust: Uber Important in the Sharing Economy," PoerPoint presentation, https://danielsethics.mgt.unm.edu/teaching-resources/ presentations.asp (accessed April 15, 2017); Maria Vega Paul, "Uber Returns to Spanish Streets in Search of Regulatory U-Turn," *Reuters*, March 30, 2016, http://www.reuters.com/ article/us-spain-uber-tech-idUSKCN0WW0AO (accessed April 15, 2017); Artyom Dogtiev, "Uber Revenue and Usage Statistics 2017," Business of Apps, November 21, 2017, http:// www.businessofapps.com/data/uber-statistics/ (accessed December 29, 2017).

Planning and Strategic Management

CHAPTER **6**

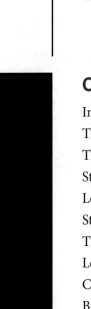

Source: Sergey Nivens/Shutterstock

Chapter Outline

After reading this chapter, you will be able to:

- Discuss the benefits that planning can bring to an organization.
- List the steps in planning.
- Describe the nature of an organization's mission and goals and how they influence planning.
- Determine the various levels of plans that organizations develop and explain how these levels are related.
- Define strategic management and strategy.
- Describe the steps involved in strategic management.
- Differentiate among the major corporate strategies and tools that managers use to develop and implement strategies.
- Analyze several common business-level strategies.
- Evaluate the importance of strategy implementation.
- Formulate actions that managers can take to improve the effectiveness of planning.
- Evaluate the goals and plans of a business.

Harley-Davidson Rolls in the New Products

Harley-Davidson has set its sights on appealing to the younger generation of bikers. Although baby boomers consist of much of Harley-Davidson's market, Harley-Davidson recognizes it must also acquire younger customers. Doing this requires it to reinvent itself so that young people do not view it as a brand for their parents. However, because the average Harley costs over $30,000, traditional Harley products remain unaffordable for many of the younger generation. For a manufacturing firm like Harley-Davidson, planning does not guarantee success, but it is necessary to achieve goals.

Harley-Davidson made the decision to address this problem by creating a stripped-down bike that carries the Harley experience and is affordable for younger people. Its Street bike is designed for smaller, younger riders with a price point of about $7,500. To keep costs low, the Street model does not have a fuel gauge, tachometer, or a clock, but it does have warning lights that will flash for low fuel or oil pressure. Once Harley implemented the decision to sell the Street bike, despite its stripped-down appearance, the product was a hit. Sales of these smaller bikes increased even as sales for customized Harleys decreased. This lower-priced model is particularly suitable for more price-conscious consumers in Brazil, South Africa, and India.

In 2014, Harley-Davidson announced it would start developing electric bicycles to appeal to younger, eco-conscious consumers. This strategy was risky for Harley-Davidson. Not only would it take years to complete the product, but electric vehicles are priced at a 10–20 percent premium. This might deter younger people from adopting them if the price is too high. However, Harley-Davidson remained undeterred. Like many car companies, Harley-Davidson recognized that electric vehicles could one day replace more traditional vehicles—particularly with consumers' and governments' growing concern over sustainability. By investing early, Harley-Davidson hoped it could create a strategic advantage over competitors.

To develop new products and achieve financial goals, a future orientation is needed at Harley-Davidson. Management's focus on various market settings and strategic goals for a product like electric bicycles requires assumptions about future technologies and how the transportation market is changing.

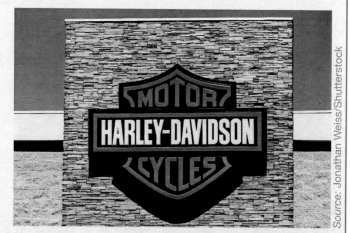

Source: Jonathan Weiss/Shutterstock

Therefore, Harley-Davidson needs to engage in the strategic planning process, analyzing opportunities and using the distinctive competence of Harley-Davidson management. The company announced its strategic goal to have two million new riders in the United States by 2027, in addition to the current three million riders.

In 2016, Harley-Davidson showed off its prototype electric bike called Livewire. The company promised to offer consumers a real electric motorcycle within five years. The motorcycle manufacturer announced its plans to make 100 new motorcycles over the next ten years, including an entire range of electric vehicles. To advance the prototypes, the company is going to have to extend the top speed and range, as well as provide a bigger battery pack. VP Bill Davidson believes that electric bikes are key to Harley-Davidson's success in the future.

Despite its success in courting younger consumers, Harley-Davidson is still struggling. To identify where the problem lies, Harley-Davidson must evaluate the gap between its current position and where it wants to be. Although it is attracting more young people to become Harley riders, many young people are choosing to purchase used Harleys over new ones from the dealer. This is requiring Harley-Davidson to adapt its plans to convert threats into opportunities. For instance, Harley-Davidson has begun encouraging its authorized dealers to sell more used bikes in their inventory. Although Harley-Davidson will likely face many challenges in the coming years, its expertise in strategic management and its willingness to adapt its goals and plans provide it with a greater chance at a comeback.[1]

Introduction

As Harley-Davidson demonstrates, planning and strategic management are essential elements in the recipe for successful management. Planning establishes the means to achieve the future. It requires that the manager or the organization specify where it wishes to go in the future and how to get there. Strategic management involves the management processes of planning, organizing, leading, and controlling, which are necessary to achieve the strategic goals and carry out the strategic plan.

In presenting this important topic, we will discuss the general steps of planning, the nature of goals, and the various types of plans used in organizations. In this chapter we will emphasize that the various types of plans should be related and that part of planning is implementing the plan. We will also take a close look at strategic planning, which relates to the crucial topic of strategic management.

The Nature of Planning

A **plan** is a set of activities intended to achieve goals, whether for an entire organization, department, or an individual. For example, Panasonic developed its Green Plan 2018 to become one of the world's top green electronics producers.[2] Planning involves determining what the organization will specifically accomplish, deciding how to accomplish these goals, and developing methods to reach the goals. At the most basic level, a plan is a road map that answers the fundamental question, "How do we get there from here?" Almost everybody agrees that a map is important; however, organizations differ greatly in how they create that map. These range from formalized, detailed steps that produce a set of written procedures to be followed to informal discussions that result in general verbal agreements. Continuing the analogy of a map, this is like comparing a U.S. Geographical Survey map prepared by trained cartographers to a map drawn by your Uncle Bud on the back of an old envelope. Both are maps but they differ greatly in the information that they provide. As it is with any organizational action, the quality of the result—in this case, implementation of the plan—will vary depending on the quality of the planning process.

Planning does not necessarily guarantee success. As we shall see, many things can go wrong with plans. Even with planning, a major economic or societal crisis can change the environment and prevent business success. For example, in the twenty-first century many financial institutions bought debt obligations, sometimes unknowingly, based on subprime loans. The collapse of this market caused many bank failures, which were likely not part of the plan. However, companies and managers who develop specific plans should have a definite head start in reaching goals and a distinct advantage over those who do not adequately plan.

Let's consider two hypothetical national rumor magazines, *All-Lies* and *Make-It-Up*. Both magazines have planning processes, yet there are important differences. *All-Lies* requires managers to submit their plans for the next year as part of their performance review. These plans include the deployment of reporters in anticipation of events of major importance. Every year senior- and middle-level managers at All-Lies have a weekend retreat dedicated to planning. Moreover, all employees are expected to participate in the planning process at their job level. *Make-It-Up* magazine, on the other hand, lives up to its name. Its plans are for the immediate future, made at the last minute, and usually involve just a few employees. Which magazine do you think will have the best chance of having one of its reporters at the next sighting of Elvis flying his UFO to a hamburger stand in Michigan? *Make-It-Up* may get lucky and have a reporter eating in the hamburger stand because she is covering the story of a 102-year-old giving birth to quintuplets. However, because of its planning, we would expect that *All-Lies* would have reporters who regularly tour this state of past Elvis sightings, which will significantly increase the magazine's chances of capturing this important story.

Planning has a significant effect on goal achievement.

Source: 287902439/Shutterstock

plan: A set of activities intended to achieve goals, whether for an entire organization, department, or an individual.

Implicit in our definition is that planning has a future orientation. All managers are concerned with some aspect of the future, but different levels or types of managers will be more concerned with different time frames. Typically, the top management of a firm, the chief executive officer for instance, is concerned with the firm's long-term future, while first-line supervisors focus on daily and weekly planning. The CEO for Honda Motor Co., Ltd., for example, may be concerned with how to expand the company's manufacturing systems into different countries, how to gain a long-term competitive edge over its main competitor Toyota, how to market its environmentally friendly cars, and how to pursue the best ways to develop new green technologies like hydrogen fuel cells. A foreman at a local automobile manufacturing facility, on the other hand, may be only slightly interested in the long-term future, but is greatly concerned about how the next quarter's demands affect his current manufacturing processes.

The Benefits of Planning

Among the benefits that arise from planning, some are economic in nature: For instance, the firm may receive a higher return on investment. Yet it should be noted that planning is not a cure-all. A company may have excellent planning and still not do well. It may have made the wrong assumptions about the economic environment such as interest rates, employment, or global competition. It also may have been incorrect in evaluating its own strengths, assuming that the company's brand equity and reputation could withstand new competition with improved products. BlackBerry Ltd.'s BlackBerry product lost market share to new technologies developed by Apple and other competitors. The company's failure to plan adequately for rival products left it struggling to compete. It is also possible to overplan—that is, to spend so much time and money formulating plans that little of either resource remains to actually accomplish anything. This warning aside, planning can benefit organizations by forcing them to focus, helping to coordinate activities and people, and motivating employees and managers.

Focus

Planning is an excellent tool for getting a company's managers to consider seriously its present status and the environment in which it operates. Forcing managers to ask basic questions about the firm's operations and customers can greatly benefit the firm. "Are we doing this operation the best way?" "How does this fit with our other business activities?" and similar queries can help individuals in an organization gain a common understanding of the firm and its purposes.

This forced focus can be especially important for large companies involved in many different industries. General Electric is a multinational corporation with thousands of employees and produces a multitude of goods and services ranging from jet engines and hybrid vehicle technology to oil drilling equipment and financial services. Because of the diversity of its different divisions, it is often difficult for managers and employees to obtain a common consensus on what is GE. However, the firm has developed and implemented a number of plans that help coordinate business units and focus on profits.

Source: alphaspirit/Shutterstock

Planning helps to focus human and financial resources to achieve organizational objectives.

Coordination

One of the major tasks of management is to coordinate the activities of groups and individuals. Proper planning provides a mechanism for meshing these different segments of the organization. For example, in many consulting companies, it is important that experts in different business areas—for example, management information systems and production—coordinate work activities. Without planning, each consultant is likely to concentrate on his or her own activities. The management information systems consultant may emphasize the need to develop sophisticated databases, while the production consultant may be more interested in tracking current product flow. Proper planning takes into account and coordinates these differing organizational priorities.

Motivation

Planning can help create an environment conducive to motivating managers and employees. Frequently, the effects of focus and coordination arising from planning can lead to higher performance levels, as organizational members recognize the firm's overall goals.

In a related manner, planning is often used to get organizational members to contribute their particular knowledge and opinions to a decision. For instance, top management may have very good reasons for banning smoking on the premises (lower health insurance, productivity, and so on). Given this goal, the company could implement a ban on smoking by erecting "No Smoking" signs and by putting special smoke detectors in the restrooms.

However, a better approach might be to incentivize employees not to smoke. For example, the Japanese company Piala, Inc., recently decided to award six extra vacation days per year to non-smoking employees. Also, getting employees involved with determining the company's approach to smoking may be very useful.[3]

Source: dizain/Shutterstock

Implementation and evaluation are key phases of the planning process.

Steps in Planning

Figure 6.1 presents the steps in planning for an organization. Although these planning steps are the same as those taken by an individual manager, the specifics, such as the nature of the goals, are different. Because planning is meant to increase the probability

FIGURE 6.1
The Steps in Planning

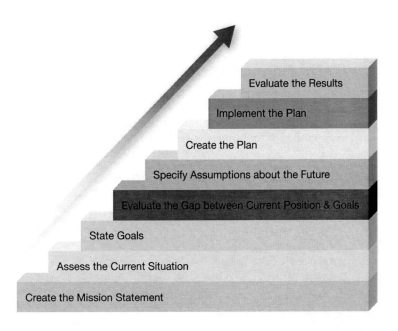

- Evaluate the Results
- Implement the Plan
- Create the Plan
- Specify Assumptions about the Future
- Evaluate the Gap between Current Position & Goals
- State Goals
- Assess the Current Situation
- Create the Mission Statement

that the organization will achieve its objectives, the process should start with the organization's mission statement. Next, the firm needs to assess how it is doing relative to its mission. Third, it should state its specific goals, which should be logically related to its mission. Then it should evaluate the gap between the goals and the current status of the organization and specific assumptions about the future. These form the basis for the next step, the creation of the plan. The last two steps in planning are called implementation and evaluation.

Creating the Mission Statement

mission: A definition of an organization's fundamental purpose and its basic philosophy.

An organization's **mission** defines its fundamental purpose. It describes, in the most primary terms, the company's basic philosophy. It should answer the questions: "What are our values?" and "What do we stand for?" The values embodied in a mission will be the synthesis of the values of a number of important organizational stakeholders: managers, owners, employees, customers, government, and interest groups. Table 6.1 lists six questions a mission statement should answer.

mission statement: A formal written declaration of the organization's mission; often includes the firm's philosophy, its primary products and markets, the intended geographic scope, and the nature of the relationships between the firm, its stakeholders, and society.

A **mission statement** is a formal written declaration of the organization's purpose that contains all, or at least most, of the following: the firm's philosophy, its primary products and markets, the intended geographic scope, and the nature of the relationships between the firm, its stakeholders, and society. Duke Energy's mission statement emphasizes improving people's lives "by providing gas and electric services in a sustainable way — affordable, reliable and clean." Its mission statement guides Duke Energy in many of its decisions, including upgrading its power plants to reduce pollution as well as investing in wind, solar, and biomass energy.[4]

In terms of planning, an important issue is the degree to which the firm has both defined and communicated its mission to its employees and other stakeholders. Many firms' mission statements are written, framed, and hung in a prominent place in the lobby or posted on a website, and never looked at again. However, a clear understanding of the mission statement reduces the ambiguity that employees may have about where the organization is trying to go and how they can help it get there. Planning, especially implementing plans, becomes more straightforward and usually is accomplished more quickly if everyone understands what the organization values. Moreover, a firm's ability to communicate its mission to its customers and other stakeholders can give that firm a tremendous competitive advantage. Conversely, the inability to convey the mission effectively, either through the lack of communication skills or because the firm is unable to define its mission, can be an enormous handicap.

Assessing the Current Situation

Before a company can make any plan, it must be aware of its present situation. This is mainly an evaluation of the current status of the internal organization. The first concern is determining the extent of the organization's resources: financial assets, employee skills, technology, and data about the work process. A second concern is the firm's working relationship with its suppliers, financial backers, and consumers.

Financial resources, employee skills, and current technologies are important because they indicate the organization's strengths and weaknesses at the present time. If these

TABLE 6.1 **Questions for Developing a Strong Mission Statement**

1. Who are we?
2. Who are our stakeholders?
3. What are our vision and values?
4. What are our core competencies?
5. What are our legal, economic, and social responsibilities to our stakeholders?
6. What are our strengths and competitive advantages?

factors are comparable to or better than those of other firms in the same markets, the organization has an advantage on which planning can be based. On the other hand, weakness usually indicates a less competitive position relative to other firms, a constraint that must be addressed in planning. Planning should not be based on goals that cannot be attained feasibly. For example, a new local toy store will probably not plan to compete against Toys 'R' Us on a national scale, at least not right away. The startup lacks the resources to open stores across the country. With that said, Toys 'R' Us has had its own difficulties, recently filing for Chapter 11 reorganization bankruptcy to help deal with burdening corporate leverage/debt.

The assessment process consists of many steps and stages that allow you to understand the current situation and make necessary changes.

Data about the work process is of immediate importance in planning. Such data are necessary to obtain an accurate assessment of present production or service delivery capability. If the company has inaccurate or incomplete data to assess its present work operations, any plans based on these data will be suspect. An airline, for example, may keep precise records of fares and total dollars of sales. However, if it does not have records of ticket sales as a function of the price of the ticket, any plan for responding to a competitor's cut in fares may be more of a guess than a planned response. Matching the competitor's fare may not do anything but retain the same level of seats that would have been sold. The price may have to be reduced to below the competitor's before enough volume can be generated to make up the lost revenue for the price cut. Thus, it should be apparent that information about financial assets, employee skills, and technology is necessary for the development of plans. These factors become the base from which the organization begins any change. It is necessary to know the current status of these factors to plan what the organization realistically can achieve.

In addition to evaluating the organization's status through its resources, it is also important to assess its relationships with suppliers, customers, and financial backers such as stockholders or financial institutions. These relationships may represent a potential limitation or a potential strength that should be addressed in planning. For example, suppose a clothing retailer decided to purchase all its apparel from only a single supplier, XYZ Fashions. The store's management must be fully aware of the problems in having a single supplier. Any change in production, distribution, or cost of XYZ Fashions' items will directly affect the retail store. If, for any reason, XYZ Fashions were forced to shut down for an extended time period, it might be necessary for the retailer to close also or change its business drastically. Many organizations have suppliers in Japan, for example. When the 2011 earthquake and tsunami hit the country and caused a nuclear emergency, their suppliers were temporarily incapacitated. A similar situation occurred when Thailand experienced massive flooding, shutting down many major firm's top manufacturing facilities.

On the other hand, by having only one supplier XYZ Fashions would enjoy a steady supply of top-quality clothing and would spend relatively little time and money planning its buying activities. Moreover, the company would need only limited marketing and advertising plans, further decreasing its costs. Most planning would thus be concentrated in the daily operation and maintenance of the stores, which would help promote a positive image with customers. The retailer's management believes that the benefits outweigh the disadvantages in this relationship. A risk assessment is needed to determine the likelihood of a disaster and the damage it would cause to the organization should it occur.

Stating Goals

In setting goals for your company, you should ask yourself: Where is my company going? A **goal** is the result that a firm wishes to achieve. A company almost always has several

goal: The final result that a firm wishes to achieve.

goals that it is pursuing simultaneously, which reflects the complex nature of business. To be stated correctly, a goal must contain several components:

- *The attribute sought:* The topic being addressed, such as profits, customer satisfaction, or product quality;

- *The target to be achieved:* The specific amount or level, such as the volume of sales or the extent of management training, to be achieved;

- *An index to measure progress:* The unit that will be used to measure the target, such as dollars for sales volume or the number of individual managers for training; and

- *A time frame:* The time period in which the goal is to be achieved, frequently a specific date.[5]

Starbucks, under CEO Howard Schultz, set its goal of expanding into the consumer packaged food industry. Although coffee would remain a main staple of the firm, Starbucks formed a goal to obtain growth by repositioning its brand as more of a consumer packaged goods firm. One way Starbucks signaled this change was by enlarging the mermaid on its logo and removing "Starbucks Coffee." In addition, Starbucks has partnered with tea company Teavana to enter the tea market. FedEx announced a plan to increase its profits by $1.7 billion over a three-year period. One step it is taking is purchasing more efficient aircraft to save on fuel costs. During one year, the firm replaced 21 Boeing 727s with more fuel-efficient Boeing 767s and Boeing 757s.[6] Simply put, it is necessary to know what is to be achieved, how much, when, and how it is to be determined whether the goal was reached or not.

Often goals are thought to be most effective if they are specific, measurable, achievable, realistic, and timely.

Source: patpitchaya/Shutterstock

Organizations set goals for a variety of activities that management thinks are essential for overall performance. Management scholar Peter Drucker, whose work has been discussed earlier, suggests that the following areas should be considered:

- *Market standing:* Refers to the percentage of the market that the firm wishes to secure; e.g., what percentage of consumers buys Nokia cameras as opposed to its competitors' cameras?

- *Innovation:* Usually refers to the nature and amount of research and development the firm is committed to carry out. This is often measured as a percentage of R&D or sales.

- *Productivity:* Usually expressed in terms of the total output—such as number of units—of the firm or of a major part of the firm (such as a division or a plant).

- *Physical or financial resources:* Refers to the amount of dollars and other assets, such as stocks, land, or buildings, that the firm is committed to possessing. In its quest to make China its second-largest market, Starbucks opened its 1000th store in the country at the end of 2013.[7]

- *Profitability:* The amount of money remaining after the expenses of operating the business has been paid.

- *Manager performance and development:* Performance refers to the level of productivity of individual managers or work groups; development refers to the additional skills a manager learns through either formal training or work experience.

- *Worker performance:* Level of productivity and the quality of activities of nonmanagerial employees.

- *Public responsibility:* Activities such as complying with laws in such areas as employment, product safety, and advertising; also includes areas that are not legislated, for example, work with civic groups and nonprofit organizations.[8]

Types of Goals

Organizations develop three types of goals: strategic, tactical, and operational. While these three types are interrelated, they differ in terms of their content and the business operations that they address.

The firm's highest-level managers set **strategic goals**, which deal with such general topics as the firm's growth, new markets, or new goods and services. Strategic goals are developed for long periods of time, usually five or more years. These goals should be central to all of the organization's planning and activities. In other words, the strategic goals establish what the firm wants to achieve in the long-term future. Logically, all the organization's other plans and activities should focus on contributing to the achievement of the strategic goals.

As an example of strategic goals, many companies like Walmart and New Belgium Brewery are integrating environmental sustainability objectives into their business. Some of these goals, such as New Belgium's goal of being 100 percent powered by renewable energy, have been achieved. However, Walmart has the same goal and has a long way to go to achieve it. Ambitious strategic goals generally take several years to fully achieve.

Tactical goals, the intermediate goals of the firm, are designed to stimulate actions necessary for achieving the strategic goals. As such, these goals are much more specific than are strategic goals. Tactical goals are usually written by and directed to middle-level managers. They are stated for shorter time periods, usually one to five years, than are strategic goals because tactical goals must be completed before strategic goals can be fulfilled. One could implement tactical goals by changing prices, closing plants, or laying off employees. For example, Merck laid off thousands of workers in an attempt to streamline the company, including its research and development area.[9] Tactical goals become the basis for tactical planning about how to carry out the functional operations, such as operations, finance, and marketing. For example, a manufacturing firm's tactical goals for reducing costs may include closing two plants and introducing robots and computer systems to its other four plants within five years. In such a case, the human resources department would also have several tactical goals to implement the strategy. Among these might be to assess the technical and computer skill levels of the firm's employees within the next 12 months. Additionally, training programs in computer programming and operations must be developed within two years. The training itself must be completed for all appropriate employees within four years. For the closing of the two plants, it would be

strategic goals: Goals set by higher managers that deal with such general topics as the firm's growth, new markets, or new goods and services.

tactical goals: The intermediate goals of the firm, which are designed to stimulate actions necessary for achieving the strategic goals.

In Holland, this biogas factory uses beet sugar pulp as a renewable form of energy.

Source: Sander van der Werf/Shutterstock

Chapter 6 Planning and Strategic Management

FIGURE 6.2
Types of Goals

necessary to determine, within one year, a system for identifying those individuals who would be offered positions at another plant and to set up an outplacement service for those employees who will be laid off at each plant within two years.

Operational goals are more specific and address activities that must be performed before tactical goals can be fulfilled. These are short-term goals that are addressed to first-line managers and usually apply to specific work operations that lead to the production of goods or services. Returning to the previous example, two of the operational goals of the human resources department would be to identify, within two weeks, the test battery that will be used to assess the skills of employees and to design the skill assessment program within seven weeks.

We can see that operational, tactical, and strategic goals and their accompanying plans are interrelated. Achieving the operational goals leads to fulfillment of the tactical goals, which leads to fulfillment of the strategic goals. One way of visualizing an organization's goal structure is through a framework like the one depicted in Figure 6.2. This framework starts with a broad view of the organization's strategy and works its way to a much narrower perspective. Each succeeding set of goals is related to the preceding ones, as are the plans that are developed and implemented in order to reach these goals.

Difficulty of Setting Goals

Setting goals can be a difficult task in an organization. Recall our discussion of stakeholders earlier in the text. Every organization has many groups of stakeholders, both internal and external, and each group has its own goals. In spite of stakeholder pleas for General Motors to hold onto its popular Saturn automobile brand, the company decided it had to sell it. In this case, satisfying all stakeholders was not achievable. Often different stakeholders' goals are in conflict with one another. Environmental groups such as the Sierra Club may contend that a chemical manufacturer's goal of cheaply disposing of chemical waste is socially irresponsible and should not be permitted. Internal stakeholder groups such as employees will almost always disagree with the firm's goal of reducing costs if implementing that goal involves laying off employees. Goals among stakeholders are a major issue in public organizations, especially governments. For example, citizens with children often wish to upgrade the school system by raising taxes to purchase better computers, school facilities, and supplies. Childless citizens, however, often object to these costs and would prefer either to reduce taxes or devote the money to other services such as police or fire protection. Both elected and appointed managers in governments are confronted with the difficult task of representing both groups in terms of planning.

Another factor affecting an organization's ability to set goals is the nature of the environment. Rapidly changing external conditions may make it extremely difficult for the firm to plan because the environment may change in an unforeseen manner and make the plans impossible to carry out. In general, companies operating in dynamic external environments set goals for shorter periods of time and review their goals more frequently. For

operational goals: Short-term goals that are addressed to first-line managers and usually apply to specific work operations that lead to the production of goods or services.

instance, Apple and Samsung release upgraded products yearly to take advantage of the rapidly changing consumer electronics industry.

Another difficulty in goal setting has to do with organizational rewards. Many managers have a short-term focus; they are attentive to this quarter's productivity or this year's return on investment. This short-term orientation is reinforced by most organizations' reward structures. Bonuses, even for upper-level executives, are often based on short-term performance, such as cost reduction during the upcoming quarter or the price of the company's stock within the next three years.

To obtain the bonus, the manager must produce results within the given time frame. However, these results may occur at the expense of long-term investments that might have had important benefits. A middle manager may reduce costs by eliminating management training for lower-level managers or reducing investments in maintenance. An upper manager may increase the profit statement of the firm by reducing research and development expenditures or the purchase of new technology. Often, such increased profitability will accelerate the demand for the stock and lead to a rise in the stock price.

Finally, good planning requires courage and risk taking. Often a firm's ability to develop a competitive advantage will depend to a great extent on making some plans that have a good deal of risk in their implementation. Managers of the hamburger chain Rally's (now merged with Checkers) thought that a restaurant offering no sit-down service and only sparse menus could prosper. Managers devoted all their energy to implementing this idea, and as the chain is still in business, it appears that they made the correct decision. A risky endeavor paid off. However, many managers are uncomfortable with risk and prefer the status quo. Planning in such a case involves a continuation of existing activities.

Evaluating the Gap between Current Position and Goals

At this point in planning, the organization has assessed its present status and set goals for the future. The next step is to determine how much difference there is between the current situation and its goals, the gap between actual and anticipated states. Are the changes needed to close this gap major or minor? Correspondingly, is it necessary to develop a plan that will require a dramatic amount of time, effort, and resources by the organization or merely an increase in the level of its present activities?

In many ways, it is much easier to develop a plan to increase present activities. For example, if a soft drink producer wishes to increase its market share, it could feasibly develop a plan that includes increasing production from its bottling plants, increasing marketing and sales promotion, and reducing prices. Obviously, the implementation of these requires the use of organizational resources. However, such activities are usually easier and less risky than those called

The process of assessing the difference between the current position and goals is often referred to as a gap analysis.

for in plans that require a major shift for the organization. Pfizer's announcement that it was restructuring into three business segments caused concern that the firm might break up. Such large-scale restructuring is deemed riskier and could hint that the firm may be struggling.[10]

Specifying Assumptions about the Future

All planning involves making some assumptions about the future of both the organization itself and the external environment. Generally, if the company can reliably assume that the organization and the external environment will remain relatively stable and similar to that of the recent past, planning is much easier because factors that may affect the appropriateness and the implementation of the plans can be anticipated with a great deal of accuracy. However, if the present status of the organization or its external environment is expected to change in an unpredictable fashion, planning obviously becomes much more difficult and complex.

For example, planning for breweries has been relatively straightforward. Laws regarding legal drinking age, amount of alcohol permissible, consumption patterns, brewing techniques, and competitors' products have all been fairly constant in the recent past and can reasonably be assumed to remain so in the foreseeable future. Planning, for the most part, can be based on previous plans and data about the relationships among these factors. However, planning for companies that produce computer software is an entirely different situation. Planners can assume that few elements of the organization or the external environment will remain constant in the future. Computer technology changes rapidly, often in unexpected directions. Competitors, their products, and their prices also change rapidly. Finally, the demand for software and systems fluctuates greatly, partially driven by the strength of the national economy. In general, organizations that cannot assume stability plan for shorter time periods and review and redesign plans more often than organizations that can make such an assumption.

Creating the Plan

The plan is the road map that shows how to get from the current state to the desired goal. If your goal is to become a chief executive officer, for example, your plan for achieving that goal will probably include getting an MBA as well as gaining management experience working at several different companies. For organizations, the plan is the document that designates methods, time frames, alternate procedures, and who is to implement it. The process of creating a plan can be broken down into four basic steps: determining alternatives, evaluating alternatives, selecting an alternative, and specifying the steps.

These steps are probably familiar to you because you use them to carry out your own personal plans and to make decisions. However, here is a brief example of how these steps may work for a men's clothing store. Max Weber's is a hypothetical clothing store operating in a medium-sized university town. Max sells traditional styles for men, including medium-priced name-brand goods. With three children getting ready for college, Max has realized that he needs more money and must increase profits by 10 percent in each of the next four years. What should he do? First, Max decides that he will not change his basic mission—to sell quality goods at reasonable prices. What are his alternatives? He could open another store just like his present one in a neighboring town. He could increase marketing and reduce prices in the hopes of taking market share from his competitors. He could broaden the type and style of items he carries. Or he could retain the men's clothing line as it is and introduce a women's line of apparel.

A successful outcome in evaluating alternatives is to find the best course of action for an organization to take to achieve its goals.

Source: Gustavo Frazao/Shutterstock

To evaluate these alternatives, Max estimates the cost of each. The opening of another store is the most expensive and costly to sustain because of the distance. Increasing marketing and sales promotions is relatively inexpensive and easy to do. Broadening the type of menswear is slightly more costly but still relatively easy because he can purchase many of the new items from the same suppliers that he currently uses. Expanding into women's garments is somewhat more expensive because it involves new suppliers and more buying trips. In addition, Max would have to hire someone who knows more about women's clothing than he does.

In selecting among these alternatives, Max examines his previous records, gathers information about the demographic trends of the area, finds data from his professional association about the buying habits of various demographic groups, and estimates potential sales. He drops the opening-an-additional-store alternative because the neighboring town is more rural and has a smaller target clientele, and the customers who live there already shop at his store. He also discards the increased-advertising-and-sales-promotion option because his research suggests that his competitors will match what he does, and no long-term advantage will result. The same is true for adding more items to his men's line. Max judges that he will attract some college students but not enough to increase profits as much as he wishes. However, the addition of women's clothing looks excellent. Max found out that women's garments are more expensive and have a higher profit margin than men's. Many of his sales are already to women who shop for their husbands or boyfriends. Finally, women spend a lot more on clothing than do men.

To specify the steps for carrying out this alternative, Max first hires Mary Follett, who works for a large department store in the area but wishes to be more in business for herself. Together the two of them draw up a list of specific activities, which includes who has authority over what purchases, who makes what decisions, the amount of space allocated for women's articles, the construction of new dressing rooms, and budgeting for buying trips and advertising. They even decide to sponsor a fashion show.

Creating a plan, as illustrated by Max Weber Clothing, shows that the process can be time consuming and involved, even for a small business. The methods used in creating the plan can be formal or informal. In this situation, Max's process is somewhere in the middle. A major force affecting the formality of a plan is the influence of outside stakeholders. Thus, in our example, if Max goes to a bank to obtain capital, the loan officer will probably require an extensive written document.

Implementing the Plan

Implementation is carrying out the steps specified in the plan. It is where the organization goes from the "thinking" mode to the "doing" mode. This stage requires the coordination of people, resources, and activities. Typically, the plan describes what steps are to be carried out but not how to carry them out, especially concerning what decisions are to be made at each step and what information must be known to make the decision. At Max's clothing store, implementation calls for purchasing the items of women's clothing to be sold. How many? What specific items? What quality and style? Decision making is a major managerial task that requires, among others, technical and interpersonal skills. In addition, it also calls for the management activities of organizing, leading, and controlling.

The implementation stage is where many plans come undone. Many managers think of implementation as being merely "administrative" or "technical" and not worthy of full managerial involvement. Nothing could be further from the truth. Thus, in our example, if Max creates a plan but Mary implements poorly—selecting poor-quality clothing that Max's customers reject—then Max will not accomplish his goals. Max must ensure that the plan is implemented fully. Lululemon faced this problem when it sold yoga pants that were too sheer (see-through). The company recalled the pants and initially blamed its suppliers for defective shipments. In this case, the plan was good but the implementation—the manufacturing, shipping, and selling of the pants—was problematic.[11]

Lululemon has successfully taken advantage of the popularity of yoga, but has faced challenges in delivering some of their clothing in a consistent quality.

The implementation stage therefore requires realistic decision making at each step of the implementation. Hasty decisions not based on facts are often very costly.

Evaluating the Results of the Plan

This step involves asking the question, "Did we get there?" Evaluating the results of planning is essential. A well-done assessment of the outcomes that resulted from the plan provides valuable feedback. The company can learn which goals are possible and which may not be, as well as which steps can be implemented easily and which cannot be. Evaluation should, in most cases, be relatively easy and straightforward. Remember that goals should include information about how much should be accomplished, when it should be accomplished, and how it should be measured. Evaluation means that the information specified in the goal statement is gathered and compared against the results of the plan. For example, one year after introducing women's clothing, Max calculates his profit and realizes that it is 25 percent higher in total dollars than the previous year, even after giving Mary a healthy commission on sales. His evaluation of the plan: "Wow! This is great! Do I really need to carry men's clothing?"

Levels of Planning

A variety of situations lead to a variety of plans, with differing attributes. One way to study the difference among plans is by looking at the level of the plan as it relates to the goals that it is developed to meet. **Strategic plans** are intended to achieve strategic goals; **tactical plans** achieve tactical goals; and **operational plans** achieve operational goals. As with goals, plans need to be complementary. Thus, operational plans are needed to achieve operational goals, which are instrumental to the completion of tactical plans. Tactical plans have the same relationship to strategic plans. Thus, in evaluating each lower-level plan, it is necessary for managers to ask themselves whether these plans are contributing ultimately to the realization of the firm's strategic goals. It is not uncommon for plans to take on a "life of their own" as functional areas adopt these plans and develop their activities around them.

At some point, as the strategic goals change, the strategic, tactical, and operational plans must be altered to accommodate the new strategic goals. Functional areas may hesitate to change their plans because they have invested much time and energy and thus feel a sense of ownership of them.

Because it is important to understand these three levels of plans and how they interrelate, we will discuss them extensively. Strategic management, a crucial aspect to successful companies, will also be discussed.

Strategic Management

We can view strategic planning as determining how to fulfill the organization's mission and maintain its long-term growth and health. **Strategic management** is a more encompassing term that refers to all the processes an organization undertakes to develop and implement its strategic plan.[12]

Central to strategic planning and strategic management is the development of a **strategy**, a course of action for implementing strategic plans and achieving strategic goals. A strategy is a general statement of actions an organization intends to take or is taking that is based on the fit of the organization with its external environment. Strategies are the means through which business goals can be attained. The creation of a firm's strategy is an entrepreneurial activity that builds from the organization's mission and goals and responds to a rapidly changing business environment. Management expert Henry Mintzberg maintains that the strategic-planning and strategy-making processes should remain somewhat intuitive in the hands of top-level managers, not deferred to overly pragmatic or structured organizational planners.[13]

The purpose of a strategy is to take advantage of what the organization does well, or hopes to do well, which will have a benefit in the external environment.[14] Strategies are the vital link as firms move from planning to implementation, from thought to action. They provide the focus needed so that the firm's mission and goals can ultimately be translated into tactical and operational plans that work and make sense. To be complete, a strategy must have four components: scope, resource deployment, synergy, and distinctive competence.

strategic plans: Plans that are intended to achieve strategic goals.

tactical plans: Plans that are designed to achieve tactical goals.

operational plans: Plans that are intended to achieve operational goals.

strategic management: All the processes an organization undertakes to develop and implement its strategic plan.

strategy: A course of action for implementing strategic plans and achieving strategic goals; a general statement of actions an organization intends to take or is taking that is based on the fit of the organization with its external environment.

You're the Manager . . . What Would You Do?

THE COMPANY: Flanagan Corporation
YOUR POSITION: New Chief Executive Officer
THE PLACE: Memphis, Tennessee

Flanagan Corporation is a national manufacturer of ready-to-eat southern-style food. Originally, the business was family-run and operated, but it grew so very quickly that family members sold out their interest over 20 years ago. At that time, the company sought to diversify and purchased a national bakery and a canned vegetable manufacturer. Flanagan's food products now dominate the market. The company's reputation is based on using the highest-quality ingredients and unique seasonings.

Twenty years ago, Flanagan was organized along two product lines: canned stews and frozen casseroles. Over the past several years, the company has adopted a more "consumer-oriented" organizational approach, developing or acquiring new health-focused products that reflect consumers' changing food consumption habits. The company has changed in many ways. It has added new product lines, streamlined operations, and taken more of a regional approach rather than a nationwide mass-market advertising approach.

However, problems arose as the company's management was stretched thin trying to manage so many diverse units. Performance and profits declined as a recession forced many consumers to save money by making meals from scratch. Jim Austerland, the chief executive officer, resigned under intense pressure from key employees and some large shareholders. Mark Johnston, with experience from a major competitor, has now taken over as CEO.

Johnston has set tough goals for the company and has taken drastic steps to meet them, closing several factories and cutting 150 jobs out of corporate headquarters. He has redefined the company to focus exclusively on stews, frozen entrees, and canned vegetables. The bakery division was sold because its product did not fit in well with Flanagan's more successful product lines. These moves have limited the technologies that Flanagan will have to manage to produce heat-processed and frozen foods.

Flanagan Corporation takes advantage of consumers' demand for "comfort foods."

Source: Antwon Mc/Shutterstock

Under the previous CEO's leadership, a single executive headed each of Flanagan's units with total responsibility for it, from developing and marketing new products to manufacturing and logistics. While some managers enjoyed the diversity, others felt stress and strain from maintaining such a broad focus. Johnston has altered the organizational structure to more of a brand management approach, giving managers total responsibility for groups or lines of products. In addition, managers have more stringent goals for production and profitability. As CEO Mark Johnston, you are now implementing this reorientation of the company.

QUESTIONS

1. What assumptions about future consumers' behaviors and attitudes are you making?

2. What role have goals played in your plans since arriving as CEO at Flanagan's?

3. What are some of the negative reactions you might have to face from employees and how would you deal with these?

Scope and Resource Deployment

Scope refers to the number of markets in which a company intends to compete or the number of products it intends to sell. A firm may have a broad or narrow scope. The McIlhenny Corporation of Louisiana, for example, sells its primary product "tabasco" in nearly every country in the world—meaning it has a broad, global scope.

Tabasco sauce is a globally popular product and has extensive global distribution.

distinctive competence: What a firm does well relative to its competitors.

Organizations may invest their resources in a number of ways. For example, one may choose to invest the majority of its funds in new manufacturing equipment or improved information systems. In a rapidly changing environment, priorities may have to be shifted and resources redeployed. As consumers continue to grow more concerned about environmental issues, sustainability and less wasteful production processes and products may be needed to satisfy the market in the future.

Synergy and Distinctive Competence

Synergy refers to the cumulative, enhanced effect of a firm's strategies. The basic idea is that an organization's resources should be linked so that the combined performance of its subunits is greater than if those units were operating alone. Although all firms strive for synergy, many focus on creating synergy as a primary intended benefit of their strategies.

A **distinctive competence** is what a firm does well relative to its competitors. The company focuses on this distinctive competence when developing its strategies. At the same time, however, it should not neglect other areas in which it is weaker relative to its competitors. MidAmerican Energy Holdings Company (a subsidiary of Warren Buffett's Berkshire Hathaway Corporation) has a distinctive competence in high-tech renewable energy. It has doubled its wind energy capacity through installing windmills and high-tech batteries to make it a "cleaner" utility company. This shift came after extensive planning about the long-term direction of utilities companies, anticipated changes to legislation, and changes in customer preferences. MidAmerican is one of the top companies in the nation for wind energy capacity.

The Strategic Management Process

A typical college student and an organization have at least one thing in common—they both have limited resources. Even the largest corporations have limits on the amount of physical, financial, and human resources they can expend. The purpose of strategy is to use the organization's resources effectively to accomplish its strategic goals. In essence, strategy is working with what you have to get where you want to be.

The development and implementation of an organization's strategy is its way of effectively focusing its direction. The strategic management process (Figure 6.3) parallels the general planning process. It entails both formulation activities—which are the major focus of planning—and implementation activities—which carry out the strategy once devised. Strategic management differs from general planning mainly in its careful attention to the external environment and the long-term goals of the firm. In fact, we have defined strategy in terms of the fit or match between an organization's resources and its environment in order to achieve its goals. It should be no surprise, therefore, that the steps in the

FIGURE 6.3
The Strategic Management Process

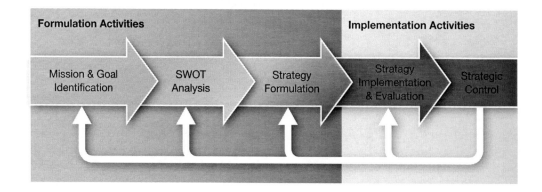

strategic management process are similar to those discussed previously with regard to general planning.[15]

Analyzing Strengths, Weaknesses, Opportunities, and Threats

After identifying the organization's mission and strategic goals (as discussed earlier), the organization must decide where it wishes to be in the long-term future. From the firm's viewpoint, there are two overriding entities or forces that determine this—the organization and its environment. Both are essential to take into consideration in strategic planning. **SWOT analysis** (Strengths, Weaknesses, Opportunities, Threats) means evaluating the organization's internal strengths and weaknesses and the opportunities and threats associated with the business's external environment. SWOT analysis emphasizes that the fit between a firm and its environment is of paramount importance, and the firm's strategy should be built around this match. Figure 6.4 demonstrates the components of a SWOT analysis.

A strength is an ability or attribute internal to the organization that has the potential of giving it a distinctive competence. Potential strengths may rest in the firm's financial capability, its management skills, cost advantages, proprietary knowledge, and/or its brand name, to name a few. Conversely, a weakness is a skill or attribute that the firm lacks or one that it has not developed and at which it performs poorly, such as failing to provide adequate customer service.

An opportunity is an environmental circumstance that is potentially beneficial for the firm. For example, the increasing proportion of older adults in the U.S. population provides an increasingly large market for organizations that offer health care and recreational services for seniors. A threat, on the other hand, is an environmental factor that could be potentially harmful to the organization. In the healthcare industry, private healthcare companies and providers often feel that different forms of government regulation of healthcare could represent a threat to their businesses.

The quality of a company's SWOT analysis depends on its ability to effectively scan its environment. Environmental scanning is the collection and analysis of important data concerning trends in the environment. Once the firm has collected and analyzed this

SWOT analysis: The evaluation of the organization's internal strengths and weaknesses and the opportunities and threats associated with the business's external environment.

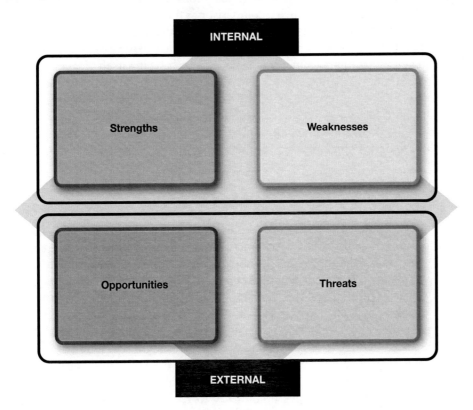

FIGURE 6.4
SWOT Analysis

data, it can then use various quantitative and intuitive forecasting methods to predict future outcomes.[16]

Strategy Formulation

Once the organization has developed its mission and goals and conducted a SWOT analysis, it can formulate a strategy through strategic planning. Top management does the formulation of a firm's overall strategy, with input from lower-level managers. Organizations formulate their strategy by determining how they will compete at the corporate, business unit, and functional level. By formulating a strategy at all levels of the organization, the firm can improve the odds that the chosen strategy will be successful.

As a rule, a firm will formulate its strategy to capitalize on its greatest strengths and to keep its organizational weaknesses from being exploited by competitors and other factors in the environment. Opportunities and threats are often the same for all firms in an industry, but a successful strategy will better exploit the opportunities and limit the environmental threats than will competitors' less successful strategies. A weak economy may affect all companies in the auto industry, but Ford's compact "Focus" automobile, now produced on a common platform throughout the world, is a clear part of Ford's strategy to appeal to value-conscious consumers and gain market share.

Evaluating the Strategic Plan

Because strategy has to do with the mission and goals of the whole organization, the implementation of strategy must also involve the entire organization as discussed in the general planning section earlier in this chapter. This means that top management must coordinate all parts of the organization in its activities and ensure that all activities are focused on implementing the firm's strategy. Simply put, strategy implementation is the actual process of executing the strategy throughout an organization. This is what we have previously referred to as strategic management.

Evaluation is the same process that we discussed relative to general planning. In this case, it involves comparing the strategic goals with the results of the implementation of strategy. The major difficulty in such a comparison is the time needed to collect data for the comparison. Both strategic goals and strategy address the long-term future, making it impossible to evaluate strategy appropriately for several years. However, no organization can wait that long to determine whether it is benefiting or harming itself. Top managers therefore evaluate strategy by using short-term indicators that can be gathered and are thought to be related to the long-term goals. If the strategic goal of Nestlé Corporation's Purina Petcare Division (formed as a result of Nestlé's purchase of the Ralston Purina Company) is to become the dominant company in pet foods, it may examine the relative change in market share and the number of prize-winning dogs that use its products at shows.

Strategic Control

After the strategy has been formulated and implemented, management needs to ensure that it is being followed. Strategic control is the feedback mechanism in the strategic management process; it compares the firm's actual performance to its intended performance. If the company fails to attain its goals, strategic control allows it to reevaluate the way the strategy was planned, formulated, and implemented. In so doing, the firm may find that a potentially successful strategy was planned well but implemented poorly. Companies can establish a variety of control systems to analyze their performance, such as profits, stock market performance, market share fluctuation, or social responsibility goal attainment. Information used in this process can come from either external or internal sources.[17]

Companies that have not attained their goals use the strategic control process as a means of feedback to help understand deficiencies in all stages in the strategic management process. This encourages a company to reevaluate its mission, goals, SWOT analysis, strategy formulation, and strategy implementation. The information also helps

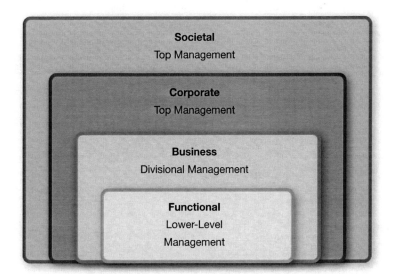

FIGURE 6.5
Levels of Strategic Management

Societal
Top Management

Corporate
Top Management

Business
Divisional Management

Functional
Lower-Level
Management

a company make improved decisions concerning all or part of the strategic management process. Even firms that have attained their goals can use the strategic control process as a means for improving their existing strategy.

Levels of Strategy

Crafting a strategy is essentially a matter of "how." How do we get there from here? How do we turn our mission and goals into action plans? Yet while "how" is at the essence of strategy making, a related matter of "who" arises. Who creates an organization's strategies? Many students (and some firms) would argue that it is only top managers who create strategy. In fact, managers at all levels, not just the top, craft strategy. Because of the changing nature of organizational environments, all managers face situations not expressly detailed in the company's "rule book." Strategy making is involved when a plant foreman responds to reports that his product output has an unacceptable amount of breakage. A sales manager is crafting strategy when she changes promotional efforts to attract new customers.

Thus, we can discuss strategic planning at a number of levels: ethics and compliance, corporate, business, and functional. These are shown in descending order of the scope of activities in Figure 6.5, which also depicts the overlapping nature of the different levels of strategies as well as which managers are usually associated with the various levels.

Ethics and Compliance

Before corporate strategic planning, the societal domain should be addressed by focusing on ethics and compliance. The ethics and compliance level of strategic planning addresses the question, "What do stakeholders expect of the organization?" This level is concerned with the legal, ethical, and social responsibilities associated with the other levels of strategic management. Although all managers are involved in some aspect of ethics and compliance, it is the domain of top managers and the company's board of directors and is associated with corporate governance responsibilities. Ethics is associated with developing principles, values, and a culture that provides guidance for responsible decisions. An example of an ethical value includes transparency in communications. Compliance requires adherence to rules and policies developed by the organization as well as laws and regulations. Compliance involves rules, policies, and training to prevent misconduct such as bribery, anti-trust, and environmental violations.

Many ethical issues in organizations relate to the misuse of technology and work time.

Chapter 6 Planning and Strategic Management 　　**177**

Corporate

corporate strategy: The scope and resource deployment components of strategy for the enterprise as a whole.

Corporate strategy is concerned with the enterprise as a whole. The basic question here is, "What business or set of businesses should we be in?" **Corporate strategy** deals chiefly with the scope and resource deployment components of strategy and focuses on determining what appropriate products/markets the firm should pursue. Top management for the entire organization handles corporate strategy. Specifically, at this level, firms make decisions about whether to create or acquire new businesses, get rid of existing ones, and establish funding priorities among their entire set of businesses. A firm like the General Electric Corporation, which actively acquires and sells businesses on an ongoing basis, deals with all of these decisions in its corporate strategic plan.

Business

business-level strategy: The area of responsibility usually assigned to the divisional-level managers.

Business-level strategy is normally the area of responsibility for the divisional-level managers (unless the organization has only one business; in that case, corporate and business-level strategies would be carried out by the same group of managers). By focusing on the synergy and distinctive competencies components, business-level strategy attempts to answer the question, "Given our particular product/market, how do we best compete?" For example, Kraft's snack division introduced new Miracle Whip dipping sauces in bacon ranch, onion blossom, and sweet tomato to gain market share in the snack industry.

Functional

Narrowing their scope, organizations must also establish strategies for functional areas such as marketing, operations, research and development, finance, and human resources management—which are unique to a given business. Managers at the functional level will typically develop short-term goals and strategies but their primary purpose is to implement selected aspects of the firm's strategic plan. For example, consider that Southwest Airlines has an overall strategy of continued growth into different markets. However, at the functional level of finance, Southwest is still concerned with a strategy of cost containment that can facilitate the growth process, in keeping with overall corporate strategy.[18]

Integrating the Levels of Strategy

Each higher strategy level serves as a constraint on the activities of lower levels. Figure 6.5 illustrates how the societal strategy of an organization can restrict corporate strategy, which restricts the business strategy, and so on. Thus, managers at the Taco Bell division could not decide, on their own, that they should go into a new business, say the Asian fast-food industry. The firm's corporate-level strategy, established by parent Yum! Brands (itself a 1997 spin-off from the PepsiCo Corporation), effectively imposes limits on the business-level managers.

Another way of distinguishing among the levels is by looking at the fraternal twins of business decisions—effectiveness and efficiency. Effectiveness is "doing the right thing," and this is normally pursued at the corporate level and the business level. Efficiency is "doing things right" and tends to predominate activities at the functional level (see Figure 6.6). Because corporate-level strategy is usually the primary time-consuming focus of top management, our discussion will begin here.

FIGURE 6.6
Strategy Levels and Business Decisions

Corporate Strategy

Remember that corporate strategy is concerned with the enterprise as a whole. Company names, such as PepsiCo, often do not tell the full story of what products they sell or have sold. Today, with major divisions in beverages (soft drinks, juices, and waters) and snack foods (FritoLay), PepsiCo Corporation is an organization with a firm grasp of savvy corporate strategy. It has identified what businesses it currently wishes to pursue and has provided an overall direction for them. Its profitable brands such as Pepsi Cola, Mountain Dew, Lays, Doritos, Fritos, Quaker, SoBe, and Tropicana serve to contribute to the success of the organization as a whole.

Strategies for Dealing with Multi-Business Organizations

A diversified company (one with many businesses) provides a special challenge for corporate managers. It must develop a strategic plan for several businesses, each facing unique environmental circumstances. Such a company has three major strategic alternatives: diversifying into new businesses, engaging in some type of partnership venture with other firms, or divesting itself of businesses it presently holds.[19] Of course, it could simply remain the same, but in our rapidly changing environment, maintaining the status quo could mean falling behind. Companies that do remain essentially the same often try to improve existing operations through organizational change and development activities or increased employee participation. Yum! Brands is the largest restaurant company in the world, counting Pizza Hut, Taco Bell, and Kentucky Fried Chicken among its many successful restaurants. Yum! Brands was, as noted above, spun off in 1997 from PepsiCo when the parent company made a decision to focus on its core competencies of soft drinks/beverages and snack foods.

Diversification

Diversification is a strategy of acquiring or developing other businesses, which must ultimately be justified by its ability to build stockholder wealth. That is, can the firm do a better job of building wealth for owners by creating a group of synergistically run companies than could an individual investor, with the same money, buying shares on the open market? A company that is contemplating diversification normally does so for one of two reasons: to gain a purely financial advantage through "playing the market" or to achieve synergy among businesses. The first reason reflects the belief that the company can buy

diversification: A strategy of acquiring or developing other businesses, which must ultimately be justified by its ability to build stockholder wealth.

Companies can grow rapidly through the acquisition of other businesses.

and run an existing company, without major changes, better than the previous management group. The second reason reflects the belief that, through synergy, it will save money in certain cost areas for one or both operations. The reason behind the strategy decision will determine what type of diversification the company will use. A company that wants to develop synergy among its various parts will probably use a **related diversification**, acquiring a business that has some connection with the company's existing businesses.

The rationale behind **unrelated diversification** is to diversify into any business that is potentially profitable for the organization. The acquired business need not be similar in any way to the existing businesses of the firm. Firms that pursue unrelated diversification strategies are normally referred to as **conglomerates**. Berkshire Hathaway, under CEO Warren Buffett, is an incredibly diversified company. It owns a wide variety of businesses including furniture stores, jewelry stores, insurance companies, the Burlington Northern Santa Fe Railroad, and, as mentioned earlier, the large MidAmerican Energy Holdings Company utility company.

related diversification: A firm's acquisition of a business that has some connection with the company's existing businesses.

unrelated diversification: The action of diversifying into any business that is potentially profitable for the organization.

conglomerates: Firms that pursue unrelated diversification strategies.

Joint Ventures

Joint ventures are contractual partnerships with other organizations in which each partner contributes to the enterprise while retaining a separate identity. A key element of such partnerships is that the partners bring unique skills to the venture, increasing the total value of the proposed endeavor. Joint ventures often provide a means for organizations to get into new markets or businesses that may be unavailable otherwise. Walmart entered into a joint venture with Bharti Enterprises in India to gain access into the country. Indian laws limit the activities of foreign companies that do not partner with domestic firms. Walmart later pulled out of India due to limitations on company activities.

Divestment

divestment: A strategy of selling off businesses that the company no longer wishes to maintain, either because they are failing or because the company has changed its corporate strategy and does not wish to be in those businesses any longer.

Divestment is a strategy of selling off businesses that the company no longer wishes to maintain, either because they are failing or because the company has changed its corporate strategy and does not wish to be in those businesses any longer. Among the reasons a company may choose to divest businesses are that the general or competitive environment has changed or that the expected synergy between business units never developed. When it became clear to General Motors that its Saab and Hummer divisions were not profitable, the company divested itself of them by selling them off.

Portfolio Analysis

As firms move from single-business entities to multi-business organizations in a variety of industries, the complexity of the strategic planning process increases. As a firm grows, it becomes important to analyze each business unit as a separate company. A **strategic business unit (SBU)** is a separate division within a company that has its own mission, goals, strategy, and competitors. PepsiCo has SBUs for its beverage units and snack foods. Since, for example, FritoLay functions as a major separate company within PepsiCo, it is an SBU. Techniques have been developed to assist individual managers in developing and analyzing the quality of their corporate strategy.

strategic business unit (SBU): A separate division within a company that has its own mission, goals, strategy, and competitors.

One such technique is **portfolio analysis**, which allows managers to visualize their businesses as a set or portfolio using certain common criteria, such as profitability or growth potential. Using a matrix, managers can position their SBUs, assess their relative attractiveness, and determine appropriate strategies for each.

portfolio analysis: A technique allowing for managers to visualize their businesses as a set or portfolio using certain common criteria, such as profitability or growth potential.

Growth/Share Matrix

Figure 6.7 shows the foursquare grid matrix first introduced by the Boston Consulting Group (BCG) as a tool for analyzing a company's SBUs. The axes for the matrix are market growth rate and relative market share. With such a matrix, it is possible for managers to more easily explore the relative strengths and weaknesses of each business, determining which ones deserve continued and perhaps greater funding and those that should be divested.[20]

Market Share

High | Low

Growth Rate — High | Low

FIGURE 6.7
Boston Consulting Group Matrix

Businesses in the upper left-hand quadrant of the matrix, called **stars**, have high market shares and operate in industries experiencing major growth. Stars represent the greatest potential opportunities for the firm, but also the greatest potential investment because increased resources are required to keep up with competitors in such rapidly expanding markets. Among Procter & Gamble's many brands, its Pampers brand has both high market share and high growth prospects, particularly in other countries.

Question marks, located in the upper right-hand quadrant, are viewed positively in the sense that they are located in attractive, fast-growing markets, but there is a question as to their ability to compete, given their low market share. Because these businesses require large amounts of capital for the same reason as the stars do, corporate managers must determine if the business's potential earnings warrant this continued investment. Herbal Essence might be classified as a question mark for Procter & Gamble.[21]

Cash cows, in the lower left-hand quadrant, are so named because they tend to generate excess cash over what is needed for continued growth. This is due to them having a high market share and being in industries that have slowly growing markets. With a strong cash cow, the firm can use the excess cash to help support stars and question marks. P&G's Bounty paper towels is an example of a cash cow.

Finally, **dogs**, in the lower right-hand quadrant, are those businesses with low market share in slow-growing markets. Because they are also low performers in their industries, these businesses have only minimal profits—sometimes even losses. Companies typically divest weaker-performing dogs because they act as a drag on the entire firm's earnings. In 2008, P&G divested itself of its Folgers coffee brand because of its slow growth.[22]

Several criticisms have been aimed at the BCG matrix. First, the labeling of businesses as stars, cash cows, question marks, and dogs tends to oversimplify the nature of these businesses. Many managers, hearing the term "dog," believe that such entities should be put to sleep. However, a firm might want to keep a dog that continues to generate profits. Second, and related to the first objection, is that a four-cell matrix neglects average-performing firms. Finally, the criteria used to classify the businesses, relative market share and market growth rate, may not be the best or only ones to apply when assessing businesses. Nevertheless, the BCG matrix is a good shorthand way for analyzing company SBUs.

stars: Those businesses that have high market shares and operate in industries experiencing major growth.

question marks: Those businesses that are viewed positively in the sense that they are located in attractive, fast-growing markets, but for which there is a question as to their ability to compete, given their low market share.

cash cows: Those businesses that tend to generate excess cash over what is needed for their continued growth due to their high market share in a slow-growing market.

dogs: Businesses that have only minimal profits or even losses due to their low market share in slow-growing markets.

FIGURE 6.8
Business Strengths/
Industry Attractiveness
Matrix

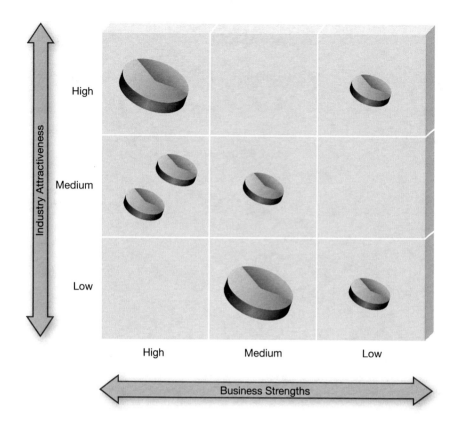

Business Strength/Industry Attractiveness Matrix

Addressing such criticisms, many organizations, most notably the General Electric Corporation, have developed newer portfolio assessment tools. The GE matrix, depicted in Figure 6.8, has nine cells. Each of its two main axes has three categories of high, medium, and low. Each axis is based on a number of different attributes. Industry attractiveness is a composite of such factors as market size, industry profit margins, and the ease of entry into the industry. Business strength is based on relative profit margins, cost position relative to competitors, and other factors. Each pie represents the relative size of each industry in terms of sales, and the "wedge" indicates the firm's relative market share.

The GE matrix allows corporate managers to visualize their organizations as a basis for plotting strategy and use in strategic planning. Businesses in the three squares in the upper left-hand quarter of the matrix are ones that the firm may wish either to continue or to earmark for increased investment levels. These are relatively strong firms in attractive industries. The three cells in the lower right-hand corner include businesses that are relatively weak in less attractive industries—prime candidates for divestiture. The firms in the three diagonal cells from lower left to upper right are the ones that frequently require careful observation by corporate managers. They are usually marginal organizations on which a decision must be made either to continue funding or to divest the businesses and divert that finding to more promising ventures.

Business-Level Strategy

If corporate-level strategy is the overall plan for what all the businesses in an organization should be doing, then business-level strategy is the plan that identifies the specific actions an individual SBU should undertake to meet corporate strategy. These individual SBUs are all seeking an edge or advantage over their competitors by attempting to create "value" for their customers. However, what good is an advantage if any one of the competitors can quickly adopt it and achieve similar results? Thus, it is important that the competitive advantage be sustainable and unique.

Types of Business Unit Strategy

Each business strategy should be a response to the particular combination of the division's resources and environment. Despite the distinct nature of business strategies, however, it is useful to think about three major types of business strategy: cost leadership, differentiation, and focus. To be used successfully, each strategy requires different sets of skills, thought processes, and priorities.[23]

Cost Leadership

Cost leadership is a business-level strategy aimed at achieving the overall lowest cost structure in an industry. The low cost is then used as a basis either for gaining market share or for undercutting competitors' prices. Cost leadership is normally attained through economies of scale, low raw materials cost, or low wages. Typically, a low-cost structure is not the result of a single action, but rather the product of a corporate attitude that attempts to cut costs on all fronts.[24] Because of its enormous size and very efficient supply chain, Walmart maintains cost leadership over competitors in a wide variety of categories from groceries and toiletries to books.

Differentiation

Differentiation is a business strategy in which the SBU offers a unique good or service to a customer at a premium price. The underlying rationale behind this approach is to identify benefits that customers consider important and for which they are willing to pay extra. Differentiation can be based on image (Chanel No. 5), unique service (Mercedes offers 24-hour tow service), high quality (Apple), and prestige (Rolex). In fact, almost any attribute that consumers value can be the basis of a differentiation strategy, from toilet paper that is extra soft (Charmin) to hot sauce that can raise blisters on your tongue (Dave's Red Hot). Note that although differentiation is based on selling unique attributes, the target market is still reasonably large. As a result, mass advertising plays an important role in persuading consumers to purchase goods and services that have a little something extra.

Focus

Focus is a business strategy in which the business concentrates on one part or segment of the market and tries to meet the demands of that segment. While some focus strategies serve the needs of a niche market seeking benefits, not all focus strategies need to have a differentiation basis.

Product Life Cycle and Business Strategy

Cassette tapes, mood rings, Chia Pets, and 8-tracks all have one thing in common: They were introduced, they flourished, they reached a saturation point in the market, and they eventually succumbed to a lack of buyer interest. This cycle of birth, growth, and decline of a product is known as the **product life cycle**. It provides a useful framework for evaluating the changing phases of a product. It also provides strategists with useful information in crafting business-level strategy.

Figure 6.9 illustrates the product life cycle as a function of time and market share. The initial stage, naturally enough, is **birth**. There the product is introduced, and for the most part, has slow growth, as the dominant design of the product is determined by the industry competition. Google has recently introduced Google Glass, a wearable computer resembling a pair of glasses. The next stage, **growth**, is characterized by dramatic increases in market share. Android phones have achieved much growth in recent years as a formidable competitor to the Apple iPhone. Slowing or no growth is typical of the **maturity** stage. Laptops are currently in the maturity stage. Growth has slowed with the introduction

Companies use advertising and promotion to help differentiate their products from those of competitors.

cost leadership: A business-level strategy aimed at achieving the overall lowest cost structure in an industry.

differentiation: A business strategy in which the strategic business unit offers a unique good or service to a customer at a premium price.

focus: A business strategy in which the business concentrates on one part or segment of the market and tries to meet the demands of that segment.

product life cycle: The cycle of birth, growth, maturity, and decline of a product.

birth: The initial stage of the product life cycle when the product is introduced.

growth: The product life cycle stage characterized by dramatic increases in the product's market share.

maturity: The product life cycle stage when the product's market share either slows or has no growth.

FIGURE 6.9
The Product Life Cycle

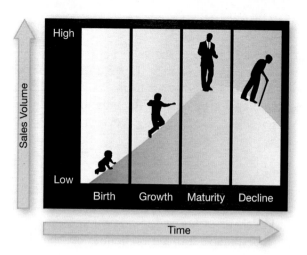

decline: The product life cycle stage marked by decreases in the product's market share.

of tablet computers. Finally, the **decline** stage is marked with decreases in the growth rate. While DVD players are still sold, demand has been decreasing as more people have turned to streaming movies directly.

Products are propelled through their life cycles by a number of factors. In some cases, technological change makes a product an anachronism. Often just changing consumer preferences will drive the life cycle. With consumers becoming more health conscious, caffeine-free and diet drinks have gained in popularity. Also, political and legal events may shorten a product's life span or increase it. After the FDA asserted that smoking causes cancer and many bars, restaurants, and cities banned smoking, the demand for cigarettes declined.

Because of the vast number of catalysts, you should not be surprised to learn that the life cycles of different products vary tremendously. Products such as Nehru jackets (go ask your Dad) may have a life cycle, as a mass-market product, of less than a year. Other products, such as automobiles, which are currently in a mature phase, have much longer life spans, particularly as they gain popularity among the growing middle class in emerging markets like China and India. Automobiles that run on alternative fuel, including hydrogen, electric, or biofuel, have also generated renewed interest.

The proper business strategy will be determined, in part, by the product life cycle. If a product is in the birth or introduction stage, the appropriate strategy may be one of focus, since at this point the price will be relatively high and the technology may be unsettled. While in the growth stage, firms can compete with just about any strategy because of the potential for continued market share increases and because the exact number of competitors is unknown. The maturity stage normally favors a cost strategy because growth is sluggish and competition is high.[25]

Implementing Strategy

Implementation is important at all levels of strategy. A firm can invest an impressive amount of time and resources into planning and formulating, but it will not achieve its mission and goals unless it effectively and expeditiously implements these strategies. Unfortunately, many top managers believe that implementation is an "administrative process," something almost routinely accomplished. In reality, it is a process that should be driven by entrepreneurial instincts. Innovation is just as important in implementing strategy as it is in formulating it. Some factors to keep in mind during the implementation phase is structure, the firm's hierarchy or pattern of the organization; systems, the procedures or guidelines that firms use in the course of doing business; and skills, discussed in more detail in the following.

Skills

The skills of the organization's members primarily consist of their knowledge of the technical aspects of the business's goods or services and how to apply this knowledge, as well as general work abilities such as communication, planning, reading comprehension, and problem analysis. Employee skills often have to change in response to changes in business strategy. The firm may have to retrain its workers, or in extreme cases, lay off workers and procure employees with more relevant skills.

Online and print ads assist businesses in filling open positions.

Staffing

Staffing involves finding and placing employees in jobs for which they have the appropriate skills. In practice this can be quite difficult. Many businesses have a wide variety of jobs with diverse knowledge and skill requirements. Staffing requires that new employees be assigned to work groups for which they have the necessary background. The difficulty is that most formal education in high school or college does not really train individuals for particular jobs in particular organizations. Even previous work experience may not be a very good indicator of the required knowledge and skills because many jobs are specific to an organization and do not closely represent those in other organizations. Facebook has job applicants perform more creative exercises such as code programming to test their skills, and many companies are beginning to use similar creative exercises to test applicants rather than focusing simply upon experience or education.

The leadership style of the firm's managers is an essential element in effective implementation. Managers who can communicate and stress the importance of strategies to employees and other stakeholders can make a tremendous difference in the implementation process.

Shared Values

You will remember that organizational culture is the set of values and beliefs shared by organizational members. A major part of the implementation process is to motivate managers and workers to "buy into" the strategy. Thus, it is important for managers to identify core beliefs and build their implementation strategies around them.

Strategic Management Pros and Cons

Much has been written, both good and bad, about strategic management. Some critics argue that strategic management is often all about planning, with little emphasis placed on implementation. It can be costly and time consuming for the organizational members involved. Also, many charge that its preoccupation with a long-term time frame is unrealistic, given the short-term expectations of stockholders and other financial stakeholders.

Tactical Plans

Before strategic management and strategic planning can take place, however, tactical and operational plans must be developed. Earlier in the chapter, we discussed tactical goals designed to stimulate the actions necessary to achieve strategic goals. Of the several important characteristics of tactical plans, one is that, whereas strategic plans address general business actions, tactical plans are concerned with specific people, activities, and resources. For example, when an information systems manager decides how many technicians to assign in developing an executive information system, he or she is implementing a tactical plan.

A second characteristic of tactical plans is that they are most commonly associated with the various functional areas of a business. That is, the planning has to do with how the activities and resources of such areas as marketing, operations, finance, R&D, and human resources may be used.

A third characteristic is that tactical plans are normally designed for a relatively shorter time period than are strategic plans. Tactical plans must be successfully completed for strategic plans to be successful. In this sense, tactical plans are stepping-stones to strategic plans (and further, for strategic management). If strategic plans are expressed for five-year time periods, then tactical plans must be expressed for shorter time periods so that the strategic time line can be met.

Finally, tactical plans are usually designed and implemented by middle-level managers. As strategic plans guide tactical planning, tactical plans guide operational planning. Middle-level managers are responsible for translating strategic plans into a form so that day-to-day plans can be related to them. They do this translation through tactical plans.

Let's look at tactical planning through the eyes of a hypothetical medium-sized company, Fayol's Sales, which for over 30 years has made wall safes for banks and other businesses. Five years of declining sales have prompted the company president, Henry Fayol, to set the strategic goal that the company should reinvent itself as a manufacturer of security systems, capitalize on its motto, "A Fayol Safe Never Fails," and have 50 percent of its sales from security systems within seven years.

To achieve this goal, the company develops strategic plans that identify potential markets, organizational resources to be developed, ways these resources should be used, and company strengths to emphasize. Once these plans are made, a number of supporting tactical plans are needed to bring Henry's visions to life. The finance department's planning is concerned with how the company may acquire capital to finance the venture. For instance, Henry's financial wizards must develop plans that address whether the company should pursue equity or debt financing.

The folks down in the marketing department are faced with the task of developing plans to sell a new product. Word of mouth and a small sales staff sold Fayol's safes traditionally. However, the security business appears to be much more competitive and seems to require a more aggressive marketing approach.

Because the technologies involved in safes and security systems are only marginally similar, the employees of the production department have their work cut out for them. Henry has decreed that since Fayol's reputation rested traditionally on its quality products, the company should keep the manufacturing of the security systems in-house. The department must, therefore, plan for entirely different production processes and contact different suppliers to fulfill materials requirements.

Thus, the number and scope of the plans that support the strategic plans can be immense. The more radical the alterations in the organization's strategic plan, the greater are the resulting change in its tactical plans. The inability of management to create and implement corresponding changes in tactical plans may result in "Fayolure" for the entire strategy.

Effective Planning

Certain approaches to planning can improve the chances that it will be successful. One of the major reasons why planning fails is that goals, plans, and actions are not constructively communicated. Sufficient information about all levels of planning—strategic, tactical, and operational—should be conveyed to organizational members. Many firms are establishing active communication programs and using technologies such as company blogs to disclose more effectively the rationale behind the firm's plans.

As we know, the environment sometimes changes between development and implementation. Assumptions on which plans are based change, and then the plan must be discarded or changed dramatically, often with little time for thought. Such issues can often be avoided by the development of **contingency plans**, which are alternate courses

contingency plans: Alternate courses of action to be undertaken if certain organizational or environmental conditions change.

General Mills Plans to Compete

In its 150-year history, General Mills has evolved from a flour mill to a packaged consumer goods company with revenues of $16 billion. More recently, General Mills has begun investing heavily in organic and natural foods with its acquisition of organic food brands Cascade Farms, Annie's, and Larabar. Sales of organic products are a $43.4 billion industry and growing. Demand for organic food is growing so rapidly, the supply has been unable to keep up. As a result, General Mills has begun underwriting the costs for farmers to convert their farms to organic crops.

All of these changes require General Mills to go through the process of strategic planning. Monitoring the environment is important to identify changes in markets and competitive threats. The products of General Mills have to meet the needs of consumers. By using organizational goals and objectives, General Mills develops plans for management to implement and control its strategy. For example, consumers have been eating less cereal and looking for quick breakfast items like yogurt and breakfast bars. This requires a plan to address those changes. As a result, General Mills has expanded into more on-the-go products such as yogurt and granola.

However, the yogurt market is becoming challenging for General Mills because of top competitors such as Chobani and Dannon. The yogurt market is a billion-dollar industry in the United States, and yogurt sales make up $1.75 billion for General Mills. Chobani, with its popular Greek yogurt, has been gaining market share. Recently, General Mills began developing a plan to revitalize its yogurt brands. As part of the planning process, General Mills set operational (short-term), tactical (mid-term), and strategic (long-term) goals. For instance, General Mills set a goal to sell more yogurt products to younger consumers. Realizing that younger consumers like more natural food, General Mills began removing artificial colors and flavors from its products. It also introduced Go Big yogurt brand targeted toward the tween audience.

Despite these changes, Yoplait slipped behind Chobani in market share. Sales of Chobani's Greek yogurt continues to increase, whereas Yoplait sales have declined. The Yoplait brand currently has 19 percent of the U.S. yogurt market, compared with Chobani's 19.8 percent and Dannon's 34 percent. On the other

Source: Ken Wolter/Shutterstock

hand, General Mills did see an increase in its Oui yogurt sales. Oui is a French-style yogurt that Yoplait has recently introduced. It is possible that this new yogurt product with its exotic brand name will help offset some of the decline General Mills is experiencing in other areas.

Perhaps as a way to meet the competition head-on, General Mills has adopted a new brand strategy: "Consumers first." The company believes this strategy will help it thrive in a highly competitive business environment. Adopting this strategy, however, requires General Mills to make costly investments to keep up with consumers' rapidly changing values.

General Mills wants its customer-centric focus to differentiate it from rival firms. In keeping with this customer emphasis, it has agreed to adopt genetically modified organism (GMO) labeling for some of its products. Although General Mills believes GMO products are safe, it wants customers to know that it is listening to their concerns. In fact, General Mills became a first mover in this endeavor by reformulating its Cheerios to be GMO-free. It was able to substitute Cheerio ingredients with non-GMO ingredients to make GMO-free Cheerios. The company looked at other cereals as well but determined that, for the time being, it would be too difficult to remove GMOs from other cereals because of the difficulties in sourcing corn and soy that are not genetically modified. However, as competitors also turn toward organic ingredients, General Mills continues to monitor consumer demand and adapt its products accordingly to maintain its competitive position.[26]

A key to effective planning is communicating goals, plans, and actions required.

of action to be undertaken if certain organizational or environmental conditions change. Organizations that create contingency plans hopefully can react more quickly and with greater thought than those that lack such plans.

Traditionally, planning was reserved for a few managers. Recently, however, it has been emphasized as appropriate for groups of managers and subordinates. One reason is that subordinates frequently have more technical knowledge about actual work steps, and are thus in a better position to evaluate the feasibility of alternative plans, saving time and cutting costs. Second, better planning frequently occurs when the managers and workers who will actually implement the plans are included in the process. This interaction permits consideration of more points of view and increases the likelihood of considering all valuable information. It also often increases the participants' understanding of the plan. They know why the plan has been designed and understand what is expected of them.

Summary and Review

■ *Discuss the benefits that planning can bring to an organization.* Planning can motivate employees to focus on the organization's present status and environment. It also provides a set of activities that coordinate the tasks of the various individuals and units. Finally, planning can help to create an environment conducive to motivating managers and employees. This can occur through the nature of the goals that are set and the process of participation in developing plans.

■ *List the steps in planning.* The first step in planning is identifying the organization's mission. The second step is assessing the present status of the organization relative to its mission. Third is establishing specific goals. Fourth is evaluating how the organization is doing relative to its goals. Fifth

is identifying the assumptions that must be made in planning, such as whether the environment will be stable or highly changeable. Sixth is developing the plan itself. The final two steps are implementing the plan and evaluating how well it achieved the goals for which it was intended.

■ *Describe the nature of an organization's mission and goals and how they influence planning.* An organization's mission defines its fundamental purpose—what it values and how it wishes to conduct itself. An organization's goals are statements of what the firm wishes to accomplish in the future. The goals of an organization should reflect and correspond to the mission of the organization. A firm's plans should be made to attain its mission and goals.

■ *Determine the various levels of plans that organizations develop and explain how these levels are related.* There are three main levels of plans. Strategic plans focus on reaching the general, long-term strategic goals of the organization and usually address the organization's relationship to its environment. Tactical plans describe how the strategic plans may be implemented and are developed for each part of the organization. Operational plans are specific descriptions of actions that must be taken by a work group to carry out the tactical plans. The three levels of plans all address the same topics and are all related to attaining the organization's strategic goals. The strategic plans are the most general statements of actions, and the operational plans are the most specific.

■ *Define strategic management and strategy.* Strategic management is the processes (organizing, leading, and controlling) an organization undertakes to implement its strategic plan and achieve its strategic goals. Central to strategic planning and strategic management is the development of a strategy, the course of action for implementing strategic plans, and achieving strategic goals.

■ *Describe the steps involved in strategic management.* The first major step is to identify the organization's mission and strategic goals, what businesses it wishes to be in, and how the businesses should be doing. Secondly, the organization should conduct a SWOT analysis—identify the strengths, weaknesses, opportunities, and threats it faces. Based on this information, the organization develops a general strategy that positions it relative to its competitors. The final steps are implementing, evaluating, and controlling the strategic plan.

■ *Differentiate among the major corporate strategies and tools that managers use to develop and implement strategies.* Corporate strategy is concerned with the organization as a whole, particularly which business or set of businesses the organization should be in. If the company operates many businesses, corporate-level strategy should account for the relationship among these. Three general corporate-level strategies are diversification (a strategy of acquiring other businesses), joint ventures (contractual partnerships with other organizations, in which each partner contributes to the enterprise while retaining its separate identity), and divestment (selling off businesses that the company no longer wishes to maintain either because they are failing or because the company has changed its corporate strategy and does not wish to be in those businesses any longer).

A major tool of corporate strategic planning is portfolio analysis. One such technique is the Boston Consulting Group's Growth/Share Matrix, a four-grid matrix that identifies strategic business units (SBUs) as stars, question marks, cash cows, and dogs, relative to the business's market growth rate and relative market share. The GE matrix places SBUs into one of nine cells of a matrix, depending on their industry attractiveness and business strength. These tools allow an organization to categorize its businesses and look at the relative performance and strength of each of these.

■ *Analyze several common business-level strategies.* Business-level strategy refers to the actions that an individual strategic business unit should take to meet corporate strategy. These actions seek to gain an advantage relative to competitors. The major, general business strategies are cost leadership (attempting to achieve the overall lowest cost structure in an industry), differentiation (offering a unique good or service to a customer at a premium price), and focus (concentrating on trying to meet the demands of one part or segment of the market). The proper business strategy will be determined, in part, by the product life cycle.

■ *Evaluate the importance of strategy implementation.* A firm will not achieve its mission and goals unless it implements its strategies effectively and expeditiously. Changing one aspect of strategy can affect many parts of a business.

■ *Formulate actions that managers can take to improve the effectiveness of planning.* Of the several actions that can be taken to facilitate planning, one is to communicate goals and plans to all members of the organization so that they have an accurate idea of what the organization is attempting to accomplish. Second is to develop contingency plans, alternatives to the original plan that allow the organization to continue to function effectively in the face of change. Finally, involving many employees in planning is effective in achieving involvement throughout the organization.

■ *Evaluate the goals and plans of a business.* Based on the materials presented in this chapter, you should be able to evaluate the planning and goal-setting efforts of the hypothetical company described in the "Business Dilemma" box.

Key Terms and Concepts

Ready Recall

1. What is planning and how does it relate to an organization's mission?
2. Why is planning necessary for the organization?
3. What are the benefits of planning to the organization?
4. What are the various types of goals that an organization may have and how are they related?
5. Which groups of managers are responsible for strategic, tactical, and operational plans?
6. How does strategic management relate to strategic planning? What is a strategy?
7. How does strategic management relate to business success?
8. What is a SWOT analysis, and why should a company conduct one?
9. What corporate strategies can managers use? Give an example of a company using each.
10. What is a strategic business unit? What business-level strategies can be applied to SBUs?
11. How does the product life cycle affect the strategy employed by an SBU?
12. Why is implementation so important to strategic management?
13. How might an organization or a manager evaluate a plan to determine if it has been effective?
14. How can an organization increase the successful implementation of its plans?

Expand Your Experience

1. Obtain copies of the mission statements of three different organizations in the same business or industry. Compare these statements in terms of what is important to the organization, how customers are addressed, and how employees are to be treated. Do you see any relationship between the mission statements and your opinion of these organizations?
2. Do a SWOT analysis for a local small business—for example, a sporting goods store, restaurant, or clothing store. If such a store is not available, interview the manager of a small business to get information about the business and its environment. Based on the SWOT analysis, what strategic plan would you recommend to the owner?
3. If your school is large enough to have separate colleges (business, engineering, arts and science, etc.), have some fun using the Boston Consulting Group's matrix to determine which colleges are stars, question marks, cash cows, or dogs. Justify your answers.
4. Go to the local mall and list 10 to 15 businesses, from the largest to the smallest. For each business, note whether you think its business strategy is cost leadership, differentiation, or focus. Be able to justify your answer. Did you see any businesses that tried to combine strategies, for instance, differentiation with low cost? Explain.
5. Find the strategic plan of your college or university. Identify the strategic goals mentioned in this document. Discuss tactical plans that academic departments might develop to reach these goals. Also discuss operational goals and plans of faculty that may be useful in achieving tactical goals.

Strategically Planning Your Career

To give you insights into strategically focusing your career, write answers to the following questions.

1. Which industries do you find to be the most interesting? How much education will you need to enter these industries?
2. Do you have the specific skills needed to advance in your preferred business? If not, what training or education do you require to develop these skills?
3. What are the greatest skills you have to offer this business?
4. Which people should you network with to give you an advantage in entering the business?
5. How can you work on your weaknesses and turn them into strengths?
6. Are there any internship or volunteer opportunities that would let me experience what it would be like to work in this business?
7. Will this job require me to work independently, or is it based more on teamwork?
8. What is the average salary for an entry-level position in this business?
9. Do you see any barriers that could prevent you from entering this business? How can you overcome them?
10. What kinds of advancement opportunities are available in this job?
11. How is the organizational culture of the business that you want to enter?

Case 6: Apple's Core Competency: Strategic Planning

Headquartered in Cupertino, California, Apple Inc. has experienced many challenges throughout its business history. In 1997, Apple's share price was $3.30. In contrast, its share price went to $176 per share, an all-time high, in 2017. Apple regularly places high on lists of "most admired companies," and to millions of consumers, the Apple brand embodies quality, prestige, and innovation. Indeed, Apple is the world's most valuable brand, with a brand value of about $170 billion. Apple is now viewed as a transformational brand, changing how we behave and how we communicate.

Apple's success can be attributed in part to the extensive and careful planning of its former CEO Steve Jobs. Although Apple started out as a computer company, Jobs had the foresight to redirect the company's strategic goal to consumer electronics. In order to meet this overarching goal, several tactical goals were set up to support the transition. Some of these tactical goals included developing and protecting intellectual property and re-creating the organizational culture from a centralized to a decentralized structure so that innovation could be nurtured and Jobs could have direct access to all projects and employees. The result was Apple's expansion into new product lines within the electronics industry. In 2001, Apple launched the iPod—a portable music player that forever changed the music industry. The company also introduced iTunes, a type of "jukebox" software that allowed users to upload songs from CDs onto their Macs and then organize and manage their personalized song libraries. Two years later Apple introduced the iTunes Store, allowing users to download millions of their favorite songs for $0.99 each online.

In 2007, Jobs announced that Apple Computer, Inc. would be renamed Apple Inc., indicating that Apple suc-

Source: KuLouKu/Shutterstock

cessfully reached its strategic goal of transitioning from being solely a computer manufacturer to becoming a driver in consumer electronics. However, in order for a company to remain competitive, it must continually focus its efforts on planning and goal setting. Apple continued to expand its product lines as part of its strategic plan. In 2007, it introduced the iPhone, which revolutionized the cellular phone industry. Apple did the same to the computer industry in 2010 with the introduction of the iPad. Under CEO Tim Cook, who has retained Jobs's executive team, Apple released the Apple Watch in 2015, a smartwatch at the forefront of wearable technology. Although the iPod was not the first MP3 player and the iPad wasn't the first tablet, these products are viewed as the industry standard, highlighting that you don't have to be the first to succeed. The company announced its first smart home speaker, HomePod, in 2017. Looking forward, Apple is working on a self-driving car and incorporating augmented reality into its iOS to stay ahead of technology trends and support the growth of those industries.

As Apple continued to introduce products, it developed and incorporated a creative tactical goal of evangelizing. The concept of evangelism has been an important component of Apple's culture, and this was particularly true under Steve Jobs. Corporate evangelists are people who extensively promote a corporation's products. Apple even had a chief evangelist whose job was to spread the message about Apple and gain support for its products. However, as the name evangelism implies, the role of evangelist takes on greater meaning. Evangelists believe strongly in the company and will spread that belief to others, who in turn will convince other people. Therefore, evangelists are not only employees but loyal customers as well. In this way, Apple was able to form what it refers to as a "Mac cult"—customers who are loyal to Apple's Mac computers and who spread a positive message about Macs to their friends and families.

The Wall Street Journal ranks Apple at number two on the Management Top 250 report, a list of the best-managed companies in the United States. In order to support the efforts of the tactical goals, Apple ensures its operational goals are set in place. One example is the design of its retail locations and the hiring of employees for these locations. Apple looks for retail employees who work well in its culture and ensures that its retail employees make each consumer feel welcome. Inside Apple retail locations are stations where customers can test and experiment with the latest Apple products. To ensure that its retail employees feel motivated, Apple provides extensive training, greater compensation than employees might receive at similar stores, and opportunities to advance. All of this planning, which includes strategic, tactical, and operational goals, has contributed to Apple's distinctive competence and success.[27]

1. What have been the benefits of planning at Apple Inc.?
2. Do you think Apple has done a good job of evaluating the gap between its current position and assumptions about the future?
3. How would you describe Apple's strategy in the highly competitive consumer electronics industry?

Notes

1. James R. Hagerty, "Can Harley Spark a Movement?" *The Wall Street Journal*, June 20–21, 2015; Bill Saporito, "This Harley Is Electric," *Time*, June 2014, 48–52; Charles Fleming, "First Times Ride: 2015 Harley-Davidson Street 750," *Los Angeles Times*, July 4, 2014, http://www.latimes.com/business/autos/la-fi-hy-first-times-ride-2015-harley-davidson-street-750-20140616-story.html (accessed November 30, 2017); Kyle Stock, "Is Harley-Davidson Losing Its Diehards?" *Bloomberg*, April 21, 2015, https://www.bloomberg.com/news/articles/2015-04-21/is-harley-davidson-losing-its-diehards- (accessed November 30, 2017); Harley-Davidson, "Our Company," http://www.harley-davidson.com/content/h-d/en_US/company.html (accessed December 5, 2017); Fred, Lambert, "Harley-Davidson Will Bring to Market Its First All-Electric Bike 'Within 5 Years,'" electrek, June 14, 2016, https://electrek.co/2016/06/14/harley-davidson-electric-bike-within-5-years/ (accessed December 22, 2017); Ankit Ajmera and Rachit Vats, "Harley Sales Recovery Far Off as Young Bikers Turn to Used Bikes," *Reuters*, August 30, 2017, https://www.reuters.com/article/us-harleydavidson-sales/harley-sales-recovery-far-off-as-young-buyers-turn-to-used-bikes-idUSKCN1BA26D (accessed December 22, 2017); Rob LeFebvre, "Harley-Davidson Embraces the Potential of Electric Motorcycles," Endgadget, May 11, 2017, https://www.engadget.com/2017/05/11/harley-davidson-electric-motorcycles/ (accessed December 22, 2017).

2. Hugh Aston, "The Quest for Hidden Treasure," *Business Week Special Advertisement Section*, 2012, http://www.businessweek.com/adsections/2012/pdf/120319_Panasonic3.pdf (accessed October 25, 2012).

3. Marguerite Ward, "This Japanese Company Is Giving Employees Who Don't Smoke 6 Extra Vacation Days," CNBC, November 2, 2017, https://www.cnbc.com/2017/11/02/this-japanese-company-is-giving-non-smokers-6-extra-vacation-days.html (accessed December 29, 2017).

4. Duke Energy, "Our Mission, Our Values," http://www.duke-energy.com/about-us/charter.asp (accessed December 29, 2017); Duke Energy, "Duke Energy Named to the Dow Jones Sustainability North America Index for the eighth consecutive year," September 12, 2013, https://news.duke-energy.com/releases/duke-energy-named-to-the-dow-jones-sustainability-north-america-index-for-the-eighth-consecutive-year (accessed December 29, 2017).

5. Charles Hofer and Daniel Schendel, *Strategy Formulation: Analytical Concepts* (St. Paul, MN: West Publishing, 1978).

6. Mary Schlangenstein, "FedEx Relies on Express Revamp to Meet $1.7 Billion Goal," *Bloomberg*, October 10, 2012, https://www.bloomberg.com/news/articles/2012-10-10/fedex-sets-1-7-billion-savings-and-profit-goal-over-three-years (accessed December 29, 2017).

7. Bruce Horovitz, "China to become No. 2 market for Starbucks," *USA Today*, September 16, 2013, http://www.usatoday.com/story/money/business/2013/09/16/starbucks-china-flagship-stores/2820885/ (accessed December 29, 2017).

8. Peter F. Drucker, *The Practice of Management* (New York: Harper & Brothers, 1954).

9. Bruce Horovitz, "Merck laying off thousands amid R&D revamp," *USA Today*, October 1, 2013, http://www.usatoday.com/story/money/business/2013/10/01/merck-layoffs/2900457/ (accessed December 29, 2017).

10. John C. Ogg, "Pfizer Restructuring May Precede Total Breakup of Empire," *YAHOO! Finance*, July 29, 213, http://finance.yahoo.com/news/pfizer-restructuring-may-precede-total-192851247.html (accessed December 29, 2017).

11. Aries Poon and Karen Talley, "Yoga-Pants Supplier Says Lululemon Stretches Truth," *The Wall Street Journal*, March 19, 2013, http://online.wsj.com/article/SB100014241278873234153 0457836981278711462.html (accessed December 29, 2017).

12. For a summary of works see James Quinn, Henry Mintzberg, and Robert James, *The Strategy Process* (Englewood Cliffs, NJ: Prentice-Hall, 1988); Cynthia Montgomery and Michael Porter, eds., *Strategy* (Boston: Harvard Business School, 1991); and Henry Mintzberg, *The Rise and Fall of Strategic Planning* (New York: Free Press, 1994).

13. Henry Mintzberg, "The Fall and Rise of Strategic Planning," *Harvard Business Review* 72 (January/February 1994): 107–114.

14. Michael Porter, "Towards a Dynamic Theory of Strategy," *Strategic Management Journal* 12 (Winter 1991): 95–117.

15. Lien Fahey, *The Strategic Planning Management Reader* (Englewood Cliffs, NJ: Prentice-Hall, 1989).

16. Lien Fahey and V. K. Narayanan, *Macro-environmental Analysis for Strategic Management* (St. Paul, MN: West, 1986).

17. Robert Simmons, "How New Top Managers Use Control Systems as Levers of Strategic Renewal," *Strategic Management Journal* 15 (March 1994): 169–189.

18. Kelvin Kelly, Aaron Bernstein, and Seth Payne, "Rumble on the Runway," *Business Week*, November 29, 1993, 36–37.

19. Richard P. Rumelt, *Strategy, Structure, and Economic Performance* (Boston: Harvard University Press, 1974); Cynthia Montgomery, "The Measurement of Firm Diversification: Some Empirical Evidence," *Academy of Management Journal* 25 (June 1982): 299–307.

20. Barry Hedley, "Strategy and the Business Portfolio," *Long Range Planning* 10 (February 1977): 9–15.

21. Powerpoint presentation by M. Hassan Shafiq, University of Central Punjab, downloaded from http://www.slideshare.net/ hasan_shafiq/head-and-shoulder-and-sunsilk (accessed December 29, 2017).

22. Jack Neff, "P&G to Divest Folgers Coffee Business," *Advertising Age*, January 31, 2008, http://adage.com/article/ news/p-g-divest-folgers-coffee-business/124788/ (accessed December 29, 2017).

23. Michael Porter, *Competitive Strategy: Techniques for Analyzing Industries and Competitors* (New York: Free Press, 1980).

24. Alan I. Murray, "A Contingency View of Porter's 'Generic Strategies,'" *Academy of Management Review* 13 (July 1988): 390–400.

25. Peter Wright, Charles D. Pringle, and Mark J. Kroll, *Strategic Management: Texts and Cases* (Boston: Allyn & Bacon, 1994).

26. Sarah Elbert, "Food for Thought," *Delta Sky*, December 2016, pp. 66–70; Annie Gasparro, "General Mills Starts Making Some Cheerios Without GMOs," *The Wall Street Journal*, January 2, 2014, http://www.wsj.com/articles/SB1000 142405270230337090457929721187427014 6 (accessed January 6, 2017); Hadley Malcolm, "General Mills to Label GMOs on Products Across Country," *USA Today*, March 18, 2016, http://www.usatoday.com/story/money/2016/03/18/ general-mills-to-label-gmos-on-products/81981314/ (accessed January 6, 2017); Stephanie Strom, "Paying Farmers to Go Organic, Even Before the Crops Come In," *The New York Times*, July 14, 2016, http://www.nytimes.com/2016/07/15/ business/paying-farmers-to-go-organic-even-before-the-crops -come-in.html (accessed January 6, 2017); John Kell, "General Mills Reveals How It Plans to 'Renovate' Yogurt Products," *Fortune*, July 14, 2016, http://fortune.com/2016/07/14/ general-mills-yogurt/ (accessed January 2, 2018); Nathan Bomey, "Slumping Yogurt, Cereal Sales Spoil General Mills' Performance," *USA Today*, September 20, 2017, https://www .usatoday.com/story/money/2017/09/20/general-mills-first -quarter-earnings/684218001/ (accessed January 2, 2018); Mary Ellen Shoup, "Chobani Beats Yoplait in Sales and Market Share as Dannon Takes No. 1 Spot in US Yogurt Market," *Dairy Reporter*, March 13, 2017, https://www.dairyreporter. com/Article/2017/03/13/Chobani-surpasses-Yoplait-in-sales -and-market-share (accessed January 2, 2018); Sean Rossman, "What Is French Yogurt and Is It the New Greek?" *USA Today*, July 6, 2017, https://www.usatoday.com/story/money/nation -now/2017/07/06/what-french-yogurt-and-new-greek/ 439935001/ (accessed January 2, 2018); Bruce Horovitz, "Cheerios Drop Genetically Modified Ingredients," *USA Today*, January 2, 2014, https://www.usatoday.com/story/money/ business/2014/01/02/cheerios-gmos-cereals/4295739/ (accessed January 2, 2018).

27. Aaron Pressman, "Why Wall Street Is Getting Worried About Apple's Stock Price," *Fortune*, November 27, 2017, http://fortune.com/2017/11/27/wall-street-apple-stock/ (accessed December 6, 2017); "The World's Most Valuable Brands," *Forbes*, https://www.forbes.com/powerful-brands/list/ (accessed December 6, 2017); Gina Hall, "These Silicon Valley Firms Make Top 10 List of the Best Managed Companies in the U.S.," *Silicon Valley Business Journal*, December 6, 2017, https://www.bizjournals.com/sanjose/news/2017/12/06/ wsj-management-top-250-amzn-aapl-goog-jnj-ibm-msft.html (accessed December 6, 2017); Kaitlyn Wang, "Tim Cook Credits Apple's Success to Two Basic Principles," *Inc.*, June 15, 2017, https://www.inc.com/kaitlyn-wang/apple-tim-cook -people.html (accessed December 6, 2017); Adam Lashinsky, "Apple's Tim Cook Leads Different," March 26, 2015, http:// fortune.com/2015/03/26/tim-cook/ (accessed December 6, 2017); "Apple Chronology," *CNNMoney*, January 6, 1998, http://money.cnn.com/1998/01/06/technology/apple_chrono/ (accessed December 9, 2017); Apple History, http://www .apple-history.com/ (accessed December 9, 2017); "Apple Introduces iTunes—World's Best and Easiest to Use Jukebox Software," Apple, January 9, 2001, http://www.apple.com/pr/ library/2001/jan/09itunes.html (accessed June 6, 2011); John Brownlee, "What It's Like to Work at Apple," Cult of Mac, July 7, 2010, http://www.cultofmac.com/what-its-like-to-work -at-apple (accessed December 9, 2017); "The evangelist's evangelist," Creating Customer Evangelists, http://www .creatingcustomerevangelists.com/resources/evangelists/guy_ kawasaki.asp (accessed June 6, 2011); "Former Apple evangelist on company's history," CNET News, March 29, 2006, http://news.cnet.com/1606-2_3-6055676.html (accessed June 6, 2011); "World's Most Admired Companies: Apple," *CNNMoney*, http://money.cnn.com/magazines/fortune/most admired/2011/snapshots/670.html (accessed December 9, 2017).

Decision Making

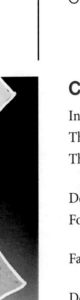

Source: Rawpixel.com/Shutterstock

After reading this chapter, you will be able to:

- Define decision making and describe the types of decisions and conditions that may affect decision making.
- Specify the steps involved in decision making.
- Contrast the decision-making models.
- Discuss the four decision-making styles.
- Examine the factors that may affect decision making.
- Summarize group decision techniques and the advantages and disadvantages of group decision making.
- Apply the decision-making models to a hypothetical situation.

To B or Not to B: Cascade Engineering Decides to Adopt B Corporation Certification

Cascade Engineering's leaders and managers make decisions that differentiate them from the competition. One major decision was to become a B corporation. B corporations are not your typical corporation. The *B* stands for *beneficial*. It is a certification awarded by the nonprofit B Lab to signal that member companies conform to a set of transparent and comprehensive social and environmental performance standards. These businesses are purpose driven and are designed to give back to communities, the environment, and employees.

Cascade Engineering makes an unlikely B corporation in that it manufactures plastic products, operating in an industry that tends to be seen as environmentally unfriendly. Most manufacturers abhor regulation and would feel constrained by the performance standards of a B corporation. Fred Keller, Cascade's founder, saw things differently. He welcomed regulation, using it as motivation to improve processes. Cascade looks at decisions based on how it can benefit the community, which often requires managers to make nonprogrammed decisions to develop unique solutions.

The company has adopted the triple-bottom-line approach of people, planet, and profits. This approach views success based not only on financial standards like profit, but also on how the firm positively impacts society and the environment. For instance, employee well-being is a major goal of the company. Management made the decision to pay a living wage to all full-time and part-time employees. More than 75 percent of employees receive health insurance coverage.

In 1999 the firm started its Welfare to Career program as a way to reach the community. Keller decided to hire lower-income individuals on welfare within his community to help them get out of poverty. This was a risky decision as it involved investing resources in a program that might not be successful. Indeed, the first few attempts to develop a program failed, requiring the company to re-evaluate its alternatives in searching for a model that worked. Eventually, the firm came across a program model that was successful, and since then its training and career program has helped more than 800 people get off welfare. Interestingly, the program has also helped Cascade financially. The company saved an estimated half a million dollars over a five-year period through tax credits, wage subsidies, and lower contracting costs as a result of the program.

Cascade Engineering values social and environmental consciousness.

Not only has Cascade made decisions to benefit the community but it has also benefited other stakeholders. The company has spent more than a decade helping customers reduce oil use and eliminate waste. It has developed a cradle-to-cradle certified product line based on a design concept that stresses reusable and safe materials, renewable energy, water quality, social fairness, and continuous improvement. Unlike many manufacturers, Cascade supports a switch to renewable energy. While this might be perceived as a risky move, Cascade is aware that this type of energy is at the forefront of innovation. Company decisions focus on sustainable solutions as the best alternative for the continued success of the company and society. Cascade Engineering has worked to develop a company culture of positive decision making when addressing the impact of the industry.

Cascade is aware of ramifications caused by plastic and is acting proactively when it comes to the subject. The company has made the decision to make sustainability the focus of its strategy in product and business development. When evaluating alternatives, therefore, sustainability is a primary consideration. To further this goal, the company produces its own alternative energy products. Although many believe companies should focus on profits first, Keller believes businesses should be analyzed not only by profit but also by how they benefit society. His efforts have netted him multiple awards, respect, and the business of like-minded companies.[1]

Introduction

One thing is certain: decisions managers make can mean the difference between success and failure of a company. Fred Keller's decision to receive B certification for his firm subjected Cascade to a set of criteria it must work hard to maintain. Although maintaining this certification requires the organization to make sacrifices, Cascade's corporate culture and organizational design have been developed to support an emphasis on sustainability and social responsibility.

In this chapter, we discuss the essence of the decision-making process by defining it, outlining the types of decisions that managers make, and analyzing conditions that affect decision making. We outline the steps involved in the decision-making process and present several decision-making models and styles. Finally, we discuss factors that affect individual and group decision making.

The Essence of Decision Making

Making decisions is widely recognized as a key aspect of management, and many managers and academicians consider it to be the most crucial element of business management. A **decision** is a choice made from alternative courses of action in order to deal with a problem. A **problem** is the difference between a desired situation and the actual situation. Decisions have to be made to resolve the barrier to a solution. Therefore, **decision making** is the process of choosing among alternative courses of action to resolve a problem.

decision: A choice made from alternative courses of action in order to deal with a problem.

problem: The difference between a desired situation and the actual situation.

decision making: The process of choosing among alternative courses of action to resolve a problem.

Types of Decisions

Managers make many different kinds of decisions, such as which employees to hire, what products to introduce, and what price to charge for them. For instance, Best Buy made a decision to implement a price-matching policy to compete against online retailers like Amazon. Managerial decisions can range anywhere from simple to complex, routine to unique. In general, however, most decisions can be classified as either programmed or non-programmed decisions.

programmed decisions: Decisions made in response to situations that are routine, structured, and fairly repetitive.

non-programmed decisions: Decisions made in response to situations that are unique, relatively unstructured, undefined, and/or of major consequence to the organization.

Programmed Decisions

Programmed decisions are made in response to situations that are routine, structured, and fairly repetitive. Such situations enable managers to develop procedures that can be applied to resolving these problems when they recur in the future.[2] Examples of programmed decisions include reordering inventory when quantities fall below a certain level, renewing the company's sponsorship of a youth softball team, or establishing what skills/requirements are needed to fill certain jobs. Many business decisions about routine procedures and basic operations are programmed decisions.

Non-programmed Decisions

Non-programmed decisions are made in response to situations that are unique, relatively unstructured, undefined, and/or are of major consequence to the organization. No standardized procedures exist to resolve these situations because the problems have never arisen before, they are complex or uncertain, or they are of such significance to the organization that they require tailor-made decisions.[3] Examples of non-programmed decisions include deciding whether to build a new plant, acquire another company, create a new position, enter into a strategic alliance, invest in enhancing operations, or develop a new product. Consider the decisions Microsoft had to make in partnering

Many manufacturing facilities, such as this bottling plant, utilize programmed decision making.

Source: MOLPIX/Shutterstock

FIGURE 7.1

The Continuum
of Certainty in
Decision Making

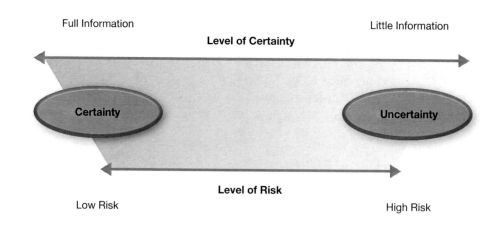

Full Information

Little Information

Level of Certainty

Certainty

Uncertainty

Level of Risk

Low Risk

High Risk

with and then acquiring Nokia. A key decision for acquiring Nokia was to gain entry into the smartphone market.

Conditions Affecting Decision Making

In an ideal business situation, managers would have all of the information they need to make decisions with certainty. Most business situations, however, are characterized by incomplete or ambiguous information, which affects a manager's decision-making process. Generally speaking, there are three conditions that affect decision making: certainty, risk, and uncertainty.[4] In Figure 7.1 we can view decisions along a continuum.

Certainty

certainty: The condition that exists when decision makers are fully informed about a problem, its alternative solutions, and its respective outcomes.

Certainty is the condition that exists when decision makers are fully informed about a problem, its alternative solutions, and its respective outcomes. Under this condition, individuals can anticipate, and even exercise some control over, events and their outcomes. Examples of decision making with complete certainty are scarce because business, like life, is filled with uncertainties. Even situations that seem certain, such as reordering supplies from the vendor who offers the best price and service, can be tinged with uncertainty because of a backorder problem, a transportation breakdown, a change in personnel, or a quality lapse. A decision relating to engineering or technical problems is usually more certain than one relating to outcomes of a marketing strategy, for example.

Risk

risk: The condition that exists when decision makers must rely on incomplete, yet reliable information.

In the context of decision making, **risk** is the condition that exists when decision makers must rely on incomplete, yet reliable information. Under a state of risk, the decision maker does not know with certainty the future outcomes associated with alternative courses of action; the results are subject to chance. However, the manager has enough information to determine the probabilities associated with each alternative. He or she can then choose the alternative that has the highest probability of success. For instance, when Starbucks introduced its Via instant coffee line, there was a risk the line would not succeed. However, Starbucks had conducted market research in the industry and felt fairly confident that the new product had the chance to be successful. On the certainty continuum, the condition of risk of a problem, its alternative solutions, and its respective outcomes lies between the extremes of being known and well-defined (certainty) and being unknown and ambiguous (uncertainty). Sometimes managers will hedge financial risks through purchasing futures contracts or using other financial instruments.

Many organizations utilize a holistic management approach to deal with risk.

Uncertainty

Uncertainty is the condition that exists when little or no factual information is available about a problem, its alternative solutions, and its respective outcomes. In a state of uncertainty, the decision maker does not have enough information to determine the probabilities associated with each alternative. In actuality, the decision maker may have so little information that he or she may be unable to even define the problem, let alone identify alternative solutions and possible outcomes.

Making decisions under the condition of uncertainty is commonplace in today's business world. Managers must acquire as much relevant information as possible and then use logic, intuition, judgment, and experience to determine the best course of action to follow. Of the conditions affecting decision making, uncertainty is the condition under which managers are the least confident about their decision making and are the most prone to error. Sometimes decisions can be very questionable with negative results, especially in the highly uncertain financial industry. Bank of America's acquisition of Countrywide Financial, for example, has been characterized as one of the worst acquisition decisions because the bank also inherited the mortgage firm's liabilities.[5]

uncertainty: The condition that exists when little or no factual information is available about a problem, its alternative solutions, and its respective outcomes.

The Steps in the Decision-Making Process

Regardless of whether a decision is programmed or non-programmed, or of the state of certainty under which it takes place, experts view decision making as a process with six steps: (1) identifying the problem, (2) generating alternative courses of action, (3) evaluating the alternatives, (4) selecting the best alternative, (5) implementing the decision, and (6) evaluating the decision (Figure 7.2). This is because some managers make quick intuitive decisions based on their experience, as we will see later in this chapter. All managers do not always go through all of these steps.

Identifying the Problem

The first step in the decision-making process is identifying the problem. We cannot place too much emphasis on this step in the process. In fact, problem identification is probably the most critical part of the decision-making process, for it is what determines the direction that the decision-making process takes and, ultimately, the decision that is made.

In identifying a problem, managers should not confuse the symptoms of a problem with the problem itself: Symptoms merely signal that a problem exists. For instance, a high level of absenteeism in a department is a symptom of a problem—not the problem itself. However, the symptom is significant because it lets the manager know that a problem exists. Then, through investigation and analysis of information, the manager can properly identify the problem. In the case of high absenteeism, the issue might be that jobs in that department are not suitably designed, the rate of pay for jobs in that department is too low, or the supervisor in charge of that department has some managerial deficiencies. The Chicago Transit Authority was able to reduce costs from absenteeism by creating a team

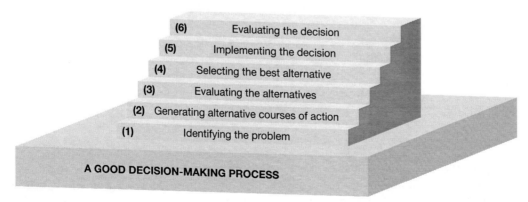

(6) Evaluating the decision
(5) Implementing the decision
(4) Selecting the best alternative
(3) Evaluating the alternatives
(2) Generating alternative courses of action
(1) Identifying the problem

A GOOD DECISION-MAKING PROCESS

FIGURE 7.2
The Steps in the Decision-Making Process

Managers like to assess a variety of strategic options to allow for adopting the best course of action for the organization.

to investigate injury fraud and other fraudulent forms of absenteeism. Additionally, many managers were replaced and others were trained in collective bargaining rules and held to higher accountability standards.[6]

Generating Alternative Courses of Action

The second step in the decision-making process is generating alternative solutions to the problem. This step involves identifying items or activities that could reduce or eliminate the difference between the actual situation and the desired situation. For this step to be effective, the decision makers must allot enough time to generate creative alternatives as well as ensure that all individuals involved in the process exercise patience and tolerance of others and their ideas.

The importance of generating alternative courses of action is often overlooked because of the time and effort involved. In the pursuit of a "quick fix," managers too often shortchange this step by failing to consider more than one or two alternatives, which reduces the opportunity to identify effective solutions. Managers need to resist the urge to begin evaluating the proposed alternative solutions (Step 3) before completing the second stage. By holding off on alternative evaluation, the manager helps ensure the generation of as many alternatives as possible, increasing the likelihood that the "best" alternative will be among those considered as possible solutions.

Let's return to the previously discussed scenario about the department plagued with a high level of absenteeism. After investigating, upper management determines that the department's supervisor has poor interpersonal skills. Solutions that might address this problem include (1) fire the supervisor, (2) transfer the supervisor to another position within the company, (3) demote the supervisor, (4) hire a new supervisor from outside the company, (5) promote an internal candidate to the position, (6) laterally move another supervisor from within the company to the position, or (7) train the supervisor in the interpersonal skill areas in which he or she has problems. It is important to realize that if decision makers do not give sufficient time to this alternative-generation phase, it could result in the supervisor being fired or transferred, when, in fact, the best alternative may be skills training.

Evaluating the Alternatives

After generating a list of alternatives, the task of evaluating each of them begins. Numerous methods exist for evaluating the alternatives, including determining the "pros and cons" of each, performing a cost-benefit analysis for each, and weighting factors important in the decision. Managers must rank each alternative relative to its ability to meet each factor and then multiply cumulatively to provide a final value for each alternative.[7] Regardless of the method used, it is during this third step of the decision-making process that the decision maker evaluates each alternative in terms of its feasibility (can it be done?), its effectiveness (how well does it resolve the problem situation?), and its consequences (what will be its costs—financial and non-financial—to the organization?).

Returning to the example of the departmental supervisor deficient in interpersonal skills, the decision makers evaluate the feasibility, effectiveness, and projected outcomes/consequences of each of the generated alternatives: firing, demoting, laterally transferring, hiring, promoting, and training.

Selecting the Best Alternative

After the decision makers have evaluated all the alternatives, it is time for the fourth step in the decision-making process: choosing the best alternative. Depending on the evaluation method used, the selection process can be fairly straightforward. The best alternative could be the one with the most "pros" and the fewest "cons"; the one with the greatest benefits and the lowest costs; or the one with the highest cumulative value, if weighting is used.

Yet even with a thorough evaluation process, the best alternative may not be obvious. It is at this point that managers must decide which alternative has the highest combined level of feasibility and effectiveness, coupled with the lowest costs to the organization. Probability estimates often come into play at this point in the decision-making process. The decision makers can analyze each alternative in terms of its probability of success; then they select the alternative with the highest probability of being successful.

In terms of the skill-deficient supervisor, an evaluation of the alternatives could reveal that the alternative with the highest probability of success—or the highest level of feasibility and effectiveness with the lowest cost—is the one that proposes training the supervisor in the area of interpersonal skills to help him improve relations with the members of his department. This alternative affords the supervisor the chance to acquire the necessary skills at a reasonable financial cost to the organization. In addition, this alternative preserves stability in the supervisory ranks by not shuffling supervisors around and promotes the philosophy that the company values training (and employees) and will provide help when necessary.

Implementing the Decision

This is the step in the decision-making process that transforms the selected alternative from an abstract thought into reality. Implementing the decision involves planning and executing the actions that must take place so that the selected alternative can actually solve the problem.

Implementation is a crucial step in the decision-making process, for the best alternative in the world cannot resolve a problem if it is not implemented properly. Many great ideas have been wasted because of breakdowns in implementation; too often managers lack the necessary resources, energy, ability, knowledge, leadership skills, or motivation to "make things happen." Successful implementation of a decision also depends on others' willingness to accept the decision and to work hard to ensure that it is carried out. Therefore, individuals affected by the decision need to be involved in the implementation stage, as well as in the rest of the steps in the decision-making process. Employee participation throughout the process engenders support for the decision and commitment to solving the problem.

Implementation is often compared to putting the pieces of a puzzle together.

In the scenario involving the departmental supervisor and the decision to provide training, implementation of the decision could involve enrolling the supervisor in a management development training program that focuses on interpersonal skills. Certainly the supervisor's superior would be involved in this process, along with possibly the human resources department.

Evaluating the Decision

In evaluating the decision, the sixth and final step in the decision-making process, managers gather information to determine the effectiveness of their decision. Has the original problem identified in the first step been resolved? If not, is the company closer to the situation it desires than it was at the beginning of the decision-making process?

If an implemented decision has not resolved the problem, the manager must determine why the decision-making process failed:

1. Was the wrong alternative selected? If so, one of the other alternatives generated in the decision-making process might be a wiser choice.
2. Was the correct alternative selected, but implemented improperly? If so, attention should be focused solely on Step 5 to ensure that the chosen alternative is implemented successfully.

3. Was the original problem identified incorrectly? If so, the decision-making process would need to begin again, starting with a revised identification step.
4. Has management not given the implemented alternative enough time for it to be successful? If so, then more time—the true test of any solution—can be allotted to the process, and the decision can be reevaluated at a later date when it has had time to prove its worth.

Returning for the last time to the supervisor with poor interpersonal skills, the manager must evaluate the decision to train the supervisor. In this case, the manager has several means of evaluating the effectiveness of the decision: (1) personal observation of whether the supervisor's interpersonal skills have improved; (2) measurement of the level of absenteeism in the department, to see if it has dropped to an acceptable level; and (3) feedback from the supervisor's employees to see if they are happier with their supervisor's level of interpersonal skills.

Decision-Making Models

Having gained an understanding of the nature of decision making and the six steps involved in the decision-making process, it will be easier to understand the basic approaches to decision making. Management theory generally recognizes three major models of decision making—the classical model, the administrative model, and the political model (see Table 7.1).

The Classical Model

classical model of decision making: A prescriptive approach—asserting that managers are logical, rational individuals who make decisions that are in the best interests of the organization—that outlines how managers should make decisions; also known as the rational model.

The **classical model of decision making** is a prescriptive approach that outlines how managers should make decisions. Also called the rational model, the classical model is based on economic assumptions and asserts that managers are logical, rational individuals who make decisions that are in the best interests of the organization. The classical model is characterized by the following assumptions:

1. The manager has complete information about the decision situation and operates under a condition of certainty.
2. The problem is clearly defined, and the decision maker has knowledge of all possible alternatives and their outcomes.
3. Through the use of quantitative techniques, rationality, and logic, the decision maker evaluates the alternatives and selects the optimum alternative—the one that will maximize the decision situation by offering the best solution to the problem.[8]

While the classical model works well in theory, events such as the Bernard Madoff Ponzi scheme scandal have made many people question anew how realistic this model is in the real world. It is prescriptive, meaning it is an ideal model of how decision making should work. However, rarely do decision makers have complete information, and sometimes they do not act in the best interests of the organization or its stakeholders. White-collar criminals such as Bernard Madoff, for instance, do not always act rationally or logically, choosing instead to adopt a decision that will profit themselves at the expense of stakeholders.

TABLE 7.1 **Three Models of Decision Making**

Classical Model	Administrative Model	Political Model
■ Attempts to maximize rewards ■ Uses facts and all information available ■ Clearly defined issues ■ Uses the best techniques for objective decisions	■ Limited understanding of alternatives ■ Incomplete information available ■ No clearly defined problem ■ More intuitive and less rational decision making	■ Applied to a specific case or situation ■ Attempts to influence others ■ Less reliance on information ■ Based more on bargaining and negotiation

The Administrative Model

In contrast, the **administrative model of decision making** is a descriptive approach that outlines how managers actually do make decisions. Also called the organizational, neoclassical, or behavioral model, the administrative model is based on the work of economist Herbert A. Simon, whose research and findings in this area resulted in a Nobel Prize in economics. Simon recognized that people do not always make decisions with logic and rationality, and he introduced two concepts that have become hallmarks of the administrative model—bounded rationality and satisficing.[9]

Bounded rationality means that people have limits, or boundaries, to their reasoning abilities. These limits exist because people are constrained by their own values and skills, incomplete information, and their own inability—due to time, resource, and capability restraints—to process all of the information needed to make perfectly rational decisions. Because managers often lack the time or ability to gather and process complete information about complex decisions, they usually wind up having to make decisions with only partial knowledge about alternatives and outcomes. This leads managers to forgo the six steps of decision making in favor of a quicker process called satisficing.

Satisficing means that decision makers choose the first alternative that appears to resolve the problem satisfactorily. Instead of going through the exhaustive process of generating and evaluating all possible alternatives in search of the best solution, managers are more likely to search only until they find an alternative that is "good enough." Thus, satisficing suggests that managers tend to implement the first satisfactory alternative that comes to their attention. Even if better alternatives are presumed to exist, managers decide that the time and expense involved in obtaining complete information are not justified.

The administrative model of decision making also has some basic assumptions:

1. The manager has incomplete information about the decision situation and operates under a condition of risk or uncertainty.
2. The problem is not clearly defined, and the decision maker has limited knowledge of possible alternatives and their outcomes.
3. The decision maker satisfies by choosing the first satisfactory alternative—one that will resolve the problem situation by offering a good solution to the problem.

The Political Model

While the classical model assumes rational decision making is based on facts, the **political model of decision making** is based on the idea that certain individuals or groups will be able to influence others to achieve their goals. In general, the political model attempts to develop coalitions to promote ideas, obtain resources, or even negotiate an advantage. Often various functional areas of business such as marketing, production, and finance may feel tension or have disagreements about a decision. The classical model assumes that everyone involved will approach the decision rationally and choose a solution based on consensus. The political model, however, recognizes that various factions or coalitions within an organization may develop, and the dominant coalition may be able to exert influence or power over others to obtain a desired decision. For example, a marketing manager may want to invest additional resources in extra services to support product sales, while the financial manager who is concerned with the next quarterly earnings report desires to cut costs. Coalitions may develop between the two functions in an attempt to influence the president of the firm to intervene and support their position.

The reality of the political model is that the dominant coalition usually emerges to obtain resources, rewards, or some type of advantage. A variety of methods can be employed in political decision making, including authority, negotiation, and the exercise of power. In some cases, there might also be a democratic approach toward making decisions involving the participation of all parties. Many industries including oil and gas, telecommunications, and healthcare are involved in political lobbying to obtain desired objectives, trying to influence government regulation decisions. Also, within firms in

administrative model of decision making: A descriptive approach, recognizing that people do not always make decisions with logic and rationality, that outlines how managers actually do make decisions; also known as the organizational, neoclassical, or behavioral model.

bounded rationality: The idea that people have limits, or boundaries, to their rationality.

satisficing: The decision maker's decision to choose the first alternative that appears to resolve the problem satisfactorily.

political model of decision making: Based on the idea that certain individuals or groups will be able to influence others to achieve their goals.

these industries, various differences of opinion are often debated, and numerous interest factors influence the position of the company on legislative issues.

So, which model is correct? As we said, the classical model of decision making is prescriptive, which means it describes how decisions should be made, not necessarily how they actually are made. Thus, it provides an example of decision making at its best—the "ideal" that managers can use to guide and enhance their own decision-making situations.

The administrative model seems to more closely describe how managers actually make decisions—especially non-programmed ones and those under conditions of risk or uncertainty. For these companies, decision making is characterized more by the satisfying behavior described in the administrative model than by the maximizing behavior described in the classical model. However, while the administrative model is "realistic," it can promote shortsightedness and a willingness to settle for "okay" in lieu of striving for "the best."

The political model describes the use of coalitions and power in decision making. Often a dominant group will attempt to influence others to secure advantages. In some cases the political model of decision making can be the best method. For instance, company survival may depend upon what the government decides, so it is important for firms to become involved in decisions through lobbying. However, overuse of this model could lead to inter-office politics, with one group dominating the entire workplace.

The decision-making models are valuable because they help managers better understand the decision-making process. The classical model illustrates how managers can strive to be more rational and logical in their decision making. On the other hand, the administrative model illustrates how managers have limits to their rationality and how these limits affect their decision making. The political model stresses the importance of bargaining and negotiation to secure desired outcomes. Thus, the information done and insight provided by these models help pave the way for managerial understanding and growth in the all-important management function of decision making.

decision styles: Determined from patterns among an individual's predispositions, such as which situations to avoid, what kind of jobs an individual enjoys, which things he or she dislikes, how an individual communicates, how an individual approaches problems, and how he or she makes decisions.

Four General Decision-Making Styles

Managers differ in the way they approach decisions. **Decision styles** reflect the way an individual visualizes and thinks about situations. Decision styles are determined from patterns among an individual's predispositions, such as which situations to avoid, what kind of jobs an individual enjoys, which things he or she dislikes, how an individual communicates, how an individual approaches problems, and how he or she makes decisions. The four decision styles are directive, analytical, conceptual, and behavioral. While these

Managers utilize a variety of decision-making styles.

decision styles are significant in describing how managers approach problems and make decisions, many managers will use different types of styles depending on the situation. Being able to adapt your decision-making style is important in making the best decisions.

Directive

Managers with a directive style of decision making dislike ambiguity and desire power.[10] These leaders base their decisions on facts and are focused upon results. Directive decision makers work better in structured environments where rules and procedures are known. Often managers with this style will make decisions based on limited information. This enables the manager to make decisions quickly. Managers with this decision-making style expect subordinates to work intensely and be committed toward achieving goals.[11]

One major advantage of directive decision making includes the speed with which decisions are made. There will be many situations where not all the information is known, and directive decision makers are able to operate in an environment that may only contain limited facts. Disadvantages include inflexibility and a more difficult time connecting with subordinates. In a study of Japanese, American, and Chinese manager decision-making styles, Chinese managers were thought to have more of a directive orientation due to the greater power distances that exist between leaders and subordinates.[12] Many managers on Wall Street have adopted a directive decision-making style because quick decisions and a strong focus on results are important for competing against other successful firms.

Analytical

Managers with an analytical style of decision making can tolerate a greater degree of ambiguity and like to tackle new challenges.[13] Analytical decision makers prefer to use logic and problem solving to make decisions. Like directive decision makers, analytical decision makers like working with facts. However, they can tolerate ambiguity and prefer to take their time analyzing data and examining different alternatives completely before making a decision.[14]

Advantages of this decision-making style include careful analysis of different alternatives and the ability to handle a variety of challenges. On the other hand, analytical decision making might not be best in situations requiring quick decisions. Much like directive decision making, the analytical decision style is more authoritative in nature. Bill Gates, founder of Microsoft, is an example of a leader who often adopted an analytical decision style.[15]

Conceptual

Conceptual skills are highly important to management as they relate to vision and creativity. Managers with a conceptual decision-making style are skilled at developing new solutions and rely on intuition. Inventors and entrepreneurs have often been placed in this category of decision making because of their willingness to take risks. Conceptual decision makers are able to think in broad terms. Unlike directive decision makers, conceptual decision makers are able to think long-term. They are more likely to desire praise and recognition for their achievements.[16]

Conceptual decision makers can make innovative decisions that can take the company in a new direction. However, some disadvantages include a longer amount of time to make decisions and a tendency to jump from one idea to another.[17] The founder and late CEO of Apple, Inc., Steve Jobs, was known for his conceptual ability to think outside of the box. Because of his vision and creativity, he was able to help save the company from bankruptcy and transform it into an electronics giant at the forefront of innovative technological consumer products.

inspiration innovative intelligent psycology brainstorming leader communication difference opportunity marketing motivation perspective idea smart research clever freedom planning success strategy **think outside the box** solution solving caucasian puzzle mindset business energy coach knowledge strength achieve optimistic overcome heart possibilities process potential emotion direction imagination aspiration attitude energy lifestyle winner idealistic thought goal brain encouragement benefit improvement bulb capability speak opinion theory invent learn document entrepreneur expert educate

Conceptual thinkers often tend to be very creative, question what others accept, and generate good ideas.

Behavioral decision makers focus more upon the individual. They tend to be supportive and empathetic to their followers, believing that satisfied employees will make satisfied customers. Behavioral decision makers are more likely to encourage employees to participate in decision making and listen to employee input. In particular, behavioral decision makers are good communicators and desire to help employees progress in their careers.[18]

Many managers have had great success adopting a behavioral decision style. Kip Tindell, co-founder and CEO of The Container Store, developed a corporate culture in which employees come first. The result has been lower turnover and more satisfied customers. Some potential disadvantages of the behavioral approach are an inability to be firm with employees and make difficult decisions.

Factors That Affect Decision Making

When you are equipped with an understanding of the decision-making models, it is easy to see how many factors can get in the way of rational decision making. The administrative model points out the realities of managerial decision making—that some circumstances can cause managers to stop short of making optimum decisions. This section will deal with some of the commonly recognized factors that affect decision making: intuition, emotion and stress, framing, escalation of commitment, and confidence and risk propensity.

These factors directly impact the way decision makers make decisions and are therefore connected to the type of decision-making style that the decision maker adopts. For instance, someone with a directive style of decision making may be less likely to take on risks, while a conceptual decision maker would rely heavily on intuition. Figure 7.3 shows the interplay between the decision-making styles and these different factors.

Intuition means immediately comprehending that something is the case, seemingly without the use of any reasoning process or conscious analysis. There are researchers who

intuition: The immediate comprehension that something is the case, seemingly without the use of any reasoning process or conscious analysis.

FIGURE 7.3

Interplay Between Decision-Making Factors and Decision-Making Styles

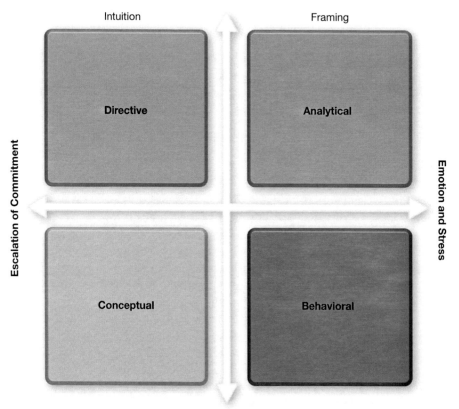

view intuition as a rather rational skill that managers *should* use in making decisions.[19] Even though the steps of the intuitive process may be buried in the subconscious part of the brain—so that we may never understand them—most experts realize the existence and importance of intuition in managerial decision making and view it as a necessary area of study.

Intuition is a hunch, a sixth sense, a flash of insight, something that "feels right," or a "gut" feeling. These descriptions could easily lead you to believe that intuitive decision making is irrational or arbitrary. However, this is not the case. While intuition refers to decision making without formal analysis or conscious reasoning, it is based on years of practice and experience that enable managers to identify alternatives quickly without conducting a systematic analysis of alternatives and their consequences. A good sense of intuition often distinguishes the truly great managers. When making a decision using intuition, the manager recognizes cues in the decision situation that are the same as or similar to those in previous situations he or she has experienced, rapidly conducts a subconscious analysis, and unconsciously makes a choice.

All of the discount retailing industry has been impacted by Sam Walton's intuition and vision.

In today's complex, dynamic business environment, managers have to make a multitude of decisions, frequently with minimal information and under time and cost constraints. The collection and analysis of data and alternative solutions can be a laborious, time-consuming, expensive process that managers do not have the luxury to undertake. Consequently, intuitive decision making becomes a necessity for managerial survival. Of course, all managers, especially inexperienced ones, should be careful not to rely too heavily on intuition. Obviously, if rationality and analytical decision making are always ignored in favor of intuition, the odds are good that managers will make poor decisions. Thus, managers need to be aware of their own use of intuition and to be careful to moderate its use with logic and analysis. Intuition is also useful when an instant decision is needed. If an employee is asked to destroy a document or engage in some other questionable conduct, a quick decisive decision is required.

Sam Walton, the founder of Walmart, exemplified the positive use of intuition. When he conceived the idea of building large discount retail stores in rural areas, he was told that the idea would never work. After all, Sears was a very successful large retailer whose success was based on stores located in urban areas. Nevertheless, Walton was sure his intuition was right … and the rest is history.

Emotion and Stress

Because most decision situations involve some element of risk, decision making can evoke anxiety, which leads to stress. Stress can derail people from following reasonable courses of action. All managers are susceptible to letting their emotions get in the way of rational decision making, and when emotions interfere with logic, managers can respond in nonproductive, even counterproductive, ways. These responses tend to be more common when decisions have to be made under time pressure.

When you consider the powerful effect that emotions such as guilt, anxiety, and embarrassment have on individuals, it is easy to understand how managers could be driven to make decisions—even bad ones—in their need to relieve the feelings plaguing them. Due to the effects of emotions and stress, decision makers have been known to respond in some predictable ways, all of which render their decisions less reasonable. Some typical responses to emotion and stress in decision making are defensive avoidance, which involves excessively delaying a decision; overreaction, making a decision impulsively to relieve anxiety; and hypervigilance, obsessively gathering more and more data in lieu of making a decision.[20] For instance, former executive of Enron Lynn Brewer describes how complacency spelled doom for the company. Although serious misconduct was occurring in the firm, perhaps the greater threat was the fact that some people knew of the fraud but decided to avoid reporting it.[21] This delayed response helped to damage the firm beyond repair.

Because the effects of emotion and stress on managers can result in faulty—even damaging—decisions, it is of paramount importance that managers realize when and how their feelings are affecting their decision making. It is during these stressful times that managers would be wise to devote time and resources to a logical decision-making process in an effort to ensure that the procedure is rational, not emotional.

Framing

Framing is widely recognized as a factor that not only affects decision making, but also contributes to many decision failures.[22] Generally speaking, framing involves the tendency to view positively presented information favorably and negatively presented information unfavorably. It refers to how information is phrased, presented, or labeled. Labels create frames of reference that serve to bias judgment—or interpretation of information—which then influences behavior. The manner in which information about a problem or possible outcomes is presented can wield a tremendous amount of influence on a decision maker's evaluation of the situation and, ultimately, on his or her decision.

For example, managers are more likely to view positively projects that have a 70 percent success rate than projects that have a 30 percent failure rate, even though these projects have the same probability of success. Because of framing, the projects presented as 70 percent successful probably seem more attractive to managers than the projects presented in terms of their failure rates. For those interested, Nobel Laureate Dr. Daniel Kahneman's recent book *Thinking Fast and Slow* provides an excellent semi-academic review of this topic.

Managers need to be aware of how easy it is to be overly influenced by the manner in which something is presented. Also, susceptibility to the power of framing is likely to increase when managers are making decisions under conditions of uncertainty. Thus, in the pursuit of sound decision making, managers must strive to analyze decision situations objectively, thereby reducing the chances that framing will unduly influence their decisions.

Escalation of Commitment

Another factor that affects decision making is an escalation of commitment to a chosen course of action. **Escalation of commitment** refers to the tendency to persist with a failing course of action.[23] In such cases, the decision makers become so immersed in their chosen course of action that they ignore or discount information that challenges the soundness of their initial decision. Caught up in the momentum of the situation, these managers lose their objectivity and seem unable to "call it quits," even though logic and rationality

The way you view a situation, or framing, has a significant impact on the outcomes.

dictates that they should. Escalation of commitment is a decision-making trap often characterized by the following descriptions or scenarios: "throwing good money after bad," a preoccupation with "sunk costs," and "too much time and money invested to quit now."

There are several reasons why decision makers fall into the trap of escalating commitment. A primary reason is their unwillingness to admit—to others or themselves—that their original decision was incorrect. Coinciding with this is unwillingness on the manager's part to accept that the resources—money, time, energy, and people—already committed to the course of action were allocated in vain. Therefore, in a need to reaffirm the wisdom of his or her original decision, the decision maker escalates his or her commitment by allocating even more resources to the attainment of the original goal. In addition, managers who have fallen into the trap of escalating commitment are often spurred to continue their seemingly faulty course of action by the feeling that the situation is bound to change for the better—because of the resources already invested, the projected favorable impact of additional resource allocation, their belief in and identification with the course of action, their unwillingness to give up or quit, and a sometimes unrealistic optimism that, despite evidence to the contrary, "things are bound to get better."[24]

One of the most egregious examples of this phenomenon occurred when Henry Ford decided to set up a rubber plantation in Brazil in the 1930s. The plantation was unprofitable from day one, plagued with disease, unruly workers, and the financial constraints of the Great Depression, but Ford continued the venture for over a decade. The company sunk hundreds of millions of dollars into Fordlandia. Ford felt that the project must succeed to satisfy his own ego and to justify the time and expense he put into it. The Fordlandia rubber project only ended when Ford passed away and his son sold the land back to Brazil. In the foreign policy area, many observers now feel that the United States' involvement in the Vietnam War, in which the United States kept committing massive resources even after it was clear that victory was highly elusive, is a good example of this phenomenon in operation.

Thus, managers must walk a fine line. On the one hand, they must be careful not to commit to an apparently faulty decision for too long, for to do so could be disastrous for the company. On the other hand, they must guard against bailing out of a decision too soon—before time and resources have had a chance to render the course of action successful. Giving up on a course of action too soon can also be disastrous for the company because of the risk that potentially successful courses of action would not be realized. Given the critical nature of escalating commitment in the decision-making process, managers should take steps to avoid the escalation trap. Some recommendations on how managers can avoid escalating commitment include the following:

1. Set limits on your involvement and commitment in advance and stick with them during the course of action. This gives the decision maker a better chance of remaining objective when evaluating the decision and subsequent course of action.
2. Do not look to other people to see what you should do. Because escalating commitment is a commonly observed behavior, it is easy to look around and see others who are escalating too, making it easier to justify your own tendency to escalate.
3. Determine why you are continuing a course of action. If there are not sound reasons to continue, then do not.
4. Remind yourself of the costs involved. Consider the added costs of continuing the course of action—not just the costs already incurred—when making your decision.
5. Be vigilant in your awareness of the tendency to escalate. It is an easy trap to fall into, and managers must be aware of this phenomenon and continually reassess the costs and benefits of continuing any course of action.[25]

Confidence and Risk Propensity

confidence: A person's faith that his or her decisions are reliable and good.

risk propensity: A person's willingness to take risks when making decisions.

Confidence and risk propensity are two factors that go hand in hand in affecting managerial decision making. **Confidence** means that a person has faith that his or her decisions are reliable and good. **Risk propensity** refers to a person's willingness to take risks when

Source: 2jenn/Shutterstock

Managers operate with different risk tolerances, with the above representing an individual with a high risk tolerance.

making decisions. Generally speaking, the higher your level of confidence in your decisions, the greater the likelihood that you will take risks in decision making.

Overconfidence is dangerous because it can lead decision makers to ignore the risks associated with a particular course of action. For example, a trader at JP Morgan, dubbed the London Whale because his large-scale trades moved the market index, often made the company money through high-risk trading. However, too many risky bets eventually led to massive losses.[26] When this happens, organizations can become vulnerable to all kinds of negative exposure, including legal and financial exposure that can spell ruin. In JP Morgan's case, overconfidence and excessive risks led to a loss of more than $6 billion. Thus, it is easy to see that an inappropriate confidence level can threaten successful decision making and implementation. Disaster is a common by-product of poor decisions made with great confidence. Yet by the same token, the potential benefits of a good decision may never be realized if the decision maker does not have, and does not project to others, enough confidence in the decision.

Similarly, there is a fine line to be walked when it comes to risk propensity. Managers who take too many and/or too great risks can lead companies to disastrous results; however, managers who are too risk averse may never lead their companies to their greatest potential. Like the other factors that affect decision making—intuition, emotion and stress, framing, and escalation of commitment—confidence and risk propensity must be scrutinized carefully to ensure that their contributions to the decision-making process are favorable and in the best interest of the organization.

Decision Making in Groups

All of the topics discussed thus far—types of decisions, conditions affecting decision making, steps of decision making, decision-making models, decision-making styles, and factors that affect decision making—apply to decisions made by both individuals and

Source: Pressmaster/Shutterstock

Because of the complexity of the decisions, most organizational decisions are made in groups.

You're the Manager . . . What Would You Do?

THE COMPANY: J&G Chemical Company
YOUR POSITION: Environmental Manager
THE PLACE: Jacksonville, FL

J&G Chemical Company, one of the largest industrial chemical producers, has always been concerned about the safe and effective disposal of chemical waste. A year ago, CEO Ken Jones hired you as an environmental manager. In your brief time with the company, you have begun implementing a new, advanced program to ensure the safety of employees, the plant site, waste-disposal areas, and the general public.

Communication to line management concerning the new program has been extensive. All line managers involved in chemical-waste disposal have attended a series of informative, instructional workshops covering safety factors, disposal guidelines, and notification procedures in the event of a potentially harmful situation. A ten-step process for crisis intervention and handling was detailed. You have conducted drills individually with the line managers to determine their understanding of the new program and to ensure that they are following the new guidelines. The line managers have presented the same information to employees under their supervision, and drills with seven of the ten teams of employees have been held. Problems in the manufacturing processes employed by Teams 8, 9, and 10 have delayed their training and drills.

On September 5, Bill Smith, a relatively new employee, discovered a hairline crack in the chemical-waste containment unit controlled by Team 9. He immediately reported the problem to the line manager and returned to his work station. Contrary to the new guidelines, the manager did not shut down the manufacturing line, and the first-shift employees left for the day. The line manager forgot to inform the incoming shift's manager of the problem. The second-shift employees continued to operate the line, sending the chemical waste into the damaged containment unit.

On September 6, Bill Smith missed work due to illness. Because Team 9 was shorthanded and rushing to meet a looming deadline, no one noticed the damaged containment unit until the second shift reported for work. By this time, the crack was substantially larger, and a small amount of chemical waste had begun seeping onto the surrounding platform and into a drain for treated

J&G Chemical Company produces industrial chemicals.

"clean" water. The pipes empty into nearby Crystal Lake, which is known for its excellent fishing and bird watching. The employee who noticed the seepage reported the problem to the line manager, who disregarded the new guidelines and empowered a stop-gap measure to allow the manufacturing process to continue.

By the time the first shift reported to work this morning, September 7, a crisis situation had developed. A disgruntled employee who had learned about the leak called a local newspaper reporter with a reputation for aggressive reporting on environmental issues. The reporter has asked to speak with you, demanding to know what J&C will do to correct the damage, if indeed environmental damage has occurred. You have politely informed her that she will be called as soon as more information is available on the situation. You have called a meeting of the line managers and asked for recommendations to defuse the crisis situation quickly, taking any necessary measures to contain environmental damage and minimize negative publicity concerning the event.

QUESTIONS

1. Trace the decision-making process you would use to handle the situation. What decision-making model would you use?

2. How should decisions be made in such a crisis environment?

3. Given the existing information, as environmental manager, what would you do?

groups. It is important to note, however, that in more and more organizations today, primarily groups rather than individuals are making decisions. In fact, in most organizations, it would be rare to find decisions being made regularly by one individual.

The reasons for the prevalence of group decision making in organizations are varied. Today's complex, dynamic business world requires more specialized knowledge than just one person can usually possess. Thus, companies are almost forced to rely on groups of individuals to obtain sufficient information and expertise needed to make sound business decisions. Moreover, once a decision has been made, the success of its implementation depends, to a great extent, on the commitment of the individuals who must carry it out. It is proven that group participation throughout the decision-making process helps create acceptance of and commitment to the decision, which go a long way toward ensuring the successful implementation of the decision. With groups such as teams, task forces, and committees becoming more commonplace in the realm of managerial decision making, it is appropriate to discuss participative management, group decision-making techniques, and the advantages and disadvantages of group decision making.

Participative Decision Making

Organizations characterized by participative, or peer-driven, decision making enable employees to provide input on organizational decisions. Managers who adopt a participative decision-making approach are willing to share power with employees when making certain decisions.[27] The goals of participative decision making are to empower employees and generate new ideas because of the diversity of input.[28] The more employees involved in the decision-making process, the greater the ability to consider alternatives and reach a decision that is most beneficial. Microsoft, Google, and other high-tech companies encourage participative decision making.

One reason why more managers favor participative decision making is that it has been shown to lead to greater job satisfaction, employee motivation, and involvement within the organization.[29] Employees involved in participative decision making often feel more secure about their jobs and less strain in the workplace.[30] How much influence participative decision making may have on employee satisfaction and productivity, however, is not as clear. While many studies have supported a positive association, others have revealed that while there is a positive relationship between job satisfaction and participative decision making, the relationship might not be practically significant.[31] Despite this fact, the complexities of the workplace and the rapidly changing business environment often create the need for groups of employees to contribute their input toward crucial decisions.

Group Decision Techniques

Group decision making is important because many business decisions are made not by individuals, but by groups or teams of employees. Whereas individual business decisions are based upon the reasoning of one person, group decisions involve the input of a number of employees. This collaboration enables employees to explore alternatives that might not be considered by a single individual. There are several decision techniques that are helpful in group decision making. In this section, we discuss two common ones: brainstorming and the nominal group technique.

brainstorming: A technique in which group members spontaneously suggest ideas to solve a problem.

Brainstorming is a technique in which group members spontaneously suggest ideas to solve a problem. Its primary purpose is to generate a multitude of creative alternatives, regardless of the likelihood of their being implemented. There are four basic rules for brainstorming:

1. Criticism is not allowed. Judgment or evaluation of ideas must be withheld until the conclusion of the idea-generation process.
2. "Freewheeling" is encouraged. The more novel and radical the idea, the better, for it is easier to "tame down" ideas than to think of them.
3. Quantity is desired. The greater the number of ideas, the greater the likelihood that a superior idea will result.
4. Combination and improvement are encouraged. In addition to contributing their own ideas, participants should suggest how others' ideas can be turned into better ideas, or how two or more ideas can be combined into yet another one.[32]

The object of brainstorming is to promote freer, more flexible thinking and to encourage group members to build on each other's creativity. By prohibiting criticism, brainstorming reduces inhibition and fears of ridicule or failure, which typically results in enthusiastic, involved participants. Brainstorming is considered to be a very effective technique for generating alternatives, the second step of the decision-making process.

Nominal Group Technique

Unlike the highly interactive, unstructured brainstorming, the **nominal group technique** involves the use of a highly structured meeting agenda and restricts discussion or interpersonal communication during the decision-making process. While the group members are all physically present, they are required to operate independently. Specifically, the following steps occur in a nominal group:

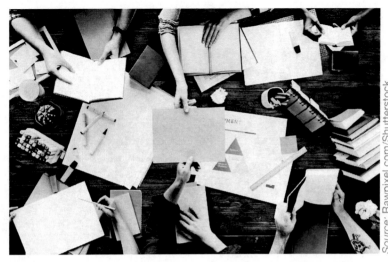

Brainstorming allows for teams to make creative recommendations for dealing with organizational challenges and opportunities.

nominal group technique: A process that involves the use of a highly structured meeting agenda and restricts discussion or interpersonal communication during the decision-making process.

1. Members meet as a group, but before any discussion takes place, each member independently writes down his or her ideas for possible problem solutions.
2. In round-robin fashion, each member takes a turn presenting a single idea to the group. This continues until everyone's ideas have been presented and recorded, usually on a flip chart or chalkboard. No discussion of the ideas occurs until all ideas have been recorded for general viewing.
3. The group then engages in an open discussion of the idea for the purpose of clarification and evaluation.
4. A secret written ballot is then taken, with each member individually and silently ranking the ideas in priority order. The idea that has the highest aggregate ranking becomes the adopted decision.[33]

The nominal group technique is useful because it ensures that every group member has equal input in the decision-making process. It also avoids some of the pitfalls—such as self-censorship, pressure to conform, group member dominance, hostility, and conflict—that can plague a more interactive, spontaneous, unstructured forum such as one using brainstorming. The nominal group technique has been an effective tool in the generation and evaluation of alternatives, the second and third steps in the decision-making process. While the size of groups may vary depending on the task, Jeff Bezos of Amazon thinks that the best group decision making occurs when two large pizzas are enough to feed the group of decision makers. Groups that are too large could prove inefficient and take too long in the decision-making process.

Individual versus Group Decision Making

So, are two (or more) heads better than one? The answer depends on several factors, such as the nature of the task, the ability of the group members, and the form of interaction. Because managers often have a choice between making a decision by themselves and including others, they need to understand the advantages and disadvantages of group decision making.

Advantages of Group Decision Making

Group decision making offers a number of advantages over individual decision making:

Organizations balance team and individual decision making.

Cultural Differences in Decision Making

There is no doubt that decision making, as well as every other aspect of organizational life, has been profoundly affected by the increasing cultural diversity that exists in today's business world. Due to changing workforce demographic trends and the increasing globalization of business, today's managers are realizing that being able to manage cultural differences is essential to the long-term success of companies.

To understand cultural differences and their impact on decision making, managers must first acknowledge that people of different ethnic backgrounds have different attitudes, values, and norms that reflect their cultural heritage. One area of cultural difference that has been extensively researched is the issue of individualism versus collectivism. Understanding individualism and collectivism is important to understanding the effects of cultural differences on decision making because cross-cultural studies suggest that certain cultures tend to favor either individualism or collectivism. For example, North Americans and northern and western Europeans tend to be individualists, and Asians, Latinos, and most eastern and western Africans tend to be collectivists. Additionally, there is evidence to support that African, Hispanic, and Far Eastern minorities in the United States tend to be collectivists.

Individualist cultures tend to place greater emphasis on the needs and goals of the individual over those of the group. Individualists consider their own beliefs and efforts of paramount importance, and they emphasize competition more than cooperation. In contrast, collectivist cultures place greater emphasis on the needs and goals of the group over those of the individual. Collectivists stress the importance of social norms, duty, and shared beliefs, and they emphasize the value of cooperation—not competition—with group members. When it comes to decision making, collectivists are more likely than individualists to sacrifice personal interests for the attainment of goals.

Equipped with an awareness of such differences, today's managers will be better prepared to under-

Source: ARENA Creative/Shutterstock

Cultural differences improve decision making in organizations.

stand how decision making—both within their organizations and between different organizations (such as joint ventures, strategic alliances, etc.)—is affected by diversity. Such an understanding of cultural diversity explains, for example, why over 90 percent of all large Japanese companies and most of the smaller ones use a decision-making process called *ringi*. This system is based on the collectivist principle that decisions are made only when a consensus is reached among team members. Conversely, American companies, with their emphasis on individualism and independent action, do not see consensus as a necessity in decision making. Understanding this difference, and others, between Japanese and American cultures can help facilitate organizational decision-making processes.[34]

1. A group can bring much more knowledge and information to bear on a problem or decision than can an individual acting alone.
2. Individuals in a group bring different experiences, perspectives, and interests that help the members see decision situations and problems from different angles.
3. Groups can typically generate and evaluate more alternatives than can one individual.
4. Within a group, discussion can serve to clarify vagueness and confusion, reduce uncertainty for those who are averse to risk, and provide an opportunity for intellectual stimulation that fosters creativity—all to a greater extent than would be possible with individual decision making.

5. People who participate in a group discussion about a decision are more likely to understand why the decision was made because they have heard the relevant arguments both for the chosen alternative and against the rejected alternatives.

6. Participants in group decision making are more likely to accept the decision ("it's 'our' decision") and, therefore, to be more committed to it, which translates into a greater motivation for ensuring successful implementation.

7. The United States values democracy, which the group decision-making process exemplifies. Thus, others may perceive a group decision as more legitimate than a decision made by a single individual.

8. Less-experienced participants in group interaction learn a great deal about group dynamics by actually being involved in the group decision-making process.

Disadvantages of Group Decision Making

Following is a list of the major disadvantages of group decision making. Table 7.2 highlights some common mistakes that are made in group decision making:

1. Groups take more time to reach a decision than would a lone individual. Group assembly and interaction take time and can result in inefficiency and increased costs.

2. One or more group members may dominate the discussion and, therefore, exert undue influence on decision selection.

3. The desire by group members to be accepted and considered valuable to the group effort can result in participants feeling pressured to conform—or not to "rock the boat." Such pressure stifles the creativity of individual contributors and encourages conformity among viewpoints.

4. To avoid the time and inherent conflict typically associated with group decision making, participants may be willing to settle for a compromise, or satisfying, decision rather than pursue an optimizing, or maximizing, decision.

5. Because the group rather than any single individual makes the decision, there is no clear focus of decision responsibility. This ambiguity can result in confusion when it comes to decision implementation and evaluation.

6. In groups, sometimes secondary considerations—such as winning an argument, making a point, saving face, defeating another's idea, or getting back at a rival—displace the primary goal of making an effective decision.

7. Groups may succumb to a phenomenon known as **groupthink**, which occurs when cohesive "in-groups" let the desire for unanimity, or consensus, override sound judgment in generating and evaluating alternative courses of action.[35] To avoid dissension, disagreement, and loss of "esprit de corps," group members may conform prematurely to poor decisions. Playing **Devil's advocate**, in which a member of the team argues for an alternative position, can be helpful in avoiding groupthink because it encourages team members to carefully consider alternative courses of action.

Equipped with the knowledge of the advantages and disadvantages of group decision making, managers should be better able to determine whether individual or group decision making is most appropriate for a particular decision situation. If choosing group

groupthink: A phenomenon occurring when cohesive "in-groups" let the desire for unanimity, or consensus, override sound judgment in generating and evaluating alternative courses of action.

Devil's advocate: When a member of the team argues for an alternative position; can be helpful in avoiding groupthink because it encourages team members to carefully consider alternative courses of action.

TABLE 7.2 Common Mistakes in Group Decision Making

1. Failure to obtain adequate information related to the decision
2. Developing conclusions based on personal bias
3. Overcommitment based on current investments
4. Succumbing to groupthink
5. Overconfidence in predicting the outcomes of a decision
6. Failure to have open discussion in resolving problems
7. Only presenting information that confirms a decision
8. Failure to delegate a decision to those with more knowledge

decision making, managers must realize that the success of the group—and, ultimately, the success of the decision—greatly depends on two factors: (1) the type of group technique used, and (2) how effectively the group capitalizes on the advantages and minimizes the disadvantages of group decision making.

Summary and Review

■ *Define decision making and describe the types of decisions and conditions that might affect decision making.* Decision making is the process of choosing among alternative courses of action to resolve a problem. Decisions may be programmed, which are made in response to situations that are routine, somewhat structured, and fairly repetitive, or non-programmed, which are made in response to situations that are unique, relatively unstructured, undefined, and of major consequence to the organization. Certainty, risk, and uncertainty often exert a significant effect on decision making.

■ *Specify the steps involved in decision making.* The decision-making process consists of six steps: (1) identifying the problem, the most critical step in the decision-making process; (2) generating alternative solutions; (3) evaluating alternatives; (4) selecting the best alternative, based on each alternative's feasibility, effectiveness, and cost; (5) implementing the decision; and (6) evaluating the decision.

■ *Contrast the decision-making models.* The classical model of decision making prescribes how managers should make decisions and asserts that managers are logical, rational individuals who make decisions that are in the best interests of the organization. The administrative model of decision making describes how managers actually make decisions. The administrative model includes the concepts of bounded rationality and satisficing. Bounded rationality means that people have limits, or boundaries, to their rationality, which lead them to forgo the six steps of decision making in favor of a quicker, yet satisficing, process—satisficing. Satisficing means that decision makers choose the first alternative that appears to satisfactorily resolve the problem situation. The political model of decision making is based on the idea that certain individuals or groups will be able to influence others to achieve their goals. In general, the political model attempts to develop coalitions to promote ideas, obtain resources, or negotiate an advantage.

■ *Discuss the four decision-making styles.* The four decision-making styles include the directive, analytical, conceptual, and behavioral styles. Managers with a directive style dislike ambiguity and desire power. These leaders base their decisions on facts and are focused upon results.

Managers with an analytical style can tolerate a greater degree of ambiguity and like to tackle new challenges. They like to use logic and problem-solving in decision making. Conceptual skills are highly important to management as they relate to vision and creativity. Managers with a conceptual decision-making style are skilled at developing new solutions and relying on intuition. Finally, behavioral decision makers focus more upon the individual. They tend to be supportive and empathetic to their followers, believing that satisfied employees will make satisfied customers.

■ *Examine the factors that may affect decision making.* Many factors affect decision making, including (1) intuition—immediately comprehending that something is the case, seemingly without the use of any reasoning process or conscious analysis; (2) emotion and stress—feelings that can derail rational decision making and result in nonproductive or counterproductive behavior; (3) framing, which refers to how information is phrased, presented, or labeled and serves to bias judgment, or interpretation, of information; (4) escalation of commitment—the tendency of individuals and organizations to persist with failing courses of action; and (5) confidence and risk propensity—the notion that the higher your confidence level in your decisions, the greater the likelihood that you will take risks in decision making.

■ *Summarize group decision techniques and the advantages and disadvantages of group decision making.* Brainstorming is a technique in which group members spontaneously suggest ideas to solve a problem. The nominal group technique involves the use of a highly structured meeting agenda and restricts discussion and interpersonal communication during the decision-making process.

The major advantages that groups offer over individuals in decision making are that they (1) provide a greater pool of knowledge and information; (2) provide more approaches and perspectives; (3) are more likely to generate more alternative solutions; (4) clarify ambiguous problems, reduce uncertainty about alternatives, and increase intellectual stimulation; (5) foster greater comprehension of the decision; (6) foster increased acceptance of and commitment to the decision; (7) have increased legitimacy; and (8) provide a training ground. On the other hand, the major disadvantages of group decision making are that groups (1) are time consuming; (2) may be dominated by one or more group members; (3) are subject to social pressure; (4) may compromise decisions, or satisfice; (5) have ambiguous decision responsibility; (6) may experience goal displacement; and (7) are subject to groupthink.

■ *Apply the decision-making models to a hypothetical situation.* Using the principles in this chapter, trace the decision-making process you would use to handle the situation described in the "Business Dilemma" box. What decision-making model would you use? How should decisions be made in such a crisis environment?

Key Terms and Concepts

administrative model of decision making 203

bounded rationality 203

brainstorming 212

certainty 198

classical model of decision making 202

confidence 209

decision 197

decision making 197

decision styles 204

Devil's advocate 215

escalation of commitment 208

framing 208

groupthink 215

intuition 206

nominal group technique 213

non-programmed decisions 197

political model of decision making 203

problem 197

programmed decisions 197

risk 198

risk propensity 209

satisficing 203

uncertainty 199

Ready Recall

1. Distinguish between the two main types of decisions, giving an example of each.
2. Describe the three conditions under which decision making may occur.
3. List the six steps of the decision-making process. Why is proper problem identification the most critical step in the decision-making process?
4. What are some of the reasons why breakdowns can occur during the decision implementation stage?
5. Contrast the three major models of decision making, outlining the assumptions associated with each.

6. Explain how the concepts of bounded rationality and satisficing affect the decision-making process.
7. Discuss the five factors that affect decision making.
8. Compare and contrast the group decision techniques presented in this chapter.
9. What are some of the advantages and disadvantages of group decision making?
10. Discuss the phenomenon of groupthink and how it affects group decision making.

Expand Your Experience

1. The shipping department of a large pharmaceutical company is experiencing slumping productivity and an increase in order-fulfillment errors. Analyze this issue by working through the steps in the decision-making process
2. A toy manufacturer makes most of its sales from a toy that has a slight safety issue. A product recall would result in the company going bankrupt. Discuss how such factors as intuition, emotion and stress, framing, escalation of commitment, and confidence and risk propensity could influence the company's decision making regarding this issue.
3. Think about decisions that you have recently made in your life or that you will need to make in the near

future. Characterize these decision situations as programmed or non-programmed and discuss how the conditions of certainty, risk, and uncertainty affect (or will affect) your decision-making process.
4. More and more businesses are using groups rather than a lone individual to make decisions. Think of two work situations that involve the need for decision making: one in which it would seem appropriate to use the brainstorming technique, and one in which it would seem appropriate to use the nominal group technique. Discuss why each of these techniques was well suited to the particular decision situation at hand.

Making Decisions

You learned from this chapter that there are four decision-making styles. Which decision-making style characterizes you? Ask yourselves the following questions to determine your primary decision-making style. Please choose the option that *most applies* to your decision-making style.

1. How do you feel about making decisions in unclear situations?
   a. They drive me nuts! Just give me the facts.
   b. They give me a chance to explore different alternatives, especially those outside of the box.
   c. They do not bother me. I explore alternatives logically before making a decision.
   d. They give me a chance to consult with others about the best approach.

2. When making a decision, what do you rely on?
   a. Concrete facts
   b. Intuition
   c. Careful attention to detail
   d. Input from others

3. What do you think is a primary strength about the way you make decisions?
   a. I use rationality and logic to quickly make a decision.
   b. I explore a broad range of alternatives and take a long-term perspective.
   c. I am careful, thorough, and well-informed when making decisions.
   d. I tend to be more team-oriented and open to suggestions.

4. If others were to identify a major weakness of your decision-making approach, they would most likely say that your decision-making style is:
   a. Autocratic
   b. Indecisive
   c. Overcontrolling
   d. Too accommodating

5. Your decision-making style is best described as:
   a. Quick and decisive
   b. Focused on the best solution in the long-term
   c. Time-consuming but thorough
   d. Time-consuming but with much advice from others

6. If you are a manager, how would you handle an employee who disagrees with your decision?
   a. As the manager, I make the decisions. I expect employees to respect that.
   b. I welcome the ability to collaborate and discuss alternatives.
   c. I will most likely go with my decision, but might hear employees out if they have good arguments.
   d. I would seriously consider the employee's position. I want to avoid conflict whenever possible.

7. You feel like you do not have all of the information needed to make the best decision. Which course do you take?
   a. Make the decision that seems best to you.
   b. Spend time brainstorming and researching creative approaches.
   c. Do not make a decision until you have explored all relevant alternatives.
   d. Consult with your team and work toward a final solution.

8. As a decision maker, you are skilled at:
   a. Making quick decisions
   b. Brainstorming for creative solutions
   c. Collecting the most relevant information
   d. Negotiating with others

9. When making a decision, you tend to trust:
   a. Your own experience
   b. Your instincts
   c. Careful analysis of alternatives
   d. Group consensus

10. You like jobs that are:
    a. Structured and well-defined
    b. Creative and thought-provoking
    c. Innovative and detail-orientated
    d. Collaborative and relational

If you selected mostly A's, your decision-making style is directive. You dislike ambiguity and prefer decision situations to be well defined. You often rely on your own experience and knowledge. You tend to make decisions quickly with the knowledge you have rather than research many additional alternatives. You also tend to be more autocratic in your decision making. Your decision-making style is beneficial in well-structured environments and when judgments need to be made quickly. To improve your decision making, try soliciting input from others in the organization and spending more time exploring alternative solutions.

If you selected mostly B's, your decision-making style is more conceptual. You love to brainstorm and think of long-term solutions. The sky is the limit in terms of creative solutions. You tend to rely more on your intuition than hard data to make decisions. You thrive in creative environments that let you use your imagination, but sometimes it is hard for you to commit to a solid decision. To improve your decision making, practice selecting and committing toward a final decision.

If you selected mostly C's, your decision-making style is more analytical. You are innovative and are willing to spend considerable time researching alternatives. You believe that approaching a decision logically is important in discovering the best solution. You are able to handle ambiguous situations well. You thrive in environments requiring detailed analysis and innovative solutions. To improve your decision making, you must learn to recognize when situations require a quick solution, when they can be explored thoroughly, and when decision making would be best served using a collaborative approach.

If you selected mostly D's, your decision-making style is more behavioral. You are very relationship-oriented and skilled at negotiation. Your team members like you because you consider their input and are committed toward the team's success. You generally dislike conflict and try to avoid it. You thrive in collaborative environments where you can interact with others. To improve your decision making, you should recognize that conflict is not always disadvantageous but could be an important means of exploring alternative solutions.

Case 7: Tony Hsieh's Decision-Making Role at Zappos

In 1999, Nick Swinmurn made the executive decision to quit his job and begin the entrepreneurial endeavor of developing a shoe website. He planned for his website to offer a vast selection of shoes and exceptional customer service. Swinmurn named the company Shoesite.com and began transferring orders between customers and suppliers. Initially, the company did not hold inventory, but not long after, the firm decided to shift its strategy and rebrand the company. The website was renamed Zappos, and in 2000 entrepreneur Tony Hsieh became the company's CEO at age 26.

Although not initially enthusiastic about becoming the CEO of a shoe website, Hsieh became CEO to lead the company in the direction he believed would provide the most benefits. After investing in the firm, Hsieh made the decision to sell his loft to pay for a new warehouse. He set his salary as CEO at $24 a year. This decision took much deliberation because of the emotion and stress involved. Hsieh realized the risk he was taking, but his intuition told him it would be a profitable decision after evaluating the alternatives. Although the company initially struggled to make a profit, things took a positive turn in 2007 after the company reached annual sales of $840 million.

Zappos has ten core values that guide its decision making and company culture. Some of Zappos's values include embracing and driving change, being adventurous, doing more with less, building a positive team and family spirit, being humble, and creating fun and a little weirdness. This not only frames the company culture but allows employees to have a customer-focused business model while making both programmed and non-programmed decisions on a daily basis. Zappos strives to make the shopping experience easy and enjoyable. It provides a 100 percent satisfaction-guaranteed return policy to ensure the organization is building and maintaining strong customer relationships.

Zappos made the decision to empower customers in their shopping experience and encourage them to order several styles and return the items that do not work out. Customers can then evaluate their decisions on products they choose. This strategy may seem expensive but tends to work in Zappos's favor. With this type of customer service, the company builds loyalty among customers. It also allows customers to feel confident when shopping with the company because they are able to return unwanted products easily.

Zappos strives to make the shopping experience easy and enjoyable.

Zappos is famous for its relaxed and wacky atmosphere. Employees have access to an employee nap room, a wellness center, and an open mic in the cafeteria. The quirkiness of the company atmosphere is not a mistake; it is strategic. Zappos encourages employees to engage in the work they do as a team. Employees are encouraged to identify problems together, generate alternative courses of action, evaluate alternatives, and then eventually select decisions that will be best for the company.

In 2009, Hsieh made an important decision. He was at a standstill with board members, who disagreed with Hsieh's management style and company culture. Hsieh evaluated potential alternatives and selected the best alternative he could think of: meet with Amazon.com and buy out the board. Hsieh approached the decision by evaluating the risk, certainty, and uncertainty factors associated with the deal. He took the proper steps of decision making and finally settled on making a deal with the world's largest online retailer. Amazon.com offered to acquire Zappos for $1.2 billion. Zappos would continue to operate independently, and Hsieh was retained as the CEO. Even though Zappos was acquired, Hsieh maintains the company's initial vision and direction. Hsieh has not looked back since and feels he made the right decision.

A more recent decision Hsieh has made involved restructuring the company. In 2015, Hsieh changed the organizational structure of Zappos from a more traditional top-down managerial hierarchy into what is called a holacracy. A holacracy redistributes power by placing it at the center of the organization. Managerial roles are eliminated, and employees become their own leaders with their own roles. Teams meet periodically to discuss the governance of the company. They have tactical meetings to discuss key issues and next actions. Hsieh made this decision because he believes it will help Zappos grow without losing productivity. Statistics show that if a company expands too much, productivity per employee tends to decrease. On the other hand, when a city expands, productivity per person tends to increase. Hsieh believes the key to sustainable growth is for Zappos's future expansion to imitate a city's growth.

Once the decision was made, employees were left to make their own choices. Recognizing that this change may not be welcome among employees—especially management—Hsieh agreed to provide severance pay for six months for employees who decided they did not want to work under the new structure. Approximately 18 percent accepted the offer.

The road to this structural change has been rough. One concern with employees making more decisions relates to the certainty that employees are fully informed about an issue or problem. In addition, to make a good decision, employees must understand the risk and uncertainty that will affect the decision-making process. This could be a challenge to some employees. In 2016, Zappos fell off *Fortune* magazine's 100 Best Companies to Work For list. However, Hsieh believes that in the long term, this decision will benefit Zappos significantly and allow it to achieve both growth and greater productivity.[36]

1. What risks did Tony Hsieh assume in the major decisions he made for Zappos?
2. How do Zappos's core values guide its decision making?
3. Describe the employee group decision-making process at Zappos.

Notes

1. Adam Bluestein, "Regulate Me. Please." *Inc.*, May 2011, 72–80; Cascade Engineering website, http://www.cascadeng .com (accessed December 23, 2017); B Corporation website, http://www.bcorporation.net (accessed December 23, 2017); "The Nonprofit Behind B Corps," http://www.bcorporation.net/ what-are-b-corps/the-non-profit-behind-b-corps (accessed December 23, 2017); Make It Right, "Cradle to Cradle®," 2017, http://makeitright.org/c2c/ (accessed December 23, 2017); Lynn Golodner, "Welfare to Career: Plastics Company Helps People Break Barriers to Success," *Corp Magazine*, December 23, 2015, http://www.corpmagazine.com/welfare-career -plastics-company-helps-people-break-barriers-success/ (accessed December 23, 2017); Tim Fernholz, "Best Practices: Cascade Engineering Makes Welfare-to-Career a Reality," *Good*, September 28, 2011, https://www.good.is/articles/ best-practices-cascade-engineering-makes-welfare-to-career -a-reality (accessed December 23, 2017); Cascade Engineering, "Welfare to Career," http://www.cascadeng.com/welfare-career (accessed December 23, 2017); B Lab, "Cascade Engineering."

2. Herbert A. Simon, *The New Science of Management Decision* (New York: Harper & Row, 1960), 5–6.

3. Simon, *The New Science of Management Decision*, 5–6.

4. K. J. Radford, *Managerial Decision Making* (Reston, VA: Reston Publishing Company, Inc., 1975), 58–61.

5. Jim Zarroli, "Looking Back on Bank of America's Country-wide Debacle," *NPR*, January 11, 2013, http://www.npr.org/ 2013/01/11/169108131/looking-back-on-bank-of-americas -countrywide-debacle (accessed December 31, 2017).

6. Mayor's Press Office, "Absenteeism at CTA Drops 22 Percent over Last Two Years," City of Chicago website, July 30, 2013, https://www.cityofchicago.org/city/en/depts/mayor/ press_room/press_releases/2013/july_2013/absenteeism_at_ ctadrops22percentoverlasttwoyears.html (accessed December 31, 2017).

7. Arthur Sondak, "How to Answer the Question, 'What Should I Do?'" *Supervisory Management* 37 (December 1992): 4–5.

8. E. Frank Harrison, *The Managerial Decision-Making Process*, 2nd ed. (Boston: Houghton Mifflin Company, 1981), 53–59; and Radford, *Managerial Decision Making*, 77, 216–218.

9. Herbert A. Simon, *Administrative Behavior* (New York: Free Press, 1947); and James G. March and Herbert A. Simon, *Organizations* (New York: John Wiley & Sons, 1958).

10. Alan J. Rowe and J. D. Boulgarides, "Decision Styles: A Perspective," *Leadership & Organization Development* 4(4), (1983), 3–9.

11. Alan J. Rowe and Richard O. Mason, *Managing with Style* (San Francisco, CA: Jossey-Bass Publishers, 1987).

12. Maris G. Martinsons and Robert M. Davison, "Strategic decision making and support systems: Comparing American, Japanese and Chinese management," *Decision Support Systems* 43(2007), 284–300.

13. Rowe and Boulgarides, "Decision Styles: A Perspective," 3–9.

14. Rowe and Mason, *Managing with Style*.

15. Carnegie Mellon Tepper School of Business, "Bill Gates Moves on to Business of Charity," http://tepper.cmu.edu/news -multimedia/tepper-stories/bill-gates-moves-to-business-of -charity/index.aspx (accessed August 9, 2013).

16. Rowe and Boulgarides, "Decision Styles: A Perspective," 3–9; Rowe and Mason, *Managing with Style*.

17. Rowe and Mason, *Managing with Style*.

18. Ibid.

19. Weston H. Agor, *The Logic of Intuitive Decision Making* (New York: Quorum Books, 1986), 5.

20. Amitai Etzioni, "Humble Decision Making," *Harvard Business Review 67* (July–August 1989), 123.

21. Lynn Brewer, Robert Chandler, and O. C. Ferrell, *Managing Risks for Corporate Integrity: How to Survive an Ethical Misconduct Disaster* (Mason, OH: Thomson, 2006).

22. Glen Whyte, "Decision Failures: Whey They Occur and How to Prevent Them," *The Executive 5* (August 1991), 25.

23. Joel Brockner, "The Escalation of Commitment to a Failing Course of Action: Toward Theoretical Progress," *The Academy of Management Review 17* (January 1992), 39.

24. Brockner, "The Escalation of Commitment," 39–61; Barry M. Staw, "The Escalation of Commitment to a Course of Action," *The Academy of Management Review 6* (October 1981), 577–587; and Max H. Bazerman, *Judgment in Managerial Decision Making* (New York: John Wiley & Sons, 1986), 67–80.

25. Bazerman, *Judgment in Managerial Decision Making*, 75.

26. Dan Fitzpatrick, Gregory Zuckerman, and Scott Patterson, "'London Whale' Sounded an Alarm on Risky Bets," *The Wall Street Journal*, February 1, 2013, http://online.wsj.com/article/SB10001424127887324156204578276113151091922.html (accessed December 31, 2017).

27. E. A. Locke and D. M. Schweiger, "Participation in Decision-Making: One More look," *Research in Organisational Behaviour* 1 (1979), 265–339.

28. Tahira M. Probst, "Countering the Effects of Negative Job Insecurity Through Participative Decision Making: Lessons from the Demand-Control Model," *Journal of Occupational Health Psychology* 10(4), 2005, 320–329.

29. Paul E. Spector, "Perceived Control by Employees: A Meta-Analysis of Studies Concerning Autonomy and Participation at Work," *Human Relations* 39(11), 1986, 1005–1016.

30. Probst, "Countering the Effects of Negative Job Insecurity Through Participative Decision Making: Lessons from the Demand-Control Model"; Susan E. Jackson, "Participation in Decision Making as a Strategy for Reducing Job-Related Strain," *Journal of Applied Psychology* 68, no. 1 (February 1983): 3–19. doi: 10.1037/0021-9010.68.1.3

31. John A. Wagner III, "Participation's Effects on Performance and Satisfaction: A Reconsideration of Research Evidence," *Academy of Management Review* 19(2), April 1994, 312–330.

32. George P. Huber, *Managerial Decision-Making* (Glenview, IL: Scott, Foresman and Company, 1980), 193–195.

33. Stephen P. Robbins, *Essentials of Organizational Behavior*, 2nd ed. (Englewood Cliffs, NJ: Prentice Hall, 1988), 114–115.

34. Taylor Cox Jr., "The Multicultural Organization," *Academy of Management Executive 5* (May 1991), 34–37; Taylor H. Cox, Sharon A. Lobel, and Poppy Lauretta McLeod, "Effects of Ethnic Group Cultural Differences on Cooperative and Competitive Behavior on a Group Task," *Academy of Management Journal 34* (December 1991), 827–847; Brian Mark Hawrysh and Judith Lynne Zaichkowsky, "Cultural Approaches to Negotiations: Understanding the Japanese," *European Journal of Marketing 25* (1991), 40–54.

35. Irving L. Janis, *Groupthink*, 2nd ed. (Boston: Houghton Mifflin, 1982), 9.

36. Adapted from "Zappos: Delivering Happiness to Stakeholders," Daniels Fund Ethics Initiative, http://danielsethics.mgt.unm.edu/pdf/Zappos%20Case.pdf (accessed November 25, 2017); Richard Feloni, "Inside Zappos CEO Tony Hsieh's Radical Management Experiment That Prompted 14% of Employees to Quit," *Business Insider*, May 16, 2015, http://www.businessinsider.com/tony-hsieh-zappos-holacracy-managementexperiment-2015-5 (accessed May 12, 2017); Rebecca Greenfield, "Zappos CEO Tony Hsieh: Adopt Holacracy or Leave," *Fast Company*, March 30, 2015, https://www.fastcompany.com/3044417/zappos-ceo-tony-hsieh-adopt-holacracy-or-leave (accessed May 12, 2017); Zack Guzman, "Zappos CEO Tony Hsieh on Getting Rid of Managers: What I Wish I'd Done Differently," CNBC, September 13, 2016, http://www.cnbc.com/2016/09/13/zappos-ceo-tony-hsieh-the-thing-i-regret-aboutgetting-rid-of-managers.html (accessed May 12, 2017); HolacracyOne, LLC, "How It Works," http://holacracy.org/how-it-work (accessed May 12, 2017); Rachel Emma Silverman, "At Zappos, Some Employees Find Offer to Leave Too Good to Refuse," *The Wall Street Journal*, May 7, 2014, http://www.wsj.com/articles/at-zappos-someemployees-find-offer-to-leave-too-good-to-refuse-1431047917 (accessed May 12, 2017); Zappos Insights, Inc., "Holacracy," http://www.zapposinsights.com/about/holacracy (accessed May 12, 2017); Zappos.com, "Company Statement from Zappos.com," YouTube, April 1, 2016, https://www.youtube.com/watch?v=3zieP6NUWL8 (accessed May 12, 2017).

Organizing: Designing Jobs, Departments, and the Overall Organization

CHAPTER **8**

Source: Rawpixel.com/Shutterstock

Chapter Outline

After reading this chapter, you will be able to:

- Discuss the concept of organizing.
- Define an organizational culture.
- Interpret an organizational chart.
- Explain why job specialization and division of labor are important for organizing.
- Assess the different approaches to grouping tasks into jobs and the advantages and disadvantages of each.
- Determine the relationships among authority, responsibility, and delegation.
- Define decentralization and describe what strengths it has for employee development.
- Describe departmentalization and organizational structure.
- Detect different types of formal structures: functional, multidivisional, matrix, network/outsourcing, and team and virtual organizations.
- Specify three characteristics that define the latent structure of the organization.
- Summarize the contingency factors that influence the type of formal structure that is best for an organization.
- Describe the different types of coordinating mechanisms that can be used to support the organizational structure.
- Distinguish among five organizational archetypes: simple structure, machine bureaucracy, professional bureaucracy, divisionalized form, and adhocracy.
- Critique a company's new organizational structure.

Best Buy Designs Plugs in Employees through Empowerment

Retail is a fast-paced environment that can be difficult to handle. Best Buy is no exception. However, the company strives to create a culture in which employees feel empowered to contribute ideas. The way Best Buy is organized is a part of its culture and provides a blueprint that guides it on a path toward goals. It provides a shared identity that impacts activities and the workplace environment. Through different approaches and organizational structures, employees have gotten involved in the company's innovation process and contribute to its profitability.

Best Buy has had to adapt to both external and internal changes over its 40-year history. The company embraced a decentralized structure in which employees were provided with greater flexibility and the opportunity to engage in company operations. Within this structure, it adopted the open-source work approach. This helped encourage employee dedication by giving them the ability to engage in projects to improve the company's operations through innovative inventions.

An important part of the company's responsiveness is its emphasis on diversity. Those at Best Buy believe that immersion and personalization are the best ways to educate managers about the need for diversity. In 2003, the company started WOLF, its Women's Leadership Forum, which aims to improve the experiences of both female employees and female customers. Today, Best Buy's leadership team is largely female. Those at Best Buy say that these methods for increasing diversity have helped the company create a more family-like atmosphere. In 2017, CEO Hubert Joly signed the CEO Action for Diversity & Inclusion™ pledge, the largest CEO-driven commitment to date for driving diversity and inclusion.

Best Buy also encourages employees to take on additional roles in the company using rewards and communication methods. For instance, at the Best Buy headquarters, one team involved with process improvement was rewarded for its efforts with a baseball game and desktop framed prints. Best Buy also holds quarterly town hall meetings. Prior to the meetings, employees are encouraged to submit questions or concerns. The questions are prioritized by Best Buy's communications team. This method provides employees with greater accessibility to the heads of the firm.

Best Buy's corporate culture serves as a compass for employees, giving them direction as to how they should represent the company.

Despite its innovative culture, Best Buy still faced challenges. Amid declining sales and increasing competition, CEO Hubert Joly was appointed to turn the company around. One immediate change was how Best Buy's Geek Squad division was organized. Recognizing that Best Buy could differentiate itself from competitors through customer service, Joly made Geek Squad services available in-store, online, or through a home advisory program. Joly also wanted to encourage employees to follow their instincts and make quicker decisions. This meant allowing employees to make mistakes but also providing them with the opportunity to fix them. Joly believes quick decision making and employee empowerment are necessary to move the company forward. Energizing employees became a key pillar of the initiative to turn around Best Buy.

These decisions were largely successful, and in 2017 Joly announced a new initiative called "Best Buy 2020—Building the New Blue." As part of this initiative, Best Buy is introducing a try-before-you-buy program that will allow customers to rent gadgets and try them out beforehand; if they want to keep the product, 20 percent of the rental fee is deducted and applied to the final cost of the product. Employee empowerment will remain a key part of this initiative to transform Best Buy into a high-growth company.[1]

Introduction

Almost any time that two or more people get together to work on a project, the issue arises of who should do what part. Dividing work into parts, assigning these parts to individuals, and coordinating the activities of these individuals are examples of organizing. Organizing work is a major activity of management. As we will discuss in this chapter, there are many ways to organize, each with its own strengths and weaknesses. Additionally, there is a variety of ways that organizations can be structured and the circumstances that dictate the form that is most suitable for any given organization.

In this chapter, we will present the major approaches to organizing tasks into jobs and, in turn, jobs into departments. In presenting these major approaches, we also discuss the strengths and weaknesses of each. Next, we examine the types of formal structures that organizations as a whole can adopt as well as the informal structures that arise as a matter of practice. We then consider extenuating factors that affect an organization's choice of formal structure and the coordinating mechanisms that are useful in helping organization members stay in contact with other elements of the company. Finally, we consider some general types of organization, such as bureaucracies, professional organizations, and small, entrepreneurial organizations.

The Nature of Organizing

In Chapter 1, we defined an *organization* as a group of people working together to achieve goals or objectives that would be difficult or impossible for them to achieve individually. By this definition, Toyota is definitely an organization. Toyota's goal to build and market well-made, relatively inexpensive cars could have been developed by a small group of individuals or even by a single person. But to implement this vision, a virtual army of employees is necessary to complete the numerous tasks involved in making and selling an automobile. Similarly, the Girl Scouts of America is an organization in the same sense that, acting as a group, the individual members can more easily accomplish their goals. These goals require them to interact and perform civic and individual assistance tasks at the local, national, and international levels.

Thought of in this way, an organization is a means of more easily performing the tasks that are essential for achieving an objective. Organizing is, therefore, the process of creating the organization. In Chapter 1, we defined organizing as the activities involved in designing an appropriate organizational structure, assigning employees duties, and developing working relationships among people and among tasks. Organizing addresses important questions such as: Who reports to whom? How are tasks linked together? Who is responsible for the completion of tasks? Who coordinates this group of people? What are the shared values and beliefs of the company?

At the most basic level, people form organizations implement their visions. Because the goals that managers often wish to pursue are difficult to reach and may encompass a number of subgoals, organizations are essential to provide certain advantages in these global markets.

Organizational Culture

In order to implement its vision, the company adopts shared beliefs, values, norms, rules, and behaviors known as organizational culture. Organizational culture is important because it impacts company activities, the workplace environment, and stakeholder relationships. Organizational culture can be considered the "blueprint" of the firm. It provides the firm with an identity and guides it on its path toward its goals. For instance, at Walt Disney World the company has adopted an organizational culture to support its vision. Its vision is "to make people happy." Disney has therefore adopted a culture that stresses customer satisfaction, and a sense of wonder among consumers. All activities—from the development of rides and rigorous hiring procedures for its theme park "characters" to movie distribution, media networks, and toys—centers around creating a "magical" experience for both parents and children.[2]

Organizational culture consists of both formal and informal expressions. Formal expressions include the company vision and mission statement, codes of ethics, ceremonies, meetings, and more. Informal expressions may include dress codes, extracurricular activities, and stories or legends. These more tangible parts of the culture are known as artifacts. The structure of the organization, including its departmentalization and authority relationships, also affect the culture. For example, some of General Electric's aviation manufacturing facilities have been run with no foremen or bosses. A plant manager sets goals, and teams of employees work to meet them. These types of organizations possess a collaborative culture in which employees not only work together but make many of the major decisions for the facility. The experience has been so successful that, in two decades, these self-managed work teams have spread from one facility to all of GE Aviation's supply chain locations.[3]

Every organization has an organizational culture, whether or not managers actively choose to influence it. For instance, managers can develop an organizational culture by modeling appropriate values, creating a transparent workplace, and ensuring that employees are familiar with company goals and expectations. Such an organizational culture will likely improve employee morale and retention. However, even if a manager does not work to actively shape an organization's culture, a culture will develop nonetheless. If the manager appears indifferent to employee conduct and employees are rewarded for getting ahead, a culture will likely form in which employees compete for rewards without concern for how they get them. Countrywide Financial had such a culture. Employees were rewarded for securing certain types of loans but were not held accountable for their behavior in getting these loans. This resulted in falsified loan information and higher-interest loans going to people with good credit scores—which in turn resulted in a number of lawsuits and the acquisition of the company by Bank of America. Also, even if a firm has formal expressions of a positive organizational culture, such as a strong ethics code or vision statement, they are irrelevant if managerial actions contradict the code. Enron, for example, had a code of conduct in place but did not adhere to its ethical policies. Thus, managers have the responsibility to establish a strong organizational culture that takes into account the needs of stakeholders and provides the firm with direction.

Formal and Informal Relationships of Organizational Structure

Formal Relationships

organizational chart: A graphic display of the official lines of authority and communication within the organization.

authority: The right to give work orders to others in the organization; associated with a position within an organization, not with the individual occupying that position.

formal organization: The arrangement of positions, as shown on an organizational chart, that dictates where work activities are completed, where decisions should be made, and the flow of information.

When we think of organizations, we normally think of an organizational chart, like the one shown in Figure 8.1. An **organizational chart** is a graphic display of the official lines of authority and communication within the organization. **Authority** is the right to give work orders to others in the organization and is associated with a position within an organization, not with the individual occupying that position. The organizational chart shows the structure of the **formal organization**, which is the arrangement of positions that dictates where work activities are completed, where decisions should be made, and the flow of information.

The boxes in Figure 8.1 represent positions in the organization, in this case the food and beverage division of a large hotel. We have included the full set of positions for only two parts of this division: beverage and restaurant operations. The higher the level of the box in the chart, the higher the level of authority that position has within the organization. The solid lines between boxes at different levels represent lines of authority and formal communication. Positions at higher levels can give work orders to those positions at lower levels if they are connected by direct lines. Horizontal lines denote communication channels between positions that are at the same authority level.

According to the organizational chart for the food and beverage division, the president and managing director of the hotel and the vice president for food and beverage occupy the two highest positions. The vice president has direct authority over the directors of catering, culinary operations, stewards, and beverage and restaurant operations. These five positions share information as indicated by the horizontal line. In addition, these five directors have authority over one to six manager-type positions who report to each one of them. Notice that the titles of these manager-type positions vary ranging from manager to steward. However, in all five operations the positions are equivalent in terms of level of duties. The managers who are connected on the chart by horizontal lines—the six restaurant managers, for example—share information and decision making. These six

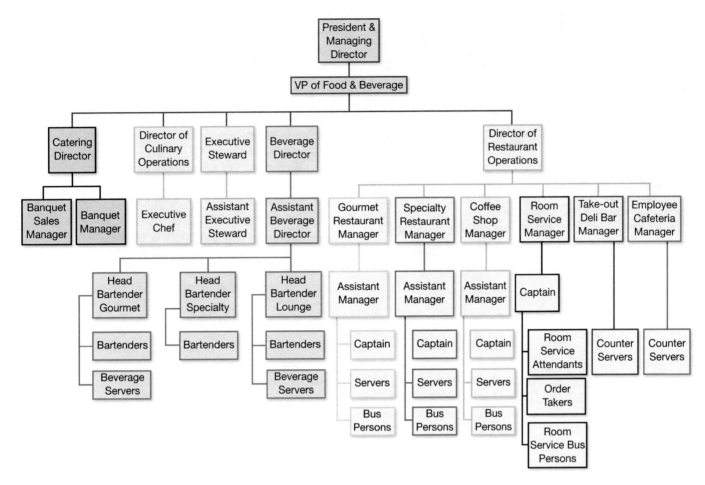

FIGURE 8.1 Organizational Chart of the Food and Beverage Division of a Large Hotel

units are the gourmet restaurant, the specialty restaurant, the coffee shop, room service, takeout and deli bar, and the employee cafeteria. Four of these have assistant managers. However, these assistant managers within restaurant operations are not formally linked on the organizational chart and, therefore, have no formal interaction.

Informal Relationships

The **informal organization** refers to the relationships among positions that are not connected by the organizational chart. These relationships occur either because the nature of the workforces the people occupying those positions to interact to complete the work more efficiently or because they have developed a friendship. The informal organization signals communication of information and decision making among positions without denoting organizational authority. As such, it is created by the employees to better accomplish their jobs.

Using the positions shown in Figure 8.1, we can describe an example of the informal organization that might develop in the food and beverage division. In reality, there is much information and decision making that occurs among all of the managers and assistant managers, because they are all affected by the same groups of customers. For example, if the hotel books a national convention with 3,500 attendees, the sequence of scheduled lunches, dinners, and cocktail parties affects all parts of the food and beverage division. When the convention has a served lunch meeting, the demand for food is increased for the banquet manager but is lessened for the other restaurant managers. Communication among all parties is used to order the appropriate amount of inventory and schedule the wait staff.

Communication and interaction are positive contributions of the informal relationships in the organization's operation. However, the informal organization can also have some

informal organization: The relationships among positions that are not connected by the organizational chart.

Source: violetkaipa/Shutterstock

Much communication is non-verbal and has an impact on organizational relationships.

negative effects, at least from the point of view of top management. In times of crisis or threat from external factors, the informal organization will communicate information about the seriousness of the crisis and possible responses by the organization. However, such information may not be accurate, particularly if it is based on incomplete or old data.

This results in the rumors that frequently circulate in organizations. Moreover, the informal organization occasionally may not hold the same goals and values as the formal organization and may actually work in opposition to the organization. For example, workers on different shifts in a manufacturing plant may agree to restrict output to protest layoffs. Informal relationships are part of every firm and should be attended to by each manager within the organization. That is, the effect of the communication of the informal organization on work outcomes should be noted and directly addressed if incorrect information is being transmitted.

The Process of Organizing

There is no one best way to organize. However, any organizing effort typically involves several activities: grouping tasks into jobs, grouping jobs into departments, and determining authority and channels of communication. Let's return to the illustration of the hotel food and beverage division for examples of each of these activities before we discuss them in detail later in the chapter. Table 8.1 lists the major tasks the directors, managers, and assistant managers of the various units carry out. Top management usually identifies these tasks when the hotel initially opens and modifies them over time. We can see that directors perform several activities that have long-term effects on the unit's employees and customers. Managers report to directors and use the directions and information provided by the director to plan the operations of a particular hotel facility or service. For example, the gourmet restaurant manager will order supplies based primarily on the monthly forecasts of convention and meeting traffic that is provided by the director, as well as on his or her own estimate of walk-in traffic. Assistant managers handle the majority of the daily

TABLE 8.1 Grouping Tasks into Jobs in the Food and Beverage Division

Director	Manager	Assistant Manager
■ Determines operational policies and procedures of unit. ■ Develops marketing and promotional campaigns both internal and external to hotel. ■ Meets with representatives of convention groups to determine food/beverage needs. ■ Forecasts monthly demand on unit for goods and services. ■ Develops weekly cost and revenue statements for unit. ■ Monitors overall service and quality of products provided by unit. ■ Selects, trains, and reviews performance of unit's managers and assistant managers.	■ Reviews inventory, sales records, and costs of food or beverage products, equipment, and lines. ■ Forecasts demand for hotel conventions and guests as well as walk-in traffic. ■ Maintains direct communication with vendors and distributors to determine quality and supply of items, places orders, and addresses all disputes between the unit and suppliers. ■ Selects, trains, and reviews performance of assistant managers.	■ Directs the daily operations of the unit. (Includes inspecting inventory for quantity and quality; maintaining and cleaning all supplies and equipment; cleaning facilities; scheduling all unit personnel; and selecting, training, and reviewing performance of all personnel.) ■ Interacts with customers to determine reactions to service and resolves any complaints. ■ Communicates information to manager concerning supplies, equipment, and personnel.

operations of a particular unit. They schedule staff inspections, maintain the facilities, interact with customers, and address any work issues with the staff.

Figure 8.1 and Table 8.1 show us that within the food and beverage division, tasks are grouped into jobs based on similarity of activity: long-term policies and planning (directors); operational policies and the monitoring of the performance of a specific unit (managers); and daily operations of a specific unit (assistant managers). Jobs are grouped into departments according to either product (beverage), service (catering, restaurant operations), or group of employees (chefs and stewards). The authority and formal communication channels follow the solid lines of the organizational chart. The tasks associated with each job indicate the activities for which that job can make decisions. For example, the assistant manager for the coffee shop can decide how to staff and serve food for that unit but not for the specialty restaurant.

Grouping Tasks into Jobs

If you needed a pair of shoes 300 years ago, you did not order shoes from Zappos.com for next-day delivery. Instead, you went to a craftsman known as a cobbler, who would measure your feet and perhaps allow you to pick out the style of shoe you desired, although in most cases you really didn't have a choice. Once you left, his work would really begin. The cobbler might do literally all the activities involved in making you a pair of shoes, from tanning the leather and crafting the soles to dyeing the material and sewing the pieces together. This craft approach resulted in a pair of custom-made shoes that were expensive and required a long time to make. For the most part, craftsmen, such as cobblers, worked alone or in very small groups; there really was no reason to organize such a manufacturing operation because each craftsman performed all the activities.

An inspector in an egg production plant has a highly specialized position.

That was the way many products were made until the Industrial Revolution. Then some businesses became concerned with producing many more products less expensively in order to deliver goods to the urban centers that were forming. They developed two basic principles of organizing during this time, which still influence present organizations: job specialization and division of labor.

Job specialization defines the division of work into smaller, distinct tasks. In the case of the hotel, examples of specialized tasks are making drinks, preparing meals, waiting on tables, and ordering food and supplies. Different individuals perform each of these tasks. Division of labor results from assigning these distinct tasks to different workers.

job specialization: The division of work into smaller, distinct tasks.

Job design is the process of grouping tasks into jobs. A job is a set of tasks common to more than one worker. In this grouping, the manager must decide how many tasks to include in a job and how complex these tasks should be. In general, as more tasks are included and the complexity of these tasks increases, the job becomes more difficult to learn and perform, and fewer workers have the necessary skills to do it successfully. There are, of course, several schools of job design, of which two are classical job design and behavioral job design.

job design: The process of grouping tasks into jobs.

Classical Job Design

Classical job design is based on the assumption that increasing job specialization and division of labor increases an organization's overall productivity. The philosopher and economist Adam Smith, in his book *The Nature and Causes of the Wealth of Nations*, showed how, even in manufacturing something as simple as a pin, it was more efficient to divide the work into specialized tasks. One individual doing all the work could, at best, make a few pins a day. However, if the labor was divided, 10 workers could produce 48,000 pins in a single day.[4] Henry Ford carried the concepts of division of labor and specialization to their extreme conclusion when he developed the assembly line for automobile production. The assembly line delivered the product so that each production worker did not have to waste time moving to the product. The worker stayed in a defined space that contained all the tools and materials necessary to complete the tasks.

When jobs are divided, they are reduced in complexity and operations until the activities of a single worker can be repeated with ease. This approach to job design was the hallmark of the Industrial Revolution and became the basis for the development of our modern production-based society. For that reason, the design of jobs based on the principles of division of labor and specialization is referred to as the **classical approach to job design**.

classical approach to job design: The design of jobs based on the principles of division of labor and specialization.

Advantages of Specialization

The classical approach has a number of advantages. Because jobs are specialized, workers can develop and use unique skills and knowledge. Instead of having to know all the details of a large operation, a single individual has to know only a small part. Work therefore becomes more efficient and costs are easier to contain. The available labor pool for any job is large because many people can perform simple jobs, and a large labor pool, according to the law of supply and demand, reduces the wages that must be paid to workers for that job. Workers can quickly learn how to perform the tasks, reducing training costs. Moreover, the workers' skills can more easily improve over time, allowing them to become experts in their set of tasks. Finally, specialized equipment can be developed profitably for two reasons. First, larger markets result in larger amounts of products being sold, and the size of the market justifies the expense of developing machines. Second, dividing work activities into specialized tasks defines specific work operations for machines to do.

Disadvantages of Specialization

However, management experts have learned that specialization has some detrimental effects on both the worker and the work being performed. Although task repetition can be seen as an advantage from the organization's point of view, from the workers' point of view, performing the exact same task over and over becomes boring. This affects quality when workers find it hard to concentrate and fail to notice variances from standards that often indicate poor quality goods. Moreover, workers often combat the monotony associated with their jobs by being absent and tardy more often. One extreme reaction to monotony is industrial sabotage, in which material or equipment is deliberately damaged by the worker. Also, repetitive movements can result in fatigue injuries—for example, carpal tunnel syndrome.

Another major disadvantage of specialization arises from one of its advantages (from the company's point of view). Job specialization essentially reduces work to its lowest common denominator, allowing the employer extreme flexibility in moving people around the factory floor because training costs will be relatively low. However, this often means insecurity for the worker, who can be easily replaced. In fact, the rise of labor unions can be traced, in part, to the fact that job specialization allowed managers to replace workers fairly quickly and relatively inexpensively.

The Behavioral Approach to Job Design

As the limitations to specialization became more apparent, both managers and researchers advocated new approaches to job design. These approaches were rooted in the idea that if a job could be made more compatible with an increasingly educated and trained workforce, the negative effects could be avoided. Whereas the classical approach to job design thought of the worker as a part of the production process—much like machinery—the **behavioral approach to job design** views workers as independent parts of the production process whose individual characteristics should be taken into account in forming jobs. Of primary concern are individuals' needs to be engaged in work that is more com-

behavioral approach to job design: The design of jobs based on the view that workers are independent parts of the production process whose individual characteristics should be taken into account in forming jobs.

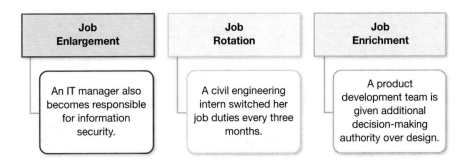

FIGURE 8.2

Behavioral Approach
to Job Design

plex, challenging, and less repetitive than that which resulted from classical job design. Behavioralists believe that if these needs are met, workers will be more efficient and motivated than those with classically designed jobs.

Several approaches to grouping tasks into jobs have been developed under the behavioral approach, including job enlargement, job rotation, and job enrichment. All of these approaches seek to decrease employee dissatisfaction. Also, by instilling the employees with a sense of accomplishment and with the feeling that the business cares about their needs, these approaches may also serve to increase employee motivation. Figure 8.2 provides examples of three major approaches.

Job Enlargement

One strategy is **job enlargement**, which is aimed at increasing the number of tasks that comprise a job. By increasing the number of tasks, workers are, theoretically, assigned more challenging and stimulating jobs. For instance, instead of merely answering the phone, a receptionist sends emails, composes correspondence, sorts mail, greets and directs visitors, and keeps track of scheduling and meetings. Over the years, many organizations have implemented job enlargement. While job enlargement has occasionally led to the anticipated improvements in worker attitudes and performance, the result has not been consistently positive. To a large part, this is because the additional tasks change the overall characteristics of the job only minimally. The worker is doing a larger variety of tasks, but all of these are about the same level in complexity and challenge. The employee is doing more of the same kind of activities. However, job enlargement has overall been more successful than job rotation, described below, in increasing employee satisfaction. IBM and AT&T have both used job enlargement.

job enlargement: A behavioral approach to job design aimed at increasing the number of tasks that comprise a job.

Job Rotation

A second behavioral job design strategy is **job rotation**, which involves a deliberate plan to move workers to various jobs on a consistent, scheduled basis. For instance, a warehouse worker may run a forklift for three months, check inventory the next three months, and load trucks for six months. This strategy still uses the classical approach to job design: the jobs consist of a few, specialized tasks. The only addition is that workers are rotated through several positions. From the organization's perspective, this is easy to implement because the jobs are both simplified and easy for new workers to learn.

This strategy has not been consistently successful as a counterbalance to the negative effects of specialization and division of labor. Presently, it is used in the cross-training of work teams that requires all members to be able to perform all the jobs of a work unit. The members of such work teams can successfully cover for one another during absences, or work together when equipment breakdowns slow a particular production step.

job rotation: A behavioral approach to job design involving a deliberate plan to move workers to various jobs on a consistent, scheduled basis.

Job Enrichment

Through **job enrichment**, jobs are designed to increase the number of similar tasks included and, more importantly, the number of tasks that require information processing and decision making. In this sense, job enrichment is a countermeasure to vertical specialization. Many of the team-building programs that have recently been started within organizations may also be regarded as job enrichment programs because they increase

job enrichment: A behavioral approach in which jobs are designed to increase the number of similar tasks involved, especially tasks that require information processing and decision making.

Job enrichment is designed to deal with boredom and a lack of satisfaction with the job.

the complexity of the team's jobs. The general results of job enrichment programs have been positive, although there is evidence that not all workers respond well. This approach intends to increase the complexity, decision making, and responsibility of the job, and workers differ greatly in their needs for these components in their jobs. Clearly, those who have a high need respond more favorably to job enrichment programs. By giving employees more challenges and responsibilities, job enrichment can increase an employee's sense of accomplishment and overall satisfaction with the job. Hyatt Hotels Corporation uses job enrichment to improve the quality of work life for employees. The benefits of job enrichment can be significant, but strategy requires careful planning.

Determining Authority Relationships

Another activity involved in organizing is determining authority relationships among employees. Usually, these authority relationships flow down an organizational chart, from high positions, such as president and vice president, down to the lower levels of the organization. For this reason, this organizing activity is sometimes known as vertical, or scalar, organization. One major purpose of establishing authority relationships is to make it easier for the organization to achieve its goals. The major tasks of managers is to direct the work of employees. For small companies, the manager can accomplish this through frequent interaction with the relatively small group of workers. As the organization matures and expands, however, this close contact is no longer possible. It is usually at this point that departments are formed. However, the organization still must coordinate and direct the activities of all employees. Therefore, all organizations must have authority and reporting relationships to specifically identify positions that serve to direct and coordinate the activities of other positions.

Authority and Responsibility

Authority is bestowed by the organization. That is, the structure of the organization indicates that some positions have authority over others, and subordinate positions must report to higher-level ones. The person who holds a position of authority gets that authority from his or her position. To reiterate, authority, mentioned earlier, involves the right to give work directives to all directly connected lower positions in the organization.

You're the Manager . . . What Would You Do?

THE COMPANY: KBJ Beef Processing Equipment
YOUR POSITION: President
THE PLACE: Casper, Wyoming

KBJ Beef Processing is one of the largest livestock equipment manufacturers in the United States. With the decrease in beef consumption over the past ten years, the company has remained successful through a redesigned organizational structure. Originally, KBJ operated with nine layers of management, which were reduced to three with the arrival of a new president, John Suede. The standing joke with employees when they learned of Suede's name and his reorganization plans was "Suede's going to turn our business inside out."

Suede's reorganization utilized teams to accomplish tasks within the organization. The company established work teams and trained them to set their own production goals and schedules, communicate with the appropriate departments and levels, evaluate and report profitability, evaluate performance, address hiring needs, and determine raises. The autonomous, empowered work teams have proved to be one of the most successful strategies that Suede implemented.

KBJ also introduced flexible work schedules for its employees, allowing them to come in earlier or later as their individual needs warranted. The flexible schedules demonstrate KBJ's vote of confidence in its employees. Suede monitored the system during the first year after implementation and found abuse to be minimal. Employees want to be on the job, working in groups they enjoy and enhancing the company's performance.

The reorganization has also given managers great opportunity because each position in the organization can be held for no more than one and a half years. Even those employees who do not enter management positions are still compensated extremely well and given opportunities to rotate jobs and cross-train. Also, the company has made a concerted effort to eliminate jobs that it does not consider intrinsically satisfying within the corporate structure. Secretarial positions, for example, were eliminated, and all employees are now responsible for processing their own work, a step which required some computer training for a small number of the employees.

Employees like the new system and gain a far greater appreciation of their productivity through the comprehensive cost/output assessments they perform. Suede makes all financial summaries available on the computers that each work group has in its station. Everyone knows exactly how the company is performing; employees work hard and are rewarded for doing so. Employee surveys indicate they especially

KBJ Processing cattle grazing near Devils Tower in Wyoming.

like the ability to solve problems on their own. Before, with all the layers of management and hierarchical reporting relationships, nothing was solved, settled, or fixed very quickly.

KBJ's new structure has allowed it to restore profitability and increase employee motivation and productivity in an increasingly pressured industry.

QUESTIONS

1. What is the significance of reducing the layers of management in KBJ?

2. Evaluate the team approach implemented in KBJ versus the approach in existence when you (Suede) became president. What caused you to implement the new structure?

3. Why is it key to have employees responsible for most aspects of their job in the team setting? What is the role of communication?

Police have the authority to enforce the law and responsibility to maintain a safe and civil society.

As an illustration, think of a classroom situation. The instructor has authority to give assignments and grades to the students. The instructor's ability to do these activities resides within the position held, as a duly authorized teacher of the university. Authority starts with the board of trustees and flows through the president, dean, department head, and finally, the instructor.

Authority is the legitimate use of power—that is, using power in areas deemed appropriate by the organization. An instructor is using legitimate power in directing students to write term papers, attend class, and complete examinations to earn credit for the course. When an organization grants a member authority, it expects something in return. Authority always carries with it the burden of responsibility. **Responsibility** means being held accountable for the attainment of the organization's goals.

responsibility: The individual's burden of accountability for attainment of the organization's goals.

French management theorist, Henri Fayol, said that authority must accompany responsibility.[5] No one in an organization can be expected to be responsible for something over which he or she has no authority. For example, if workers on the assembly line are held responsible for their tools, then they need the authority to lock the tools up—they need power over or control of the tools. If a grocery store clerk is responsible for the accuracy of the till, then others in the organization cannot be given authority to use it, even if the store becomes very busy.

Authority Relationships

Authority is a complex issue. The reporting relationships of marketing specialists and production specialists are critical to the effective performance of the organization. These reporting relationships are partly defined by the type of departmentalization the organization uses. Under product departmentalization, for example, both of these specialists may report to the same position—the product manager—and thus attend many of the same planning and review meetings. Under functional departmentalization, these two specialists would most likely report to a manager in their own areas, marketing and production, respectively. Under these circumstances, the two specialists may interact infrequently even if they are working on the same product. In addition to departmentalization, authority is affected by the span of control and the chain of command established by the structure. We discuss these types of departmentalization in more detail later in the chapter.

Span of Control

span of control: The actual number of subordinates over which a position has authority.

The **span of control** is the actual number of subordinates over which a position has authority. A broad span of control means that a manager supervises several subordinates; a narrow span of control means that she or he supervises only a few. Span of control is one of the older concepts in management and can be traced back to the early part of this century. Essentially, early theorists thought that a manager should never control more than a certain number of employees, normally five or six subordinates for higher-level managers and as many as thirty for lower-level managers. A basic assumption of such thought was that any one individual is limited in terms of available time and the amount of information that he or she can process. More subordinates mean more time demands and more information to process. However, if all subordinates are doing essentially the same job, as is the case with many lower-level managers, then more subordinates can be managed. Figure 8.3 demonstrates some of the differences between a broad and narrow span of control.

It is commonly believed today that the span of control should be determined by the particular circumstances involved. Factors such as complexity of the employees' jobs, the avail-

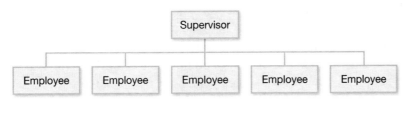

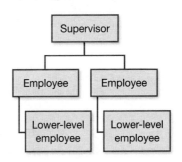

FIGURE 8.3 **Span of Control**

ability of information systems to keep track of performance data, the physical proximity of the workers, whether or not the task is self-directed, the workers' expertise, the prevalence of standard operating procedures, and the frequency of unpredictable problems should be addressed before determining the number of people whom a manager can effectively manage. For instance, in situations in which the work is relatively simple, we would expect that a broader span may be appropriate. In scenarios in which the workers are geographically dispersed, such as convenience store managers, a narrow span may be the preferred choice.

The span of control may also be affected by managerial styles. A person who manages by forging close personal relationships would probably do better with a narrow span of control. On the other hand, a person who predominantly pays attention only to performance data and intervenes with subordinates only when performance is low could operate with a broad span of control. Digital communication has also affected the span of control of many organizations. This practice adds many subordinates to the span of control because the amount of interaction between, for example, a telecommuting employee and a supervisor is reduced, and the computer system keeps records of the employee's performance.

The number of subordinates directed by each position affects the overall structure of the organization. Commonly, when narrow spans of control are needed in an organization, there must be more managers, and thus more levels of management. The structure associated with a narrow span is usually referred to as a tall organization, while the structure associated with the broad span is referred to as a flat organization. The significance of these differences is that tall organizations frequently rely on higher-level managers for decision making, and communication usually takes longer to filter through the organization. Flat organizations disperse decision making and have fewer levels of management. For example, Whole Foods retailers tend to have flatter organizations as many major decisions are made in employee teams.

Chain of Command

Chain of command is an organizing concept that ensures that all positions are directly linked in some way to top management. Such linkage means that all employees are coordinated in terms of work activities. The organizational chart depicts the chain of command. We will discuss two different types.

Unity of command is the principle that a subordinate should report to only one immediate superior. Early practicing managers argued that if an employee reports to more than one boss, conflicting orders may be given. In addition, it will be difficult to convey organizational goals effectively. This principle has been effectively ignored by some organizations in order to operate in a highly changeable environment.

Scalar chain is the principle of organizing whereby authority should flow through the organization from the top down, one level at a time. This principle is concerned primarily with the need for precise information to be transmitted through the firm. If Sally skips her immediate subordinate, Rob, and talks directly to Rob's subordinate, Mel, about a work-related topic, Rob will miss information that may affect both immediate and future work activities of his group.

chain of command: An organizing concept that ensures that all positions are directly linked in some way to top management.

unity of command: The principle that a subordinate should report to only one immediate superior.

scalar chain: The principle of organizing whereby authority should flow through the organization from the top down, one level at a time.

Chapter 8 Organizing: Designing Jobs, Departments, and the Overall Organization **235**

Another issue that must be addressed in determining authority relationships is how to divide the authority among members of the organization or department. Obviously, top managers cannot be directly involved in all decisions. There simply is not enough time nor can any one individual know enough to do this. Therefore, decision making and authority must be spread throughout the members of the organization. There are two major methods of distributing authority: delegation and decentralization.

Delegation

delegation: The assignment of work activities and authority to a subordinate.

Delegation, or empowerment, is the assignment of work activities and authority to an employee or work group. Delegation is a deliberate attempt to create efficiencies. It is intended to speed the process of work operations by reducing the demands on any one individual and therefore reducing delays in processing information, making decisions, and communicating these decisions to others. However, delegation is not a tactic to relieve managers of the responsibility for whether these work activities are performed well or not. A manager can only delegate work activities, not abdicate his or her responsibilities; therefore, it is in the manager's best interest to treat the delegation process as an important part of his or her job, one that requires careful attention and systematic review.

Essentially, delegation is like a contract between persons. An exchange of work activities and authority is made by a manager and the subordinate. The manager obtains assistance for some work tasks and can therefore use the time that these tasks would take for other important activities. The subordinate, of course, has more to do but profits because the additional tasks are usually those that can provide experience in performing the activities of the next higher-level position. The subordinate is, therefore, benefiting from one form of career training. A new working relationship between the superior and subordinate is defined by this exchange.

Table 8.2 lists some basic issues that must be addressed in delegation. The manager must assign the work tasks to the subordinate with specific goals stated. Next, the manager must grant authority to the individual. The manager should communicate this to him or her. The individual must accept responsibility for the task by agreeing to be accountable. Even though the employee is in control of the job activities, it is necessary for the two parties to meet frequently in order to keep the manager informed and to ensure that the employee has all relevant information. At this point, the manager has struck a new contract with the employee. However, this contract characterizes only the working relationship between the two people involved. The organization does not change its organizational chart or its formal authority relationships in light of delegation. As far as the organization is concerned, the manager is still ultimately responsible for the accomplishment of the delegated tasks. This is because it is possible to delegate authority, but not responsibility. Consequently, the manager will need to evaluate and control the individual's action.

Delegation has benefits for all involved. The manager is relieved of some of the daily activities necessary for getting a part of his or her work done. The employee often gets a

TABLE 8.2 Basic Issues in Delegation and Empowerment

- Include a complete set of work tasks—either a whole job or a definite part of a job.
- Set goals—the subordinate(s) should participate in developing definite end results that should be achieved.
- Include authority with responsibility—inform the subordinate and others that the subordinate has the right to make decisions for specific work activities.
- Provide information—subordinates must receive all data relevant to newly assigned job tasks.
- Communicate frequently—the subordinate should inform the manager of work on assigned job tasks. This is to provide the manager with necessary information, not to ask for direction.

chance to develop new skills and master additional tasks that will be assets in future career development. The organization benefits because the work process may be completed more efficiently and another employee gains skills in higher-level work assignments.

Despite these potentially favorable outcomes, delegation is not always used, possibly because of reluctance on the part of either the manager or the subordinate. A manager may not wish to delegate for a number of reasons. One reason is the manager may fear loss of control and not wish to be responsible for anything not done personally. Many individuals, especially if new to the position, are reluctant to accept delegated tasks because they fear making a mistake and suffering the resulting criticism.

Decentralization

An important question in the distribution of authority is to what extent authority should be spread across the organization. That is, should a few or many positions be given authority? **Centralization** is the pattern of concentrating authority in a relatively few, high-level positions. These positions must be involved in almost all decisions. Many factory environments are centralized. Conversely, **decentralization** is when authority is dispersed to several positions at various levels in the organization. Zappos has a decentralized structure where employees are empowered to make decisions and develop solutions. Many large successful firms such as General Electric and IBM are also embracing more of a decentralized structure due to the benefits involved.

centralization: The pattern of concentrating authority in a relatively few, high-level positions.

decentralization: When authority is dispersed to several positions at various levels in the organization.

In this sense, decentralization can be viewed as formalized delegation in the organization. Instead of being a personal working relationship between manager and subordinate, decentralization represents a systematic plan of the organization to spread authority. With decentralization, information and decisions are processed more quickly because there are fewer levels of employees involved. Also, more individuals receive training in how to make and implement managerial-type decisions.

Most organizations are neither completely centralized nor decentralized. In some firms, most decision making is centralized, with the exception of one or two departments that may have a great deal of decentralization like quality control and customer service. In other organizations, only certain functions are centralized, such as manufacturing. The degree to which a firm will decentralize or centralize depends on a number of factors. Generally, if an organization's environment is highly dynamic, a decentralized approach may be preferred. It allows for the faster transmission of information to those who make decisions because there are fewer levels of management to go through to reach the appropriate decision maker. Green Mountain Coffee has a flat organizational structure, which has contributed to the company's success. The structure promotes open communication and commitment among employees, which have access to all levels of management, even the CEO.

On the other hand, the degree of risk and the cost attached to a decision may affect a firm's position. Organizations will tend to be centralized if they are involved in decisions with high-risk/high-cost alternatives. A third factor is the skill and ability of the managers in the organization. Decentralization requires that managers be competent in the areas in which they are asked to assume authority. For this reason, decentralization is often accompanied by planned management development programs.

Companies like Zappos maintain a decentralized and empowered workforce, which generates significant customer satisfaction and loyalty.

Source: Adisa/Shutterstock

Organizational Structure

Organizational structure is the way that managers group jobs into departments and departments into divisions. Understanding the structure of an organization is important both

organizational structure: The way managers group jobs into departments and departments into divisions.

for the survival of the organization and for the career success of an individual. Knowing who is in charge of which processes can be crucial to your career success in any company. One of the first things we learn as new employees is who is important in this company and who is not, and we learn these things by knowing the organizational structure.

departmentalization: The grouping of related jobs to form an administrative unit—department, area, or center.

Departmentalization is closely linked to organizational structure. The grouping of jobs into departments is an activity required in organizations. **Departmentalization** means grouping related jobs to form an administrative unit—department, area, or center. Because the jobs in any one department are similar, for many purposes of the organization, each department can be considered to be a single piece of the organization. Departmentalization assists in the coordination of the jobs in an organization, and coordinating departments is easier than coordinating each job separately. Looking back at Figure 8.1, you can see that the food and beverage division has five departments: catering, culinary operations, stewards, beverage, and restaurants. Jobs in each department are grouped because they deal with the same product, service, or type of employee.

Departmentalization is also a normal stage in an organization's growth. Typically, a firm starts small, and the entrepreneur can exert a large amount of control over all aspects of operations. But as the firm's product line and geographic base expand, the owner finds it increasingly difficult to coordinate the many facets of the growing firm, and usually forms departments to maintain control. However, this grouping is not done—should not be done—in a haphazard, disorderly manner. Departmentalization should have its basis in what the firm is trying to accomplish. Departments are formed to group jobs that should be linked in order for the organization to more easily reach its objectives.

There are several ways that managers structure organizations. One way is through departmentalization, or grouping tasks into jobs and jobs into departments. A line structure is the simplest form of organizational structure and occurs when authority moves from manager down to the lowest-level employee. In small organizations that may be sufficient. In larger organizations, however, departments may proliferate until there are too many to manage. In this case, departments are clustered together, much as jobs are clustered together, to form divisions. Departments and divisions can occur as functional, customer, product, and geographic structures; however, it is important to remember that some organizations will not have divisions, only departments. Others will have many divisions, giving them a multidivisional form. Other structures include the matrix structure, the network structure, and outsourcing. The following sections will describe the different ways that organizations can decide how to group departments into larger units, either divisions or projects.

Functional Structure

When a company is relatively small or produces only one or several closely related goods or services, it usually finds that grouping jobs into departments provides as much structure as it needs. This is known as a functional, or line-and-staff, structure. While such a company can organize its departments into many forms, the most popular form is the functional structure. A **functional structure** groups jobs according to similar economic activities, such as finance, production and operations, and marketing. Pier One Imports, for example, makes use of a functional structure by grouping its functions into specific areas, including finance and administration, merchandising, stores, planning and allocations, and human resources. See Figure 8.4 for an example of functional structure.

functional structure: The grouping of jobs according to similar economic activities, such as finance, production and operations, and marketing.

Multidivisional Structure

multidivisional structure: The organization of departments together into larger groups called divisions.

A **multidivisional structure** groups departments together into larger groups called divisions. Proctor & Gamble is a huge multinational company with many different divisions ranging from home and health care to medical devices. This structure usually occurs when a firm grows so large that functional departments become cumbersome. Growing companies often diversify, which can strain a functional structure, making communication complicated and difficult.[6] When the weaknesses of the functional structure—the

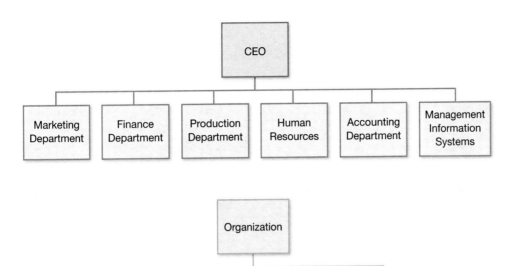

FIGURE 8.4
Functional Structure

FIGURE 8.5
**Multidivisional
Structure**

"turf wars," miscommunication, and working at cross-purposes—exceed the benefits, growing firms tend to restructure into the divisionalized form. Just as departments might be formed on the basis of geography, customer, product, or a combination (hybrid), so divisions can be formed based on any of these methods of organizing. (See Figure 8.5.)

Product Divisions

When a company uses its different products as the basis for divisions, it is using a **product division structure**. PepsiCo., for example, has product divisions for soft drinks, snack foods, and non-carbonated beverages. See Figure 8.6 for an example of a product division structure. This structure is useful when the firm's goods or services are specialized and require specific expertise for their manufacture and sale. It permits the organization to focus on its products rather than job specializations. Some pharmaceutical companies, for example, use product structure to focus on particular illnesses and group employees into product divisions to develop drugs to address these diseases.

product division structure: The organization of divisions by product.

Geographic Divisions

A firm with a **geographic division structure** creates divisions to support business operations in certain geographic regions. Multinational corporations often use this structure because the needs of customers in different parts of the world can vary substantially. By clustering into one division those people, tasks, jobs, and departments that serve a particular geographic region, the company can address the specific characteristics of the region

geographic division structure: The organization of divisions by geographic region.

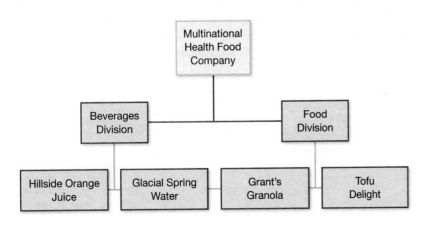

FIGURE 8.6
**Product Divisional
Structure**

Chapter 8 Organizing: Designing Jobs, Departments, and the Overall Organization

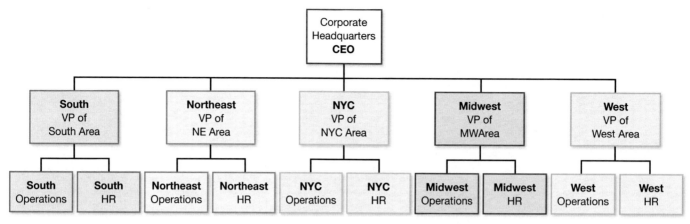

FIGURE 8.7 Geographic Divisional Structure

in the design, production, and marketing of the goods and services it plans to sell there. Such a structure permits those in the division to concentrate on the characteristics of the region rather than having their attention divided by the competing demands of providing products in a variety of widely different geographic areas.

Typically, when a multinational firm uses a geographic divisional structure, the divisional headquarters of the region are located in that region, rather than in the United States. So, for example, a company with Asian, European, and African divisions may have head offices located in Tokyo, Paris, and Johannesburg. Furthermore, the majority of employees at these locations are likely to be regional citizens rather than Americans. This increases the likelihood of success in developing, manufacturing, and marketing products suited to the consumers of the region. Failure to accommodate to the needs of a different country can have consequences ranging from product failure in that area to catastrophic events that threaten the health of the firm. (See Figure 8.7.) General Motors and Caterpillar tend to be organized by region.

Customer Divisions

customer division structure: The organization of divisions by customer.

When a firm organizes divisions by customer, it is using a **customer division structure**. Some companies may have one division for products for the private sector and another division for the public sector. Banks, like Bank of America, frequently organize their divisions to provide service to large commercial clients, small commercial clients, and individual accounts, such as personal checking or savings accounts. (See Figure 8.8.)

Holding Companies

holding company: An organization composed of several very different kinds of businesses, each of which is permitted to operate largely autonomously.

A **holding company** describes an organization composed of several very different kinds of businesses, each of which is permitted to operate largely autonomously.[7] Warren Buffett's Berkshire Hathaway can be characterized as a conglomerate holding company. Under the Berkshire Hathaway umbrella are companies as diverse as insurance, railroads, and jewelry. A corporation that has diversified into a variety of unrelated businesses is known as a conglomerate. Each of the conglomerate's businesses (divisions) is operated independently because the knowledge and expertise needed to run one business may not apply to a different business—and may even be harmful. In this structure, the parent cor-

**FIGURE 8.8
Customer Divisional
Structure**

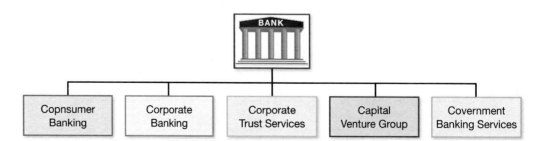

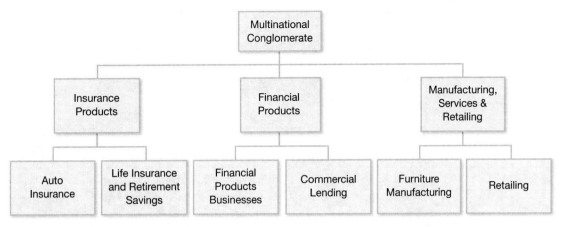

FIGURE 8.9 Holding Company Structure

poration is largely a coordinating office with few personnel; it usually tells each division what its profit contribution is expected to be, and each division has the freedom to meet these expectations as it sees fit. What is important in this structure is that each business be managed without the interference of the parent firm. (See Figure 8.9.)

Hybrid Structure

A **hybrid structure** is the combination of several different structures. It is fair to say that divisional hybrids are the most common form of organization structure. Hybrid structures can be any combination of multidivisional, functional, or holding company forms. The organization's environment, strategy, size, and primary technology all determine the best combination of structural forms for its purposes. (See Figure 8.10.)

hybrid structure: A combination of several different structures; the most common form of organizational structure.

Advantages and Disadvantages of a Multidivisional Structure

A multidivisional structure permits delegation of decision-making authority, relieving top management of the overwhelming burden of having to know everything about everything. It also permits those closest to the action to make the decisions that will affect them.

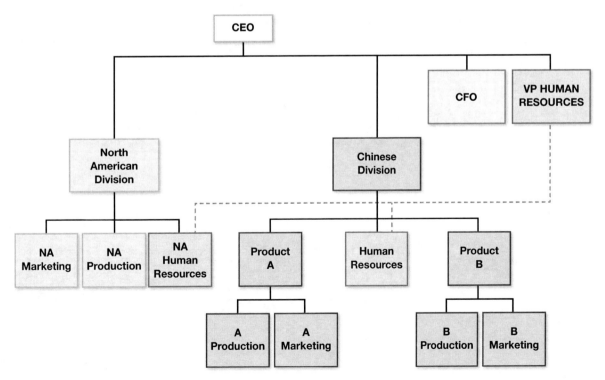

FIGURE 8.10 Hybrid Structure

Chapter 8 Organizing: Designing Jobs, Departments, and the Overall Organization

Finally, it tends to promote loyalty and commitment among those lower-level members of the organization who are making important organizational decisions. These benefits lead to other advantages. Delegation of authority and divisionalized work mean that decisions are made faster and are more likely to be good decisions, and the work tends to be more innovative and creative. By focusing each division's attention on a common denominator (geography, product, or customer), each is likely to provide goods or services that are more closely aligned with the needs of its particular geographic area or customer.

The disadvantages of multidivisional forms are that top managers may feel they are losing power, even control of their company, when they delegate decision making to others. This fear may cause top management to centralize decision making that, in effect, eliminates some of the benefits of the multidivisional structure.[8] In addition, the divisional structure inevitably creates work duplication, which makes it more difficult to realize the economies of scale that result from grouping all functions together.

For example, when each division has its own accounting department, the corporation probably employs more accountants than a centralized accounting department would require. Furthermore, a multidivisional organization may complicate consolidating the books because each division is likely to have its own unique accounting practices, some of which may be difficult to reconcile. Finally, such a structure allows each division some degree of latitude to "play" with the accounting figures, perhaps hiding some important, but negative, information from top management. This happened at AIG when its Financial Products division began to take excessive and expensive risks that nearly brought down the entire company and resulted in AIG receiving hundreds of billions in bailout money from the federal government.

Other types of organizational structures, such as the matrix structure, arose in an attempt to address the disadvantages of the multidivisional form.

Matrix Structure

matrix structure: A structure in which members of different functional departments are chosen to work together temporarily on a specific contract or project.

A **matrix structure**, also known as a horizontal design, is used when members of different functional departments are chosen to work together temporarily on a specific contract or project. The groupings or temporary departments thus formed are called project groups or teams. The matrix structure is an attempt to capture the benefits of both the functional and multidivisional forms while eliminating the disadvantages.[9] Thus, matrix structures have both a functional and divisional form, which, when combined, looks like a matrix (Figure 8.11). Pulling together employees from appropriate functional areas to work together to complete a specific project or assignment forms project groups. These employees are under the supervision of both their functional supervisor and the project supervisor.

Matrix is the structure of choice for special projects. Matrix structures permit people who do similar functional work such as accounting, computer programming, or drafting to work together, but they also allow a subgroup of these specialists to work intensely

FIGURE 8.11
Matrix Structure

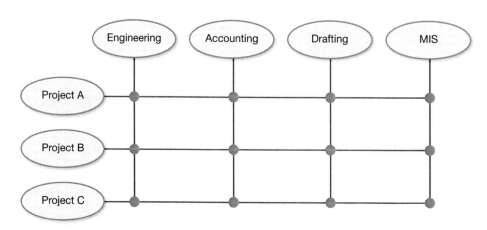

together on a specific assignment. The matrix avoids the duplication of function that occurs with the divisional structure, and it prevents the "turf wars" and miscommunication of the functional structure.

However, the matrix structure has some weaknesses. The biggest problem is that, because each team member reports to two bosses—the functional boss and the project boss—it creates ambiguity and confusion and can lead to conflicting demands being placed on team members. If not managed carefully, matrix structures can create more chaos than order. The National Aeronautics and Space Administration (NASA) was one of the first organizations to use a matrix structure.

Outsourcing involves organizational decision making about whether a process is handled internally or sourced externally.

Network Organizations/Outsourcing

The structural forms just described have been in use in the United States for some time. Some of them (functional structures) have been used in one form or another for centuries. But the world is constantly changing, and new organizational forms are often needed to meet the challenges of a new environment. In his book, *Thriving on Chaos*, Tom Peters argues that the current organizational structures most favored by large corporations are stifling their ability to compete effectively. He proposes that radical new structures are needed to address the opportunities generated by the global economy.[10] These structures are not characterized by traditional boundaries but are instead fluid and adaptable. One of the new forms that have arisen in recent years is the network form. A **network organization**, also known as a hollow structure, is primarily a command unit and does not make a good or provide a service but instead coordinates agreements and contracts with other organizations to produce, distribute, and sell products.[11] This is much like contract manufacturing. There is a core component of the organization, but most of the work is contracted to others. Oil and gas companies often use this type of structure. Network organizations utilize others to do the functional tasks involved in manufacturing and selling (see Figure 8.12).

Very recently, large companies have used a variation on the idea of network structures. In Chapter 5, we defined *outsourcing* as a strategy whereby the organization manufactures critical components, but contracts with other organizations to manufacture less important parts. Other functional tasks, such as marketing and data processing, may also be outsourced. The intent is to trim the organization down to its essential components.

network organization: A structure, primarily a command unit, that does not make a good or provide a service but instead coordinates agreements and contracts with other organizations to produce, distribute, and sell products.

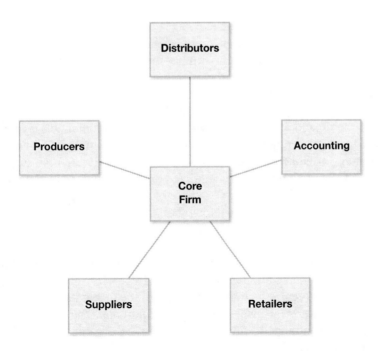

FIGURE 8.12
Network Structure

The drawback is that outsourcing gives outsiders access to potentially valuable strategic information about the firm. More and more firms are turning to outsourcing as a way of making their organizations "lean and mean" and, hopefully, more competitive.[12]

Team Structures and Virtual Organizations

Two other organizational structures that are emerging are the team structure and the virtual organization. **Team structures** occur when groups of employees are used to determine ways to allocate tasks and assign responsibilities.[13] W.L. Gore and Associates uses a team-based organizational structure of multidiscipline teams to complete projects. The technology firm does not have organizational charts or chains of command that are found in most organizations.[14] In a **virtual organization**, organizational members in different geographic areas use information technology to collaborate on projects and objectives. The Wikimedia Foundation, most famous for operating Wikipedia, is made up of contributors from across the world.[15] These organizations have few physical assets, and once the project is finished, organizational members part ways.[16] It is not uncommon for companies to create temporary virtual organizational structures to take advantage of a core competency or concern.[17] For instance, a large company such as Procter & Gamble may develop a team of product developers from different areas of the country to collaborate on new product ideas. After the team meets its goals, the structure may be dissolved.

team structure: Occurs when groups of employees are used to determine ways to allocate tasks and assign responsibilities.

virtual organization: Occurs when organizational members in different geographic areas use information technology to collaborate on projects and objectives.

Latent Structures: What the Organization Is Really Like

Up to now, we have described and discussed the formal ways in which an organization can structure itself. Another way organizations can structure is through the use of organizational charts. Organizational charts display formal flows of authority and communication. However, although the organizational chart depicts the structure of the organization, it does not necessarily tell us who makes the important decisions, how specialized are its jobs, or how rigid are its rules. These things, together, describe more of what it is really like to work for an organization than does the organizational chart. This is called the latent structure, which can be categorized according to degree of centralization, complexity, and formalization.[18]

Centralization is a pattern of concentrating decision-making authority in a relatively few, high-level positions. On the other hand, if decisions are made by the people confronted with the problem, regardless of their position in the hierarchy, then the organization is *decentralized*.

The degree of **complexity** describes how much differentiation there is between structural units; that is, how specialized the organization's jobs are, how geographically dispersed the organization is, and how tall it is. If the firm has many vertical levels and a high degree of division of labor, and is a multinational corporation, then it is a complex organization.

Formalization refers to the degree to which the organization's procedures, rules, and personnel requirements are written down and enforced. A company that rigidly adheres to the chain of command and has a two-volume personnel handbook laying out in detail every moment of every employee's work life is a highly formalized organization.

Centralization, formalization, and complexity together describe an organization's latent structure.[19] Often one finds that centralized organizations are also highly formalized and complex. American Express is an example of an organization that is all three things. A very large company with extensive division of labor and many hierarchical levels (high complexity) can become chaotic very quickly, so it makes sense to leave very little to chance, to write down all the rules and procedures and try to reduce the demands on executive time by enforcing such things as the chain of command (high formalization). Furthermore, such an organization is likely to want to preserve decision-making authority for those in command (centralization) to prevent all the disparate elements from running off into opposing directions. However, it is not a requirement that a complex organization also be formal and centralized. Indeed, some complex organizations are both informal and fairly decentralized.

complexity: The level of differentiation among structural units, including the specialization of jobs, geographical dispersion, and height of the firm.

formalization: The degree to which the organization's procedures, rules, and personnel requirements are written down and enforced.

Creating a Corporate Culture ... Virtually

It seems unlikely that businesses would encourage employees to engage in social networking, but clients of Yammer do just that. Yammer supplies internal social networking for organizations. These internal networks provide many benefits. For example, Yammer enables global employees to communicate easily in real time, cutting down significantly on email.

Yammer co-founder David Sacks believes employees using his service can more easily develop relationships and a commitment to their companies—a claim bolstered by research. Although the networks are designed for conducting business, employees often share jokes, light banter, and personal information. Many companies also use Yammer and the equivalent to track ideas from conception through production and beyond in a streamlined fashion.

The use of internal social tools like Yammer has increased significantly in the past few years. A McKinsey global study found that 72 percent of the companies in its survey used some type of internal social tool like Yammer or Chatter to facilitate communication and collaboration. After studying these tools further, McKinsey determined that employees who use these tools were 31 percent more likely to locate other employees with the expertise needed to meet job goals than those who did not use these tools. These studies demonstrate how important the virtual environment can be in increasing worldwide collaboration and advancing company goals.

Despite advantages, internal social networking has pitfalls. Disadvantages primarily affect employees, who may be too free with their comments. Anything posted on an internal social network is potentially admissible during performance reviews, promotion decisions, and legal proceedings.

However, with social media changing everyday interactions among individuals, Yammer has made an exceptional impact with its ability to organize a whole company on one network. With most companies operating in a fast-paced environment, Yammer pledges to create a private social network for companies to en-

Yammer

Yammer creates an internal social network for organizations' employees.

able productive and successful collaboration among employees. Companies that have adopted this virtual corporate culture include Ford, Orbitz Worldwide, Nationwide, and 7-Eleven, among many others.

Yammer provides a network that allows a company to self-organize and accomplish projects and tasks efficiently. Its growth potential convinced Microsoft to purchase the company for $1.2 billion in 2012. In 2017, Microsoft integrated its Office 365 Groups into its Yammer enterprise social network. This integration allows colleagues to share Office documents and projects using Microsoft tools such as OneNote, SharePoint, and Planner. As Yammer continues to evolve, its functionality has also increased. Today, employees can post inline videos and choose tools from a Yammer-specific app store. Yammer is also available on the iOS or Android mobile app for employees on the go.

At the same time, companies have realized the necessity to take precautions to prevent employee misconduct. Businesses have found that it is essential to implement user guidelines to avoid trouble and ensure employees are not misusing the software. For instance, the technology company Xerox stated that employees should use discretion, professionalism, and common sense in the tone an aunt might use with a favorite nephew. With gentle guidance, Yammer and other internal digital networks can enhance company culture and the workplace experience. As social networking continues to grow, it is likely the internal version will thrive as well.[20]

Tall and Flat Organizations

Another way of classifying the organization in terms of hierarchy of authority is through organizational layers. As we mentioned earlier, an organization with many layers of management is known as tall, and the span of management within this organizational structure is narrow. This means that each manager supervises a small number of subordinates; hence, many levels of managers are required to carry out business activities.

Organizations with few layers are known as flat organizations and have wide spans of management. This means managers supervise a large number of employees and perform a larger amount of duties. Decentralized companies often have this type of structure. In

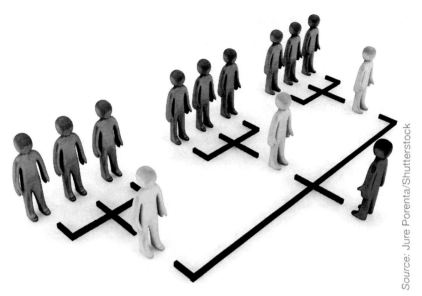

A trend in organizational design is decentralization to lower-level employees.

this scenario, individual managers may have more freedom to make decisions, and middle management positions are often eliminated.

Types of Latent Structures

mechanistic organizations:
Structures that are highly formal, complex, and centralized.

organic organizations:
Structures that are less formal, fairly simple, and decentralized.

Latent structures can be classified along a continuum (see Figure 8.13). **Mechanistic organizations** are highly formal, highly complex, and highly centralized; **organic organizations** are less formal, fairly simple, and decentralized.[21]

Mechanistic organizations tend to make decisions slowly and are easily bogged down in rules and procedures, but some employees prefer such environments because the rules are well known and well understood. A fast-food restaurant is a good example of a mechanistic organization.[22] A goal of most national fast-food chains is to have high levels of consistency across restaurants. Customers of McDonald's, Burger King, or Arby's like to know that they will get the same sandwich prepared the same way whether they are in Miami or New York City. One way to ensure this consistency is to make sure everything is done exactly the same way in each restaurant. Hence, there are strict rules for preparing every item on the menu as well as stipulations regarding what the menu must offer. Employees are often provided with extensive on-the-job training to teach them how to prepare sandwiches, fries, and shakes in exactly the right way; creativity and innovation are discouraged.

Organic organizations, on the other hand, are ambiguous, make decisions quickly, experience rapid change, and some will find them uncomfortable places to work because the rules are not clearly known or understood. One example of an organic organization is the Salvation Army. The Salvation Army does not need a complex structure. This means that different units of the organization are freer to take on new challenges, such as a new homeless shelter. Because its structure is less complex, it does not rely as much on written rules and procedures and can therefore create the procedures that will work best in a specific situation. The Salvation Army's ability to take on new tasks and to fulfill its mission regardless of the circumstances it faces is a hallmark of organic organizations.

Mechanistic   Organic

FIGURE 8.13 Mechanistic/Organic Continuum

Fast-food restaurants are very concerned about standardization of processes so that the customer experience is consistent across locations.

Both the mechanistic and organic forms are pure types, but most organizations fall in between. They can be decentralized, but very formal. They can be simple, but highly centralized. An organization can implement a latent structure anywhere along the continuum from mechanistic to organic.

Relation of Formal Structures to Latent Structures

An organization is likely to be more effective when its formal and latent structures are in harmony. For example, the purpose of using the multidivisional form is to delegate responsibility to others in the organization so that the top management team is not overwhelmed with the task of managing a very large organization. If an organization uses such a structure but then centralizes decision making and imposes overly rigid formalization, the benefits of the multidivisional structures are lost. In such a situation, the formal structure is intended to relieve those at the top of some of the burdens of management, but the latent structure puts the burden right back on them. The result is conflict, ambiguity, and, often, stagnation.

Factors Affecting Organizational Structure

Many things can affect the choice of appropriate structure for an organization. We consider five such factors in this section: organization size, organization life cycle, strategy, environment, and technology.

Organization Size

The larger an organization becomes, the more complicated its structure. When an organization is small—such as a single retail store, a two-person consulting firm, or a restaurant—its structure can be simple. In fact, if the organization is small enough there probably is not much of a structure at all.[23] A two-person consulting firm, for instance, probably has no organizational chart and no specified duties for either partner. It may have an accountant who does its taxes, and it may split the work between the managers according to tasks that each is most adept at doing. A restaurant, on the other hand, may not have an organizational chart but is likely to have a set of specific duties. There may be a hostess or maitre d', a cashier, wait staff, chefs, cooking assistants, and dishwashers. There may even be a rudimentary hierarchy, with the wait staff and cashier reporting to the hostess or maitre d'.

As an organization grows, it becomes increasingly difficult to manage without more formal work assignments and some delegation of authority. Thus, a company usually adopts a functional structure initially, but as it grows and diversifies, the weaknesses of the functional structure begin to outnumber and overwhelm the strengths and the firm shifts to a multidivisional structure.[24] Very large companies, such as *Fortune* 500 companies, use even more complicated structures such as hybrids, networks, and matrices. So, to a significant degree, the size of the organization dictates the structural forms that will be most effective. Stated another way, a small firm does not have enough members to form divisions while a very large organization would be too inefficient to survive if it used a functional structure.

Organization Life Cycle

As organizations age, they tend to progress through stages, known as a life cycle. The organization life cycle usually has five stages: birth, growth, maturity, revival, and decline. Each stage has characteristic features that have implications for the structure of the firm.[25]

Birth

In the birth phase, a firm is just beginning. The founder is typically an entrepreneur who may not yet have identified precisely the appropriate market niche. An organization in the birth stage does not yet have a formal structure, and the informal structure is characterized by a high degree of centralization but a low degree of formalization and complexity. In such a young company, the founding entrepreneur usually calls all the shots, and because there are few employees, the founder does not delegate much authority.

Growth

In this phase, the organization is trying to grow, in terms of both products offered and revenue. The emphasis in this stage is on becoming larger. Facebook and Twitter are examples of companies that are still in the growth phase. They have large, untapped potential markets and are seeking ways to grow. The company shifts its attention away from the wishes of its founder/owner and toward its customers. It has become large enough to have a formal structure, usually functionally organized departments. This permits some delegation of authority, so the latent structure is marked by somewhat less centralization, but increasing complexity and some increase in formalization.

Maturity

Once a firm has reached the maturity phase, it tends to become less innovative, less interested in expanding, and more interested in maintaining itself in a secure environment. The emphasis is on improving efficiency and profitability. The formal structure is still a functionally based departmental form; the latent structure also remains much as it did in the growth phase. There tends to be more participation in decision making, but less delegation of authority. The lack of delegation of authority is probably because there are so few changes that the same people repeatedly make those decisions. Companies can remain in the maturity phase for very long periods of time (like Dial soap), or they can transition from growth to maturity to decline fairly quickly (like compact disks).

Revival

As might be imagined, if it persists long enough, the maturity phase usually leads to decline. At some point, firms recognize that they are stagnating, usually when profit levels begin to decline, and they embark on a revival. The organization undergoes significant changes at this time. A company may decide to reengineer itself—that is, its top managers reconsider what business the organization is in and how best to organize the work processes to achieve its goals. To achieve newly set goals, the company often launches a strategy to diversify its products and increase its size. To accommodate the rapid growth, the formal structure abruptly changes from a functional structure to a multidivisional one. However, because the changes are so dramatic, top management tends to want to maintain a firm hand on the controls, resulting in a latent structure that is highly centralized, formalized, and complex. Because there is an inherent conflict in using a multidivisional formal structure and a centralized latent structure, organizations in this phase often make heavy use of coordinating mechanisms to resolve conflicts.

Decline

Organizations in decline are slowly dying. The tendency toward efficiency that characterized the maturity phase may turn into stagnation. In their efforts to become more cost-effective, firms may reduce levels of innovation, which results in stale products, which in turn results in sales declines and reduced profitability. Organizations in decline are in a vicious cycle, often attempting to improve the profit picture by reducing expenditures in the areas in which the firm most needs increased attention—R&D and new product development. In response to steady decline, companies tend to centralize their decision making even more and to become less complex but even more formalized. While the formal structure tends to stay the same, the latent structure changes, resulting in decreased communication among divisions and departments and between the organization and its environment. Decline, however, is not an inevitable stage. Firms experiencing decline may, in fact, institute the changes necessary to enter the revival stage.

The Significance of the Organization Life Cycle

An organization may proceed sequentially through all five phases of the life cycle, but it does not have to. It may skip a phase, going directly from birth to maturity, for example, or it may cycle back to an earlier phase such as going from decline to revival. A company may try to change its position in the life cycle by changing its structure. A firm in the decline phase may try to spark a revival by changing to a different kind of multidivisional structure. As the life-cycle concept implies, there is a relationship between organization

The organizational life cycle is similar to any living being's life cycle, like the Monarch butterfly.

Chapter 8 Organizing: Designing Jobs, Departments, and the Overall Organization

age and size. As organizations age they tend to get larger. Thus, there is a parallel between the structural changes a firm experiences as it gets larger and the changes it experiences as it progresses through the life cycle. Of course, there is a limit to how large a firm can become, and some firms decide to become smaller for survival purposes.

Strategy

An important decision that all firms need to make is what strategy to pursue. The strategy an organization pursues will, to some degree, suggest a structural form. Similarly, the form an organization takes needs to be consistent with the strategy it intends to pursue. If the structure does not match the strategy, it will be very difficult for the organization to implement its plan. As discussed previously, there are many different types of strategies an organization can pursue to attain its goals. A firm employing a diversification strategy, for example, will grow larger and more complex and require a more elaborate structure to manage its work effectively.

Another way to think of strategy is to think of how the organization is going to position itself in the market in terms of its product. There are two possible approaches: the company may decide always to be the first on the market with the newest and the best product (differentiation strategy), or it may decide that it will instead produce the same product more efficiently and thus more cost-effectively than its competitors (cost-leadership strategy). Each of these strategies requires a structure that will help the organization achieve its objective of either new product innovation or cost efficiency. Companies employing the cost-leadership strategy, for example, emphasize cost efficiency and generally find a functional structure most supportive of their goals. Production efficiencies are most likely achieved when job specialization is high and task variability low. Product innovation, on the other hand, requires a more flexible structure and greater coordination among organizational members. This is achieved with more complex structures such as the multidivisional or even matrix structures.

Environment

The environment, you may remember, is the external world in which the organization operates, including its stakeholders as well as the communities in which the organization maintains facilities and special interest groups. A healthy organization needs to know what expectations each stakeholder holds. While companies tend to formulate plans and strategies to deal with each stakeholder group separately (for example, marketing plans to attract customers, purchasing plans to negotiate the best supplier arrangement, public relations plans to respond to the needs of the community), taken as a whole, these disparate elements can be categorized according to whether they are beneficial or harmful and whether they are predictable.

If there is a large market for the organization's products, if the funds needed to continue operations are readily available, and if other stakeholder groups are satisfied or pleased with an organization's performance, then the organization is said to be operating in **munificent environment**.[26] An example of a munificent environment is the video-game industry, in which there is high demand for the product and capital is readily available. If the opposite is true—money is tight, the market is stagnant or declining, or stakeholder groups are making conflicting and difficult demands—then the organization is operating in a **scarce environment**. An example of a scarce environment is the automobile industry. With trust in the U.S. auto industry declining, tight resources, and the intense competition from international companies, it is increasingly hard to break into the automobile industry.

Similarly, if stakeholder demands, and specifically customer desires, are well understood and relatively stable over time, the organization has a **stable environment**.[27] An example of a stable environment is the machine tool industry. While subject to economic fluctuations, it is sensitive to little else. If customer or other stakeholders' demands are

munificent environment: An environment in which the organization has a large market for its product and has funds needed to continue operations readily available, and other stakeholder groups are satisfied or pleased with the organization's performance.

scarce environment: An environment wherein money is tight, the market is stagnant or declining, or stakeholder groups are making conflicting or difficult demands.

stable environment: An environment in which stakeholder demands, and specifically customer desires, are well understood and relatively stable over time.

In general, video games operate in a munificent environment, where demand is high and the product is widely available.

continuously changing or the primary technology of the company is constantly being improved and updated, then we are describing a **turbulent environment**. An example of a turbulent environment is the smartphone industry. Not only is the technology constantly changing, so are consumer preferences.

Organizations deal with environments that are more or less munificent (or scarce) and more or less turbulent (or stable). These features, then, occur along a continuum, and together, they have a lot to say about the types of organizational structures that will be effective. As shown in Figure 8.14, these features can be depicted as a 2 × 2 matrix.

If the environment is scarce (few resources) but stable, a company must be efficient with its resources. The stable market means that the company probably does not have to respond quickly to changes. In such an environment, a functional structure may be appropriate, as it is the most efficient and should be effective in an environment where market demands are well understood.

turbulent environment: An environment wherein customer or other stakeholder demands are continuously changing or the primary technology of the firm is constantly being improved and updated.

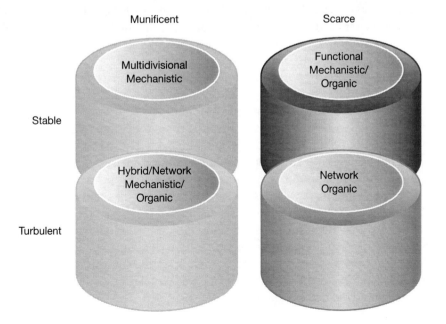

**FIGURE 8.14
Environmental
Characteristics**

If the environment is both turbulent (rapidly changing) and scarce (few resources), then an organization may use a network structure or may make heavy use of outsourcing. In such an environment, the organization faces many changing demands and few resources with which to respond to those changes. Therefore, the organization must be both flexible and efficient. Network structures permit organizations to be both. They are flexible because it is faster to negotiate new contracts that entail new specifications with new suppliers than it is to retool a factory. They are efficient because those best equipped to do the work are doing it; the organization does the one thing it does best and the rest is done by contract providers. An example is Dell Computer in Austin, Texas. The computer industry is both very turbulent and relatively scarce. Dell has responded to these challenges by operating largely as a network. It buys computer components from a variety of vendors and puts them together in configurations that match customer specifications. This structure permits Dell to be flexible, responding rapidly to new technological advances. Michael Dell also recently took the company "private" (its shares are no longer publicly traded) in an apparent effort to achieve even greater managerial flexibility.

If the environment is munificent (many resources) and stable (few changes), the organization is likely to use a multidivisional or hybrid structure. Because there are many resources, it is likely that the company will grow tall because it can afford to have many layers. It needs neither to conserve resources nor to worry about rapidly changing market conditions.

If the environment is munificent (many resources) but turbulent (rapidly changing), the form used may well be a hybrid or a matrix. If there are sufficient resources, the costs of a matrix (ambiguity) may be easily absorbed by the organization, but the form will provide the company with the flexibility needed to respond to rapidly changing market requirements.

Technology

As you may recall, technology is the process and knowledge of transforming inputs into outputs. There are three basic levels of technology in production, each of which influences an organization's structure: small-batch production, mass production, or continuous production.

small-batch technology: The production of small numbers of goods in response to a specific customer request.

In **small-batch technology**, the firm makes small numbers of goods in response to a specific customer request. Many defense contractors use small-batch production, as their contracts may specify a small number of missiles, satellites, or planes. Another example is haute couture fashion, where small numbers of designer dresses are produced.

mass technology: The production of large numbers of the same product.

Firms using **mass technology** produce large numbers of the same product. A typical mass-production operation employs an assembly line, in which the product travels down a conveyor belt with employees performing specific tasks at various stations. Many products from cars to computers to furniture are produced this way.

continuous technology: A method of production in which raw materials flow continuously through a system that transforms them into finished products.

In **continuous technology**, raw materials flow continuously through a system that transforms them into finished products. For example, oil refineries use continuous production to transform oil (raw material) into gasoline.

A British researcher, Joan Woodward, first identified these three technology types. She noted the importance of an organization's structure being consistent with its type of technology. She found that both small-batch and continuous-process technologies achieved higher performance when used in organizations with an organic latent structure, whereas mass-production technology was best used in firms with mechanistic latent structures. This is because work is customized and specialized in small-batch firms, so the specialists doing the work need to make the decisions about the work they are doing. Decision-making freedom is also necessary in continuous production because the tasks are so complex that problems are best handled at their source. Mass production, on the other hand, employs standardized technology using well-known procedures, allowing formal routines and centralized decision making.[28]

This paper processing plant in Spain uses continuous technology.

Coordinating Different Parts of the Organization

Managers intending to design or redesign an organization have many decisions to make. Not only do they have to think of the strengths and weaknesses of all the formal structural choices facing them, but they also have to consider the factors of size, organization life cycle, strategy, environment, technology, and the characteristics of the latent structure such as centralization, complexity, and formalization. In short, a designer has to coordinate many different elements to derive an organizational structure that is going to be both effective and efficient.

When you start thinking of all the things that must be decided upon, it becomes apparent that different structural elements might well create conflict. Fortunately, designers have a variety of tools they can use to help them coordinate such a complicated entity as an organization.

Coordination links jobs, departments, and divisions so that all parts of the organization work together to achieve goals. Coordination is critical to all organizations. It must be formalized and ingrained into the structure of large organizations. In small businesses, on the other hand, coordination can frequently be directed by the owner/manager of the business, who is in charge of all activities.

Coordination can be divided into two types. **Vertical coordination** is the integration of succeeding levels of the organization. An example would be using divisions to coordinate departments. **Horizontal coordination** describes linking subunits on the same level—for instance, coordination between the marketing and legal departments.

Coordinating Mechanism

Managers have developed a number of ways to help coordinate aspects of the organization, both vertically and horizontally. The goal is to link those people who must interact in the work process. For example, it is important that product development personnel talk to sales personnel so that the salespeople do not find that they have been trying to sell a product that cannot be produced. The major agents of coordination are the organizational hierarchy, rules and procedures, committees, task forces, and liaison personnel.

coordination: The linking of jobs, departments, and divisions so that all parts of the organization work together to achieve goals.

vertical coordination: The integration of succeeding levels of the organization.

horizontal coordination: The linking of subunits on the same level.

Priorities in the organization are affected by compliance, rules, regulations, and guidelines.

Source: iQoncept/Shutterstock

Organizational Hierarchy

The organizational hierarchy itself serves to coordinate subunits and employees. Managers are given the authority to make work-related decisions for those positions that report to them. At the very least, this authority allows for the coordination of the jobs held by employees. In other cases, this authority allows the coordination of departments that the employees manage. Managers coordinate authority and communication in the organization.

Rules and Procedures

Often a major coordination question confronting managers is one of priority. Rules and procedures address priority issues. Thus, in a hospital, standard operating procedures dictate that using ambulances to transport severely injured people to hospitals for emergency treatment takes precedence over the use of ambulances by the radiology department to transfer patients to another hospital that has specialized testing equipment. Rules and procedures are usually intended for commonly occurring situations in work operations. The organization cannot develop rules that will cover each possible situation, however. Codes of conduct or ethics help to establish principles and procedures that allow employees to know how to act when ethical decisions arise. The degree to which a company attempts to document every rule and procedure is the degree to which the organization is formalized.

Committees

Committees are formal, permanent groups of people brought together to monitor and keep track of ongoing situations. They usually address non-routine work situations that cannot be covered by rules and procedures. For example, corporate boards of directors usually have permanent committees on executive compensation, employee benefits, and capital expenditures. Committee membership may change over time, but the purpose of the committee remains fairly stable.

Task Forces

A task force is a temporary group of employees responsible for bringing about particular change. Task force members are usually chosen for their expertise in specific areas. Task forces will be discussed in greater detail in Chapter 13.

Liaison Personnel

Liaison personnel coordinate the efforts of different people in the organization. A systems analyst, for example, might ensure that those who will eventually use a computer system are communicating effectively with the system's designers and programmers. Liaison roles usually serve the purpose of enhanced communication. A liaison person can "speak the language" of a variety of different job specializations and can thus act as translator when specialists need to communicate with one another.

How Coordinating Mechanisms Work

Each of these coordinating mechanisms works by bringing together people from different parts and levels of the organization to solve a problem or accomplish a task that requires the cooperation of a diverse group. Such mechanisms are useful in correcting weaknesses in a particular organizational structure. In a company with a formalized, centralized functional structure, for example, management may feel that certain products are not changing as fast as consumer preferences. Such a structure lacks flexibility, making rapid change difficult. Thus, management may choose to create product teams, where specialists are brought together to manage the product. This would introduce some flexibility into an otherwise inflexible organization.

Configurations of Structural Types

Researchers have found, by examining many successful organizations, that companies tend to organize using one of five general archetypes.[29] While there are, in reality, an infinite number of ways a company can structure itself, this amazing variety tends to cluster into five general types, which are the simple structure, machine bureaucracy, professional bureaucracy, divisionalized form, and adhocracy.[30] Table 8.3 provides examples of these structural types.

Simple Structure

A **simple structure** is one with few departments, arranged by function, headed by an entrepreneur/owner, and with few technical support staff. An organization is likely to use a simple structure when it is small, probably young, and therefore entrepreneurial. The firm has few employees and little job specialization or formalization. If there are enough people to have a formal structure, it will be functional. The organization is usually in the birth or early growth phase of the life cycle and does not yet have a specific strategy.

simple structure: A structure with few departments, arranged by function, headed by an entrepreneur/owner, and with few technical support staff.

Machine Bureaucracy

A **machine bureaucracy** is a highly structured, formal organization that emphasizes procedures and rules. The formal structure is functional, and the latent structure emphasizes complexity, formalization, and centralization. The machine bureaucracy is a classic

machine bureaucracy: A highly structured, formal organization that emphasizes procedures and rules.

TABLE 8.3 Structural Types

Type of Structure	Description	Example
Simple structure	■ Few departments ■ Arranged by function ■ Common in small organizations	■ Startup company hires employees ■ A business owner hires an administrative assistant
Machine bureaucracy	■ Formal and highly structured ■ Emphasis on rules and procedures ■ Functional structured ■ Highly routinized	■ Honda car manufacturing facility ■ Housekeeping at the Marriott
Professional bureaucracy	■ Functional structure ■ Best in stable environments ■ Consists of mostly professionals ■ Provides non-routine services	■ Princeton University ■ Health and social service centers ■ Baker & McKenzie law firm
Divisionalized form	■ Departments separated into autonomous divisions ■ Decentralized latent structure ■ Multidivisional or hybrid structure ■ Common in large organizations	■ Procter & Gamble ■ Walmart ■ PepsiCo
Adhocracy	■ Decentralized and informal ■ Operates in highly turbulent environment ■ Delegation of authority is common	■ Google ■ Federal Emergency Management Association

mechanistic organization, where everything is done "by the book." It is of medium size, its environment is stable, and its favored technology is mass assembly. American car companies prior to the 1970s were classic machine bureaucracies.

Professional Bureaucracy

professional bureaucracy: An organization that has a functional structure, is medium sized, and works best in stable environments, but has primarily professional employees and a decentralized informal structure.

The **professional bureaucracy** is like the machine bureaucracy, but with some distinct differences. Like the machine bureaucracy, it has a functional structure, is medium sized, and works best in stable environments. It differs from the machine bureaucracy in that most of its employees are professionals, and it provides non-routine services. Because the employees are professionals, the latent structure tends to be decentralized, allowing those closest to the work to make the necessary decisions. Examples of professional bureaucracies include large law firms, medium-sized accounting firms, universities, and group medical practices.

Divisionalized Form

divisionalized form: A multidivisional structure or hybrid; typically a very large corporation that has organized its departments into divisions.

The **divisionalized form** is essentially the multidivisional structure or a hybrid. It is typically a very large corporation that has organized its departments into divisions. The latent structure, however, tends to be decentralized, allowing each division to make the decisions needed for its effective operation. The level of formality and complexity may vary from division to division depending on the circumstances faced. Similarly, because each division faces its own product market or geographic region, the level of environmental turbulence/stability and munificence/scarcity varies from division to division. Since each division is responsible for the production of its own goods or services, the technology can also vary substantially from one division to the next.

Adhocracy

adhocracy: A decentralized, informal, but complex organization which tries to maintain flexibility in the face of rapid environmental changes by using a matrix or network formal structure.

An **adhocracy** is a decentralized, informal, but complex organization that tries to maintain flexibility in the face of rapid environmental changes by using a matrix or network formal structure. It is a medium-sized firm operating in a highly turbulent environment requiring flexibility and ease of change. To accomplish this, the organization tends to delegate authority and does not overload itself with rules and procedures. Such firms are usually involved in complex, state-of-the-art technology and are pursuing new product strategies. Examples of adhocracies include many pharmaceutical firms, those doing business in the electronics industry, and, often, hospitals.

How Best to Structure the Organization

While organizations tend to fall into one of the five archetypes of structure just described, in reality the structures used are unique to each and every company. There are so many factors that a company must account for and so many alternate methods it may use in order to facilitate its becoming more efficient and effective that no two companies ever share exactly the same structure.

Furthermore, new structural forms are being tried all the time. It is usually true that when a company is not doing as well as expected, the first thing management does in an effort to improve performance is to change the organization's structure—to reorganize. So, companies do not choose a structure and then stay with it forever. In fact, organizational structures change almost continually, always evolving to meet the needs of changing strategies, technologies, environments, and phases of the life cycle. To remain vital and profitable, a company must be prepared to shed its skin and try on new things.

- *Discuss the concept of organizing.* An organization is a group of individuals working together to achieve goals or objectives that would be difficult or impossible for them to achieve individually. Organizing is the process of creating an organization.

- *Define an organizational culture.* An organizational culture consists of the shared values, beliefs, norms, rules, behaviors, and philosophies in an organization. Every organization has an organizational culture, whether or not managers actively choose to influence it.

- *Interpret an organizational chart.* An organizational chart is a pictorial display of the official lines of authority and communication within the organization. Vertical lines between positions indicate lines of authority; horizontal lines represent lines of communication. Positions at higher levels of the chart have authority over positions lower in the chart. The organizational chart shows the structure of the formal organization, which is the arrangement of the positions that dictates which work activities are completed, where decisions should be made, and the flow of information, but does not designate the informal relationships.

- *Explain why job specialization and division of labor are important for organizing.* Division of labor refers to the breaking down of work activities into a number of distinct steps. Specialization is assigning individuals to work on each of these steps separately. These two concepts are closely related, and both are essential for making large quantities of goods efficiently. Workers assigned to only one small part of the work process can become very knowledgeable about that part very quickly. Specialized tools and equipment can be developed. The result is that more product can be made more quickly and for less cost.

- *Assess the different approaches to grouping tasks into jobs and the advantages and disadvantages of each.* Tasks can be grouped into jobs by using either the classical approach to job design or the behavioral approach to job design. The classical approach stresses making a job very simple by including a small number of job tasks. The behavioral approach takes into account the psychological makeup of the worker and attempts to increase the number of tasks in the job and to bring the challenge of worker interest to the job.

- *Determine the relationships among authority, responsibility, and delegation.* Authority is the right to give work order to others in the organization. Responsibility refers to the accountability an individual or group is given for the attainment of goals. Delegation is the assignment of work activities and authority to a subordinate. Though the manager delegates work activities and the authority to complete them to a subordinate, the manager still is responsible for the subordinate's performance and the work activities themselves.

- *Define decentralization and describe what strengths it has for employee development.* Decentralization is the pattern of distributing authority beyond the top positions to various levels throughout the organization. Decentralization frees managers from some tasks, provides an opportunity for employees to develop new skills and master additional tasks such as managerial-type decisions, and speeds information processing and decision making because there are fewer levels of employees involved.

- *Describe departmentalization and organizational structure.* Departmentalization means grouping related jobs to form an administrative unit—department, area, or center. Organizational structure is the result of the process of creating an organization—the ways managers group jobs into departments and departments into divisions.

- *Detect different types of formal structures: functional, multidivisional, matrix, network/outsourcing, and team and virtual organizations.* An organization with departments like accounting, marketing, and engineering has a functional structure. The functional structure is efficient and useful for capturing economies of scale, but it can make communication across departments difficult and costly. In a multidivisional structure, the organization groups all the activities involved with a specific product, geographic region, customer, or some other common denominator together into a division. A matrix structure brings together employees from different functional areas to act as a team in order to complete a specific project. This avoids duplication of effort and has the efficiencies of the functional structure, but it means that each employee has two supervisors. Network organizations do not make products themselves, but contract to others the tasks of producing, transporting, and selling the product according to their designs and plans. Outsourcing means that the organization makes critical components, but contracts to others less important manufacturing or other internal tasks. Team structures occur when groups of employees are used to determine ways to allocate tasks and assign responsibilities. In a virtual organization, organizational members in different geographic areas use information technology to collaborate on projects and objectives.

■ *Specify three characteristics that define the latent structure of an organization.* The latent structure describes what the organization is really like: its degree of complexity, formalization, and centralization. Complexity refers to the degree of job specialization, vertical levels in the organization, and diversity of tasks the organization is involved in. Formalization is the degree to which the company makes use of written rules and procedures. Centralization describes an organization in which the entire decision-making process is completed in the higher echelons of the organization.

■ *Summarize the contingency factors that influence the type of formal structure that is best for an organization.* What structure is best for an organization depends on its size, strategy, environment, and technology. The larger the organization, the more complex the structure tends to become. Different types of strategy are more effectively implemented with different structures. Different structures also respond in different ways to varying levels of environmental munificence/scarcity and turbulence/stability. The more scarce and/or turbulent the organization's environment, the more organic the organization structure should become. Technology also affects the type of structure an organization should use.

■ *Describe the different types of coordinating mechanisms that can be used to support the organization structure.* Coordinating mechanisms are tools that can be used to help reduce the disadvantages of any given organizational structure design choice. Task forces are temporary groups of employees brought together to try to solve a specific problem or dilemma. Committees are more permanent groups that work on longer-range issues. Liaison personnel are people whose skill is in communicating across various functional and hierarchical levels.

■ *Distinguish among five organizational archetypes: simple structure, machine bureaucracy, professional bureaucracy, divisionalized form, and adhocracy.* New, small firms use simple structures with too few employees to require a more complex organization. The machine bureaucracy is the classic bureaucratic structure, used by medium-sized organizations in stable environments using mass-production technology. The professional bureaucracy applies to organizations whose workforce is made up of professionals. The divisionalized form is used by very large, very complex organizations that need to separate their businesses into divisions. Adhocracy organizations, which may use network or matrix structures, are highly complex, highly decentralized, and fairly informal.

■ *Critique a company's new organizational structure.* Using the principles in this chapter, evaluate the new organizational structure of the company described in the "Business Dilemma" box. Your evaluation should describe which approach to job design you used, what form of departmentalization you think would be best, the degree of employee responsibility/accountability, and the level of centralization the firm employs.

Key Terms and Concepts

Ready Recall

1. What are the advantages of organizing over having individuals complete all work tasks?
2. Why is it important for a company to have a strong organizational culture?
3. Describe the relationships depicted in an organizational chart.
4. Define division of labor and job specialization. Why are these important for organizing?
5. Compare and contrast the classical and behavioral approaches to job design.
6. What is meant by authority within an organization?
7. How are delegation and decentralization similar? How are they different?
8. What factors affect the span of control assigned to a position?
9. What is the difference between departments and divisions? Can the terms be used interchangeably? Why or why not?
10. Describe three different types of multidivisional structures. Do companies use only one of the types or can they be mixed?
11. What are the advantages and disadvantages of using the matrix structure? If you were the CEO of a small bicycle manufacturing company, would you use a matrix structure? Why or why not?
12. Is it true that the more formalized the corporate rules and procedures the better? Why or why not?
13. What is meant by organic structure, and how does it differ from a mechanistic structure?
14. A company in the decline stage of the corporate life cycle will always ultimately go out of business. True or false? Defend your answer.
15. What kind of latent structure would be best for a company in the mature stage of the life cycle?
16. The ABC Widget Company is using a cost-efficiency strategy. What formal structure is likely to work best to support that strategy? Why?
17. How is a professional bureaucracy different from an adhocracy? How are they alike?
18. Why would a company need coordinating mechanisms such as task forces or committees?

Expand Your Experience

1. Obtain an organizational chart from a medium- or large-sized company, and discuss what bases it uses to departmentalize.
2. Interview the owner of a small business with several employees to find out how he or she delegates and whether the firm tends toward centralization or decentralization. What advantages and disadvantages does this offer the owner?
3. Interview a worker and his or her supervisor in a manufacturing company about their work activities. Describe the amount of specialization and division of labor in these jobs. What are the feelings of these two workers about their jobs and the organization?
4. Talk to some of your teachers and determine the chain of command in a university or college. How many levels are in your school? What do you think your school's environment is like? Why? What structure is your school using? Is that the best structure it could use? Why or why not?
5. Interview a worker and his or her supervisor in a manufacturing company about their work activities. Describe the amount of specialization and division of labor in these jobs. What are the feelings of these two workers about their jobs and the organization?

Strengthen Your Skills

Organizational Culture

As you learned at the beginning of this chapter, every organization has a culture, whether it is actively created or it naturally emerges. There are four categories of organizational culture: apathetic, caring, exacting, and integrative. While not every organization will fall exclusively into one of these categories, it is likely that one category will predominately describe its overall culture. An organizational culture is apathetic when a company shows little concern for either employees or performance, and behaviors are based primarily on an individual's self-interest. In contrast, an organization can be described as having an integrative culture if it exhibits concern for both employees and performance. Falling between these two extremes are caring cultures, which care mainly for employees and place less emphasis on performance, and exacting cultures, which care more about performance than the people.

Below are some descriptions of organizational cultures. Identify the dominant type of culture embraced by the company.

1. Under the leadership of Al Dunlap, Sunbeam Corporation underwent an organization-wide restructuring. The principles Dunlap used to make his decisions were: 1). Get the right management team; 2). Cut back to the lowest costs; 3). Focus on the core business; and 4). Get a real strategy. As a result, the new management team was composed of people who previously worked with Dunlap at other companies, approximately half of the employees were laid off, extraneous and unprofitable product lines were eliminated, and the company's efforts were refocused on global expansion. Dunlap's actions created a culture that did not consider the long-term survival of the firm. This is an example of _____ culture.

2. Ben Cohen and Jerry Greenfield established Ben & Jerry's Ice Cream in 1978. In 1985, the company founded The Ben & Jerry's Foundation to support community projects. As the company evolved, the foundation became an integral part of the company and encourages employees to engage in philanthropy and social change activities. The philosophy of the company is that all stakeholders should benefit from the profit of the company. Ben & Jerry's is also classified as a B corporation, which is a business that uses its profits to address social and environmental problems. This is an example of _____ culture.

3. Starbucks has been expanding their product lines through acquisitions in recent years. Rather than focusing only on coffee, the company has experimented with offering food items and healthy drinks to appeal to customers throughout the course of the day and evening. Additionally, unlike most companies, Starbucks offers healthcare to both full- and part-time employees. Most companies only offer healthcare to full-time employees. This is an example of _____ culture.

4. At United Parcel Systems (UPS), employees are held to high standards to ensure maximum performance, consistency of delivery, and efficiency. These standards were conveyed to employees through extensive and exhausting training, which was so cumbersome that the Occupational Safety and Health Administration (OSHA) had to intervene on behalf of the employees. This is an example of _____ culture.[31]

5. The Boston Consulting Group (BCG) offers employees mentorship programs and in-depth training that both empowers and enables employees to succeed and contribute to the company's profit. Employees receive high compensation and the company is hesitant to lay employees off even in times of recession. The company also values external stakeholders and encourages employees to participate in philanthropic activities. This is an example of _____ culture.

Case 8: Patagonia Adopts Organizational Structure to Attract and Empower Passionate Employees

What type of organization allows employees to take off during the day to go surfing? The answer is Patagonia. When founder Yvon Chouinard first developed the company, he was not interested in pursuing profits as the firm's main goal. Instead, he wanted to contribute toward improving the planet. New employees are hired based in large part on their passion for the firm's goals, and rather than being viewed as subordinates, employees at Patagonia are considered to be partners advancing environmental preservation. To create this work environment, Patagonia uses a flat organizational structure where employees have more freedom to make decisions and pursue objectives.

The inspiration for Patagonia started more than 60 years ago. In 1953, Yvon Chouinard developed a passion for rock climbing. His passions brought him west to the San Fernando Valley in California, where he became an expert at climbing and rappelling. Unfortunately, his passion was limited by a lack of appropriate climbing gear. This led Chouinard to craft his own set of reusable iron pitons. Chouinard's invention spread by word of mouth, and demand for his gear reached an all-time high. In 1965, Chouinard decided to partner with Tom Frost to create Chouinard Equipment.

While designing tools for climbing, Chouinard realized the need for functional climbing clothing. He and his wife decided to sell clothing as a way of supporting the hardware business. In 1972, the clothing line experienced such demand and growth that it became its own business venture. They called this venture Patagonia. The name was intended to reflect the mysticism of far-off lands and adventurous places located not quite on the map. Consumers loved Patagonia's durable and brightly colored clothing.

From the beginning, Chouinard and his wife, Malinda, knew they wanted to sell items that would have a minimal impact on the environment. In 1985, the firm began donating 1 percent of its total sales to environmental or-

Patagonia designs clothing for outdoor enthusiasts.

ganizations. The couple agreed that the company would produce only products of the highest quality and manufactured in the most responsible way. They selected the following mission statement for the company: "Build the best product, cause no unnecessary harm, use business to inspire and implement solutions to the environmental crisis." Patagonia ensures its employees understand and support these values, using a mix of in-person training, video training, and online instruction to help employees learn about the company culture and increase their work skills.

Unlike many organizations, Patagonia does not want its products to wear out so that consumers will come back for more. It aims to provide durable products to allow customers the freedom of not repurchasing products from the company. While this might appear to limit sales, revenue at Patagonia has increased because consumers can trust Patagonia's products to last a long time. In fact, the firm—which constantly remarks that it places the environment over profits—has embarked upon a "Buy Less" campaign, among other initiatives that seem like they might discourage revenue growth. However, revenue has more than doubled since 2008. Employee support for these environmental initiatives is important in making them a success.

To truly make an impact, Patagonia attempts to foster synergy between all employees. Employees are committed to the organization, and Patagonia in turn tries to create a fun, informal work environment for employees. For instance, it instituted a flextime policy that allows employees to go surfing during the day if they so desire. Solar panels,

Tibetan prayer flags, and sheds full of rescued or recuperating owls and hawks are all a part of corporate headquarters. Patagonia also developed an employee internship program that enables employees to leave the company for two months to volunteer at the environmental organization of their choice.

Despite this flattened structure, there are still lines of authority at Patagonia. Patagonia employs an organizational structure that resembles a functional departmentalization type of structure. For example, Patagonia has a CEO, marketing director, and digital creative director. Other job titles are fairly unique to the type of field Patagonia participates in. For instance, the firm has a Director of Environmental Strategy that is needed for Patagonia's many environmental initiatives. Each of these department managers has employees who work under him or her to achieve departmental goals.

Despite these authority relationships, employees are encouraged to take responsibility and maintain a strong passion for their work. Yvon Chouinard desired to share authority by allowing employees to take a greater role in strategy and operations. As such, he developed an organic organization that is fairly decentralized. To encourage employee participation, Patagonia initiated a management tool that Chouinard terms the 5-15 report. Under this management tool, employees spend 15 minutes each week writing reports for management detailing their ideas, obstacles, and their views on the business. Managers then spend five minutes reading each employee's report before compiling the results and sending them to the next chain of executives. These executives respond and then send their reports up to the next chain until they reach the CEO. This not only allows employees to contribute but keeps top leaders knowledgeable about what is going on in the company.

Patagonia is a strong example of how a decentralized structure can be used to build an admired company. Its culture of encouraging employees to contribute toward its environmental goals has helped Patagonia prosper not just financially but also environmentally.[32]

1. What type of organizational structure does Patagonia use?
2. What role do employees have in the flat structure of Patagonia?
3. Why is Patagonia an employee-centered organization?

Notes

1. O. C. Ferrell, John Fraedrich, and Linda Ferrell, *Business Ethics: Ethical Decision Making and Cases*, 9th ed. (Mason, OH: South-Western Cengage Learning, 2013), 506–507; Kim Bhasin, "Best Buy CEO: 'You Need to Feel Dispensable, As Opposed to Indispensable,'" *Business Insider*, March 5, 2013, http://www.businessinsider.com/best-buy-ceo-workers-need-to -feel-disposable-not-indispensable-2013-3 (accessed November 24, 2017); "Award Reinforces Teamwork Culture at Best Buy," Successories.com, http://www.successories.com/Resources/ Motivation-Matters/success1 (accessed August 2, 2013); Jen Wieczner, "Best Buy CEO on How to Lead a Corporate Culture Turnaround (Without Making Employees Hate You)," *Fortune*, October 29, 2015, http://fortune.com/2015/10/29/ best-buy-ceo-turnaround-tips/ (accessed November 24, 2017);

Best Buy, "Hubert Joly Signs CEO Pledge for Diversity and Inclusion," July 25, 2017, https://corporate.bestbuy.com/hubert-joly-signs-ceo-pledge-diversity-inclusion/ (accessed November 24, 2017); Jen Wieczner, "The Women Who Saved Best Buy," *Fortune*, October 25, 2015, http://fortune.com/2015/10/25/best-buy-turnaround/ (accessed November 24, 2017); Jennifer Calfas, "Best Buy Wants You to Try Gadgets Before You Buy Them," *Fortune*, June 13, 2017, http://fortune.com/2017/06/13/best-buy-amazon-apple-rent-try-buy/ (accessed November 24, 2017); Business Wire, "Best Buy Investor Day Details 'Best Buy 2020: Building the New Blue' Strategy," Nasdaq, September 19, 2017, http://www.nasdaq.com/press-release/best-buy-investor-day-details-best-buy-2020-building-the-new-blue-growth-strategy-20170919-00568 (accessed November 24, 2017); Kavita Kumar, "Best Buy Moves from New Blue Turnaround to Growth Phase," *Star Tribune*, March 4, 2017, http://www.startribune.com/best-buy-moves-from-renew-blue-turnaround-to-growth-phase/415357004/ (accessed November 24, 2017); Courtney Reagan, "Best Buy CEO Sees 'Growth Opportunities' Ahead, Wall Street Isn't Buying It," *CNBC*, September 19, 2017, https://www.cnbc.com/2017/09/19/best-buy-ceo-weve-fixed-what-was-broken-now-focus-is-on-growth.html (accessed November 24, 2017).

2. "The Walt Disney Company," We Dream Business, October 11, 2012, http://wedreambusiness.org/The-Walt-Disney-Company-212.html (accessed December 31, 2017); Daniel W. Rasmus, "Defining Your Company's Vision," *Fast Company*, http://www.fastcompany.com/1821021/defining-your-companys-vision (accessed December 31, 2017).

3. "Who's the Boss? There Isn't One," *The Wall Street Journal*, June 19, 2013, https://www.wsj.com/articles/SB10001424052702303379204577474953586383604 (accessed December 31, 2017).

4. Adam Smith, *An Inquiry into the Nature and Causes of Wealth of Nations* (Hartford, CT: O.D. Cooke, 1811), 7–8.

5. Henri Fayol, *General and Industrial Management* (London: Sir Isaac Pitman & Sons Ltd., 1949).

6. John Child, *Organization*, 2nd ed. (New York: Harper and Row, 1984).

7. Richard Rumelt, *Strategy, Structure, and Economic Performance*, Harvard Business School Classics (Boston: Harvard Business School Press, 1986).

8. Gareth R. Jones and Charles W. L. Hill, "Transaction Cost Analysis of Strategy-Structure Choice," *Strategic Management Journal* 9 (March–April 1988): 159–172.

9. S. M. Davis and P. R. Lawrence, *Matrix* (Reading, MA: Addison-Wesley, 1977); J. R. Galbraith, *Designing Complex Organizations* (Reading, MA: Addison-Wesley, 1973).

10. Tom Peters, *Thriving on Chaos: Handbook for Management Revolution* (New York: Alfred A. Knopf, 1988).

11. Robert E. Miles and Charles C. Snow, "Organizations: New Concepts for New Forms," *California Management Review* 28 (Spring 1986): 62–73.

12. For more on organizational forms, see Homa Bahrami, "The Emerging Flexible Organization: Perspectives from Silicon Valley," *California Management Review* 34 (Summer 1992): 33–52; Richard A. Bettis, Stephen P. Bradley, and Gary Hamel, "Outsourcing and Industrial Decline," *Academy of Management Executive* 6 (February 1992): 7–22; C. K. Prahalad and Gary Hamel, "The Core Competence of the Corporation," *Harvard Business Review* 68 (May–June 1990): 79–91.

13. Greg L. Stewart and Murray L. Barrick, "Team Structure and Performance: Assessing the Mediating Role of Intrateam Process and the Moderating Role of Task Type," *Academy of Management Journal* 43, no. 2 (2000): 135–148.

14. "Our Culture," W. L. Gore, http://www.gore.com/en_xx/aboutus/culture/ (accessed September 10, 2013).

15. Otorowski Marcin and Surma Wojciech, "Virtual Organizations," http://www.ettighoffer.com/fr/etudes/virtual-organisations.pdf (accessed September 10, 2013).

16. "The Virtual Organisation," *The Economist*, November 23, 2009, http://www.economist.com/node/14301746 (accessed December 31, 2017).

17. Ibid.

18. Jordan Novet, "Microsoft Is Killing Yammer Enterprise Plan in January 2017, Will Start Integrating Office 365 Groups First," *Venture Beat*, September 26, 2016, https://venturebeat.com/2016/09/26/microsoft-is-killing-yammer-enterprise-in-january-2017-will-start-integrating-office-365-groups-first/ (accessed December 23, 2017); Yammer—Office Blogs, https://blogs.office.com/en-us/yammer/ (accessed December 23, 2017); Paul Leonardi and Tsedal Neeley, "What Managers Need to Know About Social Tools," *Harvard Business Review*, November–December 2017, https://hbr.org/2017/11/what-managers-need-to-know-about-social-tools (accessed December 23, 2017); Brien Posey, "Yammer Finally Grows Up," *Redmond Magazine*, June 15, 2017, https://hbr.org/2017/11/what-managers-need-to-know-about-social-tools (accessed December 23, 2017); Yammer website, https://www.yammer.com/ (accessed December 23, 2017); Ashlee Vance, "Trouble at the Virtual Water Cooler," *Bloomberg Businessweek*, May 2–8, 2011, pp. 31–32; Chris Brogan, "How to Foster Company Culture with Remote Employees," *Entrepreneur*, May 2011, www.entrepreneur.com/article/219471 (accessed December 23, 2017); "Yammer Guidelines," https://www.xero.com/blog/2011/01/yammer-guidelines/ (accessed December 23, 2017); Brad Chacos, "What the Heck Is Yammer?" *PC World*, August 7, 2012, https://www.pcworld.com/article/260517/what_is_heck_is_yammer.html (accessed December 23, 2017).

19. Robbins, *Organization Theory: Structure, Design, and Applications*; Dalton et al., "Organization Structure and Performance"; Miller and Droge, "Psychological and Traditional Determinants of Structure."

20. Stephen P. Robbins, *Organization Theory: Structure, Design, and Applications*, 2nd ed. (Englewood Cliffs, NJ: Prentice-Hall, 1987); Dan R. Dalton, William D. Todor, Michael J. Spendolini, Gordon J. Fielding, and Lyman W. Porter, "Organization Structure and Performance: A Critical Review," *Academy of Management Review* 5 (January 1980): 49–64; Danny Miller and Cynthia Droge, "Psychological and Traditional Determinants of Structure," *Administrative Science Quarterly* 31 (December 1986): 539–560.

21. T. Burns and G. M. Stalker, *The Management of Innovation* (London: Tavistock, 1961).

22. Lee G. Bolman and Terrence E. Deal, *Reframing Organizations: Artistry, Choice, and Leadership* (San Francisco: Jossey-Bass, 1991).

23. Child, *Organization*. The point is also implied in John Child, "Organizational Structure, Environment, and Performance: The Role of Strategic Choice," *Sociology* 6 (January 1972): 2–22.

24. Alfred D. Chandler, *Strategy and Structure: Chapters in the History of the American Industrial Enterprise* (Cambridge, MA: MIT Press, 1962).

25. Danny Miller and Peter H. Friesen, "A Longitudinal Study of the Corporate Life Cycle," *Management Science* 30 (October 1984): 1161–1183. See also Robert E. Quinn and Kim Cameron, "Organizational Life Cycles and Shifting Criteria of Effectiveness: Some Preliminary Evidence," *Management Science* 29 (January 1983): 33–51.

26. Gregory G. Dess and Donald W. Beard, "Dimensions of Organizational Task Environments," *Administrative Science Quarterly* 29 (March 1984): 52–73; Douglas R. Wholey and Jack Brittain, "Characterizing Environmental Variation," *Academy of Management Journal* 32 (December 1989): 867–882.

27. L. J. Bourgeois, "Strategic Goals, Perceived Uncertainty, and Economic Performance in Volatile Environments," *Academy of Management Journal* 28 (September 1985): 548–573; Kim S. Cameron, M.U. Kim, and David A. Whetten, "Organizational Effects of Decline and Turbulence," *Administrative Science Quarterly* 32 (June 1987): 222–240; Dess and Beard, "Dimensions of Organizational Task Environments."

28. Joan Woodward, *Industrial Organizations: Theory and Practice* (London: Oxford University Press, 1965).

29. Henry Mintzberg, *The Structuring of Organizations* (Englewood Cliffs, NJ: Prentice-Hall, 1979).

30. Mintzberg, *The Structuring of Organizations*; and H. Mintzberg, *Structure in Fives: Designing Effective Organizations*, 2nd ed. (Englewood Cliffs, NJ: Prentice-Hall, 1993).

31. Cliff Oxford, "Where the Happy Talk About Corporate Culture Is Wrong," *The New York Times*, May 7, 2013, https://boss.blogs.nytimes.com/2013/05/07/where-the-happy-talk-about-corporate-culture-is-wrong/ (accessed December 31, 2017).

32. Patagonia, "Environmental Internship Program," http://www.patagonia.com/us/patagonia.go?assetid=80524 (accessed on December 10, 2017); Giselle Abramovich, "Inside Patagonia's Content Machine," Digiday, January 31, 2013, http://digiday.com/brands/inside-patagonias-content-machine/ (accessed December 10, 2017); Jeff Rosenblum, "How Patagonia Makes More Money by Trying to Make Less," *Fast Company*, http://www.fastcoexist.com/1681023/how-patagonia-makes-more-money-by-trying-to-make-less (accessed December 10, 2017); Leigh Buchanan, "How Patagonia's Roving CEO Stays in the Loop," *Inc.*, March 18, 2013, https://www.inc.com/leigh-buchanan/patagonia-founder-yvon-chouinard-15five.html (accessed December 10, 2017); "Patagonia: A Sustainable Outlook on Business," Daniels Fund Ethics Initiative, http://danielsethics.mgt.unm.edu/pdf/patagonia.pdf (accessed December 10, 2017); Lynda.com, "Patagonia: Case Study," 2013, http://cdn.lynda.com/cms/asset/text/patagonia-case-study--1931751689.pdf (accessed December 10, 2017); Patagonia, "Patagonia's Mission Statement," http://www.patagonia.com/company-info.html (accessed December 10, 2017); Kyle Stock, "Patagonia's 'Buy Less' Plea Spurs More Buying," *Bloomberg*, August 28, 2013, https://www.bloomberg.com/news/articles/2013-08-28/patagonias-buy-less-plea-spurs-more-buying (accessed December 10, 2017); Sarah Max, "Everyone Gets 15 Minutes of Feedback," *Entrepreneur*, February 13, 2014, https://www.entrepreneur.com/article/231239# (accessed December 10, 2017).

Human Resource Management

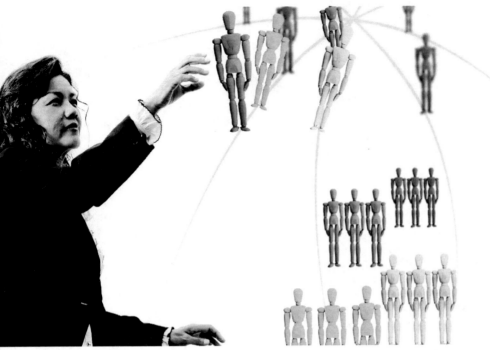

Source: Jannarong/Shutterstock

After reading this chapter, you will be able to:

- Discuss the term *human resource management* and its activities.
- Summarize how managers may plan for human resource needs.
- Specify how organizations may recruit new employees.
- Explain how companies use application forms, interviews, and tests in selecting new employees.
- Formulate the information used in designing effective training programs.
- Describe the types of performance appraisal.
- Explain the purposes of compensation systems and the basic steps in setting up these systems.
- Summarize some of the major laws that affect employment decisions.
- Explain the importance of diversity in an organization.
- Assess an organization's attempts to select, train, and appraise its employees with an improved human resource management program.

Using the Internet to Find the Best Talent

The old-fashioned "Help Wanted" sign has seen its day. The need is now being filled in cyberspace. With the advent of Monster.com, Careerbuilder.com, LinkedIn, and other job websites, businesses are increasingly posting job descriptions on the Web. On the human resources end, such sites make it easier to reach a diverse range of potential applicants. For job seekers, it allows them access to a variety of job information with a simple click of the button. Many college graduates are turning to LinkedIn, a professional social networking site, to gather information on companies and hunt for jobs.

As the Internet becomes a greater venue for job hunting, job sites have grown increasingly sophisticated in their abilities to match businesses with the best talent. For instance, LinkedIn has partnered with the online job applicant tracking system provider Taleo to make it easier to import the applicant's information from LinkedIn into the job applications for companies that use Taleo (5,000 companies use Taleo's services, including Hewlett-Packard and IBM).

Another innovative job site is Upwork, which helps businesses that are looking to outsource work to connect with a wide array of professionals. Clients post jobs on the Upwork site, specifying the job description and the skills desired, and Upwork will send the clients a list of freelance candidates it believes are best suited to the job. Clients are also free to search through Upwork's site for freelance talent or have freelancers bid for a job by submitting proposals. Common skills marketed on Upwork include user experience design, English proofreading, WordPress development, data mining, lead generation, and more. Any freelancer who can offer skills through the Internet can utilize Upwork to find clients worldwide. Sites like Upwork are likely to grow in popularity as more people are choosing freelancing as a career path. According to one survey, freelancers comprise 35 percent of the current U.S. workforce and earn $1 trillion per year.

One area of recruitment that is often underutilized is company websites. Company websites are where Internet users, including possible job candidates, turn to find out information about the company. It is not uncommon for job candidates to search the websites of companies they admire for job openings. Website recruiting also provides the company with a great opportunity to differentiate itself from competitors, especially because many organizations fail to optimize their corporate websites to recruit the best talent. An informative recruitment page on a company's website helps job candidates identify and learn about jobs that may fit their skill sets.

Online search engines and social media have greatly improved employment selection options.

Unsurprisingly, recruiters are turning to social media sites like Facebook and messaging apps to connect with candidates. Approximately 92 percent of recruiters polled in a survey claim they use social media to identify quality candidates. Many recruiters will check out a potential candidate's social media presence before hiring him or her to identify any red flags. Social media sites like Facebook are also a great way to market job opportunities due to their global reach. Although LinkedIn remains the most popular social media platform among recruiters, 35–55 percent of recruiters say they use Facebook as a recruitment tool.

Recruiters have begun using social media in more personal ways that go beyond simply checking candidate backgrounds. Social media offers recruiters the opportunity to expand their outreach and interact with potential candidates directly. The use of mobile recruiting is also increasing, with one-third of organizations claiming they use mobile recruiting to target potential candidates who own smartphones (77 percent of Americans). Recruiting through social media is an effective tool for attracting younger job seekers, as the majority have profiles on one or more social media sites. It is estimated that 86 percent of job seekers who are in their first decade of employment will turn to social media sites to look for jobs.

Companies across the world are able to use the Internet to fill their needs and locate the best talent. For the job candidate, the Internet provides the ability to research job openings and connect with recruiters. By opening opportunities for both businesses and job seekers, the Internet is revolutionizing the industry and keeping those "Help Wanted" signs in the closet.[1]

Introduction

If an organization is to be successful, it must have employees who have the appropriate skills for their jobs. Ensuring that the firm has sufficient employees with the appropriate skills is the domain of human resource management. Human resource managers are concerned with the development and growth of employees as well as employee relationships and responsibilities.

In this chapter, we will explore the role and functions of human resource management. We will begin by defining the term and discussing its importance to organizational success. Next, we will explore some human resource management programs, including planning, recruiting, selecting, orientation and training, performance appraisal, compensation, promotions, transfers, and terminations. We will look at some of the laws and regulations that affect human resource management. Finally, we examine the importance of diversity within the organization.

The Nature of Human Resource Management

Human resource management (HRM) includes activities that first forecast the number and type of employees an organization will need and then find and develop employees with necessary skills. For example, human resource planning, recruiting, and selecting are programs concerned with bringing the appropriate individuals into the organization. Orientation and training programs develop the skills required by employees to carry out the work of the company. Performance appraisals evaluate work accomplishments, while compensation can reward those who perform at high levels. Compliance with laws and regulations and with organizations' codes of conduct, policies, and required behavior are also important. A primary reason for HRM is to ensure that the organization has a sufficient number of employees who have the appropriate skills to meet the organization's needs. If these HR programs are appropriately designed and implemented, the organization will have an efficient workforce that serves as a primary strength in competitive markets. If these employees are developed and fit into a productive corporate culture, HRM will be successful. HRM must make complicated decisions about how to stay competitive.

human resource management (HRM): All activities that forecast the number and type of employees an organization will need and then find and develop employees with necessary skills.

Source: 4zevar/Shutterstock

The human resource management function is very concerned with legal and regulatory compliance.

The Importance of Human Resource Management

Organizations use HRM programs to make work-related decisions about employees. These decisions have become increasingly important to companies in recent years for several reasons, the most important of which is that industries have become more and more competitive, and many face, due to free trade and other agreements discussed earlier, foreign competitors that have low labor costs. Companies with relatively high labor costs can compete by having well-skilled employees who are rewarded for high performance. On the other hand, HR may decide to outsource some activities if the higher-cost labor pool is not sufficiently competitive. HRM addresses these issues.

Another important reason for the increased importance of HRM is that a number of federal and state laws and regulations affecting employment decisions have been introduced in the last several decades. Many of these laws are very complex in their interpretation and implementation. HR specialists are concerned with how an organization can both comply with these laws/regulations and meet its needs for an effective workforce.

Moreover, the diversity of employees in organizations is growing. Once dominated by white men, today's employees consist of significantly more women, African Americans,

TABLE 9.1 A Partial List of Tasks and Knowledge, Skills, and Abilities for the Position of Regional Sales Manager

Job Tasks

1. Use data from last year's sales, the present state of the economy, customer purchasing trends, and the number of competitors in the region to develop a sales forecast for each product item for the next six months.
2. Interview applicants for sales positions and, together with the district sales manager, decide which applicants to select. Use online training, experience forms, ability tests, and performance tests.
3. Develop promotion and sales campaigns using data from the sales forecast, recent sales, company-sponsored market surveys, and competitors' promotion and sales practices.

Knowledge, Skills, and Abilities Needed

1. Knowledge of spreadsheets and sales software.
2. Ability to use situational interviewing for selection of sales staff.
3. Ability to design a promotion campaign for each product for a six-month time period.
4. Ability to develop and analyze statistical data for sales forecasting.

Hispanics, Asian Americans, and more. Human resource managers must recognize these changes and have policies in place that will support this growing diversity.

Another reason concerns the increasing use of technology in business operations. Such technology, of course, requires employees who are skilled in its use, maintenance, and repair. The task of finding these skills in the general workforce and developing these in current employees falls primarily to human resource managers.

Information Needed for Human Resource Management

A basic activity of HR managers is collecting information to use in making job-related decisions about individuals. Most HR programs use some combination of three types of information: job characteristics, worker qualifications, and job performance. **Job analysis** is the systematic process of gathering information about important work-related aspects of a job. It identifies the first of two types of information, which includes the tasks that make up a job; the worker knowledge, skills, and abilities (KSAs) needed on the job; the information, equipment, and materials used; and the working conditions. Table 9.1 provides some example task statements and KSAs that are appropriate for the position of regional sales manager. Performance appraisal, discussed in a later section, is the process of collecting the third type of information, job performance of individual employees.

job analysis: The systematic process of gathering information about important work-related aspects of a job.

Human Resource Planning

Human resource planning involves forecasting the organization's future demand for employees, forecasting the future supply of employees within the organization, and designing programs to correct the discrepancy between the two. It serves the same purpose for human resource management as strategic planning does for other management activities. The purpose of human resource planning is to ensure that, in the future, the firm has enough employees with the appropriate skills so that it can accomplish long-term goals. Human resource planning should always start off with the organization's strategic plans and goals.

human resource planning: Involves forecasting the organization's future demand for employees, forecasting the future supply of employees within the organization, and designing programs to correct the discrepancy between the two.

Forecasting Demand

Forecasting demand for employees involves predicting how many employees the firm will need in specific jobs in the future. There are two types of forecasting methods: quantitative and qualitative.

Accurate forecasting is a key to successful human resource management planning.

Quantitative methods use statistical techniques. Two of the most often used techniques are the productivity index and regression analysis. The productivity index is the ratio of employees to unit of output. For example, suppose human resource manager Diana Taylor goes through her organization's records for the last ten years and calculates that each salesperson accounts for $85,000 in yearly sales. If she can find out the amount of sales in the strategic goal, Diana can determine the number of salespeople that will be needed. Regression analysis uses data about a number of variables that are correlated to predict sales and numbers of employees. In this case, Diana uses population of the area, number of competitors, economic strength of the community, and the number of students enrolled in the local trade school to determine the number of salespeople needed.

Qualitative forecasting methods rely primarily on the judgments of experts. These methods are used when planners cannot gather historical data to develop statistical forecasts or when they think that future business activities will be quite different from those in the past. Quantitative forecasts usually assume that what has occurred in the past will continue in the future. For example, if one salesperson produced $85,000 in yearly sales for the last five years, then this should happen for the next five. However, if more competitors start up, or the economy weakens significantly, or the firm introduces many different products, this forecast will not be accurate. In such a case, moving to qualitative methods, planners consult experts in the business operation who have a good idea about the future environment of the business, and who can provide useful judgments.

Forecasting the supply of employees involves two predictions. The first estimates how many employees there would be in the organization in specific jobs if the human resource programs currently in place continue. As with forecasting demand, both quantitative and qualitative techniques can be used. A common quantitative technique is Markov Modeling, which uses historical records to determine the probabilities, in one year, of employees in a specific job either staying in that job, moving to another job in the company, or leaving the company. These are known as transition probabilities and are calculated for each job. By using these probabilities in computer simulations, planners can determine how many individuals should be in each position at any year in the future.

The second prediction is how many individuals in the external labor market would have the necessary skills for employment in the organization at a specific time in the future. As an example of using a qualitative forecasting technique, Diana could gather experts and get their opinions, as well as collect several rounds of data concerning population trends, education levels of specific age groups, and the demand for employees by other companies. She could then use these data to estimate the number of individuals available in an external labor market. The results from both predictions will provide an estimate of the total supply of individuals with appropriate skills.

To work well, human resource planning programs must be appropriately designed and implemented. This involves reducing the discrepancies between human resource demand and supply. The next sections of this chapter will therefore discuss some of the most important HRM programs, pointing out the appropriate features of each.

Recruiting

recruiting: The process of attracting potential new employees to the organization.

Recruiting is the process of attracting potential new employees to the organization. This HR program is closely related to selection, which we will discuss in the following section, because it supplies a pool of qualified applicants from which the organization can choose those best suited for its needs.

The Purposes of Recruiting

Recruiting serves three purposes. The first is to provide enough applicants from which to select future employees. If there are too few applicants, the company's chances of hiring the best employees will be limited. The worst case occurs when the number of applicants is equal to or less than the number of available positions, possibly causing the organization to hire all the applicants regardless of their level of skills and abilities or not to fill all the open positions. The opposite problem can also occur—too many applicants are recruited. In such cases, the time and cost involved in gathering applications and reviewing applicants are considerable and may delay the schedule of hiring. The problem of too many applicants for too few jobs began to be a widespread issue in the wake of the most recent recession, as companies scaled back and cut jobs. Generally, selection specialists think that around five to ten applicants for each available position is appropriate. Again, because the supply of employees was significantly higher than demand after the most recent recession, companies had to sort through far more applications than usual for particular jobs.

The second purpose of recruiting, really an extension of the first, is to attract at least minimally qualified applicants. It does little good to have a number of applicants if most are not suited for the open positions. The processing of such applicants wastes time and resources.

The third purpose of recruiting, mandated in part by some government laws/regulations, is to attract a demographically and culturally diverse applicant pool. For example, it is difficult to achieve a diverse workforce in the organization if the recruitment process just uses certain schools, media, or mailing lists that are dominated by one or a few demographic groups.

The Internet, as noted above, has fundamentally changed the process and scale of recruiting. Companies can select from a much wider range of candidates, as they are no longer limited per se by geography or budget. As mentioned in the opening feature, online recruiting sources like Monster.com and Careerbuilder.com provide companies easy access to literally millions of résumés. Most large companies also have their own websites they use to post job openings and accept applications.

As the recruiting industry evolves, alternative means of recruitment might supplant the traditional résumé. For example, MasterCard used an internship recruiting campaign titled "Cashless Society" that required applicants to emphasize their creativity rather than education and experience. Candidates were required to use some kind of social media in order to tell a story of how they envision a cashless society. Entries came in the forms of YouTube videos and Tumblr blogs. The campaign piqued the interest of 350 applicants as opposed to the average 30 applications MasterCard usually receives. In addition to being creative, applicants had to upload their résumés on LinkedIn and follow the company on Twitter and Facebook. This is because MasterCard is interested in the applicant's brand and how he or she keeps that brand alive.

MasterCard is not the only firm using social media for recruitment purposes. Many companies have begun using new technological tools to develop their own unique recruit-

Recruiters Embrace Non-Traditional Recruitment Methods

Traditionally, recruiters have used résumés to gauge applicants' fit for a job. However, some organizations are realizing that initially judging applicants' suitability for jobs based on résumés—and immediately discarding those that do not fit the criteria—is a flawed system that can overlook talented candidates. George Anders, author of *The Rare Find: Spotting Exceptional Talent Before Everyone Else*, tells many stories of applicants with stellar résumés who have failed at jobs requiring different skill sets or character traits. And hiring the wrong person, no matter how talented he or she might appear, can cost a company greatly.

Part of the problem with using résumés and traditional recruiting methods is their inflexibility. Many recruiters insist that applicants have specific educational achievements or experience to be eligible. Unfortunately, this might eliminate inexperienced candidates who, with training, could become valuable employees. According to Anders, because employees can often learn skills on the job, character is a better predictor of employee success than experience. Some of the best candidates are not the ones with great GPAs or job backgrounds, but those who possess analytical and conceptual skills to think outside of the box.

For this reason, some businesses are changing their recruitment approaches, including using more employee referrals or accessing social networking sites like LinkedIn to search for potential candidates. Employee referrals remain the top recruitment tool, with

Innovative recruitment strategies allow companies to more accurately target successful candidates.

30 percent of all hires recruited in this way. Others are taking more unique approaches. Natural-gas company Range Resources Corp. has arranged cookouts and other events to identify candidates who have a passion for the field. Chipotle holds national hiring days when its U.S. locations hold open interviews for store positions. Facebook sends out coding puzzles for potential programmers to solve; this enables candidates interested in programming to test their abilities despite their previous work background. Several of Facebook's programmers have gotten hired after coming up with innovative solutions to puzzles.

ment campaigns. In an effort to recruit 250,000 summer employees, McDonald's created a hiring tool called "Snaplications" on Snapchat, an image messaging and multimedia mobile tool highly popular among teenagers and young adults—the type of population that McDonald's hopes to attract. McDonald's placed 10-second videos on Snapchat about how great it is to work at McDonald's and a link to its website that users could access for more information. General Mills is using the virtual reality tool Oculus Rift to give job candidates a virtual tour of the General Mills campus. Cloud computing firm Salesforce. com maintains a separate Instagram account for recruitment. The photos on the site attempt to portray what life is like as a Salesforce.com employee. Interested candidates can ask questions on the site, and Salesforce.com is quick to respond.

Although résumés will likely remain an important part of the recruitment process, employers are increasingly finding that résumés only show part of the picture. Interacting with potential candidates using nontraditional recruitment tools gives companies the opportunity to test talents that may not be readily visible in a résumé, such as creativity or problem-solving skills. As the recruiting process continues to evolve, companies are likely to use non-traditional recruitment methods to substitute for or supplement the traditional résumé.[2]

Fulfilling Recruiting Purposes

The company controls three ways of fulfilling these purposes of recruiting: the sources through which potential applicants are contacted, the information given to applicants, and the contacts between the applicants and the company. Although all three affect the number and types of applicants, companies cannot totally control recruiting. Individuals often contact companies on their own, especially well-known ones such as the Coca-Cola Company and General Electric. However, some firms refuse to respond to such applications because of the cost in staff time and resources that such responses would require.

HR managers may recruit externally or internally. External sources include the Internet, newspapers, broadcast media, employment agencies, educational institutions, brochures, flyers, and signs. Internal sources include posted notices on online bulletin boards within the organization as well as formal programs that encourage current employees to recommend that friends and family members in the job market apply to the organization. These various external and internal sources differ greatly in terms of the number of individuals and the demographic groups they attract and the costs involved.

The second factor, the information conveyed to applicants during the recruiting process, is important because applicants use this information to decide whether to pursue further contact with the company. Research has shown that, for example, at the initial stage of recruiting, lengthy ads providing relatively large amounts of information attract more applicants than do shorter ads. Announcements that describe specific job tasks and necessary KSAs also increase the percentage of appropriately qualified applicants while reducing the total number who apply. Another recruiting tactic is providing applicants with realistic job previews (RJPs), or accurate descriptions about the job and the organization that include positive points as well as negative ones. This gives any applicants who do not think the position is appropriate for them a chance to drop out of the process on their own. Utilizing RJPs benefits the company because it is better to lose such individuals before the company has invested considerable time and effort in them. Summer internships with the company are sometimes used as a way to provide full-time job applicants with RJPs.

Several aspects of contact between the organization and applicants are important. One is the promptness with which the firm gives information to the applicant, such as how quickly it schedules interviews after initial contact, when it provides information promised by recruiters, and how soon it gives evaluation messages after interviews. Another aspect is the attention given toward arranging for on-site visits. Sometimes applicants are expected to find the hotel or the company's office with very little instruction, or the details of schedules are not provided or are changed without notice. A third aspect is the interaction between recruiters and applicants. Applicants generally react favorably to the organization when there are frequent contacts, the company is receptive to visits, and recruiters are viewed as being representative of the employees of the company.

Selecting Employees

selection: The process of collecting systematic information about applicants and using that information to decide which applicants to hire.

Selection is the process of collecting systematic information about applicants and using that information to decide which applicants to hire. The major purpose of the various devices of selection—application form, interviews, testing, and reference checking—is to gather information about the applicants' job-related skills. A very important principle used in developing selection devices is that the content of the questions should reflect the activities of the job to be filled. Figure 9.1 depicts the employee selection process.

The Application

Traditional application forms ask information about educational and work history, vocational interests, and honors. However, such forms often have limitations. In the majority of cases, they have limited space, so the applicant can supply only basic information such as the names of schools attended, their respective majors, dates of attendance, and previous job titles and dates of employment. Such superficiality of information often does not give the manager sufficient detail to make sound judgments about the applicant's skills and abilities. A second limitation is that some percentage of respondents falsifies the information that they report.

One possible way to get past this limitation is through the use of online applications. Many companies no longer use traditional job applications. Instead, applicants are en-

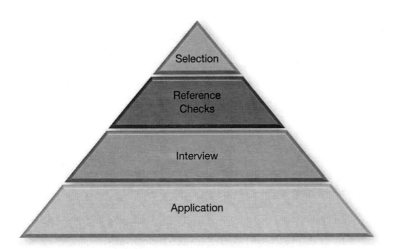

FIGURE 9.1
Employee Selection Process

couraged to apply through the company's website or at computer kiosks at company locations or retail stores. Applicants can use Procter & Gamble's employment website, for example, to search for jobs in around 100 countries.[3] By using a website, companies can easily gather more information about applicants than traditional applications can. Often these applications include lengthy lists of questions that collect data on the applicants' personality characteristics, such as confidence level and leadership qualities. These programs also provide hypothetical scenarios of situations that employees might have to deal with on the job and give a list of options that applicants must choose from. This allows the company to understand an applicant better and gauge how he or she would react to stressful situations on the job.

These new modes of collecting data are very beneficial to companies as it saves them time by screening out employees who do not "fit the bill." However, they do have a downside. For instance, they can often take considerable time for an applicant to fill out, ranging from 15-45 minutes. It is also possible for such screening questions to automatically weed out applicants who may not have, for instance, a desired confidence level, but may have other skills that could potentially make them good assets to the company. Finally, as with traditional applications, many applicants may anticipate what the company is looking for and even potentially falsify information to make them appear better candidates. Background checks are an important means of verifying information. They can be used to determine criminal records, verify financial records, and examine other pertinent information regarding the integrity of the applicant. Background checks are becoming widespread for pre-employment verification and to help identify hiring risks.

Electronic employment applications improve the efficiency of the application process.

Another device that solves some of these problems and has been used successfully is a **training and experience form**, which presents a small number—for example five—of the important tasks of the job. The form asks applicants to indicate whether they have ever performed or been trained in each of the activities. If they answer yes, they are then asked to describe briefly how to perform the activity. Thus, the questions relate directly to the major tasks of the job, satisfying the principle that the content of the questions should reflect the activities of the job to be filled. It is also more difficult to falsify answers because it is necessary to have some knowledge of the activity to respond to these questions; inaccurate answers can usually be easily detected.

training and experience form: An application device that presents a small number of the important tasks of a job and asks the applicants whether they have ever performed or been trained in each of the activities.

The Interview

The interview is, perhaps, the most often used selection device. The purpose of the interview is to allow at least one member of the organization to interact with each applicant and assess that applicant's job-related KSAs.

TABLE 9.2 Job Behavior-Based Interview Questions

1. Describe a situation in which you had to convince another person to change his or her opinion about how to perform a task. What arguments did you use? What points did the other person bring up? How did you respond to these?
2. Describe a situation in which you had to tell an individual that he or she had performed a task incorrectly. What did you tell the person? What did the person say in response? How did you end the conversation?
3. You are scheduled to attend a training session tomorrow. That night, you receive a telephone call that a close relative is seriously ill. What do you do?
4. You observe an associate abusing company resources. What do you do?

Two aspects of the interview format are especially important. First, the interview should be structured, meaning that the interviewer asks the same set of job-related questions of each candidate. This ensures that the interviewer gathers full information from each applicant, and it makes comparisons among applicants easier because they all are evaluated on the same characteristics. The second aspect of format is the nature of the questions. Questions about job-related behaviors have proven to be quite useful. Table 9.2 provides some examples of such questions. The idea behind them is that gathering information about behaviors that are performed on the job is useful in making selection decisions. The interviewer must evaluate the accuracy or completeness of the response.

Training for interviewers usually is concerned with how to conduct a job interview and how to evaluate applicants. In training for conducting interviews, topics such as legal issues, physical barriers to interaction, and how to establish rapport with the applicant are important. In training for making evaluations, interviewers can be asked to make decisions about individuals who are role-playing applicants. The use of various types of information in making these decisions is then discussed.

Tests

ability tests: Paper-and-pencil quizzes, usually multiple choice, that measure an applicant's knowledge of specific work content or cognitive ability.

performance or work-sample tests: Examinations that verify an applicant's ability to perform actual job behaviors identified from a job analysis.

assessment center tests: Programs that typically simulate managerial tasks.

integrity tests: Tests that measure an applicant's attitudes and opinions about dysfunctional behaviors such as theft, sabotage, physical abuse, and substance abuse.

personality inventories: Programs that measure the thoughts, feelings, and behaviors that define an individual and determine that person's pattern of interaction with the environment.

Many organizations use tests during the selection process to identify those applicants who have the specific KSAs needed for the available positions. Human resource managers can use many kinds of tests. The most common are the following:

- **Ability tests** are paper-and-pencil quizzes, usually multiple choice, that measure an applicant's knowledge of specific work content or cognitive ability.
- **Performance or work-sample tests** verify an applicant's ability to perform actual job behaviors identified from a job analysis. Perhaps the oldest example is a typing test. As knowledge of commonly used computer programs is also necessary for many jobs today, many companies or job centers are using tests that measure an applicant's knowledge of Microsoft Word, Excel, PowerPoint, etc.
- **Assessment center tests** are programs that typically simulate managerial tasks. One popular simulation is the In-Basket, which simulates 20 to 30 office memos, complete with an organizational chart and relevant company policy statements.
- **Integrity tests** measure an applicant's attitudes and opinions about dysfunctional behaviors such as theft, sabotage, physical abuse, and substance abuse. In the past, companies generally used paper-and-pencil, multiple-choice tests that ask about the applicant's thoughts and reactions to a number of illegal or unethical situations. Now these tests are often administered over the computer.
- **Personality inventories** measure the thoughts, feelings, and behaviors that define an individual and determine that person's pattern of interaction with the environment. Two general types of personality tests have been used in selection. One is a multiple-choice questionnaire. The second type of personality test is the projective test, which asks an applicant to write a story about ambiguous pictures or to finish partially completed sentences.

- **Physical examinations** test individuals for placement in manually and physically demanding jobs. The Americans with Disabilities Act of 1990 states that physical exams can be given only after an offer for employment has been made to the individual.

physical examinations: Tests that qualify an individual's placement in manually and physically demanding jobs.

Reference Checks

A company considering hiring a particular applicant often contacts previous employers or others who know him or her well to verify the information previously obtained. Reference checks can be handled in three ways. The first, and most often used, is through telephone conversations, in which previous supervisors of the applicant are contacted. Other ways include in-person visits, mail inquiries, and emails. Employers have even begun to use online networking sites, such as Facebook, as well as online blogs and other postings made by potential candidates as a means of checking their viability as an employee. This practice is not without controversy, however, as the individual may not represent him or herself accurately online, and many feel that it is an invasion of privacy. The organization may also obtain reference information from investigative agencies, credit bureaus, and public documents. Table 9.3 provides some general steps for checking the references of potential employees.

Employee tests can evaluate knowledge, performance, integrity, personality, and physical ability.

While checking references is popular among managers, there is very little evidence to support its use in selection. There are, in fact, a number of reasons why this information would not be useful. First, when an applicant names an individual as a reference, the company assumes that the reference meets a number of criteria: that the reference has observed the applicant in situations similar to those of the job being filled, is competent to make an evaluation, wishes to give frank and honest statements, and is able to express himself or herself adequately. Obviously, many references do not meet these requirements. This is especially true for references supplied by the applicant, which are usually chosen because of prior favorable interaction and anticipation of a positive recommendation.

Another issue is the possibility of legal action being brought by the applicant against a reference who makes negative comments. If the reference provides opinions that are not substantiated by official records, a charge of defamation of character is possible. In the case of *True v. Ladner*, for example, True, a high school teacher, won a libel and slander suit against Ladner, the school superintendent, after Ladner told a prospective employer

TABLE 9.3 Steps for Checking Employee References

1. Let the potential employee know that your company will be checking his or her references.
2. If you will be the direct supervisor of the new employee, then you should be the one to check the employee's references.
3. Contact employment references by telephone rather than by written communication. Tone of voice can often provide clues to the applicant's character and work ethic.
4. Contact personal references the employee has provided you with.
5. Check education records to determine accuracy of employee's educational background.
6. Conduct an Internet search to see if anything concerning comes up about the potential employee.
7. Keep all questions work-related! Do not ask any questions that could potentially lead to a discrimination lawsuit, including race, marital status, health conditions, and religious affiliations.

that True was not a good mathematics teacher, was more concerned with living up to his contract than going the extra mile, and was not able to "turn students on." The jury found that Ladner's reference statements were given with "reckless disregard of their truth or falsity."[4] Consequently, today some employers are refusing to give reference information for fear of possible legal liability.

With so much information available online, a quick Google search can easily bring up information on an individual's involvement in activities, religious affiliations, associations, newspaper articles about him or her, work histories, or social networking accounts. If a potential candidate was ever involved in legal trouble, this may also come up in an Internet search. For instance, many states post mug shots for arrests. However, discovering religious affiliations or health conditions may become a legal issue if an applicant claims that these were the reasons he or she was not hired.

A number of Web-based companies offer online background checks on potential applicants for a fee. These firms have purchased U.S. public records data that might be hard to collect or take too much time for the company itself to gather. As mentioned earlier, employers might also engage in online vetting by attempting to view a potential applicant's Internet and social media activities. A person's online activities (and whether they are publicly available) can give the employer an idea about the applicant's character and history. Like it or not, this information is freely available and may color a potential employer's opinion of a candidate.

Because of the risks involved with checking references or searching online, many human resource departments will only verify factual data of employment, such as dates and job title, when contacting a reference. Indeed, organizations often inform employees of such policies in the event they are asked directly for business references for present or former associates.

Orientation and Training

Once the firm has chosen the best applicants and offers have been accepted, new hires must be oriented to the organization and trained to do their jobs.

Orientation

orientation: The process of familiarizing newly hired employees with fellow workers, company procedures, and the physical properties of the organization.

Orientation is the process of familiarizing newly hired employees with fellow workers, company procedures, and the physical properties of the organization. Orientation generally includes a tour of the buildings; introductions to supervisors, coworkers, and subordinates; and distribution of manuals describing the firm's policy on vacations, absenteeism, lunch breaks, company benefits, and so on. Many companies now require online orientation and a personal session featuring procedures, facilities, and key personnel to facilitate orientation. Many companies regard orientation to be a valuable socialization device. HRM policies and the firm's code of conduct are often required reading, with job candidates being required to sign a statement of understanding and consent to comply with the documents.

Training

training: The process of instructing employees in their job tasks and socializing them into the organization's values, attitudes, and other aspects of its culture.

Training is the process of instructing employees in their job tasks as well as socializing them into the organization's values, attitudes, and other aspects of its culture. There are several reasons why training is an important human resource program. First, as we have already mentioned, it develops new employees' job skills and attitudes. Second, because jobs frequently change in organizations, especially those in which technology plays a large role, employees are frequently in need of additional training even if they remain in the same position. For example, some employees may need to learn additional software to perform successfully on the job. Several high-tech firms also might send their employees to classes or online sessions to update them on new technologies and techniques. Third, as successful individuals move up to different positions, they need training to learn requisite new tasks. For example, when non-managers are promoted to managerial positions, they need to master many of the topics presented in this textbook as part of their formal training programs. Fourth, the current organizational trend to downsize and reduce managerial layers has shifted many of the survivors to new positions, often increasing the range of tasks and requiring additional training.

The steps in training are straightforward. First, the trainer determines the employee's needs, and then develops a training program to meet these needs. Then the trainer performs an evaluation to determine if the training was successful.

Training Needs

There are two basic ways of identifying training needs. For new employees or employees moving to new positions, the job analysis is the place to start because it states the job's tasks and KSAs. Training programs are developed to teach these. For example, the

Training can involve personal emersion in training manuals, websites, and testing as well as personal or virtual training encounters.

job of a bank loan officer may require knowledge of the bank's loan procedures, of how to interview loan applicants to acquire all necessary information, and of how to analyze applicants' financial information to determine their loan risk. After the subprime meltdown and the rampant misconduct discovered in the financial sector during the most recent financial crisis, the requirements for compliance with federal and state regulations have been tightened, necessitating additional knowledge in this regard. These activities become the subject of training programs.

To determine training needs for employees who remain in the same job, it is necessary to know whether there are any substantial changes in the job and/or if the employee's job performance has declined. Changes in the job are always accompanied by new tasks, which frequently require at least minimal initial training. However, if job performance is significantly lower than before the change, extensive training may be required.

After assessing training needs, the trainer develops a detailed statement of what knowledge and skills are required and what specific objectives should be attained. For example, in training the loan officer, suitable training objectives might be (a) to know the tax laws concerning the purchase, holding, and resale of certain property and (b) to be able to gather, through the interview and the application form, all information concerning an applicant's financial status. The statement of such objectives is important because they define what should be included in the training program.

Developing the Training Program

A number of techniques are used in training. One group of training methods includes variations of **on-the-job training**, in which the employee learns the job tasks while actually performing the job. In such cases, the manager or an experienced worker conducts the training. For example, a new Pizza Hut store employee may learn how to prepare and cook pizzas by watching, and then assisting, an experienced cook. Frequent difficulties with this type of training are that trainers may not be well versed in how to teach, and they must continue to do their own jobs while they train the new employee. As a result, the employee often has to learn through trial and error or by carefully observing others. Also, if a particular situation does not arise during the training period, the trainee will be unprepared for this situation when it occurs on the job.

on-the-job training: A technique in which the employee learns the job tasks while actually performing the job.

Another group of methods involves off-job educational programs conducted by outside individuals hired by the company. Often these individuals are experienced instructors who have a wide variety of materials they can use in training. McDonald's, for example, has a training facility called Hamburger University that it uses to teach employees about restaurant management. However, it is sometimes difficult for the employee to translate the instruction directly into job actions because the nature of the learning situation is different from the work situation.

A third group of methods makes use of online instruction, which can be a good way to train a number of different skills. Job knowledge through the presentation of text material and subsequent testing is commonplace. 3-D simulations have been developed to instruct workers in how to operate machinery, and both airline pilots and surgeons are often trained with such simulations.

There are a number of training methods that are used primarily for training managers. Among the most frequent are the following:

- *Coaching*—Senior managers help guide the decisions and actions of new managers. For example, the senior manager may provide advice about how to conduct a disciplinary session. Such senior managers are sometimes referred to as mentors.

- *Committee assignments*—Organizations assign inexperienced managers to either a permanent committee or a single-project committee. The inexperienced manager interacts with others and benefits by observing how successful managers plan, organize, and direct the project.

- *Job rotation*—Companies often have a specified plan of assignments for new managers that includes jobs in various parts of the organization or department. The purpose of such training is to have the manager develop a broad knowledge of the work operations.

- *Role-playing*—Managers demonstrate how they would carry out a specific activity in the presence of others. For example, the manager might be asked to conduct a performance appraisal of an employee who has specific, deficient areas of job performance. In role-playing, the "employee" is also a manager going through the training.

- *Case study*—The manager reads written descriptions of events in an organization and must make decisions about what to do next. For example, the description may be of the initiation and administration of a total quality management program. Based on the presented information, the manager makes specific statements about such actions as training.

Evaluation of Results of Training

Managers often assume that exposing employees to training means that they have learned the material and can effectively perform the job. However, training should be directly measured to determine how well employees have, in fact, learned the material. If any deficiencies are apparent, training can be repeated. One method of evaluation is to ask employees what they thought about the training, such as whether the instructor was competent and what they think they learned. However, this has limited value because the answers may simply indicate the instructor's ability to interact with the trainees.

A better method is to give a formal test at the end of training. This could be a written questionnaire based on knowledge, or a demonstration performance of what was covered in training. Usually the instructor grades the trainees on these tests. This information can provide a very good basis for judging an individual's readiness to perform the job. A third method is to have the supervisor appraise the employee's performance shortly after the completion of training. This can also be useful in identifying job tasks for which further training is needed.

Appraising Performance

performance appraisal: A formal measurement of the quantity and quality of an employee's work within a specific period of time.

Performance appraisal is a formal measurement of the quantity and quality of an employee's work within a specific time period. Usually, performance appraisal occurs once, or at most, twice a year. There are several methods of performance appraisal, which differ in what aspects of performance are measured and how the measurement is made. Table 9.4 provides examples of the different types of measures that may be used in a performance appraisal.

TABLE 9.4 Appraising Performance

Type of Measure	Example
■ Objective Measures	■ The marketing manager reports a 16% increase in sales over the fourth quarter from last year.
■ Subjective Measures 　■ Trait Appraisals	■ The new accountant is dependable, enthusiastic, and has a good attitude toward her work environment.
■ Behavior-Based Appraisals	■ The service quality manager exhibits good leadership qualities, provides clear instruction for employees, and maintains satisfactory relationships with customers.

Objective Measures

Objective performance measures count tangible products of work performance. These could be measures of quantity—such as the dollar amount of sales or the number of garments sewn—or quality—such as the amount of scrap or the number of defect-free garments. For example, bank loan officers are evaluated on the dollar amounts of loans or the time required to process loan applications. Professional athletes are appraised variously on batting averages, tackles made, number of rebounds, and minutes played.

Many organizations prefer objective measures because they appear to be unbiased, direct gauges of work performance. This is not always true, however. One reason is that these measures are influenced by environmental conditions. The number of competitors, the economy, and the size of the territory, for example, may affect sales volume. Not all salespersons face comparable situations in this regard, so comparisons are not quite equitable. Another limitation of objective measures is that they cannot always describe all aspects of the job. For example, it is difficult and expensive to obtain measures of customer service, such as by contacting customers and asking their opinions as to how well employees have interacted with them. Good equipment maintenance is another measure that is often difficult to gather. Thus, using objective measures exclusively often means that only part of the job is appraised. Moreover, very often this results in workers devoting most of their time to the parts of their jobs that are measurable and possibly ignoring the other parts.

Subjective Measures

Subjective measures are judgments about how an employee is performing. Generally, the supervisor is the one who makes such judgments, although in some instances, they may be gathered from co-workers and subordinates as well. For example, a common performance appraisal called **360-degree feedback** is often used to get multiple perspectives on an employee's performance. This process asks co-workers from the employee's inner circle to rate the employee's strengths and weaknesses on different elements of performance. The employee will often self-evaluate him- or herself, and sometimes feedback is also solicited from customers or suppliers.[5]

360-degree feedback: Used to get multiple perspectives (employee, co-workers, customers, and/or suppliers) on an employee's performance.

Trait Appraisals

A **trait appraisal** evaluates an employee's personal characteristics such as attitude, motivation, cooperation, and dependability. Although companies commonly use these measures, they are somewhat problematic and are not always recommended as performance measures because they do not directly affect job activities.

trait appraisal: A subjective evaluation of an employee's personal characteristics such as attitude, motivation, cooperation, and dependability.

Source: alexskopje/Shutterstock

Many employee performance appraisals are based on subjective measures and evaluations.

One of the main difficulties with using trait appraisals is that there are no clear definitions of many traits. For example, some managers may define being "cooperative" in terms of whether the employee assists fellow workers in completing work assignments. Other managers may define the trait as how willingly the employee does what the manager tells him or her to do. If traits are not clearly defined, managers may find it difficult to utilize trait appraisals simply because they are not certain as to what to evaluate.

Behavior-Based Appraisals

A second type of subjective measure, **behavior-based appraisal**, evaluates how the employee performs job tasks. The items used in this appraisal must come from the job analysis. The dimensions to be evaluated are described in terms of either activities or results. The complete appraisal form contains behaviors necessary for project management, business development, customer satisfaction, and financial performance.

behavior-based appraisal: A subjective evaluation of the way an employee performs job tasks.

Advantages and Disadvantages of Subjective Measures

Subjective performance measures provide several advantages. First, they can permit the supervisor to judge all aspects of the employee's work. Even those aspects that do not result in a finished product, such as the job task of "providing information to answer customers' questions about various bank services," can be evaluated by a supervisor who monitors the interactions between the receptionist and the bank's customers. Second, the evaluation of job behaviors makes it much easier to identify deficient performance and to determine specific methods of correcting deficiencies.

The disadvantages of the use of subjective performance appraisal generally relate to the errors that supervisors may make in judging performance. For example, leniency errors refer to rating all employees very highly; severity errors result in rating all employees very low; and central tendency errors result in all employees being rated as average. A halo error occurs when the supervisor judges that, because an employee is performing very well in one job behavior, he or she is performing well in others and evaluates the employee highly in all aspects even if this is not the case. However, these errors generally can be overcome through training.

Compensating Employees

A **compensation system** is the basis on which an organization gives money, goods, or services to its employees in exchange for their work. This system is important to an organization because it serves to attract, motivate, and retain employees. If properly designed and implemented, a compensation system can help a firm reach its strategic goals and serve as a competitive advantage relative to other firms in the same industry. It can also help to motivate employees to perform at their highest levels. These behaviors may not be as common in those organizations in which compensation is based mainly on seniority.

compensation system: The basis on which an organization gives money, goods, or services to its employees in exchange for their work.

In recent years, perhaps the fastest-growing portion of executive pay has been stock options. After the fairly recent financial meltdown on Wall Street, the issue of executive compensation has come under scrutiny. A number of high-ranking executives of failed firms such as Lehman Brothers and Bear Stearns received hundreds of millions of dollars in bonuses, in spite of the unsustainably poor performance of their firms. Many critics are concerned that the compensation systems in many firms encourage excessive risk taking in order to drive up short-term stock prices. Top corporate managers thus are concerned about how to make the company highly profitable "today," without possible concern about what happens four or five years down the road. Government regulations have been exploring various ways to potentially curb excessive executive pay and/or make it more transparent.

You're the Manager . . . What Would You Do?

THE COMPANY: Turner Industries
YOUR POSITION: Human Resource Manager
THE PLACE: Jackson, Mississippi

Turner Industries, a family-operated carpeting manufacturer, was started 60 years ago just outside Jackson, Mississippi. Today, the company is the third-largest producer of carpeting in the United States. With revenue over $2 billion, Turner employs over 6,000 workers at this now-massive facility.

Five years ago, Turner developed an "Employee Initiative" program to instill commitment to customer satisfaction throughout the company. The company's employees play a vital role in this program. A flat organizational structure gives employees, working in self-managed teams, significant authority and autonomy. Production work teams can undertake training, schedule work, and determine individual performance objectives. Any production process can be halted if an employee believes that quality is suffering or safety is jeopardized.

Teams form the core of Turner's quality-improvement efforts. The company formed 25 "Proactive Teams" to address specific manufacturing and production challenges. In addition, select teams work on ways to enhance the relationship between Turner and its suppliers. Each team is asked to review the company code of ethics annually to determine how risk areas were managed over the previous year and to suggest whether new issues not covered in the code have developed. The teams, in general, respond to customers' comments, work on developing new products, and create activities that bring employees together in social situations (sporting activities, picnics, and fund-raising efforts for employee–supported charities). With diverse opportunities to affect the company, the teams demonstrate a fundamental commitment to customer satisfaction—even creating marketing opportunities that generate additional revenue.

Management and motivation of the workforce require special care on the part of Turner's management. Training and recognition is key. In a single year, the company invests $3,000 per employee in training. Recognition comes in the form of participation in teams, leadership opportunities, and interaction with top management.

Turner Industries is a family-run carpet manufacturing firm in Mississippi that implements innovative human resource programs.

Source: Offscreen/Shutterstock

Turner's efforts at improving its management and human resource practices have allowed it to reduce the number of managers; lower its overall defect rate; and increase quality, efficiency, and customer satisfaction. Revenues have increased significantly over the last four years. As a result of the focus on employees' and customers' needs, Turner has won over 20 quality awards and was voted the outstanding employer in the South in a regional competition. The company has been written about in the Top 200 Employers in the U.S., and its efforts to involve employees in determining the firm's direction have been very successful, enhancing customer satisfaction and improving business performance.

QUESTIONS

1. As human resource manager, what employee characteristics might be used in the selection of team members?

2. How might performance appraisal be done? Can team members be involved in the review of other members?

3. Identify training needs at Turner. Do you believe a company can spend too much money on training for employees? Why?

Determining Compensation

To set up a compensation system, a company must gather two sets of data. For one, it must determine, through wage and salary surveys, what comparable organizations pay certain specific jobs. Second, by using a job evaluation method, the organization must determine the worth of each job to the organization itself. Individual employees are then paid according to the worth of the job to the organization, how much comparable firms pay for the same job, and how well or how long they have done that job.

The Wage and Salary Survey

wage and salary survey: A study that tells the company how much compensation is paid by comparable firms for specific jobs the firms have in common.

A **wage and salary survey** tells the company how much compensation comparable firms are paying for specific jobs that the firms have in common. For example, a small manufacturing firm in Seattle that recruits its workforce from the Seattle metro area may exchange information on a regular basis through wage and salary surveys with other firms—usually in the same industry—that employ workers with the same skills and are within geographic regions that would allow employees to relocate or commute.

The wage and salary survey gathers information about key jobs—that is, jobs that are stable over time, are similar among the companies participating in the survey, and are at various levels in the organization. Although questions used in wage and salary surveys vary, they usually ask about direct wages, benefits and other forms of compensation, regular hours worked, and number of overtime hours. As a result of this survey, participating firms obtain data about pay in their relevant labor markets, which they can use to determine compensation for their own employees.

Job Evaluation Methods

A major principle in setting up a compensation system is that jobs, rather than the individuals who work in the jobs, are the primary basis for compensation. Some jobs, such as that of a vice president, are more valuable to the company than others and therefore are compensated at higher levels. **Job evaluation methods** determine the value of an organization's jobs and arrange these jobs in order of pay according to their value.

job evaluation methods: Techniques that determine the value of an organization's jobs and arrange these jobs in order of pay according to their value.

Although there are many job evaluation methods, the three most often used are ranking, the point method, and the job grading method. Ranking, used mainly in small companies, involves a committee of managers and compensation specialists reviewing the information gathered from job analyses and ranking each job according to its overall worth to the company. The point method evaluates jobs quantitatively, assigning points to jobs depending on how much of certain factors a job requires. For example, jobs may be assigned 50, 100, or 150 points depending on how much education is necessary to do the work. The points a job is assigned indicate its worth to the organization. The job grading method, used often by government agencies, groups all jobs into grades depending on the complexity of the job duties. Grades with more complex job duties are more highly compensated than grades with less complex job duties.

In most compensation systems, similar jobs are grouped together and treated similarly in terms of compensation. For example, in the job grading method, all jobs within the same grade receive similar compensation. In the point method, all jobs within similar points receive the same compensation.

Compensation for Individuals

The pay range for a group of jobs defines the upper and lower limits of how much every employee who has one of those jobs can earn. The compensation within this range for any one employee usually depends on either seniority or performance. Seniority is the basis for differential pay in many government and unionized work systems. Those individuals in a job grade who have more tenure usually earn more than those individuals with less tenure. Many private companies, however, try to use performance as the basis for differential pay by giving larger raises to those who receive higher performance appraisals.

A third way of paying individuals differently is skill-based pay plans, which have been introduced by both public and private institutions. Skill-based pay schemes link jobs together into hierarchies of related but increasingly difficult tasks. As a worker learns to perform more tasks, compensation increases.

Bonuses

Many employees hope to receive some bonuses as rewards for a job well done. However, among top executives the bonuses have grown to become a very large part of the total pay. Bonuses for many executives are no longer perceived as a reward, but as an expected part of the compensation package. Overall, pay for top executives is now more than 500 times that made by the average worker in the United States. Many people contend that this is an excessive differentiation no matter how large and successful the firm. Critics believe that an environment, where bonuses have been decoupled from performance has created a situation where large corporations focus on short-term performance rather than looking at the big picture over the long-term.

For example, top executives at Merrill Lynch were awarded nearly $4 billion in bonuses, even though the company had failed and had to merge with Bank of America to save it from bankruptcy. The government had to subsequently pass legislation limiting the amount of executive bonuses to $500,000 for executives at firms that received bailout money from the government. To stave off criticism, many companies have begun taking steps to tie executive pay closer to performance. If the company fares badly, executive compensation will not be as high; if it does well, then executives receive better compensation. Shareholder activists are also getting more involved in matters related to executive compensation and other company decisions.

Benefits

Among the fastest-rising costs in organizations are those associated with benefits for employees. In the 1940s, benefits accounted for approximately 5 percent of the compensation given to employees. The cost of benefits is today approaching 40 percent of total compensation in many organizations. Although benefits vary among organizations, the major categories are mandatory protection programs, pay for time not worked, optional protection programs, and private retirement plans. Table 9.5 provides a summary of these different benefits.

Some corporations have begun to look beyond traditional benefits packages. **Cafeteria benefits programs** allow an employee to choose which benefits he or she wants from a menu of different options. The advantage of cafeteria benefits is that employees can tailor a benefits program to meet their needs. **Flexible benefits programs** work by giving employees credits to spend on benefits that meet their needs, rather than forcing them to sign up for a package that is not catered to them. Both of these types of plans improve employee satisfaction by providing them with exactly the benefits that they need and want.

cafeteria benefits program: Allows an employee to choose which benefits he or she wants from a menu of different options.

flexible benefits program: Works by giving employees credits to spend on benefits that meet their needs, rather than forcing them to sign up for a package that is not catered to them.

Pay for Time Not Worked

This benefit includes pay given employees for holidays, vacation, sick leave, and personal leave. They can sometimes total up to as much as 45 days per year, depending on the organization's policies.

TABLE 9.5 Compensation Benefits

Benefit	Feature
Cafeteria	Gives employees a menu of different benefit options to choose from
Flexible	Gives employees credits to spend on benefits that meet their needs
Pay for Time Not Worked	Provides employees with paid days off, such as vacations, holidays, sick leave, and personal leave
Mandatory Protection Programs	Benefits required by law to protect the employee, including social security, workers' compensation, and unemployment compensation
Optional Protection Programs	Benefits provided to protect employees not required by law but provided to be competitive in the workplace, such as stock ownership plans, wellness programs, and educational assistance
Private Retirement Plans	Paying into pension plans for the employee's future retirement

Many employees fail to recognize the value provided by company benefits, including health benefits, insurance, and retirement.

Mandatory Protection Programs

Mandatory protection programs are those required by federal law. For many employers, Social Security is the most expensive benefit. A related benefit is unemployment compensation, which is funded by employers through a tax on a portion of the total compensation of a company's employees. A third mandatory benefit is workers' compensation, which provides prompt benefits for workers who are injured on the job regardless of fault.

Optional Protection Programs

Optional protection plans are benefits not mandated by law but offered to make the organization competitive in the labor market. Traditionally, health insurance has fallen into this category but with President Obama's Patient Protection and Affordable Care Act such insurance may now, for many employers, fall into the mandatory protection category above. Additionally, companies may elect to offer benefits such as stock-ownership and other profit-sharing plans, wellness or exercise programs, educational assistance, child care, and counseling for drug or alcohol abuse.

Private Retirement Plans

In most cases, employees and employers share the cost of funding pension plans, with the burden of payment increasingly falling on the employee. In rare cases, the employer bears the total cost. There are two major types of pension plans. Under defined benefit plans, the retirement payment depends on a formula that includes employee length of service and average income. Under defined contribution plans, regular contributions are made to investment funds, with the retirement benefits a function of the value of the investments.

Promoting, Transferring, and Terminating Employees

A major HRM concern is the movement of employees after they have been selected and trained to perform their initial job with the organization. **Promotion** is the advancement of a current employee to a higher-level job within the organization. Generally, the new position is more complex, has more responsibility, and receives more compensation. A **transfer** is the reassignment of a current employee to another job at the same level as the original job. Although the individual may receive more compensation as a result of the transfer, usually the responsibility and complexity of the new job are roughly equal to that of the original one. **Termination** is the separation of an employee from the organization. Firms use this process when they close facilities, reduce their workforce, or respond to continued poor performance.

Promotions and Transfers

We can think of promotion and transfer as being essentially the same process as selection because the central focus of all three is to match an individual's KSAs to the requirements of a job. There is one important difference, however; the nature of the data collected for transfers and promotions is different from that collected in selection because candidates for promotion or transfer already work for the organization. Consequently, managers can gather rich data from previous performance appraisals as well as opinions from current and former supervisors, with an emphasis on job activities that are similar to the activities of the new job.

Promotions and transfers that require geographical relocation are more difficult to arrange now than previously because social trends such as two-career couples, single parents with joint child-custody rights, and employees with multigenerational responsibilities, present difficulties in physical relocation.[6] As a result, companies are providing services such as career counseling for spouses, legal counseling for child-custody questions, and financial and family counseling in connection with making such a change.

promotion: The advancement of a current employee to a higher-level job within the organization.

transfer: The reassignment of a current employee to another job at the same level as the original job.

termination: The separation of an employee from the organization.

There are two major types of termination: for-cause and layoffs.

For-Cause Terminations

Termination for-cause occurs when an individual's job behavior is unacceptable. For example, an employee may be fired for poor performance or violations of the company's rules and policies. This is a complex activity that is difficult for both the company and the individual.

Well-managed terminations for-cause usually have three distinct stages. Often, particularly in unionized firms, these three stages are part of a formally stated policy. First, the manager notifies the employee, often during the performance appraisal, that his or her work behavior is unacceptable. The manager should discuss specific aspects of performance and describe the deficiencies or problems in detail. The second stage begins with the development of a program to improve the work performance. This may include additional training, regular monitoring of performance by the supervisor, and frequent feedback concerning the quality of work. If performance does not improve even after additional training and feedback, the third stage begins when the company decides that the individual is incapable of performing adequately on the job and that it is in the best interests of both the organization and the individual to terminate the relationship. The manager should record in writing all information from these stages, give a copy to the employee, and place additional copies in the employee's file. This will provide necessary data concerning the poor performance as well as attempts to improve any deficiencies in case the termination is legally contested.

Layoffs

The second type of termination is a reduction-in-force, or layoff, which ends the employment of groups of individuals or, in extreme cases, closes a complete plant or part of the organization. Layoffs are usually attributable to poor economic performance of the organization rather than the performance of the individuals involved. The most recent economic recession caused significant layoffs throughout the country. This leaves many workers with fewer options than their predecessors. Bank of America has laid off thousands of workers in its mortgage division due to slowdowns in refinancing among homeowners.[7]

Source: Andrey_Popov/Shutterstock

The decision as to whether to lay off employees is often tied directly to weakness in the economy.

There are a number of specific actions a company can take to reduce its workforce. Among them are the following:

1. *Attrition*—The organization stops recruiting and selecting new employees and allows retirements, voluntary resignations, and individual termination to reduce the number of employees. Usually, this option requires a long time to achieve a large reduction.
2. *Early retirement programs*—The organization offers a variety of incentives for senior employees to retire, such as bonuses and nearly full retirement pay for otherwise unqualified employees.
3. *Job sharing*—Two employees each work part time at a job that would require only one employee on a full-time basis.
4. *Group dismissal*—A group of employees is terminated. This may be a complete office, department, or division. Terminated employees are often, but not necessarily, given severance pay and some assistance in searching for another position.

There are no definite guidelines as to when it is appropriate to use each of these options. To a large extent, the choice depends on the severity of the economic crisis, the expected duration of the crisis, the presence of employee unions, and the relationship between the organization and the employees. Most organizations attempt to use a variety of these options, but usually use group dismissal as a last resort. Larger employers (i.e., those with 100 or more employees) are required under federal law to give employees at least 60 calendar days of notice before any layoff.

Legal Aspects of Termination

There are a number of legal issues that affect organizations' prerogative to terminate employees. Traditionally, the legal principle of employment-at-will prevailed, which holds that an employment contract is a legal agreement between free agents in which the government should not interfere, and either party may break the contract at any time, for any reason. Under strict interpretation of this principle, an organization need not show any evidence or reason to justify termination. Recently, however, a number of factors have served to limit employment-at-will.

Equal employment laws provide protection for a number of demographic groups against disproportionate termination. That is, terminations should not affect larger percentages of these groups than others. Union contracts have given some protection to union members. Often these negotiated agreements between employees and the organization limit the number of individuals who can be terminated during the life of the contract. Also, these contracts ensure that a pattern of procedures must be completed by the organization before termination. Wrongful discharge identifies four instances that are exceptions to employment-at-will: (1) the employee was discharged for reasons that contradict a fundamental principle of public policy (e.g., was fired for taking a day off for jury duty); (2) there is an expressed or implied guarantee of employment; (3) the employer's conduct violates the concepts of "good faith dealing"; and (4) other conduct interferes with a legitimate employment contract. To date, only the state of Montana, in the United States, has passed a state law formally providing employees in that state many of the above protections by way of state statute.

The Legal Environment of Human Resource Management

Over the last several decades, regulation of human resource activities has increased in terms of both areas covered and the number of laws passed. Table 9.6 contains a brief description of some of the most important laws affecting employment decisions. These are just a few of the many that affect HRM.

The equal employment opportunity laws are designed to protect individuals from unfair discrimination in employment decisions based on race, sex, age, national origin, religion, disability, and pregnancy. Unfair discrimination generally can take two forms: (1) an individual is negatively affected because of a certain demographic characteristic, such as when an applicant is denied a job because she is female, or (2) the demographic group is more negatively affected than other groups—for example, more Hispanic applicants are hired than other groups. The Civil Rights Acts of 1964 and 1991 prohibit employment discrimination on the basis of race, color, religion, national origin, and sex. President Lyndon Johnson signed the Civil Rights Act on July 2, 1964. The Age Discrimination in Employment Act of 1967 prohibits age discrimination against individuals 40 years or older. This law has had serious implications for companies' termination and selection decisions relative to cost-cutting goals. Despite the Act, however, research has shown that there is still significant discrimination against older employees, particularly in hiring procedures or during layoffs. The Americans with Disabilities Act of 1990 protects employees from discrimination based on disability, and the Pregnancy Discrimination Act of 1978 protects the rights of pregnant employees in the workplace.

Another major issue today is discrimination based on sexual orientation, which has resulted in many lawsuits by LGBT individuals against businesses who they claim discriminated against them due to sexual orientation. Federal laws do not currently explicitly protect discrimination based on sexual orientation, but some state and local government equal employment opportunity laws do provide such protection. The Americans with Dis-

TABLE 9.6 Some Major Federal and State Laws That Affect HRM

Equal Employment Opportunity Laws

- Title VII of Civil Rights Act of 1964 & Civil Rights Act of 1991—Prohibits discrimination based on race, color, religion, sex, or national origin.
- Age Discrimination in Employment Act of 1967 (amended 1978)—Prohibits discrimination against individuals 40 years of age and older.
- Americans with Disabilities Act of 1990—Prohibits discrimination based on physical or mental disabilities.

Health and Safety Laws

- Occupational Safety and Health Act of 1970—Establishes safety standards, inspections of workplaces, and citations for violations of standards.
- Workers' Compensation—Provides for payments to workers due to injury or illness, regardless of fault. Also covers rehabilitation and income loss due to death. Regulated by individual states.
- Patient Protection and Affordable Health Care for America Act of 2010—Makes health care affordable and universal so all Americans can have access to it.

Labor-Management Law

- National Labor Relations Act of 1935—Establishes the right to organize and declares that certain employer actions are unfair labor practices.
- Labor Management Relations Act of 1947—Establishes that certain union actions are unfair labor practices, and permits state right-to-work laws that make union membership non-mandatory.
- Fair Labor Standards Act of 1938—Establishes a minimum wage, requires overtime pay, and provides standards for child labor. Classifies employees as exempt (executive, administrators, professionals, and outside salespersons) or nonexempt (all others) relative to overtime pay regulations.

abilities Act of 1990 prohibits discrimination against individuals with mental or physical disabilities (including AIDS and alcoholism) that substantially limit one or more life functions. The only way a business can deny employment to a person with such disabilities is if the job has certain requirements that the employees cannot perform due to their disability (for example, some jobs require a person to be able to lift packages over 40 pounds, a task that may be difficult or impossible for some handicapped individuals).

Another set of laws is devoted to issues of employment health and safety. The Occupational Safety and Health Act of 1970 requires that organizations comply with safety standards and attempt to eliminate all hazards that affect health and safety, even if there are no existing standards. The Occupational Safety and Health Administration (OSHA) is the government agency that can set standards, inspect organizations for compliance with these standards, and issue citations for violations. State workers' compensation laws cover a number of issues that result from injury or illness, such as partial payment for income loss from partial or total disability, medical expenses, rehabilitation expenses, and death benefits. The amount of payments differs among states.

In the past decade, the topic of health care has been a growing concern. While many businesses provided health care benefits to their full-time employees, others did not. This left many Americans without health insurance. In 2010, President Barack Obama signed the Patient Protection and Affordable Health Care for America Act into law. The Act provides a "Patient's Bill of Rights" intended to make health care more accessible and allow Americans to make informed decisions about their health. The Trump Administration's Tax Reform legislation enacted in late 2017, however, sharply cuts

OSHA is concerned with workplace safety.

back on the mandates of this legislation, to the extent that its long-term viability is at this point under sharp question.[8]

Labor laws address union organization and conditions of employment. The National Labor Relations Act of 1935 (Wagner Act) established the right of workers to organize unions and bargain collectively with employers over wages, hours, and terms and conditions of employment. **Unions** are employee organizations that work with employers to achieve better pay, hours, and working conditions. Unionized employees on average earn better pay than non-unionized employees in comparable positions. On average a unionized full-time or salaried employee will earn about $200 more. However, the percentage of unionized workers is decreasing, with less than 11 percent of the workforce belonging to unions.[9] Figure 9.2 demonstrates unionization by state.

Unions and employers engage in **collective bargaining**, a process of negotiation through which management and unions reach an agreement regarding employee pay, work conditions, and hours. The intent of collective bargaining is to develop a **labor contract**, a formal, written document that describes the relationship between employees and management for a specified period of time.

The Wagner Act also set up the National Labor Relations Board (NLRB), a federal agency empowered to enforce labor-management regulations. The Labor Management

unions: Employee organizations that work with employers to achieve better pay, hours, and working conditions.

collective bargaining: A process of negotiation through which management and unions reach an agreement regarding employee pay, work conditions, and hours.

labor contract: A formal, written document that describes the relationship between employees and management for a specified period of time.

(U.S. rate = 11.3 percent)

Legend:
- 20.0% or more
- 15.0% to 19.9%
- 10.0% to 14.9%
- 5.0% to 9.9%
- 4.9% or less

FIGURE 9.2 Unionization Rate by State

Source: Bureau of Labor Statistics U.S. Department of Labor, "Union Members—2016," https://www.bls.gov/news.release/pdf/union2.pdf (accessed December 31, 2017).

Relations Act (Taft-Hartley Act) of 1947 provided further protection to organized labor by prohibiting employers from interfering with organization efforts by either implicit or overt threats, from dominating a union by providing financial assistance, or from discriminating against union members or those who file charges of labor contract violations. Another important law, the Fair Labor Standards Act of 1938, is critical with respect to compensation issues. Among many items, it establishes a minimum wage and determines which types of employees are entitled to overtime pay.

Importance of Diversity

Although most people think of diversity in terms of gender or race, diversity can also encompass age, sexual orientation, education, abilities, and more. Whereas the U.S. workforce once consisted predominately of white males, today's workforce increasingly consists of women, minorities, and employees from different generations. Rather than limiting an organization, diversity has been shown to help improve company operations. Often employees from different cultures and perspectives have unique insights that can help the organization succeed. Additionally, with an increasingly diverse consumer base, diversity in the workforce helps companies to understand their customers better and create improved ways of developing relationships with them. Diversity also helps to create better tolerance among employees as they continually interact with co-workers from different backgrounds.

Many businesses recognize the importance of supporting diversity in their workforces. Those that do not value diversity among employees risk losing insights that could increase competitiveness. Companies engaging in discrimination can face legal repercussions as well. Home Depot, Coca-Cola, and Walmart have all faced lawsuits in the past few decades claiming that the companies discriminated against women or minorities. Whether or not these allegations were true, companies can protect themselves and improve business operations by adopting policies that encourage diversity.

Affirmative action programs are legally mandated plans within organizations that attempt to increase job opportunities for traditionally underrepresented areas of the workforce. These programs set goals for increasing the number of employees from underrepresented populations with the establishment of certain hiring and promotion procedures. Lyndon Johnson established affirmative action programs in 1965 to help atone for past hiring prejudices. Affirmative action programs were upheld in 1991, but organizations were prohibited by law from engaging in reverse discrimination or hiring quotas that could place other groups at a hiring disadvantage. Some companies have claimed that affirmative action programs have prevented them from hiring the best employees due to too narrow a focus on diversity. While affirmative action programs remain controversial, organizations have benefited from increased diversity.

affirmative action programs: Legally mandated plans within organizations that attempt to increase job opportunities for traditionally underrepresented areas of the workforce.

Despite the vast improvements in diversity, many minorities continue to remain underrepresented in management positions. Among *Fortune 500* CEOs, approximately 2 percent are African American, 21 percent are Asian, 3 percent are Latino, and 6.4 percent are female.[10] However, some organizations have made great accomplishments in diversifying their workforces. For instance, PriceWaterhouseCoopers (PwC) sets strong diversity and inclusion goals. The organization has a Chief Diversity Officer that reports directly to the CEO. PwC engages in mentoring programs that often pair employees from different backgrounds together to increase understanding and knowledge generation. Approximately half of PwC's philanthropic donations go toward supporting multicultural organizations.[11]

The challenge for human resource managers is to try and understand the complex information that comes from HR laws, employee motivation, and diversity and to translate it into HRM practices. Human resource management, then, involves understanding relevant laws, recognizing the importance of forecasting and hiring good employees from diverse backgrounds, and finding the best ways to use the talents of the workforce to maximize organizational success. HR managers can use this information to design and monitor effective HRM programs to ensure that employee skills and knowledge are used to serve the organization's goals.

- *Discuss the term human resource management and its activities.* Human resource management includes those activities that forecast the number and type of employees that the organization will need and then design and implement programs that provide those individuals with necessary skills. The main programs are human resource planning, recruiting, selection, orientation and training, performance appraisal, compensation, promotion, transfer, and termination. To perform these activities, HR managers need to conduct job analyses, which identify (1) the tasks that make up a job; (2) the worker knowledge, skills, and abilities (KSAs) needed to perform the job; (3) the information, equipment, and materials used; and (4) the working conditions.

- *Summarize how managers may plan for human resource needs.* Human resource planning involves forecasting the organization's future demand for employees, forecasting the future supply of employees for the organization, and designing programs to correct the discrepancy between the two forecasts. Quantitative methods of forecasting rely on empirical data, while qualitative methods use experts' opinions and judgment to estimate the appropriate numbers.

- *Specify how organizations may recruit new employees.* Recruiting is the process of attracting potential new employees to the organization. Companies may recruit using internal sources (job postings within the organization) or external sources (employment agencies, media, social media, and broadcasting, brochures and pamphlets, college visits, and word of mouth involving current employees).

- *Explain how companies use application forms, interviews, and tests in selecting new employees.* Application forms, interviews, and tests should be designed so that they employ questions that gather information actually related to the behaviors that comprise the available job.

- *Formulate the information used in designing effective training programs.* Two basic types of information are needed to determine training needs and to design training programs. The first is a description of the tasks and the necessary knowledge, skills, and abilities of the job. The second is information about how well the employee can currently perform the job. This information should be gathered for specific aspects of the job; any part that indicates poor or marginal performance could be the basis on which to develop training programs to correct these deficiencies.

- *Describe the types of performance appraisal.* Two major types of performance appraisal are objective and subjective measures. Objective measures count tangible products of work performance such as dollar amount of sales, the number of garments sewn, or the amount of scrap produced. Subjective measures rely on the opinion of the supervisor, co-workers, or subordinates to form a judgment about the employee's work performance. Judgments can be made about the worker's traits or specific job behaviors. A common type of subjective performance appraisal is 360-degree feedback, which gets multiple perspectives from co-workers and other stakeholders on the employee's performance.

- *Explain the purposes of compensation systems and the basic steps in setting up these systems.* Compensation systems attract, motivate, and retain employees. To set up a compensation system, a company must determine what comparable firms pay specific jobs, through wage and salary surveys. Also, the company must determine how much each job should be paid through job evaluation. Individuals are then compensated according to how well or how long they have done that job.

- *Summarize some of the major laws that affect employment decisions.* Among the most important federal laws are the Civil Rights Act of 1964, the Americans with Disabilities Act, the Occupational Safety and Health Act, the Patient Protection and Affordable Care Act, and the National Labor Relations Act.

- *Explain the importance of diversity in an organization.* Employees from different cultures and perspectives have unique insights that can help the organization succeed. Also, with an increasingly diverse consumer base, diversity helps companies to understand their customers better and create improved ways of developing relationships with them. Diversity also creates more tolerance among employees as they continually interact with co-workers from different backgrounds. To encourage diversity many companies have instituted affirmative action programs, which are legally mandated plans within organizations that attempt to increase job opportunities for traditionally underrepresented areas of the workforce.

Assess an organization's attempts to select, train, and appraise its employees with an improved human resource management program. You should be able to evaluate the success of the human resource program described in the "Business Dilemma" box, including its ability to select, train, evaluate, and retain employees and give the company a competitive edge.

Key Terms and Concepts

ability tests 274

affirmative action programs 289

assessment center tests 274

behavior-based appraisal 280

cafeteria benefits program 283

collective bargaining 288

compensation system 280

flexible benefits program 283

human resource management (HRM) 267

human resource planning 268

integrity tests 274

job analysis 268

job evaluation methods 282

labor contract 288

on-the-job training 277

orientation 276

performance appraisal 278

performance or work-sample tests 274

personality inventories 274

physical examinations 275

promotion 284

recruiting 270

selection 272

termination 284

360-degree feedback 279

training 276

training and experience form 273

trait appraisal 279

transfer 284

unions 288

wage and salary survey 282

Ready Recall

1. What are human resource management (HRM) programs intended to do for the organization?
2. What information do job analyses provide and why is this information important for HRM programs?
3. What is human resource planning?
4. Define recruitment and the two major sources for recruiting.
5. What is selection? Also, what is meant by a performance test?
6. What is the purpose of training and what are the major steps in training?
7. What purpose does the performance appraisal serve? Describe what is meant by objective and subjective performance measures.
8. What is a compensation system, and what purpose does it serve within an organization?
9. What is meant by promotion, transfer, and termination of employees?
10. List some of the major laws that affect human resource management. To which HRM issues do these laws apply?
11. Describe some ways that diversity in the workforce can help an organization.

Expand Your Experience

1. Interview a human resource manager who selects both management and non-management employees. Identify the differences in the selection instruments that are used for the two types of positions, including what information about the applicants is sought.
2. Obtain a job description and a performance appraisal form from a human resource manager. Discuss whether the form directly measures essential job behaviors.
3. Interview a human resource manager about the content of a training program in his or her company for entry-level managers. Discuss the completeness of this training program from the perspective of points in the text.

Making Human Resource Decisions

Scenario:

You are the director of human resources for your company. The CEO has just informed you that the financial state of the company is dire, and as a result, he is approaching the managers of each department and asking them to reduce personnel costs. The company makes its profits primarily on services such as business consulting, cloud-based storage for large companies, and other small miscellaneous business products. The industry has become highly competitive and sales are down. There is not enough revenue at this point to pay all of the salespeople.

You are charged with devising a plan to determine how personnel costs will be reduced. After much deliberation, you decide on three options. Because this is a management dilemma, none of these options are optimal. Further, cost/benefit analysis has a role in the decision-making process, but as you are dealing with people, this type of analysis is complicated and subjective.

Options:

1. Lay off employees and use them only as needed on a project or change employment structure (i.e., move some employees to independent contractors)
2. Reduce salaries across the board
3. Reduce hours and/or benefits for lower-level staff

Instructions:

Choose one of the above options and defend this decision. Use concepts from the chapter to defend your decision. Explain why the other two options are not acceptable.

Case 9: National Football League: Not Passing Our Player Safety Expectations

Playing professional football, almost by definition, is not one of the "safest" jobs in the world, especially at the level of the U.S. National Football League (NFL) where players get injured almost every week of play. Sprained ankles, torn ligaments, concussions, and broken bones are pretty much par for the course. More than 200 concussions are reported during a typical football season.

Over the past few decades, however, retired NFL players, in particular, have been raising concerns about how repetitive head injuries/concussions sustained while playing in the NFL have deleteriously impacted them later in life. Evidence began to mount that many retired NFL players faced considerable neurological problems later in life, including issues such as permanent brain damage, dementia, and rates of Alzheimer's disease and clinical depression that are much higher than average. Some NFL players have arguably even committed suicide due to degenerative brain disease.

During 2011 and 2012, various retired NFL players brought lawsuits against the NFL with respect to this issue. The players argued that the professional football league knew or should have known the risks to NFL players due to concussions/traumatic repetitive brain injuries suffered during the NFL games and that it did not do enough to prevent these injuries. In August 2013, the NFL agreed to settle these lawsuits by paying nearly $1 billion to retired NFL players who have suffered injuries in this regard. Retired players suffering from Parkinson's or Alzheimer's diseases will receive as much as $3 million apiece, and those suffering from Lou Gehrig's disease/amyotrophic lateral sclerosis (ALS) will receive up to $5 million. All retired NFL players will be eligible for NFL-paid neurological medical monitoring and baseline testing, with $75 million allocated to pay for this. Moreover, the NFL

Professional football is greatly concerned about player safety and the effectiveness of equipment and rules in protecting players.

will also give $10 million to fund brain injury research and various education/safety programs.

Is this monetary settlement a fair one? Certainly the $1 billion number is a very significant one, with retired players potentially receiving significant individual compensation (approximately $190,000 per retired player). Also, the funds for future research could be very meaningful. Moreover, the settlement avoided potentially years of costly litigation, with likely little remedy of the situation during the ongoing litigation. That said, many felt that the NFL "got off cheap" with respect to the settlement deal. In one year, the NFL's total revenues amount to about $14 billion, and observers expect that to increase to about $25 billion by the year 2025. Clearly, the league's future revenue stream should likely be able to support these payments. Moreover, there are concerns that the agreement does not really get at the more systemic issue of making the game safer. Critics feel changes will have to start at the youth, high school, and college levels—levels of football play that involve many more individuals than the 4,800 former NFL players involved in the given lawsuits. Some also feel that the $1 billion payment will lead folks to overlook ongoing safety concerns that continue to exist. To address injuries among youth, the NFL is spending $1 million to encourage flag football at schools—a type of football that avoids collisions.

In 2017, the NFL was dealt another blow. Researchers discovered that 177 out of 202 brains from former football players who had played football sometime during their lives—including pre–high school, high school, college, and/or professional—showed evidence of brain degenerative disease. These brains were donated rather than selected at random, and the results therefore could be skewed. However, the findings suggest that concussion trauma among NFL players is much more prevalent than originally thought. This is starting to have repercussions for the football industry. The risks of suffering from permanent brain damage have already convinced some NFL players to retire early. One poll found that parents are 44 percent less likely to allow their children to play football. These additional findings may lead to more lawsuits against the NFL in the future.

Not all individuals or even NFL players feel this way, however. Some observers note that "football is football," and those playing it at all levels in a sense accept the inherent dangers involved in the game. NFL Commissioner Roger Goddell cites statistics that NFL players actually have a longer average lifespan than the average American male, although the study showing this data focused on players between 1959 and 1988. Moreover, NFL players are very well-paid professionals, with many making millions of dollars per year. Former Seattle Seahawks star cornerback Richard Sherman, for example, has strongly pointed out that NFL players have chosen their profession, and thus he feels that these types of injury concerns are to some extent overblown. Sherman observes that current NFL players are aware of all the risks and have decided to play anyway. He notes that football is a violent way to make a living, but that it is part of what is great about the game and shouldn't be watered down.

On the other hand, quarterback Brett Favre states that he has experienced memory loss that worries him, including not remembering his daughter playing youth soccer during one summer. He believes concussions have had a negative impact on his life and fears he might develop a brain disease experienced by many other athletes who have experienced hits to the head.[12]

1. To what extent should there be something of a *caveat emptor*/buyer beware when someone chooses to professionally play football in the NFL?
2. Can the NFL ever really make professional football totally safe?
3. Is playing in the NFL different from being a NASCAR driver, a police officer, or an astronaut?

Notes

1. Elaine Pofeldt, "Freelancers Now Make Up 35% of U.S. Workforce," *Forbes*, October 6, 2016, https://www.forbes.com/sites/elainepofeldt/2016/10/06/new-survey-freelance-economy-shows-rapid-growth/#3ca2d55a7c3f (accessed December 26, 2017); Upwork, "Upwork Releases First-Ever Quarterly Skills Index Revealing the Fastest-Growing Freelance Skills in the U.S.," July 7, 2016, https://www.upwork.com/press/2016/07/07/upwork-releases-first-ever-quarterly-skills-index-revealing-fastest-growing-freelance-skills-u-s/ (accessed December 26, 2017); Susan M. Heathfield, "Use the Web for Recruiting Talent," *The Balance*, February 15, 2017, https://www.thebalance.com/use-the-web-for-recruiting-talent-1918951 (accessed December 26, 2017); ZipRecruiter, "10 Simple Steps to a Great Company Career Page," ZipRecruiter blog, https://www.ziprecruiter.com/blog/10-simple-steps-to-a-great-company-career-page-on-your-website/ (accessed December 26, 2017); Jimmy Rohampton, "9 Tips for Recruiting Millennial Talent Through Social Media," *Forbes*, January 10, 2017, https://www.forbes.com/sites/jimmyrohampton/2017/01/10/9-tips-for-recruiting-millennial-talent-through-social-media/#797707c0493d (accessed December 26, 2017); Upwork, "How It Works," https://www.upwork.com/i/how-it-works/client/ (accessed December 26, 2017); Kimberlee Morrison,

"Survey: 92% of Recruiters Use Social Media to Find High-Quality Candidates," *Ad Week*, September 22, 2015, http://www.adweek.com/digital/survey-96-of-recruiters-use-social-media-to-find-high-quality-candidates/ (accessed December 26, 2017); Society for Human Resource Management, "Using Social Media for Talent Acquisition," September 20, 2017, https://www.shrm.org/hr-today/trends-and-forecasting/research-and-surveys/pages/social-media-recruiting-screening-2015.aspx (accessed December 26, 2017); Sarah K. White, "Recruiters Increasingly Rely on Social Media to Find Talent," *CIO*, May 23, 2016, https://www.cio.com/article/3073589/hiring/recruiters-increasingly-rely-on-social-media-to-find-talent.html (accessed December 26, 2017); Pew Research Center, "Mobile Fact Sheet," January 12, 2017, http://www.pewinternet.org/fact-sheet/mobile/ (accessed December 26, 2017); Laura Petrecca, "More College Grads Use Social Media to Find Jobs," *USA Today*, April 5, 2011, http://usatoday30.usatoday.com/money/workplace/2011-04-04-social-media-in-job-searches.htm (accessed December 26, 2017); Joseph Walker," LinkedIn Gets Closer to Job Seekers," *The Wall Street Journal*, September 13, 2011, http://online.wsj.com/article/SBB0001424053111904265504576568920890453258.html (accessed December 26, 2017).

2. George Anders, "The Rare Find," *Bloomberg Businessweek*, October 17–October 23, 2011, pp. 106–12; Philip Delves Broughton, "Spotting the Exceptionally Talented," *Financial Times*, October 13, 2011, https://www.ft.com/content/25dc1872-f4ba-11e0-a286-00144feab49a (accessed December 27, 2017); Joe Light, "Recruiters Rethink Online Playbook," *The Wall Street Journal*, January 18, 2011, http://online.wsj.com/article/SB10001424052748704307404576080492613858846.html (accessed December 27, 2017); Kris Maher, "A Tactical Recruiting Effort Pays Off," *The Wall Street Journal*, October 24, 2011, p. R6; Peter Cappelli, "Why Companies Aren't Getting the Employees They Need," *The Wall Street Journal*, October 24, 2011, pp. R1, R6; Jeanne Meister, "The Death of the Resume: Five Ways to Re-Imagine Recruiting," *Forbes*, July 23, 2012, http://www.forbes.com/sites/jeannemeister/2012/07/23/the-death-of-the-resume-five-ways-to-re-imagine-recruiting/ (accessed December 27, 2017); Instagram, "Salesforce.com," https://www.instagram.com/salesforcejobs/?hl=en (accessed December 27, 2017); Erin Engstrom, "Recruiting on Instagram: 4 Companies That Are Crushing It," https://recruiterbox.com/blog/recruiting-on-instagram-4-companies-crushing-it/ (accessed December 27, 2017); J. T. O'Donnell, "A Powerful Way to Use Instagram to Recruit Employees," *Inc.*, June 25, 2015, https://www.inc.com/jt-odonnell/a-powerful-way-to-use-instagram-to-recruit-employees.html (accessed December 27, 2017); Zlati Meyer and Kellie Ell, "McDonald's Looks to Snapchat to Hire 250,000 for Summer," *USA Today*, June 14, 2017, https://www.usatoday.com/story/money/business/2017/06/12/mcdonalds-hires-teens-via-snapchat/102782168/ (accessed December 27, 2017); Vineeta Sawkar, "General Mills Recruits Millennials with a High-Tech Virtual Tour," *Star Tribune*, September 15, 2015, http://www.startribune.com/general-mills-recruits-millennials-with-gopro-goggle-tour/327721891/ (accessed December 27, 2017); Dr. John Sullivan, "12 Innovative Recruiting Strategies That Savvy Companies Are Using," July 10, 2017, https://business.linkedin.com/talent-solutions/blog/recruiting-strategy/2017/12-innovative-recruiting-strategies-that-savvy-companies-are-usi (accessed December 27, 2017); Roy Maurer, "Employee Referrals Remain Top Source for Hires," *Society for Human Resource Management*, June 23, 2017, https://www.shrm.org/resourcesandtools/hr-topics/talent-acquisition/pages/employee-referrals-remains-top-source-hires.aspx (accessed December 27, 2017).

3. Procter & Gamble job website, http://us.pgcareers.com/ (accessed December 31, 2017).

4. *True v. Ladner*, 513A, 2d 257 (1986).

5. Terri Linman, "360-Degree Feedback: Weighing the Pros and Cons," http://edweb.sdsu.edu/people/arossett/pie/Interventions/3601.htm (accessed November 13, 2013).

6. Jerry Lullo, "Preparing for Relocations," *HR Magazine* 37 (October 1992): 59–63.

7. Andrew Tangel and E. Scott Reckard, "BofA cuts 1,200 mortgage jobs, with more layoffs coming," *Los Angeles Times*, October 24, 2013, http://articles.latimes.com/2013/oct/24/business/la-fi-1025-bofa-layoffs-20131025 (accessed December 31, 2017).

8. Sy Mukherjee, "The GOP Bill Repeals ObamaCare's Individual Mandate. Here's What That Means for You," *Fortune*, December 20, 2017, http://fortune.com/2017/12/20/tax-bill-individual-mandate-obamacare/ (accessed January 2, 2018).

9. Bureau of Labor Statistics, U.S. Department of Labor, "Union Members—2016," https://www.bls.gov/news.release/pdf/union2.pdf (accessed December 31, 2017).

10. Stacy Jones, "White Men Account for 72% of Corporate Leadership at 16 of the Fortune 500 Companies," *Fortune*, June 9, 2017, http://fortune.com/2017/06/09/white-men-senior-executives-fortune-500-companies-diversity-data/ (accessed December 31, 2017).

11. "PriceWaterhouseCoopers: No. 2 in the DiversityInc Top 50," *DiversityInc*, 2013, http://www.diversityinc.com/pricewaterhousecoopers/ (accessed December 31, 2017).

12. Ken Belson, "Many Ex-Players May Be Ineligible for Payment in N.F.L. Concussion Settlement," *New York Times*, October 17, 2013, http://www.nytimes.com/2013/10/18/sports/football/many-ex-players-may-be-ineligible-to-share-in-nfl-concussion-settlement.html?_r=0 (accessed December 27, 2017); Will Brinson, "Frontline PBS Doc 'League of Denial' Examines NFL Concussion Problem," *CBS Sports*, October 8, 2013, http://www.cbssports.com/nfl/eye-on-football/24051122/frontline-pbs-doc-league-o(af-denial-examines-nfl-concussion-problem (accessed December 27, 2017); Chris Chase, "NFL All-Pro Says if You Don't Like Concussions, Don't Watch Football," *USA Today*, Oct. 23, 2013, http://ftw.usatoday.com/2013/10/richard-sherman-concussions/ (accessed December 27, 2017); Andrew M. Blecher, "NFL Concussion Litigation," http://NFLconcussionlitigation.com (accessed December 27, 2017); Travis Waldron, "What Does the NFL's Concussion Settlement Mean for the Future of Football?" Think Progress, Aug. 29, 2013, https://thinkprogress.org/what-does-the-nfls-concussion-settlement-mean-for-the-future-of-football-d8650489ea7e/ (accessed December 27, 2017); Richard Sherman, "We Chose This Profession," *Sports Illustrated*, MMQB—In This Corner, Oct. 24, 2013, http://mmqb.si.com/2013/10/23/richard-sherman-seahawks-concussions-in-the-nfl/ (accessed December 27, 2017); Jacque Wilson and Stephanie Smith, "Brett Favre: Memory Lapse 'Put a Little Fear in Me,'" *CNN*, October 28, 2013, http://www.cnn.com/2013/10/25/health/brett-favre-concussions/ (accessed December 27, 2017); Michael McCann, "Will New CTE Findings Doom the NFL Concussion Settlement?" *Sports Illustrated*, August 15, 2017, https://www.si.com/nfl/2017/08/15/new-cte-study-effect-nfl-concussion-settlement (accessed December 27, 2017); Tom Huddleston Jr., "The Football Industrial Complex Is in Big Trouble," *Fortune*, September 7, 2017, http://fortune.com/2017/09/07/nfl-ncaa-football-concussion-cte/ (accessed December 27, 2017).

Organizational Change and Innovation

Source: Kheng Guan Toh/Shutterstock

After reading this chapter, you will be able to:

- Define organizational change and explain the dimensions and types of change.
- Interpret three models of change, particularly the steps involved in the comprehensive model of change.
- Determine the major causes of resistance to change and recommend how managers can deal with change resistance.
- Explain organization development (OD) and summarize the major OD interventions.
- Assess an organization's change program.

VIP Moving & Storage: More than a Moving Experience

For families and National Football League (NFL) teams, VIP Moving & Storage offers customized services to meet its customers' moving and storage needs. The company prides itself on its strong service orientation. VIP Moving offers a wide variety of moving services, including corporate moves, residential moves, packing and unpacking, furniture assembly and disassembly, and secure storage of valuables in its 50,000-square-foot storage facility. Because it is not affiliated with a major van line, it can offer personalized services in moving, packing, unpacking, storing, and setting up. It offers its customers guaranteed prices and no hidden costs.

Owner Marshall Powell Ledbetter III comes from a family of entrepreneurs. The company was started in 1932 in Columbia, Tennessee, by his grandfather under a different name. His son purchased the company, and Powell purchased the company from his father's estate in 2000 and changed the name to VIP Moving & Storage. He was only able to purchase the warehouse, however, requiring him to buy new trucks and trailers. By owning its own fleet, the company is able to offer the ultimate in customization. VIP Moving has gone from offering services in the Nashville, Tennessee, area to expanding nationwide. It has become so successful that it recently opened up a facility in Long Beach, California, in its attempt to go national.

VIP Storage tries to live up to its name by offering VIP services to all of its customers. When a client first contacts VIP Moving, a professional moving consultant from the company will work with the client to answer any questions and provide a free quote for the move. If the client chooses to use VIP's moving services, the company sends its trucks, which are equipped with state-of-the-art equipment to ensure safe transportation of all belongings. To ensure the best for the customer, VIP Moving provides the same people for the customer's move from start to finish. The customer deals with the same packers, drivers, and movers throughout the move. This hands-on continuity allows VIP Moving to provide customers with a smoother moving experience. Customer feedback for VIP Moving has been positive, and it has received an A+ rating from the Better Business Bureau.

VIP Moving & Storage is not only popular among customers moving from one house to another. It has also caught the attention of NFL teams. For more than 20 years, it has been the official mover for the Tennessee Titans and has also worked with the New York

Source: Lenka Horavova/Shutterstock

Jets, Los Angeles Rams, Seattle Seahawks, and New England Patriots. The company's movers will meet the teams at the airport to transport their equipment, set up the locker rooms, and tear down the rooms when finished. The organization is highly unique, with only a small handful of moving and transportation firms in the United States providing such a high level of customized services.

VIP Moving is an excellent role model for organizational change and innovation in small firms. The firm has seen constant change as the moving service is now in the hands of the third generation. Transportation technology and storage facilities have been updated to meet the requirements of customers. VIP Moving has acquired the most advanced and energy-efficient trucks available. Providing moving services for NFL teams has opened a new market that requires a level of service beyond what is required for moving families. There can be no delays or mistakes in getting an NFL team to the required location on time.

In addition, VIP will go to any location to move players and coaches, ensuring the same level of service as the firm shows in moving the team's equipment. Integrity best describes the organizational culture at VIP. Everything is done to assure a service quality level that is higher than that of the competition. Because the moving and storage industry is very competitive, VIP depends on a good reputation as well as social media posts to reach its customers. VIP is committed to offering the best service experience for moving and storage—one box at a time.[1]

Introduction

VIP Moving is in many ways an almost perfect paradigm of organizational change and development. As seen in that situation, change is influenced by a number of forces, both inside and outside of companies, and companies' ability to deal with and shape these forces determines their ultimate success. Jean B. Keffeler, an organizational change consultant, says that American companies can be either agents or victims of these changes: "We will either choose change or chase it."[2] Choosing change will not guarantee success, but ignoring it will almost surely guarantee failure.

This chapter deals with the process of organizational change. We will discuss briefly some of the major forces influencing organizational change and delve into the steps and techniques managers may use to deal with the process of planned change. We will conclude with a brief overview of some of the people-oriented approaches to planned change that have collectively been labeled organizational development.

The Nature of Organizational Change

There is one certainty in organizations: they must undergo change to survive. **Organizational change** can be defined as any modification in the behaviors or ideas of an organization or its units. A successful company such as Apple Inc. did not become one of the most valuable global brands by trying to maintain the status quo. Rather, it constantly monitors the environment to understand changes so it can adapt.

organizational change: Any modification in the behaviors or ideas of an organization or its units.

One important aspect of organizational change is that such modifications do not just happen: Something causes them to occur. To understand change and how best to manage it, we must be aware of some of the major forces causing change.

Forces Causing Organizational Change

Earlier in the text, we explored the various internal and external environmental forces that may affect an organization. You will remember that external forces include technological, economic, sociocultural, political-legal, and international influences, as well as customers, suppliers, competitors, substitutes, and potential new entrants to the industry. The internal forces include the owners, managers, employees, and board of directors. How managers respond to these forces may determine the success or failure of their entire business enterprise. A few examples of the pervasive impact of these forces will demonstrate the importance of responding to change.

External Forces

Examples of the influence of technology on business organizations abound. For instance, the U.S. Postal Service lost about $6 billion in fiscal year 2016, which actually was a big improvement from some earlier fiscal years. It was not all that many years ago when the Postal Service broke even each year or even made a small profit. However, as Americans increasingly turn to electronic forms of communication, first-class mail volume in particular continues to decrease by billions of pieces of mail per year. Indeed, it has only been the growth of online shopping and some delivery deals the Postal Service has made with Amazon.com and others that have helped lessen the flow of red ink.[3]

The U.S. Postal Service struggles to find a business model to address massive losses as more and more customers shop and pay bills online.

Source: Spiroview Inc/Shutterstock

Internal Forces

The major internal forces for change are owners, top management, and employees, primarily through internal feedback mechanisms. These forces, although powerful in their own right, often respond to what is happening in the external environment. Often the combination of external forces, in concert with internal forces, generates tremendous impetus for change.

Sometimes a top manager notices something in the internal operation of the business or in the external environment, and exerts tremendous forces for change. Management professor Noel Tichy says, "All corporate revolutions are started from the top. It's crucial to form from the beginning a small, tight group of people 100 percent dedicated to implementing the plan."[4] Home Depot faced major challenges under former CEO Robert Nardelli. Even during the housing boom, Home Depot's sales increased at half the rate of major competitor Lowe's. After a new CEO took over the leadership position, Home Depot implemented many internal changes, some of them revolutionary. It began marketing more toward women (Home Depot was traditionally considered a man's retailer), remodeled stores to appeal to this target market, stressed strong customer service, and invested in new technologies to create an enhanced customer and employee experience. Recently, Home Depot has not only had strong earnings, but some stock market analysts have been rating Home Depot as a slightly stronger "buy" than rival Lowe's.[5]

Sometimes the collective actions of workers, as in a strike, can start the machinery for change rolling. When the United Steelworkers Union went on strike at Globe Metallurgical, one of the largest producers of silicon metal, managers and a skeleton crew of replacement workers ran the plant, from working on the maintenance crew—as did then president Arden Sims—to running a furnace. Without the structure imposed by union rules and because of the labor shortage, Sims and his team had to be innovative in finding a more efficient way to run the plant. Within a few weeks of the strike, production had actually increased 20 percent. Self-managed work teams developed; the first-line supervisor position became unnecessary; the company began making a profit; and within a year, the plant was operating with just 120 workers, about a third of the prestrike total. All of these changes grew out of the necessity caused by the union walkout.[6]

Sometimes internal feedback mechanisms, as monitored by different organizational members, can signal that the organization needs to change in response to one or more environmental forces. Attitude surveys, performance data, employee performance evaluations, and grievances may indicate that there is a gap in performance, requiring that behaviors or activities need to be changed to close it. A **performance gap** is the differ-

performance gap: The difference between an organization's desired and actual performance levels.

Strikes can be a way for labor to let management know that they are unhappy with current working conditions or plans for hiring and layoffs.

Source: Richard Thornton/Shutterstock

ence between an organization's desired and actual performance levels. One of the best approaches to change is to set demanding standards of performance for all operations, measure performance against those standards, and hold managers accountable to them. PepsiCo, for example, has traditionally set a 20 percent profit standard for the company, with managers being held accountable for this standard. Although this may seem obvious, organizations often have both poor measures of actual performance and a weak understanding of what demanding standards should be or look like.

Dimensions of Organizational Change

Organizations change in a number of different ways, along several different dimensions that often relate to one another. When examining any organization that is experiencing a performance gap, these dimensions—extent of planning, degree of change, degree of learning, target of change, and amount of organization being emphasized—can help provide useful guidelines along which to diagnose causes and then to structure a change program.

Degree of Planning

Organizational change varies along a continuum with regard to the extent to which it is planned. At one end is **reactive change**, which occurs when organizational members react spontaneously to external and internal forces but do little to modify these forces or their behaviors. At the other end, **planned change** involves the deliberate structuring of operations and behaviors, often in anticipation of environmental forces. Most organizations fall somewhere in the middle. Businesses are too complex to have totally planned change, but at least some planning for change occurs in all organizations or the ensuing chaos would quickly destroy them.

Experts differ about how much change can be planned, and examples can be found at many points on the continuum. For example, JetBlue Airways has increasingly been working to use social media more effectively to respond to customer complaints. It started a dedicated corporate social media support team in 2010, and today that team has about 30 members. These social media experts respond to passenger complaints via both Twitter and Facebook messages (JetBlue has over 2 million Twitter followers). The airline also regularly posts relevant information on its blog. JetBlue is committed to being on the cutting edge of using new social media to help and respond to its passengers.[7] Table 10.1 describes the dimensions of organizational change involved in JetBlue's decision.

Some research suggests that many managers are fooling themselves in their belief that they can truly plan major organization transformations. However, it is still important that managers take steps to set up conditions that permit and even encourage necessary change to occur.[8]

Managers can take specific steps to facilitate change, and these steps can be learned; however, there are no guarantees that any specific action will always result in successful

reactive change: A situation in which organizational members react spontaneously to external and internal forces but do little to modify these forces or their behaviors.

planned change: The deliberate structuring of operations and behaviors, often in anticipation of environmental forces.

TABLE 10.1 Dimensions of Organizational Change for JetBlue Social Media Decision

Dimensions	Examples
Degree of Planning	Decisions regarding company use of social media
Degree of Planned Change	How extensively to use social media
Degree of Organizational Members' Involvement in Learning How to Change	How many employees are directly/indirectly involved
Target of Change	Customers/passengers
Amount of Organization Being Emphasized	Controls related to employee use of social media on-duty/off-duty, etc.

change. In any event, planned change increases the odds of success for a manager and is, thus, the focus of this chapter.

Degree of Planned Change

incremental change: A relatively small change in processes and behaviors within just one or a few systems or levels of the organization.

quantum change: A large-scale planned change in how the firm operates.

Planned change also differs along another continuum, that of degree of change. Changes may range from incremental to quantum.[9] **Incremental change**, relatively small change, involves fine-tuning processes and behaviors within just one or a few systems or levels of the organization. It occurs within the context of the organization's current structure, strategy, and culture. For example, Procter & Gamble announced that it was grouping its Global Business Units into four industry sectors to become more efficient and productive.[10] Because no major organizational restructuring occurred, this resulted in only incremental change. **Quantum change**, or large-scale planned change, involves significantly altering how the firm operates, usually by altering multiple organization levels and several of the dimensions of structure, culture, reward systems, strategy, and work design.[11]

Degree of Organizational Members' Involvement in Learning How to Change

A third dimension deals with the degree to which organizational members are actively involved in learning how to plan and implement change while engaging in solving an existing problem. Author Peter Senge describes the "learning organization," discussed earlier in chapter 2, as being engaged in continuous experimentation and feedback in an ongoing examination of the way it goes about addressing and solving problems.[12] In contrast, some organizations focus on solving immediate problems without examining the appropriateness of current learning behaviors. Using the company examples already cited, Globe Metallurgical probably comes closest to a learning organization because of its strong learn-as-you-go orientation.

Target of Change

Organizational change programs—systematic planned change efforts—can also vary with respect to the hierarchical level or functional area at which the change is targeted. Some changes are designed to influence top managers or the relationship between manager and employee. For instance, Adobe eliminated its annual performance review and instead chose more easygoing "check-in" conversations and feedback. In other words, the firm encourages managers and employees to provide ongoing feedback to one another. This change was implemented to improve relationships between managers and employees as well as help employees gain a better understanding of their strengths and weaknesses.[13] Other change programs might involve basic skills learning, such as customer service techniques, for lower-level employees only. Others could involve restructuring a marketing or R&D division without any planned change in other areas. Changes planned for one

Change in the organization can often require additional training for employees.

Archer Daniels Midland Links Farm, Factory, and Table

Archer Daniels Midland (ADM), one of the world's largest agricultural processors, is a vital link between farm, factory, and table. The Chicago-based multinational rings up almost $62 billion in annual net sales of soybeans, corn gluten, and other agricultural products provided by farmers worldwide. ADM's focus on agriculture and energy requires the adjustment of organizational behavior while operating in a very dynamic and competitive environment. External forces such as changes in technology related to innovation in the supply chain, online purchasing, and digital marketing are complex and require changes in tactics and strategy. Innovation is driven by keeping an eye on consumers and business customers and responding to their desires.

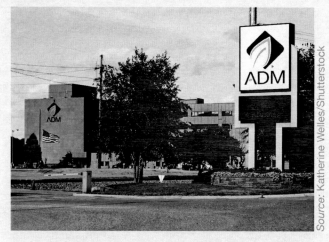

Source: Katherine Welles/Shutterstock

ADM's clients include several well-known companies. Unilever, for instance, purchases oil from soybeans procured and processed by ADM. Unilever uses this oil to produce its mayonnaise products. As ADM's executives know, Unilever and other clients are concerned with more than just price. To stay ahead of demand for sustainable agricultural processes, ADM has partnered with Unilever to enroll its farmers in the Iowa Sustainable Soy Fieldprint Project to monitor factors like soil conservation and land use. In the project's first year, 43 farms with land totaling more than 44,000 acres were enrolled. ADM also introduced a cost-share initiative to soybean farmers in Iowa to increase the pool of farms with sustainably grown soybeans and provide financial assistance to farmers. These efforts to deliberately structure operations and behaviors in anticipation of environmental forces are a good example of planned change. The initiative works hand-in-hand with Unilever's Sustainable Living Plan, which includes a commitment to source all agricultural raw materials sustainably in the coming years. These factors make ADM an ideal soybean oil supplier for Unilever's Hellmann's mayonnaise. The emphasis on documentation allows companies like Unilever to measure progress and improvements, making it easier for all parties in the supply chain to communicate with customers and stakeholders.

To support its global operations and growth, ADM buys from 220,000 suppliers and processes more than 2.5 million payments yearly. The company also manages a vast land, water, and rail transportation network to ensure that raw materials and processed products arrive when and where scheduled. Such a large organization requires ADM's management to make changes that may impact company stakeholders, both positively and negatively. Recently, ADM announced internal organizational changes likely to encounter resistance. The firm planned a series of layoffs to streamline the company's efforts and redistribute resources as it struggled with its grain-trading business. The agricultural giant employs about 32,000 employees in 160 countries, with more than 4,000 employees in Decatur, Illinois. Juan Luciano, ADM's chairman and CEO, spoke to shareholders about cutting costs and selling assets as a way to make a "strong recovery." Additionally, the company closed its energy-trading operations and changed staff in its Switzerland office, which handles commodities like wheat and soybeans. ADM emailed affected employees to tell them about the decision and claims it is handling layoffs respectfully and with consideration for employees. One way it is trying to overcome resistance is by offering some eligible employees early retirement. If these changes continue, ADM will have to work hard to overcome resistance from employees as it introduces incremental changes and makes small adjustments to fine-tune the organization.

In response to changing external forces, ADM is also making changes to its product lines. As part of its ever-changing nature, the company recently introduced Nutriance, a new range of wheat protein concentrates that are vegetarian- and vegan-friendly—a business market where it sees great potential for future profit. The increase in consumers following a more holistic approach to their health has been an ongoing external force that has prompted ADM to expand its portfolio to meet the needs of health-conscious consumers. Looking ahead, ADM is exploring natural flavors and nutritional ingredients such as protein and vitamins. By recognizing potential new areas of profitability, ADM demonstrates that it is carefully monitoring the external environment and changing accordingly.[14]

Chapter 10 Organizational Change and Innovation **301**

level or area, though, often have an impact on other parts of the organization, as we will discuss shortly.

Amount of Organization Being Emphasized

Finally, organizational change can differ with regard to the extent of "organization" being emphasized or how regulated and structured its activities may be. Some organizations are overly organized and bureaucratized and need "loosening up," while others suffer from poor coordination and may be underorganized. Fairly young and rapidly growing organizations often suffer from underorganization and may need to emphasize structure, rules, and stronger norms to lend stability to the chaos. Many organizations, for example, are struggling with to what extent employee off-duty use of social media should be controlled, particularly with respect to any off-duty references the employee may make with respect to the organization.

Types of Organizational Change

There are also several major types of planned change that vary according to the area of emphasis for the change: changes in strategy, organizational structure or design, technology, and human processes and culture. Note that these categories are not mutually exclusive.

Changing Strategy

Changing a company's strategy involves changing its fundamental approach to doing business—the markets it will target, the kinds of products it will sell, how they will be sold, its overall strategic orientation (cost, differentiation, etc.), the level of global activity, and its various partnerships and other joint-business arrangements. Changing strategy involves an attempt to align a company's resources with the various environmental forces recently discussed. Many examples abound in which companies have made major strategic changes. The Washington Post Company no longer publishes *The Washington Post* and has adopted a completely new corporate strategy, including changing its name.

Changing Structure and Design

When a company alters its structure, it may change its departmentalization, hierarchical reporting relationships, line-staff relationships, and overall design. One frequent reason for restructuring in today's environment is to meet customer needs more effectively. Sallie Mae, the largest student loan provider in the United States, broke up into two businesses. One business services government-backed student loans, whereas the more profitable business focuses on private student loans. Splitting up into two businesses helps Sallie Mae focus on two distinct target markets.[15] The quality revolution in America, increased competition, and cost consciousness will likely result in continued downsizing and streamlining of larger business, resulting in even more structural changes.[16]

Changing Technology

Many companies are introducing technological changes in their manufacturing or service operations to keep pace with massive environmental changes and competitive challenges. Computers, for example, have radically changed the very nature of business, even in very small operations, by speeding up routine activities and providing fast access to huge amounts of information. Robotics is another area that is helping many large manufacturers improve efficiency. Companies in Asia, in particular, are increasingly turning to robots to play a major role in the manufacturing process.[17]

Sometimes new technology is the focus of the business—the product itself—and not just a way to improve making a good or speed up a service. The Xerox Corporation, for example, restructured its business model to move far beyond making copier machines. Its former CEO was quick to note that the highway toll booth E-Z Pass process was developed by Xerox.[18]

Changing People Processes and Culture

Changing people processes involves changing the processes of communicating, motivating, leading, and interacting in groups. It may entail changing how problems are solved, how people learn new processes and skills, and even the very nature of how they perceive themselves, the organization, and their jobs. Major organizational change may involve altering the organization's entire culture.

Some people changes may involve only incremental changes or small improvements in a process. For example, many organizations undergo leadership training, which might teach managers how to communicate more openly with employees, use praise and other rewards to motivate performance, resolve interpersonal conflicts and deal with disruptive employees, and encourage more employee participation. Other programs might concentrate on team processes by teaching both managers and employees how to work together effectively to solve problems. Still other programs might strive to enhance union-management relations or to learn how to deal with an organization's existing power structure, which makes up what is often called the informal organization. We will take a closer look at some of these approaches later in this chapter.

Major organizational change could entail dealing with all the people processes as well as changes in such human resource systems as rewards and compensation, training and development, selection, and performance appraisal. For major change to succeed, fundamental alterations must occur in three areas: (1) coordination or teamwork, including coordination between departments and between labor and management; (2) commitment to a high level of effort, cooperation, and planned actions; and (3) competencies, meaning improved conceptual, analytical, and interpersonal skills in both labor and management. Most planned change programs target only one, or at best, two of these areas, while all three are essential for major change to occur.[19]

There are numerous examples of major change programs that have focused on changing the way people function. The U.S. Secret Service, which protects the president of the United States and other top officials, has, for example, traditionally had a somewhat laid-back approach to employee conduct while they are overseas. Recent scandals, however, involving among other things Secret Service agents hiring prostitutes while in South America, have changed the agency's culture. New rules bar agents from bringing foreign nationals back to their hotel rooms or drinking alcohol within 10 hours of their shift.[20]

Models of Planned Change

Managers who want to plan organizational change may find it helpful to have a model of how the change process works. In this section, we will briefly review two basic models of change, discuss some implications of each, and then delve more deeply into a comprehensive model that could encompass most change programs. Table 10.2 describes the models of planned change.

Lewin's Model of Change

One of the earliest and most fundamental models of change was provided by behavioral scientist Kurt Lewin. Lewin viewed the change process as a modification of the forces that

TABLE 10.2 Models of Planned Change

Model	Description
Lewin's Model of Change	Unfreezing, moving, refreezing
Congruence Model of Change	Interaction of inputs/processes causing change
Comprehensive Model of Planned Change	Step-by-step plan for change

FIGURE 10.1
Lewin's Model for Implementing Change

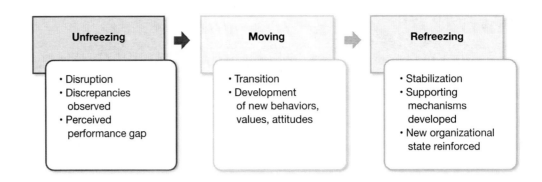

Unfreezing	Moving	Refreezing
• Disruption • Discrepancies observed • Perceived performance gap	• Transition • Development of new behaviors, values, attitudes	• Stabilization • Supporting mechanisms developed • New organizational state reinforced

keep a system's behaviors stable. He depicted the level of any behavior or attitude existing at a given time as a function of "driving forces," which are pushing for change in behavior, and "restraining forces," those striving to maintain the status quo. When these forces are about equal, Lewin said a state of quasi-stationary equilibrium exists. He devised a technique called "force field analysis" that depicts the driving and restraining forces—the real conditions of people, organization, or environment—in a situation that keeps it stable.

Lewin's model of major change grew out of this force field concept. He describes change as consisting of the following three phases (see Figure 10.1):

unfreezing: Involves disrupting the forces maintaining the existing state or level of behavior.

1. **Unfreezing** involves disrupting the forces maintaining the existing state (state A) or level of behavior. This might be done by introducing new information to show discrepancies between state A and one desired by the organization—that is, a performance gap. The performance gap for the American car manufacturers got so big that the "Big Three" finally were unfrozen.

moving: A transition period during which the behaviors of the organization or department are shifted to a new level.

2. **Moving** entails a transition period (state B) during which the behaviors of the organization or department are shifted to a new level (desired state C). It involves developing new behaviors, values, and attitudes.

refreezing: Stabilizes the organization at a new state of behavioral equilibrium.

3. **Refreezing** stabilizes the organization at a new state of behavioral equilibrium (state C). This is accomplished through the use of supporting mechanisms that reinforce the new organizational state, such as culture, norms, policies, and structures.[21] Making total quality management teams a part of standard operating procedures would exemplify refreezing.

Thus, Lewin viewed change as the adjustment of driving and restraining forces in order to facilitate movement to a new equilibrium state which is then reinforced and stabilized. This model, therefore, suggests that managers should find ways to unfreeze the existing equilibrium before any change will occur.

Congruence Model of Change

congruence model of change: An outgrowth of the systems approach to organizational theory, emphasizes the interrelationships between the various parts of an organization and how change in one part will cause reactive changes in other parts.

The **congruence model of change**, an outgrowth of the systems approach to organizational theory, emphasizes the interrelationships between the various parts of an organization and how change in one part will cause reactive changes in other parts. In the congruence model, inputs may include raw materials, environmental factors, history, customer feedback, and the organization's strategy. Processes consist of technology, human resource activities, culture, structure, and measurement systems. Outputs are all those things that reflect the firm's effectiveness: its finished products, group commitment and cohesiveness, and such individual outcomes as job satisfaction, personal performance, and attendance.[22]

The key aspect of the congruence model is that system elements, both inputs and processes, interact with one another such that changes in one part of the system can cause radical changes in another part of the system. For example, a change in the nature of raw materials or other inputs into the system may necessitate a change in the organizational and job structures, as well as in human resource processes, and may ultimately influence the outputs in terms of product quality or job satisfaction. Likewise, a change in technology may result in a change in culture, structure, and any or all of the other transformation processes.

There are several important implications of the systems approach to diagnosing and implementing change. Managers need to recognize that changes in one area may cause unintended changes in another, as the overall system seeks to regain equilibrium. Also, because systems tend to seek equilibrium, managers can expect that some changes may be resisted or even nullified by a lack of change in the rest of the system. For example, taking managers offsite for training in participative management may not result in actual change back on the job if the structure, the informal organization, and human resource systems and culture remain unchanged. A major implication is that, for significant change to occur, managers may have to intentionally change all or a number of the transformational processes simultaneously and in support of one another so that the new configurations work in harmony to exact improved outputs.

Technological improvements may result in organizational change.

A number of the organizations we have discussed thus far have attacked the change process while recognizing the interrelationship of change variables. Home Depot, for example, realized that targeting women more effectively would not only require the company to release female-oriented advertising but also to redesign stores to be more appealing to this demographic and improve customer service.

Comprehensive Model of Planned Change

The **comprehensive model of planned change**, a step-by-step plan for implementing major change, encompasses all of the facets of change discussed thus far and more.[23] It includes a set of activities managers must engage in to manage the change process effectively: recognizing the need for change, motivating change, creating a vision, developing political support, managing the transition, and sustaining momentum for the change (Figure 10.2).

comprehensive model of planned change: A step-by-step plan for implementing major change.

Recognizing the Need for Change

The change process begins with someone recognizing a need for change after scanning the organization's environment. We have already discussed some of the forces that may prompt a need for change, as well as some of the feedback mechanisms that may suggest

FIGURE 10.2

Comprehensive Model of Planned Change

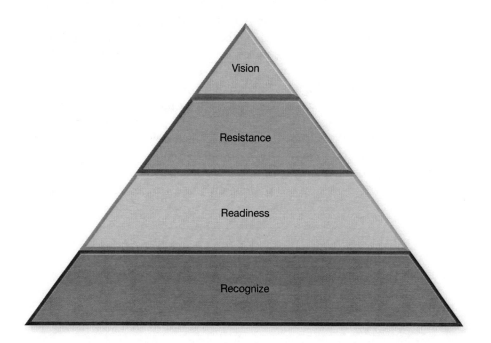

Vision

Resistance

Readiness

Recognize

needed directions for change. Recognition of the need for change may occur at the top management level or in peripheral parts of an organization, but experts disagree on where the change is most likely to start. Once the need for change is recognized, the manager must motivate change by preparing people for the changes they will face and overcoming their natural resistance to change.

Creating Readiness for Change

Preparing people for change is similar to Lewin's unfreezing step. It entails primarily bringing dissatisfaction with the current state to the surface. For instance, because of the weakening global economy, customers have been less likely to pay premium prices for intellectual technology initiatives. This puts India-based Infosys at a disadvantage as a core strategy was to sustain high profit margins. The CEO of Infosys acknowledged that changing its strategies will be rough and even painful for the company, but that it is necessary for survival.[24] Shareholder dissatisfaction with company performance in part led the Washington Post Company to sell its newspaper business. The company's recent purchase of a firm in the highly profitable healthcare industry also represents a part of the "unfreezing" in regards to the company's identity.

Preparing people for change requires direct and forceful feedback about the negatives of the present situation, as compared to the desired future state, and sensitizing people to the forces of change that exist in their environment. Managers can make themselves more sensitive to pressures for change by surrounding themselves with "devil's advocates," using networks of people and organizations with different perspectives and views, visiting other organizations in order to be exposed to new ideas, and using external standards of performance, such as a competitor's progress or benchmarks.[25]

Overcoming Resistance to Change

When change occurs, there will almost always be resistance, and understanding why resistance occurs can give managers some insight into how to deal with it.

Sources of Resistance to Change

Some of the most common reasons for resisting change include uncertainty and insecurity, reaction against the way change is presented, threats to vested interests, cynicism and lack of trust, perceptual differences, and lack of understanding.

People need a certain amount of stability and security in their lives, and change can present unknowns that produce anxiety. Employees may worry about their ability to meet new job demands or even fear losing their jobs. Given the recent era of company downsizing, it is logical and understandable that most employees view change negatively. They may believe they will be unable to learn new required skills, or they may simply have personalities that cause them to dislike ambiguity. Change often results in altered work practices and work group relationships. Workers may resist restructuring attempts and continue to conduct business as they did before if the fabric of their social relationships is threatened.

Resistance to change may grow out of a reaction against being controlled or loss of autonomy. If a change seems arbitrarily imposed or unreasonable, if management uses little tact in implementing or announcing it, or if it is poorly timed, negative reactions may result. If a company had encouraged participation and empowerment but stopped because of a tough economy or bad business cycle, that kind of change is likely to be severely resented.

Some changes may result in employees losing their positions of power; labor union situations provide an excellent example of concern over such loss. A top executive of the Inland Steel Company described the painstakingly slow progress in trying to implement a total quality management (TQM) program at his company as the United Steelworkers scrutinized every move management tried to make to improve operations.

Employees who have been treated unkindly or at best indifferently by management over the years are likely to face any change with skepticism. At Inland Steel, workers

Whereas empowerment of employees to make more decisions can be a positive in many organizations, a dramatic change in leadership and employee responsibilities can be met with resistance.

were cynical because they were accustomed to hearing management pay "lip service" to employee empowerment without seeing any meaningful change. Years of traditional hierarchical management may cause workers anywhere to be very skeptical when management proposes moving into more progressive organizational practices, such as TQM and empowerment. At Inland Steel, employees were eventually empowered to find ways to improve yields. Internal reforms, along with a weak dollar and a long-term value orientation, helped Inland Steel bounce back to profitability. Inland Steel Company caught the attention of Ispat International N.V., which later acquired the company.[26]

Sometimes people resist change because they perceive the situation differently from those trying to institute the change. They may perceive that no change is warranted or that a different type of change would be more effective based either on a different diagnosis of a problem or a different opinion about what should be done. Employees and supervisors in one large manufacturing plant told their corporate engineers that the new design for a production line would not work. The company spent nearly $300,000 changing the line anyway and, sure enough, the new line did not work. Managers should recognize that workers' perceptions of a situation may be more accurate than their own because of their proximity to it. In some cases, resistance to a bad change can ultimately save the company much in time and money.

One situation where there might be particular resistance to change is when an organization attempts to introduce a new **innovation**, or a new product, method, process, or approach. In order for any innovation to successfully occur in an organization, significant organizational change needs to occur. For instance, the successful Apple innovations of today, such as iTunes, the iPad, and the iPod, were not developed without significant organizational change. Although Apple started off in the 1970s as an innovative company with revolutionary new products, it stagnated in the late 1990s. When co-founder Steve Jobs returned as CEO, he recognized that major organizational changes were needed to return Apple to its status as an innovative company. He simplified product matrixes, placed renewed emphasis on product development, and created a top-down culture of accountability. As part of this change, employees were made to feel as if they were part of something greater than themselves. These changes helped Apple branch out into the consumer electronics market and develop revolutionary innovations that would change the music, computer, and mobile phone industries (among others). Later, the firm changed its name from Apple Computer to Apple Inc. to signify its move into consumer electronics.[27]

innovation: The act of introducing a new product, method, process, or approach.

Chapter 10 Organizational Change and Innovation   307

Finally, resistance may stem from a lack of understanding of the change, including its need, nature, or implications for individuals. When the change process is not clearly presented, people tend to fill in the information gaps with rumors and speculation, often assuming the worst in terms of personal impact. On the other hand, as Inland Steel and Apple demonstrate, informing employees of reasons for the change, providing them with more responsibilities, creating a shared vision, and developing a strong corporate culture are a few of the ways managers can overcome resistance to change.

Reducing Resistance to Change

Research has identified a number of different strategies that managers may apply to deal with resistance to change, including education and communication, participation and involvement, facilitation and support, negotiation and agreement, manipulation, co-optation, and coercion (Table 10.3). Managers *try* to match a strategy to the demands of a situation to overcome resistance or to manage it with minimal disruption. Factors worth considering are the amount and type of change being attempted; the power of the resisters; the nature, cause, and form of the resistance; and the short- and long-term effects of the strategy.

One of the primary tactics used to help people deal with the anxiety of change is education and communication. Consultant Jean Keffeler says that "the amount of communication required to allay organizational anxiety in times of unusual change, even if the change is perceived as positive, is enormous. People have an insatiable need to hear what's going on and what it means to them?"[28] Communication is key.

In the long run, getting employee participation in change decisions and increased involvement in all aspects of the change may be the single best method to overcome resistance. Participation increases understanding of the change process, enhances feelings of control and autonomy, and provides for employee input that can make the change work better. It reduces uncertainty and often allows for the maintenance of social relationships during the change. Once the change is finally complete, a sense of ownership discourages resistance and increases commitment to making the change successful. At the Xerox Corporation, for example, some employees historically resisted the company's movement away from its nuts-and-bolts copier machine business. To change people's minds in this regard, company executives said they had to get employees to "align and feel engaged" and get "passionate" about what they do.[29]

TABLE 10.3 Methods for Dealing with Resistance to Change

Method	Description
Education and communication	Inform employees about the need for change and communicate the potential positive outcomes
Employee participation	Get employees involved in change decisions to increase understanding and increase commitment
Managerial support	Provide stress counseling, special training, and simply good listening to reduce fear of change
Negotiation	Making concessions in an area not related to the change, or distributing perks that help make the change easier
Manipulation	Selectively distributing information to control the perception of a change
Co-optation	Having resistant individuals join the change team—specifically to reduce their power to resist, rather than to truly participate
Coercion	Threaten punishment for resistance to change

When anxiety and fear cause resistance, management can offer support in the form of stress counseling, special training, and simply good listening. Unfortunately, most organizations do a bad job with respect to stress counseling and listening. Managers should acknowledge the legitimacy of the anxiety and discomfort, whereas many managers intensify anxiety by acting startled that employees would not readily accept a change. Accepting employees' discomfort and helping them deal with it can help management gain commitment to the change. Training in change management, coping mechanisms, stress management, and career self-management will facilitate the change process.[30]

Sometimes management can negotiate an exchange of something in return for acceptance of a change. Making concessions in an area not related to the change, or distributing perks that help make the change easier, can help overcome resistance. Because of strong union resistance, changes at Inland Steel were negotiated at almost every phase of change and over nearly all issues related to job design, work team design, the compensation system, and even transition team makeup. Although changes took longer under these conditions, management recognized the real power of the union to undermine any change attempt of which it disapproved, as well as the union's power to help change occur. Negotiation and participation slowly overcame some of the resistance.[31]

Manipulation and co-optation are sometimes used when other tactics will not work or have been tried unsuccessfully. Manipulation occurs when information and decisions are selectively distributed to control the perception of a change. Co-optation involves having resistant individuals join the change team—specifically to reduce their power to resist, rather than to truly participate. If employees recognize the manipulation or co-optation, however, even greater resistance can occur and ultimately make the change even more difficult. In universities, it is a common practice for deans to appoint faculty "troublemakers" to advisory committees in areas where they might resist a dean's proposed change. This co-opting makes the resisters part of the change process and minimizes their impact, but keeps them from complaining about not being involved or about their loss of autonomy. There is sometimes a fine line between participation in the change process and co-optation. A real danger occurs with this tactic if it is obvious or superficial. Imagine the reaction if John or Robert Kennedy had tried in 1963 to co-opt the resistance of Martin Luther King, Jr., by offering him a government job during the civil rights movement.

Coercion is sometimes used when managers will not or cannot take the time to implement less authoritarian tactics. The obvious danger with the use of real or implied threats or punishment is the antagonism and further resistance that are generated—sometimes very subtly—and the damage that it can do to the relationship between the change agent and those resisting the change. Many progressive managers reject the use of coercion, as well as manipulation and co-optation, on moral and ethical, as well as practical, grounds. These techniques are not consistent with the more open, ethical, and positive climates their companies are trying to create.

Creating a Vision

Managers can facilitate change by clearly defining and communicating their vision of where their firms are headed. Applying Lewin's model, this means knowing what the desired future state C will look like. That mental picture can be fairly general—perhaps being a lean, flexible organization—or it can be quite specific—such as one multinational company's vision of having sales forces of a certain size placed on each of five major continents by the year 2020.

The Washington Post Company, for example, has created a vision of being a more diversified corporation than it has been in the past. Transformational leaders, as discussed elsewhere in the text, inspire with their visions of the future. John F. Kennedy said in 1961 that we would reach the moon in that decade, inspiring a space program and a nation. Martin Luther King, Jr.'s, "dream" of equality in his lifetime inspired an entire race.

A research study that surveyed several hundred change agents (those who initiate or foster change) found that the single most positive facilitator of a change program is

Employees can be motivated by tying rewards to performance and educating them about the mission of the organization.

"creating a shared vision with employees of what the organization will look like when the program is completed."[32] The ability to visualize and communicate the desired future state is therefore crucial to planned change. Helpful mechanisms include a clear mission statement, a specific statement of desired performance and human outcomes, a clear explanation of processes that will facilitate the outcomes (for example, rewards being based on performance), and midpoint goals to keep motivation high and to provide feedback.[33]

Developing Political Support

We can picture organizations as political systems composed of different groups competing for power. Managers of different functional areas compete for resources and influence, so each develops his or her own sources of power. Workers compete with management over who will determine the structure of jobs and overtime and other work issues. For change to be successful, leaders of change must identify key stakeholders and then develop support within the key political groups.[34] They can use various sources of power and change strategies to generate support from these players. Once the key leaders are brought on board, they can in turn generate energy in support of a change. Raymond Smith, former CEO of Bell Atlantic (now Verizon), used the term "shadow of the leader" to depict the role of leaders who were to cast their shadows over the organization by modeling desired behaviors. JetBlue has made its ability to respond to customers with complaints on a "real time" basis via social media a part of its whole corporate "DNA," with support directly from the top of the organization all the way down.

Leaders can also use symbols and language to facilitate change. Researchers are now exploring the importance of the use of metaphors to diagnose organizational functioning.[35] For example, picturing a top executive group as "a basketball team that sometimes plays together, but often has one player hog the ball," can help the group understand a problem it may be having with one strong member dominating the group and its subsequent effects on other group members. Using symbolic team names can also help people focus on change.

Managing the Transition

transition state: The period during which the organization learns the behaviors needed to reach the desired future state.

While the organization moves from the current state to its desired future state, it will go through a period of change, or "moving" in Lewin's terminology. This **transition state** is the period during which the organization learns the behaviors needed to reach the desired future state. This can be a period of extreme disruption and must be effectively managed, or chaos can occur and the desired future state never met. During the transition, the organization needs to develop and use feedback mechanisms to ensure that changes really are happening as planned. These can include surveys, sensing groups, and consultant interviews, as well as existing informal communication channels. Three major activities are required during the transition: activity planning, commitment planning, and management structures.[36]

Activity Planning

Activity planning refers to designing the road map and noting specific events and activities that must be timed and integrated to produce the change. Change expert David Nadler says that, at this stage, change leaders should use "multiple and consistent leverage points." Growing out of systems theory and the congruence model, his idea is that a number of different processes (leverage points) must be changed so that they support one another and the overall desired state.[37] If greater customer service is the goal, then the organizational structure might be changed to empowered teams. Team members could be sent to visit key customers personally to assess their needs, and reward systems could be changed to encourage new ideas for customer service and to reduce defects that cause customer dissatisfaction. Such activities must be sequenced and integrated to form a consistent system. Using Lewin's terminology, this would mean reducing many of the "restraining forces" and increasing the "driving forces" all at once or in the proper sequence. There must be a "fit" or "alignment" of these key processes.

Commitment Planning

Commitment planning starts with identifying key political powers in the organization. It also entails planning specific ways to get them involved in the transition activities in order to gain their support. Singapore-based nonprofit International Rubber Study Group consists of more than 30 governments, producer groups, and consumers of rubber. A new goal for the group is to create a plan of sustainability standards for the rubber industry. However, creating and implementing these standards requires commitment from purchasers of rubber—particularly top officials at tire companies, which are some of the largest rubber consumers. The nonprofit has hosted summits that include representatives from companies such as Bridgestone Corp., Michelin, and Semperit A.G. Bridgestone has committed to having tires made from 100 percent sustainable raw materials by 2050.[38]

Management Structures

Management structures (such as individual appointees, teams, or ad hoc committees) must be used to help run things during the transition, plan the direction of the changes, and keep ongoing operations running smoothly as the change occurs. Management structures for handling the transition can include the chief executive officer or other top manager, a project manager to coordinate the transition, representatives of major constituencies involved in the change, natural leaders who have the confidence and trust of large numbers of affected employees, a cross-section of people representing different functions and levels, and/or a cabinet, representing people with whom the chief executive consults and in whom the CEO confides.[39]

Our example companies have used different structures. Sometimes these structures are temporary, created to meet special needs. Xerox's board reserves the right to create ad hoc committees when considered necessary.[40] After Bob McDonald retired from Procter & Gamble (P&G) as CEO, he worked closely with P&G's leadership team and with the new CEO to ensure a smooth leadership transition.[41] It was important for the company to gain the confidence of consumers and reassure them that P&G leadership was pursuing the best courses of action for the firm.

Sustaining the Momentum of the Change

Once a change has begun, initial excitement can dissipate rapidly in the face of everyday problems. However, managers can help sustain the momentum for change by providing resources, developing new competencies and skills, reinforcing new behaviors, and building a support system for those initiating the change. Extra resources may be needed for training, consultation, data collection and feedback, special meetings (even off-site retreats), and to provide a financial buffer if performance drops during the transition period. Managers usually underestimate both the time and extra resources needed to execute a major change. Changes often require new skills of organizational members: problem-solving skills for group members, interpersonal skills for line workers suddenly asked to talk to customers, and software skills for employees using new technology. The new skills employees are required to learn and new resources go hand in hand.

The entire organization must reinforce not only the learning of new behaviors but also those persons initiating the new learning. When top managers are the agents of change, the reinforcement and support must come from the network of persons who understand and support the change. An internal consulting group or external consultant can reinforce

You're the Manager . . . What Would You Do?

THE COMPANY: Preston County Transportation
YOUR POSITION: Transportation Director
THE PLACE: Portland, Oregon

Preston County Transportation was a highly centralized organization with authority concentrated at upper levels. Low-level employees had to go through their superiors and fill out reams of paperwork to accomplish anything. Even simple repairs took days or even weeks, and, as a result, morale was very low. Maintenance on the county's buses was substandard, in part due to employee apathy because mechanics were not held accountable for the condition of the buses. Poor maintenance led to low-quality service with high levels of pollution, poor internal seating and conditions, and breakdowns.

The county brought in a retired military general, Jim Barnes, as the new transportation director to assess the problems and provide a detailed recommendation of how to change the situation. After weeks of study and interviews, Barnes suggested decentralizing the department and delegating responsibility to the lowest levels of the organization. He recommended creating maintenance teams and giving team members responsibility for the maintenance of all buses under their control. Barnes also suggested moving maintenance teams to several locations throughout the county to provide greater accessibility to major routes and bus traffic. The key to Barnes's plan is creating a feeling of personal interest and pride in each team's success.

The county decided to accept and implement Barnes's plan. The results were outstanding. Teams developed very strong identities and began to compete with each other for safety and duration awards, indicating length of time between major service problems. The plan made maintenance and lower-level employees feel important and necessary for the success of the organization.

With morale, involvement, and performance improving, Barnes next set out to address the problem of the mounds of paperwork required to accomplish anything in the department. Bus repairs had been slowed

Preston County Transportation works to improve employee morale with significant reorganization.

because upper-level authorities had to approve all major work. This system was changed by giving employees greater opportunity to make repair decisions and greater access to parts (inventories were dramatically expanded). New computer software programs were used to list available parts at each repair facility and vans were utilized to shuttle parts to needed locations. After the reorganization, parts could be shipped to most locations within one hour.

Finally, Barnes ordered that all county transportation facilities be painted and completely cleaned and refurnished, and that new uniforms be provided for employees. This was intended to enhance employees' pride in working for the county bus system.

QUESTIONS

1. As new transportation director, evaluate your plans to change this organization.

2. What are the inherent benefits and risks with decentralization?

3. What do you see as your long-term priorities in managing this new system? How do you maintain morale and productivity?

the executives and provide a sounding board for their decisions. New organizational structures may have to be devised for support. Top management must reinforce lower-level managers and workers by linking formal rewards to the desired behaviors. One major auto company for instance, in trying to improve quality, linked 40 to 60 percent of its managers' bonuses to product quality. Recognition, encouragement, and praise are informal rewards that can be tied quickly to desired behaviors. Even the good intrinsic feeling associated with achievement of goals can help maintain momentum when early successes are built into the change program.[42] Campbell Soup Corporation's top executives, for example, have been historically well known for throwing impromptu parties (or so-called "wingdings"!) to celebrate company performance improvements.

Organizational Development

One general approach to planned change that has gained prominence over the last 30 years or so focuses primarily on people processes as the target of change. This approach—called organization development—is grounded largely in psychology and other behavioral sciences, although more recently it has evolved into a broader approach encompassing such areas as organizational theory, strategy development, and social and technical change.

The Nature of Organizational Development

Organizational development (OD) can be formally defined as "a system-wide application of behavioral science knowledge to the planned development and reinforcement of organizational strategies, structures, and processes for improving an organization's effectiveness."[43] This definition reflects several important features of organizational development. First, OD deals with whole systems (company, department, work group) as opposed to a single individual or a single function within a system. Second, OD uses behavioral science knowledge, as in the areas of leadership, motivation, team functioning, rewards, conflict resolution, and change. This distinguishes it from such things as computer-systems or operations-research types of change approaches. Third, OD involves planned change, but not in the more rigid sense of organizational planning. Rather, it involves more of an adaptive, flexible, ongoing process of diagnosing and solving people-related problems. Fourth, it involves the creation and reinforcement of change with all the implications we have discussed thus far. Fifth, it can encompass strategy, structure, and process changes—although, traditionally, OD has focused on the people processes almost exclusively. Finally, OD focuses on improving organizational effectiveness, in terms of both productivity and quality of work life. An important aspect of the practice of OD is that effectiveness implies that organizations learn to solve their own problems and ultimately deal successfully with issues without the help of an outside consultant who specializes in OD.

Organizational development is often carried out with the aid of a consultant, either from outside the company or from within, who is separate from the team or group being assisted. An OD practitioner, often called a change agent, facilitates the change process by structuring learning experiences, diagnosing problems, helping to generate and implement solutions, and encouraging certain types of interaction processes. The actions of these agents of change are generally referred to as interventions because they attempt to hinder the erosion of the organization's effectiveness by modifying the ways its members function. Although OD practitioners usually have specialized training in the behavioral sciences, many have supplemented that expertise with training in other areas to give them the broader perspectives that are useful in facilitating change in today's complex organizations.

The focus of OD is often the hidden or more subtle features of an organization. Although an OD intervention might change more visible features, such as structure, formal authority relationships, policies, and technology, OD tacitly recognizes the impact of the more hidden, informal organization and deals with many of these features to promote organizational effectiveness.

Most OD interventions use an **action research** approach to change, which encompasses and further defines the steps of the Lewin change model (see Figure 10.3) and involves an ongoing process of joint (consultant with clients) problem discovery, diagnosis, action planning, action implementation, and evaluation. The evaluation uncovers further problems on which to focus, using the action steps again. As problems are successfully addressed, the organization, over time, learns the skills necessary to properly conduct the action research process without an OD practitioner's assistance, and the client-consultant relationship is eventually terminated. This model provides the basic format through which a number of varied OD interventions are implemented.

organizational development (OD): A system-wide application of behavioral science knowledge to the planned development and reinforcement of organizational strategies, structures, and processes for improving an organization's effectiveness.

action research: Encompasses and further defines the steps of the Lewin change model and involves an ongoing process of joint (consultant with clients) problem discovery, diagnosis, action planning, action implementation, and evaluation.

FIGURE 10.3

Comparison of Action
Research Model to
Lewin's Change Model

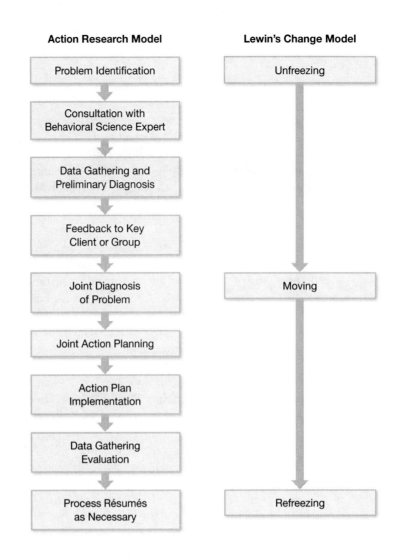

Action Research Model

- Problem Identification
- Consultation with Behavioral Science Expert
- Data Gathering and Preliminary Diagnosis
- Feedback to Key Client or Group
- Joint Diagnosis of Problem
- Joint Action Planning
- Action Plan Implementation
- Data Gathering Evaluation
- Process Résumés as Necessary

Lewin's Change Model

- Unfreezing
- Moving
- Refreezing

OD Interventions

The following overview of OD interventions, although not exhaustive, reflects the varied nature of the OD approach to change, as well as the different levels at which change might be targeted. Many OD interventions use some combination of these different approaches, with the number and variety of techniques, tools, and facilitative experiences being limited only by the art, skill, and imagination of the many practitioners. Table 10.4 describes the different types of organizational development interventions.

Survey Feedback

survey feedback: Involves gathering data through questionnaires and personal interviews.

Survey feedback involves gathering data through questionnaires and personal interviews. The data are tabulated, organized, and returned to the surveyed group by the change agent in anonymous summarized form and used as a vehicle to stimulate discussion about problem areas that the group should address. The content or focus of the survey is usually the behavioral processes that make up this section of your management textbook (leadership, motivation, and so on) although other problems that surface may also be addressed. Data may consist of facts, perceptions, attitudes, and opinions, but tend to be most helpful when they are specific, accurate, limited, relevant, important, and inspiring. How the data are used is as important as the nature of the data itself. Data must be fed back to the client group in such a way as to be accepted as valid, cue the group into important areas, stimulate movement or change, promise a reward if behavior is successfully changed, and generate present and future learning.[44]

An example of survey feedback occurred in a 15-year-old engineering company whose president felt that some top managers and key employees resisted attempts to make neces-

TABLE 10.4 OD Interventions

Type of Intervention	Example
Survey feedback	Use questionnaires to get information
Process Consultation	Consultant focuses directly on client and goals
Team Building	Helping two or more groups work together
Role Negotiation	Negotiating role behaviors/expectations
Life and Career Planning	Structured counseling for employees
Third-Party Peacemaking	Outside-party conflict resolution
Techno-Structural Redesign	Restructuring reporting and other relationships
Job Redesign	Changing the nature of tasks
Grid OD	Six-phase overall organizational intervention

sary changes, seemed to lack a sense of urgency about performance, and in general did not function well as a team. A consultant conducted personal interviews with the top managers and discovered that the president's authoritarian and often sarcastic leadership style was a root cause of many of the symptoms the president had perceived. These data were presented during an off-site retreat exercise in which the president was allowed to listen to and to seek clarification of the summarized data but not to defend reported actions. The employees' perceptions were accepted as valid, verified during the exercise, and treated as important. The group, with the consultant's help, designed a program to help the president improve in key interpersonal areas. This example, as well as a number of the other techniques discussed below, should emphasize the importance of the behavioral science training of the change agent. The potential damage, for individuals and the overall organization, is severe if these activities are not planned, structured, and implemented with skill and understanding. Untrained amateurs have no business engaging in this type of endeavor.

Surveys help managers understand employees' attitudes and can identify problems which need to be addressed.

Process Consultation

During **process consultation**, a consultant focuses on the dynamic task-related processes—how a client or group sets goals, gathers information, solves problems, and allocates work—and assists the client organization in diagnosing how to enhance these kinds of processes. Again, such areas as communication, conflict resolution, leadership, and decision making may be examined and targeted for improvement. A key difference between process consultation and survey feedback is that the consultant is involved in more direct behavioral observation in the former, while asking others about their perceptions, attitudes, and feelings in the latter.[45] Feedback, diagnosis, action planning, implementation, and evaluation are still a part of both interventions.

Team Building

Team building involves using structured group experiences to help ongoing work teams function more effectively through better decision making, goal setting, and intragroup communications. It may also deal with group leadership patterns, roles members perform

process consultation: A consultant focuses on the dynamic task-related processes—how a client or group sets goals, gathers information, solves problems, and allocates work—and assists the client organization in diagnosing how to enhance these kinds of processes.

team building: Involves using structured group experiences to help ongoing work teams function more effectively through better decision making, goal setting, and intragroup communications.

in the group, and group norms and values. Team building may be part of process consultation or grow out of a diagnosis conducted through the survey-feedback process. FMI is an outside consultant firm that often provides team-building services for projects in the construction industry.[46]

Intergroup team building is designed to facilitate functioning between two or more groups by helping the groups understand and deal with areas of conflict; debilitating interaction patterns; perceptual discrepancies; norm, goal, and value differences; and lack of coordination. The Transportation Security Administration (TSA), which provides security screening in U.S. airports, has put special emphasis on employee team building in recent years.

Role Negotiation

Role negotiation entails structuring interactions between interdependent persons or groups to clarify and negotiate role behaviors and expectations. Role negotiation helps groups and individuals know what their responsibilities are, what actions they should take at different times in dealing with certain issues, and, in general, how they are to work together. This intervention can be a primary focus in itself or part of a broader team-building or intergroup team-building program.

Life and Career Planning

Life and career planning involves the use of structured counseling and group discussions, often accompanied by skill and interest testing, to assist employees in planning career paths and integrating life and career goals. These activities can be planned and combined with an overall education and employee development program.

Third-Party Peacemaking

Third-party peacemaking involves a consultant who facilitates conflict resolution between two individuals. It may entail structuring meetings, facilitating discussions, interpreting communications, pacing interactions, and suggesting compromises or integrative solutions.[47]

Techno-Structural Redesign

Techno-structural redesign is a large-scale intervention that involves redesigning the organizational structure—reporting relations, division of labor, departmentalization, functions, and the like—to better address environmental contingencies and better utilize information and process technologies. A self-designing organization intervention involves employees in the ongoing process of self-examination and redesign to meet rapid environmental changes.

Job Redesign

Job redesign, you will remember from elsewhere in the text, focuses on changing the nature of how tasks are performed and often entails job rotation, job enrichment, and/or job enlargement. Job redesign attempts to enhance not only productivity but also job involvement and organizational commitment.

Grid OD

Grid OD is a six-phase overall organizational intervention that comprehensively and systematically attempts to enhance personal management style, team functioning, intergroup problem solving, overall organizational functioning, and the ability of the organization to continually improve how it solves its own problems, resolves conflicts, and makes decisions.

Using OD Interventions Successfully

The success of OD interventions depends on matching the correct intervention to the organizational need, the skill of the OD practitioner at implementing the program, and the

intergroup team building: Designed to facilitate functioning between two or more groups by helping the groups understand and deal with areas of conflict; debilitating interaction patterns; perceptual discrepancies; norm, goal, and value differences; and lack of coordination.

role negotiation: Entails structuring interactions between interdependent persons or groups to clarify and negotiate role behaviors and expectations.

life and career planning: Involves the use of structured counseling and group discussions, often accompanied by skill and interest testing, to assist employees in planning career paths and integrating life and career goals.

third-party peacemaking: Involves a consultant who facilitates conflict resolution between two individuals.

techno-structural redesign: A large-scale intervention that involves redesigning the organizational structure to better address environmental contingencies and better utilize information and process technologies.

job redesign: Focuses on changing the nature of how tasks are performed and often entails job rotation, job enrichment, and/or job enlargement.

grid OD: A six-phase overall organizational intervention that attempts to enhance the ability of the organization to continually improve.

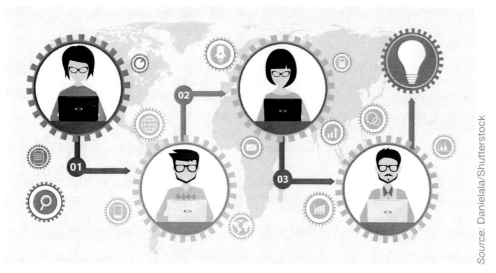

Job rotation involves giving employees different responsibilities within the organization.

readiness of the client organization to accept the intervention. Because OD emphasizes joint diagnosis and action planning, acceptance of the process and the ultimate change strategies is often very high.

It should be apparent from the information presented in this chapter that organizational change is both a complex and pervasive phenomenon. Understanding the process of planned change and developing skills in various change techniques and processes will likely be a key competency for successful managers of today's intricate business organizations.

Summary and Review

■ *Define organizational change and explain the dimensions and types of change.* Organizational change refers to modifying the behaviors or ideas of an organization or its units. Organizational changes are often a result of reactions to internal or external environmental forces. These change varies in how extensively it is planned (reactive to planned change), how extreme the change is (incremental to quantum change), how much members are involved in learning how to conduct future change, where the change is targeted (level and/or functional area), and in whether the organization needs to be loosened up or more highly organized. Different types of change reflect an overall focus on different features of organizational functioning. Strategy changes focus on the nature of how the organization will conduct its business and meet its market demands. Organizational structure and design changes deal with how work will be organized, delegated, and managed. Technology changes focus on changing machinery or equipment that enhances either the products of the company or its means of producing the good or service. Human process changes focus on the interpersonal processes and overall cultural components that influence or make up the way people interact in the organization.

■ *Interpret three models of change, particularly the steps involved in the comprehensive model of change.* Kurt Lewin's model of change views change as a process of "unfreezing" the forces that keep an organization functioning at a certain level (state A), "moving" or changing to new behaviors (state B), and then "refreezing" the behavior into a new equilibrium or behavioral level (state C). The congruence model characterizes change as an interrelated set of transformational processes and structures that turn organizational and environmental inputs into organization, group, and individual outputs.

The comprehensive model of planned change involves a sequence of management activities that are important for quantum change. Managers first must recognize a need for change by scanning the internal and external environments. Then they must motivate the change by preparing people for change (unfreezing) and overcoming the resistance to change that inevitably arises. Managers must also create and communicate a vision of the future that inspires commitment to the change process and the desired future state, and develop political support for change with powerful constituencies.

The transition must also be successfully managed through activity planning, commitment planning, and use of management structures to control the process. Finally, momentum for the change must be maintained by providing resources for the change, developing new competencies and skills, reinforcing new behaviors, and building support for the change agents.

■ *Determine the major causes of resistance to change and recommend how managers can deal with change resistance.* Resistance to change may occur because of uncertainty and insecurity, reaction to the way change is presented, threatened vested interests and real loss, cynicism and lack of trust, perceptual differences, and a simple lack of understanding. One situation where there might be particular resistance to change is when an organization attempts to introduce a new innovation, or a new product, method, process, or approach. Specific tactics for addressing resistance include education and communication, participation and involvement, facilitation and support, negotiation and agreement, manipulation, co-optation, and, when all else fails, explicit and implicit coercion.

■ *Explain organizational development (OD) and summarize the major OD interventions.* Organizational development is a system-wide application of behavioral science knowledge to the planned development and reinforcement of organizational strategies, structures, and processes for improving an organization's effectiveness. OD often involves the use of change consultants or practitioners who help the organization implement an action research approach to change by jointly discovering and diagnosing problems, developing and implementing action plans, and evaluating results and repeating the process. Specific OD interventions that typically use the action research approach include survey feedback, process consultation, team and intergroup development, role negotiation, life and career planning, third-party peacemaking, techno-structural redesign, job design, and grid OD.

■ *Assess an organization's change program.* Based on what you've learned in this chapter, you should be able to assess the change program implemented in the "Business Dilemma" box and project future actions for the department.

Key Terms and Concepts

action research 313

comprehensive model of planned change 305

congruence model of change 304

grid OD 316

incremental change 300

innovation 307

intergroup team building 316

job redesign 316

life and career planning 316

moving 304

organizational change 297

organizational development (OD) 313

performance gap 298

planned change 299

process consultation 315

quantum change 300

reactive change 299

refreezing 304

role negotiation 316

survey feedback 314

team building 315

techno-structural redesign 316

third-party peacemaking 316

transition state 310

unfreezing 304

Ready Recall

1. What external forces necessitate changes in the way companies do business? What internal forces can cause a change in the way a company does business? Supply examples of how these forces prompt change.
2. Explain the five dimensions of change along which organizations can be analyzed to determine causes and solutions to problems.
3. Name and briefly explain four different types of organizational change.
4. Compare and contrast Lewin's model of change with the congruence model of change. Compare and contrast these changes to the models of change discussed in the text—in particular, the comprehensive model of planned change. (This would be a good project to do with one or two fellow classmates.)
5. What are the major steps in the comprehensive model of planned change?
6. What are the major sources of resistance to change in organizations? List seven major strategies for overcoming resistance to change.
7. What is organizational development (OD)?
8. List and explain at least seven major types of OD interventions.

Expand Your Experience

1. Think about the external and internal forces that have affected your college or university in the recent past, are affecting it now, and will affect it in the not-too-distant future. What changes have you seen and what ones do you think will be necessary in the future in the areas of strategy, structure and design, technology, and people processes or culture to deal with these forces of change?

2. Find and interview the owner of a fairly small business (10 to 20 employees) in your community that has been in existence for at least ten years. Discuss the major changes he or she has made in the business and analyze how the changes came about and how they were implemented and sustained.

3. Many employees in business have been asked to undergo radical changes in how they do their jobs. Find an employee who has faced a major change (it could be a friend, relative, classmate, etc.) and discuss his or her resistance to the change, including why he or she felt resistance. How was it overcome? How did the company try to overcome resistance? Think of a similar change you've been asked to make and analyze your own sources of resistance to change.

Strengthen Your Skills

Change from a Management Standpoint

Instructions: The following scenario is designed to help you think about some of the various challenges one faces when managing a change process. Imagine yourself as the manager in the scenario. After reading the scenario, answer the questions below. Keep the concepts of organizational change and innovation in mind as you answer the questions.

Scenario:

Comestibles Natural, a New Mexican restaurant, makes the best salsa and hot sauce in the state. The condiments are so popular that the restaurant began bottling 8-ounce and 16-ounce jars under the brand name Comestibles Salsa with the tag line "Natural" to sell directly from the location. This simple act created larger demand for the products. Increasingly more customers pour into the restaurant every day to purchase jars of salsa and hot sauce. While this may seem like a good thing, overall it is negatively contributing to the entire operation of the restaurant. Too much congestion in the lobby is creating too much noise pollution for the diners, and people are constantly bumping into each other in the lobby. Just last week a fire marshall came in for a meal, and, after seeing the conditions, warned the manager of safety violations. Additionally, the restaurant cannot keep up with the demand. In fact, the chefs are becoming disgruntled because they constantly have to make salsa on top of the regular orders. The manager has received increasingly more complaints from dining customers regarding the decreasing quality of food. Some say that their orders are served cold while others claim that their sides of beans and rice are smaller than usual. Not surprisingly, most of the complaints refer to the lack of free salsa refills on the tables. The manager knows something needs to change, but he is unsure how to go about it. He is also unsure how the employees will react to change since they are accustomed to their routines.

Questions:

1. Why is change needed? What organizational issues does this change seek to address?
2. Who will be affected by this change?
3. Where in the organization would you expect to experience the most resistance to this change?
4. What types of resistance do you anticipate? What will the resistance look like?
5. What can you do to proactively manage those who are resistant?
6. What specific behaviors do you need from the employees to address the resistance?
7. What type of personal support or assistance will you need to implement the change?

Case 10: Organizational Change at Starbucks

Starbucks—the Seattle-based company that popularized the "coffee culture"—is brewing up higher sales through new beverages and new cafés in global markets. A stop at Starbucks has become part of many consumers' daily routines. Some are attracted by the variety of high-quality, brewed-to-order coffee and tea, whereas others look forward to relaxing and socializing in the "third place" between home and work. Today, there are more than 24,000 Starbucks stores in 70 countries.

As with all firms, Starbucks must undergo change to be successful. Consumer preferences change rapidly, and Starbucks must adapt if it wants to avoid being left behind. Changes in consumer preferences, as well as changes in technology and the economy, are external forces the

Starbucks experiences significant organizational change.

company must face. Starbucks also experiences internal organizational change, such as changes in management and employees. This requires Starbucks to understand competition and changing market conditions, as well as changes resulting from employee turnover and corporate culture. Of particular importance is how these changes impact the customer experience. When the financial crisis occurred in 2008–2009, the change in income levels and employment led to a drop in sales. A combination of overexpansion and declining revenues required Starbucks to make organizational changes quickly, including hiring back its founder Howard Schultz as CEO. Under Schultz's leadership, Starbucks closed some of its stores and focused on enhancing the customer experience to create more value for customers. This emphasis on the customer helped Starbucks rebound, but it continues to face challenges as it adapts to internal and external organizational forces. Because the consumer is the most important focus at Starbucks, managing the quality of the coffee experience that Starbucks provides is essential for Starbucks management.

Starbucks continues to refine the retail environment to increase customer value. It has researched and refined every aspect of the customer experience, from the size of its coffees ("tall" is actually "small") to the number of minutes that customers spend waiting in line. To speed up purchases, it offers the options of paying by cell phone and ordering ahead. To pay with the Starbucks app, consumers with iPhone, Android, or Windows cell phones simply download the app and let cashiers scan the Starbucks code on the screen during checkout. The app links to the customer's Starbucks Card, which combines the rewards of a loyalty program with the convenience of a prepaid card, for making purchases. The Starbucks mobile wallet is a big hit: nearly a third of its sales volume now comes through its mobile wallet.

One major change Starbucks has encountered in recent years is its saturation in the United States. Well established in the intensely competitive U.S. market, Starbucks is growing much more quickly in Asian markets. This is requiring the firm to place more emphasis on how it targets Asian consumers. The company has 3,000 cafés in 135 cities in China, where consumers drink, on average, just three cups of coffee every year. By opening more locations and encouraging consumers to bring their friends for coffee and conversation, Starbucks aims to increase demand and boost sales throughout China. Long-term growth in China is one of the company's top priorities. In Japan, where Starbucks now has more than 1,300 cafés, consumers have long enjoyed the tradition of meeting in neighborhood coffee shops.

After more than 30 years as CEO, co-founder Howard Schultz stepped down from the helm in 2017, replaced by former COO Kevin Johnson. Often when the founder steps down—especially one as popular as Howard Schultz—the move creates internal turmoil within the company. One way Starbucks is overcoming resistance to this change is by replacing Schultz with a seasoned executive who has worked with Schultz during key changes at the firm. It also helps that Schultz is not leaving the company entirely. Not only will he remain executive chairman, but he is also planning to focus his energy on expanding the company's premium coffee segment.

The company considers restaurant industry studies, credit card data, and same-store sales trackers to set financial forecasts. Starbucks aims to open 12,000 additional stores, refocus on its coffee beverages, and expand its focus on technology and its rewards program to lead the organizational change and exceed growth targets. The company announced plans to sell its Tazo tea brand to Unilever, close all 379 Teavana locations, and end its e-commerce platform. Sometimes a key part of change involves eliminating less profitable segments that take away from the company's core focus.

With company food sales reaching 21 percent of total sales in the United States, Starbucks aims to elevate its food offerings. The company invested in high-end Italian bakery Princi and opened a bakery inside the company's flagship Reserve Roastery and Tasting Room in Seattle. This bakery features more than 100 menu items, including croissants, sandwiches, salads, and more. The company's roasteries are designed to be larger than its traditional café concept and will incorporate Princi bakeries, including those slated for Shanghai, Milan, New York, Tokyo, and Chicago. Part of Schultz's job now that he is no longer CEO will be to focus on these roasteries, which sell premium coffee products that Starbucks believes will become a lucrative industry in the coming years.

Taking note of consumer interest in energy drinks, which has blossomed into a $27.5 billion market, Starbucks launched Starbucks Refreshers to take advantage of this growing trend. Starbucks Refreshers is a line of carbonated drinks with more than half the caffeine content of an espresso shot. Available in supermarkets and in Starbucks cafés, these all-natural drinks combine green, unroasted coffee with fruit juices for a fruity, non-coffee flavor. To gain significant market share, Starbucks must battle against Red Bull, Rockstar, and other well-known marketers of energy drinks. In undertaking this endeavor, Starbucks must deliberately structure its operations and strategies to anticipate environmental forces, including the changing behavior of consumers and competitors.

When it comes to innovation, Starbucks clearly engages in planned change. It is proactively embracing innovative changes it believes will help it to become a more successful firm. This is the opposite of reactive change, in which organizations react spontaneously to external and internal forces but do little to modify their behavior. The company's many successful initiatives, as well as its not-so-successful ones, demonstrate that the firm is ready and willing to make changes to maintain its competitive advantage and gain market share.[48]

1. Describe how Starbucks introduced technological changes to speed up purchases.
2. What external and internal forces are causing Starbucks to refocus on its coffee beverages?
3. Describe the organizational changes Starbucks has had to undertake to continue its success.

Notes

1. Conversation with Marshall Powell Ledbetter III; VIP Moving & Storage website, http://www.vipmovingandstorage .com/ (accessed July 14, 2015); Better Business Bureau, "VIP Moving & Storage Inc.," https://www.bbb.org/losangeless iliconvalley/business-reviews/moving-and-storage-company/ vip-moving-and-storage-in-pacoima-ca-1023815 (accessed January 28, 2018).

2. Jean B. Keffeler, "Managing Changing Organizations: Don't Stop Communicating," *Vital Speeches*, November 15, 1991, 92–96.

3. United States Postal Service, "U.S. Postal Service Reports Fiscal Year 2016 Results," November 15, 2016, https://about .usps.com/news/national-releases/2016/pr16_092.htm (accessed December 31, 2017).

4. Brian Dumaine, "Times Are Good? Create a Crisis," *Fortune*, June 28, 1993, 127.

5. Paula Rosenblum, "Home Depot's Resurrection: How One Retailer Made Its Own Home Improvements," *Forbes*, August 21, 2013, https://www.forbes.com/sites/paularosenblum/2013/ 08/21/home-depots-resurrection/#257d281258c3 (accessed December 31, 2017).

6. Bruce Rayner, "Trial-by-Fire Transformation: An Interview with Globe Metallurgical's Arden C. Sims," *Harvard Business Review* 70 (May-June 1992): 117–129.

7. "Jet Blue, Social Media All-Stars," *Fortune*, September 16, 2013, p. 136.

8. Michael Beer, Russell A. Eisenstat, and Bert Spector, "Why Change Programs Don't Produce Change," *Harvard Business Review* 68 (November-December 1990): 158–166.

9. Thomas G. Cummings and Christopher G. Worley, *Organization Development and Change*, 5th ed. (St. Paul: West Publishing Company, 1993), 63.

10. Business Wire, "Procter & Gamble Announces Organization Changes," *The Wall Street Journal*, June 5, 2013, http:// online.wsj.com/article/PR-CO-20130605-911270.html (accessed December 3, 2013).

11. Teresa Joyce Covin and Ralph H. Kilmann, "Implementation of Large-Scale Planned Change: Some Areas of Agreement and Disagreement," *Psychological Reports* 66 (June 1990): 1235–1241.

12. Peter Senge, *The Fifth Discipline: The Art and Practice of the Learning Organization* (New York: Doubleday, 1990).

13. Phyllis Korkki, "Invasion of the Annual Reviews," *The New York Times*, November 23, 2013, http://www.nytimes .com/2013/11/24/jobs/invasion-of-the-annual-reviews.html (accessed December 31, 2017).

14. Archer Daniels Midland Company, "ADM Expands Portfolio with Range of Wheat Protein Concentrates," November 28, 2017, https://www.adm.com/news/news-releases/adm -expands-portfolio-with-range-of-wheat-protein-concentrates (accessed December 2, 2017); Tony Reid, "ADM Planning Layoffs," *Herald & Review*, July 20, 2017, http://herald-review .com/business/agriculture/adm-planning-layoffs/article _26e525e5-f10d-5a5f-a4ae-fab3958340d8.html (accessed December 2, 2017); Javier Blas, "Commodity Trading Arm in Sleepy Swiss Village Trips Up ADM Again," *Chicago Tribune*, February 8, 2017, http://www.chicagotribune.com/business/ ct-archer-daniels-midland-commodity-trading-20170208-story .html (accessed December 5, 2017); "Partnerships Across the Supply Chain Drive Continuous Improvement, Helping Meet Corporate Commitments," *Field to Market*, December 19, 2016, https://fieldtomarket.org/case-studies-series/partnerships -across-supply-chain/ (accessed December 5, 2017); Leah Guffey, "ADM Helps Unilever Bring Out the Best," *AgWired*, September 18, 2014, http://agwired.com/2014/09/18/adm-helps -unilever-bring-out-the-best/ (accessed July 6, 2015); Paul Demery, "Archer Daniels Midland Cultivates Its Handling of Purchase Orders and Invoices," *InternetRetailer*, September 9, 2014, https://www.internetretailer.com/2014/09/09/archer -daniels-midland-cleans-its-handling-purchase-orders (accessed December 23, 2017); Gregory Meyer, "Archer Daniels Midland Buys Wild Flavors for €2.3 bn," *Financial Times*, July 7, 2014, http://www.ft.com/intl/cms/s/0/636b8732-05b4-11e4 -9baa-00144feab7de.html#axzz3LYqkltWg (accessed July 6, 2015); Archer Daniels Midland website, http://www.adm.com (accessed December 23, 2017); "ADM Announces Layoffs Across the Country: 175 in Decatur," IllinoisHomePage.net, http://www.illinoishomepage.net/news/local-news/adm

-annouces-layoffs-across-the-country-175-in-decatur/93355620 (accessed December 23, 2017).

15. Danielle Douglas, "Sallie Mae to Split into Two Companies," *The Washington Post*, May 29, 2013, http://articles .washingtonpost.com/2013-05-29/business/39603758_1_ private-student-loans-ffelp-john-remondi (accessed December 31, 2017).

16. Keffeler, "Managing Changing Organizations."

17. Paul Mozor & Eva Dov, "Robots May Revolutionize China's Electronics Manufacturing," *The Wall Street Journal*, September 24, 2013, http://online.wsj.com/news/articles/ SB10001424052702303759604579093122607195610 (accessed December 4, 2013).

18. Carol Hymowitz, "Xerox's Ursula Burns on Her Career Path and Changing Company Strategy," *Bloomberg Business Week*, August 8, 2013, http://www.businessweek.com/articles/ 2013-08-08/xeroxs-ursula-burns-on-her-career-path-and -changing-company-strategy (accessed December 31, 2017).

19. Beer, Eisenstat, and Spector, "Why Change Programs Don't Produce Change."

20. "Secret Service Facing Another Sex Scandal," *USA Today*, November 14, 2013, http://www.usatoday.com/story/news/ politics/2013/11/14/secret-service-sex-scandal/3554007/ (accessed December 31, 2017).

21. Cummings and Worley, *Organization Development and Change*, 53.

22. Adapted from Cummings and Worley.

23. Cummings and Worley, 145.

24. Shilpa Phadnis and Anshul Dhamija, "Tough Decisions Needed to Rebuild Desirable Infosys: N R Narayana Murthy," *The Times of India*, June 16, 2013, https://timesofindia.india times.com/business/india-business/Tough-decisions-needed -to-rebuild-desirable-Infosys-N-R-Narayana-Murthy/ articleshow/20611203.cms (accessed December 31, 2017).

25. Cummings and Worley, 147.

26. "The Modern History of Inland Steel, Northwest Indiana Steel Heritage Project," 2009, http://www.nwisteelheritage museum.org/inland-history.htm (accessed December 31, 2017).

27. Ryan Faas, "How Steve Jobs Changed Apple…" *Computerworld*, August 26, 2011, http://www.computerworld.com/s/ article/9219496/How_Steve_Jobs_changed_Apple...?taxon omyId=214&pageNumber=1 (accessed December 31, 2017); Adam Lashinsky, "How Apple Works: Inside the World's Biggest Startup," *CNNMoney*, August 25, 2011, http://tech .fortune.cnn.com/2011/08/25/how-apple-works-inside-the -worlds-biggest-startup/ (accessed December 31, 2017); "The Apple Revolution: 10 Key Moments," *Time*, http://content.time .com/time/specials/packages/article/0,28804,1873486_1873491 _1873530,00.html (accessed December 31, 2017); Thomas Ricker, "Apple Drops 'Computer' from Name," engadget, January 9, 2007, https://www.engadget.com/2007/01/09/ apple-drops-computer-from-name/ (accessed December 31, 2017).

28. Keffeler, 96.

29. Hymowitz, supra note 5.

30. Ronald Elliot, "The Challenge of Managing Change," *Personnel Journal* (March 1990): 40–49.

31. Alan L. Wilgus, "Forging Change in Spite of Adversity," *Personnel Journal* 70 (September 1991): 60–67.

32. Covan and Kilmann, "Implementation of Large-Scale Planned Change."

33. Cummings and Worley, 151.

34. David A. Nadler, "Managing Organizational Change: An Integrative Perspective," *The Journal of Applied Behavioral Science* 17 (April-June 1981): 191–211.

35. Catherine Cleary and Thomas Packard, "The Use of Metaphors in Organizational Assessment and Change," *Group and Organization Management* 17 (September 1992): 229–241.

36. Cummings and Worley, 156–157.

37. David A. Nadler, "Managing Organizational Change: An Integrative Perspective," *The Journal of Applied Behavioral Science* 17 (April-June 1981): 191–211.

38. Huileng Tan, "Rubber Study Group Looks for Sustainability Plan," *The Wall Street Journal*, September 3, 2013, http:// blogs.wsj.com/searealtime/2013/09/03/rubber-study-group -looks-for-sustainability-plan/ (accessed December 31, 2017); David Shaw, "Sustainability: Not Just a Buzz Word," Rubber News, July 6, 2012, http://www.rubbernews.com/article/ 20120706/NEWS/307069995/sustainability-not-just-a -buzzword (accessed December 31, 2017).

39. Cummings and Worley, 157.

40. Xerox, "Corporate Governance Guidelines (As Amended May 23, 2017)," https://www.xerox.com/en-us/about/corporate -citizenship/guidelines (accessed December 31, 2017).

41. "'Was Mr. McDonald Fired?': P&G's Cryptic Memo on CEO Switch," *The Wall Street Journal*, May 23, 2013, http:// blogs.wsj.com/corporate-intelligence/2013/05/23/pg-memo/ (accessed December 31, 2017); "2013 Best Companies for Leaders," ChiefExecutive.net, January 10, 2013, http:// chiefexecutive.net/2013-best-companies-for-leaders-top-5 (accessed December 31, 2017).

42. Graves, "Leaders of Corporate Change."

43. Cummings and Worley, 2.

44. David A. Nadler, *Feedback and Organization Development: Using Data-Based Methods* (Reading, MA: Addison-Wesley Publishing Company, 1977).

45. Edgar H. Schein, *Process Consultation Volume II: Lessons for Managers and Consultants* (Reading, MA: Addison-Wesley Publishing Company, 1987).

46. FMI, "Project Partnering and Team Building," http://www .fminet.com/mc/productivity-project-management -improvement/projectpartneringteambuilding.html (accessed December 4, 2013).

47. Richard E. Walton, *Managing Conflict: Interpersonal Dialogue and Third-Party Roles*, 2nd ed. (Reading, MA: Addison-Wesley Publishing Company, 1987).

48. "Starbucks Coffee International," *Starbucks*, https://www .starbucks.com/business/international-stores (accessed November 28, 2017); Jackie Wattles, "Starbucks: Nearly a Third of

Sales Were Made Digitally Last Quarter," *CNN*, April 27, 2017, http://money.cnn.com/2017/04/27/news/companies/starbucks -digital-sales/index.html (accessed November 28, 2017); Cathaleen Chen, "Starbucks Is Betting Big on China and It Makes Perfect Sense," TheStreet, November 5, 2017, https:// www.thestreet.com/story/14374987/1/starbucks-is-still-betting -big-in-china.html (accessed November 28, 2017); Starbucks Coffee Japan, "About Us," http://www.starbucks.co.jp/en/ company.html (accessed November 28, 2017); Sarah Whitten, "Starbucks Opens First Princi Location, Teases More to Come in 2018," *CNBC*, November 7, 2017, https://www.cnbc.com/ 2017/11/07/starbucks-opens-first-princi-location-teases-more -to-come-in-2018.html (accessed November 28, 2017); Lauren Hirsch, "Starbucks Tanks on Revenue Miss, to Sell Tazo Tea Brand to Unilever," *CNBC*, November 2, 2017, https://www .cnbc.com/2017/11/02/starbucks-earnings-q4-2017.html (accessed November 28, 2017); Marguerite Ward, "3 Ways CEO Kevin Johnson's Leadership Style Could Shape Star-bucks," *CNBC*, April 3, 2017, https://www.cnbc.com/2017/04/ 03/3-things-you-need-to-know-about-new-starbucks-ceo-kevin -johnson.html (accessed November 28, 2017); Sarah Whitten, "Starbucks Shares Up as CEO Says He's 'Optimistic' He Can Exceed New Growth Targets," *CNBC*, November 3, 2017, https://www.cnbc.com/2017/11/03/starbucks-ceo-says-hes -optimistic-he-can-exceed-new-growth-targets.html (accessed November 28, 2017); Bruce Horovitz, "Starbucks to Jolt Consumers with Refreshers Energy Drink," *USA Today*, March 22, 2012, http://usatoday30.usatoday.com/money/industries/ food/story/2012-03-21/starbucks-energy-drink-refreshers-red -bull/53693616/1 (accessed July 6, 2015); Jennifer Van Grove, "Starbucks Apps Account for 42M Payments," *VentureBeat*, April 9, 2012, http://venturebeat.com/2012/04/09/starbucks -42m-mobile-pay/ (accessed July 6, 2015); Roemmele, "Why Is the Starbucks Mobile Payments App So Successful?" *Forbes*, June 13, 2014, http://www.forbes.com/sites/quora/ 2014/06/13/why-is-the-starbucks-mobile-payments-app-so -successful/ (accessed July 6, 2015); Mike Esterl, "Coke Looks for Energy-Drink Boost from Monster," *MarketWatch*, August 15, 2014, http://www.marketwatch.com/story/coke-looks-for -energy-drink-boost-from-monster-2014-08–15 (accessed July 6, 2015); Trefis Team, "Here's How Starbucks Will Be Impacted by a Change in Management," *Forbes*, December 5, 2016, https://www.forbes.com/sites/greatspeculations/2016/12/ 05/here-how-starbucks-will-be-impacted-by-a-change-in -management/#639879401f56 (accessed December 22, 2017); John Kell, "Starbucks CEO Howard Schultz Is Stepping Down," *Fortune*, December 1, 2016, http://fortune.com/2016/ 12/01/starbucks-howard-schultz-steps-down/ (accessed December 22, 2017).

Effective Leadership in the Organization

CHAPTER **11**

Source: Palto/Shutterstock

After reading this chapter, you will be able to:

- Differentiate leadership from the concept of management.
- List the sources of power leaders use to influence others' behavior.
- Distinguish successful leaders from less successful leaders and non-leaders, according to their traits.
- Compare and contrast the major dimensions of leadership behavior used in the behavioral theories.
- Summarize the contingency factors covered in Fiedler's contingency theory, Blanchard's situational leadership theory, and path-goal theory.
- Determine what may neutralize, or substitute for, leadership behavior.
- Specify the leadership practices that can contribute to successful transformational leadership and that distinguish it from transactional leadership.
- Evaluate a leader's efforts to manage a crisis situation.

Sheryl Sandberg: Wonder Woman

Sheryl Sandberg, chief operating officer (COO) of Facebook, is a shining example of a transformational leader. She does not just lead employees using reward power and negotiation. Instead, she lives the values and vision that she proclaims. In the process, Sandberg's charisma and authenticity inspire not only employees at Facebook but also women everywhere who want to make a difference.

Sandberg provides an excellent leadership role model for gender equality. Sandberg often asks why there are so many more men in leadership roles than women. She even wrote a book, *Lean In*, to start a critical discussion to address the empowerment of women in leadership positions. Globally, the book has created 34,000 Lean In circles, in which small groups of women meet regularly to provide education, expert advice, and discussion about leadership. The idea is to gain new skills and expand the ability to influence others.

Sandberg's story is empowering to women who want to pursue management positions. Prior to Facebook, Sandberg was the vice president of online sales and operations at Google. Before Google, she was chief of staff for the U.S. secretary of the treasury. After her graduation from Harvard Business School, with an MBA of the highest distinction, she worked as a management consultant for McKinsey Company. Sandberg met Mark Zuckerberg, and the next year he hired her away from Google to serve in the role of COO of Facebook. In this role, she helped make Facebook profitable by focusing on advertising. She became the first woman on the Facebook board of directors in 2012. She has also served on the board of Starbucks and the Walt Disney Company.

Many experts credit Sandberg's leadership as one of the reasons Facebook is so successful. Despite his innovativeness, expertise, and leadership qualities, experts believe that Chief Executive Officer (CEO) Mark Zuckerberg lacks some of the human relations and marketing skills that Sandberg possesses. When Sandberg first became COO, she personally introduced herself to hundreds of employees throughout the company. She tries to solicit feedback from employees and encourage debate. Her strong communication skills, interpersonal engagement with employees, and information sharing have led workers to identify with and admire Sandberg. This type of referent power encourages employees to work hard because they like and admire Sandberg. Her strengths have complemented Zuckerberg's to help make Facebook such a powerful company. Sandberg was ranked as the fifth most powerful woman in business by *Fortune* magazine in 2017.

Sandberg is not only concerned with gender equality but also with helping others through hardship. Her

Source: Krista Kennell/Shutterstock

latest cause is to help those who have suffered a loss in life. Her husband passed away while on vacation in Mexico in 2015 at the age of 47. She coauthored a book, *Option B*, with Wharton Professor Adam Grant in 2017 to help people deal with grief, illness, or adversity of any kind. In coming to terms with her grief, Sandberg acknowledges that employees are often expected to leave their emotions at the door when they enter the workplace. Sandberg believes leaving humanity out of the workplace is a mistake. She now has Option B groups on Facebook that provide resources to those dealing with grief. Sandberg acknowledges that her own tragedy has taught her important things about sympathizing with others, such as simply listening to the person and being with him or her. She publicly credits Mark Zuckerberg and his wife Priscilla with helping her through the aftermath of her husband's death, showing how important other people's support was to her during this difficult time. Sandberg's vulnerability is an important leadership trait because it demonstrates that leaders do not have to cover up their feelings to lead effectively.

Only 20 percent of executives are women, and less than 4 percent are women of color. Many challenges for gender equality in the workplace have hindered women in assuming leadership roles. More recently, publicized cases of sexual harassment have inundated the news. There is even concern that some organizations dealing with sexual harassment may be trying to create distance between men and women. There is much more work to be done for women to have the opportunity to advance in organizations. This is another opportunity for Sheryl Sandberg to play a leadership role in promoting equality in the workplace. With her strong background and leadership ability, Sandberg is clearly up to the challenge.[1]

Introduction

Leadership is one of the most fascinating and widely discussed aspects of management. Because of its intangible, elusive nature, writers and practitioners have been interested in what makes good or bad leaders for centuries: scientists have been studying it for around 100 years. The number of approaches to and definitions of good leadership are nearly as numerous as the writers who have studied it. In this chapter, we define leadership and distinguish it from management, and then examine different sources of leadership power. Next, we explore several theories that attempt to determine what makes an effective leader. We conclude with a discussion of some of the approaches in the study and practice of leadership.

The Nature of Leadership

Leadership is the process of influencing the activities of an individual or a group toward the achievement of a goal. This definition reflects three elements: the leader, the followers, and the process of influencing goal-directed behavior. Sam Walton, the late founder of Walmart stores; Mahatma Gandhi; and President John F. Kennedy are examples of strong leaders who influenced different kinds of groups of followers to accomplish goals.

> **leadership:** The process of influencing the activities of an individual or a group toward the achievement of a goal.

Leadership versus Management

Management is a broad concept that encompasses activities such as planning, organizing, staffing, and controlling, as well as leading—as we have seen throughout this book. Leadership, on the other hand, focuses almost exclusively on the "people" aspects of getting a job done—inspiring, motivating, directing, and gaining commitment to organizational activities and goals. Leadership accompanies and complements the management functions, but it has more to do with coping with the dynamic, ever-changing marketplace, with rapid technological innovation, increased foreign competition, and other fluctuating market forces. In short, management influences the brain, while leadership encourages the heart and the spirit.[2]

Organizations need both management and leadership, and some leaders can provide both. Others manage but cannot lead, while still others seem born to lead, but cannot manage. Managers provide and maintain stability and predictability within the organization by setting goals, implementing appropriate action steps to achieve those goals, and allocating resources accordingly. Leaders are less reactive. They formulate and develop the vision and strategies that guide the company into the future. Additionally, managers take care of the more pragmatic matters related to employees such as job structuring, training, and delegating, whereas leaders appeal to the emotions of the employees. Leaders will connect with different employees with the organization to reinforce the company's vision, incite motivation, and encourage learning and risk taking. In this way, one can see that managers and leaders complement each other and provide a healthy balance between reason and emotion and rational behavior and risk-taking. Unfortunately, most U.S. companies today appear to be over-managed and under-led.

When Fred Smith founded the Federal Express Co., he was acting as a leader. His vision of overnight package delivery represented a quantum leap forward in the industry, and he had to inspire acceptance of and commitment to that vision by all employees, customers, and investors. Now FedEx has grown into a gigantic organization, with hundreds of complex systems. Smith and the company's executives spend much of their time managing these systems in order to provide stability and avoid chaos. Smith still spends time communicating his vision to his workers by emphasizing the need for quality and service to meet the competition.

Sources of Power

Understanding leadership requires insight into the possession and use of power. **Power** refers to a person's capacity to influence the behavior and attitudes of others. We can think

> **power:** A person's capacity to influence the behavior and attitudes of others.

of it as potential ability attributed to a person. Bosses can fire employees but seldom do on a regular basis. We can also think of power as actively attempting to influence someone to do what you want. A boss actively directing an employee's behavior represents the use of power.

In either case, power is inherent in a relationship between two people and is based on one's ability to satisfy or deny satisfaction of some need of the other. That ability may be based on a formal contractual relationship between an organization and an individual, called **organizational power**, or it can be based on an interpersonal relationship between individuals or on one's personal characteristics, called **personal power**.[3] There are eight major sources of power: legitimate, reward, coercive, expert, referent, charisma, information, and affiliative.[4]

Legitimate Power

Legitimate power comes from a person's formal position in an organization and the authority that accompanies that position. The contractual relationship between employees and managers, for example, grants managers legitimate power to influence certain kinds of behavior. However, this kind of power may be limited by the formal contract—for example, when an employee refuses to do anything more than what the specific job description dictates. Thus, using a "do it because I'm the boss" approach may limit a manager's capacity to lead.

Reward Power

Reward power stems from a person's ability to bestow rewards. This, too, is an organizationally based source of power because companies generally grant managers the right to assign formal rewards, such as bonuses, days off, and promotions. Managers can also use social rewards, such as praise and recognition. Effective leaders learn that the creative use of informal rewards along with formal ones enhances their ability to lead. For example, one company gives a ticket to employees who get their projects done well ahead of the deadline. The employees can then "cash in" their ticket for a paid day off during designated times of the year. Such rewards can serve to increase both productivity and employee morale.

Coercive Power

Coercive power, another organizationally based source of power, is derived from a leader's control over punishments or the capacity to deny rewards. Leaders who demote, berate, withhold an expected pay increase, or threaten someone with a poor job assignment are using coercive power. Physical coercion was common in many businesses prior to the twenty-first century, and regulations were passed against it. Psychological and emotional coercion are more commonly used forms of negative influence today. Although regulations and laws limit a leader's ability to use coercive power, it is still all too common in many business settings. For instance, it is estimated that one in three workers have been a victim of bullying sometime during their careers. The use of punishment to gain compliance has the negative side effect of creating hostility and resentment toward the punisher and possibly reduced dedication to an organization. For instance, Enron had adopted what was termed a "rank and yank" system in which employees in the lowest 20 percent of performance levels were systematically fired. This led employees to compete against one another rather than work together, which served to create a highly competitive culture where success and profitability surpassed a concern for ethical conduct. While some still cling to the model of the hard-nosed executive boss, many CEOs see the use of coercion diminishing in favor of more positive sources of power.[5]

Source: ever/Shutterstock

Recognition can be one of the more effective forms of reward for employees.

---

organizational power: A person's ability to satisfy or deny satisfaction of another's need, based on a formal contractual relationship between an organization and the individual.

personal power: A person's ability to satisfy or deny satisfaction of another's need, based on an interpersonal relationship between individuals or on his or her personal characteristics.

legitimate power: The influence that comes from a person's formal position in an organization and the authority that accompanies that position.

reward power: Organizational power that stems from a person's ability to bestow rewards.

coercive power: An organizationally based source of power derived from a leader's control over punishments or the capacity to deny rewards.

Expert Power

Expert power is derived from a person's special knowledge or expertise in a particular area. The mechanic fixing a piece of equipment would probably have more expert power in that technical area than would a CEO. Professors and researchers rely mostly on expert power. Managers who also wish to be leaders learn to develop and use this personal source of power more than the formal sources. Bill Gates had tremendous expert power because of his computer knowledge, in addition to the formal, legitimate power that he had as founder and former CEO of Microsoft.

expert power: Power or influence derived from a person's special knowledge or expertise in a particular area.

Referent Power

Referent power results when one person identifies with and admires another. Referent power cannot be granted by organizations; it is a personal source of power you develop on your own. Through friendly communication, sharing of information, and mutually rewarding and close interpersonal relations, even friendships may develop. In such relationships, the employee may want to please the manager or some other person simply because it gives both of them pleasure or satisfaction. We do things for our friends that we will not do for others, simply because we like them.

referent power: Personal power that results when one person identifies with and admires another.

Charisma

People with **charisma**, another personal source of power, inspire admiration, respect, and loyalty. People desire to emulate them based on some intangible set of personality traits. Charismatic leaders are often distinguished by two characteristics: They are usually excellent communicators, the proverbial "silver-tongued devils," and they make people feel more secure and more powerful in themselves. Martin Luther King, Jr. and Malcolm X made their followers feel strong enough to resist racism and segregation. John F. Kennedy beseeched U.S. citizens to "ask not what your country can do for you, ask what you can do for your country." More recently, former U.S. President Barack Obama inspired similar loyalty and excitement around the world. These charismatic leaders empowered their followers to serve their causes. Like referent power, charisma cannot be granted by an organization. See Table 11.1 for more examples of leaders who use these sources of power.

charisma: The ability to inspire admiration, respect, loyalty, and a desire to emulate, based on some intangible set of personality traits; a personal source of power.

Information Power

Information power requires having access to important information that is not common knowledge, or having the ability to control the flow of information to and from others.

information power: Power that is a result of having access to important information that is not common knowledge, or of having the ability to control the flow of information to and from others.

TABLE 11.1 Different Power Sources and Examples of Leaders

Source	Example
Legitimate	Jeff Bezos, CEO of Amazon, has become respected as a result of his revolutionary business savvy.
Reward	James Dimon, CEO of J.P. Morgan, offers several types of rewards to employees.
Coercive	Charlie Ergen, former chairman of Dish Network Corporation, is known for influencing employees' behavior aggressively.
Expert/Information	Jack Welch, former CEO of General Electric, is widely followed for his precise knowledge of business management.
Referent	Warren Buffett, CEO of Berkshire Hathaway, is admired by many for his integrity and decision-making skills.
Charisma/Affiliative	Richard Branson, CEO of Virgin Group, is authentic and inspirational to the people around him.

The information may come from formal organizational sources or informal reciprocal relationships. People at all levels of an organization can have this source of power; indeed, it is not uncommon for a CEO's secretary to be one of the most influential and powerful employees in the company. Information power may be organizational or personal.

Affiliative Power

affiliative power: Power that is derived by virtue of a person's association with someone else who has some source of power.

Affiliative power comes by virtue of a person's association with someone else who has power. It works only when those being influenced are aware of the association and recognize the power of the person from whom the power is being "borrowed." A substitute teacher, for instance, is essentially "borrowing" the power of the teacher for a day.

The Use of Power

Managers and leaders exercise power to garner an appropriate response from subordinates. Indra Nooyi, CEO of PepsiCo., ranks among the most powerful women in the world because of her high position within the company, which is legitimate power, but also because of the personal power she possesses in the form of expert power and charisma.[6] Responses to power from subordinates fall into three major categories: commitment, compliance, or resistance. Commitment means the subordinate does what the leader wants because he or she really wants to and is dedicated to successfully fulfilling the request. Commitment comes about because of a desire to please the other person (referent power), respect for the leader's knowledge and the belief that the desired action is the best thing to do (expert power), or the inspiration or empowerment to engage in what might be perceived as a noble behavior (charisma power). Compliance means the subordinate does only what is required and nothing more. Compliance is the likely response when a manager exercises the formal authority of his or her position (legitimate power), offers special inducements contingent on fulfilling the request (reward power), or threatens punishment (coercive power). Resistance can take many forms, from the subtle (such as working slowly) to the obvious and extreme (such as destroying products or personal belongings and systematic employee theft). Although resistance is possible with any of the sources of power, it is least likely with the personal power sources and very likely when coercion is used. Information and affiliative power may have various effects, depending on how they are exercised.

empowerment: The process of providing employees with the ability to contribute input and take on responsibilities for organizational decisions.

If managers want to foster employee commitment to tasks, they should develop and use personal sources of power as the primary means of influencing their employees' behavior. Organizational power sources—particularly legitimate and coercive—should be used selectively, such as when there is little time to explain rationally or encourage commitment or when the dangers of noncompliance are severe. Personal sources of power are essential when extra effort is required, when close surveillance is impossible, and when the manager has no legitimate authority or control over rewards and punishments.

Empowerment

While power is an essential component to leadership, employee empowerment has been used to encourage an innovative and productive organization. **Empowerment** is the process of providing employees with the ability to contribute input and take on responsibilities for organizational decisions. Some leaders adopt an employee-centered approach to empower employees to take on more leadership

Employees may try to resist certain types of power, but their efforts are usually addressed by managers.

Source: ArtFamily/Shutterstock

responsibilities. Although it is up to leaders to make the final decisions, they realize that involving employees in the decision-making process is beneficial to the firm. For instance, research suggests that employee empowerment and effective communication from managers leads to greater employee satisfaction.[7] Other benefits of employee empowerment include increased productivity by encouraging employees to contribute their unique ideas and accept responsibilities; better customer service because employees are empowered to adjust their customer relationship strategies to different situations; and a greater ability to embrace change because empowered employees are encouraged to challenge the status quo.[8] Employee empowerment also takes some of the burden off of leaders, allowing other employees to take on greater roles in the decision-making process within the organization.

To create employee empowerment, leaders must establish a transparent workplace where employees feel encouraged in contributing ideas and communicating with managers. However, this requires leaders of the organization to allow for dissent. Some managers find that they have a difficult time sharing power and permitting employees to challenge the status quo. Employees themselves often feel uncomfortable taking on additional roles due to worries about failure or getting on the wrong side of company leaders. As a result, many organizations are instituting leadership programs to help train employees to become more effective leaders. Such programs are important for both managers and employees. Managers can be trained in employee empowerment and empathy, while employees can learn leadership skills such as teamwork, conflict resolution, and communication.[9]

Trait Approach to Leadership

The earliest approaches to the study of leadership focused, not on the process of influencing others, but on the personal characteristics of the leaders themselves. Psychologists and researchers alike tried to determine what traits—physical, intellectual, and personal—distinguish leaders from followers. Early studies revealed a perplexingly large number of traits related to leadership success. Researchers have analyzed over 300 of these studies and found a few traits to be fairly consistent characteristics of leaders.[10] However, because researchers found no definable set of traits that consistently predicts leadership success in a variety of situations, the trait approach lost credibility by the 1950s and 1960s. Experts now recognize that certain traits increase the likelihood that a person will be an effective leader, but they do not guarantee effectiveness, and the relative importance of different traits depends on the nature of the leadership situation.[11] The trait approach has not fully died out, but the focus has shifted more to what leaders do to be successful, rather than on what kinds of personalities or physiques they might have. Table 11.2 highlights some skills that leaders need to be effective.

A published analysis of leadership traits condensed the important primary ones into six core-trait categories:

Drive: Leaders desire to achieve and are ambitious about their work; they take initiatives and show energy and tenacity in accomplishing chosen goals.

Motivation: Leaders want to lead; they possess a socialized or positive need for power and are willing to take charge.

Honesty and Integrity: The best leaders are honest and truthful, and they do what they say they will do.

TABLE 11.2 Skills for Successful Leaders

Empathy	Sense of humor
Truthfulness	Attracts and motivates strong employees
Poise and confidence	Commitment
Communication	Competency
Delegation	

Self-Confidence: Leaders project their confidence by being assertive and decisive and taking risks. They admit mistakes and foster trust and commitment to a vision. They are emotionally stable, rather than recklessly adventurous.

Cognitive Ability: Leaders tend to be intelligent, perceptive, and conceptually skilled, but are not necessarily geniuses. They show analytical ability, good judgment, and the capacity to think strategically.

Business Knowledge: Leaders tend to have technical expertise in their businesses.[12]

Emotional Intelligence

emotional intelligence: The capacity to be aware of, control, and express one's emotions, and to handle interpersonal relationships judiciously and empathetically.

Although researchers have found no definable set of traits that consistently predicts leadership success, many agree that emotional intelligence is important to being a good leader. **Emotional intelligence** involves being able to manage oneself as well as form relationships with others. Emotionally intelligent leaders such as Warren Buffett are self-aware and are able to control their emotions, enabling them to handle conflicts and challenging situations. Emotionally intelligent leaders are also able to empathize with employee concerns and make employees feel like they are important contributors to the organization.[13] Because emotional intelligence impacts how one relates to others in the organization, some employers consider it to be a better predictor of success than IQ.[14]

Psychologist Daniel Goleman classified leadership styles based upon emotional intelligence. He developed six categories for leaders: coercive, authoritative, affiliative, democratic, pacesetting, and coaching. The coercive style generally uses threats and punishments to control people, whereas the authoritative style incites followers' confidence in the leader. Leaders who employ the affiliative style hold relationships in high regard as a way to connect with others. The democratic style allows everyone to take part in important decisions. Pacesetters may intimidate their followers with their high standards, while coaches have the opposite effect by helping others achieve their goals.[15] Richard Boyatzis and Annie McKee used Goleman's categories as a jumping off point to come up with the idea of a resonant leader. Resonant leaders are aware of themselves and their emotions, have a strong passion and belief in the outcome of company objectives, and adopt a caring attitude toward employees.[16] These types of leaders also have the ability to change their leadership styles to adapt to different situations. Resonant leaders inspire employees to believe in the firm and take ownership of the company goals and mission.

Behavioral Models of Leadership

As the trait approach waned, researchers began trying to identify the behaviors that distinguish effective from less effective leaders. Two major dimensions of leader behavior emerged from this body of research: One deals with how leaders get the job done, and the other deals with how leaders treat and interact with their subordinates. In this section, we will discuss three models that developed from this research: the Ohio State model, the University of Michigan model, and the leadership grid model.

Source: Krista Kennell/Shutterstock /Shutterstock

Emotional intelligence involves a sensitivity and understanding of how to use and manage emotions.

The Ohio State Studies

In an effort to describe what leaders actually do, researchers at Ohio State University analyzed the results of questionnaires they administered to a sample of leaders and followers. From this, they concluded that leadership behavior consists of two broadly defined dimensions they labeled "consideration" and "initiating structure."[17] **Consideration behaviors** involve being friendly and supportive by listening to employees' problems, supporting their actions, "going to bat" for them, and getting their input on a variety of issues. **Initiating-structure behaviors** involve defining and structuring leader-subordinate roles through activities such as scheduling, defining work tasks, setting deadlines, criticizing poor work, getting employees to accept work standards, and resolving problems. The dimensions seem to be relatively independent of each other, so leaders may rank high on one dimension and low on another at the same time.[18]

Early studies found that "Hi-Hi leaders," those ranking high in both dimensions, are most effective, although results were inconsistent. Subsequent research found that there may not be a simple relationship between the two dimensions and effectiveness. The only reliable finding has been that leaders exhibiting consideration behaviors tend to have more satisfied subordinates. Relationships between the two dimensions and effectiveness appear to depend on the situation. That "Hi-Hi" leaders are always the best leaders appears to be myth.[19]

The University of Michigan Studies

At about the same time the Ohio State studies were being conducted, researchers at the University of Michigan were also studying leadership effectiveness from a behavioral perspective. They too compared effective leaders to less effective leaders and came up with two dimensions of leadership behavior, which they labeled "task-oriented behaviors" and "relationship-oriented" behaviors.[20] The researchers found that effective managers engage in **task-oriented behaviors** such as planning and scheduling work, coordinating employee activities, and providing necessary supplies, equipment, and technical assistance—all designed primarily and specifically to get tasks completed and goals met. This task-oriented behavior appears to correspond to the initiating-structure dimension identified in the Ohio State studies. Martha Stewart could be considered a task-oriented leader. A self-proclaimed "control freak," Martha Stewart's ability to plan, coordinate, and provide her expertise created a media empire.[21]

The researchers also found that effective managers employ **relationship-oriented behaviors**, such as being considerate, supportive, and helpful to subordinates by showing trust and confidence, listening to employees' problems and suggestions, showing appreciation for contributions, and supporting employees' careers. Tony Hsieh at Zappos has developed a corporate culture focused on relationships and employee well-being. Employees at Zappos are encouraged to hang out together even outside of the workplace. These relationship-oriented behaviors correspond to the consideration behaviors of the Ohio State research.

Rensis Likert, a management theorist and leader of the Michigan Institute for Social Research, summarized the research by concluding that the most effective managers engage in both dimensions of leadership behavior by getting employees involved in the operation of their departments or divisions in a positive and constructive manner, setting general goals, providing fairly loose supervision, and recognizing their contributions. He called these managers **employee-centered leaders**.

Less effective managers are mostly directive in their approaches and more concerned with closely directing employees, explaining work procedures, and monitoring progress in task accomplishment; these he called **job-centered leaders**.[22]

Adaptation of the Leadership Grid

The leadership grid grew out of the two-dimensional behavioral approach to leadership. Developed originally as a managerial network by consultants Robert Blake and Jane

consideration behaviors: Patterns of being friendly and supportive by listening to employees' problems, supporting their actions, "going to bat" for them, and getting their input on a variety of issues.

initiating-structure behaviors: Defining and structuring leader-employee roles through activities such as scheduling, defining work tasks, setting deadlines, criticizing poor work, getting employees to accept work standards, and resolving problems.

task-oriented behaviors: Behaviors—such as planning and scheduling work, coordinating employee activities, and providing necessary supplies, equipment, and technical assistance—designed primarily and specifically to get tasks completed.

relationship-oriented behaviors: Behaviors such as being considerate, supportive, and helpful to employees by showing trust and confidence, listening to employees' problems and suggestions, showing appreciation for contributions, and supporting employees' concerns.

employee-centered leaders: The most effective managers, who engage in both dimensions of leadership behaviors by getting employees involved in the operation of their departments or divisions in a positive and constructive manner, setting general goals, providing fairly loose supervision, and recognizing employees' contributions.

job-centered leaders: Less-effective managers, who are mostly directive in their approaches and more concerned with closely supervising employees, explaining work procedures, and monitoring progress in task accomplishment.

FIGURE 11.1
Continuum of People vs. Operations

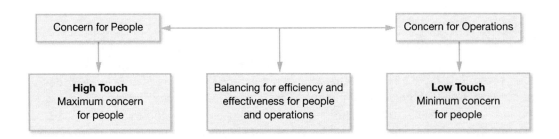

Mouton, this model builds on the Ohio State and University of Michigan studies and describes a leader's style as a position on a continuum between concern for operations and concern for people.[23] We have adapted the original model into a continuum shown in Figure 11.1. Concern for operations, which parallels task-oriented behavior and initiating structure, is on one end of the continuum, while concern for people is at the opposite end of the continuum.

There are three major styles in the continuum reflected by differing levels of the two leadership behaviors. Each extreme of the continuum represents a disproportionate management style. For example, the high touch management style represents a concern for people but little concern for operations. Google, while not completely fitting into this extreme, has some practices that cater to employees while not necessarily contributing to overall goals. The low-touch management style reflects concern for operations at the expense of concern for people. For example, Charlie Ergen, former CEO of Dish Network Corporation, was known for his harsh leadership. In order to address employee tardiness, he instituted fingerprint scanners to replace employee badge scanners to enter the building. If they were even one minute late, employees were reprimanded and not allowed to offer an explanation for their tardiness. Despite the fact that this practice left employees feeling dispirited, Ergen appeared to care more about employees being to work on time than their morale. It is rare for any company, however, to fit into these two extremes because neither type usually lasts very long. A concern for people at the expense of operations will result in goals not being met, which impacts the bottom line. A concern for operations at the expense of people will lead to a dissatisfied workplace with high turnover and low productivity.

The trick for managers is to balance these two extremes to consider both people and operations. This balance is often considered the ultimate style. Those that are able to bal-

An emphasis on operations and production can lead to employee dissatisfaction and turnover.

ance these two styles will achieve both efficiency and effectiveness in their operations and management. Goals are accomplished through the joint efforts of managers and employees working closely together for the good of the company and all employees. Evernote functions at a level similar to this. Employees work in teams, and while there is a team manager, hierarchic ranks are not emphasized. Additionally, the company takes steps to take care of employees with benefits such as unlimited vacation time, $1,000 spending money for vacation, and paid housecleaning two times per month for each employee.[24]

Two additional styles of leadership, not considered on the continuum, are paternalism and opportunism. *Paternalistic*, or "father knows best," management raises a high level of concern for people to reward for compliance, or punish for rejection. The paternalist strives for high results. The *opportunistic*, or "what's in it for me?" management style describes a leader who uses whatever grid style needed to obtain selfish interests and for self-promotion. These managers adapt to situations to gain maximum advantage. Performance by the manager occurs according to a system of exchanges, and effort is given only for an equivalent measure of effort from employees.

The continuum approach has as an underlying assumption that one approach—balancing between operations and people—is best. The contradictory results of the research into this style, however, suggest that some flexibility is needed in the application of this and other models.

Contingency Theories of Leadership

Neither the trait nor the early behavioral approaches to leadership were able to identify conclusively a single best style of leadership. In fact, the most effective leadership style depends on the situation a leader faces. Whether to be task- or people-oriented, or job- or employee-centered, or even how much employees should be allowed to participate in decision making is contingent on certain situational characteristics. In this section, we will examine several leadership models that address contingency factors, including situational leadership theory, Fiedler's contingency theory, and path-goal theory.

Situational Leadership Theory

Probably the most popular leadership model, and the one most frequently applied in leadership development and training, was originally developed by Paul Hersey and Ken Blanchard as the "life cycle theory of leadership."[25] It evolved through several versions into the **situational leadership theory**, the premise of which is that a leader's style should be contingent on subordinates' skills and dedication.[26]

To understand situational leadership theory, we must define several concepts. *Directive behaviors* involve telling a subordinate the how, what, when, and where of a task and closely supervising task accomplishment. *Supportive behaviors* entail listening to subordinates, supporting and encouraging their progress, and involving them in decision making. Levels of directive and supportive behaviors are shown in Figure 11.2, with a leader's style falling into one of the four areas. Hersey and Blanchard suggest that the levels of directive behavior (akin to task-oriented or initiating structure behaviors) and supportive

situational leadership theory: A leadership model whose premise is that a leader's style should be contingent on subordinates' competence and commitment.

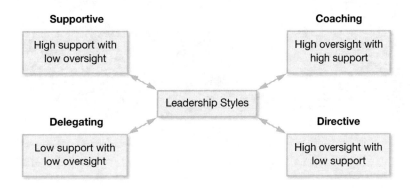

Supportive
High support with low oversight

Coaching
High oversight with high support

Leadership Styles

Delegating
Low support with low oversight

Directive
High oversight with low support

FIGURE 11.2
Alternative Situational Leadership Styles

behavior (akin to people-oriented or consideration behaviors) that a leader uses should depend on the development level of the subordinates. *Development level* refers to a subordinate's skills or ability in setting and attaining goals related to a specific task and his or her dedication toward accepting responsibility for those goals.

According to this theory, managers assess an employee's development level and ascertain the appropriate levels of directive and supportive behaviors based upon how much support and oversight is needed. A directive leadership style involves high oversight with low support. Managers assuming this style tell the employee what to do and when, where, and how to do it, to guide the employee in properly carrying out the task. This style may be appropriate with new employees unfamiliar with how to perform. A coaching leadership style involves both high oversight and high support. Employees at this level have gained some, but not full knowledge of their tasks and have low dedication because they have not figured out a strategy for the long-term. Managers can coach employees with fairly high levels of direction as well as a high level of support to deal with their waning dedication.

Employees that require a mainly supportive management style require high support but not much oversight. The manager may listen to complaints, show support, and help talk through personal issues, but seldom needs to provide direction in task areas. This occurs when employees have been around the organization a while and have the skills, motivation, and desire to perform their job duties. Finally, the most highly competent employees are both competent and committed. For these employees, a delegating style of leadership characterized by low support and low oversight is appropriate. It provides subordinates full rein to determine how to perform their tasks.

The biggest takeaway of this theory is that management styles depend on the situation of where employees are at in their development. Therefore, a manager might assume a delegating leadership style to an employee that has been at the organization for a long time while assuming a directive leadership style with new hires.

For example, in a football team of 11 players, only 1 or 2 might be superstars like Tom Brady or Peyton Manning, who need little coaching because they have both high skills and high dedication. Six or seven players might have varying levels of skills or dedication; they perform well but require the appropriate motivation and direction to do so. One or two players may not show much ability and have little dedication to the team. In order to be successful, coaches need to focus on the middle six or seven who make up the bulk of the team and should probably avoid those without strong skills or dedication.[27]

Athletes can exhibit a broad range of needs in terms of the amount of coaching required.

Application of the situational leadership model is not easy. Managers must first observe and communicate with employees to determine their level of development. Managers must also be flexible in applying direction and support because employees vary from one to another, as well as within themselves, over time and from task to task. Some managers are inflexible in their leadership style. Moreover, employees may not initially agree with a manager's assessment of their development level, thus requiring a leader's skill in arriving at an assessment consensus and an agreed-upon leadership style, a process called **contracting for leadership style**. It is also important for a leader to be constantly aware of the need to develop team members by gradually moving ahead of them on the leadership curve and pulling them along the development continuum. Yet another difficulty with the model is that it deals with only one aspect of a situation, the subordinates, and ignores other possibly important factors.

Fiedler's Contingency Theory

While Blanchard's theory calls for leaders to adjust their behaviors to meet the situational needs of subordinates, Professor Fred Fiedler took a different approach in his earlier **contingency theory**, suggesting that successful leadership requires matching leaders with primarily stable leadership styles to the demands of the situation.[28] If a leader's style does not match the situation, then either the situation should be changed or another leader should be found who does match the situation.

Leadership Style

A major, often controversial aspect of Fiedler's theory is how he characterizes and measures leadership style. Fiedler asserts that a leader tends to be either relationship-oriented (similar to the consideration or employee-centered styles) or task-oriented (comparable to the initiating structure and directive styles). He considers a leader's style, like a trait, to be rooted in his or her personality and to be stable, regardless of the situation. Task-oriented leaders consistently emphasize getting the job done without much concern for their subordinates' feelings; relationship-oriented leaders are most concerned about their people across all kinds of tasks. However, Fiedler's critics counter that people are capable of learning and changing their behaviors, even leadership behavior.[29]

To measure a leader's style, Fiedler devised a **Least Preferred Coworker (LPC) Scale** consisting of a series of adjective continuums. Low-LPC leaders view and describe their least preferred co-workers negatively and are thought to be task-oriented. High-LPC leaders view even their least preferred co-worker in a relatively favorable light and are thought to be relationship-oriented. Fiedler's LPC scale to measure leadership style is also controversial, with some researchers questioning the scale's validity.[30]

Situational Contingencies

Whether a relationship-oriented or task-oriented leader will be successful depends on the favorability of the situation—that is, the extent to which the situation gives the leader control over subordinate behavior. Favorability is defined by three aspects of the situation:

Leader-member relations—The extent to which the leader is accepted by group members and has their support, respect, and goodwill is the most important determinant of favorability.

Task structure—The degree to which a task is well-defined or has standard procedures for goal accomplishment. Creative or ambiguous tasks would be less structured.

Position power—The extent to which a leader has formal authority over employees to evaluate their work, assign tasks, and administer rewards and punishment.

By combining these three situational variables, Fiedler's Contingency Model derives eight different situations, called octants. The most favorable situation (octant 1) is one in which leader-member relations are good, the task is structured, and the leader has strong

contracting for leadership style: A process whereby employees may not initially agree with a manager's assessment of their developmental level, thus requiring a leader's skill in arriving at an assessment consensus and an agreed-upon leadership style.

contingency theory: The suggestion that successful leadership requires matching leaders with primarily stable leadership styles to the demands of the situation.

Least Preferred Coworker (LPC) Scale: A measurement of a leader's style consisting of a series of adjective continuums.

position power. The least favorable situation (octant 8) is one where a leader has poor relations with subordinates, an unstructured task, and little formal power.

Style Effectiveness

In his research, Fiedler found that task-oriented leaders tended to be most effective (have higher group productivity) in the three most favorable and the very least favorable situations (octants 1, 2, 3, 8), while relationship-oriented leaders were most effective in the situations of moderate favorableness. If the leader's style does not match the situational demands, Fiedler would advise the leader to alter the situation, perhaps by restructuring the task or seeking more position power.

There has been considerable research on Fiedler's model, generating both support and criticism for his ideas. Criticisms of the model include its neglect of leaders who score in the middle on the LPC scale, the use of the LPC scale itself, the fact that many leaders can and do change their behaviors, and the relative lack of consideration of other situational characteristics related to the followers.[31] Nonetheless, Fiedler's contingency theory was one of the first to recognize the importance of the situation to leadership effectiveness, and it sensitized managers and researchers alike to the ineffectiveness of the one-best-way approach to leadership.

Path-Goal Theory

Another contingency model of leadership was developed by Robert House as an outgrowth of the expectancy theory of motivation. **Path-goal theory** is so named because it is concerned with how leaders affect subordinates' perceptions of their personal and work goals and the paths to goal attainment. It considers leaders effective to the degree that their behavior increases employees' attainment of goals and clarifies paths to these goals. What behaviors will help to accomplish these positive results depend on two aspects: leader behavior and situational factors.[32]

Leader Behavior

Path-goal theory recognizes four major types of behavior:

Directive Leadership: As with situational leadership theory, directive behaviors include giving task guidance, scheduling work, maintaining standards, and clarifying expectations.

Supportive Leadership: Leaders concentrate on being approachable, showing concern for employees' well-being, doing little things to make the work environment more pleasant, and helping to satisfy employees' personal needs.

Participative Leadership: Leaders consult with subordinates, solicit suggestions, and seriously consider their input when making decisions.

Achievement-Oriented Leadership: Leaders set challenging goals, expect high performance, constantly seek improved performance, and show confidence in employees' ability to accomplish goals.

At different times and under different conditions, any of these leader behaviors may be most effective. Unlike Fiedler's model, path-goal theory assumes that leaders can adapt their styles to meet the demands of the situation or needs of subordinates to gain favorable outcomes. See Table 11.3 for examples of these four types of leader behavior.

Situational Factors

Path-goal theory proposes that two classes of situational factors affect what leadership behaviors are appropriate: (1) employees' personal characteristics, and (2) environmental pressures and demands with which the employee must cope to accomplish the goal.

One important personal characteristic is an individual's locus of control (LOC), the extent to which a person believes he or she has control over what happens to him or her in life. Individuals who have an internal LOC believe they largely control what happens to

Fiedler's contingency approach to leadership indicates that leaders must adjust their styles when the circumstances dictate change.

Source: Peshkova/Shutterstock

path-goal theory: A model concerned with how a leader affects employees' perceptions of their personal and work goals and the paths to goal attainment.

TABLE 11.3 Examples of Path-Goal Theory Behaviors

Behavior	Example
Directive	Anne Mulcahy, former CEO of Xerox, successfully guided the company through the 2008 recession by setting new standards and reorienting employees.
Supportive	Mark Zuckerberg, CEO of Facebook, sits among his employees, who see him as approachable and concerned for them.
Participative	Marissa Mayer, former CEO of Yahoo!, held regular office hours for employees to give feedback or offer new ideas.
Achievement-Oriented	Wendy Kopp, Founder of Teach for America, wanted to create educational equality and has been successful by setting goals and inspiring others.

them; those with an external LOC believe that their lives are more controlled by fate, luck, chance, or significant other people. Consider Sarah, who has done poorly on a management test. If Sarah has an internal LOC, she will probably say that her poor grade is due to not studying hard enough, but if she has an external LOC, she may attribute the poor grade to bad luck or an excessively difficult test. An individual with an internal locus of control may require less directive behavior than one with an external LOC. Another personal factor is an employee's belief in his or her own ability to perform the task at hand. People with low confidence in their ability will likely respond better to directive behavior.

Environmental characteristics include (1) the nature of the task structure, (2) the formal authority of the situation, and (3) the nature of primary work groups. Although there are many propositions concerning how situational characteristics, personal characteristics, and leader behaviors interact to influence employees, the general premise of the path-goal theory is that the leader should apply whatever behavior helps to provide more positive rewards for employees, to strengthen employees' beliefs that their efforts will lead to goal accomplishment and positive rewards, or to make rewards more contingent on goal accomplishment.

Path-goal theory has been very beneficial by pointing out a number of important situational contingency variables not covered in other theories; it also points out the important motivational consequences of leader style on subordinate attitudes, beliefs, and behaviors.

Current Trends in the Study and Practice of Leadership

Although the contingency approach is still used, a number of other approaches to the study of leadership have been introduced in recent years. In this section, we will discuss the leader substitute approach, the leader-member exchange theory, charismatic leadership, authentic leadership, servant leadership, transactional and transformational leadership, gender and leadership, and leadership challenges, none of which totally abandons the contingency approach.

Leadership Substitutes Theory

The contingency models discuss conditions that call for certain leadership behaviors. Some situational aspects have an even greater effect by severely limiting the ability of a leader to influence outcomes. Two such situational factors have been identified as substitutes and neutralizers.[33] Some other situational aspects actually have a positive impact on the leader behaviors; hence, they are called enhancers.

Leadership substitutes are aspects of the task, subordinates, or organization that act in place of leader behavior and thus render it unnecessary. For example, unambiguous, routine tasks or employees' knowledge, ability, and experience can substitute for task-oriented or directive behaviors. For example, Whole Foods allows service employees to form teams and make independent decisions.

leadership substitutes: Aspects of the task, subordinates, or organization that act in place of leader behavior and thus render it unnecessary.

You're the Manager . . . What Would You Do?

THE COMPANY: Academy Oil
YOUR POSITION: Base Commander
THE PLACE: Altus, Ohio

Academy Oil is a small oil production company owned and operated by the U.S. Army. The facility supplies the oil to a major petroleum refinery and receives credit toward future purchases. The oil production facility has been in operation for 25 years. Recently, a crisis occurred when a storage tank ruptured while being filled. Thousands of gallons of crude oil spilled into a nearby river, the major source of drinking water for the area. The oil spill had immediate negative effects on wildlife, fish, and local residents.

The military base assembled a crisis management team to go to the scene of the incident and direct the cleanup operation. The Army's crisis management teams are ready and prepared to deal with just such disasters. The teams plan worst-case scenarios and analyze past public relations and other problems in prior incidents to assess what could have been done better. The team knows how to disseminate information and serves as a center for outside sources to contact. In this disaster, the base's commander, Col. Jim Briggs, did not make a public statement until he had collected enough information and had enough support activities engaged to honestly assure the public that everything possible was being done.

The situation worsened when cleanup efforts failed to contain the oil spill. Already fearful city residents were warned that the city's water systems would be shut down and they would be without water for several days. Reporters on the scene collected enough information to levy serious charges against the base's managers. They discovered inadequate training procedures and old, ill-maintained equipment, including the 25-year-old tank that had ruptured.

Briggs then held a press conference with the media in which he acknowledged that problems had existed

Academy Oil Company exhibits leadership in a crisis situation.

at the base in operating the oil production facilities, apologized, and took full responsibility. He also indicated that an oil company would be purchasing the oil production facilities and rights and the base would no longer be involved in the oil business.

The crisis team worked to get volunteers from major oil companies to donate their efforts to help clean up the spill. The team also worked closely with the media to keep them informed, as did Col. Briggs. Briggs brought water tankers into city areas to provide emergency water supplies. The spill was contained and water service reconnected in the area within three and a half days.

QUESTIONS

1. Evaluate Briggs' effectiveness in managing the crisis.

2. What type of leadership skills did Briggs use in this situation?

3. Describe the function of the crisis team and how this assisted Briggs in dealing with the public in this situation.

In other situations, leaders may not even be necessary. If a cohesive work team of trained professionals performs structured tasks in a highly formalized environment, then little direct supervision and involvement by a leader may be warranted. Indeed, the understanding and creative use of leadership substitutes may be integral to the success of self-managed work teams.

Leadership neutralizers are aspects of the task, subordinates, or organization that either paralyze, destroy, or counteract the effect of a leadership behavior. For example, if employees, such as those at FedEx and UPS, are indifferent to organizational rewards, then a supervisor engaging in the supportive leadership behavior of praising and rewarding would likely have little positive effect on employee satisfaction or motivation. In such a situation, the supervisor may have to stick to task-oriented behaviors, try other support-

leadership neutralizers:
Aspects of the task, subordinates, or organization that have the effect of paralyzing, destroying, or counteracting the effect of a leadership behavior.

Training programs can address team building and successful collaborative techniques.

ive (but non-reward-oriented) behaviors, or replace these employees with ones who will work within the system.

In some situations, other changes might be made that enhance the effectiveness of a leader's behavior. **Leadership enhancers** are aspects of the task, subordinates, or organization that amplify a leader's impact on employees. For example, if a nonperformance-based reward system is neutralizing a leader's impact, then changing the system to give the leader more power to influence rewards can make the same leadership behavior more effective. FedEx has an award that can be given on the spot for doing something outstanding. Likewise, having team-building exercises as part of a training program may aid in fostering positive group norms and values that help employees accept the task-oriented behaviors of a fairly directive leader. Dig This is a company offering team-building and motivational leadership exercises. The company uses heavy equipment, such as tractors and bulldozers, as tools to teach groups of employees how to work together. The company has been successful because it combines training with elements of fun. The creation of leadership enhancers can work very well when a leader has the necessary skill and appropriate organizational goals but is prevented by one or more neutralizers from being effective.[34]

In general, understanding how substitutes, neutralizers, and enhancers influence the effectiveness of leadership behavior can help an organization when a leader cannot be changed for political, financial, ethical, or other practical reasons. It can also play an important role when leadership is in transition.

Leader-Member Exchange Theory

The **Leader-Member Exchange (LMX) Theory** describes how leaders develop "unique" working relationships with each of their subordinates, based on the nature of their social exchanges.[35] Each leader-subordinate relationship differs in terms of both the feelings present and the behaviors demonstrated. Higher-quality relationships are reflected by

leadership enhancers: Aspects of the task, subordinates, or organization that amplify a leader's impact on employees.

Leader-Member Exchange (LMX) Theory: A description of how leaders develop "unique" working relationships with each of their employees, based on the nature of their social exchanges.

more positive attitudinal statements, closer emotional ties, and stronger mutual commitment and loyalty, as well as more employee influence and autonomy.[36] Based on these relationships, leaders tend to develop *in-groups*—those subordinates who are part of their "team"—and *out-groups*—those who are not.

Research has found that in-group members perform better, have higher levels of satisfaction, are promoted more quickly, and have lower turnover rates. This implies that employees should try to be in the in-group if they desire more rewards. Managers need to be aware that these two distinct groups can develop, with both positive and negative consequences. If the in-group includes virtually every employee, then all workers will be more likely to receive these positive outcomes. Out-group members, though, will often feel disenchanted and resentful and lose their team identification and commitment.

Although the theory is somewhat vague on how leader-member exchange relationships develop, some recent research suggests that friendship and the process of forming friendships may parallel the LMX relationship development process and have similar effects. Simply becoming and remaining friends on the job may be the essential element of positive LMX relationships and may assist the leader in motivating employees.[37]

Charismatic Leadership

Much has been written about charismatic leaders in nearly all phases of public life. Sam Walton, the founder of Walmart; Michael Dell of Dell Inc.; Peyton Manning, the former quarterback of the Denver Broncos; and the late George Steinbrenner, the shipbuilder who became a Yankees baseball team owner—all are examples of charismatic leaders. Charisma has become even more important as competition has grown; today's companies need to inspire employees to higher levels of performance in order to meet stiff competition. If we can find out what makes a leader charismatic, then we may be able to advance our organizations and motivate employees like never before. Thus, a closer look at charisma is warranted.

Charismatic leaders inspire followers to a higher level of performance, instill confidence in themselves and other leaders, empower employees and subordinates, and generate tremendous devotion and obedience.[38] This devotion can sometimes rise to the level of cult leaders. Charismatic leaders have a strong sense of dominance, self-confidence, a need to influence, and a belief in the value and righteousness of their causes.[39] They are typically eloquent speakers who can clearly express a vision or ideology, and convince people of its value no matter how extreme.[40] Howard Schultz of Starbucks had to return as CEO to lead the coffee chain after the company declined under new leadership. The first thing he did was to re-communicate the vision and values of Starbucks.

For our purposes, it is more important to know what charismatic leaders actually do, especially in the business world. They tend to promote causes that deviate greatly from the status quo, yet still fall within the realm of acceptance by followers. They take personal risks that often appear heroic and engage in unconventional behavior to achieve the changes they desire. They assess the environment realistically and implement innovative strategies when the environment appears favorable. Finally, they engage in self-promotion to inspire employees or followers, often by presenting the status quo as negative and their vision and themselves as the solution. They exert personal power (expert and referent) that may involve elitist, entrepreneurial, and exemplary behaviors that position them as reformers, rather than administrators or managers.[41] Finally, charismatic leaders maintain intensely personal relationships with their followers, based on emotional rather than rational grounds.

Contrary to traditional beliefs, not only can many of these behaviors be learned, but they represent a separate dimension of leadership behavior, distinct from consideration or initiating structure, that enhances employees' task performance and satisfaction. Charismatic leadership may help convey the importance of a given task, while initiating structure conveys the orderliness of the task, and consideration expresses the shared responsibility (supportiveness) for the task.[42] Table 11.4 provides some steps for successful leadership.

TABLE 11.4 Steps for Effective Leadership

1. Act as a role model for employees.
2. Clearly communicate company expectations and mission.
3. Encourage employee participation and creativity.
4. Communicate core values.
5. Listen as much as you speak and encourage feedback.
6. Empower employees to make decisions.
7. Identify and guard against ethical risks.
8. Build sincere relationships.
9. Evaluate employee successes and failures.
10. Engage the workforce in continuous improvement.

Authentic Leadership

Another form of leadership that is gaining acceptance is authentic leadership. **Authentic leaders** are passionate about company objectives, model corporate values in the workplace, and form strong relationships with stakeholders.[43] In other words, authentic leaders "practice what they preach." Other characteristics of authentic leaders include self-awareness, a drive to achieve the company's mission, strong connections with stakeholders, and the ability to adopt a long-term perspective.[44] Kim Jordan, co-founder and former CEO of New Belgium, is an example of an authentic leader. When she co-founded the company, she collaborated on a set of values that would direct the company's corporate culture. Among these values was a strong emphasis on employee involvement and sustainability. As a leader, she tries to ensure that every activity performed by New Belgium Brewing aligns with its core values. Today NBB engages in numerous sustainability initiatives. It purchases wind credits to offset its energy use, investigates ways to recycle packaging and other materials, and even provides employees with a bicycle after one year of employment to reduce gas emissions from driving. It is also 100 percent employee-owned, and employees actively participate in company operations.

authentic leader: A leader who is passionate about company objectives, models corporate values in the workplace, and forms strong relationships with stakeholders.

Source: Lightfield Stuido/Shutterstock

New Belgium Brewing in Fort Collins, CO, operates with open book management and has an authentic leader who embraces the culture, values, and environmental sensitivity of many Americans.

Warren Buffett: The Oracle of Omaha's Leadership Style

Warren Buffett did not change his life plans when he was rejected by Harvard. An avid reader with a photographic memory, he persevered. He then researched other universities and discovered that Benjamin Graham, the author of *The Intelligent Investor*, was a professor at Columbia University. He immediately enrolled there, was accepted, and became the star pupil and eventual partner of the famous Graham. His investment philosophy of *value investing*, a concept created by Graham, served him well throughout his career.

Value investors invest in stocks they believe are underpriced compared to their value. These investors carefully study a firm's financials to determine what they think the business is truly worth. If the stock is being sold at a price lower than its value, the value investor purchases the stock. Eventually, when the market realizes the firm's worth and the stock price increases, the investor profits.

Buffett's approach was to take ownership in companies that he believed would do well in business. His firm, Berkshire Hathaway, has become a conglomerate with ownership in well-performing companies, including Geico, Heinz, Benjamin Moore, and See's Candies. Buffett believes in these firms and their value, a strategy that has made him one of the ten richest people in the world. He is known as the Oracle of Omaha because he has lived there for most of his life and many investors follow his advice and decisions.

Source: Krista Kennell/Shutterstock

Leading such various companies is not easy. Companies require leaders who know the business and have specialized expertise, something nearly impossible for one person to do with so many different business areas. For this reason, Buffett is more of a democratic leader. Rather than micromanaging the managers of his companies, Buffett's leadership style is a free-rein, hands-off approach, allowing managers to do their jobs. He believes giving his managers autonomy allows them to achieve their highest performance. He wants his managers to "own" their jobs. By hiring knowledgeable managers and empowering them to run the companies as they believe best, Buffett is able to lead his vast business conglomerate successfully.

(continued)

Servant Leadership

servant leader: A leader who leads by example and forms strong relationships with employees.

Servant leadership is not mutually exclusive of authentic leadership, as servant leaders also lead by example and form strong relationships with employees. Servant leadership was first coined by Robert K. Greenleaf in his 1970 essay "The Servant as Leader." According to Greenleaf, servant leaders try to ensure that the highest priorities of their followers are met. Effective servant leaders help followers to grow.[45] In an organization, a servant leader would not measure success solely by productivity but also by how employees are growing in their skills, well-being, and career opportunities.

Servant leaders model servant leadership for their followers, are people-centric, treat others with respect and integrity, demonstrate humility, and remain vigilant and disciplined.[46] Former CEO of ServiceMaster, William Pollard modeled this type of leadership. During one particular board meeting, when Pollard spilled a cup of coffee, he got down on his hands and knees to clean the spill himself rather than letting someone else do it.[47] TD Industries and Synovus Financial Corporation have adopted servant leadership as the foundation and philosophy of their companies. Employees at TD Industries are considered to be partners rather than subordinates and own most of the stock, while Synovus has instituted family-friendly policies to encourage employees to have a healthy work-life balance.[48]

Warren Buffett: The Oracle of Omaha's Leadership Style *(continued)*

Buffett's organizational leadership philosophy includes *focusing on the business*. At his headquarters, 25 people run the organization. He admonishes entrepreneurs "to focus on the business and not growing a large staff."

Some of the other leadership practices that Buffett acknowledges made him so successful include the following:

1. **Token Fees.** His board members are paid token fees and are not provided liability insurance. Buffett wants his board members to take risks so that they can relate to the shareholders they represent.

2. **Character and Integrity First.** Buffett is not given to ego; all employees must think of the company first before their own interests. He stresses that Berkshire's reputation must be guarded, and managers must report any bad news immediately.

3. **Stay Humble.** Buffett avoids hiring people who are egotistical, bureaucratic, and complacent. He believes these characteristics lead companies to falter.

4. **Trust Your Managers.** Managers should run their own businesses. They can call Mr. Buffett, if needed; otherwise, they receive a letter from him every two years.

5. **Admit Your Mistakes.** Buffett admits mistakes and failures while acknowledging that some of his managers can do things better than he can.

6. **Importance of Giving Back.** Buffett is a generous philanthropist, and his children run many of his foundations that support health, art, education, and service organizations. Managers and all employees are encouraged to give back with service and financial support; they get to choose their projects based on the needs of their communities.

7. **Praise.** Buffett believes in praising his managers and staff and mentioning them by name, publicly acknowledging their successes and achievements. Positive feedback improves performance.

8. **Stay Focused on Your Career Goals.** Buffett advises entrepreneurs to make a list of their goals and work toward the top five because the others become a distraction.

Although Buffett is complex and a financial genius, he is also a humble person. Buffett tops the list of philanthropists, having given away 71 percent of his fortune since 2000. He advocates life-long learning and is resolved to go to bed each night a little wiser than he was that morning.[49]

Transactional versus Transformational Leadership

The discussions of leader-member exchanges and charismatic leadership highlight the contrast between two major leadership styles currently being discussed by leadership experts: transactional and transformational leadership.[50] Although these two leadership styles differ, studies have shown that both forms of leadership can have positive outcomes. One study, for instance, found that transactional and transformational leadership decreased the likelihood for unethical communication (bullying) in the workplace.[51]

Transactional leadership is more traditional, with managers engaging in both task- and consideration-oriented behaviors in an exchange manner—you do things for me, and I'll do things for you. Transactional leaders get things done by promising and providing recognition, praise, pay increases, and advancements in return for higher performance. They also impose punishments on workers who perform poorly. Some managers actively engage in these types of transactions by seeking out opportunities to take action to improve performance and thus reward employees. Other less effective managers use a more passive management-by-exception approach and often concentrate on punishing non-standard performance.[52] Although the active-reward approach has shown better results than the passive-punishment approach, both can result in mediocre performance. In a path-goal fashion, these two approaches require the manager to clarify subordinate

transactional leadership: A more traditional approach in which managers engage in both task- and consideration-oriented behaviors in an exchange manner.

TABLE 11.5 Transactional versus Transformational Leadership

Transactional Leadership Characteristics	Examples	Transformational Leadership Characteristics	Examples
■ Use of reward power ■ Negotiates for performance ■ Emphasis on required conduct ■ Good for rapidly changing situations	■ U.S. Army ■ General Motors ■ New Orleans Saints ■ Delta Airlines ■ Bank of America	■ Uses charisma to inspire employees ■ Communicates a shared vision ■ Promotes change ■ Strong support for an ethical culture	■ Whole Foods ■ Amazon ■ Apple ■ Berkshire Hathaway ■ 3M

roles, define subordinate needs, and clarify how those needs will be met in exchange for valued outcomes. The leaders' effectiveness is limited in many cases by lack of control over organizational rewards and punishments as well as the inability to excite, inspire, or foster commitment in employees.[53]

transformational leadership: A style that goes beyond mere exchange relationships by inspiring employees to look beyond their own self-interests and by generating awareness and acceptance of the group's purposes and mission.

Transformational leadership goes beyond mere exchange relationships by inspiring employees to look beyond their own self-interests and by generating awareness and acceptance of the group's purposes and mission. Transformational leaders often appeal to higher ideals and ethical values such as truthfulness, transparency, fairness, and diversity. Transformational leaders have tremendous power to do good things, however. In business, they can excite employees to perform beyond what they thought they were capable of doing. Employees in these organizations work in order to satisfy the higher-order needs identified in Maslow's hierarchy. Research has shown that transformational leadership is even more effective than servant leadership in organizational learning.[54] Examples of transformational leaders would be Ursula Burns, who led Xerox out of a major crisis; Michael Dell, whose vision and inventory strategies caused his company to rapidly grow into a multi-billion-dollar firm; and Steve Jobs, who transformed a struggling Apple into the world's most valuable brand. Table 11.5 compares transformational leadership with transactional leadership.

A number of characteristics seem to distinguish transformational leaders from the more traditional transactional leaders:

Transformational leaders help employees to achieve goals and accomplish tasks they otherwise would not have been able to do.

Source: MJgraphics/Shutterstock

Charisma: Transformational leaders provide a vision and mission, instilling a sense of trust and respect in followers. Charisma is a necessary condition for transformational leadership, but it is insufficient without the remaining traits. Tony Hsieh of Zappos is charismatic with his emphasis on WOW customer service and his ability to motivate employees.

Inspiration: Transformational leaders communicate through images, conveying a simple yet powerful message that inspires followers to a higher purpose. Google's corporate motto, "Don't be evil," which was later changed to "Do the right thing," is a result of this aspect of transformational leadership.

Intellectual Stimulation and Empowerment: Transformational leaders stimulate their followers' intellectual process by promoting rationality and problem solving. They are willing to take risks and get their followers thoroughly involved in their purpose. Steve Jobs of Apple Inc. led his company with these characteristics.

Individual Consideration: They give individualized and personal attention to followers. They act as coaches, developers, and supporters, admonishing when necessary, but emphasizing the positive. John Mackey, CEO of Whole Foods (now a part of

Amazon.com), embodies individual consideration by making sure his employees and their families are taken care of.

Change Facilitation: They recognize the need for and promote change. They see themselves as agents of change who are willing to commit themselves and their subordinates' involvement to the future they envision. Jeff Bezos is a change facilitator. He left his job to start an online bookstore company and refused to stop there. Today, Amazon sells everything from media to electronics.

Integrity: They promote the higher-order values noted above and model honesty and integrity with their own behavior.[55] Warren Buffet tries to hire managers with integrity and a concern for ethics.

Transformational leadership, although not common in business and government, is certainly not restricted to a few "born" charismatics. Moreover, research has found that transformational leadership exists at all levels of organizational hierarchies and is positively related to a number of different performance criteria in an extremely broad range of organizations: senior U.S. Navy officers, business and industry leaders in many countries, educational administrators, and religious leaders.[56] Perhaps the most exciting aspect of transformational leadership is that there is increasing evidence that it can be learned.

Gender and Leadership

With more and more women advancing to higher managerial positions, it is natural to examine the relationship between leadership and gender. Numerous studies over the years have shown that while male and female leaders may have different leadership styles, overall both are equally effective in leading others.[57] However, there continues to be a gap between female top managers and male top managers in business. Female CEOs such as Marillyn Hewson of Lockheed Martin, Indra Nooyi of PepsiCo, and Virginia Rometty from IBM make up a much smaller percentage than their male counterparts. Approximately 5 percent of CEOs at *Fortune* 500 companies are women.

However, recent studies are showing that female leaders actually score higher on many leadership dimensions.[58] For instance, women leaders tend to score higher on interpersonal skills, teamwork, empathy, and mentoring.[59] As collaboration becomes increasingly important in organizations, demand for these types of leadership skills is rising. More

Source: Syda Productions/Shutterstock

Female leaders exhibit many successful leadership characteristics in the workplace.

attention is being paid to "soft" leadership skills including self-awareness, empathy, motivation, and social skills.[60] Many of these skills have traditionally been thought of as feminine and therefore less useful to management. Yet in recent years the business landscape has begun to shift from a hierarchal leadership style to one built upon relationships and collaboration. The more masculine qualities of assertiveness, vision, and ambition continue to remain important,[61] and both genders should try to incorporate both "soft" and "hard" skills into their management styles.

Despite the equal leadership effectiveness of the two genders, women remain underrepresented in leadership roles. Due to popular stereotypes, women tend to be characterized as nurturers and selfless, traits that have not been traditionally looked upon with favor in terms of leadership qualities. Even female leaders who adopt more "masculine" traits of aggressiveness, ambition, and dominance may be looked down upon for acting "too masculine."[62] However, as the business environment continues to evolve, more women are being recognized for their leadership abilities. Evidence also suggests that women might have advantages in transformational leadership due to their ability to connect with followers.

Sheryl Sandberg, the corporate operations officer at Facebook, has exemplified the woman as a leader. Named as one of the "50 Most Powerful Women in Business," Sandberg is in charge of maintaining positive relationships with stakeholders, expanding Facebook into other markets, and anticipating threats to the company such as new regulation. Her previous job as vice president of online sales at Google helped hone her leadership abilities, enabling her to take on a major managerial role when she arrived at Facebook. Sandberg also appears to possess some people skills that CEO Mark Zuckerberg may at times lack.[63] Sandberg demonstrates how ambition, interpersonal skills, and collaboration can successfully lead a firm to greater opportunities. In the next section, we present a set of behavioral practices that leaders of all kinds in all types of situations can develop in themselves and help to develop in others.

The Leadership Challenge

James Kouzes and Barry Posner list five major leadership practices—each with two behavioral subcategories—that they found present in successful leaders.[64] These five practices are quite similar to the characteristics of transformational leadership and, moreover, are behaviors that nearly any manager (or aspiring manager) can learn. Kouzes and Posner challenge managers to become true leaders by:

Challenging the Process

Leaders act as pioneers by changing the status quo. They do this by searching out opportunities to change, grow, and improve, as well as experiment, take risks, and learn from their mistakes. They actively look for things to change, and they encourage subordinates not to fear taking a calculated risk with them. Former Target CEO, Bob Ulrich, began a process of reinventing Target to be perceived as hipper and more stylish, as well as affordable enough to compete directly with Walmart. Current CEO Gregg Steinhafel has continued this mission to provide low-cost yet stylish items.

Inspiring a Shared Vision

Leaders begin to inspire by envisioning the future—perhaps a new facility, a major process innovation, or a new product or market. They then enlist others in the common vision by appealing to their values, interests, hopes, and dreams. They paint a picture with language, using metaphors and symbols to give life to their vision and attract others to it. Steve Jobs and Michael Dell epitomize the visionary leader.

Enabling Others to Act

Leaders build successful teams and make others feel like owners of the vision by fostering collaboration and strengthening others. They encourage collaboration by emphasizing cooperative, instead of competitive, goals, by seeking integrative solutions, and by building relationships based on trust, mutual respect, and individual dignity. They empower others by involving them in planning and decision making, along with granting autonomy and discretion.

Modeling the Way

Leaders epitomize what they want others to do, and they encourage them to do it. First, they set the example by developing a set of values. They then reflect those values in decisions they make and actions they take. They also plan small wins by dividing tasks into smaller chunks and experimenting frequently, giving people a sense of choice and accomplishment along the way. They build commitment to the goal and the process. Bill Gates modeled the work ethic of Microsoft by working long hours when he led the company.

Encouraging the Heart

Leaders make people feel good about what they are doing by recognizing contributions and celebrating accomplishments. Effective leaders use a variety of rewards and strive to link them to performance. Leaders who encourage the heart also cheerlead, have public ceremonies and rituals, stay personally involved, and build caring social networks. They give heart to others. Vince Lombardi said that love—which he defined as loyalty and teamwork—was at the core of his success as a coach.

Additionally, leaders must be able to influence others to follow them. Good interpersonal skills and the ability to persuade others are therefore important components of leadership. Figure 11.3 shows some of the ways that leaders can build influence within an organization. Managers who engage in these leadership practices are more likely to be perceived as leaders and gain the personal sense of achievement that accompanies the accomplishment of important goals through people.

FIGURE 11.3

Steps for Building Persuasion

■ *Differentiate leadership from the concept of management.* Leadership is the process of influencing the activities of an individual or a group toward the achievement of a goal. While leadership involves inspiring and motivating change in people through a shared vision, management involves organizing processes logically to achieve goals by adding stability.

■ *List the sources of power leaders use to influence others' behavior.* Power is a person's capacity to influence the behavior and attitudes of others. Leaders can use several sources of power to gain commitment and/or compliance from followers while not generating resistance: legitimate authority of their position, expertise, charisma, referent relationships, rewards, punishments, information they possess, or their affiliations with other powerful people.

■ *Distinguish successful leaders from less successful leaders and non-leaders, according to their traits.* Leaders tend to be higher than followers in many trait areas, such as intelligence, sociability and even height, but the differences are often small. Recent research has found that leaders tend to possess six core traits: drive, motivation to lead, honesty and integrity, self-confidence, cognitive ability, and business knowledge in their disciplines. Emotional intelligence also appears to be an important characteristic of leaders.

■ *Compare and contrast the major dimensions of leadership behavior used in the behavioral theories.* The behavioral theories of leadership all include two major dimensions of leadership behaviors. In each, one dimension involves getting the job done by directing employees; by scheduling, monitoring and controlling work; and by providing resources. The other dimension involves maintaining good leader-subordinate relationships, employee commitment, and satisfaction by listening, supporting, praising, and involving subordinates in work decisions. The Ohio State studies labeled these two dimensions "initiating structure" and "consideration," while the University of Michigan studies called them "task-oriented behaviors" and "relationship-oriented behaviors." Many other major leadership theories and models, such as situational leadership theory, Fiedler's contingency theory, and the leadership grid, use some form of these two behavioral dimensions.

■ *Summarize the contingency factors covered in Fiedler's contingency theory, Blanchard's situational leadership theory, and path-goal theory.* Situational leadership theory, Fiedler's contingency theory, and path-goal theory all maintain that the appropriate leadership style depends on, or is contingent upon, certain characteristics of the situation, usually related to the nature of the followers, the leader-follower relationship, or the nature of the task environment. Situational theory contends that the skill levels and dedication of followers are the key variables. Fiedler's theory says the quality of leader-member relations, the level of task structure, and the position power of the leader are the key components. Path-goal theory maintains that such things as employees' locus of control, task structuring, the leader's formal authority, and the nature of the work group should determine leader behavior.

■ *Determine what may neutralize, or substitute for, leadership behavior.* Leadership substitutes are aspects of the task, subordinates, or organization that act in place of leader behavior and thus render it unnecessary. Leadership neutralizers are aspects of the task, subordinates, or organization that have the effect of paralyzing, destroying, or counteracting the effect of a leadership behavior.

■ *Specify the leadership practices that can contribute to successful transformational leadership and that distinguish it from transactional leadership.* Transactional leadership is more traditional, with managers engaging in both task- and consideration-oriented behaviors in an exchange manner. Transformational leadership inspires employees to look beyond their own self-interests and generates awareness and acceptance of the group's purposes and mission. Good leaders challenge the process, inspire a shared vision in followers, enable others to act by fostering collaboration and empowering others, model the way by epitomizing the values they encourage in others, and encourage the hearts of their followers by recognizing their contributions and celebrating their accomplishments.

■ *Evaluate a leader's efforts to manage a crisis situation.* You should be able to evaluate the effectiveness of the manager described in the "Business Dilemma" box, applying the various management theories discussed in this chapter.

Key Terms and Concepts

Ready Recall

1. Discuss how leaders and managers differ.
2. Do you think a person can be a successful leader and manager at the same time? Why?
3. What are the different sources of power a manager can use? Which tend to be the best? Why?
4. What are the contingency variables or situational characteristics in the situational leadership theory and Fiedler's contingency theory?
5. What are the four leadership styles used in the situational leadership theory and when should they be used? What are some of the difficulties associated with applying the model?
6. What are the four major types of leader behaviors discussed in the path-goal theory of leadership?
7. Name some personal and situational factors that can enhance or neutralize the effect of a leader's actions or can in some cases substitute for his or her actions.
8. Describe charismatic, authentic, and servant leadership.
9. Contrast transactional and transformational leaders.
10. How do path-goal theory and leader-member exchange theory parallel transactional leadership?
11. Name the five leadership practices that Kouzes and Posner challenge managers to develop within themselves and within subordinate managers and supervisors.

Expand Your Experience

Take any local leader in business, politics, or education (your school's president may be a good one) who appears frequently in the newspaper. Peruse whatever articles you can find on this individual and, using Kouzes's and Posner's five categories, discuss whether this person qualifies as a transformational leader.

Listed below are some political, military, and business leaders, sports and entertainment personalities, characters in TV shows, and other well-known personalities. For each person that you recognize, list in rank order the three most prominent sources of power you believe the person possesses. Use the number corresponding to the source of power.

| Sources of Power: | 1 = Expert | 2 = Legitimate | 3 = Referent | 4 = Reward |
| | 5 = Charisma | 6 = Coercive | 7 = Affiliative | 8 = Information |

Bill Gates, founder of Microsoft _____ _____ _____

Barack Obama, U.S. president _____ _____ _____

Hillary Rodham Clinton, secretary of state _____ _____ _____

Dr. Martin Luther King, Jr., civil rights leader _____ _____ _____

Sarah Palin, former governor of Alaska _____ _____ _____

Joe Montana, famous football quarterback _____ _____ _____

Adolf Hitler, leader of the Nazi party _____ _____ _____

John F. Kennedy, late U.S. president _____ _____ _____

Barbara Walters, journalist _____ _____ _____

Michael Jordan, basketball star _____ _____ _____

James Bond, fictional spy _____ _____ _____

Arnold Schwarzeneggar, actor/politician _____ _____ _____

George Patton, U.S. general _____ _____ _____

Madonna, singer/actress _____ _____ _____

Perry Mason, fictional attorney _____ _____ _____

Michael Phelps, Olympic gold medalist _____ _____ _____

Bernie Marcus, Home Depot co-founder _____ _____ _____

Strengthen Your Skills

Leadership Skills

Read each of the short paragraphs about selected leaders. Answer the questions concerning their leadership styles.

Larry Ellison is a visionary leader who has turned Oracle into a highly successful company. However, he is also known for ruffling feathers and acquiring other organizations despite the obstacles. A professed admirer of Genghis Khan, Ellison successfully implemented a takeover of PeopleSoft after fighting in federal court. Ellison was convinced PeopleSoft would help Oracle achieve long-term growth. In the process of the takeover, Ellison demonstrated that he was willing to adopt tough tactics that earned animosity from some. Does Ellison appear to have more of a concern for people or operations?

a. Concern for people
b. Concern for operations
c. A balance between the two

The military is known for a very directive leadership style. Orders are given, and soldiers are expected to obey. General George Patton was a strong military man, but he was also known for leading from the front and giving his troops inspiring speeches before battle tinged with vulgarity. He is most known for his Speech to the Third Army, in which he stresses teamwork, patriotism, honor, and the importance of every soldier's contribution no matter how small. Which leadership style did Patton most likely embody?

a. Authentic leadership
b. Transactional leadership
c. Servant leadership
d. Coercive leadership

Starting from the time he was in college, Blake Mycoskie started a number of small businesses. During a trip to Argentina, Mycoskie noticed that many of the children in rural areas did not have shoes. This inspired him to start TOMS Shoes with the goal to provide shoes to children in need. He created the One for One business model; for every pair of shoes sold, a pair would be provided for a child in need. After his highly successful business model took off, Mycoskie decided to expand the One for One model to eyewear. For every pair of sunglasses sold, people in need would receive glasses or eye surgery. Mycoskie is a highly driven individual who desires to make a difference. Which path-goal theory behavior most describes Mycoskie?

a. Participative
b. Directive
c. Achievement-oriented
d. Supportive

Archbishop Desmond Tutu is known for his work in social rights in South Africa. In his work, he exhibited a commitment to alleviating the effects of the apartheid on his people. This was a dangerous endeavor, and even more so as Tutu took a peaceful approach. He was able to inspire fear in the most fearsome people through words alone, and made gains on helping his people through this terrible time. People clung to Tutu as a leader because the authenticity of his words was evident in his actions, and he took the burdens of the people on as if they were his own. What kind of leadership does Archbishop Desmond Tutu exhibit?

a. Charismatic leadership
b. Servant leadership
c. Authentic leadership
d. Transformational leadership

Jeff Bezos, CEO of Amazon, is a respected and successful entrepreneur who built his company from the ground up and is about to celebrate its 20th anniversary. He has laid out 10 clearly defined principles that the company strictly follows. While his employees are intimidated by him, they also admire him for his incredible knowledge and understanding of every aspect of business. Oftentimes, Bezos will speak harshly to his employees and a few minutes later will act as if he was not angry. Which of the following traits does Jeff Bezos exhibit?

a. Team building and listening
b. Persuasiveness and self-awareness
c. Business knowledge and influence
d. Adaptability and self-monitoring

Case 11: Blake Mycoskie Provides Leadership for TOMS and Social Entrepreneurship

Most firms do not want other companies to copy their successful business model. However, the shoe retailer TOMS is not your typical retailer. Although many organizations try to incorporate cause-related marketing into their business operations, TOMS takes the concept of philanthropy one step further by blending a for-profit business with a philanthropic component in what it terms the One for One® model. For every product purchased, TOMS donates products or resources to help those in need. Under Mycoskie's inspirational leadership, the company's One for One concept has inspired other firms—such as eyeglass retailer Warby Parker—to adopt similar models as a way to give back to society. Rather than feel threatened, Mycoskie is funding social entrepreneurship firms with similar missions.

Unlike many nonprofits, TOMS's for-profit business enables the company to support its philanthropic component, which keeps the company from having to solicit donations. The idea for TOMS occurred after founder Blake Mycoskie witnessed the immense poverty in Argentinean villages, poverty so bad that many families could not afford to purchase shoes for their children. Recognizing the importance of shoes to health and education, Mycoskie decided to create a new for-profit business with a socially focused mission. For each pair of shoes TOMS sold, it would deliver a free pair of shoes to children in need across the world.

For his original product, Mycoskie decided to adopt the alpargata shoe worn in Argentina. The alpargata is a slip-on shoe made from canvas or fabric with rubber soles. After a *Los Angeles Times* article featured Mycoskie's new business, demand for the shoes exploded. Unfortunately for Mycoskie, he did not have enough shoes to fill the orders. He was able to work out the product shortage, and today TOMS is a thriving business.

Mycoskie demonstrates a number of traits that have made him an effective leader, including empathy, commitment, and passion. His skills in planning, organizing, staffing, and controlling TOMS's operations allowed him to turn his vision into a reality. Mycoskie also adopted a transformational leadership approach by inspiring employees to look beyond their self-interests to embrace the company mission of helping others. He has the ability to influence others and create leaders in the TOMS organization. His charisma attracted not only employees but customers as well. Mycoskie wanted customers to become active participants in the One for One movement by using their pur-

Source: Kathy Hutchins/Shutterstock

chases to change the world. This inspirational business model provided TOMS with a competitive advantage, and the company was able to distribute its one-millionth pair of shoes in 2010.

After distributing its one-millionth pair of shoes, TOMS began to consider other products that could be used in the One for One model. "When I thought about launching another product with the TOMS model, vision seemed the most obvious choice," Mycoskie explained. Because 80 percent of vision impairment in developing countries is preventable or curable, TOMS decided that for every pair of eyewear it sold, the company would provide treatment or prescription glasses for those in need. TOMS chose Nepal as the first country in which to apply its One for One model.

In 2012, Mycoskie took a sabbatical from TOMS, moving to Austin, Texas, with his wife to reflect on his "why" for leading the company. After recommitting to his original mission to improve the lives of others with his business, he returned with a renewed sense of passion and energy. The desire to help others resonates with both TOMS employees and customers, so Mycoskie recognized how important it was to return to a purpose-focused mindset. Customers who do business with TOMS feel committed to the company because they know that their purchases are going toward a good cause, even if they might pay a bit more in the process. TOMS also goes to great lengths to educate the public about the importance of its mission. Every year, the company promotes the One Day Without Shoes campaign, in which participants spend one day without shoes to understand what children in developing countries must undergo daily. These events have been supported by celebrities such as Charlize Theron, Kris Ryan, and the Dallas Cowboys Cheerleaders.

In 2014, TOMS made the decision to expand the One to One model into the coffee business and started TOMS Roasting Co. Each purchase of a bag of TOMS Roasting Co. Coffee provides an entire week's supply of safe drinking water to a person in need. However, as TOMS expanded, it began to experience problems that plague more traditional firms, such as slower decision making and more internal conflict. Because Mycoskie's long-term goal is for TOMS is to be recognized as "the most influential, inspirational company in the world," he knew the company needed someone to tackle management so he could focus on leadership. He sold half of the business to Bain Capital in 2014 and hired Jim Alling as CEO to improve stability and strategic thinking. Mycoskie then used $100 million from the sale of his share to start TOMS Social Entrepreneurship Fund. This fund provides financial support to like-minded companies that want to focus on social entrepreneurship. Mycoskie continues to demonstrate authentic leadership with his passion for TOMS's objectives and his willingness to model corporate values and form relationships with customers, employees, and other social entrepreneurs in using business as a force for good.

Led by Mycoskie's vision, TOMS has provided more than 35 million pairs of shoes to children in need in over 60 countries, restored sight to more than 250,000 people across 13 countries, and provided 175,000 weeks of clean drinking water to people in five countries. Despite its success, TOMS's mission is far from complete. As its expansion into coffee demonstrates, the company is looking for new opportunities to apply its One for One model. It has even adopted a new logo, "For One, Another," to demonstrate the importance of caring for one another. TOMS demonstrates how transformational leadership, an innovative concept, and a vision supported by employees and customers can create a successful company that makes a difference.[65]

1. How has strong leadership at TOMS created a successful organization?
2. What are some ways that Blake Mycoskie created a shared vision for employees and customers?
3. Which of the five major leadership practices are present in Blake Mycoskie's leadership?

Notes

1. Sarah Elbert, "Modern Super Hero," *Delta Sky*, December 2017, pp. 78–81, 178–179; Henna Inam, "Sheryl Sandberg on Being Human," *Transformational Leadership: Coaching & Leadership Development*, June 21, 2015, http://www.transformleaders.tv/sheryl-sandberg-on-being-human/ (accessed January 14, 2018); Shawn Doyle, "What Every Boss Can Learn About Leadership from Sheryl Sandberg from Facebook," *Inc.*, September 7, 2017, https://www.inc.com/shawn-doyle/what-every-boss-can-learn-about-leadership-from-sh.html (accessed January 14, 2018); Alexandra Topping and Decca Aitkenhead, "Sheryl Sandberg Credits Mark Zuckerberg with Saving Her Life," *The Guardian*, April 15, 2017, https://www.theguardian.com/technology/2017/apr/15/sheryl-sandberg-credits-mark-zuckerberg-with-saving-her-life (accessed January 14, 2018).

2. James M. Kouzes and Barry Z. Posner, *The Leadership Challenge: How to Get Extraordinary Things Done in Organizations* (San Francisco: Jossey-Bass Publishers, 1987).

3. See Gary Yukl, *Leadership in Organizations*, 2nd ed. (Englewood Cliffs, NJ: Prentice-Hall, 1989) for a thorough discussion of the subtleties surrounding the definitions and approaches to the study of power.

4. Adapted from Gary Yukl, *Leadership in Organizations*; and Robert C. Benfari, Harry E. Wilkinson, and Charles D. Orth, "The Effective Use of Power," *Business Horizons* 29 (May-June 1986): 12–16.

5. Thomas A. Stewart, "New Ways to Exercise Power," *Fortune*, November 6, 1989, 52–64; and Benfari, Wilkinson, and Orth, "The Effective Use of Power."

6. "The World's 100 Most Powerful Women," *Forbes*, 2013, http://www.forbes.com/power-women/list/ (accessed September 6, 2013).

7. Soonhee Kim, "Participative Management and Job Satisfaction: Lessons for Management Leadership," *Public Administration Review* 62 (March/April 2002): 231–241.

8. Leigh Richards, "What Are the Benefits of Employee Empowerment?" *Small Business Chronicle*, http://smallbusiness.chron.com/benefits-employee-empowerment-1177.html (accessed January 6, 2018).

9. Craig L. Pearce and Charles C. Manz, "*The New Silver Bullets of Leadership:* The Importance of Self- and Shared Leadership in Knowledge Work," *Organizational Dynamics, 34* (2005): 130–140; S. Holt and J. Marques, "Empathy in Leadership: Appropriate or Misplaced? An Empirical Study on a Topic That Is Asking for Attention," *Journal of Business Ethics, 105* (2012): 95–105.

10. Ralph M. Stogdill, *Handbook of Leadership: A Survey of the Literature* (New York: Free Press, 1974).

11. Bernard Bass, *Handbook of Leadership: A Survey of Theory and Research* (New York: Free Press, 1981) as summarized in Yukl's *Leadership in Organizations*.

12. Shelley A. Kirkpatrick and Edwin A. Locke, "Leadership: Do Traits Matter?" *The Academy of Management Executive* 5 (May 1991): 48–60.

13. Robert Kerr, John Garvin, Norma Heaton, and Emily Boyle, "Emotional Intelligence and Leadership Effectiveness,"

Leadership & Organizational Development Journal 27 (2006): 265–279.

14. "Seventy-One Percent of Employers Say They Value Emotional Intelligence over IQ, According to CareerBuilder Survey," CareerBuilder, August 18, 2011, http://www.career builder.com/share/aboutus/pressreleasesdetail.aspx?id=pr652&sd=8/18/2011&ed=08/18/2011 (accessed January 6, 2018).

15. Daniel Goleman, "Leadership That Gets Results," Harvard Business Review, March-April 2000, pp. 82–83.

16. Richard Boyatzis and Annie McKee, *Resonant Leadership: Renewing Yourself and Connecting with Others Through Mindfulness, Hope and Compassion* (Boston: Harvard Business Review Press, 2005); Bruce Rosenstein, "Resonant leader is one in tune with himself, others," *USA Today*, November 27, 2005, http://usatoday30.usatoday.com/money/books/reviews/2005-11-27-resonant-book-usat_x.htm (accessed January 6, 2018).

17. Chester A. Schriesheim and Barbara J. Bird, "Contributions of the Ohio State Studies to the Field of Leadership,' *Journal of Management* 5 (Fall 1979): 135–145; Carroll L. Shartle, "Early Years of the Ohio State University Leadership Studies," *Journal of Management* 5 (Fall 1979): 126–134.

18. Steven Kerr, Chester A. Schriesheim, Charles J. Murphy, and Ralph M. Stogdill, "Toward a Contingency Theory of Leadership Based Upon the Consideration and Initiating Structure Literature," *Organizational Behavior and Human Performance* 12 (August 1974): 62–82; L. L. Larson, J. G. Hunt, and R. N. Osburn, "The Great Hi-Hi Leader Behavior Myth: A Lesson from Occam's Razor," *Academy of Management Journal* 19 (December 1976): 628–641.

19. Paul C. Nystrom, "Managers and the Hi-Hi Leader Myth," *Academy of Management Journal* 21 (June 1978): 325–331.

20. Bass, *Handbook of Leadership*.

21. Patty LaNoue Stearns, "Martha Stewart consorts with fans," *Herald-Journal*, July 12, 1995, E3.

22. Rensis Likert, "From Production—and Employee—Centeredness to Systems 1-4," *Journal of Management* 5 (Fall 1979): 147–156; and Rensis Likert, *The Human Organization* (New York: McGraw-Hill Book Company, 1967).

23. Robert R. Blake and Anne Adams McCanse, *Leadership Dilemmas-Grid Solutions* (Houston: Gulf Publishing Co., 1991).

24. Adam Bryant, "Phones Are Out, but the Robot Is In," *The New York Times*, April 7, 2012, http://www.nytimes.com/2012/04/08/business/phil-libin-of-evernote-on-its-unusual-corporate-culture.html?mtrref=www.google.com&gwh=85A60CD5966B292711FA9AE6E8A8A088&gwt=pay (accessed January 6, 2018).

25. Paul Hersey and Kenneth Blanchard, "Life Cycle Theory of Leadership," *Training and Development Journal* 2 (May 1969): 4–6.

26. Kenneth Blanchard, Patricia Zigarmi, and Drea Zigarmi, *Leadership and the One Minute Manager* (New York: William Morrow & Company, 1985).

27. Richard Rapaport, "To Build a Winning Team: An Interview with Head Coach Bill Walsh," *Harvard Business Review* 71 (January-February 1993): 110–120.

28. Fred E. Fiedler, "Engineer the Job to Fit the Man," *Harvard Business Review* 53 (September-October 1965): 115–122.

29. Yukl, *Leadership in Organizations*.

30. Ramadhar Singh, "Leadership Style and Reward Allocation: Does Least Preferred Co-Worker Scale Measure Task and Relation Orientation?" *Organizational Behavior and Human Performance* 33 (October 1983): 178–197; and Chester A. Schriesheim and Steven Kerr, "Theories and Measures of Leadership: A Critical Appraisal of Current and Future Directions," in *Leadership: The Cutting Edge*, eds. J.G. Hunt and L.L. Larson (Carbondale, IL: Southern Illinois University Press, 1977).

31. Yukl.

32. Robert J. House and Terence R. Mitchell, "Path-Goal Theory of Leadership," *Journal of Contemporary Business* 3 (Autumn 1974): 81–97.

33. Steven Kerr and John M. Jermier, "Substitutes for Leadership: Their Meaning and Measurement," *Organizational Behavior and Human Performance* 22 (December 1978): 375–403.

34. Jon F. Howell, David E. Bowen, Peter W. Dorfman, Steven Kerr, and Phillip M. Podsokoff, "Substitutes for Leadership: Effective Alternatives to Ineffective Leadership," *Organizational Dynamics* 19 (Summer 1990): 21–38.

35. Fred Dansereau, Jr., George Graen, and William J. Haga, "A Vertical Dyad Linkage Approach to Leadership Within Formal Organizations: A Longitudinal Investigation of the Role Making Process," *Organizational Behavior and Human Performance* 13 (February 1975): 46–78.

36. Gary Yukl, "Managerial Leadership: A Review of Theory and Research," *Journal of Management* 15 (June 1989): 251–289.

37. Nancy G. Boyd and Robert R. Taylor, "The Influence of Leader-Subordinate Friendship on the Evaluation of Subordinate Performance," *1992 Southern Management Association Proceedings*, 164–166.

38. Jay A. Conger and Rabindra N. Kanungo, "Toward a Behavioral Theory of Charismatic Leadership in Organizational Settings," *Academy of Management Review* 12 (October 1987): 637–647.

39. M. Potts and P. Behr, *The Leading Edge* (New York: McGraw-Hill, 1987).

40. Conger and Kanungo, "Toward a Behavioral Theory of Charismatic Leadership."

41. Conger and Kanungo.

42. Jane M. Howell and Peter J. Frost, "A Laboratory Study of Charismatic Leadership," *Organizational Behavior and Human Decision Processes* 43 (April 1989): 243–269.

43. Bill George, Peter Sims, Andrew M. McLean, and Diana Mayer, "Discovering Your Authentic Leadership," *Harvard*

Business Review, February 2007, http://hbr.org/2007/02/
discovering-your-authentic-leadership/ar/1 (accessed January 6, 2018).

44. Kevin Kruse, "What Is Authentic Leadership?" *Forbes*, May 12, 2013, https://www.forbes.com/sites/kevinkruse/2013/05/12/what-is-authentic-leadership/ (accessed January 6, 2018).

45. Robert K. Greenleaf, *The Servant as Leader* (Westfield, IN: Robert K. Greenleaf Center, 1982).

46. Edward D. Hess, "Servant Leadership: A Path to High Performance," *The Washington Post*, April 28, 2013, https://www.washingtonpost.com/business/capitalbusiness/servant-leadership-a-path-to-high-performance/2013/04/26/435e58b2-a7b8-11e2-8302-3c7e0ea97057_story.html?utm_term=.a6a2f7d5f4bd (accessed January 6, 2018).

47. Jim Heskett, "Why Isn't 'Servant Leadership' More Prevalent?" *Harvard Business School Working Knowledge*, May 1, 2013, http://hbswk.hbs.edu/item/7207.html (accessed January 6, 2018).

48. Sen Sendjaya and James C. Sarros, "Servant Leadership: Its Origins, Development, and Application in Organizations," *Journal of Leadership & Organizational Studies* 9 (Fall 2002): 57–64; Clay Brewer, "Servant Leadership: A Review of Literature," *Online Journal of Workforce Education and Development* 4 (Spring 2010): 1–8, http://opensiuc.lib.siu.edu/cgi/viewcontent.cgi?article=1008&context=ojwed (accessed January 6, 2018).

49. Jena McGregor, "The Leadership Wisdom of Warren Buffett," *The Washington Post*, March 2, 2015, https://www.washingtonpost.com/news/on-leadership/wp/2015/03/02/the-leadership-wisdom-in-warren-buffetts-letter/?utm_term=.4fcedcb25aff (accessed January 19, 2018); Robert Frank, "Warren Buffett Is the Most Charitable Billionaire," *CNBC*, September 21, 2017, https://www.cnbc.com/2017/09/21/warren-buffet-is-the-most-charitable-billionaire.html (accessed January 19, 2018); Investopedia Staff, "Warren Buffett: How He Does It," *Investopedia*, August 30, 2017, https://www.investopedia.com/articles/01/071801.asp (accessed January 19, 2018); "10 Top Brands Warren Buffett's Berkshire Hathaway Owns," *CNBC*, May 5, 2014, https://www.cnbc.com/2014/05/05/10-top-brands-warren-buffetts-berkshire-hathaway-owns.html?slide=7 (accessed January 19, 2018); "What Is Value Investing?" BuffetBooks, http://www.buffettsbooks.com/howtoinveststocks/course1/investing-for-beginners/what-is-value-investing.html#sthash.HPn7R7Gn.dpbs (accessed January 19, 2018); Joseph Chris, "9 Warren Buffett Leadership Style Doctrines," Driving Business Connections blog, September 15, 2015, http://www.josephchris.com/9-warren-buffett-leadership-style-doctrines (accessed January 4, 2018); Tanza Loudenback, "24 Mind-Blowing Facts About Warren Buffett and His $87 Billion Fortune," *Business Insider*, January 10, 2018, http://www.businessinsider.com/facts-about-warren-buffett-2016-12 (accessed January 19, 2018); Andrew Hill, "Buffet's Exceptional Style of Leadership," *Financial Times*, February 28, 2011, https://www.ft.com/content/73e667a8-436b-11e0-8f0d-00144feabdc0 (accessed January 3, 2018); Jory MacKay, "This Brilliant Strategy Used by Warren Buffett Will Help You Prioritize Your Time," *Inc.*, November 15, 2017, https://www.inc.com/jory-mackay/warren-buffetts-personal

-pilot-reveals-billionaires-brilliant-method-for-prioritizing.html (accessed January 4, 2018); posted by Practical Wisdom, "Charlie Munger—Advice for the Young Generation—This Is What You Need to Know in Your Youth," *YouTube*, September 6, 2017, https://www.youtube.com/watch?v=Qf4trOzMy2I (accessed January 4, 2018); Juno Tay, "Warren Buffet's Speech to the University of Georgia Students Part 1 (Archive 2001)" Nasdaq, April 21, 2013, http://www.nasdaq.com/article/warren-buffett-speech-to-university-of-georgia-students-part-1-cm238914 (accessed January 3, 2018); posted by Texas Business Hall of Fame, "Warren Buffett and Charles Munger Class of 2016," *YouTube*, January 23, 2017, https://www.youtube.com/watch?v=-ARcxChbVHQ (accessed January 19, 2018);; posted by Motivation Madness, "Warren Buffett's Life Advice Will Change Your Future," *YouTube*, September 11, 2017, https://www.youtube.com/watch?v=PX5-XyBNi00 (accessed January 19, 2018).

50. James M. Burns, *Leadership* (New York: Harper and Row, 1978).

51. Aysegul Ertureten, Zeynep Cemalcilar, and Zeynep Aycan, "The Relationship of Downward Mobbing with Leadership Style and Organizational Attitudes," *Journal of Business Ethics* 116 (2013): 205–216.

52. Bernard M. Bass, "From Transactional to Transformational Leadership: Learning to Share the Vision," *Organizational Dynamics* 18 (Winter 1990): 19–31.

53. Bernard M. Bass, "Leadership: Good, Better, Best," *Organizational Dynamics* 13 (Winter 1985): 26–40.

54. "Impact of Transformational and Servant Leadership on Organizational Performance: A Comparative Analysis," *Journal of Business Ethics* Vol. 116, No. 2 (2013): 433–440.

55. Bass, "From Transactional to Transformational Leadership."

56. Bass, "From Transactional to Transformational Leadership."

57. Alice H. Eagly, S. J. Karau, and M. G. Makhijani, "Gender and the effectiveness of leaders: a meta-analysis," *Psychological Bulletin* 177 (January 1995): 125–145.

58. Herminia Ibarra and Otilia Obodaru, "Women and the Vision Thing," *Harvard Business Review*, January 2009, http://hbr.org/2009/01/women-and-the-vision-thing/ar/1 (accessed January 6, 2018).

59. Judy B. Rosener, "Ways Women Lead," *Harvard Business Review*, November 1990, http://hbr.org/1990/11/ways-women-lead/ar/ (accessed January 6, 2018); Rochelle Sharpe, "As Leaders, Women Rule," *Bloomberg Businessweek*, 2000, https://www.bloomberg.com/news/articles/2000-11-19/as-leaders-women-rule (accessed January 6, 2018).

60. Joan Marques, "Understanding the Strength of Gentleness: Soft-Skilled Leadership on the Rise," *Journal of Business Ethics* 116 (2013): 163–171.

61. Leigh Buchanan, "Between Venus and Mars," *Inc.*, June 2013, pp. 64–74.

62. Alice H. Eagly and Linda L. Carli, "The female leadership advantage: An evaluation of the evidence," *The Leadership Quarterly* 14 (2003): 807–834.

63. Brad Stone, "Everybody Needs a Sheryl Sandberg," *Bloomberg Businessweek*, May 16–22, 2011, pp. 50–58; Ken

Auletta, "A Woman's Place," *The New Yorker*, July 11, 2011, https://www.newyorker.com/magazine/2011/07/11/a-womans-place-ken-auletta (accessed January 6, 2018); "Mark E. Zuckerberg," *The New York Times*, updated January 3, 2011, http://topics.nytimes.com/topics/reference/timestopics/people/z/mark_e_zuckerberg/index.html (accessed August 4, 2011); Jefferson Graham, "Facebook Wants to Be Big among Small Businesses," *USA Today*, September 16, 2011, p. 3B.

64. Kouzes and Posner, *The Leadership Challenge*.

65. Blake Mycoskie, "The Founder of TOMS on Reimagining the Company's Mission," *Harvard Business Review*, January/February 2016, pp. 41–44; Ashley Fahey, "TOMS Founder Reflects on Conscious Capitalism, Entrepreneurship Ahead of Talk in Charlotte," *Charlotte Business Journal*, November 22, 2017, https://www.bizjournals.com/charlotte/news/2017/11/22/toms-founder-reflects-on-conscious-capitalism.html (accessed November 30, 2017); Patrick Cole, "TOMS Free Shoe Plan, Boosted by Clinton, Reaches Million Mark," *Bloomberg*, September 15, 2010, http://www.bloomberg.com/news/2010-09-16/toms-shoe-giveaway-for-kids-boosted-by-bill-clinton-reaches-million-mark.html (accessed November 30, 2017); TOMS, "One for One," http://www.toms.com/one-for-one-en/ (accessed November 30, 2017); Booth Moore, "TOMS Shoes' Model Is Sell a Pair, Give a Pair Away," *Los Angeles Times*, April 19, 2009, http://www.latimes.com/features/image/la-ig-greentoms19-2009apr19,0,3694310.story (accessed December 10, 2017); Stacy Perman, "Making a Do-Gooder's Business Model Work," *Bloomberg Businessweek*, January 23, 2009, http://www.businessweek.com/smallbiz/content/jan2009/sb20090123_264702.htm (accessed November 6, 2014); Michelle Prasad, "TOMS Shoes Always Feels Good," *KENTON Magazine*, March 19, 2011, http://kentonmagazine.com/toms-shoes-always-feel-good/ (accessed November 6, 2014); Craig Sharkton, "TOMS Shoes—Philanthropy as a Business Model," sufac.com, August 23, 2008, http://sufac.com/2008/08/toms-shoes-philanthropy-as-a-business-model/ (accessed June 3, 2011); Mike Zimmerman, "The Business of Giving: TOMS Shoes," *Success Magazine*, September 30, 2009, http://www.successmagazine.com/the-business-of-giving/PARAMS/article/852 (accessed June 3, 2011); "TOMS Founder Shares Sole-ful Tale," *North Texas Daily*, April 14, 2011, http://www.ntdaily.com/?p=53882 (accessed March 5, 2012); Scott Gerber, "Exit Interview: Blake Mycoskie," *Inc.*, December 2014/January 2015, p. 144; PR Newswire, "TOMS Is on a Mission to Brew Something Greater: TOMS Roasting Co. Launches as the Next One for One® Product," *Cision*, March 12, 2014, https://www.prnewswire.com/news-releases/toms-is-on-a-mission-to-brew-something-greater-toms-roasting-co-launches-as-the-next-one-for-one-product-249740051.html (accessed December 10, 2017); Rick Tetzeli, "Behind TOMS Founder Blake Mycoskie's Plan to Build an Army of Social Entrepreneurs," *Fast Company*, January 11, 2016, https://www.fastcompany.com/3054929/behind-toms-founder-blake-mycoskies-plans-to-build-an-army-of-social-entrepr (accessed December 10, 2017).

Motivating People

Source: Moopixel/Shutterstock

After reading this chapter, you will be able to:

- Define *motivation* and explain its importance to managers.
- Compare and contrast the content theories of Abraham Maslow, Clayton Alderfer, Frederick Herzberg, and David McClelland.
- Analyze the process theories relating to how managers can motivate employees, including equity theory and expectancy theory.
- Determine how managers may use learning theories to motivate employees to behave as expected.
- Explain how goal-setting theory can be used to enhance employee motivation.
- Specify how managers may design jobs or apply strategies to motivate employees.
- Evaluate a company's efforts to motivate its sales team.

King Arthur Flour—Where Employees Love Their Flour!

You might think flour is boring, but at King Arthur Flour, employees love the stuff! The company was founded in 1790—the year after George Washington was elected president. It has grown slowly from 5 employees beginning in 1790 to over 300 today. What makes these employees so passionate about flour? They own the business. Although King Arthur Flour operated as a family-owned business for five decades, it is now 100 percent employee-owned.

Therefore, employees control their fate and have a true stake in their flour. The company practices an open-book form of management in which employees-owners are provided access to financial information. Employees are openly encouraged to provide input on new innovations and solutions to potential issues. For instance, when King Arthur Flour experienced a difficult month due to rising flour prices and supplier cancellations, employees were informed about the situation and asked to collaborate on how to address it. Together, the employees came up with plans to help the company bounce back. This transparency invites employees to take an active role in the management of the company.

In 1990, King Arthur was essentially a mail-order business. Today it sells to bakeries and grocery stores, runs a retail store in Vermont, and excels in public relations and marketing. Employees throughout the business are honored as valuable members of a team. All employees are offered training and development opportunities, such as baking/cooking workshops, along with free products and store discounts. The company has won awards based on its structure: number four on Best Places to Work in Vermont in the large employer category and part of *The Wall Street Journal*'s Top Small Workplaces.

By owning the business, employees are motivated to produce premium products and provide excellent service. To ensure success, King Arthur Flour looks for responsible, driven, and self-motivated individuals who are committed to the organization. Although some might view this type of ownership as too much responsibility, at King Arthur Flour, it is just the opposite. Employees are motivated to create a positive work environment and improve on all aspects of the company to achieve goals. If an employee has a suggestion for an improved product or process, he or she is encouraged to share it with management.

Employees at King Arthur are also dedicated to sustainability and the environment. The company ad-

At King Arthur Flour, employees control their fate because the business is now 100 percent employee-owned.

vocates sustainable living by recycling, composting, decreasing energy consumption, and reducing its use of toxic products. King Arthur does not use chemical additives in its flour, nor does it use genetically modified wheat. The company is a member of the Vermont Business Environmental Partnership (promoting improved environmental and economic performance) and Green Up Day. It is also a B Corporation, which stands for *beneficial*. This certification is awarded by the nonprofit B Lab to signal that member companies conform to a set of transparent and comprehensive social and environmental performance standards.

Giving back to the community is also important at King Arthur Flour. Employees are given 40 hours of paid time off each year to volunteer in their communities. It hosts a Bake for Good: Kids program in which it sends instructors to schools nationwide to teach students about baking. The company donates all materials so that the program is free for the schools involved. The bakery also supports charities with a number of social objectives, from helping train low-income and immigrant women in the art of baking to providing fresh produce to consumers in need. Encouraging employees to take an active role in their volunteering allows them to see the company as not only a thriving business but also an integral part of its communities.

Overall, King Arthur appears to be a fun place to work—where those who love cooking, baking, and sustainability can come together in partnership to run their own company.[1]

Introduction

Because employees have the ability to influence the achievement of organizational goals, most top managers agree that employees are an organization's most valuable resource. To achieve organizational objectives, employees must have the ability (appropriate knowledge and skills), the tools (proper training and equipment), and the motivation to perform their jobs. Managers who understand how to motivate and address their employees can help them be more productive and thus contribute to the achievement of organizational goals.

In this chapter, we examine a number of theories regarding motivating employees. First, we define motivation and discuss its importance and how managers have traditionally viewed it. Next, we discuss several theories that attempt to identify what motivates employees, followed by theories that look at how employees' motivation is directed and controlled. Finally, we explore how managers may design jobs to better motivate employees.

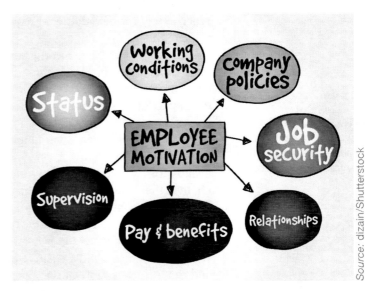

Managers who understand how to motivate and address their employees can help them be more productive and thus contribute to the achievement of organizational goals.

What Is Motivation?

Motivation is an inner drive that directs behavior toward goals. A need—the difference between a desired state and an actual condition—is a major influence on motivation, and thus is a component of many motivation theories. A goal is a desired end result that, when attained, may help satisfy a need. Both needs and goals can be motivating. Motivation explains why we do what we do; at times, a lack of motivation explains why we avoid doing what we should do. If you feel that you can afford to get a D on the final for this class and still have a B average overall, you may be less motivated to study for the test. A person who recognizes or feels a need will be motivated to take action to satisfy that need and achieve a subsequent goal (Figure 12.1).

Consider a mother who needs money to pay for her child's educational expenses. Because of the difference between her current pay and the amount of money she requires in

motivation: An inner drive that directs behavior toward goals.

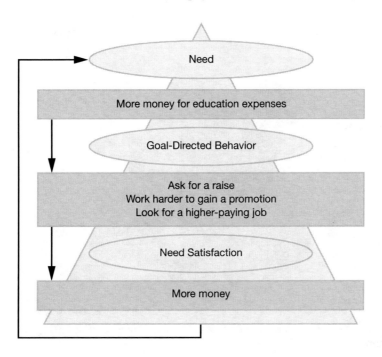

FIGURE 12.1
The Motivation Process

order to pay for the additional expenses, she recognizes a need. To satisfy the need and achieve the goal of gaining more money, she may ask for a raise, work harder to differentiate her performance in order to gain a promotion, seek a higher-paying job, or even steal from the company. Human resource managers, as with managers in general, are concerned with the needs of employees, their goals and how they try to achieve them, and the impact of these needs and goals on job performance.

One important individual characteristic that affects motivation is **morale**, the sum total of employees' attitudes toward their jobs, employer, and colleagues. When New Belgium Brewery won the Better Business Bureau's Business Ethics Award, along with other awards for its green business strategies, employees' pride in the organization increased. On the other hand, low morale may cause high rates of absenteeism and turnover. Before Washington Mutual bank's failure, employees had very low morale. Many were already looking for new jobs and using up their remaining sick and vacation leave. Respect, appreciation, adequate compensation, involvement, promotion opportunities, a pleasant work environment, and a positive organizational culture are all potential morale boosters and can influence motivation.

The Importance of Motivation

A major goal of management is to help employees satisfy their needs in ways that benefit both the individual and the organization. Dissatisfied employees can be costly for a firm, resulting in decreased productivity and potentially high turnover. The cost to hire and retrain individuals is high in many firms.

Motivation is more than a tool that managers can use to foster employee loyalty and boost productivity. It is a process that affects all the relationships within an organization and influences many areas such as pay, promotion, job design, training opportunities, and reporting relationships. Fundamentally, employees are motivated by the nature of the satisfying relationships they have with their supervisors, by the nature of their jobs, and by characteristics of the organization (Figure 12.2). In particular, supervisor qualities that support motivation include honesty, supportiveness, empathy, accessibility, fairness, and openness. Companies can motivate employees by paying equitably, rewarding dedication, and recognizing exceptional performance and creativity.[2] Southwest Airlines has an annual employee recognition dinner that some people call the "Academy Awards of

Source: Dmytro Zinkevych/Shutterstock

Dissatisfied employees can be costly for a firm, resulting in decreased productivity and potentially high turnover.

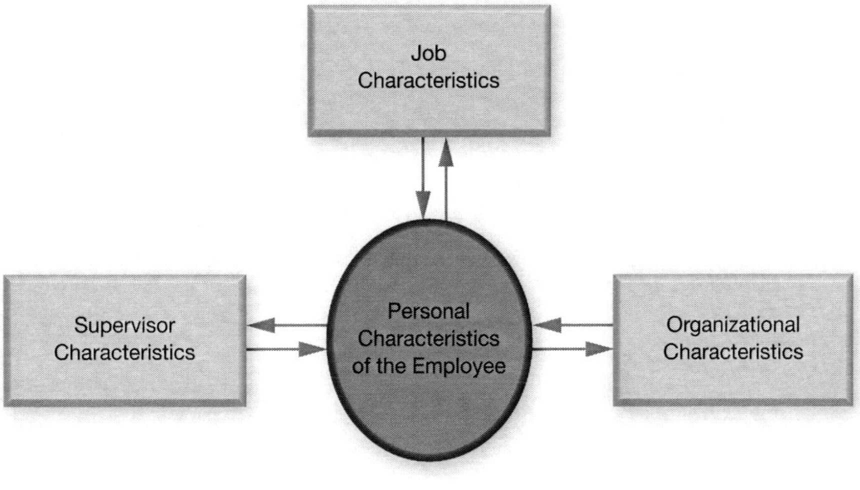

FIGURE 12.2
Internal Employee Motivation

Aviation." These elements are in turn influenced by the nature of employees' motivation in a dynamic relationship.

Efforts to motivate employees should consider organizational and individual needs to be successful. A recent trend has been to empower or give employees greater autonomy in decision making within the organization. Many employees enjoy the challenge and vote of confidence such decision-making autonomy can bring. The Ritz-Carlton, for example, gives employees up to $2,000 of discretion money to address employee concerns. In these situations, the employees are provided with the ability to resolve customer concerns as they see fit.[3] However, research has found that certain occupations, such as service representatives (for example, hotel personnel), dislike increased empowerment and the resulting responsibility.[4] Perhaps these employees have found that with increased decision-making autonomy comes increased accountability that they do not want.

Managers certainly recognize the importance of motivation. However, during an economic downturn, firms look for more creative methods to motivate their employees, particularly amidst an environment of layoffs and pay cuts. Some companies, for example, are offering employees stock options in the company in lieu of raises. Other non-financial incentives include establishing an environment of open communication between managers and employees, giving productive employees more of a leadership role (such as putting them in charge of a work team), and praising employees for a job well done.

Efforts to motivate employees may have negative effects on the organization as well, such as putting the wrong person in charge of a project. Financial institutions such as J.P. Morgan can send the wrong messages to employees by rewarding them with bonuses and other financial incentives for making risky decisions. In the case of J.P. Morgan, a trader engaging in high-risk trades caused the firm billions of dollars in losses. This high-risk environment resulted in disaster. Thus, managers need to evaluate all motivation plans carefully to ensure that they are realistic and will generate the desired results.

Historical Perspectives of Motivation

Our current understanding of motivation comes from three distinctive historical approaches: the traditional approach, the human relations approach, and the human resources approach. The contributor of each has uniquely shaped our current philosophy. Table 12.1 summarizes these three perspectives.

The Traditional Approach

Frederick Taylor, the "father of scientific management," was one of the first to address formally the issue of worker motivation. As we discussed in Chapter 2, scientific management was concerned with analyzing job tasks to develop more efficient and productive workers. Taylor's approach to employee motivation was based on the principle of

TABLE 12.1 Historical Perspectives of Motivation

Traditional Approach (economic)	Human Relations Approach (social)	Human Resource Approach (social and economic)
■ Concerned with efficiency ■ Based on principle of hedonism ■ Employees generally dislike work ■ Emphasizes wages as a motivating factor ■ Limited concern for employees' welfare	■ Concerned with providing employee feedback ■ Emphasizes social needs of employees ■ Employees want their performance to be appreciated ■ Employee satisfaction is related to the social work environment	■ Emphasizes both social and economic needs of employees ■ Workers are complex, valuable entities that contribute to the firm ■ Employee skills and abilities are important for maximizing utility ■ Uses pay and other benefits to motivate employees

hedonism, which maintains that people are motivated to seek pleasure and avoid pain. He suggested that incentives would provide pleasure and motivate employees to be more productive. Punishments were also common in the Taylor system. Taylor and his peers believed that work was generally distasteful to employees and that earning money and avoiding punishment were the employees' primary goals. The concepts that emerged from this time include incentive pay systems, which are quite visible today in many organizations. Incentive pay systems are associated with issues related to short-term profits, such as misconduct and excessive risk taking.

The Human Relations Approach

In contrast with Taylor's output-driven theories, Harvard Professor Elton Mayo felt that giving employees feedback and some level of self-esteem and appreciating their performance would best motivate them. Mayo's Hawthorne studies at the Western Electric plant (discussed in Chapter 2) showed that social needs are of great importance in motivating employees. The evolution of personnel departments has been attributed to Mayo. As the belief was established that the social environment influences general employee satisfaction and therefore work satisfaction, personnel departments arose to systematically address workers' needs and desires. NetApp strongly believes in the benefits of employee recognition. The vice chairman of the company encourages managers to inform him when an employee does something right. The vice chairman then personally calls up the employee to thank him or her. This simple recognition shows employees that their efforts are appreciated.[5]

The Human Resource Approach

The human resource approach goes beyond the traditional and human relations approaches. It considers both the economic and social needs of the individual as well as the need to feel like a positive contributor to an important undertaking.

This perspective views workers as complex entities who are valuable resources to the organization as well as important in their own right. It maintains that the maximum utility for both the company and the workers lies in using as much of the employee's skill and ability as possible to accomplish organizational goals. Companies' efforts to provide benefits beyond stock options and health insurance address such needs. Many companies, for example, now provide on-site day care for children, flexible scheduling, and company-paid health club memberships. Facebook offers employees benefits including 100 percent coverage of medical, dental, and vision premiums; on-site daycare; and concierge services.[6] Employee trust, loyalty, commitment, and productivity can be influenced by a firm's efforts to consider what the employees might actually want and need to function optimally in the work environment. This motivates employees to do their best for the organization while satisfying the maximum number of employee needs. Companies such as Google and Microsoft have focused on creating work environments that make employees feel as if they are each the most important part of the organization.

Content Theories of Motivation

Throughout the twentieth century, researchers have sought ways to motivate workers to increase productivity. Their studies have generated theories of motivation that have been applied with varying degrees of success. Among these are the **content theories**, a group of theories that assume that workers are motivated by the desire to satisfy needs and seek to identify what those needs are. In other words, content theories try to determine the content of activities or rewards needed to motivate individuals. Taylor's traditional view of motivation, for example, suggests that money to satisfy financial obligations motivates employees. In this section, we discuss the content theories of Abraham Maslow, Clayton Alderfer, Frederick Herzberg, and David McClelland.

content theories: A group of theories that assume that workers are motivated by the desire to satisfy needs and that seek to identify what their needs are.

Maslow's Hierarchy of Needs

Psychologist Abraham Maslow theorized that people have five basic needs: physiological, security, social, esteem, and self-actualization.[7] **Maslow's hierarchy of needs** shows the order in which people strive to satisfy these needs.

Physiological needs are the essentials for living—water, food, shelter, and clothing. According to Maslow, people devote all their efforts to satisfying these physiological needs until they are met. For example, if you are struggling to get a job to provide food and shelter for your family, you will probably be concerned more with a job's pay than with whether the employees are nice or the company has an exercise facility. Only when physiological needs are met do people focus their attention on satisfying the next level of needs—security.

Security needs relate to protecting yourself from physical and economic harm. Examples of actions that a person may take to satisfy security needs include reporting a dangerous workplace condition to management, maintaining safety equipment, and purchasing insurance with income protection in case the person becomes unable to work. Once security needs have been satisfied, people strive for social goals.

Social needs include love, companionship, and friendship—the desire for acceptance by others. To fulfill social needs, a person may try many things—making friends with a co-worker, joining a professional organization, or throwing a party. Once their social needs have been satisfied, people attempt to satisfy their need for esteem.

Maslow's hierarchy of needs: The order in which people strive to satisfy the five basic needs as theorized by Maslow—physiological, security, social, esteem, and self-actualization.

Source: Kaspars Grinvalds/Shutterstock

The human resource approach considers both the economic and social needs of the individual; for example, providing on-site day care for children and company-paid health club memberships.

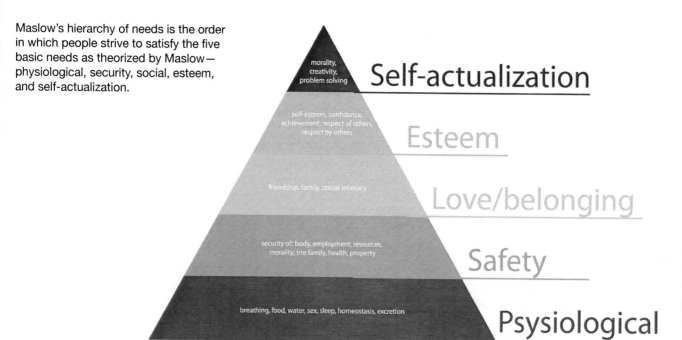

Maslow's hierarchy of needs is the order in which people strive to satisfy the five basic needs as theorized by Maslow—physiological, security, social, esteem, and self-actualization.

Self-actualization

morality, creativity, problem solving

Esteem

self-esteem, confidence, achievement, respect of others, respect by others

Love/belonging

friendship, family, sexual intimacy

Safety

security of: body, employment, resources, morality, the family, health, property

Psysiological

breathing, food, water, sex, sleep, homeostasis, excretion

Maslow's Hierarchy of Needs

Source: Antonina Tsyganko/Shutterstock

Esteem needs relate to respect—both self-respect and respect from others. One aspect of esteem needs is competition—the need to feel that you can do something better than anyone else. Competition often motivates people to increase their productivity. Esteem needs are not as easily satisfied as the needs at lower levels in Maslow's hierarchy because they do not always provide tangible evidence of success. However, these needs can be realized through rewards and increased involvement in organizational activities. When people feel they have achieved some measure of respect, self-actualization becomes the major goal of life.

Self-actualization needs derive from a desire to be the best you can be, to maximize your potential. A self-actualized person feels that she or he is living life to its fullest in every way. For actor George Clooney it might mean winning an Oscar, or for Tiger Woods it may have meant winning more PGA Tournaments than any other golfer. Although such milestones reflect the need to self-actualize, Maslow believed that this need is never fully realized. Rather, it represents an ongoing lifelong striving for self-improvement that not all individuals desire to achieve.

Maslow's theory states that people must satisfy the needs at the bottom of the hierarchy before working toward higher-level ones. Thus, people who are hungry and homeless are not very concerned with obtaining respect from their colleagues. Only when physiological, security, and social needs have been more or less satisfied do people seek esteem. This theory also suggests that if a low-level need such as security is suddenly reactivated, the individual will try to satisfy that need rather than higher-level needs. Managers should learn from Maslow's hierarchy that employees will be motivated to contribute to organizational goals only if they are able first to satisfy their physiological, security, and social needs through their work.

Maslow's hierarchy, although intuitively appealing and frequently used in management training, has not found widespread support from management researchers. Many experts believe that, beyond the first two basic needs, people vary in their need emphasis. Some may seek social-need satisfaction, while others may emphasize esteem needs or even self-actualization. Thus, each individual may respond differently to organizational characteristics. Moreover, the steps in Maslow's hierarchy are not necessarily experienced in a sequential manner: People can have more than one need at the same time. Situations dictate which needs are most important at a given point in time. If a woman is pregnant, for example, and knows she will be taking a maternity leave from her job, causing money to be tight, she is likely to be more conscious of security and physiological needs, whereas before, with two well-paying jobs, she and her husband had no financial concerns. Because of the overly simplified nature of Maslow's model, it provides little to help managers motivate employees. Nevertheless, it functions best in enhancing managers' awareness of individuals' needs and the complex and broad nature of these needs.

Alderfer's ERG Theory

Several alternative theories have been proposed based upon Maslow's hierarchy. One of the most well-known is the Alderfer ERG Theory. Clayton Alderfer used the ERG Theory to fill holes in Maslow's hierarchy of needs. Alderfer classified needs into three categories: (E)xistence, (R)elatedness, and (G)rowth. Existence needs coincide with Maslow's physiological and security needs. In an organization, wages would meet existence needs. Relatedness needs coincide with Maslow's social and esteem needs. Relationships with co-workers can help fulfill an employee's relatedness needs. However, whereas Maslow combined external (from other people) and internal esteem needs into one category, Alderfer believes that internal esteem needs have more to do with self-actualization. He therefore combines internal esteem needs with Maslow's concept of self-actualization as growth needs. In an organization, this might translate into an employee trying to pursue higher work goals because of the satisfaction he or she receives from them.

Despite the similarities between Alderfer's ERG Theory and Maslow's Hierarchy of Needs, the ERG Theory has some important differences. First, it simplifies Maslow's five levels into three. Alderfer also makes a distinction between external and internal esteem needs. Additionally, Alderfer does not see his categories as a necessarily step-by-step process. While Maslow believed that a person needs to satisfy their lower-level needs before they aspire to satisfy higher-level needs, Alderfer proposed that a person can desire to satisfy more than one type of need at the same time. He also proposed that when people are frustrated in settling higher-level needs, they double their efforts to settle the next lower-level needs in the hierarchy. For instance, if a person cannot satisfy growth needs, he or she would increase efforts to fulfill relatedness needs. If an employee has personal work goals that cannot be fulfilled, for instance, he or she might try to compensate for this by achieving relatedness needs such as friendlier relations with co-workers.[8]

Herzberg's Two-Factor Theory

In 1959, psychologist Frederick Herzberg proposed a theory of motivation that focuses on the job and on the environment where work is done. In his study, Herzberg asked engineers and accountants to relate what job-related issues made them feel good about their jobs and which ones made them feel bad. He also asked them to describe the conditions that led to these positive or negative feelings. From this, Herzberg identified two categories of job factors, which he called maintenance factors and motivational factors (Table 12.2).

Herzberg's **maintenance factors**, which relate to the work setting, include adequate wages, comfortable working conditions, fair company policies, and job security. These factors do not necessarily motivate employees to excel, but their absence may be a potential source of dissatisfaction, low morale, and high turnover. Many people feel that a good salary is one of the most important job factors, even more important than job security and the chance to use one's mind and abilities. Salary and security, two of the maintenance factors identified by Herzberg, make it possible for employees to satisfy the physiological and security needs identified by Maslow. However, the presence of maintenance factors is unlikely to motivate employees to work harder. For instance, not many children likely want to be gastroenterologists—doctors who specialize in the digestive system—when they grow up even though the average pay is more than $250,000 a year.[9] According to

maintenance factors: Those aspects of a job that relate to the work setting, including adequate wages, comfortable working conditions, fair company policies, and job security.

TABLE 12.2 Herzberg's Maintenance and Motivational Factors

Maintenance Factors	Motivational Factors
Company policy	Achievement
Supervision	Recognition
Working conditions	Work itself
Relationships with peers, supervisors, and subordinates	Responsibility
Salary	Advancement
Security	Personal growth

motivational factors: Those aspects of a job that relate to the content of the work, including achievement, recognition, the work itself, involvement, responsibility, and advancement.

Herzberg's theory, while high pay is likely to help keep employees from dissatisfaction, it does not by itself lead to satisfaction.

Motivational factors relate to the content of the work and include achievement, recognition, the work itself, involvement, responsibility, and advancement. They promote higher levels of performance. The absence of motivational factors may not result in dissatisfaction, but their presence is likely to motivate employees to excel. Thus, the higher-level goals in Maslow's hierarchy and the motivational factors identified by Herzberg are important factors in motivating employees to work harder. One reason companies such as Google, Apple, Amazon, Dreamworks, and Mattel receive so many job applicants is because they are known for their exciting job environments.

Herzberg's theory is not without its critics. One criticism is that the original study was limited to professional engineers and accountants and that the results may not be generalizable to blue-collar workers.[10] Subsequent studies by Herzberg and other researchers conducted on a variety of blue- and white-collar jobs have yielded inconsistent results.[11] Another criticism is that the theory oversimplifies the nature of the relationship between motivation and sources of job satisfaction or dissatisfaction.[12] Nevertheless, Herzberg's ideas have had a significant impact on the practice of management by making managers aware of the importance of motivation.

Herzberg's motivational factors and Maslow's esteem and self-actualization needs are similar. Workers' low-level needs (physiological and security) have largely been satisfied by minimum-wage laws and occupational-safety standards set by various government agencies and are therefore not motivators. Consequently, to improve productivity, management should focus on satisfying workers' higher-level needs (motivational factors) by providing opportunities for achievement, involvement, and advancement and by recognizing good performance. Many companies combine both motivational factors and maintenance factors to maximize employee motivation.

McClelland's Achievement Theory

Psychologist David McClelland categorized needs differently than did Maslow or Herzberg: achievement, affiliation, and power. The need for achievement refers to an individual's desire for goals that are well-defined and moderately difficult and include employee participation and feedback. People with a high need for achievement are motivated, show great initiative, and are goal-oriented. How do you increase employee needs for achievement and instill characteristics valuable to the organization? McClelland suggests a training course called "total push," within which employees are given role models with a high need for achievement to emulate. Short-term work goals are set, and exercises and techniques are provided to encourage employees to analyze their hopes, aspirations, fears, successes, and failures.[13]

Facebook Knows How to Motivate Employees

According to a Glassdoor study, Facebook is the second-best company to work for in America, with a ranking of 4.5. This success largely stems from Facebook's leadership, specifically CEO Mark Zuckerberg, who was awarded a 99.3 percent approval rating by nearly 19,000 Facebook employees. There are many reasons for Zuckerberg's high approval rating, including his promotion of innovativeness and workplace openness and flexibility.

Source: vlsoft/Shutterstock

At Facebook, employees are encouraged to take risks and stay innovative. Zuckerberg is also open to listening to any ideas that employees have, no matter how long the employee has been with the company. He has been known to meet with entry-level employees and hear any ideas they may have. Engineers are encouraged to consistently create new software builds and can test this software on 10,000 to 50,000 users. More importantly, engineers are not punished if their innovation testing leads to mistakes or failures in the company. A former intern once crashed Facebook when testing a solution for a bug and was later hired by the company, which is a great example of Facebook encouraging innovation. Not only are engineers and employees given free rein on their work, but they are also given the ability to choose the team with which they would like to work. Under the direction of Zuckerberg, Facebook sets clear, unwavering goals for employees and the company. These are signs of an engagement-focused culture, which leads to greater motivation when working. A key success factor of Facebook is that the company focuses on an individual's strengths rather than fixing his or her weaknesses. This encourages employees to find their "best fit" in the company, leading to a happier workplace. This is a primary factor in an employee's performance and intent to stay with the company.

Facebook has great employee benefits, including free lunches, laundry services, and shuttle buses. It also allows for flexible work hours and the ability to work at home when needed. However, the benefits offered at Facebook are common in Silicon Valley. The difference-maker in the Silicon Valley talent war is a company's reputation for job satisfaction. According to analysis conducted by a recruiting site, Facebook pulls employees from Apple 11 times more than Apple does from Facebook, and Facebook holds a 15:1 advantage over Google and 30:1 over Microsoft. This proves that Facebook's high reputation of job satisfaction is drawing more professionals to the company rather than to other companies.

Facebook is also home to one of the largest open-office spaces in the world. This office structure increases collaboration and bonding among co-workers, allows for easier communication, and increases idea cross-pollination, which clearly aids in the innovative nature of the company. Open offices are very common in Silicon Valley, and many are prone to having drawbacks such as workplace distractions and lack of boundaries. Facebook has worked to overcome any negative aspects of an open office. Employees are given a laptop that gives them the ability to move around the office. Different spaces are provided for the employees to meet or work, including libraries, one-person offices, and meeting rooms that come in a variety of sizes. Employees are also provided 27-inch monitors at their desks with the option of noise-canceling headphones, as needed, to limit office distractions.

The mission of Facebook is to make the world more open and connected at all levels of the company, which is proven by its own internal focus on an open and innovative work environment. Zuckerberg has also said that the company's strategy is to learn as quickly as possible what the Facebook community wants; this leads to a culture that encourages people to try new things without a fear of failure. Creativity and flexibility in the workplace lead to happier employees, which is clearly demonstrated by Facebook's high employee satisfaction rating.[14]

The need for affiliation is the desire to work with others in the organization rather than alone. Individuals with a high need for affiliation want to interact with others, guide others, and learn from those with whom they work. The need for affiliation relates to the social needs identified by Maslow. Employees with a high need for affiliation would probably be most effective working in an office with co-workers rather than working at home alone.

The need for power is a function of the influence and control an individual has over others. What people are able to contribute is often limited or constrained by the organizational environment that allocates power. To successfully utilize power within the organization, the individual must be accepted, forceful, and capable.

Process Theories of Motivation

process theories: A set of theories that try to determine "how" and "why" employees are motivated to perform.

Whereas content theories try to determine "what" motivates employees, the **process theories** try to determine "how" and "why" employees are motivated to perform. This group of theories attempts to describe the processes that motivate behavior. Process theories differ from content theories in that they attempt to determine the reasons for why employees become motivated, whereas content theories look only at what motivates the individual. Process theories include equity theory and expectancy theory.

Equity Theory

equity theory: A theory stating that the extent to which people are willing to contribute to an organization depends on their assessment of the fairness of the rewards they will receive in exchange.

Equity theory developed from the research of J. Stacy Adams, who suggested that individuals strive to engage in equitable exchanges or relationships.[15] According to **equity theory**, how much people are willing to contribute to an organization depends on their assessment of the fairness of the rewards they will receive in exchange. In an equitable situation, a person receives rewards proportional to the contribution he or she makes to the organization. In practice, equity is a subjective notion.

According to equity theory, each of us regularly develops a personal input-outcome ratio, taking stock of our contribution (inputs) to the organization in time, effort, skills, and experience and assessing the rewards (outcomes) offered by the organization in pay, benefits, recognition, and promotions. We then compare our ratio to the input-outcome ratio of some other person—a "comparison other," who may be a co-worker, a friend working in another organization, or an "average" of several people working in the organization.

$$\frac{\text{Inputs (Self)}}{\text{Outcomes (Self)}} = \frac{\text{Inputs (Other)}}{\text{Outcomes (Other)}}$$

If the two ratios are close, then we will probably feel that we are being treated equitably.

Consider two salespeople, one who earns $50,000 per year and the other $65,000. The lower-paid salesperson has less experience in sales and generates lower volume than the one earning $65,000; therefore, she is likely to perceive overall equity as fair. As she gains experience and brings in greater sales, there should be increases in her salary. If the higher-paid salesperson were to decrease her productivity over a sustained period, her salary should not increase and possibly should even decrease to maintain equity within the organization.

Because of the subjective and comparative nature of the evaluation, a person will feel either equitably compensated, overcompensated, or undercompensated. The result of this perception will be one of several outcomes. The person may increase performance or productivity to remedy the perception of overcompensation, decrease performance or productivity to remedy the perception of undercompensation, or do nothing if the situation is perceived as being equitable. Unfortunately for managers, workers often have trouble communicating their feelings of inequity and instead decrease the quantity or quality of their work or increase their absenteeism.

Because almost all the issues involved in equity theory are subjective, as they are based on employee evaluations, they can generate problems. Managers should try to avoid equity problems by ensuring that rewards are distributed on the basis of performance and that all employees clearly understand the basis for their pay and benefits.

Source: Orla/Shutterstock

Process theories try to determine "how" and "why" employees are motivated to perform.

Expectancy Theory

Psychologist Victor Vroom developed **expectancy theory**, which says that motivation depends not only on how much a person wants something but also on the person's perception of how likely he or she is to get it.[16] A person who wants something (a particular outcome) and has reason to think he or she will actually get it by putting effort toward performance will be strongly motivated. Consider, for example, a salesperson at a BMW dealership that has been told that if he can increase his average sales by 30 percent, he will receive double the commission on his overall sales. However, because he knows that sales are usually much slower in this quarter, and thus increasing his sales would be nearly impossible, he does not change his selling behavior or effort to achieve the goal. A more realistic goal would have the salesperson attempting to maintain his sales average in a period in which he generally sells less. Such a goal is more realistic, attainable, and has motivational potential for the employee.

According to expectancy theory, if a car salesperson believes that extra effort will help him attain a bonus or a higher commission, then he will probably be motivated to strive for that goal.

Expectancy theory is illustrated in Figure 12.3. **Expectancy** refers to a person's expectation that effort will lead to high performance. If the car salesperson believes that extra effort will help him attain a bonus or a higher commission, then he will probably be motivated to strive for that goal. On the other hand, if the salesperson lacks the ability or the opportunity to reach high performance, his expectancy will be low and so will his motivation.

Instrumentality is a person's expectation that performing a task will lead to a desired outcome. If the salesman believes that studying competitive cars (performance level) will increase his ability to sell cars (outcome), he will probably be more motivated to do so. But if he believes that BMW buyers are highly educated and have conducted extensive research themselves, then he may not be motivated to investigate the competition.

Each potential outcome has a value, or **valence**, which describes its importance. Employees are likely to be more motivated to perform at higher levels if they consider the resulting outcomes valuable; conversely, they are less likely to work hard to achieve outcomes that hold little value to them. If our BMW salesman is trying to put his daughter through college, for example, he may be quite motivated to try to sell more cars to gain double the commission on his overall sales despite a slow quarter, but he may be less motivated to perform if the outcome of his efforts will merely be a certificate of appreciation

expectancy theory: A theory stating that motivation depends not only on how much a person wants something but also on the person's perception of how likely he or she is to get it.

expectancy: A person's expectation that effort will lead to high performance.

instrumentality: A person's expectation that performing a task will lead to a desired outcome.

valence: The value of each potential outcome which describes its importance.

LEVEL OF EFFORT ● **QUALITY OF PERFORMANCE** ● **VALUE OF THE OUTCOME** *to the employee*

FIGURE 12.3
Expectancy Theory

from his employer. Each individual places different values on each potential outcome, so an outcome desired by one employee may hold little interest for another.

Expectancy theory suggests that managers can influence an employee's motivation in three ways—first, by helping the employee to believe he or she can achieve successful performance; second, by having faith in the employee; and third, by providing needed support such as training and guidance. In addition, it is important to determine the kinds of outcomes that have high value for different individuals, which recognizes employee diversity. Finally, managers should relate outcomes to performance.

Goal-Setting Theory

goal-setting theory: A theory which recognizes the importance of goals in improving employee performance.

One of the most discussed theories in management has been **goal-setting theory**, which recognizes the importance of goals in improving employee performance. In other words, goals can act as motivators by focusing employees' efforts on specific activities. Thus, employees operating with goals outperform those without goals. The particular advantages of goals include directing attention and action, mobilizing effort, creating patterns of persistent behavior, and developing strategies for goal attainment.[17]

Merging the individual's and the organization's needs is the most important step to getting employees to attain organizational goals. Employees ask such key questions as, "Will this benefit just management, or will it benefit me?", "Is this behavior rewarded?", or "Do I have the support, equipment, facilities, time, budget, and staff to attain this goal?" For goals to motivate effectively, these issues must be addressed. Researchers have found five key characteristics that improve employees' commitment to and acceptance of goals: specificity, difficulty, feedback, participation, and competition.[18]

Goal specificity means goals should be clear and well-defined. They should serve as a call to action and specify a preferred outcome, a deadline, and a budget. For example, goals for an advertising manager might be to launch a new microwavable frozen pizza in national supermarket chains, and establish market presence with a 2 percent share of the frozen pizza market within one year on a budget of $5 million. The advertising manager will obviously need more information to achieve the goal, but the broad considerations have been established and provide a starting point for goal achievement.

Difficulty of goals refers to challenge. Easy goals do not motivate employees because they provide no challenge. At the other extreme, very difficult goals discourage and frustrate employees. Goal difficulty must be assessed by looking at the individual's (or group's) skills, knowledge, and ability.

Feedback on goals may occur at varying times in the process of achievement. You can receive feedback on your plan for goal achievement, or on an ongoing basis throughout the process and upon completion of the goal(s). Feedback can both motivate the employee and assist in effectively achieving the goal. If an employee is "off track," he or she needs feedback as soon as possible.

Very difficult goals discourage and frustrate employees; goal difficulty must be assessed by looking at the individual's skills, knowledge, and ability.

Source: sezer66/Shutterstock

Participation in the process of setting goals gives employees insights and controls and deepens their commitment. Competition in goal attainment can involve pitting one individual against another (as in individual sales goals) or pitting one group against another (as in cost-efficiency for one team or division versus another). Competition, however, can have negative side effects if employees engage in unethical behavior or behavior that could harm the organization in the long run.

Learning Theories

Learning theories attempt to explain how employees learn to perform desirable behaviors within an organization. Learning theories postulate that employees can be motivated to achieve goals by associating outcomes with certain types of behavior. Managers can therefore use motivational techniques to teach employees what is acceptable and unacceptable within the organization. While reinforcement theory often involves firsthand experience with the outcomes of a particular action, social learning theory is based upon observation, behavioral outcomes, and beliefs.

Reinforcement Theory

Reinforcement theory is a theory which assumes that behavior may be reinforced by relating it to its consequences. The most widely discussed application of reinforcement theory is **behavior modification**, which involves changing behavior and encouraging appropriate actions by relating the consequences of behavior to the behavior itself. The concept of behavior modification was developed by psychologist B. F. Skinner, who showed that there are two types of consequences that can modify behavior: reward and punishment. Skinner found that behavior which is positively reinforced, or rewarded, will tend to be repeated, while behavior that is punished will tend to be eliminated.

Types of Reinforcement

There are four types of reinforcement: positive reinforcement, negative reinforcement or avoidance, punishment, and extinction. Table 12.3 provides examples of each of these types of reinforcement.

Positive reinforcement strengthens a desired behavior by rewarding it or through providing other positive outcomes. Traditional employment rewards include praise and recognition, raises, bonuses, and promotions for doing a good job; such rewards reinforce behavior because the desirable consequences encourage employees to continue the behavior.

Avoidance strengthens a desired behavior by allowing individuals to avoid negative consequences by performing the behavior. For example, employees are likely to come back from lunch on time to avoid being reprimanded or docked for taking long lunch breaks.

Punishment weakens or eliminates an undesired behavior by providing negative consequences. An employee who frequently uses work time to shop online for personal items, for example, may be reprimanded, have his or her pay reduced, or even be fired if the situation becomes severe enough. Unfortunately, more managers have access to methods of punishment than access to rewards; consequently, punishment activities are more prevalent.

reinforcement theory: A process theory which assumes that behavior may be reinforced by relating it to its consequences.

behavior modification: An application of reinforcement theory, which involves change in behavior and encouraging appropriate actions by relating the consequences of behavior to the behavior itself.

positive reinforcement: The act of strengthening a desired behavior by rewarding it or providing other positive outcomes.

avoidance: The act of strengthening a desired behavior by allowing individuals to avoid negative consequences by performing the behavior.

punishment: The act of weakening or eliminating an undesired behavior by providing negative consequences.

TABLE 12.3 **Types of Reinforcement**

Reinforcement Type	Example
Positive Reinforcement	A car salesman gets a bonus for exceeding his quota of cars sold.
Avoidance	A graphic designer works late to avoid getting reprimanded for missing a project deadline.
Punishment	A city worker is demoted after receiving a DWI conviction.
Extinction	An ethics officer eliminates bonuses for employees who exceed work objectives in an unethical manner.

extinction: Weakening an undesired behavior by not providing positive consequences.

Extinction weakens an undesired behavior by not providing positive consequences. It occurs when positive reinforcement is withdrawn from a previously positively reinforced behavior. When the behavior is not reinforced, it will subside and eventually stop. A manager faced with an employee who complains needlessly and endlessly may reduce the complaints by ignoring the behavior.

Schedules of Reinforcement

According to reinforcement theory, the timing of reinforcement is just as important as what kind of reinforcement is used. A **fixed-interval schedule** provides reinforcement at specified periods of time, regardless of behavior. The weekly paycheck is an example. This method does not provide a great deal of incentive because employees know they will receive the paycheck regardless of the level of work performance. A **variable-interval schedule** varies the period of timing between reinforcements. The boss who brings donuts for the office staff from time to time, but on no set schedule, and not related to performance, is using a variable-interval schedule of reinforcement. Although this act may help morale, it does little to motivate work behavior because it is not tied to performance.

fixed-interval schedule: A pattern of reinforcement at specified periods of time, regardless of behavior.

variable-interval schedule: A pattern whereby the period of reinforcement varies between one reinforcement and the next.

fixed-ratio schedule: A pattern offering reinforcement after a specified number of desired performance behaviors, regardless of the time elapsed between them.

variable ratio schedule: A pattern whereby the number of behaviors required for reinforcement is varied.

Two additional reinforcement schedules are based on the frequency of behavior rather than time. A **fixed-ratio schedule** offers reinforcement after a specified number of desired performance behaviors, regardless of the time elapsed between the behaviors. One example is giving salespeople a bonus for every fourth sale made. The fixed-ratio schedule is a strong motivator because the reward is linked directly to the performance behavior.

A **variable-ratio schedule** varies the number of behaviors required for reinforcements. For example, praising an employee after completing the third, eighth, fourteenth, and twentieth circuit boards completed is an example of using a variable-ratio schedule. While it is difficult to keep track of when and whether employees have been rewarded, the variable-ratio schedule can be quite a powerful motivator. An unusual application of a variable-ratio schedule of reinforcement is using poker to improve workplace attendance. Employees who are at work on time each day can draw a card from a deck. By Friday, each employee with perfect attendance has a poker hand, and top hands can win prizes. The fun of playing and potentially winning are all reinforcers randomly tied to desired performance behavior.

Applying Reinforcement Theory

Managers who want to motivate employees to behave appropriately should carefully consider the long-term effects of punishment and reward before selecting a policy. Punishing unacceptable behavior provides quick results but may lead to undesirable long-term side effects such as employee dissatisfaction and increased turnover. Consequently, punishment must occur only in certain situations in which the nature of the offense is so serious, dangerous, or in violation of corporate codes of ethics that a message must be sent to all employees. For example, an employee might be demoted or terminated for organizational expense account abuse. Punishment tells the person what not to do, but does not prescribe appropriate behavior. Research does suggest that, when applied judiciously, punishment can be used in the workplace without undesirable side effects. In the long run, however, rewarding appropriate behavior will generally be more effective in modifying behavior.

To encourage employees to behave appropriately, most firms use internal or external rewards. For example, Avon sales representatives who exceed their sales goals receive praise from their supervisors and become eligible for cruises and gifts. Successfully managing employees requires balancing internal and external rewards in making the job challenging enough and acknowledging the appropriate behavior with external rewards. To teach its Chinese employees about ethical behavior and its importance, Walmart offers ethics awards to outstanding employees. It does this because understanding of business ethics is not as widespread in China.

Some managers work to find alternatives to punishment. For example, one company manager found an alternative to punishment that motivates employees to admit to their mistakes and provides a lesson to the rest of the staff. Of course, in this situation, managers

You're the Manager . . . What Would You Do?

THE COMPANY: Eagle Pharmaceuticals
YOUR POSITION: Director of Sales
THE PLACE: St. Louis, MO

Eagle Pharmaceuticals is the second-largest prescription drug manufacturer in the United States. The St. Louis–based company has recently been recognized for its innovative and effective techniques for motivating its sales force. The company newsletter, the "Touchdown," which uses many analogies from sports, highlights the salesperson that has been the most successful during the previous quarter. Besides being named in the company newsletter, the employee receives a football jersey with the company name and logo on the front and his or her name on the back, and an engraved plaque. The employee also receives $1,000 worth of Eagle stock.

Beyond the recognition and gifts, Eagle tries to capture some of the successful tactics and strategies the winning salesperson uses via Skype; an interview with the winning salesperson is broadcast among the managers of the other four regional offices. The regional managers summarize the ideas and then discuss them with the salespeople they manage.

Sales managers feel strongly that programs such as this are important and that, by sharing strategies and tactics with one another, they can be a successful team. Eagle's sales organization does not heavily use such a team orientation because of the individualized nature of goals, objectives, and performance. Thus, Eagle has worked hard to break down the barriers and have employees communicate freely with one another through emails and biannual meetings. Vice President Hal Brenner says, "When the team scores, the individual scores. We recognize the individual and allow him or her to share his success with everyone else. That's how we succeed. The employees like it and the stock prizes give them an even greater incentive to make the company a success."

Other programs Eagle uses to motivate employees include a "Super Bowl Club" for those employees who reach or exceed their sales goal. And the top 20 salespeople (in terms of goal achievement, not in comparison to one another) each year (out of a sales force of 250) win a "Heisman Award," which includes an all-expenses-paid vacation to the Caribbean. Excellence in performance is acknowledged by top management. In addition, Eagle gives its employees great autonomy in decision making, empowering salespeople and

Source: Luis Louro/Shutterstock

Eagle Pharmaceuticals uses many analogies from sports to successfully motivate its sales force.

district managers. This has led to higher-quality work, increased productivity, and lower turnover for the company.

QUESTIONS

1. From the sales manager's perspective, what is the importance of getting employees to compete against a goal instead of against one another?

2. What do you think are the most effective motivational rewards Eagle uses? Critique the practices currently used.

3. As a sales manager, if you had to go to a university introduction to management class and talk about the use of motivational theories in your company's practices, which would you discuss and why?

Over time, rewarding appropriate behavior will generally be more effective than punishing unacceptable behavior in modifying behavior.

must be careful to reinforce the admission of errors, not the act of causing errors. This motivational technique can increase productivity because the employees know that most of their mistakes will be used as a learning experience and not as grounds for dismissal.

Social Learning Theory

social learning theory: A theory stating that employees learn not only through direct experience but also through observation and personal qualities.

Social learning theory maintains that employees learn not only through direct experience but also through observation and personal qualities. Interacting with others in the organization teaches employees about what is acceptable and unacceptable.[19] Three important components to social learning theory include vicarious learning, self-reinforcement, and self-efficacy.

Vicarious learning is learning through observation. In an organizational context, an employee sees somebody performing a certain behavior and imitates him or her. This often occurs when an employee sees somebody else in the firm as a role model. Employees take their cues from these figures and model their behavior.[20] To become a role model a person must be trustworthy, competent, and credible, which is why authority figures such as managers are usually the primary role models in an organization. Ethical decision making in an organization is significantly influenced by role models and organizational members that are observed making decisions. Yet in order for the modeling process to take place, the following steps must occur:

1. *Attention:* The employee must observe and pay attention to the modeled behavior.
2. *Retention:* The employee must accurately recall the behavior.
3. *Reproduction:* The employee must have the necessary skills to reproduce the behavior.
4. *Motivation:* The employee must be motivated to model the behavior. This often occurs when the employee observes that the modeled behavior received positive reinforcement.[21]

Table 12.4 provides some examples of this step-by-step process.

Consider what happened when a Nordstrom customer lost the diamond from her wedding ring in the store. A security worker helped her search and got two other workers to open up the bags of the retailer's vacuum cleaners, where the diamond was found. The

TABLE 12.4 Components of Vicarious Learning

Steps in Vicarious Learning	Examples
Attention	A new manager notices how an older manager seems to motivate employees through positive feedback.
Retention	When meeting with her subordinates, the new manager recollects how the older manager motivated employees.
Reproduction	The new manager has the ability to provide positive feedback.
Motivation	Remembering the positive impact the older manager seemed to have, the new manager provides positive feedback to her subordinates for activities they have done well.

employees were later introduced at the annual shareholders meeting to demonstrate how Nordstrom exhibits exemplary customer service.[22] Other Nordstrom employees who witnessed the event and saw the employees' actions rewarded might be inclined to demonstrate similar service in their jobs.

Self-reinforcement occurs when employees regulate their behavior by offering themselves rewards for achieving desired performance.[23] In other words, rather than having managers provide reinforcement, employees are able to motivate themselves to achieve objectives. Sometimes providing employees with additional responsibilities or decision-making authority could lead them to set their own goals and reward themselves when they are achieved.

Self-reinforcement works best with skilled employees who receive internal satisfaction when personal goals are achieved. At Apple Inc., employees work in a secretive internal culture. The security measures at Apple's facilities are extensive and can prove frustrating. However, Apple is consistently rated as a top workplace. Employees at Apple believe their efforts are changing the world and receive self-satisfaction from working hard and improving the firm.[24]

Self-efficacy refers to an employee's confidence that he or she can perform a task or behavior successfully.[25] Training to improve employee skill levels as well as positive reinforcement can greatly enhance employee self-efficacy.[26] A heightened self-efficacy can motivate an employee to address challenges and improve performance. For example, a salesperson who is provided with adequate training and encouragement may feel motivated to strive for increasingly higher sales goals.

Motivation and Job Design

The various theories on motivation have helped managers develop strategies for motivating their employees to achieve organizational objectives and for boosting morale within their organizations. Many of these techniques involve job design, which applies motivational theories to the structuring of jobs in order to increase productivity and morale.

Herzberg identified the job itself as a motivational factor. Managers have several strategies that they can use to design jobs and thereby promote employee motivation. Among these strategies are job design techniques such as job rotation, job enlargement, and job enrichment, which were discussed in Chapter 8. In this section, we will look at a job characteristics model, flexible scheduling strategies, and pay for performance.

Hackman and Oldham's Job Characteristics Model

J. Richard Hackman and Greg Oldham took a different approach to job design by trying to identify how managers can motivate workers by helping them to achieve more of their higher-level needs.[27] They first identified five job characteristics that determine a job's potential to motivate:

1. *Skill variety* is the number of diverse activities and skills an employee performs in a job. Jobs perceived as challenging are probably high in variety.
2. *Task identity* is the degree to which an employee performs a complete job with a recognizable beginning and ending. When workers perform only one part of the entire job, as is common with specialization, they may fail to feel a sense of completion or accomplishment. Expanding the job's tasks may both help workers gain that sense of completion and increase task identity.
3. *Task significance* is the degree to which an employee perceives the job as important and having an impact on the company or consumers. Feeling that they are doing something worthwhile is important to most people.
4. *Autonomy* is the degree of control (freedom and discretion) employees have in performing the job. It fosters a sense of responsibility.
5. *Feedback* is the extent to which employees know how well they are performing the job. People need to know how they are doing so that they can modify their performance appropriately.

Oldman and Hackman's theory suggests that the more of these five characteristics managers can design into jobs, the higher will be employees' motivation.

The job characteristics model also identified three psychological states that affect workplace motivation. When any of these psychological states is low, so is employee motivation.

1. *Experienced meaningfulness* is the degree to which employees perceive their work as satisfying and rewarding. If you feel, for example, that soldering circuits onto circuit boards is a trivial task, your motivation to perform that task won't be very high, regardless of how much responsibility or feedback you get from that task. Experienced meaningfulness is influenced by skill variety, task identity, and task significance.
2. *Experienced responsibility* is the extent to which employees feel personally responsible for the quality of their work. It is influenced by autonomy.
3. *Knowledge of results* is the extent to which employees receive feedback about their performance. It is influenced by feedback.

Feedback is important for employees to let them know how they are doing so that they can modify their performance appropriately.

The influence of the five job characteristics on employees' psychological states results in high work motivation, high work performance, high satisfaction, and low absenteeism and turnover.

Additionally, Oldham and Hackman identified *growth-need strength*, the extent to which an employee desires a job that provides personal challenges, a sense of accomplishment, and personal growth. Different individuals bring different needs to the workplace. One employee may need to satisfy only low-level needs, while another may need to satisfy the highest-level needs. Managers need to identify employees' needs and design jobs accordingly; this is particularly important when dealing with a culturally diverse workforce. For those employees with high growth-need strength—those who are seeking the greatest challenges and personal growth—job enrichment programs may enhance motivation. Conversely, for those employees with low growth-need strength, such job enrichment programs may frustrate rather than motivate.

Flexible Scheduling in Work Design

While many Americans continue to work a traditional 40-hour workweek—consisting of five 8-hour days with fixed starting and ending times—many companies are turning to flexible-scheduling strategies as solutions to motivation issues as well as to meet the needs of an increasingly diverse workforce. These strategies include flextime, compressed workweeks, job sharing, part-time work, and working at home.

Flextime allows employees to choose their starting and ending times as long as they are at work during a specified core period (Figure 12.4). This helps employees better maintain a healthy work-life balance. Understandably, flextime does not reduce the total number of hours that employees work; rather, as its name suggests, it gives them flexibility in selecting the hours they work. Employees are free to schedule their work around core times in which all employees must be present. A firm may specify that employees must be present from 10:00 A.M. to 3:00 P.M. One employee may come in at 7:00 A.M. and leave at the end of the core time, perhaps to attend classes at a nearby college after work. Another employee may come in at 9:00 A.M. in order to have time to drop off children at a day-care center and commute by public transportation to the job.

flextime: A work schedule that allows employees to choose their starting and ending times as long as they are at work during a specified time period.

Flextime may help in the service industry by making employees available over more hours, while workstations and facilities can be better utilized by staggering employee usage, and in congested areas, flex schedules may even reduce rush-hour traffic. Moreover, flexible schedules may also contribute to healthier lifestyles such as increased physical activity and better sleep habits. For instance, Cisco offers flexible work schedules as well as day care, mentoring, and a school-age child assistance program. The company has been nominated as one of the 100 best companies for working mothers.[28]

The **compressed workweek** is a four-day (or shorter) period in which an employee works 40 hours. Under such a plan, employees generally work 10 hours per day and have a three-day weekend. The compressed workweek reduces an organization's operating expenses because its actual hours of operation are reduced. It is also a benefit to parents who want to have more days off to spend with their families. The U.S. Bureau of Labor Statistics states that positions such as transcription, financial managers, database

compressed workweek: A four-day (or shorter) period in which an employee works 40 hours.

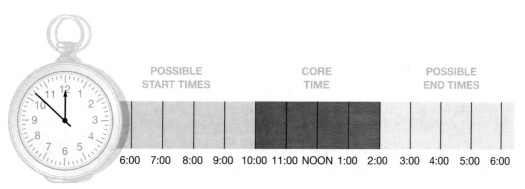

FIGURE 12.4
Flextime, Showing Core and Flexible Hours

administration, or graphic designer tend to offer more flexibility in scheduling and are easily adapted to the above scheduling alternatives.

Job sharing occurs when two people do one job. For example, one person may work from 8:00 A.M. to 12:30 P.M., and the second person would come in at 12:30 P.M. and work until 5:00 P.M. Job sharing gives both people the opportunity to work and time to fulfill other obligations, such as parenting or education. With job sharing, the company has the benefit of the skills of two people for one job, often at a lower total salary cost than one person working eight hours a day would be paid.

Two other flexible scheduling strategies that have grown popular are allowing full-time workers to work part-time for a certain period and allowing workers to work at home. Some firms are allowing employees to work only part-time for six months or a year so that they can care for a new baby or an elderly parent or just slow down for a little while to "charge their batteries." When the employees return to full-time work, they are usually given positions comparable to their original full-time position. Other firms are experimenting with having employees work at home part-time or even full-time. These employees are frequently connected to their workplace through computers, fax machines, and telephones. Telecommuting has helped many employees to ease parenting responsibilities, and some have discovered that they are more productive at home without the distractions of the workplace. About 90 percent of employees regularly telecommute at international consulting firm Deloitte. At Cisco, employees spend 80 to 90 percent of their time outside of the office. Companies are turning to flexible work schedules to give more options to employees who are trying to juggle their work duties and family responsibilities.

While telecommuting can be a boon for many, some employees have discovered that they are not suited for working at home. Work-at-home programs do help reduce overhead costs for businesses, but they may cause problems when the absence of home-bound employees slows operations. Working-from-home policies have become increasingly controversial. Former Yahoo CEO Marissa Mayer eliminated Yahoo's work-from-home policy because she felt that working from home hinders collaboration, which is important for innovation and creativity.[29] Other companies such as Bank of America and Best Buy are following similar practices. It is important for companies that adopt telecommuting policies to ensure that employees are personally accountable and have the ability to work without the need to be monitored.[30]

Flexible-scheduling strategies are among the benefits that certain employees value more than others. Companies are hearing that employees are not necessarily aware of the value of many of their basic benefits. Communicating the value of employee benefits can reduce the pressure to increase the benefits package, reduce turnover, increase employee motivation, and increase overall productivity and profits.[31]

Paying for Performance

How much and how employees are compensated for their performance obviously has some influence on their motivation and effort, but the issue of how much pay motivates may cause problems for managers seeking ways to enhance motivation. Maslow and Herzberg show that pay (money) enables an employee to satisfy his or her basic needs. While Herzberg sees money as a maintenance factor that does not necessarily motivate an employee to perform at higher levels, his theory indicates that low or inadequate pay may result in dissatisfied, unmotivated employees. Equity theory suggests that employees must be paid at least fairly, and that they need to perceive that they are earning what their efforts are worth. Skinner's behavior modification theory shows that employees need to be rewarded for their efforts, but suggests that the weekly paycheck (a fixed-interval positive reinforcement) may not be as effective at motivating employees as other methods of reinforcement.

With this in mind, managers can create pay plans that motivate if they

1. show employees that good performance leads to high levels of pay,
2. minimize any negative consequences of good performance, and
3. create conditions that provide desired rewards other than pay for good performance.[32]

So-called merit pay, which rewards employees according to their performance contributions, is a natural product of expectancy and reinforcement theories because it links pay increases to work performance. In the past few years, compensation for company executives has been criticized because stakeholders did not feel that certain compensation packages were worth the performance. The controversy came to a head after the most recent financial crisis, when some executives at failing firms took home millions in total compensation. As a result of this pressure, more firms are beginning to align executive compensation to performance.

Companies today are increasingly striving to relate pay to performance at both the hourly and managerial level. Incentives don't always have to be cash-based, either. Noncash incentives include merchandise, travel, recognition, and status. Noncash rewards can be related to the goal. For example, if an employee is the top manager in a region, a new luxury car would reinforce the value of the employee to the organization.

After the most recent financial crisis, more companies are aligning compensation with performance.

Integration of Motivation Theories

To understand motivation, it is best to look at all the theories of motivation we have discussed in conjunction with one another. Content, process, goal-setting, and learning theories can all be integrated, as demonstrated in Figure 12.5. This is because many of the ideas and relationships are similar from model to model, and the ultimate benefit comes from their synergy. Expectancy theory provides the foundation for an integrated model of motivation. Effort directly affects performance and is directly affected by goals. Performance will be high if employees perceive a relationship between their performance level and rewards. Performance level can also be impacted through benefits or workplace variables, such as Herzberg's hygiene and motivational factors. Although effort directly affects performance, ability has a moderating effect: The more training, experience, or raw talent a company has, the greater the performance level.

According to expectancy theory, performance level is directly related to outcome rewards. Performance evaluation must be fair and equitable (equity theory) for employees to view the outcome rewards favorably. The rewards serve to reinforce the behavior or performance level. Inequitable or low-level rewards may inhibit maximum productivity of employees.

Individual goals and McClelland's need for achievement determine how goal-directed the individual is. These factors also take into account equity theory and reinforcement. The higher the employee's need for achievement, the greater his or her goals and the more defined his or her goal-directed behavior. According to Maslow's hierarchy of needs

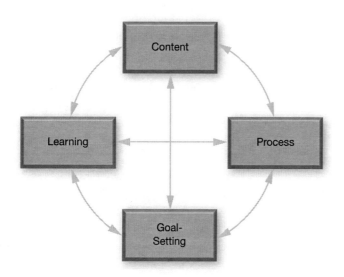

FIGURE 12.5
Integration of Different Theories

and Alderfer's ERG theory, employee goals depend largely on what stage the employee occupies. For instance, employees concerned about their job security will have different goals than employees in a stable job who are looking for advancement opportunities. The need for achievement is an internal drive, and individual goals may also take into account external needs, such as a larger home or a new car.

Reinforcement theory acknowledges the importance of the interaction between performance level and the outcome rewards. It becomes a self-fulfilling prophecy. The more appropriate the level of rewards, the higher the level of performance. Closely related is social learning theory, in which the employee learns acceptable and unacceptable behavior by observing and interacting with others. This integrated model provides insights identifying key areas to address in increasing employee motivation.

Summary and Review

■ *Define motivation and explain its importance to managers.* Motivation is an inner drive that directs behavior toward goals. It is more than a tool manager can use to foster employee loyalty and productivity; it is a process that affects all the relationships within an organization and influences many areas.

■ *Compare and contrast the content theories of Abraham Maslow, Clayton Alderfer, Frederick Herzberg, and David McClelland.* Abraham Maslow defined five basic needs and arranged them in the order in which they must be satisfied: physiological, security, social, esteem, and self-actualization. Clayton Alderfer classified needs into three categories: (E)xistence, (R)elatedness, and (G)rowth. Frederick Herzberg identified two types of factors that relate to motivation. Maintenance factors, such as adequate wages and comfortable working conditions, relate to the work environment; they must be present for employees to remain in a job. Motivational factors—recognition, responsibility, advancement, and the job characteristics—relate to the work itself; they encourage employees to be productive. Herzberg's maintenance factors can be compared to Maslow's physiological, security, and social needs; motivational factors may include Maslow's esteem and self-actualization needs. David McClelland identified three needs: achievement, affiliation, and power.

■ *Analyze the process theories relating to how managers can motivate employees, including equity theory and expectancy theory.* Equity theory suggests that how much people are willing to contribute to an organization depends on their assessment of the equity of the rewards they will receive in exchange. Each person develops a personal input-outcome ratio of the rewards (outcomes) offered by the organization divided by his or her contribution (inputs) to the organization. The worker then compares his or her ratio to the input-outcome ratio of some "comparison other" and adjusts effort accordingly. Expectancy theory states that motivation depends not only on how much a person wants something but on the person's perception of how likely he or she is to get it. Expectancy is a person's expectation that effort will lead to high performance. Expectancy theory suggests that the entire set of outcomes of any given act, and the person's subjective probability of attaining these outcomes, determines motivation.

■ *Determine how managers may use learning theories to motivate employees to behave as expected.* Reinforcement theory assumes that behavior may be strengthened by relating it to its consequences. Behavior modification involves changing behavior and encouraging appropriate actions by relating the consequences of behavior to the behavior itself. Four types of reinforcement are positive reinforcement, negative reinforcement or avoidance, punishment, and extinction. Four schedules of reinforcement are fixed-interval schedule, variable-interval schedule, fixed-ratio schedule, and variable-ratio schedule. Managers who want to motivate employees should consider the long-term effects of punishment and reward. Social learning theory maintains that employees learn not only through direct experience but also through observation and personal qualities. According to the theory, employees often find role models in the company who they wish to emulate. Often these role models are authority figures such as a manager. Modeling acceptable behavior is one way managers can use the social learning theory to motivate employees to behave as expected.

■ *Explain how goal-setting theory can be used to enhance employee motivation.* Goal-setting theory recognizes the importance of goals in improving employee performance. Specificity, difficulty, feedback, participation, and competition improve commitment to and acceptance of goals.

■ *Specify how managers may design jobs or apply strategies to motivate employees.* Hackman and

Oldham's job characteristics model takes a different approach to job design by trying to identify how managers can motivate workers by helping them to achieve more of their higher-level needs. It identified four core job characteristics that determine a job's potential to motivate—skill variety, task identity, task significance, autonomy, and feedback—which lead, in turn, to three psychological states that affect workplace motivation: experienced meaningfulness, experienced responsibility, and knowledge of results. Growth-need strength is the extent to which an employee desires a job that provides personal challenges, a sense of accomplishment, and personal growth. It determines whether or not a more enriched job will actually motivate a worker. Managers may also employ flexible scheduling strategies (flex-time, compressed workweeks, job sharing, work sharing, part-time work, or working at home) and effective pay-for-performance strategies.

■ *Evaluate a company's efforts to motivate its sales team.* You should be able to apply the various theories discussed in this chapter to evaluate the effectiveness of the manager described in the "Business Dilemma" box and make recommendations for future programs to maintain morale.

Key Terms and Concepts

avoidance 373	fixed-ratio schedule 374	motivational factors 368
behavior modification 373	flextime 379	positive reinforcement 373
compressed workweek 379	goal-setting theory 372	process theories 370
content theories 365	instrumentality 371	punishment 373
equity theory 370	job sharing 380	reinforcement theory 373
expectancy 371	maintenance factors 367	social learning theory 376
expectancy theory 371	Maslow's hierarchy of needs 365	valence 371
extinction 374	morale 362	variable-interval schedule 374
fixed-interval schedule 374	motivation 361	variable-ratio schedule 374

Ready Recall

1. Why do managers need to understand the needs of their employees?
2. Describe the motivation process.
3. Explain Maslow's hierarchy of needs. Why is it important?
4. What are Herzberg's maintenance and motivational factors? How can managers use them to motivate workers?
5. Differentiate between the content and process theories of motivation. Which do you think are most useful to managers looking for ways to motivate their employees?
6. Compare and contrast equity theory and expectancy theory. How can managers apply these theories to promote higher levels of motivation?
7. Explain the significance of behavior modification in motivating employees.
8. Describe the four types of reinforcement. Which of the four schedules of reinforcement do you think would be most effective at motivating employees to work harder?
9. Discuss some of the job-design strategies mentioned in the chapter. How can managers use these to increase the motivation of shop-floor employees?
10. Name and describe some flexible-scheduling strategies. Why would a business use a flexible-scheduling strategy?

Expand Your Experience

1. Consider a person who is homeless: How would he or she be motivated and what actions would that person take? Use the motivation process to explain. Which of the needs in Maslow's hierarchy are likely to be most important? Least important?
2. Look at your college or university's football or other athletic team and interview managers and players. What is its level of morale? How does the team currently motivate players to perform? Based on the theories you've learned in this chapter, recommend changes to enhance motivation and morale.
3. Visit a local business and interview managers and employees there. What is the level of morale? How does the firm currently motivate employees to work toward company goals? Based on the theories you've learned in this chapter, recommend changes to enhance motivation and morale.

Motivating

You will use the three illustrations below to complete a story in pictures and words about motivation. Please refer to Figure 12.5 for a description of the four types of major motivational theories covered in the text. A scenario is provided to set the stage for your story. Each of the subsequent figures is titled so you can relate the motivational theories to your storytelling as you see fit. You and your group will write a script for the figures to complete the story about motivation. Your team of scriptwriters is to base the script on what you have learned about motivation and your collective experiences about how motivation works.

Scenario

You and your co-workers have just completed an employer-sponsored training on motivation. The next day at work, while on break, you all are discussing the motivational theories and how they apply to your everyday work life. The discussion reveals that most employees are not motivated because they never see their boss. While most employees consistently show up for work, they are disheartened by the inefficiencies of processes and inadequate equipment in the office. There are many occasions wherein employees discuss how these issues can be solved. However no one of authority is around to hear their comments, so they continue on in their routine and do the minimum work that is expected of them.

The View from the Back of the Dog Sled

Source: gorillaimages/Shutterstock

Describe all aspects of your workplace as if you were seeing it from the back of the dog sled.

Visions from the Front of the Dog Sled

Source: Anna Silanteva/Shutterstock

Describe all aspects of your workplace as if you were seeing it from the front of the dog sled.

Shared Visions and Missions

Source: COLOMBO NICOLA/Shutterstock

Conclude your story with how shared values and mission can affect motivation.

Wyndham Worldwide is a leading global provider of travel-related services, including lodging, timeshare exchange, and rentals. The company consists of more than 8,100 franchised hotels that include Days Inn, Howard Johnson, Wyndham Hotels & Resorts, Super 8, Ramada, and Planet Hollywood. Stakeholders view Wyndham Worldwide as a company with high integrity. The company's leadership and strong compliance program act as a model for ethical practices within the hotel and motivate employees to employ goal-directed behavior.

To maintain a strong, motivated, and ethical corporate culture, Wyndham has implemented an extensive compliance program to reinforce and motivate employees to act ethically. The company has drafted a thorough Code of Business Conduct that has received top scores from the Ethisphere Institute for its comprehensiveness and availability to stakeholders. Wyndham encourages employees to acquaint themselves with the code of conduct to familiarize them with the company's expectations and motivate them to make the right decisions when facing an ethical dilemma.

Wyndham positively reinforces employees by encouraging favorable work behavior to ensure success for overall operations. The company aims to keep employee morale high and emphasizes the experienced meaningfulness each employee should feel when interacting with guests. The corporate culture at Wyndham Worldwide focuses extensively on employee well-being due to the company's view that motivated employees are crucial to the success of the business.

Employees are extremely valuable to the Wyndham brand; as a result, Wyndham offers a range of employee benefits. These include health and welfare benefits, retirement planning, employee discounts, education assistance, employee assistance, adoption reimbursement, flexible work arrangements, and domestic partner benefits. The firm's 401(k) plan is ranked highly among corporate retirement plans. Wyndham will match up to 6 percent of employee contributions after only one year of employment. Its 401(k) plan has been ranked in the top 15 percent of plans for Company Generosity. The firm also provides employees with a discount of up to 40 percent when staying at Wyndham hotels on their travels. By encouraging employees to stay at its Wyndham properties, Wyndham has turned its employees into some of its most loyal customers.

Attaining and maintaining these benefits motivates employees to increase overall productivity of everyday operations. Not only does Wyndham incentivize employees through benefits, it also keeps employees motivated by reinforcing the mindset of taking pride in the services the company offers. Wyndham focuses extensively on embracing the triple-bottom-line business approach, which takes

Wyndham positively reinforces employees by encouraging favorable work behavior to ensure success for overall operations.

into consideration the social, financial, and environmental factors of a potential decision. Employees are encouraged to consider these three criteria before making decisions that could increase or decrease value for the company, its customers, and society. The triple bottom line serves as an added extraneous motivational factor because employees feel more strongly that their decisions have an impact.

In an effort to achieve organizational objectives, management aims to motivate employees to motivate each other. For instance, the firm has a peer-to-peer employee recognition program. Employees can nominate their co-workers for recognition for performing outstanding work. Another program rewards employees who demonstrate exceptional Count on Me! service. This program emphasizes stellar customer service through responsiveness, respect for the customer, and delivering a great customer experience. Employees who go above and beyond these criteria are awarded gift cards and invitations to go on company trips at some of Wyndham's more beautiful locations. Rewarding employees not only motivates them to display desired behavior, but it also increases Wyndham's reputation and customer satisfaction—which in turn improves its bottom line.

In addition to great customer service, management aims to motivate employees to support the environment and society. As part of its triple-bottom-line approach, Wyndham measures success not only by how it does financially but also by how its operations impact people and the planet. To encourage employees to practice environmentally friendly behaviors, Wyndham holds celebrations for "green" dates like Arbor Day, Earth Day, and Wyndham Worldwide Green Day. Wyndham developed an online learning module for employees called Introduction to Sustainability. Wyndham Hotel Group and Wyndham Vacation Ownership also created a more comprehensive program called

Achieving Everyday Sustainability with modules that apply to specific jobs or functions, allowing employees to customize their sustainability training according to their position in the firm. Wyndham's attempts to get employees involved in sustainability appear to be succeeding; the company has been recognized as an industry leader in excellent sustainability performance.

To help support local communities, Wyndham encourages employees to participate in a number of philanthropic programs. Wyndham Worldwide works to support charities that help women and children through donations, volunteerism, fundraising, and raising awareness. The Wyndham Worldwide Charitable Foundation donates to both well-known charities and local outreach programs. In 2016 Wyndham partnered with the charity Save the Children to hold giving events, provide disaster relief, and support the Save the Children sponsorship program.

Wyndham also gives employees the chance to volunteer with the charities that they prefer. The company provides employees with a paid day off to volunteer in their communities. Wyndham will match employee gifts to charitable institutions up to a certain amount. Additionally, the company encourages employees to get customers involved by giving them a chance to donate their reward points to charity. By participating in these programs, employees are able to see the difference they make. This in turn helps motivate employees to continue as a part of the Wyndham family through excellent service for those who stay at any of the company's locations.[33]

1. What are some ways that Wyndham demonstrates that it values its employees?
2. Describe how Wyndham motivates its employees to practice more sustainable behaviors.
3. How might contributing to philanthropic initiatives help to motivate employees at Wyndham?

Notes

1. Kelly K. Spors, "Top Small Workplaces 2008," *The Wall Street Journal*, February 22, 2009, https://www.wsj.com/articles/SB122347733961315417 (accessed December 30, 2017); King Arthur Flour website, www.kingarthurflour.com (accessed December 30, 2017); "King Arthur Flour Leads the Way with B-Corp Logo," CSRwire, February 15, 2008, www.csrwire.com/press/press_release/14672-King-Arthur-Flour (accessed December 30, 2017); "2013 Best Places to Work in Vermont," http://bestplacestoworkinvt.com/index.php?option=com_content&task=view&id=50 (accessed December 30, 2017); "About the White House: Presidents. 1. George Washington," https://www.whitehouse.gov/about-the-white-house/presidents/george-washington/ (accessed December 30, 2017); Bruce Edwards, "VEDA Aids King Arthur Expansion," *Rutland Herald*, June 12, 2013, https://www.timesargus.com/articles/veda-aids-king-arthur-flour-growth/ (accessed December 30, 2017); King Arthur Flour, "Why Employee Ownership Matters," https://www.kingarthurflour.com/our-story/article/employee-owned.html (accessed December 30, 2017); King Arthur Flour, "Our Story—Community," https://www.kingarthurflour.com/our-story/community/ (accessed December 30, 2017); King Arthur Flour, "Bake for Good: Kids," https://www.kingarthurflour.com/our-story/article/bake-for-good-kids.html (accessed December 30, 2017).

2. Carolyn Wiley, "Create an Environment for Employee Motivation," *HR Focus* 69 (June 1992): 14–15.

3. Micah Soloman, "A Ritz-Carlton Caliber Customer Experience Requires More Than Just Empowered Employees," *Forbes*, September 18, 2013, https://www.forbes.com/sites/micahsolomon/2013/09/18/empowered-employees-vs-brand-standards-the-customer-experience-needs-both/#3ccfd5825b8d (accessed January 6, 2018).

4. Michael Hartline, "The Socialization of Customer-Contact Employees in Service Organizations: Effects on Employee Behaviors and Service Quality Outcomes," unpublished dissertation, University of Memphis, 1993.

5. *Fortune*, "100 Best Companies to Work For," 2013, http://money.cnn.com/magazines/fortune/best-companies/2013/snapshots/6.html?iid=bc_sp_list (accessed January 6, 2018).

6. Scott Martin, "Perksville, USA," *USA Today*, July 5, 2012, 1A–2A.

7. Abraham Maslow, *Motivation and Personality* (New York: Harper & Row, 1954).

8. Clayton P. Alderfer, *Existence, Relatedness, and Growth* (New York: The Free Press, 1972); Clayton P. Alderfer, "Theories Expressing My Personal Experience and Life Development," *The Journal of Applied Behavioral Sciences* Vol. 25, No. 4 (1989): 351–365.

9. Kerry Miller, "Worst Jobs with the Best Pay," *Businessweek*, https://www.bloomberg.com/news/articles/2006-09-13/worst-jobs-with-the-best-pay (accessed September 20, 2013).

10. Robert J. House and Lawrence A. Wigdor, "Herzberg's Dual-Factor Theory of Job Satisfaction and Motivation: A Review of the Evidence and a Criticism," *Personnel Psychology* 34 (Winter 1967): 369–389; Victor H. Vroom, *Work and Motivation* (New York: Wiley, 1964).

11. Frederick Herzberg, *Work and the Nature of Man* (Cleveland: World Publishing, 1966); Marvin D. Dunnette, John P. Campbell, and Milton D. Hakel, "Factors Contributing to Job Satisfaction in Six Occupational Groups," *Organizational Behavior and Human Performance* 43 (May 1967): 143–174; C. L. Hulin and P. A. Smith, "An Empirical Investigation of Two Implications of the Two-Factor Theory of Job Satisfaction," *Journal of Applied Psychology* 61 (October 1967): 396–402; Vroom, *Work and Motivation.*

12. House and Wigdor, "Herzberg's Dual-Factor Theory of Job Satisfaction and Motivation."

13. David McClelland, "The Urge to Achieve," in Louis E. Boone and Donald. D. Bowen, *The Great Writings in Management and Organizational Behavior* (New York: McGraw-Hill, 1987): 386.

14. Tanner Christensen, "How Facebook Keeps Employees Happy in the World's Largest Open Office," *Inc.*, March 9, 2016, https://www.inc.com/tanner-christensen/how-facebook-keeps-employees-happy-in-the-worlds-largest-open-office.html (accessed December 5, 2017); Catherine Clifford, "How Mark Zuckerberg Keeps Facebook's 18,000+ Employees Innovating: 'Is This Going to Destroy the Company? If Not, Let Them Test It,'" *CNBC*, June 5, 2017, https://www.cnbc.com/2017/06/05/how-mark-zuckerberg-keeps-facebook-employees-innovating.html (accessed December 5, 2017); Mike Hoefflinger, "How Facebook Keeps Its Employees the Happiest, According to a Former Insider," *Business Insider*, April 11, 2017, http://www.businessinsider.com/how-facebook-keeps-employees-happy-2017-4 (accessed December 5, 2017); Steve Kux, "10 Reasons Why 99% of Facebook Employees Love Mark Zuckerberg," *Lifehack*, http://www.lifehack.org/articles/work/10-reasons-why-99-facebook-employees-love-mark-zuckerberg.html (accessed December 5, 2017); Marguerite Ward, "The 25 Best Companies to Work for in America," *CNBC*, December 7, 2016, https://www.cnbc.com/2016/12/07/the-25-best-companies-to-work-for-in-america.html (accessed December 5, 2017).

15. J. Stacy Adams, "Toward an Understanding of Inequity," *Journal of Abnormal and Social Psychology* 67 (November 1963): 422–436; J. Stacy Adams, "Injustice in Social Exchange," in *Advances in Experimental Social Psychology*, 12th ed., L. Berkowitz, editor (New York: Academic Press, 1965).

16. Vroom, *Work and Motivation*.

17. Edwin A. Locke, K. M. Shaw, and Gary P. Latham, "Goal Setting and Task Performance: 1969-1980," *Psychological Bulletin* 90 (1981): 125–152.

18. J. R. Hollenbeck, J. R. Williams, and H. R. Klein, "An Empirical Examination of the Antecedents of Commitment to Difficult Goals," *Journal of Applied Psychology* 74 (1989): 18–23.

19. Arthur Bandura, *Social Learning Theory* (Englewood Cliffs, NJ: Prentice-Hall, 1977); Arthur Bandura, *Social Foundations of Thought and Action* (Englewood Cliffs, NJ: Prentice-Hall, 1986); Tim R.V. Davis and Fred Luthans, "A Social Learning Approach to Organizational Behavior," *Academy of Management Review*, Vol. 5, No. 2 (1980); 281–290.

20. Arthur Bandura, *Social Foundations of Thought and Action*, M. E. Brown and Linda K. Treviño, "Ethical Leadership: A Review and Future Directions," *The Leadership Quarterly*, 17 (2006); 595–616.

21. Albert Bandura, *Social Learning Theory*; Davis and Luthans, "A Social Learning Approach to Organizational Behavior."

22. Amy Martinez, "Tale of Lost Diamond Adds Glitter to Nordstrom's Customer Service," *Seattle Times*, May 11, 2011, http://seattletimes.com/html/businesstechnology/2015028167_nordstrom12.html (accessed January 6, 2018).

23. Albert Bandura, "Self-Reinforcement: Theoretical and Methodological Considerations," *Behaviorism*, Vol. 4, No. 2 (1976): 135–155.

24. Neil Hughes, "Former Employees Shed Light on Apple's Internal Corporate Culture," *Apple Insider*, July 7, 2010, http://appleinsider.com/articles/10/07/07/former_employees_shed_light_on_apples_internal_corporate_culture (accessed January 6, 2018).

25. Albert Bandura, *Self-Efficacy: The Exercise of Control* (New York: W.H. Freeman, 1997); Albert Bandura, "Self-Efficacy: Toward a Unified Theory of Behavioral Change," *Psychological Review* 84 (1977): 191–215.

26. Marilyn E. Gist and Terence E. Mitchell, "Self-Efficacy: A Theoretical Analysis of Its Determinants and Malleability," *Academy of Management Review* Vol. 17, No. 2 (1992): 183–211.

27. J. Richard Hackman and Greg R. Oldham, *Work Redesign* (Reading, MA: Addison-Wesley, 1980).

28. "2011 Working Mother 100 Best Companies," *Working Mother*, http://www.workingmother.com/best-companies/cisco-5 (accessed September 20, 2013).

29. Julianne Pepitonne, "Marissa Meyer: Yahoos Can No Longer Work from Home," *CNN Money*, February 25, 2013, http://money.cnn.com/2013/02/25/technology/yahoo-work-from-home/index.html (accessed January 6, 2018).

30. Cy Wakeman, "Is Yahoo Right to Ban Working from Home?" *Forbes*, March 7, 2013, http://www.forbes.com/sites/cywakeman/2013/03/07/is-yahoo-right-to-ban-working-from-home/ (accessed January 6, 2018).

31. Kathleen Pease, "Selling with Employee Benefits Communication," *Life and Health Insurance Sales* 135 (February 1992): 12–13.

32. George T. Milkovich and Jerry M. Newman, *Compensation*, 2nd ed. (Plano, TX: Business Publications, 1988); and Edward E. Lawler III, *Organizational Effectiveness* (New York: McGraw-Hill, 1971).

33. Harvey Chipkin, "Thinking Green," *Lodging*, January 18, 2010, http://www.lodgingmagazine.com/PastIssues/PastIssues/Thinking-Green-1218.aspx (accessed July 31, 2013); "Wyndham Worldwide Excels at Stakeholder Management," Daniels Fund Ethics Initiative, http://danielsethics.mgt.unm.edu/pdf/Wyndham%20Case.pdf (accessed December 29, 2017); "Wyndham Vacation," Glassdoor, https://www.glassdoor.com/Benefits/Wyndham-Vacation-US-Benefits-EI_IE356401.0,16_IL.17,19_IN1.htm (accessed December 29, 2017); BrightScope Inc., "Wyndham Worldwide Corporation," https://www.brightscope.com/401k-rating/66718/Wyndham-Worldwide-Corporation/67807/Wyndham-Worldwide-Corporation-Employee-Savings-Plan/ (accessed December 29, 2017); Wyndham Worldwide Corporation, "Wyndham Hotel Group," http://www.wyndhamworldwide.com/category/wyndham-hotel-group (accessed December 29, 2017); Wyndham Worldwide Corporation, "Education," http://www.wyndhamworldwide.com/category/education (accessed December 29, 2017);

Wyndham Worldwide Corporation, "Wyndham Worldwide's Global Sustainability Performance Results in Achieving 2016 Industry Leader and Gold Class Distinction for Excellent Sustainability Performance by RobecoSAM," *PR Newswire*, February 11, 2016, https://www.prnewswire.com/news -releases/wyndham-worldwides-global-sustainability -performance-results-in-achieving-2016-industry-leader-and -gold-class-distinction-for-excellent-sustainability-performance -by-robecosam-300218766.html (accessed December 29, 2017); Wyndham Worldwide Corporation, "Wyndham Raises $66,000," February 22, 2016, http://www.wyndhamap.com/ wps/wcm/connect/wyndham/home/about-wyndham/media -centre/news/wishes-wyndham-fundraising (accessed December 29, 2017); Wyndham Worldwide Corporation, "Wyndham Worldwide Releases 2016 Corporate Social Responsibility Report," January 18, 2017, http://www.wyndhamworldwide .com/news-media/press-releases/wyndham-worldwide-releases -2016-corporate-social-responsibility-report (accessed December 29, 2017); Wyndham Worldwide Corporation, "Philanthropy," http://www.wyndhamworldwide.com/category/ philanthropy (accessed December 29, 2017); Wyndham Worldwide Corporation, "Employee Benefits," http://www .wyndhamap.com/wps/wcm/connect/Wyndham/home/about -wyndham/Careers/LifeAtWyndham/EmployeeBenefits (accessed December 29, 2017); Wyndham Worldwide Corporation, "Count on Me! Service," http://www.wyndhamap.com/ wps/wcm/connect/Wyndham/home/about-wyndham/Careers/ OurVision/CountOnMeService (accessed December 29, 2017); "Wyndham Worldwide Hotel Group Matching Gifts," Double the Donation, 2017, https://doublethedonation.com/matching -gifts/wyndham-worldwide-hotel-group (accessed December 31, 2017).

Effective Team Management

CHAPTER 13

Source: Rawpixel.com/Shutterstock

Chapter Outline

Introduction

The Nature of Groups and Teams

Structural Influences on Group Effectiveness

Process Influences on Group and Team Effectiveness

Contextual Influences on Group Effectiveness

Problems in Groups

After reading this chapter, you will be able to:

- Distinguish between the terms *group* and *team*.
- Summarize a general model of group effectiveness, including its primary components.
- Describe the types of groups and teams that exist in organizations.
- Specify five stages of team development.
- Discuss how group size, norms, cohesiveness, and trust affect group performance.
- Determine different roles that members can play in a group.
- Relate some of the problems associated with group functioning.
- Analyze a business's use of teams.

Timberland Is All about Teamwork and Sustainability

Timberland is all about teamwork and collaboration. From its product development team to its Global Stewards, Timberland is committed to using teamwork to advance its goals of sustainable product offerings. In addition to teamwork among its employees, Timberland has also partnered with suppliers and even competitors to create solutions for positively impacting the environment.

Timberland is headquartered in Stratham, New Hampshire. The firm grew out of the Abington Shoe Company founded in 1955, becoming Timberland Company in 1978. The firm began by manufacturing footwear and later expanded into clothing and accessories. Timberland is known for its eco-friendly products. It is estimated that one-third of the company's footwear is made at least partially from recycled materials. Timberland products are sold through its own network of stores, department stores, and websites. The firm was so successful that it was acquired by VF Corporation for $2.3 billion.

From the beginning, Timberland leaders recognized that they could positively impact the sustainability movement through teamwork. In 2001, the company started a cross-functional team made up of employees from different areas in the company to determine how it could contribute toward sustainability. This was just the beginning of Timberland's green teams. For instance, one team monitors the conditions of Timberland's factory suppliers to ensure they are complying with the social and environmental management systems described in Timberland's code of conduct. Another team monitors the authenticity of Timberland's green corporate messages to ensure that the firm is not greenwashing, or making unsubstantiated claims about its sustainability as a firm. Its corporate social responsibility team works toward advancing sustainability and social responsibility.

As an example, every year Timberland participates in Serv-a-palooza, a corporate social responsibility initiative where employees take a work day and use it to volunteer in their communities. During its 18th Serv-a-palooza, Timberland employees participated in approximately 70 service projects in 10 countries, ranging from helping to maintain forests around Tokyo to conducting outdoor activities with youth at a park in Italy. Timberland also formed its Global Stewards Program. Global Stewards are teams of passionate vol-

Timberland is committed to using teamwork to advance its goals of sustainable product offerings.

unteer employees at Timberland locations throughout the country who take the time to participate as civic leaders within their communities, empower employees, and lead social responsibility projects in their communities. Additionally, Timberland launched its Earthkeepers campaign that works to bring people into groups on a global scale to address environmental issues. In addition to this initiative, Earthkeepers became a shoe line that is designed to be disassembled so that 50 percent of the materials can be recycled.

Timberland realizes that even with dedicated employees, making a difference requires the firm to team up with other important stakeholders. Timberland partnered with its leather suppliers to decrease energy and water usage at its leather tanneries. Timberland also teamed up with consultants and academia to develop its own green index for its products. The green index caught the attention of other retailers, including Timberland's competitors. Timberland thereby saw the opportunity to work with its rivals to create a more thorough green index that could be applied to the footwear and apparel industry. The company worked with Nike and many other firms to create the Higg Index, a green index for apparel. It has also worked with Adidas on developing a green index for footwear.

Timberland believes that collaboration is an important way to make a difference for the environment. It recognizes that by developing teams among various stakeholders, including employees, suppliers, and competitors, it can realize its goals and create a major difference within its industry.[1]

Introduction

Being able to manage in a team environment—and to direct groups in general—has become an important skill for today's managers. Although a company may be broken up into different areas, these areas tend to be interdependent. For instance, the marketing department of a large corporation might want to invest money in developing a new product. However, input from the finance department is needed to determine whether the company has enough funds to pursue the project. It is not unusual for teams to consist of members from a variety of areas within the organization. Therefore, knowledge about how to operate in teams effectively is important for the successful functioning of the organization.

In this chapter, we examine aspects of group behavior in organizations with an emphasis on understanding how work groups develop and function, what potential pitfalls they can face, and how managers can make groups function more like teams. First, an important distinction should be made between groups and teams.

The Nature of Groups and Teams

Although some management experts do not make a distinction between groups and teams, there is a difference. In the workplace, there has been a gradual shift over time to an emphasis on teams and managing them to enhance individual and organizational success. Some experts now believe that the highest productivity results occur only when groups become teams. They see the two concepts as fundamentally different, with groups being the more general of the two.[2] All teams are groups, but not all groups are teams.

A **group** has traditionally been defined as two or more individuals who communicate with one another, share a collective identity, and have a common goal. A group can be virtually any size over one, as long as the members engage in some form of communication, maintain that they are a group, and have some common objective, be it weakly or strongly held. The U.S. Congress is a group, although few would call it a team. A **team** is a "small number of people with complementary skills who are committed to a common purpose, set of performance goals, and approach for which they hold themselves mutually accountable."[3] Classmates taking a course together are a group, but classmates may subdivide into a team to perform a project. In business, several salespeople working together to close a key account would be a sales team.

group: Two or more individuals who communicate with one another, share a collective identity, and have a common goal.

team: A small number of people with complementary skills who are committed to a common purpose, set of performance goals, and approach for which they hold themselves mutually accountable.

Work teams share leadership roles, have both individual and mutual accountability, and create collective work products.

TABLE 13.1 Differences between Groups and Teams

Work Group	Team
Has a strong, clearly focused leader	Has shared leadership roles
Has individual accountability	Has individual and group accountability
Has the same purpose as the broader *organizational* mission	Has a specific purpose and the team delivers a project
Creates individual work products	Creates collective work products
Runs efficient meetings	Encourages open-ended discussion and active problem-solving meetings
Measures its effectiveness indirectly by its effects on others (e.g., financial performance of business)	Measures performance directly by assessing collective work products
Discusses, decides, and delegates	Discusses, decides, and does real work together

Groups versus Teams

Table 13.1 points out some important differences between groups and teams. One major difference revolves around how work gets done. Work groups emphasize individual work products, individual accountability, and even individual-centered leadership. In contrast, work teams share leadership roles, have both individual and mutual accountability, and create collective work products. In other words, a work group's performance is a function of what its members do as individuals, while a team's performance is based on collective products, what two or more workers accomplish jointly.

One useful way to picture any work group is the extent to which it functions like a team. If you were to draw lines between items in the left and right columns in Table 13.1, you could then treat the items as continuous dimensions along which groups could vary, from very individualistic groups, such as a company's geographically dispersed salespersons, to collective teams. Throughout this chapter, we will discuss factors that influence the effectiveness of groups and teams wherever they fit on this continuum.

Benefits of Teams

So what is all the excitement over teams? In the rapidly changing, highly competitive environment businesses face today, teams contribute to the bottom line in a number of ways:

1. *Teams help to motivate workers.* Teams motivate by providing both internal rewards in the form of an enhanced sense of accomplishment for employees as they achieve more and external rewards in the form of praise and certain perks.
2. *Teams can be a major part of the quality effort.* At Whole Foods, teams work together to come up with ways the company can improve operations and address issues that are important to the organization.[4]
3. *Teams help companies be innovative.*
4. *Teams enhance productivity and cut costs.*
5. *Teams can enhance worker involvement, information sharing, and perceived task/job significance.* Research comparing traditional workers with those in self-directed work teams, where workers manage the team largely without supervision, found the latter to be higher in all of these dimensions, as well as in innovation.[5]

In a general sense, teams tend to have and use greater knowledge than individuals do, and when working together they create a greater number of approaches to problems than individuals do.

Consider a NASCAR or Indy Racing League pit crew. When a problem occurs, the collective experience and skills of the entire team can quickly repair a malfunctioning race car. Furthermore, team participation enhances employee acceptance of, understanding of, and commitment to team goals.[6] Teams are important in the U.S. Marines because in each unit members depend on each other to help accomplish their goals. Because so much organizational activity occurs in teams, managers need to understand how teams develop and operate if they are to realize these benefits and help their organizations function efficiently and effectively.

The collective experience and skills of the entire pit crew team can quickly repair a malfunctioning race car.

Organizational context and group structure and processes interact to influence the effectiveness of work groups. Work groups are influenced in turn by feedback over the group's outcomes.[7] Obviously, factors within the organization itself—culture, task design/technology, mission clarity, autonomy, level and type of feedback mechanisms, reward and recognition systems, training and consultation, and physical environments—will have an influence on the effectiveness of work groups. However, the primary focus of this chapter is the structure and processes that occur within the group or team. It is important to see how organizational context influences other group variables.

The factors that influence the effectiveness of work groups most directly are those found within the group or team, including its structure and process. Structural factors include team or group type, size, and composition of skills and abilities. Group processes include stages of development, norms, roles, cohesiveness, and interpersonal processes such as trust development, facilitation, influence, leadership, communication, and conflict resolution.[8]

Performance and personal outcomes demonstrate effectiveness. Products made, number of ideas generated, customers served, number of defects per thousand items produced, overtime hours, items sold, or customer satisfaction levels are all performance measures. Personal outcome measures include employee satisfaction, commitment, and willingness to stay on the team. Both are important for the long-term viability as well as the short-term success of a team.

Structural Influences on Group Effectiveness

The type, size, and composition of groups and teams are structural factors that influence their effectiveness, so we will take a closer look at them now.

Types of Groups and Teams

We can classify groups and teams along a number of dimensions, including how they develop, from which parts of the organization they draw their members, and their purpose, duration, and level of empowerment—the extent of their authority and ability to make and implement work decisions. For example, the Ritz Carlton hotel chain gives employees the authority to make decisions that resolve service issues. The type of groups an organization develops depends on the tasks it needs to accomplish and other contextual variables already noted. How successfully these groups will function depends on a number of other structural and process characteristics.

formal groups: Groups created by the organization that generally have their own formal structure.

informal groups: Groups that arise naturally from social interaction and relationships and are usually very loosely organized.

functional groups: Groups that perform specific organizational functions, with members from several vertical levels of the hierarchy.

cross-functional groups: Groups that cut across the firm's hierarchy and are composed of people from different functional areas and possibly different levels.

Groups and teams can be *formal* or *informal*. Most groups or teams with a title or group designation are **formal groups** created by the organization as part of its formal structure. These groups generally have their own formal structures as well. **Informal groups** arise naturally from social interaction and relationships and are usually very loosely organized. A friendship group or a clique is an example of an informal group. A departmental athletic team, although titled, often grows informally out of social relationships. Even more formal groups at organizations like Hewlett-Packard encourage considerable informal communication throughout their organizations to enhance the dissemination of knowledge.

Groups can also be functional or cross-functional. **Functional groups** (sometimes called command groups), as the name suggests, perform specific organizational functions, with members from several vertical levels of the hierarchy. Accounting, personnel, and purchasing departments are examples of functional groups. **Cross-functional groups** (sometimes called horizontal groups) cut across the firm's hierarchy and are composed of people from different functional areas and possibly even different levels. While functional groups are usually permanent, cross-functional groups are often temporary, lasting for as little as a few months to as long as several years, depending on the group task being performed.

Most groups can also be classified as having one of three purposes: (1) Some groups make recommendations, for instance by suggesting ways to improve quality; (2) some groups make products or perform certain functions, such as teams formed for product development; and (3) some groups direct activities, such as functional groups that conduct business in their area of operations.[9] Obviously, the latter two group types would tend to be more autonomous than the first.

Given these general categorizations, we can now examine the nature of some specific kinds of teams: top management team, task forces, committees, project teams, research and development teams, quality-assurance teams, self-directed work teams, and virtual teams. Table 13.2 summarizes these different types of teams.

TABLE 13.2 Types of Teams

Type of Team	Description
Top management team	Consists of higher-level executives of the organization whose responsibilities include setting strategic goals for the firm
Task force	Team of temporary employees responsible for bringing about a particular change
Committee	A permanent formal team that does some specific task
Project team	Similar to task forces, but responsible for running their operations and are totally in control of a specific work project
Product development team	A special type of project team that is formed to devise, design, and implement a new product
Research and development (R&D) team	A team formed to conduct basic and applied research to discover new approaches that will add to the company's profitability
Quality-assurance team	Team formed to recommend changes that will positively affect the quality of the organization's products
Self-directed work team	Team of employees who are responsible for a process or segment of a job that delivers a good or service to a customer, either internal or external
Virtual team	Team consisting of people from different locations that communicate on projects through technology such as email, videoconferencing, faxing, and other forms of digital communication

Top Management Team

Top management teams consist of the higher-level executives of the organization, such as the chief executive officer, the chief financial officer, the chief operations officer, and the chief marketing officer. Top management teams set strategic goals for the company. They are concerned with the direction of the company and opportunities for achieving the firm's vision. For example, Facebook's CEO Mark Zuckerberg and COO Sheryl Sandberg might meet with other executives to discuss expansion opportunities for the company. Interestingly, though, some countries in the world actually try to ban Facebook.

Task Forces

A **task force** is a temporary group of employees responsible for bringing about a particular change. They may be formed within a functional area, but are most frequently cross-functional, temporarily pulling workers from throughout the organization. Task force membership is usually a function of someone's expertise rather than hierarchical position. For example, Apple Inc., might put together a task force to explore developing new educational applications for the iPad. Coca-Cola developed a five-year task force to evaluate pay and promotion opportunities for minorities. This task force was comprised of employees from different departments within the company.[10]

task force: A temporary group of employees responsible for bringing about a particular change.

Committees

A **committee** is usually a permanent formal group that does some specific task; it may be functional or cross-functional. A loan committee in a bank, for instance, may have members from several areas besides the loan department to help provide outside expertise. A grievance committee resolves grievances in a union environment, while a graduate studies committee in a university determines the graduate curriculum. Because committees often make formal decisions, they usually have official members of the formal hierarchy as part of the group, unlike a task force.

committee: A permanent formal group that does some specific task; may be either a functional or cross-functional group.

Project Teams

Project teams are similar to task forces, but usually they are responsible for running their operation and are totally in control of a specific work project. They are often cross-functional and almost always temporary, although a large project, such as designing and building a new airplane at Boeing Corporation, may last for years. Project teams, such as those at Boeing, are often the guts of the organization or the central business function.

project teams: Groups similar to task forces, but usually responsible for running an operation and in control of a specific work project.

product-development teams: A special type of project team formed to devise, design, and implement a new product.

Product-Development Teams

Product-development teams are a special type of project team formed to devise, design, and implement a new product. Sometimes product-development teams exist within a functional area—such as research and development—but now they more frequently include people from numerous functional areas and may even include customers to help ensure that the end product meets the customers' needs. The development of a new electric plug-in hybrid automobile, such as the Chevy Volt, could use a product-development team to design and implement the product. Amvac Chemical Corporation has product-development teams consisting of agronomists and scientists to develop the company's products.[11] Many product-development teams today utilize the Internet to collect customer feedback on new product ideas as the Internet offers a fast, easy way to collect customer opinions and gauge demand for product ideas.

Source: Tom Wang/Shutterstock

A product-development team would probably be used to design and implement a new electric plug-in hybrid automobile.

Research and Development (R&D) Teams

Research and development teams are formed to conduct basic and applied research. Basic research is conducted to discover new technologies or expound upon established knowledge of existing technologies, whereas applied research takes known technologies and applies them to real-world problems or situations. These activities should assist the company in remaining current or ahead of its competitors in terms of new technologies that have the potential to be commercialized, new approaches to old products through technology, and contributions to the company's profits.

Quality-Assurance Teams

Quality-assurance teams are generally fairly small groups formed to recommend changes that will positively affect the quality of the organization's products. Quality circles are the most common form of quality-assurance team. Quality circles (QCs) are groups of workers brought together from throughout the organization to solve specific quality, productivity, and service problems. Although the "quality circle" term is not as popular as it once was, the quality movement is stronger than ever. Comcast uses quality-assurance teams to ensure the quality of its product offerings. The use of teams to address quality issues will no doubt continue to increase throughout the business world.

Self-Directed Work Teams

A **self-directed work team (SDWT)** is a group of employees who are responsible for a process or segment of a job that delivers a good or service to a customer, either internal or external.[12] Sometimes called self-managed teams or autonomous work groups, SDWTs are designed to give employees a feeling of "ownership" of a whole job. With shared team responsibility for work outcomes, team members often have broader job assignments and cross-train to master other jobs, which permits greater team flexibility.

The defining characteristic of an SDWT is the extent to which it is empowered by management. A team that its somewhat empowered might do its own housekeeping, have members who train each other, repair and maintain equipment, and perhaps schedule production. A team takes on additional functions normally reserved for managers, professionals, and other specialists as the level of empowerment increases. For example, a highly empowered team might also manage suppliers, schedule vacations, hire new employees, choose team leaders, and even be responsible for the purchase of new equipment. Naturally, the functions and their order will vary across organizations and teams. Some leadership roles always exist, even in the most highly empowered teams.[13]

We pay special attention here to self-directed work teams because so many organizations today are desperately searching for ways to cut costs and to adjust to changes in our highly competitive and increasingly global marketplace. Work teams hold the promise for meeting these challenges. SDWTs reduce the need for extra layers of management and thus can help control costs. They also provide the flexibility, through facilitation of communications and reduction of bureaucracy, to change rapidly in order to meet the competition or respond to customer needs.

Virtual Team

A virtual team is a team consisting of people from different locations that communicate on projects through technology such as email, videoconferencing, faxing, and other forms of digital communication. Virtual teams encompass all types of teams and can be used for product development, quality assurance, task forces, and so on. One study found that nearly half of the companies polled use virtual teams.[14] BP, Nokia, and Ogilvy & Mather have all used virtual teams.[15] Virtual teams are particularly important for global businesses where team members might be located in different areas throughout the world.

Virtual teams may require some adjustment for employees used to meeting face-to-face. However, in some cases virtual teams are more productive than traditional teams. One study of software development teams from across the world found that virtual teams led to greater efficiency and results. This is because virtual teams allow experts from across the world to collaborate on projects, time constraints are less limiting because members have a greater ability to work during times that are more convenient for their schedule, and the diversity of team members can increase the organization's understanding of different consumers.[16]

To make the most of these benefits, however, virtual team members should take the following steps, including clarifying tasks and processes, establishing strong communication channels, conducting regular meetings, tracking commitments, sharing leadership, and interacting frequently with team members.[17] In terms of clarifying teams and processes, it is important that teams agree upon who is responsible for which task and make sure everyone understands their responsibilities.[18] Strong channels of communication are essential for virtual team success. Organizations such as Cisco offer virtual solutions with high-quality video for companies whose team members collaborate over long distances.[19] Interacting with members frequently through regular meetings and other forms of interaction is important to build relationships, monitor progress, and collaborate on innovative solutions. Tracking commitments is necessary to ensure that each team member is doing his or her tasks. Additionally, sharing leadership encourages involvement in the process and requires team members to make sure the team is on track.[20]

Virtual teams are particularly important for global businesses where team members might be located in different areas throughout the world.

Source: Rawpixel.com/Shutterstock

Size of Groups

Much research into group decision making has suggested that the ideal group size is about seven. Fewer members might make faster decisions but are less likely to have the optimum mix of skills and abilities. With much larger groups, decisions can get bogged down with too many inputs or individual contributions are minimized or lost entirely. Jeff Bezos at Amazon.com has a two-pizza rule. He believes that the ideal group should be no larger than the 7–10 people required to consume two pizzas.

Recently, many companies have developed more flexibility in determining group size, with as many as 12 members being viewed as a desirable number for most of the types of teams discussed thus far. Traditional work groups performing fairly routine, repetitive tasks requiring little coordination might function well with only one supervisor for a group of 50 to 75 employees. However, groups of this size tend to break naturally into smaller, informal groups, whether the formal structure dictates such a break or not.

In fact, for most groups trying to function as teams, 20 may be about as many members as the team can use effectively. Motivation may wane as meetings drag on. Even the difficulty of finding an adequately sized meeting space makes larger teams less effective. A major problem in larger groups is **free-riding**, the tendency for some individuals to perform at less than their optimum levels in groups. They instead rely on others to carry their share of the workload. Free-riding tends to increase as group size increases.[21] Students are often annoyed by problems with free-riders on group projects, but this is a problem that will persist throughout their working life.

free-riding: The tendency of some individuals to perform at less than their optimum in groups, relying instead on others to carry their share of the workload.

Composition of Groups

Regardless of the type or size of a group, none will be successful without the right mix of skills and abilities. Ensuring that group members have the necessary technical skills to

You're the Manager . . . What Would You Do?

THE COMPANY: Jones' Pizza
YOUR POSITION: Director of Operations
THE PLACE: Madison, WI

The success of home-delivered pizza companies led Jane Jones to open the first Jones' Pizza store in 2004. Jones' Pizza has grown rapidly and now has annual sales of more than $1.5 billion, 1,200 corporate-owned stores, and additional franchise stores. Such success created a need for effective employee training and a system for maintaining quality. Jones maintains that training is the responsibility of each person in the organization. Store managers shoulder the task of making sure their employees are successful by serving as a resource for them.

Promotions at Jones' Pizza are based not only on successes but also on each employee's ability to train someone to take over his or her position. The hourly positions at the store level include order taker, pizza maker, oven tender, router, and driver. Most store managers cross-train their employees to compensate for absences and expected, as well as unexpected, rushes. Jones' Pizza supplements on-the-job training with Internet training that demonstrates pizza making and safety, service, and security tips. Employees are well rewarded for their successes and implemented suggestions. Thus, Jones' Pizza gains the benefit of creative ideas, and employees are encouraged to be constructive and independent.

Because Jones' Pizza offers and promotes "the fastest delivery service in town," driver-safety training has become an important focus in the overall training program. Last year, 20 drivers for a major competitor were involved in accidents, and an Indiana teenager was killed while making a delivery for a competitor.

There is growing concern that there has been an overemphasis on performance for employees who work together in self-managed work teams. In the highly competitive home-delivery pizza industry, customers want quality and speedy delivery. The major advantage of getting employees to work together in teams is quick response time. The team's self-regulating nature allows for greater error detection, and, through supportive

Source: stockyimages/Shutterstock

Promotions at Jones' Pizza are based not only on successes but also on each employee's ability to train someone to take over his or her position.

team relationships, corrections are possible as the order moves through the hands of the hourly employees.

On the surface, it appears that the teamwork allows one employee to compensate for another employee's weakness. In the case of Jones' Pizza, top management is concerned that the close, cohesive work teams have achieved high efficiency but not other organizational goals. An overemphasis on speed or delivery may create legal, ethical, and social responsibility concerns and problems for the organization.

QUESTIONS

1. As director of operations, how would you describe the type of groups that exist at Jones' Pizza? What is the relationship between informal or friendship groups and the formal organizational structure?

2. How is the work group utilized at Jones' Pizza to increase product quality, including delivery speed?

3. Discuss the possibility of work groups becoming so internally focused and concerned with efficiency that legal, ethical, or social responsibility issues emerge. What are the legal, ethical, and/or social responsibility issues you face in this situation?

perform a job may be one of a manager's or group leader's most important functions. In team-oriented work environments, ensuring optimal team composition can be a massive task. Striving for demographic diversity is one way of broadening viewpoints and experiences in a group.

Although the right mix of talents is important, in general, the more heterogeneous a group, the better it is to solve problems. Groups with diverse membership may take longer to become cohesive, but are likely to be more productive in the long run. Avoiding individuals who are not cooperative or are unwilling to listen to others' perspectives will help the groups be more productive.

Process Influences on Group and Team Effectiveness

How a team functions once it is formed largely determines its likelihood of success. The most highly talented sports teams must "gel" or they won't be successful. The same holds true for teams in business. Their success depends on how they develop, the norms that evolve in the group, the roles that members perform, and how well they perform a number of important group processes.

Stages of Group and Team Development

Groups and teams, like people and even organizations, have life cycles. They are born, they develop, and are eventually terminated. During this progression, groups pass through certain stages, although the stages may vary in duration from one situation to another, and sometimes even the sequence may be changed. Understanding how groups make progress can give a manager insight into behaviors needed to help the group function successfully at each stage. Although there are several models of group development, emphasizing different types of behaviors and orientations, one very useful depiction of the process includes five phases: forming, storming, norming, performing, and adjourning.[22] Table 13.3 summarizes these different stages. The leader's role is to help facilitate task and social interactions throughout the stages.

Forming

Group members meet for the first time or two in the **forming stage** and become acquainted with each other and familiarize themselves with the group's task. They may "test" others for potential friendships and mutual interests and see how others approach the task at hand. Emerging leadership functions and interdependencies are often a concern here. A formal group leader might encourage some informal interaction among group members at this stage. Many groups start, even within the first minute of group interaction, to form a strategy for addressing the group's task. This strategy often lasts through the first half of the group's allotted time to deal with the task.[23] The manager or team leader can sometimes facilitate this task approach by giving some thought and preliminary work to the task before the group meets, and by withholding the setting of the formal agenda for a period of time.

forming stage: The stage when group members meet for the first time or two, become acquainted, and familiarize themselves with the group's task.

TABLE 13.3 **Stages of Group and Team Development**

Stages	Description
Forming	Group members meet for the first time, become acquainted, and become familiar with the group's tasks
Storming	The stage where conflict occurs as team members assert their roles, jockey for leadership positions, and make known their feelings and thoughts about the tasks
Norming	The stage where conflicts are largely resolved and harmony ensues
Performing	Members have reached a level of maturity that facilitates total task development
Adjourning	The tasks are completed and the team or group disbands

During storming, some members may challenge the leader's position or show hostility to those with whom they disagree, while others may psychologically withdraw from the group.

Storming

storming stage: The stage when conflict usually occurs and in which group members begin to assert their roles, jockey for leadership positions, and make known their feelings about a task.

Conflict generally occurs during the. **storming stage** as group members begin to assert their roles, jockey for leadership positions, and make known their feelings and thoughts about the task. Some members may challenge the leader's position or show hostility to those with whom they disagree or have personality clashes. Others may psychologically withdraw from the group. Cliques may form and subgroups may argue over task or relationship issues. The group leader should strive to keep everyone involved and maintain communication lines. These tasks emphasize the importance of reasonably sized groups. He or she should also encourage members to manage and resolve conflict constructively rather than allowing it to escalate or be subdued, only to rise again later. If member roles and group norms are not successfully negotiated during the storming stage, then the group may never advance to a more productive level of functioning. It is during this stage that the groundwork for having a true team is laid because interaction patterns start evolving at this time.

Norming

norming stage: The stage when conflicts are largely resolved and harmony ensues.

Conflicts are largely resolved and harmony ensues during the **norming stage**, sometimes to the detriment of giving full consideration to minority opinions, as we shall see later. In this stage, a sometimes tenuous balance of interpersonal forces is achieved. Members accept their roles, divide work tasks, have largely resolved leadership issues, and mostly share mutual expectations. The leader must promote a balance between maintaining harmony and continuing to strive to achieve the task at hand. The danger for a group at this time is that members may feel good, but may not be getting the job done. Most of the time, groups move through this stage fairly quickly.

Performing

performing stage: The stage in which members have reached a level of maturity that facilitates total task involvement.

A group reaches the **performing stage** when members have reached a level of maturity that facilitates total task involvement. Members concentrate on solving the problem or performing the task, and they listen and provide important inputs and feedback on issues. They are not afraid to offer suggestions, and they help other group members express their opinions. Conflicts at this stage are over legitimate task concerns rather than petty personality or power issues. Issues are confronted, not ignored. Members are clear on the goals of the group and the means for accomplishing the goals. During this stage, the leader should concentrate on task-oriented behaviors, while maintaining relationships through encouragement, rewards, and positive communication. Many groups never fully reach the performing stage. Research has found that in temporary groups with designated time frames, the group starts "performing," or actually making good progress on the task, at almost exactly the midway time point on the task regardless of how much time is allotted.[24]

Adjourning

The **adjourning stage** occurs when task forces, project teams, and committees complete their task and disband. At this stage, heightened emotions and some depression over separation from the group and its members are accompanied by positive feelings associated with task accomplishment. The leader may want to commemorate this stage with a ceremony to recognize not only the group's accomplishments, but also the positive associations and friendships. This emphasis on the positive should help promote future cohesiveness should the team or some of its members be reunited.

adjourning stage: The stage in which task forces, project teams, or committees complete their task and disband.

Group Norms

Group **norms** are important because they prescribe appropriate behavior for group members and help reduce the disruption and chaos that would ensue if group members didn't know how to act. Groups enforce norms to facilitate group survival, establish what behavior is expected of group members, help the group avoid embarrassing interpersonal problems, express the central values of the group, and clarify what is distinctive about the group.[25] Norms can influence nearly all aspects of group functioning, from how members carry out a task to how they dress, eat, and talk to the boss.

norms: Prescriptions for appropriate behavior of group members that help reduce the disruption and chaos that would ensue if group members didn't know how to act.

Norms can be very positive in that they can support the goals, mission, and success of the organization. At Whole Foods, for example, voting on whether to retain or dismiss a new employee is a widely accepted norm among all teams. This norm helps ensure that teams are made up of competent individuals that are most likely to help the groups, and thereby the business as a whole, succeed. At most Ritz Carlton hotels, a widely held norm is that a customer's problem or request is "owned" by the person who receives it regardless of whose job it might involve. The employee will strive to resolve the problem within 10 minutes of receiving it. This norm of customer service makes the Ritz Carlton distinctive among major hotel chains and helps ensure its success.

However, norms can also be a negative influence on a group by encouraging dysfunctional behavior. Occasionally, some group members may form a subgroup, called a shadow organization, that has norms contrary to those of the greater group or organization.[26] For example, workers may establish standards of production far below what is desired by management.

Levels of Norms

Norms tend to be of three levels: pivotal, relevant, and peripheral.[27] Figure 13.1 demonstrates these three norms, from the most important norms for team success to the less important. **Pivotal norms** are critical for success within a group. If a group member rejects a pivotal norm, then his or her stay in the organization is likely to be very limited. When Apple CEO Tim Cook meets with product-development teams, he asks some very pointed questions about both the technical and financial aspects of the project. Team leaders and members must be prepared to answer these questions or they may not last long at Apple. Thus, being prepared is a pivotal norm at Apple. A pivotal norm would also include being present at meetings and being engaged in decision making.

pivotal norms: Standards that are critical for group success.

Relevant norms are fairly important, but not as critical as pivotal norms are. It is generally important for a salesperson to be on time for work (relevant norm) but with productivity (pivotal norm) as the highest goal in the department, the salesperson might be able to come in late more often with minimal repercussions if he or she is a highly productive employee. The use of computers or smartphones in meetings to conduct personal affairs not associated with the meeting may be acceptable if the individual remains productive in the meeting. Overuse of personal electronic devices or leaving the meeting to make multiple phone calls may be viewed as unacceptable behavior.

relevant norms: Norms that are important, but not as critical as the pivotal norms.

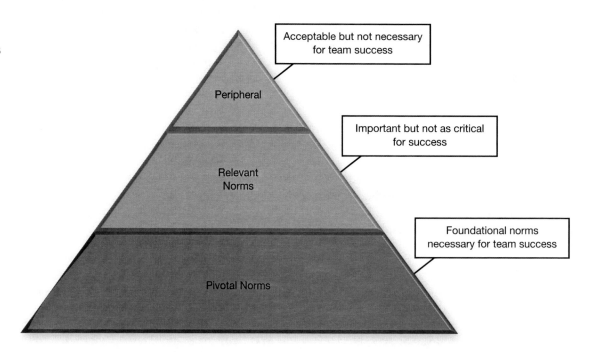

FIGURE 13.1
Levels of Norms

Acceptable but not necessary for team success

Peripheral

Important but not as critical for success

Relevant Norms

Foundational norms necessary for team success

Pivotal Norms

peripheral norm: A norm that is accepted by some, but is not important for organizational success.

A **peripheral norm** is one that some people accept, but that is not important for success in an organization. Managers in one engineering company meet every Friday after work for a beer at a nearby pub. Although most show up all the time, some seldom show up and a few never go at all. Status at work is not affected by this peripheral norm.

Of course, what is peripheral in one group may be relevant or pivotal in another. For managerial success in most Japanese organizations, the kind of after-work "schmoozing" the engineers were doing is absolutely essential. At some companies, such as Levi Strauss & Company, mode of dress is peripheral because the norm for even the top executive team is—you guessed it—Levi's jeans. At other firms, such as IBM or Procter & Gamble, dress code is more likely to be a relevant norm.

The Development of Norms

There are four methods through which norms develop over time.[28] One way is through the explicit statements of group leaders. The founder of Mars Candy Co. once brought into a meeting of his top executives a box of stale Mars candy bars he had found at a store. He went around the room, threw a candy bar at each team member, and told them he would hold each of them responsible if he ever found another stale Mars candy bar in a store. However, most explicit statements are not as extreme. For instance, a dean's comment to a faculty member that he stopped by during office hours and did not find him there might be enough to enforce a norm that professors are expected to honor office hours.

A second way norms develop is through some critical event in a group's history. The Mars example above could be one. Another is a common tale about Ray Kroc, the founder of McDonald's. Kroc once ordered the backs of the chairs of McDonald's store managers to be cut off to remind them that their job was to be out in the restaurant managing, not lounging in their offices. A university ethics committee's vote to sanction a faculty member for having an affair with a student sends a message that lasts for years about the values and norms the group holds.

Sometimes the first behavior pattern that emerges in a group sets group expectations for subsequent ones. If, during the first meeting, a team leader cracks a joke and then asks for every member's opinion about an issue, then the norms of casual interaction and full participation may be initiated within the team.

The final method through which norms may evolve is through a carryover from past experiences. You and your instructor know the basic norms for your management class simply from having been participants in previous classes.

ATA Engineering: Award-Winning Teamwork

How often do you see genuine and effective teamwork in your day-to-day life? At least in the workplace, the call for teamwork often remains unheard. Not so at ATA Engineering Inc., a San Diego–based provider of analysis and test-driven design solutions for structural, mechanical, electromechanical, and aerospace products. When managers from a larger engineering firm formed ATA Engineering in 2000, they wanted to create a decentralized organization with few organizational layers—in other words, a flat, equalized business culture.

In 2004, the company went further, making ATA entirely employee-owned via a stock ownership plan. Thanks to this flat structure and transparent culture, large and small decisions alike are made through employee consensus. All employees are also granted a high level of trust, making it possible for them to make decisions and lead projects without first receiving approval from those higher up. At times, senior employees find themselves working under lower-level employees, but that's the way they like it. The entire company is dedicated to the outcome of a project rather than to catering to egos and titles. Salary and compensation are part of the culture as well. All employees receive the same percentage of their salaries as an annual bonus. There is no separate executive bonus system.

Today, ATA Engineering has 120 employees at eight offices throughout the United States. When looking for new candidates to hire, a strong work ethic, mutual respect, and teamwork are important qualities that ATA Engineering wants new hires to possess. It is important for new employees to fit into ATA's unique and decentralized corporate culture. Management believes these factors are crucial in building an organization that offers both exceptional value to customers and a fun, rewarding workplace for employees.

Not only does ATA focus on teamwork within its own offices, but ATA also wants to help other businesses do the same. ATA is a value-added reseller for Siemens PLM Software's Teamcenter. Teamcenter is software that aims to improve productivity and promote creativity by connecting different co-workers at a company through one program. Essentially, Teamcenter allows

At ATA, the entire company is dedicated to the outcome of a project, rather than to catering to egos and titles.

Source: Pressmaster/Shutterstock

separate technical groups such as engineering and development to communicate through this software. The technology improves communication across different disciplines and departments. It also keeps information from becoming isolated and enables knowledgeable workers to collaborate on projects.

The many facets of ATA's culture create a system that eliminates the resentment and frustration common to the organizational systems of other companies. ATA Engineering has been recognized as one of the Most Innovative Companies by the National Center for Employee Ownership, and the Beyster Institute at the University of California–San Diego awarded the company the Innovations in Employee Ownership Award. The company has also been named one of San Diego's 100 fastest-growing companies and one of *The Wall Street Journal*'s Top Small Workplaces. ATA was also awarded the George M. Low Award, the quality and performance award from the National Aeronautics and Space Administration (NASA). As a NASA contractor, ATA was recognized for its ability to solve problems in the design of NASA's Mars Science Lab and its commitment to teamwork. ATA Engineering is dedicated to creating a working environment in which every employee matters and feels valued.[29]

Socializing and Modifying Norms

Regardless of how norms are established, it is the manager's job to help new employees learn the group's norms and values. This is called **socialization**, the process by which an individual learns the norms, values, goals, and expectations of an organization. All employees at Disney World go through both formal training and socialization to become knowledgeable and proactive in providing quality service. The manager must also support prevailing positive norms and try to change dysfunctional or negative ones. There are some techniques managers can use to maintain, change, and teach organizational

socialization: The process by which an individual learns the norms, values, goals, and expectations of the organization.

norms. These include providing a formal and informal orientation program; establishing a mentoring system; conducting training (which communicates norms as well as develops skills); modeling the desired behaviors; sanctioning positive behaviors and weakening negative ones, through speech and action; using formal evaluations to support positive norms; using the rewards system to reinforce norms, such as paying for performance; using informal and formal communication and feedback to discuss norms and how well group members are meeting the norms; recruiting and selecting individuals who already have exhibited positive norms; gaining the support of the group's informal leaders to promote positive norms; and developing standard operating policies and procedures that clarify and support desired norms.[30] Because teams need to be adaptable, these techniques should be used to socialize members to the pivotal norms, but not to stifle their creativity by forcing them to conform to every relevant and peripheral norm the group may hold.

Group Roles

role: A description of the behaviors expected of a specific group member.

While norms relate to rules and expectations shared by all group members, a **role** is the behaviors expected of a specific person in the group. For example, the managerial position includes roles that are supposed to provide leadership, direction, and motivation to achieve goals. Other members of a group will have different responsibilities. A work team may share a norm related to quality customer service, but individual group members may engage in different behaviors relative to that norm. Some may interact with customers on a daily basis, while others serve the customer behind the scenes. Problems can result if roles are not clear in a group. It is a manager's job to ensure that necessary roles are performed, that people understand their roles, and that resolutions are reached when role behaviors come into conflict.

Role behaviors can be described by examining the role senders and the target persons. Role senders, who may include a person's manager, fellow group members, customers, suppliers, and even the formal organization, send messages through a job description about what they expect from the target person. The target person perceives (filters) this sent role and develops the received role, what she thinks others want her to do. She mixes this role with her own personal attributes and self-expectations to determine the role behaviors in which she will engage.[31] At Disney World, all employees (role receivers) are viewed as part of the entertainment offered by the park (the managers at which are role senders), and are encouraged to be creative as well as to carry out their assigned roles.

These role concepts are easy to see in sports teams. The coach, teammates, fans, and even the position description send role expectations. In baseball, the pitcher is the only position expected to throw the ball to batters, while all players share the common role behavior of catching the ball. Everyone bats, but expectations vary as to how they will perform. Historically, Hank Aaron played the role of home-run hitter, as do present-day stars. His personal attributes and self-expectations allowed him to develop special role behaviors. If Tom Brady does not perform his respective roles, or does so relatively poorly, then his team is not likely to be successful, and its fans will be disappointed.

The same kinds of phenomena occur in work groups, although they may be less obvious. Some role behaviors are apparent. The team leader, for example, sets the agenda, calls the group to order, and directs the discussion by calling on various members. Each member also may perform certain behaviors dictated by her or his job title: salespeople call on customers, accountants deal with financial data, and so on. Other less apparent role behaviors evolve in a group and are particularly relevant during meetings and discussions. Two important roles are leadership roles and boundary-spanning roles.

Leadership Roles

task-specialist roles: Behaviors oriented toward generating information and resolving problems.

Two kinds of roles emerge in groups: task-specialist roles and group-maintenance roles.[32] Although these are often called leadership roles, this is somewhat of a misnomer in a group because these roles are performed by all group members at various times. **Task-specialist roles** are behaviors oriented toward generating information and resolving problems. These include initiating activity to get the group started, giving information and opinions, seeking information and opinions from others, summarizing the group's inputs in concise form, elaborating on others' inputs to facilitate comprehension, and testing group consensus. For example, the task specialist leadership role at Dell might be filled by the product manager when developing a new marketing strategy. These roles are obviously aimed at getting the job done. **Group-maintenance roles** help the group to engage in constructive interpersonal relationships and help members fulfill personal needs and derive satisfaction from group participation. These behaviors include encouraging inputs from all members, harmonizing the group to deal with conflict, setting standards of group operation, gatekeeping to ensure that everyone has a chance to speak, relieving tension through suggesting breaks or using humor, and testing group feelings. The group maintenance role would be an important one at healthcare facilities such as St. Jude Children's

In baseball, the pitcher is the only position expected to throw the ball to batters, while all players share the common role behavior of catching the ball.

Hospital because so many variables must be considered when dealing with children and healthcare issues. Some group members tend to be task specialists while others tend toward maintenance roles. Unfortunately, some tend to perform dysfunctional roles called antigroup behaviors. The characteristics of each of these roles are shown in Table 13.4.

Antigroup roles include behaviors that disrupt the group, draw attention to individual rather than group functioning, and detract from positive interactions. These include blocking the discussion of others, seeking recognition through side discussions or inappropriate joking, dominating the conversation, or avoiding group interaction entirely. Most groups will have at least one member who engages in some of these actions. When antigroup role behaviors are present, leaders and others must utilize the task and maintenance behaviors to get the group back on target. Control measures, such as limiting the number of time any one person can speak, may be helpful in discouraging antigroup behavior. At some meetings, participants are all granted equal amounts of time for their comments.

group-maintenance roles: Behaviors that help the group engage in constructive interpersonal relationships, and help members fulfill personal needs and derive satisfaction from group participation.

antigroup roles: Behaviors that disrupt the group, draw attention to individual rather than group functioning, and detract from positive interactions.

Boundary-Spanning Roles

Boundary-spanning roles involve interacting with members in other units of the organization or even outside the organization. The group leader who acts as a link with upper-level bosses is in a boundary-spanning role. Many members in quality teams go visit and work with client organizations to help learn how to serve the client better. Some group members act as liaisons with other teams or have membership on other teams, thus sharing information across the boundaries among the groups. As the use of teams grows, change accelerates, and demands for customer service and quality become even more pronounced, such boundary-spanning roles will become ever more important. The increase in the use of cross-functional teams is a reflection of these changes.

boundary-spanning roles: Group behaviors involving interaction with members in other units of the organization or outside the organization.

TABLE 13.4 Group Role Behavior

Task-Specialist Role	Group-Maintenance Role	Antigroup Role
■ Initiating activity	■ Encouraging	■ Blocking
■ Giving information and opinions	■ Harmonizing	■ Seeking recognition
■ Seeking information and opinions	■ Setting group standards	■ Dominating
■ Summarizing	■ Gatekeeping	■ Avoiding
■ Elaborating	■ Tension relieving	
■ Consensus testing	■ Testing group feelings	

cohesiveness: The tendency of group members to unite in their pursuit of group goals and to be attracted to the group and each other.

Cohesiveness refers to the tendency of group members to unite in their pursuit of group goals and to be attracted to the group and each other. This definition includes both an individual element—members attracted to each other and to the group itself—and a group element—members united in pursuit of a goal. These two elements reflect a "synergistic" effect of a cohesive group as being greater than the sum of its parts.

How groups get to be cohesive and how managers can facilitate that process has been a topic of interest to researchers and practitioners for some time. The more opportunities group members have to interact and communicate with one another, the better they will get to know each other and the more likely they will develop close relationships. Having to work together on tasks also tends to promote group cohesiveness. Thus, if a group is too large or geographically dispersed, such opportunities will be minimized. If the members see themselves as similar in attitudes, values, and personal characteristics, initial attraction to the group may be stronger and can foster cohesiveness. In more diverse groups, a manager may have to identify and promote similarities to speed along the bonding process. One extremely important method of doing this is developing agreement around a common goal. At New Belgium Brewing in Fort Collins, CO, all employees are bound to and support an organizational culture based on striving for greater sustainability. The more specific and clear the goal and the more it can be shown to fulfill important member needs, the greater the likelihood that cohesiveness will occur. At New Belgium, employees voted to power the brewery using wind energy, even though it might reduce their pay gained through profit sharing. Agreeing on a common mission, such as the customer service mission of the Ritz Carlton or the "absolutely positively overnight" delivery mission of FedEx, enhances cohesiveness.

Sometimes that goal can be directed externally in the form of competition against another group. Pitting one group against another is a potent force promoting internal solidarity. Retailers such as Home Depot and Lowe's are competitive and encourage employees to identify with their companies in order to provide more internal cohesiveness and better services. On the other hand, "competition" within the group tends to damage cohesiveness. In sports, it is often the case that the stronger the opponent, the greater the team's desire to work together to win it. In business, the exhortation to "beat the competition" is used to motivate and foster team cohesiveness. Moreover, if external groups and others within the broader organization recognize its success, the team becomes more cohesive. In football, the Baltimore Ravens franchise is a strongly united and successful team. Its players take pride in the fact that other teams see them as fierce competitors. Management uses this to promote the "us against them" mentality.

Understanding group cohesiveness is important because of the direct impact it has on a group's functioning and work output. In general, research has shown a positive relationship between overall productivity and group cohesiveness.[33] Moreover, highly cohesive groups tend to engage in more internal social interaction and communication; have more positive, cooperative, and friendly interactions; exert greater influence on their members; have greater member satisfaction; and are more effective in achieving goals they set for themselves.[34]

Figure 13.2 demonstrates the interaction between group cohesiveness and performance norms. Groups tend to be most productive when they are highly cohesive and have high performance norms. Members agree on a spe-

Source: wavebreakmedia/Shutterstock

In business, the exhortation to "beat the competition" is used to motivate and foster team cohesiveness.

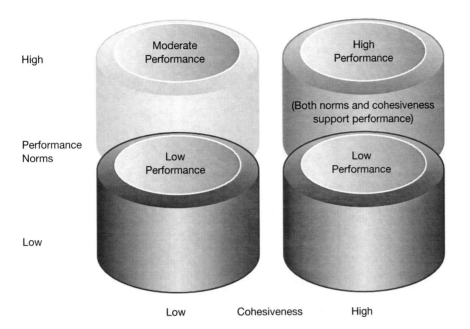

FIGURE 13.2
Effect of Group
Cohesiveness and
Norms on Performance

cific goal of high performance, and their cohesiveness helps them accomplish it. A group with high norms but low cohesiveness is moderately successful because individual members are striving for success but may not be working together as a team. Groups with low performance norms and high cohesiveness may provide the most severe challenge for a manager, because they have set low standards and members are strongly in agreement on the production level due to their cohesiveness. One frequently finds this problem in government agencies, where job security is very high. The manager must try to raise standards, possibly through a pay-for-performance system or through interpersonal intervention in the group, such as by establishing relationships and gradually modeling high productivity. In government agencies, rewards or recognition may help to model expected performance levels. If these attempts fail, the manager could reduce the work interdependency of team members or even break up the group on certain tasks. If the group is complacent, then competition within the group could have a positive impact. All of these techniques may be resisted by the cohesive group, but without some action the group has little chance for improvement.

Additional Interpersonal Processes

A number of interpersonal processes influence the effectiveness of groups. Processes such as open communications, power and influence, leadership, and change are discussed in some detail in other chapters of this text. Three other processes that seem particularly important are managing conflict, building trust, and encouraging group facilitation.

Conflict Resolution

Although conflict has traditionally been viewed as negative, the more modern view is that conflict is both inevitable and in many cases desirable if properly managed.[35] Managing conflict is an essential skill for team success because conflict has the potential to immobilize virtually any group. Conflicts grow almost naturally out of individual interaction and can be defined as antagonistic interaction in which one person blocks the goals, intentions, or behaviors of someone else. Conflicts can be caused by different individual goals, scarce organizational resources such as money or personnel, power and status differences, personality clashes, personal

The widespread practice of using email to communicate, rather than face-to-face interactions, has increased the potential for conflicts arising from poor communication or misunderstandings.

Source: Antonio Guillem/Shutterstock

TABLE 13.5 Conflict Management Styles

Style	Examples
Competing	A new CEO comes into a struggling company and uses aggressive management tactics to fire hundreds of workers without the advice of the management team.
Avoiding	The leaders of an organization ignore employee concerns about potential misconduct because they do not want to interrupt performance.
Accommodating	The supervisor of a department allows her employees to engage in flex-time and spend more time with their families.
Compromising	A union and a major company negotiate on a cost-of-living adjustment in a way that both parties find acceptable.
Collaborating	Two companies in a joint venture work together to share technology without compromising their trade secrets.

aggressiveness, ambiguous roles or job boundaries, faulty communications, differences in values or perceptions, inadequate authority or power, and even management's oppressive behavior. The widespread practice of using email to communicate, rather than face-to-face interactions, has increased the potential for conflicts arising from poor communication or misunderstandings.

Management experts generally recognize five major styles for dealing with conflict, although subtle variations may be observed. These styles evolve from different levels of the individual in an attempt to satisfy both his or her own goals or concerns and those of the other person (see Table 13.5).

competing style: A management style involving a stance of high assertiveness with low cooperation.

1. The **competing style** involves a stance of high assertiveness with low cooperation. A person using a competing style wants to get his or her way or to win and doesn't care much about the other person's feelings or about a long-term relationship. You might adopt this style when negotiating your best deal on a home mortgage. While this style is important to use in certain situations, managers that use this style exclusively tend to be self-serving and may not always pursue the best interests of the organization. Some believe former Lehman Brothers CEO Dick Fuld adopted this style in his refusal to accept offers from Warren Buffett and other potential buyers for the struggling company because he thought the offers did not reflect Lehman's value. The investment bank ended up going bankrupt. Many criticized Fuld's hubris and accused him of not putting company interests first.[36]

avoiding style: A style displaying low assertiveness and low cooperation.

2. The **avoiding style** displays low assertiveness and low cooperation. Here the individual is not much concerned about personal goals and may not care enough about the larger goal to fight about it. This style might be appropriate on trivial matters and when there is little chance of winning the conflict. This could be a good strategy for dealing with the company "know-it-all." Sometimes this approach results in the issue going away, or at least not escalating. However, managers should exert caution in overusing this approach. Avoiding issues that should be addressed could spell doom for the company. For instance, Enron's leaders largely avoided learning about and addressing ethical issues within the firm. As a result, the company failed and many employees and investors lost their investments.

accommodating style: A style exhibiting low assertiveness and high cooperation.

3. The **accommodating style** exhibits low assertiveness and high cooperation. You allow the other person's needs to be satisfied at the expense of yours. This is a good strategy when the relationship is more important than your needs—for instance, in discussing the resources for a new computer system or providing administrative

assistance for a top salesperson. However, a manager should never sacrifice the company's values and ethics policies. Managers that are too accommodating are not likely to resolve conflicts in ways beneficial to the firm.

4. The **compromising style** reflects moderate concern for both your goals and the other person's. You both give up something in order to reach agreement and, at least partially, to attain desired outcomes. This strategy is common when goals are diametrically opposed and no resolution appears to be otherwise attainable—for example, the case of what department will receive what percentage of a travel budget. Some experts criticize the tendency to settle for a compromise too willingly (a trait seen in certain managers) as each party loses something in the exchange.

> **compromising style:** A style that reflects a moderate concern for both your goals and the other person's goals.

5. The **collaborating style** shows both high assertiveness and high cooperation. Both parties win as they work through issues and reach an optimal solution that meets everyone's needs to the fullest. This style is appropriate for most important organizational decisions where goals are important and relationships must be maintained. For example, each department or group might provide some centralized services such as improved computer technical support.

> **collaborating style:** A style displaying both high assertiveness and high competition.

Conflicts over important issues generally can have a beneficial outcome when everyone collaborates. Team members should care enough about their own goals, the goals of others, and certainly the overall organizational goals to work through problems.

Negotiation skills often come into play during conflict resolution. **Negotiation** occurs when two or more parties discuss a problem with the intent to resolve differences and come up with a solution. In an ideal situation, team members will discuss the issue, come to an understanding, and resolve their differences to come up with an agreed-upon solution. However, this is not always the outcome. The outcome of negotiation can result in all parties feeling satisfied, some parties feeling satisfied while others are dissatisfied, or all parties feeling partially satisfied and partially dissatisfied. This last outcome is likely to occur during situations in which compromise represents the best solution.

> **negotiation:** Occurs when two or more parties discuss a problem with the intent to resolve differences and come up with a solution.

Negotiation can be broken down into two strategies. *Distributive negotiation* takes the view that there are only so many resources to go around (a "fixed pie"). Therefore, each side must haggle in an attempt to get as much of the pie as possible. Distributive negotiation is closer to a competing conflict management style as it tends to view the process from a win-lose perspective.[37] *Integrative negotiation*, on the other hand, takes the perspective that successful integration between the parties can enlarge the pie, creating

Negotiation occurs when two or more parties discuss a problem with the intent to resolve differences and come up with a solution.

Source: Pressmaster/Shutterstock

TABLE 13.6 Tips for Successful Negotiation

1. Focus on the issue, not the people.
2. Take a collaborative approach to the problem.
3. Listen to the other party's argument.
4. Encourage the other party's participation.
5. Diffuse escalating behaviors by returning to the issue.

beneficial solutions for both parties. In integrative negotiating, the parties attempt to find common ground and use shared interests to reach outcomes that are mutually beneficial.[38] Integrative negotiation is more equivalent to a compromising or collaborating style of conflict management. Integrative negotiation is often the preferred method of negotiation in a team setting, although distributive negotiation may be required in certain situations. Table 13.6 provides some tips for successful negotiation.

Problems abound where conflicts have not been successfully worked through and negative consequences result. The negative side of conflict can result in restricted communication, personal attacks, dysfunctional organizational behaviors, an inappropriate test of wills, and disrupted groups. Abusive behavior is widely reported as a major problem. In a "National Business Ethics Survey" conducted by the Ethisphere Institute, 18 percent of respondents reported suffering from or witnessing abusive behavior in the workplace.[39] Handled properly, though, conflict can result in enhanced creativity and innovation along with improved organizational efficiency as issues are resolved. It can keep people motivated and involved as they meet the challenges of team functioning.

Trust

Trusting someone is not only believing that he or she is honest, straightforward, and sincere but also believing in that person's ability to perform.[40] Trust underlies the entire concept of empowerment and self-directed work teams. Managers must trust that employees will honestly and capably handle the increased responsibility given them. Trust is the foundation of effective business ethics initiations in organizations. Employees must believe that management truly cares about them, trusts them, has faith in them, and will not undermine their empowered efforts.

Because management has the power, managers are the ones who must establish relationships of trust. They cannot expect trust or demand it from employees, but they can do some things to facilitate and earn it: Communicate information openly and honestly; listen; be consistent in feelings, expressions, words, deeds, and missions; demonstrate sincere regard and concern for self and others; treat others fairly; be consistent and predictable with others; show respect for employees by empowering them through delegation and listening to their opinions and suggestions; and demonstrate competence. Do these things, and trustworthiness is nearly ensured.[41]

Group Facilitation

facilitators: Leaders who help the group overcome internal obstacles or difficulties so that it may achieve desired outcomes.

The team environment in which managers find themselves in modern organizations calls for a new kind of leadership. No longer can a manager be the highly directive, all-knowing autocrat or straw boss. Because knowledge is widely shared and decisions are being made in groups, managers must also be **facilitators,** helping the group overcome internal obstacles or difficulties so that it may achieve desired outcomes efficiently. In the role of facilitator, managers or group leaders focus the group's energy on defining and accomplishing goals. They also help the group communicate efficiently; foster an atmosphere that encourages all team members to participate; encourage group decision making at every appropriate opportunity to ensure member support and commitment; anticipate emergencies which require rapid decisions (along with establishing procedures to handle emergencies so that group support is maintained); and encourage self-discovery and experimentation by protecting members' ideas from attack so that they can feel secure in sharing and exploring new ideas, proposals, thoughts, and opinions.[42]

Remember that it is possible, even desirable, that all members of the group share in the facilitation responsibilities to ensure a group works successfully.

Contextual Influences on Group Effectiveness

A number of factors within the overall organization and environment have a major impact on how groups function. These factors include culture, task design/technology, mission clarity, autonomy, feedback mechanisms, reward and recognition systems, training and consultation, and physical environments. Of these, culture, organizational missions, and training are discussed elsewhere. The other characteristics warrant a brief discussion due to their impact on group and team functioning.

The nature of the task determines to a large extent whether a group or team is called for. A claims adjuster at State Farm Insurance, for example, is largely independent of other adjusters and works directly with clients. The position requires some information sharing, but not a high degree of coordination. Technology has affected group behavior as well. With webinars that allow for live meetings or presentations to be conducted via the Internet, even geographically dispersed workers function more like teams. Technology has enabled team members to work together without ever meeting face-to-face, leading to the development of virtual teams in which members communicate through electronic forms of communication.

The level of autonomy in decision making that is fostered by top management also influences group functioning. If top managers have centralized decision making, then using empowered or self-managed work teams will be virtually impossible. Many of the early failures of quality initiatives resulted from a perceived lack of real impact on the problems considered, due to top management's required approval of all changes. The increasing use of self-directed work teams requires that teams have greater autonomy to carry out their tasks and goals.

Feedback mechanisms—the amount and nature of information that individuals and teams receive about their performance—affect team functioning in a number of ways. Feedback may indicate that groups are not sufficiently cohesive to sustain commitment and

Feedback mechanisms—the amount and nature of information that individuals and teams receive about their performance—affect team functioning in a number of ways.

retain employees, or customer satisfaction measures may indicate that project teams are not advancing rapidly enough through the stages of development to be performing adequately. Feedback mechanisms may be informal, such as electronic social network interactions with customers, or they can be quite sophisticated. If feedback mechanisms are inadequate, then teams can flounder for months or even years without realizing that change is required.

Reward and recognition systems also determine group functioning. Some experts point out that individuals and departments are expected to interact frequently and meaningfully with other individuals and departments, yet are rewarded totally on the basis of individual accomplishments rather than for their interdependent performance—which diminishes interaction and mutual aid.[43] Players for the Chicago Bulls, for example, would probably be very reluctant to pass the ball to a teammate, even if he had an easier shot, if all of their rewards and their future on the team were based solely on their personal scoring averages at the end of the season. Thus, reward systems should encourage team efforts, not hinder them.

A final factor often neglected in examining work group functioning is the physical environment. Office arrangement and layout can influence work and communication flow or send powerful messages about organizational values and norms. Artifacts in the culture such as documents, codes of conduct, websites, even logos and artwork in the physical environment can help set the tone for group functioning.

Problems in Groups

Obviously, groups and teams can be powerful forces for satisfying employee needs and accomplishing organizational goals. However, there are difficulties associated with groups and teams that can derail organizational success. Some of these have been discussed already—problems with role ambiguity and role conflict; difficulties in establishing positive group norms consistent with the organizational culture; hardships in getting the right mix of skills, abilities, and traits; free-riding; and various antigroup behaviors. Other problems in groups that must be worked through are personality clashes and other conflicts over jurisdiction, scarce resources, or power and status differences. Observed misconduct can also create problems in groups. In a business ethics survey, approximately 33 percent of respondents reported seeing misuse of company time, the number-one specific form of misconduct that year.[44] Many employees do not report misconduct and may even engage in the same conduct if they feel that others are doing it and the risk of being caught is low. This can result in a poor ethical work environment for the group. Observing misconduct by a group member can also create tension and problems with lack of trust. In completing this chapter, we will explore some additional problems that may occur in group interaction.

Conformity and Agreement

conformity: Adherence to the group's norms, values, and goals.

One common problem many teams face is dealing with the related issues of conformity and agreement. In the context of a group, **conformity** means adherence to the group's norms, values, and goals. While member acceptance of pivotal norms is important for both individual and group success, too much conformity—especially to the point of blind adherence even to all peripheral norms—can result in reduced creativity and objectivity in addressing issues and solving problems. For example, in a set of experiments in which subjects were asked to judge whether three lines were equal or different in length, many individuals conformed to the consensus of a group, judging lines that were obviously different in length to be the same just because the rest of the group said they were.[45] This kind of conformity, when applied to work situations, can detract from the generation of new ideas and from a group member's tendency to disagree with inappropriate behaviors that the group might be demonstrating. This phenomenon occurred at Countrywide Financial when loan officers started granting so-called "liar loans" to borrowers who were encouraged to falsify application documents in order to secure a larger loan than they would otherwise be eligible for.

Experts have identified two special cases of group conformity. We defined the concept of groupthink in Chapter 7 as a condition in which poor decision making occurs because the desire to maintain group cohesiveness precludes the critical evaluation of alternative courses of action.[46] For example, to avoid "rocking the boat" or upsetting the positive shared feelings of group solidarity, members may withhold information or opinions that would go against an apparent group consensus. The result is that decisions are made and implemented without considering all possible alternatives, or the alternatives offered are given less than full examination.

Irving Janis, who coined the term *groupthink*, identified eight symptoms of the phenomenon:

1. Illusion of invulnerability—members become convinced that they are invincible, and their overconfidence results in a willingness to take great risks.
2. Illusion of morality—members believe that whatever they do is good, ethical, and morally correct, when in fact, it may not be.
3. Illusion of unanimity—members falsely believe they are all in agreement.
4. Collective rationalization—members justify any concerns about the value of what they are doing or challenges to their decisions.
5. Mind guarding—some members protect the group by preventing adverse information from being presented.
6. Shared stereotypes—members negatively stereotype outsiders who may present a threat to the group and its decisions.
7. Self-censorship—members consider disagreement with the group inappropriate, so they don't speak out.
8. Direct pressure—members who voice objections to the apparent group consensus are pressured by other members to conform.[47]

One common problem many teams face is dealing with the related issues of conformity and agreement.

These groupthink symptoms can be prevented through specific techniques, including assigning the role of critical evaluation to everyone in the group, appointing a specific individual to be a "devil's advocate" to challenge the group consensus, breaking the group into smaller subgroups to discuss issues, having the leader withhold his or her opinion about the issue, and bringing in outside experts to challenge the group's thinking. Within the broader organization, ways to preclude groupthink include establishing an organizational culture that encourages original thinking and challenges, training leaders, and conducting organizational development activities such as team building and creative problem solving. Most firms are developing ethics programs to encourage appropriate conduct and systems for reporting of misconduct. It is important that leaders establish cohesive groups with norms that encourage rather than discourage critical evaluation of ideas within the context of appropriate conduct.[48]

A special case of groupthink called the **Abilene Paradox**—a term derived from originator Jeny Harvey's family's unwanted, but agreed upon, automobile trip to Abilene—occurs when members of a group publicly agree on a course of action even though there is an underlying consensus agreement that an alternative course is preferred.[49] Each person incorrectly assumes that everyone else wants the publicly chosen alternative. An example would be when an executive team continues to approve expenditures for a project that each member privately believes ought to be scrapped. The unwillingness of members to bring up their true feelings and beliefs results in an escalating commitment to a bad decision. This phenomenon can result from some combination of the desire not to "step on someone's toes" or to humiliate the original project advocate.

Abilene Paradox: A situation occurring when members of a group publicly agree on a course of action even though there is an underlying consensus agreement that an alternative course is preferred.

Politics

Yet another problem endemic to groups is **politics**, which in this context refers to maneuvering to try to gain an advantage in the distribution of organizational rewards or

politics: The maneuvering by an individual to try to gain an advantage in the distribution of organizational rewards or resources.

resources. Although most people view this pursuit of self-interest at work negatively, many see it as necessary for individual success.[50]

Political maneuvering is considered negative because it consumes valuable time better spent on productive matters, often subverts organizational goals, diverts human energy, and can result in the loss of valuable employees who cannot or do not wish to "play the game." Such maneuvering includes a full range of activities, from the fairly benign and acceptable—such as helping others to gain favor and developing a network of positive relationships—to the dastardly and dangerous—such as backstabbing. Other common political tactics include generating destructive competition, using ingratiating language, spreading rumors, using scapegoats, leaking confidential information outside the group, blaming others, sabotaging others' projects, circumventing a boss, playing it safe by not being associated with projects that might fail, playing dumb, playing favorites, or even intentionally escalating commitment to a collapsing project so that immediate failure will not be acknowledged. In highly politicized organizations, members advance not based on individual merit but due to how those in authority feel about them. This environment decreases cooperation between employees and increases competitiveness.[51] All of these activities are associated with abusive behavior, a form of unethical conduct that can hurt productivity and create a negative group work environment. A full list of political behaviors is almost endless, but the point is clear. Playing politics in most cases is negative and should be avoided if possible.[52]

On the other hand, it is important for managers to possess political skills. There is a major difference between possessing political skills to navigate challenging situations and developing a highly politicized workplace environment. Managers that are adept at navigating ambiguous situations can create positive change for their firms.[53] Additionally, political skills can be used to reduce ambiguity among employees and guide them in workplace decisions.[54] A manager with political skills can avoid developing a highly politicized environment by advocating for a participative corporate culture, adhering to organizational values, and distributing awards in a fair manner.

As a manager, you can minimize the effects of politics by establishing a trusting and honest communication climate and promoting team goals and rewards. An ethical culture that offers rewards for open and transparent communication and interaction can help eliminate or reduce misconduct. Discouraging competition for limited outcomes, rewarding those who help others instead of competing with them, basing performance evaluations on productivity and not personalities, reducing favoritism, using job rotation and highly interdependent tasks to promote group member cooperation, and having upper management model nonpolitical behavior should help reduce negative politics in the workplace.

Despite the costs and problems associated with teams, their benefits can far outweigh any negatives. Harnessing the power of the group will likely be the management imperative for many years to come.

Summary and Review

- *Distinguish between the terms* group *and* team. A group is two or more persons who communicate, share a collective identity, and have a common goal. A team is a small group whose members have complementary skills as well as a common purpose, goals, and approach, and who hold themselves mutually accountable. The major distinction is that individual performance and outcomes are most important in groups, while collective work group performance and outcomes are what count most in teams.

- *Summarize a general model of group effectiveness, including its primary components.* Effectiveness is measured by performance outcomes, such as units produced, as well as personal outcomes, such as member satisfaction and commitment to the group. These outcomes are influenced by group structure—including the group type, size, and composition of skills and abilities—as well as the processes of group development, cohesiveness, norms, roles, conflict management, trust, and facilitation. Also important are aspects of the organization itself, such as culture, task design and technology, mission clarity, autonomy, feedback mechanisms, reward and recognition systems, training and consultation, and the physical environment.

■ *Describe the types of groups that exist in organizations.* The many types of groups and teams in organizations vary by composition, duration, degree of autonomy, development and function. Special kinds of groups include top management teams, task forces, committees, project teams, new-product development teams, research and development teams, quality-assurance teams, self-directed work teams, and virtual teams.

■ *Specify five stages of team development.* Groups tend to develop through the stages of forming, storming, norming, performing, and adjourning.

■ *Discuss how group size, norms, cohesiveness, and trust affect group performance.* Work teams function best when limited to between 7 and 20 members, but the optimal number depends on the circumstances. They also function better when expectations about appropriate behavior within the group norms are positive and clear, when members trust one another, and when they are cohesive.

■ *Determine different roles that members can play in a group.* Roles are the behaviors expected of and demonstrated by specific individuals in groups. Some members emphasize task-oriented roles, some group-maintenance roles, and others roles that span the boundaries of the group.

■ *Relate some of the problems associated with group functioning.* Difficulties associated with groups and teams include role ambiguity and role conflict; problems in establishing positive group norms consistent with the organizational culture; problems getting the right mix of skills, abilities, and traits; free-riding; personality clashes; conflicts over jurisdiction, scarce resources, power, and status differences; and various antigroup behaviors. Other problems relate to excessive conformity to group norms, which can reduce creativity and objectivity in addressing issues and solving problems. Groupthink and the Abilene Paradox are two examples. Another problem in groups is politics, or maneuvering to try to gain an advantage in the distribution of organizational rewards or resources, because it consumes time, may subvert organizational goals, diverts energy, and can result in the loss of valuable employees.

■ *Analyze a business's use of teams.* In the "Business Dilemma" box, you encountered a hypothetical business having difficulties with its team environment. You should be able to analyze the teams' effectiveness, using the model presented in this chapter, and make recommendations for a future course of action.

Key Terms and Concepts

Abilene Paradox 413	facilitators 410	pivotal norms 401
accommodating style 408	formal groups 394	politics 413
adjourning stage 401	forming stage 399	product-development teams 395
antigroup roles 405	free-riding 397	project teams 395
avoiding style 408	functional groups 394	quality-assurance teams 396
boundary-spanning roles 405	group 391	relevant norms 401
cohesiveness 406	group-maintenance roles 405	role 404
collaborating style 409	informal groups 394	self-directed work team (SDWT) 396
committee 395	negotiation 409	socialization 403
competing style 408	norming stage 400	storming stage 400
compromising style 409	norms 401	task force 395
conformity 412	performing stage 400	task-specialist roles 404
cross-functional groups 394	peripheral norm 402	team 391

Ready Recall

1. Explain the difference between groups and teams.
2. What are some of the assets of teams?

3. What are the two outcomes in the group effectiveness model? What factors affect these outcomes?

4. What are self-managed work teams and what tasks might they perform that traditionally are performed by managers?
5. How are norms formed and taught or altered in an organization or group?
6. How are team cohesiveness, norms, and performance related?
7. What major roles do group members perform?
8. Discuss the way teams develop over time.
9. What are some problems that may crop up in groups and teams?
10. What are the symptoms of groupthink and how can team leaders prevent it from happening?

Expand Your Experience

1. If teams are being used in any of your classes this term, try to identify the stage of development each of the teams is in. Describe each team in terms of cohesiveness, trust levels, and norms.
2. In your fraternity, sorority, school athletic team, or workplace, see if you can identify instances of political behavior. Have these behaviors had positive or negative effects on group functioning?
3. Interview the department chairperson in charge of one of the academic departments in your college or university. Using Table 13.1 as a guideline, explore whether the professors function more like a group or a team. Contrast what you find here with what you see on your school's basketball, football, or baseball team.
4. Find and interview the owner of a local small business or the manager of a fairly large department in a larger company. Ask this manager to describe some of the norms in their operations.

Strengthen Your Skills

Teamwork

The research and development team at O'Collin's Corporation is faced with an issue. It has been developing an electric vehicle to compete with the Chevy Volt, and after months of testing, has determined that there is a 40 percent chance of the battery catching on fire if the casing is bumped at certain speeds. The team approaches the team leader with their concerns and he calls for a meeting. Team member one argues that there is no issue as the chances are not high of this occurring. He argues that their product is not any more vulnerable than other electric vehicles and votes for the project to continue as is. Team member two is worried about safety and proposes that the team work on building a protective casing for the battery that would eliminate shock if bumped. This would delay the project and increase costs. Team member three suggests that the project should be suspended until further tests can be done and more information can be gathered.

Instructions:

Break into groups of four and have each person take on the role of the team leader and team members. Assume that position for your debate/discussion. Before you begin, take a moment to assume the character of your role. What kind of attitude/approach do you imagine your character having during the product development process that led to this situation? Then begin a discussion, taking into consideration the costs, benefits, and any potential consequences of each decision. Once your team has come to a decision, each person will evaluate the team in terms of how well they worked together. Give each field a score: 1 = Disagree; 2 = Neutral; 3 = Agree. Add them up and see how well your team worked together.

1. Team was open to all ideas expressed
2. Each member gave their opinion and defended it
3. The team shared in a common goal without conflict
4. There was an element of respect to each interaction
5. Every member was involved in making the final decision

If your score is 5, the team did not work together well. If your score was 15, your team worked together well. If your score falls between 5 and 15, there is room for improvement among team members to work well together.

Case 13: Whole Foods "Teaming Up" to Improve Profitability

In 1978, two entrepreneurs, John Mackey and Rene Hardy, began a challenging venture to create a company that incorporated the values of healthy living and conscious capitalism, all with a $45,000 loan. Their efforts led them to open a small natural foods store named SaferWay, founded in Austin, Texas, in 1980. The two founders had a difficult time beginning the company and later merged with Clarksville Natural Grocery, which culminated in the two companies becoming the world's largest retailer of organic and natural food and personal care products. The

Whole Foods team members are highly regarded and are given personal stakes in the company through stock options.

new company was called Whole Foods. Whole Foods has grown not only domestically but also internationally since its initial expansion in 1984.

Starting the business was no easy feat; the company has faced many challenges along the way. Less than a year after opening, a devastating flood hit Austin, which wiped out the store's entire inventory. The company faced over $400,000 worth of damages. After weighing options, the company banded together to work as a team. With the help of the community, they were able to reopen their store in four weeks. From the beginning, Mackey instilled company core values in all aspects of the organization.

The core values embraced by Whole Foods have enabled it to turn its mission into a reality. The company's values involve meeting customer needs and describe the company's commitment toward selling the highest-quality natural and organic products. Whole Foods aims to create positive and ethical ongoing partnerships with suppliers while simultaneously creating wealth through profits and growth as well as caring about the community and environment. The company also aims to delight customers by promoting the health of all stakeholders through healthy-eating education. Along with management striving to implement these core values, employees help to create this environment through daily interactions with customers. Employees are highly valued at Whole Foods and are labeled team members to empower them through their everyday contributions.

Whole Foods team members are highly regarded and are given personal stakes in the company through stock options. Company leaders realize that the success of the company depends on Whole Foods Market team members and believe in motivating and rewarding them for quality performance. At each Whole Foods store, individuals are divided into eight to ten teams and are the backbone of the store. Initially, when an individual is hired, he or she is hired on a provisional basis. Before candidates are hired on a provisional basis, they undergo a 60-day pro-

cess of interviews on the phone, with team members, and with leaders. If two-thirds of the team members vote in favor of the candidate at the end of the provisional period, the candidate becomes part of the team. Those who do not receive two-thirds of the votes can redo the provisional period with another team or choose to leave the company.

This element is an important part of the Whole Foods culture because the company believes that working together is the most important thing that occurs during business hours. This team approach has been adopted throughout the entire chain of command. Regional leaders are arranged into teams, and even founder John Mackey shares his CEO title with fellow co-CEO Walter Robb. Hard work and positive attitudes are essential for team members because additional pay and profit sharing are based on team performance. Each individual relies on the productivity of the members in his or her team to receive these benefits; employees cannot reach them alone.

Whole Foods also uses the talents of employees to improve company operations. It implements an open-door policy that allows employees to provide feedback to managers and other team members, which ensures that clear and concise communication is constantly occurring in the store. In addition to this, Whole Foods strives to enrich the lives of Whole Foods employees and incentivizes employees to participate in a healthy discount incentive program for team members. The company rewards employees for living healthy lifestyles when employees and team members reach certain benchmarks. To reach the goals of the program, team members are prompted to work together while simultaneously encouraging one another through positive reinforcement.

Self-directed work teams consisting of employees make many of the decisions in the day-to-day operations of the different stores. For instance, teams have control over their scheduling and aim to work with each other to provide an optimal schedule for everyone. The company provides its team members with extensive training and educational resources, including information on the company's gain-sharing program and the company's quality standards. By empowering its employees through teams, perks, and education, Whole Foods has been able to turn its workers into significant contributors of value for the company.

Despite the success of Whole Foods, the company has struggled to get rid of its "whole paycheck" reputation in recent years. Many consumers viewed Whole Foods products as unaffordable. Even its 365 Everyday Value brand failed to shake off this image. Due to financial struggles, Amazon.com acquired Whole Foods in 2017 for $13.7 billion. How Amazon.com's management of Whole Foods will impact team decision making is unclear, but there are signs that Whole Foods is becoming a more centralized company. For instance, rather than allowing local stores to decide whether to carry regional items, these decisions will now be made by Whole Foods executives at headquarters.

These changes might take away some of the team autonomy that has been practiced at individual stores. Amazon.com and Whole Foods will need to find a balance between a more centralized approach—which might lead to decreased costs, greater control, and faster and more consistent decision making—and the team approach practiced at individual stores that has provided Whole Foods with its own distinctive flair and made it a great place for employees to work.[55]

1. Describe some of the ways Whole Foods encourages teamwork among employees.
2. Why does the use of teams allow Whole Foods to tap into a variety of talent?
3. How does Whole Foods make use of self-directed work teams?

Notes

1. Mindy S. Lubber, "How Timberland, Levi's Use Teamwork to Advance Sustainability," *Green Biz*, May 9, 2011, https://www.greenbiz.com/blog/2011/05/09/how-companies-court-stakeholders-accelerate-sustainability (accessed December 31, 2017); Timberland Company, "Engaging Employees: Timberland's Global Stewards Program 2009 Report," http://responsibility.timberland.com/wp-content/uploads/2011/05/Stewards_Program_2009.pdf (accessed August 6, 2013); Betsy Blaisdell and Nina Kruschwitz, "New Ways to Engage Employees, Suppliers and Competitors in CSR," *MIT Sloan*, November 14, 2012, https://sloanreview.mit.edu/article/new-ways-to-engage-employees-suppliers-and-competitors-in-csr/ (accessed December 31, 2017); Timberland Company, "Focus—Corporate Social Responsibility Report 2001," http://responsibility.timberland.com/wp-content/uploads/2011/05/2001-CSR-Report.pdf (accessed August 6, 2013); Chuck Scofield, "Sharing Strength: Lessons About Getting By Giving," *LiNE Zine*, http://www.linezine.com/7.2/articles/cssslagbg.htm (accessed December 31, 2017); David Hellqvist, "Timberland: 40 Years of the Yellow Boot," *The Guardian*, April 16, 2013, https://www.theguardian.com/fashion/2013/apr/16/timberland-40-years-yellow-boot (accessed December 31, 2017); Timberland, "About Us," https://www.timberland.com/about-us.html (accessed December 31, 2017); Timberland, "Responsibility," https://www.timberland.com/responsibility.html (accessed December 31, 2017); Timberland, "Timberland Employees Around the Globe Take Part in 18th Annual Serv-a-Palooza Service Event," September 17, 2015, https://www.timberland.com/newsroom/press-releases/timberland-18th-annual-serv-a-palooza-service-event.html (accessed December 31, 2017).

2. Jon R. Katzenbach and Douglas K. Smith, "The Discipline of Teams," *Harvard Business Review* 71 (March/April, 1993), 111–120.

3. Katzenbach and Smith, "The Discipline of Teams."

4. Whole Foods, "Why We're a Great Place to Work," http://www.wholefoodsmarket.com/careers/workhere.php (accessed January 6, 2018).

5. Richard S. Wellins, William C. Byham, and Jeanne M. Wilson, *Empowered Teams: Creating Self-Directed Work Groups That Improve Quality, Productivity, and Participation* (San Francisco: Jossey-Bass Publishers, 1991).

6. Norman F. Maier, "Assets and Liabilities in Group Problem Solving: The Need for an Integrative Function," *Psychological Review* 74 (9 July 1967), 239–249.

7. Eric Sundstrom, Kenneth P. DeMeuse, and David Futrell, "Work Team: Applications and Effectiveness," *American Psychologist* 45 (February 1990), 120–133.

8. Sundstrom, DeMeuse, and Futrell, "Work Teams."

9. Katzenbach and Smith.

10. Patrick J. Kiger, "Task Force Training Develops New Leaders, Solves Real Business Issues and Helps Cut Costs," Workforce Management, May 2007, www.workforce.com (accessed September 9, 2013); Duane D. Stanford, "Coca-Cola Woman Board Nominee Bucks Slowing Diversity Trend," *Bloomberg*, February 22, 2013, https://www.bloomberg.com/news/articles/2013-02-22/coca-cola-s-woman-director-nominee-bucks-slowing-diversity-trend (accessed January 6, 2018).

11. "Global Product Development Team," Amvac Chemical Corporation, http://www.amvac-chemical.com/AboutUs/ProductDevelopmentTeam/tabid/69/Default.aspx (accessed January 6, 2018).

12. Richard S. Wellins, William C. Byham, and Jeanne M. Wilson, *Empowered Teams: Creating Self-Directed Work Groups That Improve Quality, Productivity, and Participation* (San Francisco: Jossey-Bass Publishers, 1991).

13. Wellins, Byham, and Wilson.

14. Theresa Minton-Eversole, "Virtual Teams Used by Global Organizations, Survey Says," Society for Human Resource Management, July 19, 2012, https://www.shrm.org/resourcesandtools/hr-topics/organizational-and-employee-development/pages/virtualteamsusedmostbyglobalorganizations,surveysays.aspx (accessed January 14, 2018).

15. Lynda Gratton, "Working Together...When Apart," *The Wall Street Journal*, June 16, 2007, https://www.wsj.com/articles/SB118165895540732559 (accessed January 6, 2018).

16. Keith Ferrazzi, "Virtual Teams Can Outperform Traditional Teams," *Harvard Business Review*, March 20, 2012, http://blogs.hbr.org/2012/03/how-virtual-teams-can-outperfo/ (accessed January 6, 2018).

17. Michael Watkins, "Making Virtual Teams Work: Ten Basic Principles," *Harvard Business Review*, June 27, 2013, http://blogs.hbr.org/2013/06/making-virtual-teams-work-ten/ (accessed January 6, 2018).

18. Ibid.

19. Cisco, "Optimize Team Performance," http://www.cisco.com/en/US/solutions/ns1007/IndCS_Virtual_Teams.html (accessed January 6, 2018).

20. Michael Watkins, "Making Virtual Team Work."

21. Robert Albanese and David D. Van Fleet, "Rational Behavior in Groups: The Free-Rider Tendency," *Academy of Management Review* 10 (April 1985), 244–255.

22. Bruce W. Tuckman and Mary Ann C. Jenson, "Stages of Small Group Development Revisited," *Group and Organizational Studies* 2 (December 1977), 419–427.

23. Connie J. G. Gersick, "Time and Transition in Work Teams: Toward a New Model of Group Development," *Academy of Management Journal* 31 (March 1988), 9–41.

24. Gersick, "Time and Transition in Work Teams."

25. Daniel C. Feldman, "The Development and Enforcement of Group Norms," *Academy of Management Review* 9 (January 1984), 47–53.

26. Richard F. Allen and Saul Pilnick, "Confronting the Shadow Organization: How to Detect and Defeat Negative Norms," *Organizational Dynamics* 2 (Spring 1973), 13–17.

27. Edgar H. Schein, "Organizational Socialization and the Profession of Management, The Third Douglas Murray McGregor Lecture of the Alfred P. Sloan School of Management, Massachusetts Institute of Technology, reprinted in David A. Kolb, Irwin M. Rubin, and James M. McIntyre, *Organizational Psychology: Readings in Human Behavior in Organizations*, 4th ed. (Englewood Cliffs, NJ: Prentice-Hall, Inc., 1984).

28. Feldman, "The Development and Enforcement of Group Norms."

29. Kelly K. Sports, "Top Small Workplaces 2008," *The Wall Street Journal*, February 22, 2009, https://www.wsj.com/articles/SB122347733961315417 (accessed January 1, 2018); ATA Engineering, "ATA Engineering Named as One of San Diego's 100 Fastest Growing Companies," October 2, 2008, http://www.ata-e.com/news/ata-engineering-named-one-san-diegos-100-fastest-growing-companies/ (accessed January 1, 2018); "This Year's Most Innovative Employee-Owned Companies Awarded in Chicago Last Week," National Center for Employee Ownership and the Beyster Institute, http://www.ata-e.com/news/ata-wins-most-innovative-employee-owned-company-award/ (accessed January 1, 2018); Michelle Strulzenberger, "Employee Ownership Results in Better Workplace for ATA Engineering Inc.," Axiom News, January 16, 2009, http://axiomnews.ca/node/456 (accessed June 24, 2013); ATA Engineering, "Siemens PLM Software," http://www.ata-e.com/software/siemens-plm-software (accessed January 1, 2018); ATA Engineering, "ATA Engineering Recognized by *Wall Street Journal* as One of the Top Small Workplaces for 2008," October 13, 2008, http://www.ata-e.com/news/ata-engineering-recognized-wall-street-journal-one-top-small-workplaces-2008/ (accessed January 1, 2018); ATA Engineering website, http://www.ata-e.com/ (accessed January 1, 2018); ATA Engineering, "ATA Engineering Wins Top NASA Quality Award," June 26, 2013, http://www.ata-e.com/news/ata-engineering-wins-top-nasa-quality-award/ (accessed January 1, 2018).

30. Schein, "Organizational Socialization and the Profession of Management."

31. Daniel Katz and Robert L. Kahn, *The Social Psychology of Group Behavior* 2nd ed. (New York: John Wiley & Sons, 1978).

32. Adapted from Thomas A. Kayser, *Mining Group Gold* (El Segundo, CA: Serif Publishing, 1990).

33. Charles R. Evans and Kenneth L. Dion, "Group Cohesion and Performance: A Meta-Analysis," *Small Group Research* 22 (May 1991), 175–186.

34. Marvin Shaw, *Group Dynamics: The Psychology of Small Group Behavior* (New York: McGraw-Hill, Inc., 1971).

35. Kenneth Thomas, "Overview of Conflict and Conflict Management: Reflections and Update," *Journal of Organizational Behavior* (May 1992), 263–274.

36. Christian Plumb and Dan Wilchins, "Lehman CEO Fuld's hubris contributed to meltdown," *Reuters*, September 14, 2008, http://www.reuters.com/article/2008/09/14/us-lehman-backstory-idUSN1341059120080914 (accessed January 6, 2018).

37. "Distributive Negotiation," Program on Negotiation Harvard Law School, http://www.pon.harvard.edu/tag/distributive-negotiation/ (accessed October 10, 2013).

38. "Integrative Negotiation," Program on Negotiation Harvard Law School, http://www.pon.harvard.edu/tag/integrative-negotiation/ (accessed January 6, 2018).

39. Ethics Resource Center, *National Business Ethics Survey of the U.S. Workforce* (Arlington Virginia: Ethics Resource Center, 2014), p. 39.

40. Stephen R. Covey, *Principle Centered Leadership* (New York: Summit Books, 1991).

41. Derived from Covey; Marsha Sinetar, "Building Trust into Corporate Relationships," *Organizational Dynamics* 16 (Winter 1988), 73–79; Fernando Bartolome, "Nobody Trusts the Boss Completely—Now What?" *Harvard Business Review* 67 (March/April 1989), 137–139; and Dale E. Zand, "Trust and Managerial Problem Solving," *The Administrative Science Quarterly* 17 (June 1972), 229–239.

42. Kayser, *Mining Group Gold*, 17.

43. Gregory O. Shea and Richard A. Guzzo, "Group Effectiveness: What Really Matters?" *Sloan Management Review* 28 (Spring 1987), 25–31.

44. Ethics Resource Center, "2011 National Business Ethics Survey" (Arlington, VA: Ethics Resource Center, 2012), p. 39.

45. S. E. Asch, "Effects of Group Pressure upon the Modification and Distortion of Judgments," in *Groups, Leadership, and Men*, H. Guetzkow, ed. (Pittsburgh: Carnegie Press, 1951), 177–190.

46. Irving Janis, "Groupthink," *Psychology Today* 5 (November 1971), 43–46, 74–76.

47. Janis, "Groupthink."

48. Janis, "Groupthink."

49. Jerry B. Harvey, "The Abilene Paradox: The Management of Agreement," *Organizational Dynamics* 3 (Summer 1974), 63–80.

50. Victory Murray and Jeffrey Gandz, "Games Executives Play: Politics at Work," *Business Horizons* 23 (December 1980), 11–23.

51. K. Michele Kacmar, Martha C. Andrews, Kenneth J. Harris, and Bennett J. Tepper (June 16, 2012). "Ethical Leadership and Subordinate Outcomes: The Mediating Role of Organizational Politics and the Moderating Role of Political Skill." *Journal of Business Ethics* 115 (June 2013), http://www.springerlink.com/content/yu5570k436347857/ (accessed January 6, 2018).

52. This list and the subsequent one on techniques to reduce politics were compiled from Dan Farrell and James C. Petersen, "Patterns of Political Behavior in Organizations," *Academy of Management* 7 (July 1982), 403–412; Murray and Gandz, "Games Executives Play"; Don R. Beeman and Thomas W. Sharkey, "The Use and Abuse of Corporate Politics," *Business Horizons* 30 (March–April 1987), 76–130; Blake E. Ashforth and Raymond T. Lee, "Defensive Behavior in Organizations: A Preliminary Model," *Human Relations* 43 (July 1990), 621–648; and Jerry B. Harvey, "Some Thoughts About Organizational Backstabbing: or, 'How Come Every Time I Get Stabbed in the Back, My Fingerprints Are on the Knife?" *The Academy of Management Executive* 3 (November 1989), 271–277.

53. J. Pfeffer (1992). "Understanding power in organizations." *California Management Review* 34, 29–50.

54. K. Michele Kacmar, Martha C. Andrews, Kenneth J. Harris, and Bennett J. Tepper, "Ethical Leadership and Subordinate Outcomes: The Mediating Role of Organizational Politics and the Moderating Role of Political Skill," *Journal of Business Ethics* 115 (June 2013), http://www.springerlink.com/content/yu5570k436347857/ (accessed January 6, 2018).

55. Whole Foods, "Why We're a Great Place to Work," http://www.wholefoodsmarket.com/careers/why-were-great-place -work (accessed December 30, 2017); Whole Foods, "Whole Foods Market's Core Values," http://www.wholefoodsmarket .com/values/corevalues.php#supporting (accessed December 30, 2017); "100 Best Companies to Work For: Whole Foods Market," *CNN Money*, 2011, http://money.cnn.com/magazines/ fortune/bestcompanies/2011/snapshots/24.html (accessed December 30, 2017); "100 Best Companies to Work For: Whole Foods Market," *CNN Money*, 2013, http://money.cnn .com/magazines/fortune/best-companies/2013/snapshots/71 .html?iid=bc_fl_list (accessed September 9, 2013); Kerry A. Dolan, "America's Greenest Companies 2011," *Forbes*, April 18, 2011, www.forbes.com/2011/04/18/americas-greenest -companies.html (accessed December 30, 2017); Joseph Brownstein, "Is Whole Foods' Get Healthy Plan Fair?" *ABC News*, January 29, 2010, http://abcnews.go.com/Health/w_ DietAndFitnessNews/foods-incentives-make-employees -healthier/story?id=9680047 (accessed December 30, 2017); Deborah Dunham, "At Whole Foods Thinner Employees Get Fatter Discounts," That's Fit, January 27, 2010, http://www .thatsfit.com/2010/01/27/whole-foods-thin-employees-get -discounts/ (accessed September 9, 2013); David Burkus, "Why Whole Foods Builds Its Entire Business on Teams," *Forbes*, June 8, 2016, https://www.forbes.com/sites/david burkus/2016/06/08/why-whole-foods-build-their-entire -business-on-teams/#47872abc3fa1 (accessed December 30, 2017); Kate Taylor, "Here Are All the Changes Amazon Is Making to Whole Foods," *Business Insider*, November 15, 2017, http://www.businessinsider.com/amazon-changes-whole -foods-2017-9/#whole-foods-immediately-slashed-prices-and -announced-another-round-of-price-cuts-in-november-1 (accessed December 30, 2017).

Communicating in Organizations

Source: Rawpixel.com/Shutterstock

After reading this chapter, you will be able to:

- Define *communication* and explain its importance to managers.
- Describe the communication process and the factors that affect it.
- Compare and contrast the various communication forms and channels and the "richness" of each.
- Distinguish between formal and informal communication in an organization.
- Determine how groups and teams communicate.
- Describe common gender differences in communication style.
- Detect the barriers to effective communication and specify potential ways to overcome them.
- Critique an organization's communication efforts.

Keurig Green Mountain Brews More Effective Communication

Keurig Green Mountain, formerly Green Mountain Coffee Roasters Inc., based in Waterbury, Vermont, is a leader in the specialty coffee industry. The company sells coffee and beverage selections through a coordinated, multi-channel distribution network of wholesale and consumer-direct operations. It also sells Keurig single-pack coffee packets and Keurig brewers, which are single-cup brewing systems that have exploded in popularity.

Keurig Green Mountain is interesting in the way its 5,700 employees communicate within the organization. The company is decentralized and has a flat organizational structure with few layers of management. Although it has functional departments that vary across the company, there is an openness of communication that allows employees regular access to all levels of the organization. The company uses digital communication channels such as voicemail or email to inform groups of decisions and encourages employees to voice their opinions and ideas in response. Verbal communication is used at meetings, and employees are encouraged to share their views. Written forms of communication, such as agendas, outline the results of these meetings and serve to guide efficient and seamless decision making across the company. This communication across channels ensures that the collaborative nature of getting things done is spread equally throughout the company.

However, communication also involves listening, which is especially important in decentralized organizations. All members of the organization must be careful to choose the most appropriate form of communication and ensure they are listening to the responses. This can be done by not looking at one's computer or smartphone while others are talking. This will ensure channel richness, which is vital to the company's success.

Feedback is another important aspect of communication. As part of the Keurig Green Mountain evaluation and control system, a process called the after-action review—adapted from the U.S. Army—is utilized. The goal of the review is to answer four key questions: What did we set out to do? What happened? Why did it happen? What are we going to do about it? Most of the effort is spent on the last question to ensure that the company learns from its successes and failures. Employees are empowered to apply these lessons and encouraged to share their views in a "constellation of communication" that ensures a collaborative style of getting things done.

Corporate social responsibility is a major objective of Keurig Green Mountain. Keurig Green Mountain invests in sustainably grown coffee initiatives, and the company is developing K-cup pods that are increasingly recyclable. This is particularly important, as one major criticism of Keurig Green Mountain is the large amounts of waste its pods can create over time.

Green Mountain Coffee Roasters improves organizational communication.

Keurig Green Mountain announced the pods would be 100 percent recyclable by 2020. To ensure employees are on board with these initiatives, Keurig Green Mountain must communicate this objective effectively.

The company also developed a program called Community Action for Employees that provides full-time employees with up to 52 paid hours to volunteer in their communities. Employees are also encouraged to donate their volunteer time in areas where they have specific skills. For instance, some of Keurig Green Mountain's information technology employees volunteer with the organization Technology for Tomorrow, which teaches senior citizens how to use technological tools like the Internet and smartphones.

Decentralized forms of communication tend to work better in smaller organizations. Therefore, as Keurig Green Mountain expands, it must carefully manage the richness of communication channels to ensure that employees will continue to be heard and that managers are aware of activities within the company. For example, Keurig Green Mountain has faced accusations of becoming less transparent regarding some accounting practices. This is a result of a failure in decentralized communication. In order to address this problem, the company must strengthen communication systems among all departments.

In 2016, JAB Holding Company purchased Keurig Green Mountain for $13.9 billion. The company was also taken private. A privately held company with fewer owners might make it easier for management to strengthen communication channels both internally and externally. Communication that keeps employees informed has been crucial to Keurig Green Mountain's past success. The company must continue to display effective communication skills, including listening and asking for feedback, to ensure a collaborative corporate culture focused on developing specialty coffees sustainably and responsibly.[1]

Introduction

Communication is of vital importance. If we were unable to indicate that we were hungry or in serious danger, for instance, our survival could be at stake. The role of communication is also critical for an organization and its managers. Most managerial activities—email, social networking via services like Twitter or Facebook, meetings, phone calls, and talking with employees and customers—involve communication skills. Thus, management and communication go hand in hand.

For managers to become effective communicators, they must first understand what communication is. They must also recognize that communication is subject to misunderstandings and distortion. Thus, in this chapter, we will explore the concept of communication by discussing the communication process, identifying the various types and forms of communication, and exploring some common barriers to effective communication—as well as possible ways to overcome them.

What Is Communication?

Some may think of communication as one person telling another person something, either orally in person or over the phone, or in writing, email, or text message. However, it entails much more. **Communication** is the process through which information and meaning are transferred from one person to another. The information and meaning can be transferred in various forms (such as written or oral), and the methods used to transfer the information and meaning can vary (for example, face to face, telephone, memo, or report). A combination of methods may even be used to help ensure that a message is received properly. Your supervisor, for example, may choose to have a face-to-face meeting concerning your promotion and then follow up with a written memo that reiterates the main points of the meeting.

communication: The process through which information and meaning are transferred from one person to another.

In general, people communicate because they want to achieve a goal, satisfy a personal need, or improve their immediate position.[2] It is very important to note that real communication has not occurred until the person for whom a message is intended has both received and understood the information sent. In other words, it is not enough simply to send a message. Let's say, for example, that your professor displays the answer to a complex accounting problem in a PowerPoint, but offers neither a verbal explanation for how he arrived at the answer nor the opportunity for questions. In this instance, the professor has sent a message (via the PowerPoint presentation); however, the chances are very good that many students do not fully understand what the message means. Thus, communication has not taken place. Therefore, communication is a process of "sharing," rather than simply sending, information. In the business world, this sharing of information allows companies to accomplish diverse goals. An effective manager fosters the interactive sharing of ideas to create mutual understanding. Communication is made more complex and difficult in a global, multicultural business environment.

The Importance of Communication in the Business World

Communication is of vital importance to managers because it allows them to engage in the planning, organizing, leading, and controlling functions. Managers must be able to communicate their visions, goals, and directions to others. These others must be able to communicate back to managers to let them know whether goals and objectives are being achieved. For instance, a goal in connection with covering this chapter is to enrich your understanding of communication. However, the professor who does not allow questions to be asked or does not ask questions of you

Organizational communication faces challenges in the global, multicultural environment.

Source: Sergey Nivens/Shutterstock

cannot be sure that this goal has been attained. Research shows that both organizational and individual performance improves when managerial communication is effective.[3] Indeed, communication competency is a fundamental aspect of job performance and managerial effectiveness.[4] Most human resource executives who have managed to climb the corporate ladder to top management positions attribute a great majority of their success to "good communication skills." Today, many have a tendency to overly rely on electronic communication forms like email, websites, and text messages, which can challenge "good communication skills."[5]

The Communication Process

We can think of communication as a process consisting of a chain of identifiable links, with the ultimate objective being to influence behaviors, attitudes, and beliefs. And, like a chain, it is only as strong as its weakest link. A baseball team, for example, can consist of many strong hitters, but if there are no good pitchers, the team is not likely to win many games. Each position on a baseball team is critical, just as is each element of the communication process, which consists of definite and identifiable components: the sender, encoding, channel, the receiver, decoding, and feedback (Figure 14.1).

The **sender**, the person who wishes to relay or share particular information and meaning, initiates the communication process. For example, let's say your friend misses a day at work. It was announced that day that an important project would be due sooner than expected.

To communicate that important information to your friend, you assume the role of sender and initiate the communication process. First, you perform the process of **encoding**, or transforming your information into understandable symbols, typically spoken or written words or gestures. Next, you choose an appropriate **channel**—the medium or method used to transmit the intended information and meaning (such as leaving an email or telling her face to face). The **receiver**, the person to whom the information and meaning are sent—in this case, your friend—then attempts to "decode" the sender's message. **Decoding** is the process of interpreting and attaching personal meaning to the message. In other words, during the decoding process the receiver attempts to understand what the encoded symbols mean, whether they are type in an email or words coming out of your mouth.

sender: The person who wishes to relay or share particular information and meaning, and initiates the communication process.

encoding: The process of transforming information into understandable symbols, typically spoken or written words or gestures.

channel: The medium or method used to transmit the intended information and meaning (such as leaving an email or telling a person face to face).

receiver: The person to whom the information and meaning are sent.

decoding: The process of interpreting and attaching personal meaning to the message.

FIGURE 14.1

The Communication Process

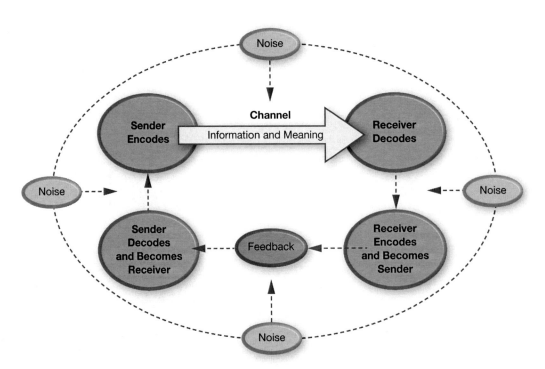

Feedback, the receiver's response to the sender's communication, is another important component of the communication process. For example, if you choose to communicate to your friend about the project by sending her an email, she may later provide feedback in the form of a reply message or a verbal "thank you" for the information. Feedback can be thought of as sort of a return message that lets the sender know the message has indeed been received, as when a colleague requests an RSVP for a business luncheon.

feedback: The receiver's response to the sender's communication.

The processes of encoding and decoding are potential sources for communication errors. As symbols are being translated into meanings, knowledge, attitudes, and other factors can act as information filters and create noise. **Noise** is anything that interferes with the message being communicated effectively and can be of various types. Differences in educational level, experience, and culture can impede the communication process. For example, much of the difficulty encountered when U.S. managers try to implement traditional American management styles (autocratic leadership) in foreign countries is due to cultural differences. Physical noise (such as loud equipment or loud talking) can also inhibit effective communication, as does being preoccupied with another thought (as with a supervisor who is too rushed to meet a deadline). We will look at ways of overcoming noise later.

noise: Anything acting as an information filter, such as knowledge, attitudes, and other factors, that interferes with the message being communicated effectively.

Effective communication, therefore, can be defined as the process of sending a message in such a way that the message received is as close in meaning as possible to the message intended. The process is cyclical in nature. Once a message is decoded into meaning by the receiver, some sort of response is often desired. Then, a new message is sent by the receiver (now the sender) to the original sender (now the receiver) and the process starts over again. Restated then, effective communication requires (1) the message to be encoded into symbols that will accurately convey it to the receiver (a good rule of thumb is to keep symbols simple and relevant), (2) the message to be conveyed in a well-organized manner, and (3) distractions to be eliminated.[6] For example, when a supervisor discusses a performance evaluation with an employee, the supervisor should do so in a quiet, private place with no disruptions, and should strive to use both language the employee can understand and explain the evaluation clearly.

Many factors affect the communication process, including the form and channel of communication chosen, perception, and the state of communication within organizations. We will explore these topics in the next few sections.

Forms of Communication

Essentially, you can think of the way in which a message is communicated as being two-dimensional. One dimension has to do with the form of communication you choose—verbal, written, or nonverbal. The second dimension has to do with the medium or channel of communication employed. Within each form, there are several channels of communication from which to choose. For instance, verbal communication may take place face to face, over the telephone, or over a two-way radio. When choosing the form and channel of communication, it is important to keep in mind the ultimate objective of the communication. If your goal is to reduce the uncertainty of a particular situation, for example, then you should choose a communication form and channel that permit and encourage information exchange, such as face-to-face verbal communication.[7] In this section, we will first take a closer look at the different forms of communication and then move to a more detailed discussion of the various channels of communication. Table 14.1 summarizes these different channels of communication.

The type of communication should have an impact on where and how the communication occurs.

TABLE 14.1 Channels of Communication

Verbal	Words spoken to convey information and meaning
Written	When information and meaning is transferred through recorded words
Digital	When meanings and symbols are transmitted through digital devices
Nonverbal	Information conveyed by actions and behaviors rather than by spoken or written words
Listening	Accurately receiving and understanding information

Verbal Communication

verbal or oral communication: Words spoken through various channels to convey information and meaning.

We can think of **verbal or oral communication** as words spoken to convey information and meaning. Verbal communication can take place through various channels (such as face to face, over the telephone, or Internet connection) and can take place on different levels (individually or in a group). Verbal communication is a significant part of a manager's job. For example, most managers hold meetings, talk on the telephone, and give speeches. Thanks to videoconferencing and other forms of technology, face-to-face communication is also possible for people separated by long distances.

Verbal communication offers both benefits and drawbacks. Among its greatest benefits are that it encourages immediate feedback—through questions or verbal confirmation—and allows the integration of nonverbal communication, such as head nodding and voice tone. In addition, verbal communication tends to be easier to use than other forms of communication. It does not require the complex skills that are needed in writing a report or typing a memo on a computer. Among the drawbacks of verbal communication are that incorrectly chosen words invite inaccuracies. Telling an employee that he or she is making good progress but still needs to improve could mean different things to sender and receiver. Leaving out important information (the sender) or forgetting or "selecting out" part of the message (the receiver) are other disadvantages. Noise is another, more prevalent problem in oral communication. Additionally, oral communication does not accommodate the need for formal documentation or written records, which might be needed in a court dispute covering an employee's termination, for instance.

Written Communication

written communication: Information and meaning transferred as recorded words, such as memos, reports, and email.

Written communication, or information and meaning transferred as recorded words—such as memos, reports, and email—tends to be more accurate than verbal communication, as senders take more time to collect, organize, and send the information. Written communication also has the benefit of providing a permanent record of communication, an important consideration in the business world. For example, when an employee needs to be informed of a new policy, it is often done in a written form. Most large organizations have written codes of conduct that communicate to employees about the organization's ethical expectations. However, written communication also has its serious drawbacks. It tends to inhibit immediate feedback and exchange and is more difficult, complex, and time consuming than is oral communication, in most cases.

One exception to this is email. Many businesspeople today are opting to send emails rather than letters or memos as it is quicker and more convenient to use. With the click of a button, your message is sent. Almost instantaneously, the recipient receives the message. Email is highly effective and easy to use. The problem is that email has become such an informal and easy-to-use form of communication (think of the various emails you send your friends) that many people send emails without proofreading them thoroughly. This can be a problem. It doesn't look very professional to your boss, for example, if the email you sent him is filled with typos and emoticons. Additionally, because email is so easy to use, some people send messages without thinking through what they are saying. For instance, say you are angry with your boss. While still angry, you rattle off an email and push the send button. Only afterward do you realize that your email, written in anger, is highly offensive and will likely make things worse. This may not have happened if you had written an actual letter, as the effort required may have given you time to sort through your emotions and calm down. These are just a few examples of the dangers of email. A businessperson should therefore treat professional emails as any other form of formal written communication in the workplace.

Email presents unique challenges in its immediacy and ability to be shared with others, suggesting caution and care in its use.

Digital Communication

We feel that digital communication is so important that it merits a section of its own. Digital communication is when meanings and symbols are transmitted through digital devices, including the Internet, electronic billboards, and mobile devices. Digital communication can consist of both written and verbal communication. As we have already mentioned, email is a common form of written communication in today's workplace. Other forms include reviews, blogs, and social media postings. Videoconferencing, podcasts, and online video make it possible for verbal communication to take place over the Internet as well. It is important for managers to understand the significance of digital communication. Younger employees are likely to be well-versed in digital technologies and may be more comfortable using these technologies than more traditional forms such as memos or talking on the phone.

Digital media can also help employees communicate internally. Intranets increase communication among different departments and management levels. The internal social network Yammer is helpful for employees who need to collaborate from different areas of the company. Cloud computing allows employees to access resources and information over a network rather than having to use physical resources. Salesforce.com offers cloud computing resources to help companies improve their communications and information management. Additionally, companies are now using social networks to communicate with consumers. Customer service employees might use Facebook or Twitter to address customer concerns quickly. Some organizations such as Southwest Airlines constantly monitor their Twitter feeds to detect and answer customer concerns.

Despite the benefits of digital communication to the workplace, it is necessary for managers to ensure that it is not being abused. With the digital world literally at employees' fingertips, it can be tempting for employees to use digital communication such as Facebook for purposes that are not beneficial to the organization. In one survey, 64 percent of respondents stated that they use websites during work hours for non-work purposes.[8] Some companies have tried to prevent this misuse by banning certain websites and social networks. However, bans could limit productivity and make employees feel as if the company does not trust them. As a result, many organizations have adopted policies which specify how much time can be spent on digital sites for non-work purposes.

Nonverbal Communication

In general, **nonverbal communication** refers to information conveyed by actions and behaviors rather than by spoken or written words. Nonverbal communication plays a critical role in shared understanding and meaning because it influences messages sent and received. In fact, most shared understanding comes from nonverbal messages, such as facial expressions, voice, hand gestures, and even clothing worn. If verbal and nonverbal communication contradict one another, the receiver is likely to become confused and give more weight to the nonverbal communication. Nonverbal communication also conveys the emotional state of the sender, which can often be the most important part of the

nonverbal communication: Information conveyed by actions and behaviors rather than by spoken or written words.

There are some highly effective nonverbal communications that can support verbal or written communication.

Source: JooFotia/Shutterstock

message. If your boss claims not to be angry, but is turning red, has clenched fists, and is standing tense and stiff as a board, you may want to walk softly, because the nonverbal cues are expressing extreme anger.

Much nonverbal communication is unconscious or subconscious. In fact, quite a bit of information sharing can take place without a word ever being spoken. Assume, for example, that you are in a weekly meeting at your job. However, you cannot hear very well because there is a group of employees just behind you talking about their after-work plans (noise). The boss notices the distraction and throws a nasty glare at the talking employees, who immediately stop. A message was sent (stop talking) and received (the employees stopped) without a word being spoken. Far too often we think that effective communication requires the written or spoken word, but in reality, neither is required.

Research suggests that managers typically send two types of nonverbal communication.[9] One type of nonverbal communication is sent by the setting or the physical properties of the context in which the message is sent. These properties include such things as boundaries, how familiar the area is to the sender and receiver, or whether or not it is "home turf." For example, many executives place visitors in front of their desks while they sit behind them. The desk serves as a boundary beyond which the guests are not to go. The second and most popular form of nonverbal communication is **body language**, the broad range of body motions and behaviors—from facial expressions to the distance one person stands from another—that send messages to a receiver. For instance, hourly employees may stand farther away from their company president in an elevator than from each other, indicating that the employees feel more comfortable with one another than with the company president. The distance maintained can also be a reflection of the power or status of the boss relative to others.

body language: The broad range of body motions and behaviors, from facial expressions to the distance one person stands from another, that send messages to a receiver.

There are a number of different forms that communication using body language can take. One is kinesic communication, which is communication through the movements of head, eyes, arms, hands, legs, or torso. Winking, head nodding, hand gestures, and arm motions are forms of kinesic communication. Proxemic communication is a less obvious means of communicating messages through the relative body position and distance between those having a discussion. It involves varying the physical distance separating a salesperson and customer, for example. Touching, or tactile communication, is another form, although it is less popular in the United States than in other countries. Handshaking is a common form of tactile communication around the world. Table 14.2 demonstrates these different forms of body language.

TABLE 14.2 Different Forms of Body Language

Type of Communication	Example
Kinesic communication	Waving side-to-side is a common way of saying hello and goodbye in the United States and Europe.
Proxemic communication	Direct face-to-face communication can be confrontational or intimate, and so many conversations are held with people sitting or standing at an angle to one another.
Tactile communication	Handshaking is a common form of tactile communication around the world.

One of the hardest skills to master is the ability to effectively listen to colleagues.

Because nonverbal communication has such a dramatic influence, managers should pay close attention to their nonverbal actions and behaviors when communicating. In particular, they should ensure that their nonverbal messages agree with their verbal or written messages. Managers should also pay attention to the nonverbal messages sent by others; research suggests that the more effective managers tend to be those who are sensitive to nonverbal cues.[10]

Listening

Listening is a valuable, and often underestimated, component of communication. **Listening** involves accurately receiving and understanding information. Without listening a conversation between two or more people will be one-sided and ineffective. For managers, listening to employees is important in understanding employee concerns and gathering their input. Listening also impacts employee morale; employees list a failure to have their concerns taken seriously as being among their top complaints in the workplace.[11] Listening is crucial for a manager to be able to make important decisions.[12] Managers often receive critical information from other people in the workplace, including co-workers, superiors, and subordinates. Failing to listen therefore limits the manager's ability for effective decision making.

Conversely, managers who make it a priority to listen establish credibility and trustworthiness among themselves and employees of the organization.[13] Employees can be assured that managers will listen and carefully consider their input.[14] This helps the manager identify areas of strengths and weaknesses in the organization. Showing respect to employees through listening encourages them to reciprocate. The better a manager is at listening, the more employees will feel encouraged to communicate with them and with others.

listening: Accurately receiving and understanding information.

Communication Channels

As stated earlier, choosing the appropriate channel (face to face, the telephone, written reports, etc.) is an important consideration when communicating information. One critical aspect of choosing an effective channel is **channel richness**, a channel's ability to transmit information. Channels differ in their ability to handle multiple cues simultaneously, to encourage immediate feedback, and to focus personally on the receiver. We can view communication channels as falling along a continuum of richness (Figure 14.2), with face-to-face communication as the richest medium and impersonal written communications (like reports) as the least rich.[15]

channel richness: A channel's ability to transmit information, including the ability to handle multiple cues simultaneously, encourage feedback, and focus personally on the receiver.

FIGURE 14.2
A Continuum
of Channel Richness

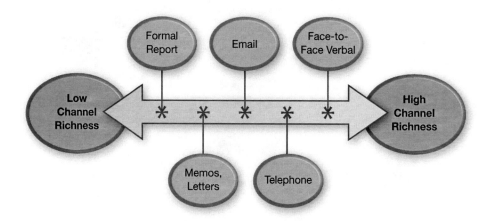

The face-to-face channel is the richest medium because it can handle many cues simultaneously (for example, the spoken word, facial expression, and voice tone), prompt immediate feedback, and create and maintain personal focus on the communication. For instance, a one-on-one conversation between you and your supervisor concerning your work performance allows you to ask specific questions and allows the supervisor to better determine what are your particular strengths and weaknesses. At OpenAir.com, all staff members meet daily at 9:30 A.M. to share information and anecdotes about customer calls from the previous day. No chairs are allowed, and everyone is encouraged to participate.

The telephone or Internet media are not quite as rich as face-to-face communication because they do not permit the communicators to see each other's body language. Communicating over the telephone tends to prompt greater immediate feedback than written channels, but not as much as face-to-face communication. Like face-to-face communication, the telephone or Internet are personally focused channels. Although written channels can be personally focused as well, they can handle only one cue (e.g., no body language, no voice tone). Because written channels can convey only the message on paper or computer terminals, they are slow to prompt feedback. For instance, it is easy to allow a memo that requires a response to be buried underneath a stack of other papers, all the while thinking, "I'll respond to that later." It is even easier for an email to get buried in your mailbox when you receive dozens every day!

The message and the particular situation, not the sender's whim or preference, should guide the selection of a particular channel. Like decisions, communication can be classified as routine or non-routine. Routine communication tends to be simpler, more straightforward, already agreed upon, and well understood. Therefore, routine messages can be effectively communicated through less rich channels, such as written memos. Non-routine communication is characterized by ambiguity, time pressure, and surprise. Because non-routine communication has a high potential for misunderstanding, it should be communicated through richer channels that can handle more cues simultaneously and encourage immediate feedback. For example, a contract negotiation between a company and its union representatives is an example of a non-routine communication. There are many subtle issues that make such communication ambiguous, so they should be done face to face. On the other hand, the daily production numbers in a plant are often simply posted on a chart on the bulletin board or sent to various managers' offices on computer printouts.

Perception and Distortion

perception: The process through which we receive, filter, organize, interpret, and attach meaning to information taken in from the environment.

Perception, the process through which we receive, filter, organize, interpret, and attach meaning to information taken in from the environment, is an important behavioral component of the overall communication process. Physical systems (for example, our eyes and ears) take in and filter information, while our mental processes further filter, organize, interpret, and attach meaning to that information. Information inputs are not only verbal, but include sensations received through sight, taste, hearing, smell, and touch. When we hear a manager speak or touch a product, we receive information inputs. Increasingly, businesses are employing scent to help attract customers who may be in the information-search stage of the buying decision process. Some Westin hotels use a fragrance that blends green tea, geranium, green ivy, black cedar, and freesia to evoke a sense of tranquility in their lobbies, whereas Sony uses an orange-vanilla-cedar scent in some Sony Style stores to make female shoppers feel more comfortable. **Distortion** occurs when there is a deviation between the sent message and the received message. In major distortions, the received message may bear little resemblance to the actual message. Because the perception process involves so many manipulations of incoming information, it is common for distortions to result from our perceptions. Even art or other objects in a manager's office could distort the received message.

distortion: A deviation between the sent message and the received message.

Filtering or screening, often referred to as **perceptual selection**, involves choosing stimuli from the environment for further processing. Perceptual selection has to do with a person's willingness or unwillingness to receive information. It may occur for three basic reasons: (1) The receiver is uncomfortable with the information; (2) he or she does not want to bother with the information; or (3) there is simply too much information to process fully, a condition called "information overload." Unfortunately, managers often ignore certain information (for example, a downturn in sales figures) because they do not want to hear it or they "hope" things will change. Also, managers may engage in perceptual selection because they discern a threat. Managers who sense a threat may display "defensive behavior," which inhibits the communication process because it requires that they defend themselves rather than concentrate on the communication at hand. Consider, for example, the manager who just learned that he received a very poor evaluation from his employees and in ten minutes is having a conference with one of those employees concerning her performance evaluation. Often in this undesirable situation, the offensive sender has sent multiple cues and the defensive listener distorts what he has received.[16]

perceptual selection: The choosing of stimuli from the environment for further processing; also known as filtering or screening.

The process of organizing, interpreting, and attaching value to the selected stimuli is called **perceptual organization**. This is a natural and essential process that handles the information we take in more efficiently and effectively. By organizing diverse information into fewer conceptual categories, we can better understand and capitalize on the information. Sometimes, though, such categorizing can have negative effects. One all-too-familiar form of perceptual organization is **stereotyping**, which occurs when we categorize people into certain groups based on an attribute such as race, sex, or education level and then make generalizations about them according to their group membership. For example, many people assume that men are better at performing mathematical exercises than women. A manager might therefore view men as being better at number-oriented tasks than women in the organization, when in fact a woman may be better. Men also tend to be more open and confident about their achievements than women, which could cause managers to view a male employee who frequently mentions his accomplishments as a higher performer than a female employee who prefers to let her work speak for itself. We discuss gender communication differences later in this chapter. For these reasons, managers must be particularly sensitive to perceptual organization, as it can inhibit open and honest communication because of the distortions it might cause at any point in the communication process.

perceptual organization: The natural and essential process of organizing, interpreting, and attaching value to the selected stimuli.

stereotyping: A type of perceptual organization in which we categorize people into groups based on certain characteristics such as race, sex, or education level, and then make generalizations about them according to their group.

Managers have an enormous amount of information to deal with, especially with management and computer information systems. To be more effective, managers and decision makers need to understand how people select and organize this information.

Communicating in Organizations

Communication within an organization can flow in a variety of directions and from a number of sources, each using both oral and written forms. In addition, organizational communication comes in many forms, such as plans, performance appraisals, future projections, open-door policies, reports, meetings, and compensation packages.[17] Traditionally, formal communication patterns in an organization were classified as vertical and horizontal. With the increased use of matrix structures and various types of teams, formal communication may occur in a number of patterns. There are also informal communication patterns used by managers as well as employees.

At Matsuhita, for example, executives are required to file reports to the president by email and are provided the technology needed in order to do so. Companies use intranets or internal computer networks to share information and to increase collaboration. Intranets help employees quickly find or view information, subject to security provisions. Capital One, IBM, and Staples have been recognized as having some of the best intranets in corporate America. At many companies, however, such communications technology has contributed to information overload for some employees, who spend more time than ever managing online content, email, and other electronic communications. As mentioned earlier, email and Internet abuse, wherein employees use work computers for purposes other than work, is becoming more problematic.

Formal Communication

Formal channels of communication are intentionally defined and designed by the organization. They represent the flow of communication within the formal organizational structure. Typically, communication flows in three separate directions: upward, downward, and horizontally, though diagonal communication has become common more recently (Figure 14.3).

Upward Communication

upward communication: Communication flowing from lower to higher levels of the organization, such as progress reports, suggestions, inquiries, and grievances.

As indicated, **upward communication** flows from lower to higher levels of the organization. Examples of upward communication include progress reports, suggestions for improvement, inquiries, and grievances. Researchers have found that upward communication is more often subject to distortion than downward communication. For example, workers are more likely to distort or even withhold information that may make them look bad. This tendency increases as the receiver's status increases or distrust in the receiver increases.[18] According to the Ethics Resource Center, around 37 percent of people who observe misconduct do not report it.[19] Many employees do not report observed misconduct or violations of organizational policy because they fear retaliation or becoming involved.

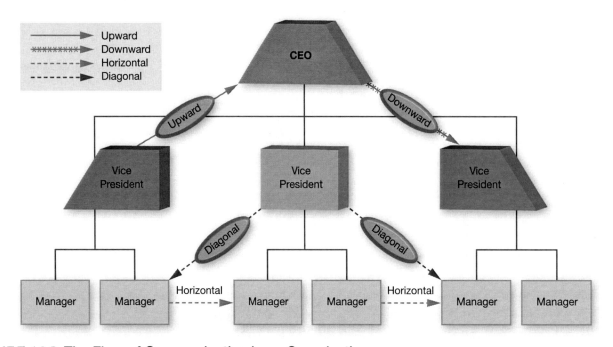

FIGURE 14.3 The Flow of Communication in an Organization

Downward Communication

Downward communication refers to the traditional flow of information from upper organizational levels to lower levels. Typically, this type of communication involves job directions, assignment of tasks and responsibilities, performance feedback, and certain information concerning the organization's strategies and goals. Speeches, policy and procedure manuals, employee handbooks, codes of conduct, websites, and job descriptions are all examples of downward communication.

The main problem with downward communication is that, as information gets passed from one level to the next, message content may be distorted or lost, usually more through natural filtering than through the intentional distortion that characterizes some upward communication. A major problem with managers and downward communication is their assumption that employees don't need or want to know much about what is going on. For instance, many times after an acquisition has taken place, management tends to neglect explaining to employees what they can expect next. For example, when Southwest Airlines merged with Air Tran, many Air Tran employees wanted rapid communications about their employment status.

Horizontal Communication

Horizontal communication involves the exchange of information among individuals on the same organizational level, such as across or within departments. Thus, it generally involves colleagues and peers. Horizontal information informs, supports, and coordinates activities both intra-departmentally and interdepartmentally. At times, the organization will formally require horizontal communication among particular organizational members, as is the case with task forces or project teams. In general, horizontal communication should be increased when tasks are non-routine and high in uncertainty. However, when tasks are more routine in nature, communication is typically more formal and follows the chain of command.

Diagonal Communication

Some organizational structures, particularly matrix structures, employ teams comprised of members from different functional areas, even different levels of the hierarchy. When these individuals from different units and organizational levels communicate, it is **diagonal communication**. With more and more firms reducing the number of management layers and increasing the use of self-managed work teams, many workers are being required to communicate with others in different departments and on different levels to solve problems and coordinate work. At 3M, for instance, a team might be formed of workers from all functional areas (accounting, marketing, operations, and human resources) to work on a specific product project to ensure that all points of view are considered. Diagonal communication will likely continue to increase in importance.

Informal Communication Channels

Informal communication channels are not deliberately designed and, therefore, do not abide by the formal organizational hierarchy or chain of command. This does not mean that informal communication channels are unimportant. Some of the most significant information might be gleaned in casual elevator or cafeteria conversations. In this section, we will look at two types of informal communication channels: the grapevine and the process of "management by walking around." Technology and social media have facilitated more casual forms of informal communication.

The Grapevine

Informal communication channels are typically referred to as the **grapevine**, which exists in virtually all organizations. Research has identified two common types of grapevines. In a **gossip chain**, one person spreads information to many other people. A **cluster chain** involves one person or a selected few people exchanging information with only a few others.

downward communication: The traditional flow of information from upper organizational levels to lower levels, such as job directions, assignment of tasks, performance feedback, and information concerning the organization's goals.

horizontal communication: The exchange of information among individuals on the same organizational level, either across or within departments.

diagonal communication: The flow of information, often in matrix structures, between individuals from different units and organizational levels.

grapevine: Informal communication channels, found in virtually all organizations.

gossip chain: The spreading of information by one person to many others.

cluster chain: An exchange in which one person or a selected few share information with only a few others.

Technology and texting have created some very informal communication that filters into the workplace.

In other words, the information and its exchange "clusters" around a selected few, rather than many individuals.[20]

In the past, the accuracy of grapevine information was of great concern, particularly to managers. Today, many managers view the quality of communication through formal organizational channels as being poor. Thus, the grapevine can serve dual purposes for a manager: (1) the manager can receive accurate information from grapevine sources, and (2) the manager can use the grapevine to communicate information to organizational members.

Attempts to eliminate an organization's grapevine are useless. In fact, informal communication is increasing.[21] A more practical way to deal with an organization's grapevine is to accept it and control it where and when possible. For example, maintaining open communication channels throughout the organization can help determine what is being said on the grapevine, as well as the information's accuracy. Managers can also use the grapevine to their advantage—as a "sounding device" for possible new policies, for example. People love to gossip, and managers need to be aware that grapevines are present in every organization. Managers who understand how grapevines function can use them to their advantage by disseminating information to squelch rumors and dispel incorrect information. Managers can also use the grapevine to obtain valuable information that could improve decision making.

Management by Walking Around

Another form of informal communication that has evolved is "management by walking around" (MBWA), in which managers informally interact and exchange information with employees by simply circulating around the office or plant on a regular basis.[22] MBWA involves managers (at all levels) developing positive relationships with employees and talking with them directly to find out about their particular jobs, departments, or divisions. MBWA also allows managers to utilize the richest communication channel (face-to-face verbal communication), while breaking down some of the common barriers to communication, such as distance and formality.

Communication in Groups and Teams

People tend to communicate differently in group or team situations than they do individually.[23] With the current trend of using groups to aid in decision making and a greater focus on team management, today's managers must know and understand these special communication patterns and behaviors.

Three basic communication patterns within groups have been observed (Figure 14.4). The wheel pattern is highly centralized, with all communication in the group flowing through one person. In other words, one person distributes necessary information to group members and, in turn, all group members must communicate through this one person to make decisions or solve problems. The Y pattern is a little less centralized in that two persons tend to be the focal points of communication processes. The most decentralized pattern is the network pattern, in which communication flows freely among all group members and all group members participate equally.

The nature and degree of task complexity play an important role in determining which communication pattern is more effective. The centralized pattern seems to be more effective when group tasks are simple, routine, and require very little interdependency, as is the case with a traditional assembly line. On the other hand, tasks that are highly interdependent, non-routine, and complex—such as when a management team analyzes potential

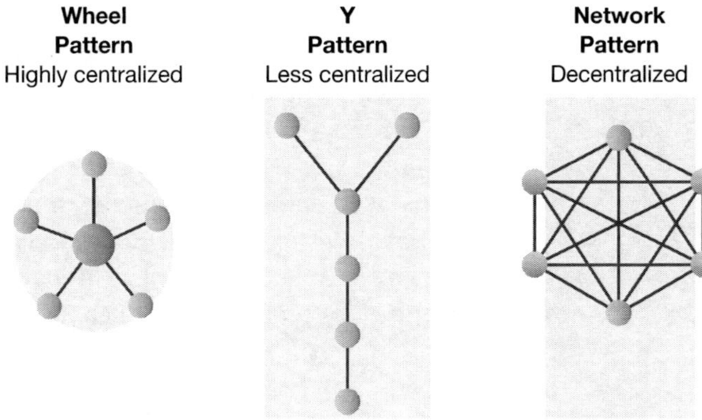

FIGURE 14.4
Group Communication
Patterns

Wheel Pattern
Highly centralized

Y Pattern
Less centralized

Network Pattern
Decentralized

companies for acquisition—tend to require a more decentralized group communication pattern.[24]

Each pattern of group communication has unique benefits and drawbacks. A centralized pattern, due to the dominance of one person, tends to discourage members from contributing input and discourages openness and honesty. By the same token, a decentralized pattern may create confusion and ill will and be too time consuming because everyone participates equally. Of course, seldom in the real world do all individuals contribute equally, even in a fully decentralized work team.

Managers should be alert to the concerns of group communication and attempt to structure the communication pattern appropriately. Technology can help address some of these concerns. For instance, group decision support systems combine communication and online support to facilitate group decision making. Such systems can help manipulate communication patterns among group members so that information flows more effectively. Research shows that management information systems are improving communication flow and efficiency.[25] Thanks to technology such as social media, companies have the ability to communicate with stakeholders like never before. For instance, direct sellers have often used Facebook and Twitter to update their followers on company news or products and answer questions in realtime.

Gender Differences in Communication

Managers should recognize that employees of an organization have different ways they communicate. Some differences result from personality. Extroverts, for example, will likely communicate differently than introverts. Other communication differences occur when employees come from different cultures. In Thailand and Japan, for instance, people try to avoid telling someone "no" directly, using words such as "we'll see" or "ask me later." In some cultures it may be customary to avoid eye contact with a superior. While the person might be trying to convey respect, in the United States a manager might perceive a lack of eye contact as a sign that the person is not listening. Gender differences, however, tend to receive more attention, particularly as more women move into executive positions and the nature of management continues to evolve.

Gender studies on communication have often been conducted to determine whether differences in communication might somehow contribute to wage or promotion disparities. Indeed, studies have revealed that women appear to have a harder time negotiating and are more likely to avoid competition. Male employees, on the other hand, have been characterized as overconfident, direct, and competitive.[26] While female employees might rely upon their hard work and dedication to earn them recognition, male employees are more likely to ask for what they want. These characteristics might give male employees a competitive edge when it comes time for promotion. Women also tend to be more relationship-oriented and tend to be uncomfortable with the appearance of superiority, while men are more comfortable appearing superior and in making decisions without consulting others.[27]

Gender differences are more discussed as women, increasingly, move into executive leadership positions.

Does this mean female employees are at a disadvantage when it comes to management positions? As the concept of what makes a good manager evolves, many characteristics generally thought feminine are growing in importance. For instance, studies have shown that female employees tend to be stronger in empathy, influence, self-awareness, and conflict management—all important skills for managing employees.[28] Women leaders are often more likely to encourage participation from others, and participatory management has been found to increase morale and innovation.[29] It is not our intention to argue for more masculine or feminine characteristics among managers. Indeed, many of the characteristics common to both male and female managers are effective in managing others, such as assertiveness, empathy, teamwork, and ambition. Probably the best managers are the ones that can adapt their communication styles according to the situation.

Barriers to Effective Communication

To be effective, managers need not only to understand the communication process, but also to understand and strive to overcome the barriers to effective communication. Communication barriers occur at three levels: personal, organizational, and environmental.

Personal Barriers

Personal communication barriers are often the result of differing individual characteristics, semantics, channel selection, consistency of signals, credibility problems, and incrimination. Individual characteristics have to do with personality, background, basic beliefs and attitudes, and even mood. For instance, extroverts are likely to communicate differently than introverts. People from one country may have trouble understanding someone from another country. These differences can sometimes hinder effective communication.

Individual Characteristics

Individual characteristics that affect communication have to do with personality, background, basic beliefs and attitudes, and even mood. These elements not only affect how a person chooses to communicate, but may cause a person to misunderstand, distort, or even block out a message. For instance, if your professor is in a really bad mood when you ask for an extension on a project deadline, she may ignore your request or blast you for procrastinating, rather than waiting for you to explain that someone has stolen your car, which contained your paper.

Several dimensions of personality may affect communication. For example, if you are an extrovert, then you probably prefer face-to-face communication, whereas an introverted person may prefer written forms of communication. Another personality dimension is "sensing" types" versus "intuitive types." A sensing type prefers to deal with concrete facts and details, and has a here-and-now orientation, whereas an intuitive type favors broader overviews and general information while having a future orientation.[30] From a communication perspective, a sensing-type person is likely to send very detail-oriented messages; however, an intuitive type will probably tend to send, and prefer to receive, only the essential general information and its implications. In addition, a sender who has a "feeling" type personality would be much more concerned with how a message affects the receiver than would one leaning toward the "thinking" personality type. For instance, if a subordinate asks you for feedback on a task he or she did inadequately, your reaction might be different depending on personality type. If you are more of a thinker, you might be straightforward and blunt about the issues with his or her work. If you are more of a feeling type, you might choose to compliment them on things they did well first or try to soften the criticism. Thus, our basic core personality significantly influences the way in which we send and receive information.

As we briefly touched upon, our ethnic, national, and cultural backgrounds also affect how we communicate: Words and symbols have different meanings. For example, it is perfectly acceptable for heterosexual males to kiss each other in France, but this practice is not as readily acceptable in the United States. Another example is the use of the word *diet*. In most European countries, the term is strictly prescriptive or medicinal in nature. In the United States, though, the term can be used both prescriptively and to mean reduced calories. Consequently, U.S. beverage producers do not use the word *diet* on labels of products exported to some countries to indicate reduced calories, but instead use the word *light*. Thus, a person's background can influence how he or she perceives a communicated message.

The mood of employees and managers has an impact upon the nature and flow of communication within the organization.

Another important individual characteristic that influences communication is social background, which plays a critical role in the formation of attitudes and beliefs. For example, our particular social background tends to determine how we stereotype other people or groups (occupations, genders, races, departments, customers, employees). If, for instance, employees have the attitude that customers are a "pain in the neck," then they will probably perceive information received from customers as "complaining" or "whining," instead of as valuable feedback on which to base product-change decisions. In addition, managers who believe that employees are lazy and need to be told what to do (Theory X managers) will communicate quite differently with employees than will managers who believe that employees want to work and need autonomy (Theory Y managers). For example, a Theory X manager may use more written communication in the way of rules and policies than a Theory Y manager.

Finally, even a person's mood at the time of the communication can influence its effectiveness. For example, the division sales manager who has just had an argument with a spouse is not likely to receive a quarterly sales report showing a downturn in sales with much sensitivity or to be open to explanations as to why sales are low. However, it is possible that, with time to cool off, the manager will be more willing to listen to reasons for poor sales. Mood, as indicated earlier, involves a time element, as people's moods change over time.

Semantics

Semantics refers to the different uses and meanings of words. Sometimes words take on different meanings depending on the person, which can create confusion in a message. In terms of channel selection, some people lean toward a channel they are more comfortable with even though a more effective one exists. For example, a shy person might want to inform her boss that she is quitting through email, even though face-to-face communication is most appropriate. Consistency refers to whether a message matches with body language and spoken words. This also affects credibility, or whether the sender can be trusted. Finally, there are times when people may be apprehensive and, therefore, reluctant to transmit information because they think they may incriminate themselves (make themselves look bad).

semantics: The different uses and meanings of words, often influencing the effectiveness of a message.

You're the Manager . . . What Would You Do?

THE COMPANY: Star Quest Manufacturing
YOUR POSITION: Vice President of Production
THE PLACE: Bismarck, ND

Like many manufacturers in the United States, Star Quest (SQ) took a hard look at the techniques used by Japanese firms to gain dominance in world markets. As one of the few manufacturers of microwave ovens in the United States, SQ saw firsthand the importance of the total quality process and other strategies American factories used to compete against the Japanese. So in 2003, SQ developed a quality program for its Iowa plant. From the beginning, SQ saw communication as a vital element to the quality drive.

SQ launched a new program called "Intracommunication Leadership Initiative," which gave employees tasks once handled by first-line managers. At first, however, employees viewed the program as just another management fad. Therefore, the company had to do some "damage control," reemphasizing top management's commitment to the new program and the potential benefits to employees. Once employees got the message, their attitude toward the program changed quickly.

The fundamental purpose of the Intracommunication Leadership Initiative program was to flatten the layers of management. Instead of having a supervisor overseeing many employees, the system relies on teamwork and peer pressure to accomplish the plant's goals. Employees who handle similar tasks meet regularly with each other and the manager who has ultimate responsibility for their duties. For example, SQ's human resource manager meets weekly with the 17 employees assigned the tasks of human resources for their groups. Employees make all decisions within the boundaries of their responsibilities, ranging from electing representatives to changing jobs. One team was given the task of replacing the policies and procedures handbook with a one-page list of guiding principles. Another team reviews issues and makes recommendations to management. Yet another team evaluates ways to improve on-the-job safety.

Employees who are not self-motivated team players or who cannot get used to their peers' authority have difficulty within this system. Also, the remaining upper-level managers face additional stress and frus-

Star Quest Manufacturing improves communication and increases product quality while reducing costs.

tration; in addition to their regular management duties, they must also train workers to supervise themselves.

By improving communications and empowering workers to take control of increasingly more aspects of their jobs, the company not only motivates them to work harder but also saves money on supervisory expenses. All employees are now highly knowledgeable about what occurs within their group as well as how their group is linked to the total quality processes and strategies SQ has adopted in its efforts to compete against Japanese microwave oven manufacturers.

QUESTIONS

1. At SQ, how is the communication process linked to a desire to improve product quality? What could have happened had you, as vice president of production, and other upper-level managers not reacted quickly to employees' initial negative attitude toward the program?

2. Within each work group, an employee is elected, drafted, or persuaded to assume one of the supervisory duties. What techniques or skills do you look for in individuals to achieve the appropriate communication with, and motivation of, the work group?

3. What are the communication problems you face in dealing with many team representatives who are being trained to supervise themselves?

Channel Selection

Communication channels can be personal barriers in that some individuals always seem to lean toward a particular channel even though a more effective one exists. Consider, for example, a supervisor who uses a written memo to let you know about the recent denial of a promotion. The more effective channel in this case might have been a face-to-face meeting in which you could ask questions. However, the supervisor, perhaps uncomfortable in one-to-one situations, chose the written memo. It is also possible that the organization itself dictates the use of certain channels over others. At most universities, professors are notified of their tenure status via a written letter, even though a meeting with the tenure-peer committee might be a more appropriate channel to allow the professor to ask for additional information and elaboration on the group decision. Managers who desire to communicate effectively should be aware of their own communication channel preferences, as well as the organization's, which may or may not be the best to use in a given situation.

Consistency

It is important to ensure that communication symbols and signals are consistent. If the words chosen to communicate a message do not match the sender's body language, the potential for misunderstanding and confusion increases. Inconsistency may even cause the receiver to mistrust the sender and the message being sent, which gives rise to credibility issues. For example, if a supervisor assures an employee of a high performance rating, but the employee later learns that a request for a raise in pay was denied because of a lower performance rating by the supervisor, the employee most likely will not trust the supervisor in the future.

Credibility

A sender's credibility plays an important role in how a message is received and understood. If the receiver does not consider the sender trustworthy or knowledgeable about the subject being communicated, he or she will most likely be reluctant even to listen to the message. For example, if you learn that your professor has no practical management experience, you may feel that she has little knowledge concerning the area of management and, thus, place little weight on anything she tells you concerning the subject. Likewise, a sender may limit what he or she communicates to a receiver who is not considered trustworthy. For instance, if an employee offers an idea for a more efficient way to perform a job and his supervisor takes credit for it, then the employee is more likely to withhold future information from the supervisor, as he will probably not trust the supervisor with such information. A survey revealed that 97 percent of executives considered transparent communication by leaders to be one of the top methods of building trust among employees.[31]

Incrimination

Finally, we should point out that there are times when people may be apprehensive and, therefore, reluctant to transmit information because it is likely to anger a supervisor or make the transmitter look bad. Such reluctance will increase if the sender believes that the incriminating information will not be acted upon appropriately or sensitively. Managers need to be aware of such situations and make adjustments accordingly.

Organizational Barriers

Organizational characteristics can also inhibit effective communication. The more prominent of these are power and status problems, goal and priority differences, and organizational structure.

Power and Status

People in upper areas of the organization, those who have more status and power, may be hesitant to listen to those individuals lower in the hierarchy, feeling, for example, that people of lower status and power do not possess any useful information. By the same token, individuals of lower status and power may be reluctant to share information because they believe that people with higher status and power will not listen.

Goal and Priority Differences

Goal and priority differences among organizational functions, departments, or divisions may influence how effectively a message will be sent and/or received. Obviously, each department or unit will view problems and concern from its own perspective. Consequently, departments may feel less inclined to be receptive to others' messages. The use of cross-functional decision making or project teams helps overcome this barrier.

Organizational Structure

Finally, the structure of an organization can dramatically influence the effectiveness of communication. For example, if the firm's organization does not provide sufficient upward, downward, and horizontal communication channels, then not only the quality but the quantity of information sharing could be reduced. The structure can also influence which channels are used. A more centralized structure, for example, tends to make greater use of written communication, whereas a more decentralized structure encourages more face-to-face communication. In recent years, there has been a trend toward eliminating middle-management layers, and a by-product of this trend has been improved communication effectiveness. This is because centralized structures—those with several layers between top management and first-line supervisors—tend to inhibit effective communication flow from the bottom of the organization up. Companies are also restructuring to facilitate communications between and among organizational units and/or divisions to overcome communication barriers.

Environmental Barriers

Factors inherent in the environment in which a message is transmitted can also disrupt the communication process. These factors include noise, information overload, and physical barriers within the environment.

Earlier, we defined noise as anything that interferes with a message being communicated effectively. A mother who works at home, for example, may find her efforts to communicate with clients on the telephone distracted by an active toddler.

Information overload refers to the condition of having too much information to process, as is the case when a worker is given too many jobs to perform. The implication is that individuals can effectively process only a certain amount of information. An example would be if your professor gave you too much information, too quickly, concerning a term paper's requirements or if a manager gave an employee too much information at one time

information overload: The condition of having too much information to process.

Information overload means an employee has so much communication that the important messages to process can get lost, as a driver might experience in the above setting.

about a report's requirements. In either situation, the receiver probably does not receive the message. Managers need to be aware of the potential for information overload and to make appropriate adjustments, such as providing written instructions to back up verbal instructions.

Finally, there are physical structures in the environment that can inhibit effective communication. For example, firms that locate managers' offices on floors separate from where employees are working tend to reduce communication flow between the two. Likewise, a large desk that separates students from a professor tends to inhibit open and honest communication. In an effort to overcome these kinds of communication obstacles, many companies are locating managers' offices in the middle of employee work areas and even having managers eat their lunch in the employee cafeteria; many professors now lecture to students who are sitting in circularly arranged desks.

Overcoming Communication Barriers

There is no sure way to guarantee effective communication, but there are several techniques available for improving the chances that it will occur. These include listening, providing feedback, being aware of cultural diversity, choosing an appropriate channel, structuring the organization appropriately, and improving interpersonal relationships.

Listening

Unfortunately, ours is not a society that practices good listening skills, and many communication breakdowns can be attributed to poor listening. Many factors both inside and outside organizations demonstrate that today's managers need to acquire good listening skills. For example, currently many organizations are decentralizing, which means that information is flowing upward much more so than in more traditionally structured organizations. And, as new technology develops, customers' preferences change, societal concerns intensify, and more companies globalize, receiving accurate information is critical to survival. Such changes require that managers and employees become better listeners.

Organizations are recognizing the increased importance of good listening habits. Consider, for example, the alert salesperson who recognizes that listening often involves sorting out complex relationships in a client company. Only by listening can he or she determine the one person or department who is the key in the final purchasing decision.[32]

In general there are four levels of listening and four levels of related responses, as illustrated in Table 14.3. The first level is *unrelated listening and responding*, when the receiver does not listen to anything the sender says. Consequently, the response is completely different or unrelated to the message. The second level is *tangential listening and responding*, where the receiver hears a small portion (perhaps a word or two) of the sender's message and then goes off on a tangent. The amount of the message actually heard, however, is not enough to provide a fully appropriate response. At the third level, *furthering listening and responding*, the sender is encouraged by the receiver (either verbally or nonverbally) to continue with his or her message. In other words, the receiver is actively listening; however, full understanding of the message has not been attempted. At the fourth level, *feeling listening and responding*, the receiver attempts full understanding of the information and meaning. He or she focuses not only on the words but also on the feelings or emotions being expressed or implied. Often the receiver will express his or her own feelings while acknowledging the feelings of

If an employee is distracted by music or texting, they may not be receiving the information that co-workers are sharing.

TABLE 14.3 Levels of Listening and Responding

Level 1 Unrelated Listening and Responding
Receiver does not listen to sender's message.
Example: *Sender:* I had a car accident this morning.
Receiver: Did you hear about Mary and Charlie getting divorced?
Level 2 Tangential Listening and Responding
Receiver listens to a small portion of a sender's message.
Example: *Sender:* I had a car accident this morning.
Receiver: Cars can really be a pain. I put mine in the shop twice last week.
Level 3 Furthering Listening and Responding
Receiver signals the sender that he or she is listening and encourages the sender to continue with the message.
Example: *Sender:* I had a car accident this morning.
Receiver: Where did it happen?
Level 4 Feeling Listening and Responding
Receiver fully attempts to understand the message.
Example: *Sender:* I had a car accident this morning.
Receiver: I'm so sorry! Were you or anyone else hurt?

the sender. Acknowledging these levels of listening and responding should demonstrate that for communication to reach its maximum effectiveness, good listening requires being sensitive to others' feelings.[33] After all, successful communication requires points both to be made and to be learned.

Perhaps the most important asset to effective communication is *active listening*, which involves giving and receiving feedback concerning the information contained in the message. Characteristics of active listening include asking questions, showing interest, paraphrasing, making direct eye contact, and consciously eliminating noise. In short, active listening allows for two-way communication. To help make sure that you are an active listener, try going through the following steps:

1. Maintain frequent eye contact.
2. Be sensitive to nonverbal messages (body language).
3. Know yourself (your perceptions and biases).
4. Eliminate both physical and mental noise.
5. Remain open-minded and sensitive.

Providing Feedback

Closely related to listening well is the ability to give effective feedback. The tendency to pass judgment or evaluate others is a common cause of communication breakdown. It can cause the receiver to become defensive or resentful, which may distort the sender's message and intentions (noise). Effective feedback enhances and facilitates the communication process. For instance, U.K. supermarket chain Sainsbury provides a guarantee that all employee feedback and suggestions will be considered. Employees can also discuss issues with managers in what the firm calls its "daily huddle." The company has received thousands upon thousands of communication messages from employees because they feel that their feedback is considered important.[34] Effective feedback:

1. Focuses on description, not judgment; managers should describe the situation, for instance, rather than label a person.
2. Focuses on behavior, not personality: managers should talk about what a person actually does rather than what they think or imagine the person is like.

3. Incorporates the receiver's needs; in other words, managers should provide beneficial, not harmful, feedback.
4. Addresses behavior that the receiver can do something about or has control over.
5. Is asked for, not imposed.
6. Involves sharing information, not making demands.
7. Is given at the appropriate time, preferably as soon as possible.
8. Does not result in information overload. Managers should think in terms of how much information can be used, rather than how much they would like to give.
9. Is concerned with *what* actually happened rather than *why* it happened. In other words, managers should not assume they know someone else's intentions or motivations.[35]

Being Aware of Cultural Diversity

Communicators should also be aware of the increasingly diverse nature of today's workforce. Recognizing and being sensitive to others' needs and perspectives can help reduce semantic problems and noise, increase objectivity, and generally enhance communication.

Choosing an Appropriate Channel

Different channels of communication have advantages and disadvantages, and certain types of information warrant specific types of channels. Firing an employee, for example, should be done face to face. Thus, choosing an appropriate communication channel can be conducive—even essential—to effective communication.

Structuring the Organization for Communication

Organizations can take specific steps to enhance the communication process. For example, providing employees with proper communication training should benefit the communication processes within the organization. Fostering a climate of trust and openness should also encourage frequent and open communication. Moreover, the communication process can be facilitated by ensuring that formal communication channels are available in all directions (upward, downward, horizontal, diagonal). Finally, the use of multiple channels should be encouraged, including both formal and informal communications. For example, a written code of ethics can be beneficial, but if it is not backed up by training and verbal support for management, it will probably be ineffective. Thus, the structure of the organization should fit the communication needs of its members.

Improving Interpersonal Relationships

Perhaps one of the most important ways to improve the communication process is to view it as a people process. This improves interpersonal relationships and reduces defensive communication. Suggestions for improvements in this area include not using judgmental language or behaviors, regarding the sender or receiver as being an equal, not trying to control the sender or receiver (for example, by imposing certain values or points of view), not having hidden motives (being open and honest at all possible times), not using gimmicks or tricks, being spontaneous, showing empathy (not neutrality), and approaching every communication situation with an open mind.[37]

One of the most important messages in this chapter is the critical nature of communication. Communication is vital both personally and professionally. It is particularly vital to managers, as it is integral to every part of a manager's job and responsibilities. Additionally, the very success of the entire organization hinges on effective communication, both internally and externally.

Communication strategies and tactics vary based on the composition and location of the workforce.

The Rainforest Alliance: Communicating a Commitment to Sustainability

When you think of the phrase "non-profit organization," you likely think of a bare-bones operation run by people who are so dedicated that they do not mind working for peanuts. However, the Rainforest Alliance, a highly recognized non-profit aiming to conserve biodiversity and promote sustainability, defies this mold. In fact, the company works hard to ensure a great workplace with fair compensation and open communication among its employees and stakeholders. With thousands of members and supporters, the Rainforest Alliance has been fighting globally for wildlife, wild lands, workers, and communities since 1987. To pursue its mission, the Rainforest Alliance needs dedicated employees, so it makes sense that the company promotes a motivational, encouraging work environment.

Rainforest Alliance has grown rapidly to over 300 employees worldwide. Thanks in part to its widespread growth, the Rainforest Alliance is a decentralized organization that empowers employees of all ranks to take charge of projects. Thus, the Rainforest Alliance adopts a network pattern of communication. Employees are encouraged to attend staff meetings for senior-level staff, a way for lower-level employees to "learn the ropes" and better communicate with all members of the organization. The organization prefers internal promotion when positions open up, rather than outside recruiting. This allows employees to feel like they have a stake in the organization and a real chance for advancement, which builds morale. The company also offers employees opportunities to work in foreign offices, which provides the chance to travel, communicate with stakeholders from other countries, and learn more about the company's vision.

Communication with key stakeholders is critical to the Rainforest Alliance's success. For example, employees are in continual contact with landowners throughout the world in an attempt to show them the benefits of Rainforest Alliance certification (which indicates that certified forests are maintained sustainably). The organization also boasts several educational websites, including its Eco-Index, a bilingual website that connects users with over 1,000 profiles of conservation projects in the Americas and the Caribbean. Its communication efforts have helped spread the Rainforest Alliance mission worldwide.

The Rainforest Alliance also has communication and marketing resources for businesses that partner with the organization. The Rainforest Alliance provides auditing and certification services for businesses—such as agricultural, tourism, and forestry organizations—that wish to display the Rainforest Alliance certification seal. The Rainforest Alliance blog describes how sustainabil-

The Rainforest Alliance communicates with key stakeholders to strengthen relationships.

Source: Laurens Hoddenbagh/Shutterstock

ity can positively impact a business, and its seal is one way businesses can inform consumers that they have incorporated sustainability principles into their operations. The Rainforest Alliance even has its own business unit called RA-Cert involved with auditing, evaluation, and certification decisions. Certification means little, however, if consumers do not realize it exists. For this reason, the Rainforest Alliance offers communication and marketing advice on how to spread awareness and reach consumers. Additionally, the Rainforest Alliance offers resources to businesses that want to educate their own employees about sustainability.

Like other non-profits, however, the Rainforest Alliance is not without critics. Some complain that the company's certification criteria are too lenient, citing Fair Trade certification as a better option. Yet advocates of Rainforest's methods say that it encourages growers and businesses to engage in continuous improvement. Stakeholders generally have a positive image of the Rainforest Alliance. A survey cited in the *Economist* noted that coffee drinkers were likely to spend extra on coffee certified by the Rainforest Alliance due to the quality of taste, although the company has also been taken to task for putting its seal on coffee containing only 30 percent certified coffee beans. Rainforest Alliance argues that this motivates companies to purchase more from certified growers, which in turn ensures that these growers remain sustainable. Although the company has been called Fair Trade Lite, it has the support of the *Economist* and *Consumer Reports* and is aligned with a number of sustainably focused organizations worldwide. For individuals looking to aid the environment and support small growers, the Rainforest Alliance is making a positive difference with its desirable model workplace and large-scale communication efforts.[36]

As we have seen, communication is essential to the proper functioning of an organization. However, even with the best communication, companies are going to face barriers and obstacles throughout their lifetimes. Sometimes these barriers cannot be overcome through the companies' traditional way of doing things. Instead, companies, particularly successful ones, have to institute organizational change in order to adapt to changing market circumstances. The effective implementation of organizational change often means the difference between company death or survival.

Summary and Review

- *Define* communication *and explain its importance to managers.* Communication is the process through which information and meaning are transferred from one person to another. Managers must communicate in order to perform their organizational roles and the functions of planning, organizing, leading, and controlling. Communication is necessary for managers to convey their goals and visions to employees and to see if employees correctly understand, accept, and are achieving those goals and visions.

- *Describe the communication process and the factors that affect it.* The communication process can be thought of as a chain of identifiable links with the ultimate objective of influencing behaviors, attitudes, and beliefs. It consists of a number of distinct components: A sender encodes a message that is sent across some channel to a receiver who decodes the message and sends a return message, called feedback, letting the sender know the message was received and how it was interpreted. Many factors, called noise, can interfere with the process, including differences in educational level, experience, and culture as well as various types of physical noise such as machinery running or background talk. Other factors that may influence the communication process include perception, perceptual distortions, and the form and channel of communication used.

- *Compare and contrast the various communication forms and channels and the "richness" of each.* Major forms of communication are verbal, written, digital, nonverbal, and listening. Various channels can be utilized for each form. Verbal communication may be face to face, over the telephone, and even on two-way radios. Written channels include letters, memos, reports, and email. Digital communication occurs when meanings and symbols are transmitted through digital devices. This information can be either verbal or written. Nonverbal communication consists of messages sent by actions or behaviors, rather than by spoken or written words. Listening involves accurately receiving and understanding information. Channels vary in richness or in the ability to transmit information. Face-to-face verbal communication is the richest medium because verbal, visual, and even other sensory cues can be used during communication. Written channels are the least rich.

- *Distinguish between formal and informal communication in an organization.* Formal communication is intentionally defined and designed by the organization and represents the flow of communication throughout the formal hierarchy. Formal communication may be upward, downward, horizontal across functional areas, or even diagonal across functions and hierarchical levels, but is usually within the context of formal organizational functioning. Informal communication channels—the grapevine—are not deliberately designed and do not abide by formal organizational hierarchy or other arrangement.

- *Determine how groups and teams communicate.* Within groups, individuals develop specific patterns of communication, depending on how centralized or decentralized the communication is. In a wheel pattern, the messages flow only through a centralized person or "spoke." This highly centralized pattern contrasts sharply with the decentralized network pattern, in which communication flows freely among all group members. The pattern of group communication should reflect the complexity of the issue being discussed or decision being made.

- *Describe common gender differences in communication.* Studies have revealed that women often appear to have a harder time negotiating and are more likely to avoid competition. This is likely because they are more relationship-oriented and prefer to avoid the aura of superiority. Female employees tend to rely more on their work to speak for itself. Male employees, on the other hand, have been characterized as overconfident, direct, and competitive. They are more likely to ask for what they want and make decisions without necessarily consulting with others. Female employees tend to be stronger in empathy, influence, self-awareness, and conflict management. Many of these characteristics are important for effective management.

■ *Detect the barriers to effective communication and specify potential ways to overcome them.* Barriers to effective communication may be classified as personal, organizational, and environmental. Personal barriers include individual characteristics, semantics, inappropriate communication channels, inconsistent symbols and signals, and credibility issues. Organizational barriers include power and status, goal and priority differences, and organizational structure. Environmental barriers include noise, information overload, and physical barriers. Techniques to overcome

these barriers include listening, providing more effective feedback, being aware of cultural differences, making better channel choices, and certain organizational actions such as worker-communication training and improved interpersonal relationships.

■ *Critique an organization's communication efforts.* Evaluate the communications process at Star Quest as described in the "Business Dilemma" box. Your evaluation should include a discussion of how the firm's unique structure dictates communications.

Key Terms and Concepts

body language 428	feedback 425	perceptual selection 431
channel 424	gossip chain 433	receiver 424
channel richness 429	grapevine 433	semantics 437
cluster chain 433	horizontal communication 433	sender 424
communication 423	information overload 440	stereotyping 431
decoding 424	listening 429	upward communication 432
diagonal communication 433	noise 425	verbal or oral communication 426
distortion 431	nonverbal communication 427	written communication 426
downward communication 433	perception 430	
encoding 424	perceptual organization 431	

Ready Recall

1. Define *communications* and explain its importance to management.
2. Describe the communication process.
3. Give examples of how perceptions might influence the communication process.
4. What is meant by defensive communication?
5. Compare and contrast formal versus informal communications.
6. How do groups/teams communicate differently than individuals?
7. List some barriers to effective communication and discuss ways managers can minimize them.
8. Discuss the characteristics of effective feedback.
9. Explain the concept of "good listening."
10. Discuss how "information overload" can inhibit effective communication.

Expand Your Experience

1. Divide into groups of two. Have one person give and one person receive at the four different levels of listening and responding. Have the receiver describe his or her feelings. Then reverse the roles.
2. Explain the statement, "The communication process can be thought of as being a chain, made up of definite and identifiable links—and like any chain is only as strong as its weakest link."
3. Go to a local organization and interview the person most responsible for the company's public relations. Find out the various forms and methods of communication used and report them back to your class.
4. Interview local businesspeople at various organizational levels concerning their communication roles and responsibilities. In addition, ask them to describe their view of communication and how it may change in the future. Report these findings to the class.

Identifying and Evaluating Communication in Organizations

Instructions:

Divide the class into teams of four or five. Have each team read the scenario below. After each team has read the scenario, answer and discuss the questions.

Scenario:

At a recent staff meeting there were concerns addressed about one of the company's manufacturing facilities in Oklahoma. A few months ago, the CEO issued a memo explaining there may be a relocation of manufacturing to another building. The reasons for this potential relocation were not stated, and there has been no other discussion of it since. There was a rumor, however, that the facility was acquired by a relative of one of the board members, and that the company is paying excessive leasing fees for use of the building. Employees in the corporate office claimed to have knowledge that the new owner of the facility has a very large insurance policy on the building. In addition, it was mentioned that the manufacturing facility is very old, might have asbestos, and does not meet the fire safety code. Many of these concerns are discussed only in the manufacturing facility among workers. One of the plant managers overheard the workers' discussion and talked it over with some of his fellow managers. Finally, it is a known fact that the factory is infested with highly rare Socorro doves. The creatures are causing a lot of problems and are depositing large amounts of guano. The State Wildlife Commission has warned the company that the Socorro doves are rare and usually only exist in captivity. Recently, a number of the Socorro doves were found dead

The Socorro doves are rare and usually only exist in captivity.

in the factory, and it is suspected that the plant manager may have poisoned them.

QUESTIONS

1. What forms of communication are managers and employees using in this organization? Evaluate the richness of the channels chosen.
2. In what directions are the pathways of communication flowing? Evaluate the effectiveness of these pathways.
3. Is the content of the communication credible? Why or why not?
4. Does the form of communication contribute to its credibility? Why or why not?

Case 14: Best Buy Excels in Communication

At Best Buy, communication with stakeholders is a pivotal element in the firm's success. Best Buy ranks number 72 on the Fortune 500 and is the largest consumer electronics retailer in the world. Best known for its discounted high-quality products, customer-centered approach, sustainable outreach, and extensive recycling program, Best Buy is listed as a "socially responsible" company. Best Buy's reputation as a high-quality, socially responsible retailer would not be possible without its ability to communicate with the proper audiences and adapt its communication strategies to take advantage of newer trends that increase its reach.

Best Buy was founded by Richard Schulze in 1966. Its initial target market was college students who wanted

higher-end electronics. In 2000, when sales growth slowed, Best Buy acquired Geek Squad, a repair service. This acquisition led to its Concept 5 stores, where products are sold and customers are taught how to use them. This required significant investment on Best Buy's part because it not only had to train its employees on how to use the products but also teach them how to communicate these products' services to customers in a way they could understand. Its additional investment paid off. It led to improved service turnaround time and increased customer satisfaction. By 2009, the company became the primary online and brick-and-mortar provider of consumer electronics.

Best Buy views itself as a customer-centered organization. The company uses www.BestBuy.com to learn more about its customer needs and preferences. Customers can use that website to rate every product purchased. This feedback is essential for Best Buy to understand customer needs and communicate on a more individual level. In fact, it was this type of communication that led Best Buy to develop its first Corporate Social Responsibility Report in 2007. The report was a response to its customers' repeated concerns over sustainability, particularly in the area of electronics. It showed customers that the company had received and understood their concerns. Electronic waste was filling landfills, and customers wanted to see this problem addressed. In response, Best Buy implemented a wide-scale electronics recycling program. In 2009, Best Buy set a goal to reduce carbon emissions by 45 percent; by the end of 2016, it had reached nearly 47 percent.

In terms of communication, Best Buy focuses on listening and engaging employees and customers using both formal and informal communication channels. Best Buy has a public affairs office that monitors Best Buy communications and external relationships such as government affairs, corporate responsibility, and community relations. Best Buy hired Matt Furman as chief communications and public affairs officer. An experienced professional in communication, Furman leads a team of communications managers and specialists to create positive relationships between Best Buy and its stakeholders.

Besides human capital, Best Buy invests in different platforms to foster its communication with employees. The company has forums like Geek Squad Forums and a Best Buy community where Best Buy's employees can exchange information and share ideas. Best Buy uses a digital tool that encourages employees to develop and communicate their new ideas. The company also implements an employee listening system to discover the unmet needs of employees.

On a more informal level, Best Buy actively engages customers on social media. Its blog keeps its technology fans updated with the latest technologies on the market. Best Buy uses Facebook creatively as well. Best Buy Facebook gives consumers the ability to ask questions and receive answers, search for products and gifts, and learn about Best Buy events. Best Buy's use of technology like social media not only engages customers but also utilizes the social networks of employees and customers to spread its message to others.

Best Buy also believes effective communication is necessary to create an ethical organizational culture. Today Best Buy employs a chief ethics officer and maintains a blog for company employees. This blog covers ethical lapses and related issues. Employees can visit the website and read about company policy regarding ethically questionable behaviors. Best Buy shares lessons learned from past experiences with employees to teach them how to best defend themselves from crossing ethical boundaries.

After a period of stagnant growth, Best Buy hired a new CEO, Hubert Joly. Under Joly, Best Buy once again became a growth company. Joly recognized the need for innovative new products, but he also knew that without communication, stakeholders would not know about them. When he implemented Best Buy's "Renew Blue" marketing strategy, he made sure the company communicated with stakeholders about new product lines as well as in-store and online customer opportunities. Its Geek Squad division began an in-store, online, and home advisory program. By utilizing these different communication channels, Best Buy was able to extend its reach and customer service opportunities.

In another attempt to improve customer service, the Geek Squad hours were expanded to provide 24-hour service on site, at home, or through the Internet. Now Best Buy technology experts can communicate with customers during any hour of the day in person or online. Walmart and Amazon, its biggest competitors, do not offer comparable at-home services.

In 2017, Joly announced at an investor conference that the company will implement "Best Buy 2020—Building the New Blue." Communicating this strategy to investors is important in getting them to support Best Buy's marketing focus. Research has shown that Best Buy's advertisements tend to be more impactful when they highlight products, which is prompting the company to engage in more product-oriented advertising campaigns. For example, Best Buy is introducing a new service called "Assured Living," a service that uses smart-home technology that allows millennials/caregivers to look in on their aging parents while permitting the seniors to live independently. To communicate this new service to consumers, Best Buy has developed a website and has advisors who can offer more detailed information to customers about the technology. Best Buy also posts weekly advertisements on its deals website that highlight discounted products and other deals for customers.

By listening to customers, Best Buy is able to discover their desires and develop innovative products to meet their needs. In addition to customers, Best Buy knows it must communicate with other stakeholders such as employees and investors to gain their support for the company's initiatives. Best Buy has proven that it listens to its stakeholders and will implement initiatives based on their feedback. This communication has been integral in facilitating Best Buy's development of strong stakeholder relationships, allowing it to compete against online rivals and adapt to an increasingly digital world.[38]

1. How does Best Buy engage in the communication process?
2. Describe some ways Best Buy uses formal and informal communication.
3. How has listening to stakeholder feedback helped Best Buy compete in an increasingly digital world?

Notes

1. Jena McGregor, "Online Extra: Learning on the Front Lines," *Bloomberg Businessweek*, July 10, 2006, http://www.businessweek.com/stories/2006-07-09/online-extra-learning-on-the-front-lines (accessed January 1, 2018); Keurig Green Mountain website, http://www.keuriggreenmountain.com/ (accessed January 1, 2018); Dun & Bradstreet, Inc., "Keurig Green Mountain," Hoovers Online, http://www.hoovers.com/company-information/cs/company-profile.keurig_green_mountain_inc.09ca839579577b55.html (accessed January 1, 2018); "Green Mountain Coffee Roasters Brews Formula for Success," in O. C. Ferrell, Geoffrey Hirt, and Linda Ferrell, *Business: A Changing World*, 6th ed. (New York: McGraw-Hill Irwin, 2008), 233–234; Leslie Patton and Nikolaj Gammeltoft, "Green Mountain Drops as David Einhorn Says Market 'Limited,'" *Bloomberg Businessweek*, October 17, 2011, http://www.businessweek.com/news/2011-10-17/green-mountain-drops-as-david-einhorn-says-market-limited.html (accessed November 6, 2013); Christopher Faille, "Green Mountain Coffee's Trouble with Bean Counting," *Forbes*, June 23, 2011, https://www.forbes.com/sites/greatspeculations/2011/06/23/green-mountain-coffees-trouble-with-bean-counting/#2578180296dc (accessed January 1, 2018); *GMCR Fiscal 2012 Annual Report*, http://files.shareholder.com/ downloads/GMCR/2774887737x0x630863/FDBC5F63-78E8-493C-9BB9-8F33000C0465/GMCR_2012_ANNUAL _REPORT.pdf (accessed November 6, 2013); "Green Mountain Coffee: Starbucks Bursts Its Bubble," Seeking Alpha, March 9, 2012, http://seekingalpha.com/article/422241-green-mountain-coffee-starbucks-bursts-its-bubble (accessed January 1, 2018); Keurig Green Mountain, "2016 by the Numbers," January 3, 2017, https://www.keuriggreenmountain.com/en/OurStories/Business/2016ByTheNumbers.aspx (accessed January 1, 2018); Keurig Green Mountain, "Sustainability," http://www.keuriggreenmountain.com/en/Sustainability/Overview.aspx (accessed January 1, 2018); Steven Bruce, "HRWorks Sits Down with Keurig Green Mountain Coffee," HR Daily Advisor, October 9, 2017, http://hrdailyadvisor.blr.com/2017/10/09/hrworks-sits-keurig-green-mountain-coffee/ (accessed January 1, 2018); "World's Most Innovative Companies: #43 Keurig Green Mountain," *Forbes*, May 2015, https://www.forbes.com/companies/keurig-green-mountain/ (accessed January 1, 2018).

2. David R. Kolzow, "Communication and Leadership: The Critical Foundation for an Effective Economic Development Program," *Economic Development Review* 8 (Summer 1990): 19–23.

3. Robert Snyder and James H. Morris, "Organizational Communication and Performance," *Journal of Applied Psychology* 69 (August 1984): 461–465.

4. Larry E. Penley, Elmore R. Alexander, I. Jernigan, and Catherine I. Henwood, "Communication Abilities of Managers: The Relationship to Performance," *Journal of Management* 17 (June 1991): 57–76.

5. John H. Telford, Jr., "What Does It Take to Get a Plum HR Job?" *Human Resources Professional* 5 (Winter 1993): 36–38.

6. Ken G. Smith and Curtis M. Grimm, "A Communication-Information Model of Competitive Response Timing," *Journal of Management* 17 (March 1991): 5–24.

7. Diana Stork and Alice Sapienza, "Task and Human Messages Over the Project Life Cycle: Matching Media to Messages," *Project Management Journal* 23 (December 1992): 44–49.

8. Martha C. White, "You're Wasting Time at Work Right Now, Aren't You?" *TIME*, March 13, 2012, http://business.time.com/2012/03/13/youre-wasting-time-at-work-right-now-arent-you/ (accessed January 20, 2018).

9. Michael B. McCaskey, "The Hidden Messages Managers Send," *Harvard Business Review* 57 (November-December 1979): 135–148.

10. Penley, Alexander, Jernigan, and Henwood, "Communication Abilities of Managers."

11. Susan M. Heathfield, "Top Ten Employee Complaints," *About.com*, http://humanresources.about.com/od/ retention/a/emplo_complaint.htm (accessed July 10, 2012).

12. Gary T. Hunt, *Communication Skills in the Organization*. Upper Saddle River, NJ: Prentice Hall, 1989).

13. Ibid.

14. R. E. Freeman and L. Stewart, "Developing Ethical Leadership," *Business Roundtable Institute for Corporate Ethics*, 2006, www.corporate-ethics.org.

15. Stork and Sapienza, "Task and Human Messages."

16. Jack R. Gibb, "Defensive Communication," *Journal of Communication* 11 (September 1961): 141–148.

17. Tony Alessandra and Rick Barrera, "Motivating to Excellence," *Security Management* 36 (November 1992): 20, 22; John M. Wellborn, "Productivity and Pay," *LIMBRA'S Market Facts* 10 (November/December 1991): 1–4.

18. Walter Kiechell III, "Breaking Bad News to the Boss," *Fortune* (April 9, 1990): 111–112.

19. Ethics Resource Center, *National Business Ethics Survey® of the U.S. Workplace* (Arlington, VA: Ethics Resource Center, 2014).

20. Keith Davis, "Management Communication and the Grapevine," *Harvard Business Review* 31 (September-October 1953): 43–49.

21. "Spread the Word: Gossip Is Good."

22. Thomas J. Peters and Robert H. Waterman, Jr., *In Search of Excellence: Lessons from America's Best Run Companies* (New York: Harper & Row, 1982); Tom Peters and Nancy Austin, *A Passion for Excellence* (New York: Random House, 1985).

23. Jerry Wofford, Edwin Gerloff, and Robert Cummins, *Organizational Communication* (New York: McGraw-Hill, 1977).

24. Wofford, Gerloff, and Cummins, *Organizational Communication*.

25. Virginia M. Cerullo and Michael J. Cerullo, "Operations Audits of Computer Information Systems: A General Framework," *Internal Auditing* 8 (Winter 1993): 44–52.

26. Maria Gamb, "Nice Girls Still Don't Ask for What They Want! Why Women Fall Short at the Negotiating Table," *Forbes*, July 2, 2012, http://www.forbes.com/sites/womens media/2012/07/02/nice-girls-still-dont-ask-for-what-they-want -why-women-fall-short-at-the-negotiating-table/ (accessed January 20, 2018); Muriel Niederle and Lise Vesterlund, "Do Women Shy Away from Competition? Do Men Compete Too Much?" *The Quarterly Journal of Economics*, 2007, 1067–1101.

27. Gamb, "Nice Girls Still Don't Ask for What They Want! Why Women Fall Short at the Negotiating Table"; "Male and Female Communication: Differences Worth Noting," *Value Options*, July 12, 2013, https://www.achievesolutions.net/ achievesolutions/en/Content.do?contentId=10241 (accessed January 20, 2018).

28. John Baldoni, "Few Executives Are Self-Aware, But Women Have the Edge," *Harvard Business Review*, May 9, 2013, http://blogs.hbr.org/2013/05/few-executives-are-self -aware/ (accessed January 20, 2018);

29. Judy B. Rosener, "Ways Women Lead," *Harvard Business Review*, November 1990, http://hbr.org/1990/11/ways-women -lead/ar/ (accessed January 20, 2018).

30. Sandra G. Hirsh and Jean M. Kimmerow, *Introduction to Type in Organizational Settings* (Palo Alto, CA: Consulting Psychologists Press, 1987).

31. Deloitte, *Trust in the workplace: 2010 Ethics and Workplace Survey*, 2010, https://www.bentley.edu/files/2015/04/07/ Trust%20in%20the%20Workplace-2010%20Ethics%20and %20Workplace%20Survey.pdf (accessed January 20, 2018).

32. Bruce Bond, "'Listening' as a Sales Function," *Telephone Engineer and Management* (May 15, 1993): 70.

33. David Lindo, "Say It with Feeling," *Office Systems* 9 (November 1992): 14, 16.

34. Katie Allen, "Companies That Put Employee Engagement Policy into Practice," *The Guardian*, August 21, 2010, http:// www.guardian.co.uk/business/2010/aug/22/top-companies -employee-engagement (accessed July 11, 2012).

35. George Manning and Kent Curtis, *Communication: The Miracle of Dialogue* (Cincinnati, OH: South-Western Publishing Co., 1988).

36. Rainforest Alliance, "Annual Report 2012," http://www .rainforest-alliance.org/sites/default/files/about/annual _reports/ AR2012_spreads-optimized.pdf (accessed June 24, 2013); Rainforest Alliance, "About Us," http://www.rainforest-alliance .org/about (accessed January 1, 2018); Kelly K. Spors, "Top Small Workplaces 2008," *The Wall Street Journal*, February 22, 2009, https://www.wsj.com/articles/SB122347733961315417 (accessed January 1, 2018); Richard Donovan, "Rainforest Alliance Launches TREES," Forest Stewardship Council, www.fscus.org/news/index.php ?article=169 (accessed May 29, 2009); Rainforest Alliance, "Marketing Your Commitment to Sustainability," https://www.rainforest-alliance.org/business/ marketing (accessed January 1, 2018); Rainforest Alliance, "Raising Awareness…Among Employees," https://www .rainforest-alliance.org/business/marketing/awareness/ employees (accessed January 1, 2018); Rainforest Alliance, "What Does Rainforest Alliance CertifiedTM Mean?" October 25, 2016, https://www.rainforest-alliance.org/faqs/what-does -rainforest-alliance-certified-mean (accessed January 1, 2018).

37. Gibb, "Defensive Communication."

38. O. C. Ferrell, John Fraedrich, and Linda Ferrell, *Business Ethics: Ethical Decision Making and Cases*, 9th ed. (Mason, OH: South-Western Cengage Learning, 2013), 506–507; Business Wire, "Best Buy Investor Day Details 'Best Buy 2020: Building the New Blue' Strategy," Nasdaq, September 19, 2017, http://www.nasdaq.com/press-release/best-buy -investor-day-details-best-buy-2020-building-the-new-blue -growth-strategy-20170919-00568 (accessed November 24, 2017); Kavita Kumar, "Best Buy Moves from New Blue Turnaround to Growth Phase," *Star Tribune*, March 4, 2017, http://www.startribune.com/best-buy-moves-from-renew-blue -turnaround-to-growth-phase/415357004/ (accessed November 24, 2017); Courtney Reagan, "Best Buy CEO Sess 'Growth Opportunities' Ahead, Wall Street Isn't Buying It," *CNBC*, September 19, 2017, https://www.cnbc.com/2017/09/19/best -buy-ceo-weve-fixed-what-was-broken-now-focus-is-on- growth.html (accessed November 24, 2017); Adrianne Pasquarelli, "Why Best Buy Is Reorganizing Its Marketing Team," *Ad Age,* April 21, 2017, http://adage.com/article/cmo -strategy/buy-reorganizes-marketing-team/308756/ (accessed December 17, 2017); Jeff Bullas, "How Best Buy Energized 170,000 Employees with Social Media," http://www.jeffbullas .com/how-best-buy-energized-170000-employees-with-social -media/ (accessed December 17, 2017); John Vomhof Jr., "Best Buy Scraps Twelpforce, Shifts Twitter Support to Geek Squad," *Minneapolis/St. Paul Business Journal*, May 7, 2013, https://www.bizjournals.com/twincities/news/2013/05/07/ best-buy-scraps-its-twelpforce.html (accessed December 17, 2017).

Management Control Systems

CHAPTER 15

Source: Sashkin/Shutterstock

Chapter Outline

Introduction
Control in Organizations
The Control Process
Forms of Management Control
Managing the Control Process

After reading this chapter, you will be able to:

- Define *management control* and explain why it is necessary.
- Examine the process through which managers develop and implement control.
- Distinguish among the various forms of control.
- Summarize the elements of effective control.
- Determine why control is sometimes met with resistance and how managers may overcome this resistance.
- Assess an organization's control program.

Coca-Cola Changes Controls to Adapt to Mexican Soda Tax

The country of Mexico is the biggest per capita consumer of soda in the world. The Coca-Cola Company controls 73 percent of the Mexican market for carbonated beverages, compared to 42 percent in the United States. Indeed, purchases in Mexico comprise about 5 percent of the company's overall global sales, a significant percentage for a company of Coca-Cola's global scope and magnitude. A strategy can achieve its desired results only if implemented properly. When actual performance is different from expectations, there are a number of causes for this difference. The external environment can change substantially and be a significant issue in implementation and control.

On the surface, Mexico seems like an ideal market for Coca-Cola, but significant health consequences have resulted from its citizens' preferences for sweeter beverages. Mexico has one of the highest death rates from diabetes of any of the 35 members of the Organization of Economic Cooperation and Development (OECD). About 15.8 percent of consumers in Mexico suffer from diabetes compared to the 7 percent OECD average. Also, according to Mexican government statistics, about 70 percent of adults in the country are overweight or obese, which ranks them number two in the world and 18.6 percent higher than the other OECD countries. To deal with this problem, the Mexican government introduced a special tax of 10 percent on sugary soft drinks and various sweetened packaged foods. Consumption of sugary drink purchases was reduced by 12 percent, whereas sales of water beverages increased. This change in the political environment is affecting planning and controlling mechanisms at Coca-Cola.

Coca-Cola has established itself in the country with ubiquitous billboards and signage in the streets and sporting events. Additionally, FEMSA, Coca-Cola's largest bottling facility, is located in Mexico. Disruption could therefore seriously impact Coca-Cola's presence in the country—and, due to its large market in Mexico, its financial bottom line as well. Coca-Cola also faces allegations from critics that it promotes unhealthy behaviors through sales of its soft drinks.

As a measure of controlling the deviation in its plan, the company has advertised with slogans such as "Movement = Happiness" in order to promote responsible drinking of its product. Another tactic Coca-Cola has taken is not to associate with the soft drink lobbyists who are trying to do away with the extra tax. This move might seem to be disadvantageous to Coca-Cola

Coca-Cola has begun to advertise with slogans such as "Movement = Happiness" in order to promote responsible drinking of their product.

from a financial standpoint. However, the company believes not opposing the tax will be perceived as a responsible move due to the influence the company has in the country. These actions could help Coca-Cola's reputation because it takes more of a triple-bottom-line approach by considering the social implications of its products. Coca-Cola also announced that it would invest $8.2 million in Mexico by 2020.

Unfortunately, to control its market share and pay the tax on its soft drinks, Coca-Cola FEMSA management must make some hard decisions. Prices for its drinks—and for sugary drinks across the board—increased. This in turn is impacting consumption of soda products. On a more positive note, Coca-Cola has been able to mitigate the decrease in soda purchases with an increase in sales of its bottled water and juice brands. The company is therefore focusing more on its other brands not subject to the tax. For instance, Coca-Cola's Ciel brand controls 19.4 percent of the bottled water market in Mexico (Pepsi's Epura brand controls 7.1 percent). This provides Coca-Cola with opportunities to expand its market reach. In 2017, Coca-Cola announced it would purchase the premium bottled water brand Topo Chico, a fast-growing brand sourced and bottled in Mexico. Coca-Cola hopes to expand sales of this brand into both the United States and Mexico. These changes in internal controls will ideally help the firm to cope with changing environmental conditions without significantly impacting the bottom line.[1]

Introduction

Coca-Cola is faced with adapting to and implementing organizational controls related to government concerns about population obesity and diabetes. Businesses throughout the world are constantly adopting organizational controls for and adapting to a wide range of issues. The word *control* sometimes conjures up images of a totalitarian state devoid of personal freedom where everything is preordained by a faceless, all-knowing, all-powerful being who often fails to have the best interests of those being controlled in mind. Consequently, individuals, in their roles as organizational employees, often resist being controlled and changing as situations merit. However, as we will discuss in this chapter, control is vital for efficient and effective organizational operations. The challenge to managers is to understand both the purpose and importance of control and to use it so that it does not infringe on employees' personal freedoms.

In this chapter, we explore management control systems. As you will see, control is closely associated with many of the other managerial functions discussed throughout this book. We begin by examining the nature of management control, including its purpose, importance, areas, responsibilities, and how it relates to planning. Next, we explore both the control process, as well as the various forms of control most important in organizations. Finally, we look at how to manage the control process and present some common ways in which to ensure its optimal implementation and use.

Control in Organizations

Any company, without effective control, has no way of knowing how well it is doing relative to its goals. **Management control** includes all activities an organization undertakes to ensure that its actions lead to achievement of its objectives. A **management control system** is a planned, ordered scheme of management control. It allows managers to readily assess where the firm actually is at a point in time relative to where it wants or expects to be. Managers at Coca-Cola will now have to adapt its sales goals in Mexico to new government regulations concerning its products. This is an example of the need to monitor changing external environmental trends.

Internal controls refer to processes that are developed to provide assurance that an organization reaches its objectives relating to operational efficiency, accuracy of financial reporting, and regulatory compliance.[2] Internal regulations within a business likely cover a wide range of issues. A company will likely have a per diem allowance for food when employees travel on company business. For example, an organization might have a limit of $85 per day, and individuals will not be reimbursed above this amount absent extenuating circumstances. Other internal controls will be designed to limit risk. For instance, a bank may allow any officer of the rank of vice president or above to approve a loan up to $10,000, but mandate that loans above this amount must be approved by multiple bank officers. Company financial budgets are also an important element of internal control.

management control: Includes all activities an organization undertakes to ensure that its actions lead to achievement of its objectives.

management control system: A planned, ordered scheme of management control that allows managers to readily assess where the firm actually is at a point in time relative to where it wants or expects to be.

internal controls: Processes that are developed to provide assurance that an organization reaches its objectives relating to operational efficiency, accuracy of financial reporting, and regulatory compliance.

The Importance of Control

All the good planning efforts and brilliant ideas in the world do little good if a firm has no system of management control. Control, therefore, is an essential part of effective organizational management. In today's dynamic, unpredictable global business world, control plays a more crucial role than ever before. Specifically, control helps an organization adapt to changing conditions, limits the magnification of errors, assists in dealing with increased complexity, and helps minimize costs. Walmart allegedly paid bribes to Mexican officials to expand stores. This resulted in a violation of the Foreign Corrupt Practices Act (FCPA). Walmart must increase its internal controls related to financial and regulatory matters to prevent similar acts of misconduct in the future.

Adapting to Changing Conditions

Change itself is about the only thing that can be predicted with any degree of certainty in turbulent markets. While change is inevitable, it is the nature of change that defies accurate forecasting. Who would expect a government to tax sugary soft drinks specifically? A properly designed management control system can allow managers to effectively anticipate, monitor, and respond to often constantly changing environmental conditions. Most firms monitor financial performance as a key quantitative control measure. A decrease in earnings per share would be a significant benchmark for adjustment. But some things, like employees being killed on the job, may be much harder for companies to adapt to than a quarterly miss on company earnings per share.

Limiting the Magnification of Errors

Generally, a small error or mistake does not adversely affect organizational operations. However, a small error or mistake left uncorrected—perhaps one undetected as a result of a lack of control—may be magnified with the passage of time, eventually harming the whole company. For example, a report that underestimates the number of product defects within a manufacturing company may easily lead to perpetuation of a flawed production system, and, with time, tarnish the organization's image. An effective management control system would enable production managers to pinpoint the problem before further damage is done.

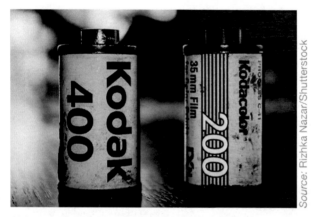

Although Kodak had started developing its digital photography business in the 1970s, it was slow in putting any internal emphasis on this operation since its traditional film business was considered too profitable.

Dealing with Organizational Complexity

Today's businesses must contend not only with an increasingly complex external environment, but with increasing internal complexity as well, particularly in highly diversified or rapidly growing organizations. For example, for many decades the Eastman Kodak Corporation had a virtual monopoly in the U.S. photographic film business—in the late 1970s controlling nearly 90 percent of this business. The phrase "A Kodak Moment" became part of the American lexicon. However, Kodak did not take seriously the threat in the film business from the Fuji Company of Japan. Moreover, although it had started developing its digital photography business in the 1970s, it was slow in putting any internal emphasis on this operation (its traditional film business was considered too profitable). Its delayed response hurt the firm, and by the year 2000, Kodak was struggling. It fired its CEO and began a broad corporate restructuring too late. In 2012, the venerable Kodak Company, started in the late 1800s by George Eastman, filed for bankruptcy. Today, having recently emerged from the bankruptcy process, the firm is only a shell of its former self, and is in the digital printing and graphics business.

Minimizing Costs

A properly designed system of control can often allow a firm to enjoy considerable cost reductions. For example, Seattle-based Boeing, the world's leading aircraft manufacturer, fairly recently announced that it intended to cut the cost of designing and building a plane by no less than 25 to 30 percent. Boeing proposed to accomplish this objective by designing and implementing a more efficient system of control over the company's $8 billion inventory stock, including adopting the just-in-time inventory management concept. After a few years, Boeing's tighter control helped it reduce inventory stocks by $700 million. More recently the firm has announced plans to reduce costs through decentralizing certain business functions, reducing supplier costs, and expanding service revenue (service revenue is usually more profitable than production).[4] This is an example of an internal control that helps the firm achieve its objectives.

Safety and Control Standards at SeaWorld

All organizations require control systems to regulate organizational activities to maintain performance at acceptable levels. An organization has to adapt to changes in the environment, as well as deviations that occur in internal operations. Control can focus on any area of an organization, and the following incident at SeaWorld Orlando illustrates the need for vigilance in setting standards and taking corrective action.

Historically, the "Dine with Shamu" show at the 11 different SeaWorld amusement parks was a big-time attraction. The interaction between trainers and killer whales drew millions of visitors to the theme parks annually. However, in 2010, Dawn Brancheau, a 40-year-old SeaWorld Orlando trainer, was drowned by the whale Tilikum (Tili) toward the end of a show.

What exactly happened remains unclear. Some have argued that the trainer might not have been careful enough. Animal rights activists have asserted that holding killer whales in captivity is an inherent recipe for disaster. Others, including the U.S. Occupational Safety and Health Administration (OSHA), placed the blame on SeaWorld, stating that the amusement park should have had more controls in place to protect its trainers. OSHA felt, in part, that SeaWorld thought it could accurately predict the behavior of the killer whales, when the evidence for this was not compelling.

Government regulators also felt that past issues involving Tili should have put SeaWorld on special notice. For example, the 12,000-pound whale had at least partially contributed to the deaths of two other people, one of them a trainer at Sealand in British Columbia, Canada. Nevertheless, SeaWorld Orlando purchased him in 1992, and he became a major hit at the amusement park.

Given Tili's past, one might ask why trainers were allowed in the water with him. Tili also resumed performing 13 months after Brancheau's death. However, OSHA ruled that while SeaWorld Orlando committed serious safety violations, its violations were not "willful." SeaWorld was ordered to pay $12,000 in fines.

SeaWorld has undergone some major adaptations since Brancheau's death. First, it suspended in-water interactions between the trainers and the whales. Instead of riding on, hugging, and being thrust into the air by the whales while in the water, trainers today deal with the whales from out of the water, usually standing behind physical barriers. New walkways were built around

How the entertainment parks will adapt to the competing goals of pleasing their patrons and maintaining safety is a challenge that SeaWorld must constantly address.

the Shamu stadium, and trainers started wearing safety vests. A later settlement at the San Diego park also regulated how close trainers could be to the pool's edge and when trainers could safely touch the whales.

Today's "Dine with Shamu" show, however, is less exciting than in the past. Initially, SeaWorld argued for getting the trainers back into the water with the whales, saying it had new safety protocols that can more effectively protect trainers while they are interacting with the whales. On the other hand, critics pointed out that dangerous conditions will always exist when interacting up close with such large and unpredictable animals. A documentary called *Blackfish* further solidified public opinion against the breeding of orcas in captivity. SeaWorld announced that it would stop breeding orcas in captivity and that the generation of orcas currently at SeaWorld would be its last.

Although SeaWorld has announced it would no longer breed orcas in captivity, its safety controls remain crucial in protecting the well-being of employees. Like all companies, SeaWorld must take into account the safety of its employees, and these controls take on greater importance when working with unpredictable animals. How the entertainment parks will adapt to the competing goals of pleasing patrons and maintaining safety is a challenge that SeaWorld must constantly address. Workplace safety should be a high priority in setting standards and taking corrective action to minimize risks employees face in their performance of job activities.[3]

Responsibilities for Control

Traditionally, managers have been responsible for the control process. Most large organizations employ individuals, often called *controllers* (also comptrollers), whose chief responsibility is to coordinate and supervise financial and other control activities. Recent developments in management practices, however, have led to more sharing of responsibility for control activities with lower-level employees. For example, increasing degrees of employee empowerment—allowing operational-level employees more input into organizational policies and procedures—are intended to take advantage of the fact that the people who actually do the work know it better than anyone else does. These workers, especially those with lengthy and specialized experience, can contribute innovative ideas and other useful input about how best to get things done that others not so intimately familiar with the operations processes could not provide.

Ironically, increasing control and control-related responsibilities at lower levels may create the need for still more control. Managers at one of Corning Corporation's ceramics plants, for example, grouped production workers into teams and gave them new authority to decide, among other things, how production should be scheduled—a form of control in itself. Contrary to their expectations, however, management found that worker performance declined and that a general state of confusion prevailed over the new system. On investigation, they found that the solution lay in more control in the form of additional employee training. Corning management had empowered employees to say how things should be done, but failed to prepare them for that power or for the resulting working environment. After a training program was implemented and workers were allowed to get used to the new system, performance increased, waste declined, and product defects were significantly reduced.[5]

The Link between Planning and Controlling

For control to be effective, it must be integrated with planning so that managers can readily compare actual results with planned projections. Moreover, the ability to control activities must be considered during the planning process. When developing marketing plans, for example, marketing managers should focus not only on measurable performance criteria such as sales and market share to facilitate effective management control, but also on performance in terms of more subjective and difficult-to-quantify criteria such as company image and employee morale. Although these criteria are less quantifiable than other performance measures, they are controllable and should be closely managed.

The relationship between planning and controlling continues as a long-term cycle. Managers make plans and then use control to evaluate the effectiveness of organizational activities relative to those plans. For example, the Patient Protection and Affordable Care Act (ObamaCare) required many organizations to reexamine their health plan programs and make adjustments in this important benefit to employees. If the control system indicates that things are proceeding as they should, the current plan should be maintained. However, managers may find the firm is not making adequate progress, in which case, they should revise the current plan. Or, the control system may indicate that the situation—for example, the competitive or economic environment—has changed, warranting the development of a new plan.

The Control Process

The control process consists of four basic steps: establishing performance standards, measuring performance, comparing performance against standards, and evaluation and corrective action (Figure 15.1). The dotted lines in the figure indicate feedback communication.

Establishing Performance Standards

performance standards: The first step in the control process; targets set by management against which actual performance is compared at a future date.

The first step in the control process is to establish **performance standards**, targets set by management against which actual performance is compared at a future date. Without such standards, managers cannot accurately gauge the effectiveness of the company's efforts. For example, management consulting, technology, and outsourcing firm Accenture made a commitment to reduce carbon emissions per employee by 35 percent its 2007 baseline.[6] Accenture managers will use these performance standards as benchmarks to track the effectiveness of the company's ongoing efforts toward carbon emission reduction.

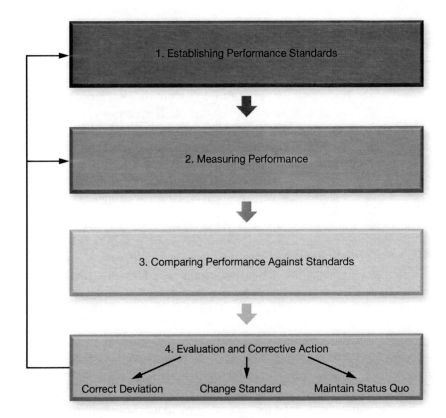

FIGURE 15.1
The Control Process

1. Establishing Performance Standards

2. Measuring Performance

3. Comparing Performance Against Standards

4. Evaluation and Corrective Action

Correct Deviation   Change Standard   Maintain Status Quo

Ideally, performance standards will be closely related to organizational goals. Like goals and objectives, performance standards should be stated in very clear, easily measurable terms, and they should be realistic given both the internal and competitive environment in which the organization operates.

Performance standards should also reflect organizational strategy and therefore be expected to vary widely among organizations and even internally within a particular organization with respect to different products or markets. A well-established market leader such as Procter & Gamble might set performance standards related to maintaining its market-share leadership position in each of the many product categories in which it competes, while a smaller, less well-known company might set standards related to gaining initial entry and acceptance in a limited number of geographical markets. In international markets where Procter & Gamble is not a market leader to such an extensive degree, its performance standards are likely to reflect different strategic considerations. For instance, the company might set a performance standard for a "new" brand of shampoo introduced in Peru to attain a 4 percent market share in the first six months, even though the same shampoo has long led the domestic market—where the standards reflect the company's objective to maintain its relative competitive position. Similarly, Coca-Cola may have to adjust its market share goals in Mexico somewhat lower (i.e., below the current 5 percent) given government policies. Thus, as Coca-Cola's situation in Mexico illustrates, control standards must reflect marketplace realities to facilitate meaningful comparisons with actual performance.

Measuring Performance

The second step in the control process is measuring actual performance in the context of the specific activities that management wishes to control. In most organizations, this assessment occurs continually. For example, if a company establishes as a performance standard a certain maximum acceptable product defect rate, managers must measure the rate continually to ensure that all products fall below it.

It is sometimes difficult to measure performance accurately. For example, a pharmaceutical company such as Amgen, which concentrates its efforts on relatively "high-risk"

Performance evaluation calls not only for quantitative and diagnostic skills, but also for subjective yet crucial decision making.

Source: Denis Rozhnovsky/Shutterstock

drugs in many developing fields of medicine that some of its competitors often avoid, may spend years developing and testing a potential product that may never actually make it to the market. Although it can be difficult to measure performance in such a case, a valid method must be developed to facilitate effective control. The company might measure performance by looking at reviews and testing done on its ongoing projects by other scientists or medical associations, or it could consider performance in terms of successfully combatting individual symptoms of certain diseases in the laboratory, regardless of whether the drug gets to the market.

Comparing Performance against Standards

The third step in the control process involves comparing measured actual performance against the standards established in step one. Actual performance may match the performance standard exactly, or it may be higher or lower than the target. Management must decide how much deviation from standards will be tolerated before considering corrective action. In some cases, this decision is quite straightforward. If Procter & Gamble sets a standard of being the market-share leader in each product category in which it competes, then it is easy to determine if it has met that standard. In other situations, the decision may not be nearly so simple. If Amgen sets standards for a drug related to combatting specified symptoms of a disease, and the drug fails to meet those standards but receives a number of unexpected positive reviews from experts in the scientific community, Amgen may decide that it has made acceptable progress anyway. Or, a sales manager might find that while an annual sales increase of 10 percent falls short of the 12.5 percent performance standard, no action is warranted because of unexpected environmental circumstances—such as the surprise introduction of a strong competitive product—during the measurement period or new government regulation/taxes. Managers should be constantly aware that unforeseen conditions that may influence control decisions can occur at any time.

Evaluating Performance and Taking Corrective Action

In the final step of the control process, managers evaluate actual performance relative to standards and then take appropriate action. Performance evaluation calls not only for quantitative and diagnostic skills, but, as already mentioned in the previous step, also for subjective yet crucial decision making. Before deciding how to respond to deviations between performance standards and actual performance, managers in charge of control must determine the reason(s) for the deviation. Specifically, they must determine whether the plan previously laid out was properly implemented and failed to work, or if it was not implemented properly. As illustrated in Figure 15.1, once managers have evaluated the firm's performance, they must decide which of three basic options is the appropriate response: correct the observed deviation, change the performance standards, or simply maintain the status quo. Table 15.1 highlights these different options.

TABLE 15.1 Evaluating Performance and Action

Options for Evaluating Performance	Examples
Correct the Deviation	Provide better customer service training
Change Standards	Set a lower sales goal
Maintain the Status Quo	Keep the current product defect standard

Correct the Deviation

When actual performance deviates significantly from the performance standard, managers will ordinarily take steps to correct the discrepancy. For example, faced with a higher-than-acceptable number of customer complaints, managers at a service firm such as McDonald's may decide, after careful investigation, that certain employees or groups of employees need additional customer service training. Corrective action may be called for when performance standards have been exceeded as well. For example, a restaurant that easily surpasses its profit or number-of-customer-related performance standards may decide to expand physical facilities, increase hours of operation, or even raise menu prices in an attempt to bring actual performance more in line with standards.

Change Standards

A second option available when there is a discrepancy between actual performance and the performance standard is to change the initial performance standards. This option is the likely choice when observation of actual performance leads managers to conclude that the original standards were unrealistic given environmental conditions. Standards may have been set too low or too high, requiring modification for future control activities to be effective.

Nintendo's introduction of its Wii console in 2006 was so popular that it sold out with each new shipment. The consoles were popular throughout the world. However, Nintendo did not realize how popular the Wii consoles would be in the United Kingdom. In 2007, Nintendo estimated that it would sell 14 million units. Toward the end of the year, it adjusted the figure to 17.5 million units. Even these new standards were not sufficient to keep up with demand. European customers—particularly those who had pre-ordered the Wii console in advance for Christmas—were frustrated after Nintendo was not able to ship enough to the stores in the area.[7] Years later Nintendo's latest Wii console, the Wii U, faced similar shortage problems.[8] Such an unexpected success requires that managers increase future performance standards to more realistic and challenging levels for effective control; otherwise, the passive standards may encourage suboptimal performance when objectives are achieved far too easily. On the other hand, if the Wii had not fared so well, Nintendo managers might have had to decrease future performance standards.

Maintain the Status Quo

When performance standards are either met or nearly met, maintaining the status quo—the current course of action—may be the best response. If production managers set an optimistic performance standard of a 50 percent decrease in product defects, and actual performance indicates a 48 percent reduction, the company has obviously made significant progress. Maintaining current production control policies and procedures is generally the proper course of action to take in such a case. Moreover, managers should reward employees for "a job well done," and otherwise encourage them to continue on their current course of action.

Forms of Management Control

In this section, we will look at three levels of control—organizational, operations, and strategic—and then discuss financial control techniques. **Organizational control** oversees the overall functioning of the whole firm. It is a broad-based form of control that guides all organizational activities. The two dominant forms of organizational control are bureaucratic and clan control. While some companies adopt one form to the complete exclusion of the other, most exhibit characteristics of both forms with one exerting noticeably more influence than the other. Figure 15.2 illustrates the characteristics of and differences between the two forms of organizational control.

Bureaucratic Control

Bureaucratic control, sometimes called hierarchical control, attempts to control the firm's overall functioning through formal, mechanistic structural arrangements. It seeks

organizational control: A broad-based form of control that guides all organizational activities and oversees the overall functioning of the whole firm.

bureaucratic control: Attempts to control the firm's overall functioning through formal, mechanistic structural arrangements; sometimes called hierarchical control.

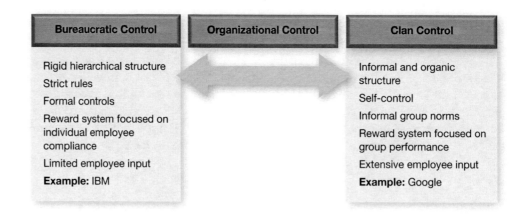

FIGURE 15.2
Forms of Organizational Control

Bureaucratic Control — Organizational Control — Clan Control

Bureaucratic Control
Rigid hierarchical structure
Strict rules
Formal controls
Reward system focused on individual employee compliance
Limited employee input
Example: IBM

Clan Control
Informal and organic structure
Self-control
Informal group norms
Reward system focused on group performance
Extensive employee input
Example: Google

to gain employee conformance through strict administration of rigid, straightforward policies and procedures, and its reward system focuses on individual employee compliance with either an implied or formal, written code of behavioral standards. As such, bureaucratic control allows limited employee input into organizational activities.

Although its corporate culture has become much less bureaucratic in recent years, IBM Corporation was for many years known for exhibiting strong bureaucratic control tendencies. As stated by one former IBM sales representative, the longstanding traditional dress for male managers at IBM was ". . . a dark blue pinstriped suit with a freshly starched white shirt; a conservative, striped tie—with the stripes pointing to the heart; and heavy, polished, black wing-tip shoes."[9] Using its formal control system, IBM was able to develop such a distinctive, respected, and effective way of conducting business that countless organizations copied it, with varying degrees of success, down nearly to the very last detail.

Clan Control

clan control: Seeks to regulate overall organizational functioning through reliance on informal, organic structural arrangements; also referred to as decentralized control.

Clan control, also referred to as decentralized control, seeks to regulate overall organizational functioning through reliance on informal, organic structural arrangements. It tries to foster strong employee commitment by vigorously encouraging employee input and group participation. Rather than setting strict behavioral standards as in bureaucratic control systems, clan control relies on self-control and informal group norms to *effectively* create a relaxed yet sharply focused working environment.

Google has been recognized for its relatively informal, easygoing, clan-controlled atmosphere. Google has traditionally allowed employees to take work time to focus on their own individual projects. The corporate headquarters (Googleplex) has a variety of benefits, including free meals, arcade games, and a fitness center. Google desires to give its employees freedom to design a working environment in which they feel most comfortable and best able to function productively. Google's rapid rise to the top of its industry and its long-term stay there can be attributed in no small part to its effective use of clan control.

Bureaucratic or Clan Control?

Although one form of organizational control is not necessarily "better" than the other, managers should keep several issues in mind when deciding on what form to apply. First, companies seldom use one form of organizational control to the complete exclusion of the other. For example, the formerly highly bureaucratic IBM always permitted some employee participation, and Google, the classic example of a company exhibiting clan control, has formal rules that employees must follow. Second, control that is too bureaucratic may result in employee alienation as well as failure to recognize and use potentially good ideas often better generated in a more informal setting. Third, control that is too clan-oriented might result in an organization with no idea where it is going or one heading in so many different directions that it fails to accomplish anything. Finally, consistency of control orientation is vital. Not only will employees resist drastic change—especially to extreme bureaucratic control—but, after working under one form of organizational control, they may have a hard time adjusting to a change in control. If Google were to decide suddenly to move to a more radically bureaucratic form of control, managers and subordinates used to the more informal atmosphere would likely have great difficulty adapting to the change.

Operations Control

Operations control regulates one or more individual operating systems within an organization. Most companies practice three basic forms of operations control—preliminary, screening, and feedback—with the forms differentiated primarily by the focus of the control itself. Operations will be discussed in greater detail in Chapter 16.

operations control: Regulates one or more individual operating systems within an organization.

Preliminary Control

Preliminary control (sometimes also referred to as feed-forward or steering control) monitors deviations in the quality and quantity of the firm's resources to try to prevent deviations before they enter the system; its focus is on inputs to the good or service production process. In the area of human resources, for example, preliminary control techniques include employee selection, placement, and, where it occurs before formal employment, training of newly hired personnel. Such activities help management eliminate job candidates who are unsuitable for the company's needs. Other preliminary control techniques include inspection of incoming materials used in the production process, as well as capital and financial budgeting—financial control techniques that will be dealt with in more detail later.

preliminary (or feed-forward or steering) control: Monitors deviations in the quality and quantity of the firm's resources to try to prevent deviations before they enter the system; its focus is on inputs to the product or service production process.

Nowhere is the importance of preliminary control more important than in the total quality management (TQM) movement. Although TQM focuses on achieving superior levels of quality and customer value at all levels of the operations process, high-quality inputs are essential for overall organizational quality because they reduce the need for costly inspections (i.e., feedback control) and allow managers to pay more attention to quality problems occurring within internal firm operations.[10] This helps explain why so many organizations have consistently been reducing the number of suppliers of parts and materials to the production process, while at the same time building deeper and more permanent relationships with those vendors they retain.[11]

Screening Control

Screening control (also called yes/no or concurrent control) regulates operations to ensure that they are consistent with objectives; the focus is on the transformation process that converts inputs into outputs. Managers supervising the work of their subordinates, for example, are exerting screening control to ensure that employees' activities will result in achievement of objectives. Delegation of authority provides managers with the power to use both financial—pay raises and promotions or demotions—and nonfinancial—praise or verbal reprimand—incentives to carry out screening control.

screening (or yes/no or concurrent) control: Regulates operations to ensure that they are consistent with objectives; the focus is on the transformation process that converts inputs into outputs.

In addition to supervisory direction, screening control includes quality and production control measures such as ongoing training programs designed to update continually the skills and knowledge of both managers and non-managers. These programs serve as control in that well-trained employees consistently require less formal supervision and control by other means as compared to their less-trained counterparts. The rapid pace of change, caused by technological advances and an increasingly global business environment, has made training-based control programs more popular. Some corporations run such programs on an in-house basis, while others contract with universities and other entities for such training.

Another form of screening control is statistical process control (SPC), which employs "control charts" such as the one depicted in Figure 15.3 to continuously track performance variation over time. The charts provide employees with readily accessible information with which to monitor their work and predict when they are about to exceed control limits and possibly waste organizational resources. Developed by Walter Shewart at Bell Labs

statistical process control (SPC): Another form of screening control which employs "control charts" to continuously track performance variation over time.

FIGURE 15.3

Hypothetical Statistical
Process Control Chart
of the Manufacturing
Process of Steel
Castings

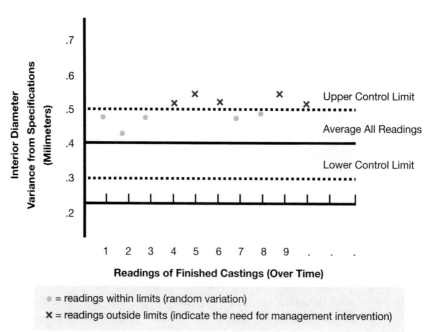

Readings of Finished Castings (Over Time)

● = readings within limits (random variation)
✗ = readings outside limits (indicate the need for management intervention)

in the 1930s and later refined by W. Edwards Deming, SPC is a key TQM tool with which to explain the variation that inevitably occurs in every production process.[12] In short, SPC serves to determine whether work processes can effectively be brought under control or if they should be left alone, as well as when manager intervention is necessary.

According to Shewart, management intervention is called for only when the limits of random variation—that occurring strictly by chance—have been exceeded. Otherwise, the level of variance does not significantly affect the performance of the production process and should be left alone, at least for the time being and contingent upon ongoing SPC efforts.[13] Faced with the production process depicted in the SPC control chart in Figure 15.3, managers in charge of screening control should at least be concerned with the specific causes of the intermittent, nonrandom variation, and may want to take immediate action to bring the system back into control. As with all other forms of management control, SPC works best when those individuals being controlled understand the nature and purpose of the control process.

Feedback Control

feedback (or post-action) control: Monitors the firm's outputs, the results of the transformation process.

Feedback control (also known as **post-action control**) monitors the firm's outputs, the results of the transformation process. Feedback control techniques include: (1) the analysis of financial statements to evaluate the actual costs relative to expected (standard) costs through use of standard cost accounting systems, (2) quality control efforts to determine whether the manufacturing process is producing output of an acceptable quality level, and (3) employee performance evaluations to determine whether or not actual performance, in terms of productivity or number of errors, is acceptable. The results of these analyses are fed back into the operating system, where they then affect future output. If, for example, after completing a production run, a company's analysis of cost accounting data indicates that its manufacturing output has cost more than anticipated, management will be alerted to the situation and can take corrective action to prevent the costly deviation from recurring on future production runs.

Multiple Control Systems

In practice, most companies do not employ the three forms of operational control in isolation. Instead, most use a multiple control system, often using all three forms simultaneously to effectively achieve control of operating systems. For example, computer firms employ multiple control systems in assembling personal computers: Integrated circuits must conform to prescribed quality standards before being installed (preliminary control); various circuit configurations are tested during assembly (screening control); and the completed units are stringently tested before being packed for shipment, pinpointing or correcting operational errors in the system if necessary (feedback control).

In general, operations control methods employed earlier in the production process are less costly than those performed at later stages. For example, while concerned with minimizing deviations from quality standards at all stages in the production process, TQM focuses primarily on controlling the quality of various inputs to the system—i.e., on "doing things right the first time."[14] As we have said, companies have found that the costs associated with correcting mistakes already made far outweigh the costs of controlling initial product quality.[15] Errors first detected by feedback control not only cost the company in terms of product repair or replacement, but they also often result in high long-term costs associated with losing customers who experience poor product quality. When errors are detected early on in the production process by preliminary control, both the short-term and long-term costs associated with poor product quality can be avoided.

Strategic Control

The purpose of **strategic control** is to ensure that the organization effectively understands and responds to the realities of its environment. Effective strategy leads to the attainment of organizational objectives; effective strategic control should tell managers if their strategies are appropriate given the actual circumstances faced. Without strategic control, managers have no way of knowing—other than eventual goal attainment or failure—if their company is headed in the right direction. Conducting business in such "blind" fashion is sure to lead to less than optimal use of valuable organizational resources as well as missed competitive opportunities.

Effective strategic control is especially important for companies operating in highly complex and dynamic environments; they require more detailed, continuous control than those operating in more stable environmental conditions. For instance, high-technology companies such as General Electric are likely to place great emphasis on control techniques designed to stay abreast of industry developments that might affect organizational strategy or attainment of their strategic goals.

> **strategic control:** Ensures that the organization effectively understands and responds to the realities of its environment.

Financial Control

Pure financial control does not exist in the same sense as do operations, organizational, or strategic control, but control of financial resources is so closely related to the use of other resources that financial control is exercised, in part, through proper control in these other areas. For example, if a lack of control in purchasing results in the inefficient use of physical resources—perhaps by not having the right raw materials on hand when needed—the organization's financial resources will not have been used efficiently. Thus, it is important to understand techniques that companies commonly employ to control financial resources. Organizations typically use a number of financial control techniques, many of which are beyond the scope of this book. Here, we focus on the most commonly used and basic methods: budgetary control, analysis of financial statements, and financial audits.

> **budgeting:** The principal means of controlling the availability and cost of financial resources.

> **budgets:** Formal, written plans for future operations in financial terms.

Budgetary Control

The principal means of controlling the availability and cost of financial resources is through **budgeting**, the process of establishing formal, written plans—called **budgets**—for future operations in financial terms. Budgeting allows companies to anticipate and control financial resource needs. In a manufacturing company, for example, a cash-flow budget tracks and controls financial resource needs as the firm purchases materials, produces and inventories finished goods, sells goods, and receives cash for them.

There are two main forms of budgeting. **Operating budgeting** deals with relatively short-term financial control concerns, including having sufficient cash on hand to cover daily financial obligations such as routine purchases and payroll. Cash-flow budgeting, as described above, is a form of operating budgeting. In contrast, **capital budgeting** is

> **operating budgeting:** Deals with relatively short-term financial control concerns, including having sufficient cash on hand to cover daily financial obligations such as routine purchases and payroll.

> **capital budgeting:** Concerned with the intermediate and long-term control of capital acquisitions such as plants and equipment.

Budgeting allows companies to anticipate and control financial resource needs.

concerned with the intermediate and long-term control of capital acquisitions such as plants and equipment.

Companies have traditionally developed control budgets in one of three ways. With **top-down budgeting**, top managers establish budgets and hand them down to middle- and lower-level managers for review and implementation. Although top-down budgeting has the advantage of being able to take a broad, corporate perspective and is relatively quick and inexpensive because it involves relatively few people, it fails to consider the input of those employees closest to and most knowledgeable of actual work responsibilities. **Bottom-up budgeting**, on the other hand, flows up from lower levels of an organization for review by top management. Bottom-up budgeting involves those more directly engaged in the actual tasks covered by the budget; however, its disadvantage is the possibility that those same people may have a somewhat narrow view of their specific tasks, leading them to ignore the effects of their proposed actions on the overall organization. In practice, a form of negotiated budgeting is usually called for. As its name implies, **negotiated budgeting** involves a degree of give and take between upper and lower levels of management to develop the most appropriate form of budgetary control for a given situation.

Regardless of the type or process of budgeting in use, budgeting in general has both advantages and disadvantages as a form of financial control. Its advantages include the fact that it can lead to better coordination of organizational activities because the budgeting process often involves employees from various organizational areas, allowing conflicts to be discovered and discussed before they become actual problems. When done properly, budgetary control also serves as a means of bringing together diverse organizational members to determine overall objectives as well as a means of communicating these plans to the organization as a whole. Finally, in theory, budgeting, especially operating budgeting, implies a need for the organization to adapt continually in the face of constant environmental change.

Disadvantages of traditional budgeting as a means of control include the unavoidable fact that it is difficult to do. Managers must successfully allocate scarce organizational financial resources among many departments and subunits, all with projects that they feel are worthy of full organizational backing. Furthermore, in actual practice, budgeting often involves the extensive use of *incremental budgeting*, the process of merely adjusting the previous period's budget to arrive at the new plan of control. Overreliance on incremental budgeting greatly increases the probability that managers will fail to consider current—and likely changed—environmental conditions. Budgeting also suffers when it is used as a method of legitimizing current power structures, when upper-level managers slash or redistribute financial resources in order to reinforce their power—possibly "paying back" or "rewarding" a subordinate manager—rather than basing their decisions on matters more directly related to overall operational performance.

To overcome these disadvantages, many firms have turned to **zero-based budgeting (ZBB)**, a method of budgeting in which managers thoroughly reevaluate organizational activities to determine their true level of importance. The key elements of ZBB include identifying objectives, evaluating alternative means of accomplishing each activity, evaluating alternative funding levels (maintain current level or raise or lower levels), evaluating workload and performance levels, and establishing priorities.[16] As a form of financial control, ZBB forces managers to view budgeting as a true management process rather than a simple matter of recycling and adjusting the budget for the previous planning period. As a means of budgetary control, ZBB requires managers to reevaluate all activities

top-down budgeting: Top managers establish budgets and hand them down to middle- and lower-level managers for review and implementation.

bottom-up budgeting: Flows up from lower levels of an organization for review by top management and involves those more directly engaged in the actual tasks covered by the budget.

negotiated budgeting: Involves a degree of give and take between upper and lower levels of management to develop the most appropriate form of budgetary control for a given situation.

zero-based budgeting (ZBB): A method of budgeting in which managers thoroughly reevaluate organizational activities to determine their true level of importance.

to determine their true level of importance and resulting funding level as compared to alternative uses of limited financial resources. This thorough reevaluation of activities and alternative uses of financial resources gives ZBB its name: Everything is considered as if it is a completely new—zero-based—matter. Such an approach is especially appropriate for today's increasingly dynamic marketplace.

Regardless of how effective budgetary control may actually be, it should never be the sole means of a company's financial control. Overreliance on this one—or any other one—method of control may lead managers to ignore other pertinent information that can be uncovered only through the use of other financial control methods. By relying on several forms of financial control, a firm can discover trends through complementary and supportive information that pinpoints potential problems requiring management attention.

Financial Statements and Analysis

Financial statements allow a firm to classify the effects of the many varied transactions that occur in the course of conducting business. The two principal financial statements used in management control are balance sheets and income statements. The **balance sheet**, a snapshot of the organization's financial position at a given moment, indicates what the firm owns and what proportion of its assets are financed with its own or borrowed money. The **income statement**, which shows the profitability of an organization over a period of time—a month, a quarter, or a year—and helps managers focus on the organization's overall revenues (from sales and investments) and the costs incurred in generating those revenues. A detailed analysis of such statements helps management determine the adequacy of the organization's earning power and its ability to meet current and long-term obligations.

Analyzing balance sheets and income statements as a form of financial control answers two basic questions: (1) How much money did the organization make or lose? and (2) What is a measure of the organization's worth based on historical values found on the balance sheet? Using **ratio analysis**, managers take information from the two financial statements so that they can measure the company's efficiency, profitability, and sources of finances relative to those of other organizations. Ratio analysis allows an organization to determine its levels of liquidity and solvency. *Liquidity ratios* indicate an organization's ability to meet short-term (less than one year) debt obligations as they come due. Establishing minimum and maximum performance standards will serve to alert the organization that it has either too little or too much invested in liquid assets—those that can be converted into cash quickly. *Solvency ratios* allow a company to assess its ability to meet long-term obligations. The two ratios reflect the claims of creditors and owners on the organization's assets. Table 15.2 describes some common financial ratios used to measure an organization's financial health.

As previously mentioned, analysis of financial statements may occur as a form of feedback control, where managers use information provided in such statements to evaluate the organizational output—actual past performance—and to determine the need for changes in future resource acquisitions or operational activities. For example, after analyzing its income statement, Boeing Corporation might decide to employ an alternative supplier of a certain component part if it determines that the current supplier's products have generated less-than-optimal results; for another firm, higher-than-anticipated levels of defects in a current supplier's product, for example, may have reduced the profitability of a production process.

Financial Audits

A **financial audit** is a periodic and comprehensive examination of a firm's financial records. As a control technique, audits can tell managers whether the information on which they have been basing decisions has been accurate, a sort of "double-checking" technique of financial control. Audits may be internal, performed by the organization's own accounting staff, or external, done by qualified independent agencies. External auditing carries the advantage of objectivity; an outsider is unlikely to be so accustomed to the way that things are routinely done within an organization as to overlook common errors. Also,

balance sheet: A snapshot of the organization's financial position at a given moment; indicates what the firm owns and what proportion of its assets are financed with its own or borrowed money.

income statement: Shows the profitability of an organization over a period of time—a month, a quarter, or a year—and helps managers focus on the organization's overall revenues (from sales and investments) and the costs incurred in generating those revenues.

ratio analysis: Managers take information from the two financial statements (balance sheets and income statements) so that they can measure the company's efficiency, profitability, and sources of finances relative to those of other organizations.

financial audit: A periodic and comprehensive examination of a firm's financial records.

TABLE 15.2 Ratio Analysis

Liquidity Ratios		
Type of Ratio	*Equation*	*Description*
Current Ratio	Current Assets/Current Liabilities	Measures an organization's ability to pay short-term obligations
Quick Ratio	(Current Assets – Inventory)/Current Liabilities	How well an organization can meet its short-term obligations without selling its inventory
Solvency Ratios		
Debt to Equity Ratio	Total Liabilities/Shareholders' Equity	How much the organization is using its equity to finance its assets
Debt to Assets Ratio	(Debt × Total Liabilities)/Total Assets	How much the firm is financed by debt
Times Interest Earned Ratio	(EBIT)/Interest	Measures the safety margin of an organization with respect to the interest payments it must make to its creditors

Assets: Items of value a firm owns, such as cash, land and equipment, and intellectual property. Current assets are those that can be converted into cash within a year. Long-term assets are those that represent a commitment of at least one year. Inventory is a current asset, but it is harder to turn into cash than other types of current assets.
Liabilities: Debts the firm owes to others, such as bank loans and employee wages. Current liabilities are debts that must be paid within one year. Long-term liabilities are debts that have longer repayment terms.
Shareholders' Equity: Contains all of the money that has ever been contributed to the company and which the firm does not have to pay back. Stock is a form of shareholders' equity.
EBIT: Earnings before interest and taxes are paid out.
Interest: Fee paid by the borrower as compensation for using the lender's assets.

an external agency may be in better touch with new or innovative accounting methods and thus be better able to suggest alternative means of enacting more effective financial control. Additionally, an outside auditor is less likely to encounter a conflict of interest.

Nonfinancial Control

nonfinancial controls: Provide a company with a method to measure nonfinancial performance such as ethics and compliance activities as well as those related to sustainability.

Nonfinancial controls provide a company with a method to measure nonfinancial performance such as ethics and compliance activities as well as those related to sustainability. It is a way for a company to balance its behaviors and resulting impact on the communities it serves. Companies that focus solely on financial measures tend to be more consistently shortsighted because they make decisions based on the immediate fluctuations in the bottom line. Those that give equal weight to financial and nonfinancial measures alike have a long-term perspective of how their actions will impact others. Since the implementation of the Sarbanes-Oxley Act, regulators are increasingly asking for information other than financial measures to judge the character of a company's operations. Those who have instituted some form of nonfinancial accounting are looked well upon even when they become involved in financial or ethical violations. We will discuss two of the more popular nonfinancial control methods in the following section: the Balanced Scorecard and the triple bottom line.

Balanced Scorecard

Balanced Scorecard: A management control system customized for a company's industry, technology, mission, and strategy.

The **Balanced Scorecard** is a management control system customized for a company's industry, technology, mission, and strategy. The scorecard scores four categories: financial, customers, internal processes, and innovation and improvement activities. These

You're the Manager . . . What Would You Do?

THE COMPANY: Aerodyne Corporation
YOUR POSITION: Vice President of Ethics
THE PLACE: Bethesda, MD

Aerodyne Corporation is the fourth-largest aircraft manufacturer in the United States. Nearly 50 percent of Aerodyne's sales come from government contracts and the remainder from commercial airlines. Over the past ten years, airlines have experienced intense scrutiny as a result of labor problems, bankruptcies, consolidation, and plane crashes. Aerodyne has been the subject of two investigations that examined the use of defective parts and lack of quality control in certain aspects of the production process. In addition, Aerodyne has come under scrutiny because of expense padding on government contracts. These incidents probably occurred as a result of the company ignoring the potential impact of ethics training and control systems.

Tracy Reynolds was hired two years ago to head an ethics department, with the goal of establishing training systems for the entire company. Tracy's first step was to develop a comprehensive code of ethics, a formal statement of what the company expects in terms of ethical behavior from its employees. Following the development of the code of ethics, employees were provided training on the code's requirements. Additionally, employees were encouraged to report violations without any fear of retribution. A special 24-hour, 800-number, ethics hotline was installed to allow employees to ask anonymous questions about any issue or policy.

Tracy also helped establish systems to monitor compliance with federal procurement laws and installed procedures for the voluntary disclosure of violations to the appropriate authorities. Once these systems were in place, training was done on a region-by-region

Source: aapsky/Shutterstock

Aerodyne is no longer ignoring the potential impact of ethics training and control systems.

basis, with Tracy and her four assistants conducting three-hour seminars. Part of each seminar involved discussing ethical issues in the industry, situations that have plagued the company in the past, and procedures for avoiding unethical decisions. Many who reviewed the content of the ethics training seminars felt the frank group discussions of issues and dilemmas were perhaps the strongest part of the training. They helped employees recognize ethical issues and gave them outlets through which to obtain additional information to assist them in making ethical decisions.

QUESTIONS

1. How does the ethical program provide control for Aerodyne?

2. Defend the investment in training and development required by an ethics program.

3. What are the potential benefits of this program?

---

features are chosen by the manager and reflect a direct relationship with the company's overall strategy. The balance in the Balanced Scorecard comes from the measurement of both financial and nonfinancial aspects of the company's operations such that one complements the other. In this way, the Balanced Scorecard reveals the trade-offs resulting from the company's decisions, which allows managers to evaluate the future course of the company. In contrast to using only financial measures—which give a picture of the company's past—the Balanced Scorecard gives a picture of the company's current state and future performance with indications as to how to improve.[17]

Nike, Inc. uses the Balanced Scorecard for its social and environmental sustainability initiatives. The main focus for Nike in this area is in manufacturing. The scorecard is divided into three sections. The first measures lean manufacturing objectives such as physical changes to the production process, leadership capabilities, and employee empowerment. The second measures health, safety, and the environment by ensuring the company's code of conduct is being practiced so that factories are safe and operating at the highest energy-efficient levels. The third section relates to human resource management, or the treatment of employees. The scorecard is scored by a team from Nike as well as a team from a third party. This reduces bias, increases transparency, and provides balanced information for the company to evaluate.[18]

Triple Bottom Line

The **triple-bottom-line approach** (also known as people, planet, profit) focuses on the social, environmental, and economic impact of a company's operations equally and simultaneously. Usually, all of these aspects are integrated into each other and can be measured in different ways. Because measuring social and environmental initiatives is difficult, it is important for companies to standardize measurements validly and consistently.[19]

For example, actress Jessica Alba founded The Honest Company after realizing there was a shortage of non-toxic products for babies such as diapers, lotions, etc. She established the company with a mission that views social and environmental goals just as important as profits. The company has five methods of measuring their contribution to each goal. First, a portion of proceeds from products sold are donated to charities improving the health and social situations of children and families. Second, products are made from natural, organic, sustainably harvested, renewable, and pure raw materials. Third, materials are tracked so the company knows where they end up. Fourth, the company uses renewable sources of electricity. Finally, the company established a code of conduct for the supply chain to encourage humanitarian treatment of workers, as well as environmental and transparency standards.[20]

Source: patpitchaya/Shutterstock

The triple-bottom-line approach (also known as people, planet, profit) focuses on the social, environmental, and economic impact of a company's operations equally and simultaneously.

Many public companies do not post their Balanced Scorecard results for all to see since they directly correspond to the company's strategic roadmap. This is not the case for the triple bottom line, however. One indication that a company is employing the triple-bottom-line approach is that they apply to become a benefit corporation, or B corp. This certification from the nonprofit B Lab signifies that the companies are acting responsibly when it comes to impacting social, environmental, and economic conditions.[21]

Managing the Control Process

As with other processes occurring within a company, control must be carefully managed to be successful. To facilitate effective control, managers must understand how to develop the process as well as to overcome resistance to it. To ensure that control systems continue to operate in smooth fashion, managers must be able to identify signs of inadequate control.

Developing the Control Process

Because of differing circumstances faced by individual organizations, what makes the ideal control system for one is not necessarily appropriate for another. However, effective control systems are typically well-integrated with planning and are flexible, accurate, timely, and objective.

Integration with Planning

As we said earlier, if control is to be effective, it must be closely linked with the planning process. Specifically, managers must set objectives that may readily be converted into performance standards that will reflect how well plans are being carried out. For example, Boeing managers might set a performance standard of never holding more inventory than is necessary to complete outstanding orders in an effort to evaluate the effectiveness of the company's ongoing operations. Such standards represent an attempt not merely to save a certain amount of money, but also to meet the company's goal of reducing costs. Such a close link with planning ensures that efforts at increased control may be easily and accurately evaluated in terms of meeting organizational objectives.

Flexibility

Flexibility is an important factor in the development of an effective management control system to allow the company to respond to changes in the business environment. The more turbulent or complex the environment, the more flexible the control system should be. For example, consider a manufacturing organization such as Xerox (copiers and other office automation equipment) that employs a complicated, multistep production system incorporating hundreds or even thousands of raw materials or component parts. Because each step in the production process must follow the successful completion of the previous step, the production control system must be able to monitor and manage each successive step in the process. Likewise, inventory control must account for current and expected levels for each of a multitude of parts and materials. If changes occur in either the production process or the required quantity of materials needed—perhaps due to new technology or changing consumer demand—control must be flexible enough to readily accommodate modifications while remaining effective. Inventory control will be discussed in greater detail in Chapter 16.

Accuracy

Control systems are useful only to the extent that the information on which they rely (and therefore produce) is accurate. Just as with management information systems, system output can be only as good as system input. If a quality control system somehow permits workers an opportunity to hide product defects, the control system is useless because it cannot accurately measure or report on what it is supposed to.

Timeliness

An effective management control system provides performance information when it is needed. In general, the more uncertain and unstable the situation, the more often information will be needed. Marketing managers, for example, will require control-related information pertaining to the sales performance of a new product much more often than they will need such information on a mature, stable product that has been on the market for several years. For instance, a few years ago Microsoft wanted to develop a tablet to compete against the iPad. To compete, marketing managers at Microsoft would have required more information at shorter intervals than they would have for more established products. The firm needed to find out how it could improve upon the iPad and provide customers with features they most desired. Ultimately, Microsoft was successful in developing a very competitive new product.[22]

Objectivity

To be effective, the control system must provide unbiased information. The manager who plays favorites with certain subordinates and "lets them off the hook" by submitting information that does not reflect actual performance deficiencies does no one, including the organization as a whole, any favors. If production workers allow defective products to slip through the system, bypassing control, not only might the company's image suffer as consumer complaints surface, but the production unit deemed responsible for the errors may be unfairly reprimanded. Moreover, objective, control-related information calls for managers to assess qualitatively the information they receive. Rather than simply report unusually high sales figures for a region or individual salesperson, a sales manager should look beyond the numbers into how the sales were made. It could be that drastic and unauthorized price concessions or unrealistic guarantees were provided to buyers in hopes of gaining sales. Information pertaining to such deviations must be uncovered and reported in detail to facilitate effective management control.

Source: Pieter Beens/Shutterstock

When Microsoft wanted to develop a tablet to compete against the iPad, their marketing managers would have required more information at shorter intervals than they would have for more established products.

TABLE 15.3 Reasons for Resistance to Control

	Examples
Overcontrol	The manager of an engineering department insists on being a part of every project, including the small ones.
Inappropriately focused control	An accountant is rewarded for getting a major business account finished by the deadline, although he had to skip sections of the audit.
Controls that award inefficiency	A consultant must fill out an hour of paperwork just to file a short report.
Creation of enhanced accountability	Employees are angry because they have been told their computers are being monitored.

Understanding Resistance to Control

Implementation of new control systems often implies modified management philosophies as well as new responsibilities for organizational workers. As with other forms of change, such alterations of control systems are likely to be met with resistance. Additionally, common perceptions of control as a force restraining individual or group action add to the likelihood of employee resistance. In short, managers charged with developing a control system should recognize that employees may resist control. While some employees may be less likely to resist change than others because of personal factors such as what might be called a "zone of indifference," or differing levels of acceptance of authority, common reasons for resistance to control include overcontrol, inappropriately focused control, control that rewards inefficiency, and the creation of enhanced accountability. Table 15.3 describes these in more detail.

Overcontrol

The issue of the appropriate level of control to apply is situational in nature. Levels that might seem overly aggressive or restrictive for management of a team of administrative office workers may very well be essential to the effective control of a sports team or military unit. However, a fine line often exists between the proper level of control and overcontrol, and companies sometimes try to control employees' activities more than they should. For example, an organization that explicitly tells its employees what to wear, when to eat, what social media they can use, and what they can and cannot generally do during their free time away from the workplace is likely to experience employee resistance to such overly aggressive practices.

Most employees recognize that control is necessary to the regulation of activities directly related to job performance. In fact, it is the responsibility of management to make sure that this understanding exists.[23] However, when control creeps into the realm of non-job-related behavioral matters, many employees may feel that the organization is overstepping its bounds. Some people, for example, argue that random testing for employee drug or alcohol use is wrong because they feel that companies should not be able to tell them what to do in their free time unless it has a direct, noticeable impact on actual work performance. One general problem today, though, is that the lines between on-duty work requirements and some off-duty activities can sometimes be blurred.

Managers must carefully balance the level of control against both situational demands and employee rights. Control for the sake of controlling workers will likely be unproductive from a long-term perspective; it must be firmly founded in terms of actual and relevant job performance in a manner that makes sense to the person being controlled. Overcontrol will likely result not only in low employee morale and commitment, but also

Source: AC Rider/Shutterstock

Avoid production control systems that cause workers to feel they must sacrifice product quality to meet the system's quantity standards.

in mistrust and even legal hassles with labor-related regulatory agencies, rather than the improved organizational performance desired.

Inappropriate Focus

A production control system that places an extremely high priority on the number of units produced may result in workers who feel they must sacrifice product quality to meet the system's quantity standards. Not only will that company waste resources having to rework defective units, but it may also lose loyal customers who find substandard products. Firms can ill afford to place themselves in such situations, as research has found that it is increasingly more profitable for companies to retain loyal current customers by providing consistently high product quality than to recruit new customers through promotional efforts.[24]

Workers are much more likely to be motivated by a control system that seems to make sense. The principal means by which to achieve this ideal situation is to properly focus management control efforts. For example, a company's operations and financial control efforts might be supported by extensive training programs in which each and every employee learns to read financial statements and to understand the impact of his or her work activities on the company's profit structure. Also, employees can be given broad access to financial information. Only when control systems are focused on relevant issues in terms that clearly make sense to those being controlled can they be expected to function optimally.

Rewards for Inefficiency

A former product marketing manager for a major banking company told the authors of his disappointment over the bank's decision to reclaim and redistribute resources that had been earmarked for use in his department in the upcoming final quarter of the year. The manager felt that executive management had merely transferred the resources to another, less-efficient department that had already used up its allotted funds because it "needed" the money more than his department did. In effect, the department receiving the additional resources was rewarded for inefficient performance. The manager responded by structuring his department's budget for the following year so that all resources would be expended before the scheduled fourth-quarter executive budgetary review. While the manager's response may be understandable, it was a misguided strategy devised to counter an ineffective control system, resulting in inefficient use of scarce departmental resources. Regardless of the specific response in this case, a system of budgetary control that rewards inefficiency is likely to be met with resistance because it appears to be unfair, arbitrary, and, most importantly, nonsensical.

Accountability

Even properly designed control may be resisted because it creates additional levels of accountability. Effective control allows managers to pinpoint departmental or individual employee deficiencies. A worker who has been performing inefficiently is likely to resist a control system that shows that he or she is not performing up to standards. However, technological advances—such as the ability to monitor computer activities in the workplace—that may enhance a company's ability to monitor employees' activities and increase accountability have led to both employee abuse and worker concern and distrust. Managers must carefully consider the possible ethical implications of attempting to secure additional levels of accountability through increased control.

Overcoming Resistance to Control

Although employees may resist control because of, among other factors, management misuse, control remains a necessary managerial function. Without it, the organization is unlikely to achieve its objectives. The challenge to managers is to exercise control so that employees understand the need for control but are not unduly inconvenienced by it. In general, there are four things managers can do to overcome resistance to control: create effective control, encourage employee participation, and use both management by objectives (MBO) and a system of checks and balances.

Create Effective Control

Probably the best way to avoid resistance to control is to establish effective control in the first place. This requires both careful planning before implementation, as well as continual monitoring of the effectiveness of the control system, rather than simply doing what has always been done before or what works best for some other organization. Only with thorough planning and maintenance can a control system be properly integrated with overall organizational planning and be as flexible, accurate, timely, and objectively meaningful to those most directly controlled as it should be.

Encourage Employee Participation

More and more companies are realizing the benefits of allowing non-managerial employees increased say in the establishment of organizational policies and procedures. Such empowerment can be applied effectively to planning for and implementing a system of control, as employees are less likely to resist a system that they themselves helped to create.

Earlier, we mentioned the use of employee empowerment and increased control through additional levels of training at one of Corning Corporation's ceramics plants. In this instance, Corning managers worked closely with the plant's unionized assembly workers to jointly and radically change the way work was done. To control the level of

Employees are less likely to resist a system that they themselves helped to create.

product quality, they decided to eliminate 21 separate job classifications and replace them with one highly trained product specialist. Managers grouped most of the workers into teams and gave them authority to decide where machines should be placed, who should work on them, and how production should be scheduled. Corning's effort at increasing employee participation in the control process resulted in an increase in productivity and a decrease in product defects.[25]

Employee empowerment is a form of control in itself in that empowered employees who know their jobs better, have more responsibility, and exhibit higher levels of commitment simply need to be monitored—controlled—less. Although control in this manner is ordinarily considered in a positive light, some organizational management researchers question the motivation behind increased employee empowerment, arguing that modern quality control efforts in particular are little more than covert attempts on the part of management to extract as much labor as possible from employees with a minimum amount of supervision—that is, management effort. While perceptions such as these may be warranted in some cases, they can be avoided in other instances by carefully educating controlled employees about how the process works and how their work activities affect overall organizational performance.

Use MBO

Another way to overcome resistance to control may be through the use of management by objectives (MBO), a management philosophy based on converting organizational objectives into individual objectives. Working closely in concert with management, workers set their own goals, which in turn serve as standards against which to evaluate their actual performance. MBO assumes that allowing employees to set personal objectives will gain their commitment to those objectives, leading to increased performance. Also, employees know before starting work that they *will* be rewarded on the basis of how well they satisfy and maintain these personal goals and standards. Moreover, MBO links planning and control closely, lessening the likelihood that resistance to control *will* occur.

Use Checks and Balances

When properly employed, a system of checks and balances should provide documentation for managerial control decisions. For example, if a production worker is reprimanded for poor-quality work, a properly designed quality control system should provide information pertaining to the exact cause of the inadequate work. Resistance to control decreases because an effective system of checks and balances serves to protect employees as well as management. A reprimanded production worker, for example, should be able to refer to information provided by the control system to see if the cause of the poor-quality work is truly something under his or her control; the worker can use the system of checks and balances to "prove" his case and hopefully help correct the deviation should he or she not be directly at fault.

Signs of Inadequate Control Systems

In addition to understanding ways to overcome resistance to control, managers also need to be aware of the basic signs of a control system that is not operating effectively. Following are some indicators of possible control-related difficulty:

1. *A high incidence of employee resistance to control.* A control system that employees continually resist may simply not be right for the specific situation. This is likely to be the case after repeated attempts at either improving the control system or trying to explain or justify it to employees. It may be that employees consider the system excessive, or that the control is inappropriately focused. In this situation, managers must work closely with employees to determine the cause of the resistance and take appropriate action to remedy the situation.

2. *A unit meets control standards but fails to achieve its overall objectives.* In this case, it is likely that the link between planning and control is poor. If Boeing, for example,

Anytime an organization appears to be losing ground from a competitive or financial standpoint, it is wise to examine its control system.

meets its performance standard of reducing the cost of manufacturing aircraft by 25 to 30 percent but finds that it has not met its overall objective of making it more economical for customers to buy new planes instead of maintaining old ones, it is probable that the control standards established did not realistically reflect what it would take to meet the objective. Additionally, the control may be unable to measure what it is supposed to measure or perhaps is not being enforced stringently enough.

3. *Increased control does not lead to increased or adequate performance.* The extra control may simply not be needed or it may not be appropriate for the situation. Adding control where it is not needed runs the risk of alienating those controlled and should be avoided.

4. *The existence of control standards that have been in place for an extended period of time.* When an organization becomes stagnant in this day and age, it cannot remain competitive. As the environment inevitably changes, so should the organization and its system of management control. Changes in the U.S. health-care system and evolving federal mandates are requiring companies to continually update control mechanisms in this critical area.

5. *Organizational losses in terms of sales, profits, or market share.* Declining performance is a clear indicator of trouble. Anytime an organization appears to be losing ground from a competitive or financial standpoint, it is wise to examine its control system. Effective control should allow the company to pinpoint the cause of the problem before major losses occur. Inadequate control itself may have, as we saw earlier in the chapter, played a role in the downfall and ultimate bankruptcy of the venerable Eastman Kodak.

Although an essential managerial function, controlling the complex activities of organizational members is seldom a simple undertaking. The challenge to managers is to understand the purpose and importance of control, and to use it so that it does not infringe on employees' personal freedoms, but maximizes organizational performance. As part of this process, it is the responsibility of management to convey the need for control to employees in a manner that facilitates active and voluntary participation in the control process. For this ideal situation to occur, managers must structure and communicate the objectives of the process throughout the organization so that conforming to clearly defined control guidelines makes sense to those being controlled. Responsibility for control does not end after system implementation, nor does it involve the simple inspection of the output of the production process. Through control, managers must constantly look for sometimes hidden signs of inadequate performance at all stages and levels of organizational activity, and they must enact corrective action when warranted.

■ *Define* management control *and explain why it is necessary.* Management control includes all activities an organization undertakes to ensure that its actions lead to achievement of its objectives; a management control system is a planned, ordered scheme of management control. Internal controls refer to processes that are developed to provide assurance that an organization reaches its objectives relating to operational efficiency, accuracy of financial reporting, and regulatory compliance. Management control allows managers to readily assess where the firm actually is relative to where it wants or expects to be. It also serves to help an organization adapt to changing conditions, limit the compounding of errors, deal with increased complexity, and minimize costs.

■ *Examine the process through which managers develop and implement control.* The control process consists of four steps: establishing performance standards (targets set by management against which to compare actual performance at a future date), measuring performance, comparing performance against standards, and evaluating and taking corrective action. Should discrepancies occur between desired and actual performance, a firm can decide to correct the deviations, change the performance standards, or maintain the status quo.

■ *Distinguish among the various forms of control.* Four forms of control are organizational, operations, strategic, and financial. Organizational control regulates the overall functioning of the organization. It includes bureaucratic control (control through formal, mechanistic structural arrangements) and clan control (control through more informal, organic structural arrangements), which can be viewed as opposite levels of organizational control, though most firms make use of both to varying degrees. Operations control regulates one or more individual operating systems within an organization, and can be subdivided into preliminary, screening, and feedback control. Preliminary control monitors deviations in the quality and quantity of the organization's inputs with the objective of preventing deviations before they enter the system. Screening control regulates the transformation process to ensure that it is consistent with objectives. Feedback control monitors the firm's outputs. Strategic control ensures that the organization effectively understands and responds to the realities of its environment. Financial control includes budgeting (the process of establishing formal, written budgets for future organizational operations), analysis of financial statements (balance sheet and income statement), ratio analysis (measures of the company's efficiency, profitability, and sources of finances relative to those of other organizations using information provided by financial statements), financial audits (periodic and comprehensive examinations of a firm's financial records), and nonfinancial controls including tools such as the Balanced Scorecard and the triple-bottom-line approach.

■ *Summarize the elements of effective control.* Effective control systems are well-integrated with planning and are flexible, accurate, timely, and objective. Most importantly, control systems should make sense to those individuals being controlled.

■ *Determine why control is sometimes met with resistance and how managers may overcome this resistance.* Common reasons for resistance to control include overcontrol, inappropriately focused control, control that rewards inefficiency, or control that results in enhanced accountability. To overcome resistance to control, managers may create effective control from the outset, encourage employee participation, and employ both management by objectives and a system of checks and balances. Often, workers must be educated about the purpose and function of control, as well as about how their activities relate to control objectives.

■ *Assess an organization's control program.* Based on the material presented in the "Business Dilemma" box and throughout this chapter, evaluate the vice president's efforts to control Aerodyne's ethical decision making. You should be able to describe the forms of control being used and address how these efforts will help improve the organization's performance.

Key Terms and Concepts

Ready Recall

1. Why is control important? What do you think would happen without it?
2. Why must control be closely integrated with organizational planning?
3. List the four steps in the control process.
4. List and define the four types of control. How do organizational, operations, and strategic types of control differ from one another? How do they relate?
5. Differentiate between bureaucratic and clan organizational control. Which is the better form of control?
6. How does operating budgeting differ from capital budgeting?
7. How is a financial audit used for purposes of control?
8. What are some common reasons for resistance to control?
9. How can managers combat resistance to control? What is the most important factor in this process?
10. How can managers recognize inadequate control systems?

Expand Your Experience

1. Take a look at your own place of employment (if you are not employed, apply the question to your college or university). Who is responsible for the control function? Cite specific examples of the four forms of control used in your workplace.
2. How effective are control systems that are based on meeting objectives stated in the same terms for both the finance and production departments? Why might control of this nature prove less than optimal? How would you alter the system to be more meaningful for the individual functional departments?
3. Analyze the control system of a local small business (you may have to interview some managers and employees to get enough information). Identify examples of each of the forms of control as practiced within the company. Is the control system adequate? Why or why not? If you judge the control to be inadequate, make some recommendations for improving it.

Strengthen Your Skills

Controlling

Instructions:

Read the following scenario and apply the concepts of the triple-bottom-line approach to Tamboran's control systems, which are designed to direct a company's actions toward its goals. Tamboran is an innovative explorer for hydrocarbon shale gas in onshore basins that tries to be ethical in its practices.

Scenario:

Companies that emphasize the triple bottom line in their operations focus on social, environmental, and financial concerns. Companies often refer to the state of their bottom line, which means that they are concerned about the health of their profits. The decisions these companies make are often based on the extent to which their profits are affected by these decisions. The triple bottom line, on the other hand, measures the impact the decisions have on social and environmental concerns in addition to profits. These additional factors are a form of nonfinancial auditing. This approach is especially important for companies whose activities can be seen as controversial.

Tamboran is a company that specializes in alternative energy resources such as hydraulic fracturing or fracking, and it incorporates a triple-bottom-line approach to its methods. Fracking is the process of using a high-powered mixture of water and rocks or chemicals to fracture the areas where natural gas is abundant in order to release and capture the gas. This process is viewed by many as harmful to the environment and those living in the areas where drilling occurs. The use of millions of gallons of water as well as the use of certain chemicals do create environmental and health concerns. However, others claim that fracking is a better alternative to traditional oil drilling. Furthermore, the use of natural gas compared to fossil fuels is often deemed better for the environment.

Tamboran is sensitive to these issues, as is evidenced by its corporate values: wealth creation, providing for a "low carbon" energy future, environmental responsibility, health and safety, and community engagement and partnership. The company, which operates in Ireland, the United Kingdom, Botswana, and Australia, has also issued a commitment statement to each region outlining what these communities can expect from them. They propose that their actions not only meet mandatory regulations but go beyond them. Some of the topics in these statements include monitoring groundwater and air quality, noise pollution, and seismic activity before, during, and after operations; public displays of information regarding operations; use of steel surface and intermediate casings lined with

advanced, engineered cement from the base of the well to the surface to ensure safety of groundwater; use of a Cement Bond Log across the entire surface casing to ensure stability, which will be inspected by the appropriate regulatory agency before drilling begins; abstaining from the use of chemicals; and recycling as much water as possible. Please see the following link: http://www.tamboran.com/ for more information on the company.

QUESTIONS

1. Evaluate Tamboran's concern for social issues.
2. Evaluate Tamboran's concern for environmental issues.
3. What information can you find that gives you some indication of Tamboran's profitability?

Case 15: Home Depot Forms Effective Management System

When Bernie Marcus and Arthur Blank opened the first Home Depot store in Atlanta in 1979, they forever changed the hardware and home-improvement retailing industry. Marcus and Blank envisioned huge warehouse-style stores stocked with an extensive selection of products offered at the lowest prices. Home Depot has a history of powerful leaders who helped the company become a mega-corporation. Home Depot is now the largest home-improvement retailer in the world, with over $78 billion in revenues. Because of Home Depot's leadership, the company continues the tradition of doing things on a grand scale.

Marcus and Blank were successful leaders who built a strong culture at Home Depot based on the concept of the inverted pyramid: placing customers and store associates at the top and executives at the bottom. Home Depot's store-centric culture put emphasis on the satisfaction of the customer and the associate, which led to Home Depot's many successful years in business. However, the company encountered a period of challenges when the founders decided to bring on a new leader who would grow Home Depot's infrastructure and technology. After this decision, Blank stepped down as CEO and joined Marcus as co-chairman of Home Depot. Blank was replaced by Robert Nardelli, a high-level executive at General Electric (GE). The store-centric culture of Home Depot was very different from the performance-focused culture of GE. This cultural divide became an issue when Nardelli tried to run Home Depot in a way similar to how he ran his branch of GE. Rather than follow the inverted pyramid established by founders Blank and Marcus, Nardelli took a top-down approach to running Home Depot: executives at the top and customers and store associates at the bottom.

During the Nardelli years, many resources were invested into implementing new technology to streamline Home Depot's operations. However, with the technol-

Source: Billion Photos/Shutterstock

ogy improvements in the storefront came staffing cuts. These staffing cuts demonstrated to stakeholders that the inverted pyramid was no longer a focus of Home Depot. Nardelli was also critical of associates and store managers, leading employees to fear for their jobs if they did not follow his directions perfectly. Because of Nardelli's strict management style, he replaced store managers with former military officers, a tactic he learned during his time at GE. With these changes, Home Depot went from a relatively laid-back work environment to a militant work environment. Staffing cuts also led to consistent customer complaints regarding customer service. Home Depot was ranked last among major U.S. retailers in the University of Michigan's annual American Consumer Satisfaction Index. Former managers at Home Depot blamed the company's service issues on a culture that operated under principles reminiscent of the military.

The new Home Depot culture created a hostile work environment for executives as well. Nardelli announced that he would measure everything that happened in the company and hold executives accountable for their numbers. There was a large turnover of executives during this time—both from termination and resignation. Executives who did not meet their goals were often fired and replaced with former GE executives. Other executives, such as former Chief Marketing Officer John Costello, often quit because of the in-your-face management.

Nardelli's tenure at Home Depot was not all negative. Sales doubled from $46 billion to $81.5 billion over a five-year period, and many successful technology initiatives were implemented. The board was pleased with these results; however, the negative feedback from stakeholders and the cultural shift led to Nardelli's termination. Frank Blake became the new CEO. Blake immediately distanced himself from Nardelli's militant ways. After a short time as CEO, it was clear that Blake would bring Home Depot back to the founders' original vision. Blake quickly refocused on the inverted pyramid and began to restore the customer experience.

Not only was Blake responsible for restoring the original culture of Home Depot, he was also tasked with leading the company through the housing crisis. While staffing cuts were inevitable, and almost 11,000 employees were laid off, Home Depot's management tried to minimize the loss for current associates by keeping wages and bonuses consistent. To do this, Home Depot executives centralized the company and refocused on Home Depot's most profitable business: existing retail outlets. Home Depot invested in its people. To regain associates' trust, Home Depot often consulted with Blank and Marcus to make sure the current vision of Home Depot was on par with the original vision. Homer Awards were brought back to reward employees for hard work, and assistant store managers were granted restricted stock. It also became easier for store employees to win bonuses. Slowly but surely, morale was being restored.

When Nardelli was fired from Home Depot, customer satisfaction was at an all-time low. The company's Twitter feed was inundated with comments from dissatisfied customers about the service they encountered in stores. Blake quickly admitted to the customer service problems the company faced, apologized for the inconvenience it caused, and encouraged customers to continue to leave feedback so it could make improvements. Each one of the complaints was addressed; some angry followers were appeased by phone calls from store managers and personal emails responding to their specific issues. The responsiveness of Blake and the former senior manager of social media, Sarah Molinari, not only transformed angry protesters into enthusiastic fans but also resulted in a strategic advantage for the company in how it deals with customer feedback. These changes proved Home Depot had effectively shifted back to its core culture: recognizing employees for hard work and satisfying customers.

After seven years with the company, Blake stepped down as CEO and was replaced by Craig Menear. The succession was smooth, so well planned that it had a minimal effect on Home Depot's stock price. Much like Blake, Menear proved that he would continue to focus on the core culture of Home Depot. This is being put to the test as brick-and-mortar retailers like Home Depot are experiencing huge changes in how they do business because of competition from online retailers like Amazon. Innovation and growth are more important than ever for Home Depot. Because of this, strong leadership is essential. Home Depot executives have accepted the challenge to lead Home Depot through the "Amazon-era." Although many companies have struggled because of online retailing, Home Depot has continued to be successful, with increases in revenue, profits, and customer spending, partly because of its new e-commerce strategy. The company's online sales have increased 21.5 percent since Menear became CEO. Home Depot seems to be surviving the "Amazon-era" with the help of its powerful and committed managers.

Home Depot has experienced rapid growth and success, and its leaders have used organizational controls to adapt to changing conditions. Its leaders have used a planned, ordered system of management control to allow managers to assess the firm at a point in time and then take corrective action to obtain objectives. Top management has been pushed back on course by monitoring performance and making changes. Managers have re-embraced the founders' original vision of continuously putting the needs of consumers and associates above the needs of the executive team. This customer-focused culture would not be possible without a history of strong, transformational leaders.[26]

1. What type of organizational controls did Nardelli use as a manager? What about Frank Blake?
2. Why do you think there was so much resistance to control when Nardelli became CEO of Home Depot? Use Table 15.3 to describe some of these reasons.
3. What are some methods Frank Blake used to restore morale and overcome resistance to control?

Notes

1. Sarah Boseley, "Mexico's Sugar Tax Leads to Fall in Consumption for Second Year Running," *The Guardian*, February 22, 2017, https://www.theguardian.com/society/2017/feb/22/mexico-sugar-tax-lower-consumption-second-year-running (accessed January 1, 2018); Luc Cohen, "PepsiCo, Coca-Cola Still Sparkle in Mexico After Fizzy Drinks Tax," *Reuters*, July 7, 2016, https://www.reuters.com/article/us-pepsico-mexico-tax/pepsico-coca-cola-still-sparkle-in-mexico-after-fizzy-drinks-tax-idUSKCN0ZO0B5 (accessed January 1, 2018); OECD, "List of OECD Member Countries—

Ratification on the Convention on the OECD," http://www.oecd.org/about/membersandpartners/list-oecd-member-countries.htm (accessed January 1, 2018); Astrid Rivera, "OECD: Mexico, Highest Obesity Rate in People Aged 15–74 Years," *El Universal*, November 11, 2017, http://www.eluniversal.com.mx/english/ocde-mexico-highest-obesity-rate-people-aged-15-74-years (accessed January 1, 2018); OECD, "Obesity Update 2017," https://www.oecd.org/els/health-systems/Obesity-Update-2017.pdf (accessed January 1, 2018); Sarah Butler, "Coca-Cola and Other Soft Drink Firms Hit Back at Sugar Tax Plan," *The Guardian*, March 17, 2016, https://www.theguardian.com/business/2016/mar/17/coca-cola-hits-back-at-sugar-tax-plan (accessed January 1, 2018); "Mexico's Sugary-Drink Tax Cut Consumption by Almost 10% Last Year," *Fast Company*, March 1, 2017, https://www.fastcompany.com/3068611/mexicos-sugary-drink-tax-cut-consumption-by-almost-10-last-year (accessed January 1, 2018); Tina Rosenberg, "How One of the Most Obese Countries on Earth Took on the Soda Giants," *The Guardian*, November 3, 2015, https://www.theguardian.com/news/2015/nov/03/obese-soda-sugar-tax-mexico (accessed January 1, 2018); Nicole Perlroth, "Spyware's Odd Targets: Backers of Mexico's Soda Tax," *The New York Times*, February 11, 2017, https://www.nytimes.com/2017/02/11/technology/hack-mexico-soda-tax-advocates.html (accessed January 1, 2018); Jay Moye, "Topo Chico Sparkling Mineral Water Joins Coke's Venturing & Emerging Brands Portfolio," October 2, 2017, http://www.coca-colacompany.com/stories/coca-cola_s-venturing---emerging-brands-welcomes-topo-chico-spar (accessed January 1, 2018); "Mexico Leads World in Bottled Water Use," *Mexico News Daily*, June 16, 2015, https://mexiconewsdaily.com/news/mexico-leads-world-in-bottled-water-use/ (accessed January 1, 2018); Nathaniel Parish Flannery, "Why Are Mexico and Mike Bloomberg Battling Coca-Cola?" *Forbes*, October 28, 2013, https://www.forbes.com/sites/nathanielparishflannery/2013/10/28/why-are-mexico-and-mike-bloomberg-battling-coca-cola/#71150378192f (accessed January 1, 2018); Tim Walker, "Mexico's Coke Wars Ignite as the Government Places a Tax on 'The Real Thing,'" *The Independent*, November 5, 2013, http://www.independent.co.uk/news/world/americas/mexicos-coke-wars-ignite-as-the-government-places-a-tax-on-the-real-thing-8923253.html (accessed January 1, 2018); Elinor Comlay, "Coke FEMSA Shares Fall as Mexico Passes Food, Drink Taxes," *Reuters*, October 31, 2013, http://www.reuters.com/article/2013/10/31/us-mexico-sodatax-idUSBRE99U16120131031 (accessed January 1, 2018).

2. Committee of Sponsoring Organizations of the Treadway Commission, *Internal Control–Integrated Framework*, May 2013, https://na.theiia.org/standards-guidance/topics/Documents/Executive_Summary.pdf (accessed January 20, 2018).

3. Lizette Alvarez, "For Safety, Ballet Between Human and Killer Whale Loses Some Intimacy," *The New York Times*, June 7, 2012, http://www.nytimes.com/2012/06/08/us/killer-whale-shows-restricted-at-seaworld-orlando.html (accessed December 23, 2017); Randy Dotinga, "Risky Business at Shamu Stadium," July 13, 2012, *Voice of San Diego*, https://www.voiceofsandiego.org/topics/news/risky-business-at-shamu-stadium/ (accessed December 23, 2017); "Whale Kills Trainer as Horrified Crowd Watches," *Fox News*, February 24, 2010, http://www.foxnews.com/us/2010/02/24/whale-kills-trainer-horrified-crowd-watches.html (accessed December 23, 2017); Jo Tweedy, "'Shamu' Killer Whale Drowns Trainer at SeaWorld Orlando in Florida," *Daily Mail*, February 25, 2010, http://www.dailymail.co.uk/travel/article-1253738/Sea-World-killer-whale-Shamu-kills-trainer-Dawn-Brancheau.html (accessed December 23, 2017); SeaWorld, "Educational Encounters and Experiences That Matter," SeaWorld Cares, https://seaworldcares.com/en/future/educational-encounters (accessed December 23, 2017); SeaWorld, "Last Generation," SeaWorld Cares, https://seaworldcares.com/Future/Last-Generation/ (accessed December 23, 2017); Associated Press and Daily Mail Reporter, "SeaWorld Introduces New Safety Vests Four Years After Trainer Was Dragged Underwater by Killer Whale and Dismembered," *Daily Mail*, April 28, 2014, http://www.dailymail.co.uk/news/article-2615349/Sea-World-orca-trainers-begin-using-safety-vests.html (accessed December 23, 2017); Lori Weisberg, "SeaWorld Settles Orca Trainer Safety Citations," *Los Angeles Times*, January 6, 2016, http://www.latimes.com/business/la-fi-seaworld-osha-20160106-story.html (accessed December 23, 2017).

4. Kevin Michaels, "Opinion: OEMS Increase Production, Squeeze Suppliers," *Aviation Week*, November 25, 2013, http://aviationweek.com/awin/oems-increase-production-squeeze-suppliers (accessed January 20, 2018).

5. Ronald Henkoff, "Companies that train best," *Fortune* (March 22, 1993), 62–75.

6. Accenture, *Accenture CDP 2013 Response*, 2013, http://www.accenture.com/SiteCollectionDocuments/PDF/Accenture-CDP-2013.pdf (accessed November 27, 2013).

7. "Nintendo warns of Wii shortages," *BBC News*, November 14, 2007, http://news.bbc.co.uk/2/hi/7094069.stm (accessed January 20, 2018); "Wii shortages frustrating gamers," *BBC News*, December 8, 2006, http://news.bbc.co.uk/2/hi/technology/6161717.stm (accessed January 20, 2018).

8. Louis Bedigian, "Nintendo Wii U Sales to Exceed Predecessor," *Forbes*, November 14, 2012, http://www.forbes.com/sites/benzingainsights/2012/11/14/nintendo-wii-u-sales-to-exceed-predecessor/ (accessed January 20, 2018).

9. Author's personal interview with a former IBM typewriter salesperson, April 6, 1994, Memphis, Tennessee.

10. Jeannette A. Davy, Richard E. White, Nancy J. Merritt, and Karen Gritzmacher, "A derivation of the underlying constructs of just-in-time management systems," *Academy of Management Journal* 35(August 1992): 653–670.

11. Myron Magnet, "The New Golden Rule of Business," *Fortune* (February 21, 1994), 60–64; Davy, White, Merritt, and Gritzmacher, "A Derivation of the Underlying Constructs of Just-In-Time Management Systems"; Joseph L. Cavinato, "A total cost/value model for supply chain competitiveness," *Journal of Business Logistics* 13(2), (1992), 285–301; Arthur R. Tenner and Irving J. DeToro, *Total Quality Management: Three Steps to Continuous Improvement* (Reading, MA: Addison-Wesley, 1992).

12. Tenner and DeToro, *Total Quality Management: Three Steps to Continuous Improvement*; Artemis March and David

A. Garvin, "A Note on Quality: The Views of Deming, Juran, and Crosby," *Harvard Business School Reprint 9-687-011*, (1986), 1–13.

13. Tenner and DeToro.

14. Tenner and DeToro; Chapman Wood, "The prophets of quality," *Quarterly Review*, American Society for Quality Control, Fall 1988; Philip Crosby, *Quality Is Free: The Art of Making Quality Certain* (New York: Mentor Books, New American Library, 1979).

15. Joseph M. Juran, "Made in U.S.A.: A renaissance in quality," *Harvard Business Review 71*(July-August 1993), 42–50; Frederick F. Reichheld, "Loyalty-based management," *Harvard Business Review 71*(March-April 1993), 64–73; Benson P. Shapiro, V. Kasturi Rangan, and John J. Sviokla, "Staple yourself to an order," *Harvard Business Review 70* (July-August 1992), 113–122; Tenner and DeToro.

16. H.W. Allen Sweeny and Robert Rachlin, *Handbook of Budgeting* (New York: John Wiley and Sons, 1987), 649.

17. Robert S. Kaplan and David P. Norton, "Putting the Balanced Scorecard to Work," *Harvard Business Review*, September 1993, http://hbr.org/1993/09/putting-the-balanced-scorecard-to-work/ (accessed November 26, 2013).

18. Nike, Inc., "Manufacturing," www.nike.com, 2012, http://www.nikeresponsibility.com/report/content/chapter/manufacturing (accessed November 26, 2013).

19. Environmental Leader, "Companies Increasingly Pursue the 'Triple Bottom Line,'" May 1, 2013, http://www.environmentalleader.com/2013/05/01/companies-increasingly-pursue-triple-bottom-line/ (accessed January 20, 2018).

20. Anne Field, "Jessica Alba: Triple-Bottom-Line Entrepreneur," *Forbes*, May 30, 2012, http://www.forbes.com/sites/annefield/2012/05/30/jessica-alba-triple-bottom-line-entrepreneur/ (accessed January 20, 2018).

21. "About B Lab," B Corporation, http://www.bcorporation.net/what-are-b-corps/about-b-lab (accessed January 20, 2018).

22. Microsoft, iPad vs. Windows, 2013, http://windows.microsoft.com/en-us/windows-8/compare#T1=surface-2 (accessed November 12, 2013).

23. Willard I. Zangwill, "Focusing all eyes on the bottom line," *The Wall Street Journal* (March 21, 1994), A12.

24. James L. Heskett, Thomas O. Jones, Gary W. Loveman, W. Earl Sasser, Jr., and Leonard A. Schlesinger, "Putting the service-profit chain to work," *Harvard Business Review 72* (March-April 1994).

25. Henkoff.

26. Brad Tuttle, "Why Home Depot Is Immune to the 'Amazon Effect,'" *Time: Money*, August 16, 2016, http://time.com/money/4453962/home-depot-amazon-effect-sales/ (accessed September 17, 2017); "How Home Depot Overcame a Difficult Cultural Shift: A Q&A with CFO Carol Tome," Greenleaf Center for Servant Leadership, July 10, 2015, https://www.greenleaf.org/how-home-depot-overcame-a-difficult-cultural-shift-a-qa-with-cfo-carol-tome/ (accessed September 27, 2017); Heidi N. Moore, "Chrysler: The end of Bob Nardelli. Again," *The Wall Street Journal*, April 21, 2009, https://blogs.wsj.com/deals/2009/04/21/chrysler-the-end-of-bob-nardelli-again/ (accessed September 27, 2017); Home Depot, "CEO Craig Menear Talks Innovation: Follow the Consumer," Home Depot, October 19, 2016, https://corporate.homedepot.com/newsroom/ceo-craig-menear-talks-innovation-aspen-institute (accessed September 27, 2017); Internet Retailer, "Home Depot Builds Out Its Online Customer Service," June 4, 2010, https://www.digitalcommerce360.com/2010/06/04/home-depot-builds-out-its-online-customer-service/ (accessed September 27, 2017); Joann Lublin, Matt Murray, and Rick Brooks, "Home Depot Names GE's Nardelli as New CEO in a Surprise Move," *The Wall Street Journal*, December 6, 2000, https://www.wsj.com/articles/SB976051062408860254 (accessed September 27, 2017); John Kell, "Home Depot's Former CEO Frank Blake to Retire as Chairman," *Fortune*, January 16, 2015, http://fortune.com/2015/01/16/home-depot-former-ceo-retires-as-chairman/ (accessed September 27, 2017); Julie Creswell and Michael Barbaro, "Home Depot Ousts Highly Paid Chief," *The New York Times*, January 4, 2007, http://www.nytimes.com/2007/01/04/business/04home.html?mcubz=3 (accessed September 27, 2017); Louis Uchitelle, "Home Depot Girds for Continued Weakness," *The New York Times*, May 18, 2009, http://www.nytimes.com/2009/05/19/business/19depot.html (accessed September 27, 2017); Nathan Owen Rosenberg, "The Key to Home Depot's Success Is Transformational Leadership," Insigniam, http://insigniam.com/blog/the-key-to-home-depots-success-is-transformational-leadership/ (accessed September 27, 2017); Parija B. Kavilanz, "Nardelli out at Home Depot," *CNN Money*, January 3, 2007, http://money.cnn.com/2007/01/03/news/companies/home_depot/ (accessed September 27, 2017); Wharton School, "Home Unimprovement: Was Nardelli's Tenure at Home Depot a Blueprint for Failure?" *Knowledge@Wharton*, http://knowledge.wharton.upenn.edu/article/home-unimprovement-was-nardellis-tenure-at-home-depot-a-blueprint-for-failure/ (accessed September 27, 2017); Rachel Tobin, "Frank Blake Is Home Depot's 'Calmer-in-Chief,'" *Seattle Times*, September, 4, 2010, https://www.seattletimes.com/business/frank-blake-is-home-depots-calmer-in-chief/ (accessed September 27, 2017); Rachel Tobin Ramos, "Home Depot Laying Off 1,000 Nationwide," *Atlanta Journal-Constitution*, January 26, 2010, http://www.ajc.com/business/home-depot-laying-off-000-nationwide/ADq8GoBrxpX5h37LIxBxyM/ (accessed September 27, 2017).

Managing Operations and Increasing Productivity

CHAPTER 16

Source: Romolo Tavani//Shutterstock

Chapter Outline

Introduction

The Nature of Operations Management

Planning and Designing Operations Systems

Managing the Supply Chain

Managing Inventory

Managing Quality

Managing Productivity

After reading this chapter, you will be able to:

■ Define *operations management* and identify the activities associated with it.

■ Determine the elements involved in planning and designing an operations system.

■ Specify how managers manage the supply chain.

■ Assess the importance of quality in the operations management process.

■ Define *productivity*, explain why it is important, and propose ways to improve it.

■ Evaluate operations issues in a franchise operation.

Trader Joe's: Operational Success

First founded in 1967 in California, Trader Joe's is composed of more than 470 stores in 41 states. Despite its large reach, Trader Joe's exudes the same neighborhood-store atmosphere that it did back in 1967. Trader Joe's excellent operations and customer service have generated a loyal customer following that has made it a success.

One of Trader Joe's biggest assets is uniqueness. In addition to maintaining a neighborhood-store feel, Trader Joe's maintains smaller facilities and product lines than comparable stores—a deliberate operational move to create its specialty image. Trader Joe's stocks about 4,000 items compared to the 50,000 stocked by the typical grocery store. Inventory control has been a key advantage in reducing costs and focusing on a limited number of quality products. Whereas many markets sell as many as 50 selections of one food item, Trader Joe's sells only a few. Products that have low demand or high production costs often do not last long. Because Trader Joe's stores are smaller than those of competitors, managers recognize the importance of selecting products that have a high turnover ratio. The combination of lower inventory and higher product turnover creates greater efficiency in store operations.

With sales of roughly $13 billion, Trader Joe's also sets itself apart with its private-label products. More than 80 percent of Trader Joe's stock consists of private-label products. This gives Trader Joe's management more control over the supply chain. Trader Joe's private-label products keep it from relying too extensively on any one supplier; Trader Joe's can therefore keep prices lower than rival Whole Foods because it can solicit more competitive bids from suppliers. Trader Joe's is particularly well known for its deals on alcoholic products and frozen foods. These deals are advantageous for Trader Joe's because it attracts customers to its locations.

Other attributes that set Trader Joe's apart from the competition are its operations and productivity. The company has an efficient philosophy when viewing its supply chain: the less, the better. At any given time, management aims to minimize the number of hands that touch a product. Trader Joe's will purchase directly from manufacturers, ship straight to distribution cen-

Trader Joe's has crafted its distribution process to create efficiency and reduce cost.

ters, then send products to stores. In comparison to competitors, Trader Joe's has crafted its distribution process to create efficiency and reduce costs. This efficiency increases productivity and allows customers to receive premium products consistently. The company also aims to minimize employee turnover, which allows for maximum productivity. Trader Joe's seeks to develop a collaborative culture where managers will help with stocking shelves or sweeping floors if the need arises. By retaining employees, Trader Joe's is able to provide knowledgeable employees for customers. This also allows for less recruiting, training, and employee start-up costs. Trader Joe's management operations and productivity have proved profitable thus far.

Additionally, Trader Joe's excels at quality and supplier relationships. It employs product developers who travel the world in search of best product/price combinations. Suppliers covet contracts with Trader Joe's, which charges less in fees and is known for on-time payments. Trader Joe's made the decision to sell only sustainable seafood starting in 2012 and refuses to carry products containing genetically modified ingredients. Its responsible measures have caused it to be consistently recognized as an ethical company. Trader Joe's expands only into areas that can support this streamlined distribution system. With its popularity continuing to rise, customers seem impressed by the way Trader Joe's is redefining the grocery-shopping experience.[1]

Introduction

As the opening vignette illustrates, the operations function of an organization is crucial to success. Operations management is a continual process that should never become stagnant. Environmental changes (for example, in consumer demand) make it necessary for the operations function to change as well. Frequently, these environmental changes will affect the resources the organization needs to attain its goals. In all societies, there is a limited supply of resources such as land, labor, capital, knowledge, time, and raw materials. Using these resources efficiently is critical not only to fulfilling social needs and demands (such as education and health care) and maintaining competitiveness but also to sheer survival. These conditions also hold true for businesses and other organizations. If a company uses its resources wastefully, more efficient competitors are likely to gain an advantage in the marketplace and possibly even put the less efficient company out of business. Within an organization, the operations function is responsible for ensuring that the firm uses resources as effectively and efficiently as possible.

In this chapter we discuss the role of operations management in acquiring and managing the resources necessary to create goods and services, in planning the processes that will transform those resources into finished products, in overseeing the transformation process, and in ensuring that the products are of the quality expected by customers. Additionally, we look at the way technology has changed production and operations and the increasing importance of productivity.

The three main functions within a business are finance, marketing, and operations. **Operations management (OM)** is the development and administration of the activities involved in transforming resources into goods and services. Operations managers oversee the transformation process, the planning and designing of operations systems, and the managing of inventory, quality, and productivity. Operations management is the "core" of most organizations because it is responsible for the creation of the organization's products.

operations management (OM): The development and administration of the activities involved in transforming resources into goods and services.

The Nature of Operations Management

At the heart of operations management is the transformation process through which **inputs** (resources such as labor, money, materials, information, and energy) are converted into **outputs** (goods, services, and ideas). The transformation process combines inputs in predetermined ways using different equipment, administrative procedures, and technology to create a product (Figure 16.1).

Transformation may take place through one or more processes. In a business that manufactures oak furniture, for example, inputs pass through several processes before being turned into the final outputs—furniture to sell to customers (Table 16.1). The furniture maker must first strip the oak trees of their bark and saw them into appropriate sizes—one step in the transformation process. Next, the firm dries the strips of oak lumber, a second form of transformation. Third, the dried wood is routed into its appropriate shape and made smooth. Fourth, workers assemble the wood pieces, then treat and stain or varnish the piece of assembled furniture. Finally, the completed piece is stored until delivery can be made.

inputs: Resources such as labor, money, materials, information, or energy that are transformed by a process to become an output.

outputs: The amount of goods, services, or ideas produced by a machine, factory, company, or an individual in a period.

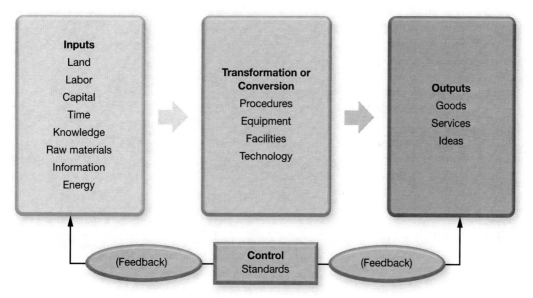

FIGURE 16.1 The Transformation Process of Operations Management

TABLE 16.1 Inputs, Outputs, and Transformation Processes in the Manufacture of Oak Furniture

Inputs	Transformation	Outputs
oak trees	cutting or sawing	oak furniture
labor	routing	
information/knowledge	measuring	
stain or varnish	assembling	
router and saw	staining/varnishing	
warehouse space/time	storing	

Different types of transformation processes take place in organizations that provide services, such as banks, colleges, and most nonprofit organizations. A bank transforms inputs such as employees, time, money, and equipment by way of processes such as filling out loan applications and repayment agreements, cashing checks, and accepting deposits. Outputs of these processes include automobile loans, home mortgages, checking and savings accounts, and other financial products. In your college or university, inputs such as information, classrooms, and teachers are used to produce well-educated students, hopefully, who possess the necessary skills and qualifications to successfully enter the professional job market. In this setting, transformation processes include lecturing, textbook reading, and computer simulations. Transformation processes occur in all organizations, regardless of what they produce or their objectives. For most organizations, the ultimate objective is for the produced outputs to be worth more than the combined costs of the inputs.

Note, in Figure 16.1, that the operations manager is concerned with all activities that directly relate to the production of outputs. To ensure that this process takes place within acceptable standards of quality and rate of output, managers control the production process by taking measurements (feedback) at various points in the transformation process and comparing them to previously established standards. If there is any deviation between the actual and desired outputs, the manager may wish to take some sort of corrective action.

Today, OM includes a wide range of organizational activities and situations outside of manufacturing, including entertainment.

Historical Perspective

Historically, operations was known as "production management," or "manufacturing," primarily because of the view that operations was limited to the manufacture of physical goods. The focus was on methods and techniques required to operate a factory efficiently. The change from "production" to "operations" represents a broadening of the discipline to include the increasing importance of service organizations. Additionally, the term *operations* reflects managers' interest in viewing the operations function in its totality—including procedural considerations—rather than simply as an analysis of inputs and outputs.

Today, OM includes a wide range of organizational activities and situations outside of manufacturing, such as health care, food service, banking, entertainment, retailing, education, transportation, and government. Thus, we use the terms **manufacturing** and **production** interchangeably to represent the activities and processes used in making *tangible* products, whereas we use the broader term **operations** to describe those processes used in the making of both *tangible* and *intangible* products.

Operations in Service Businesses

Manufacturers and service providers are similar, yet different. For example, both types of organizations must make design and operating decisions. An automobile manufacturer must determine where to locate its factory and how large the factory should be; a bank must determine where to locate its main office and how large a building is required. Manufacturers and service providers must both schedule and control operations as well as allocate necessary resources. Though manufacturers and service providers often perform similar activities, they also differ in several respects. We can classify these differences in five basic ways.

First, manufacturers and service providers differ in the nature and consumption of their output. For example, the term *manufacturer* implies a firm that makes tangible products, such as radios, basketballs, or watches. A service provider, on the other hand, produces intangible outputs such as airline travel or photo processing. The very nature of the service provider's output requires a higher degree of customer contact than does the output of the manufacturer. Also, the actual performance of the service typically occurs at the point of consumption. When you go to a doctor for an illness, for example, you must be physically present for the doctor to make the exam and issue a diagnosis and prescription. Because services typically occur at the point of consumption, it is impossible to store them for later use. For instance, an airline cannot save empty seats for use on a later flight. Ford and other automakers, on the other hand, can separate the production of a truck from its actual use. Consequently, manufacturing can occur in an isolated environment, away from the customer; whereas service providers, due to their need for customer contact, are often more limited than manufacturers in selecting work methods, assigning jobs, scheduling work, and exercising control over operations.

A second way to classify differences between manufacturers and service providers has to do with the uniformity of inputs. Manufacturers typically have more control over the amount of variability of inputs than do service providers. For example, each customer entering a bank is likely to require different services due to differing needs and wants, whereas many of the tasks required to manufacture a truck are the same across each unit of output, such as painting the truck or putting tires on it. Because of this variability, the products of service organizations tend to be more "customized" than those of their manufacturing counterparts. Consider, for example, a haircut versus a bottle of shampoo. The haircut is much more likely to incorporate your specific desires (customization) than is the bottle of shampoo.

Manufacturers and service providers also differ in the uniformity of their output. Because of the human element inherent in providing services, each service tends to be performed differently. Not all bank tellers, for example, wait on customers in the same way.

manufacturing: The activities and processes used in making tangible products; used interchangeably with the term *production*.

production: The activities and processes used in making tangible products; used interchangeably with the term *manufacturing*.

operations: The processes used in the making of both tangible and intangible products.

"De Vegetarische Slager"—The Vegetarian Butcher

De Vegetarische Slager (DVS) is a Dutch vegetarian food producer. DVS started with Jaap Korteweg's initiative toward an organic and animal-friendly diet. At the end of the twentieth century, swine fever and mad cow disease had killed many people in the Netherlands. During this period, Jaap tried to find vegetarian alternatives, but he, as a meat lover, missed the taste and texture of meat. Not being satisfied with vegetarian foods at the time, Jaap spent ten years searching and developing meat-like vegetarian products. In 2010, he founded DVS to market his products to the world. His success in developing and managing the firm's operations involved transforming raw materials into plant-based food products that taste like meat.

Since its launch in 2010, DVS has become a sizable business with 3,500 stores in 15 countries. To earn such an achievement, DVS has focused extensively on product quality. From day one, the development team at DVS committed to producing plant-based products resembling meats without compromising taste or texture. With the right focus on quality, DVS has convinced not only vegetarian customers to purchase its products but also many meat eaters. According to Jaap, the company receives letters from vegetarians complimenting the company on the taste of its products, as well as letters from meat lovers who have stated they prefer DVS's vegetarian chicken alternative over the taste of real chicken. In addition to customer testimonials, the "meatiness" of DVS's products has been proven in various food taste contests. In a Best Meatball contest, for instance, DVS's product was awarded third place, which ranked above many meat-based products.

The vegetarian food market is promising for companies like DVS. First, the plant-based product is a sustainable solution to global warming and climate change. Worldwide, livestock farms emit about 18 percent of human-caused greenhouse gases. Hence, switching from a meat-based diet to a plant-based one reduces the pressure of livestock production on the environment. Second, the global market has a growing number of environmentally conscious consumers who are willing to sacrifice their personal interests for sustainable development. This is an opportunity for vegetarian food manufacturers to capitalize on the trend and increase profitability. Finally, more people are becoming vegetarian or semi-vegetarian for health benefits. In short, changing consumer values and a growing concern for the environment are creating a great demand for vegetarian food production.

Despite the tremendous success and the macroenvironmental advantages, DVS still needs to overcome challenges. The meaty quality of its products allows

Source: Allik/Shutterstock

DVS to take advantage of a unique market niche that targets both vegetarians and meat lovers. However, it also places greater pressure on DVS to maintain high quality-control standards. There are many challenges in developing a vegetable product that tastes like meat. To ensure the unique taste and texture of each meat type, DVS has to set up production for each product line. Thus, expanding product lines while ensuring the meat-like experience is an operational challenge.

To remain innovative, DVS must also develop new products. This requires the firm to invest heavily in product development to make exciting new plant-based meats. One of its biggest challenges is a vegetable-based steak. The inputs involved with developing a plant-based steak product are different from its other products like vegetarian meatballs and chicken, requiring DVS to experiment in order to develop a vegetable product with the perfect steak flavor. DVS has partnered with Wageningen University and large multinationals like Unilever and Givaudan to find the solution for its steak production. DVS is also facing a legal and branding issue. The Dutch Food and Consumer Product Safety Authority (NVWA) has accused DVS of misleading consumers with meat names. In 2012, the Dutch authorities required DVS to change its product name "minced meat" (or *Gehakt* in Dutch) because the word is reserved for meat products only. After one consumer complained that DVS is using meaty terms for its plant-based products, the NVWA decided to force DVS to change all of its product names. Otherwise, the authorities will fine the firm. Despite these drawbacks, vegetarian food manufacturing is a profitable industry. As with most profitable industries, new competitors are increasingly entering the market. Innovations in managing products and the supply chain is necessary for DVS to maintain its competitive advantage for meat-

"De Vegetarische Slager"—The Vegetarian Butcher (continued)

like products—especially since the Dutch authorities have placed limitations on how these "meat-tasting" vegetarian products can be marketed. Yet DVS is up to the challenge. The firm has been an innovative leader in establishing standards and managing quality. As its fans will attest, the company has brought the taste and texture of plant-based food to a higher level. If DVS can overcome the current operational and political challenges, global consumers can expect to have more tasty vegetarian "meats" in the future.[2]

Therefore, a service output tends to have high variability. If a barber or stylist performs 15 haircuts in a day, it is unlikely that any two of them will be exactly the same. In manufacturing, the high degree of automation available allows manufacturers to generate uniform outputs; thus, the operations are more smooth and efficient.

A fourth point of difference is the amount of labor required to produce an output. Service providers are generally more labor-intensive (require more labor hours) because of the high level of customer contact, perishability of the output (must be consumed immediately), and high degree of variation of inputs (customization). A manufacturer, on the other hand, is likely to be more capital-intensive because of the machinery and technology used in the mass production of highly similar goods.

The final classification of differences between service providers and manufacturers involves the measurement of

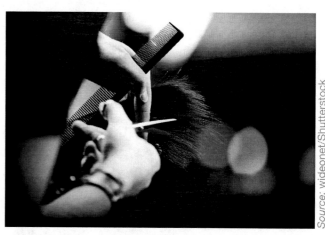

While manufacturing produces greater uniformity in their inputs and outputs, services such as haircuts tend to have high variability in their inputs and outputs.

productivity for each output provided. Manufacturers find measuring productivity much more straightforward because of the tangibility of the output and its high degree of uniformity. For the service provider, variations in demand (for example, higher demand for home loans in some months than in others), variations in service requirements from job to job, and the intangibility of the product make productivity measurement more difficult. Consider, for example, how much easier it is to measure the productivity of employees involved in the production of 100 automobiles as opposed to serving the needs of 100 bank or barbershop customers.

It is convenient and simple to think of organizations as being either manufacturers or service providers, as we have been doing here. In reality, however, most organizations are a combination of the two, with both tangible and intangible qualities embodied in what they produce. For example, automobile manufacturers provide customer services such as toll-free hotlines and warranty protection, while banks may sell checks and other tangible products that complement their primarily intangible product offering. Thus, we consider "products" to include both tangible physical goods as well as intangible service offerings. It is the level of tangibility of its principal product that tends to classify a company as either a manufacturer or a service provider. From an OM standpoint, this level of tangibility greatly influences the nature of its operational processes and procedures.

Planning and Designing Operations Systems

Before a company can produce any output or product, it must first decide what it will produce and for what group of customers. It must then determine what processes it will use to make these products as well as the facilities it needs to produce them. These decisions make up operations planning. Although planning was once the sole realm of the production and operations department, today's more successful companies involve all departments within an organization, particularly marketing and research and development, in these decisions.

Planning the Product

Before making the product, a company must determine what consumers want and then design a product to satisfy that want. Most companies use marketing research to determine the kinds of goods and services to produce and the features they must possess to satisfy consumers. Marketing research can also help gauge the demand for the product and identify how much consumers are willing to pay for it. Once management has developed an idea for a product that customers will buy, it must then plan how to produce the product.

Within a company, the engineering or research and development department is charged with turning a product idea into a workable design that can be produced economically. In smaller companies, a single individual (perhaps the owner) may be solely responsible for this crucial activity. Regardless of who is responsible for product design, planning does not stop with a blueprint for a product or a description of a service; it must also work out efficient production of the product to ensure that enough is available to satisfy consumer demand. How does an automobile company transform steel, aluminum, glass, and other materials into a new car design? How does a day-care center use toys, educational materials, and human labor to teach and care for children while their parents work? Operations managers must plan for the types and quantities of materials needed to produce the product, the skills and quantity of people needed to make the product, as well as the actual processes through which the inputs must pass in their transformation to outputs.

Designing the Operations Processes

Before a firm can begin production, it must first determine the appropriate method of transforming resources into the desired product. Often, consumers' specific needs and desires dictate a process. Customer needs, for example, require that all 3/4-inch bolts have the same basic thread size, function, and quality; if they did not, engineers and builders could not rely on 3/4-inch bolts in their construction projects. A bolt manufacturer, then, will likely use a standardized process so that every 3/4-inch bolt produced is like every other one. On the other hand, a bridge often must be customized so that it is appropriate for the site and expected load; furthermore, the bridge must be constructed on-site rather than in a factory. It should be noted that various processes are used when manufacturing a product. For example, though most automobiles are made on an assembly line, some of the lines are highly automated while others are highly labor intensive. Planning the operational processes for the organization involves two important areas: capacity planning and facilities planning.

Planning Capacity

capacity: The maximum load that an organizational unit can carry or operate at a given point in time.

The term **capacity** refers to the maximum load that an organizational unit can carry or operate at a given point in time. The unit of measurement may be a worker or machine, a department, a branch, or even an entire plant. Maximum capacity can be stated in terms of the inputs or outputs provided. For example, an electric plant might state plant capacity in terms of the maximum number of kilowatt hours that can be produced without causing a power outage, while a restaurant might state capacity in terms of the maximum number of customers that can be effectively—comfortably and courteously—served at any one particular time.

Capacity-planning decisions can be both long term and short term. Long-term decisions tend to focus on overall capacity levels, such as with building a new plant. Short-term capacity decisions relate more to the effects that variations in demand have on capacity, as with the fluctuating demand of a seasonal product (such as snow sleds). Usually, long-term capacity decisions are based on demand that has been forecasted over some time horizon. This forecasted demand is converted into capacity needs or requirements. Short-term capacity decisions are based more on deviations from the norm or average demand. Such deviations are critical to the operations system as they may result in ideal capacity at some points in time while resulting in the inability to meet demand at others. For example, automakers are tentatively developing electric cars to meet future regulation and growing demands for sustainability. However, automakers are carefully analyzing consumer demand for the cars, recognizing that a desire for greater sustainability does not always translate into willingness to pay a higher price for a more sustainable vehicle. Automakers are therefore being careful in expanding capacity due to fears that expanding too quickly in this product area will result in too many cars and too little demand.

Source: Dmytro Zinkevych/Shutterstock

Automakers are carefully analyzing consumer demand for the electric car and expanding capacity slowly to avoid producing too many cars and having too little demand for them.

Efficiently planning the organization's capacity needs, whether for the long or short run, is an important process for the operations manager. Capacity levels that fall short can result in unmet demand, and consequently, lost customers. On the other hand, when there is more capacity available than needed, operating costs are driven up needlessly due to unused and often expensive resources. To avoid such situations, organizations must accurately forecast demand and then plan capacity based on these forecasts. Another reason for the importance of efficient capacity planning has to do with long-term commitment of resources. Often, once a capacity decision—such as factory size—has been implemented, it is very difficult to change it without incurring substantial costs.

Planning Facilities

Once a company knows what process it will use to create its products, it then can design and build an appropriate facility in which to make it. Many products are manufactured in factories, but others are produced in stores, at home, or where they ultimately will be used. Manufacturers must decide where to locate their operations facilities, what layout is best for producing their particular product, and even what technology to apply to the transformation process.

Facility Location

Where to locate an organization's facilities is a significant question because, once the decision has been made and implemented, the firm must live with it due to the high costs involved. When a company decides to relocate or open a new facility at a new location, it must pay careful attention to the alternatives for such a move. Choosing the right site takes time, patience, and agreement among top managers, and veterans of site searches have learned that the process requires a lot of homework and solid objectives.[3] Though the critical location factors vary by firm, the following are among the most common concerns: proximity to market, availability of raw materials, availability of transportation, availability of power, climatic influences, availability of labor, community characteristics (quality of life), and taxes and inducements.

The facility-location decision is complex because it involves the evaluation of many factors, some of which cannot be measured with precision. Because of the long-term impact of the decision, however, it is one that cannot be taken lightly.

Facility Layout

Arranging the physical layout of an organization is a complex, highly technical task. Some industrial architects specialize in the design and layout of certain types of businesses. There are three basic layouts: fixed-position, process, and product.

A company using a **fixed-position layout** has a central location for the product and brings all resources required to create the product to that location. The product—perhaps an office building, a microwave relay station, a house, a hydroelectric plant, or a bridge—does not move. Companies relying on fixed-position layouts are typically involved in large, complex tasks such as construction or exploration. They generally make a unique

fixed-position layout: A company has a central location for the product and brings all resources required to create the product to that location.

product, rely on highly skilled labor, produce very few units, and have high production costs per unit.

Firms that use a **process layout** organize the transformation process into departments that group related processes. A metal fabrication plant, for example, may have a cutting department, a drilling department, and a polishing department. A hospital may have an X-ray unit, an obstetrics unit, and so on. Organizations using a process layout deal with smaller-scale products than those requiring a fixed-position layout. Their products are not necessarily unique but significantly different. Doctors, custom-made cabinet makers, commercial printers, and advertising agencies are examples. Such firms tend to create products to customers' specifications and produce relatively few units of each product. Because of the low level of output, the cost per unit of product is generally high.

The **product layout** design requires that production be broken down into relatively simple tasks assigned to workers positioned along the line. Workers remain in one location, and the product moves from one worker to another. Each person in turn performs his or her required tasks or activities. An assembly line is the classic example of a product layout. Examples of products produced on assembly lines are automobiles, television sets, vacuum cleaners, toothpaste, and meals from a cafeteria. Organizations using a product layout are characterized by their standardized product, the large number of units produced, and the relatively low unit cost of production.

Many companies actually use a combination of layout designs. For example, an automobile manufacturer may rely on an assembly line (product layout) but may also use a process layout to manufacture parts. A commercial sign manufacturer may rely on the process layout but also use an assembly line to assemble the components of a sign. No matter which facility layout is used, the cost and efficiency of operations depend on the degree to which the layout works effectively.

Technology

Technology is the application of knowledge (tools, processes, procedures) to solve problems. Every industry has a basic, underlying technology that dictates the nature of its transformation process. The steel industry continually tries to improve steelmaking techniques; the health care industry performs research into medical technologies and pharmaceuticals to improve the quality of health care service. Two developments that have strongly influenced the operations of many businesses are computer applications and robotics.

Computer Applications

Computers have been used for decades and on a relatively large scale since IBM introduced its 650 series in the late 1950s. Most of the early applications were of a recordkeeping nature—for example, processing payrolls and maintaining inventory records. Today many businesses would not be able to exist without computers.

The operations function uses computers in the product-design phase as well as in the actual manufacturing of products. These applications are generally referred to as **computer-assisted design (CAD)** and **computer-assisted manufacturing (CAM)**, which are computerized approaches that link the design and manufacturing areas, making information readily available. For instance, CAD is used in 3D printing. Using CAD software, a 3D image is developed. The CAD file is sent to the printer, which uses layers of liquid, powder, paper, or metal to construct a 3D model. Thanks to CAD and CAM applications, new innovations such as 3D printing are becoming more common.[4]

Companies may also use computers to monitor the transformation process, gathering information about the equipment used to produce the product, as well as about the product itself, as it goes from one stage of the transformation process to the next. The computer provides information to an operator who may, if necessary, take corrective action. In the monitoring mode, the computer itself does not take the corrective action, although in some highly automated systems, computers can control the production process. A computer compares data generated by the transformation process concerning the operation of the equipment and certain product characteristics with predetermined standards. If these

process layout: Firms organize the transformation process into departments that group related processes.

product layout: Requires that production be broken down into relatively simple tasks assigned to workers positioned along the line.

computer-assisted design (CAD): The use of computer systems to assist in the creation, modification, analysis, or optimization of a design.

computer-assisted manufacturing (CAM): The use of computer software to control machine tools and related machinery in the manufacturing of products.

comparisons are favorable, the process continues; if they are unfavorable, the computer is programmed to take corrective action. No direct intervention by human beings is needed.

In **flexible manufacturing**, computers can direct machinery to adapt to different versions of similar operations. For example, with instructions from a computer, one machine can be programmed to carry out its function for several different versions of an engine without shutting down the production line to refit the machines. Also, an athletic shoe manufacturer might invest in a flexible manufacturing system that allows it to make ten different styles and sizes of shoes on the same machinery.

Robotics

The industrial robot is less glamorous and considerably less sophisticated than fictional robots such as R2D2 and C3PO in the *Star Wars* movies. An **industrial robot** is a machine designed to move materials, parts, tools, or specialized devices through variable programmed motions, for the performance of a variety of tasks.[5] These "steel-collar" workers have become particularly important in industries such as nuclear power, hazardous-waste disposal, ocean research, and space construction and maintenance, in which human lives would otherwise be at risk. For instance, the Bechtel Corporation employed robots to clean up a contaminated nuclear reactor at Three Mile Island, the site of a much-publicized nuclear accident in 1979.[6]

Robots are used in numerous other production and operations environments by companies all around the world. They are especially prevalent in the automobile industry, where they are used to move materials as well as in assembly operations such as spot welding and painting. As a matter of fact, many assembly operations—not just of cars, but of television sets, telephones, stereo equipment, and many other products—depend on industrial robots. Researchers continue to make more and more sophisticated robots, and some speculate that, in the future, robots will not be limited to space programs and production and operations, but will also be able to engage in farming, laboratory research, and even household activities. Some speculate that the industrial era for robots is ending as they become more sophisticated. Increasingly, robots are being operated independently of direct human control.[7]

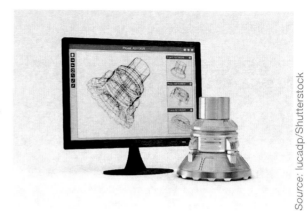

Computer applications such as CAD and CAM are used in the product-design phase and in the actual manufacturing of product respectively.

flexible manufacturing: Computers can direct machinery to adapt to different versions of similar operations.

industrial robot: A machine designed to move materials, parts, tools, or specialized devices through variable programmed motions, for the performance of a variety of tasks.

Robots are especially prevalent in the automobile industry, where they are used to move materials as well as in assembly operations such as spot welding and painting.

You're the Manager . . . What Would You Do?

THE COMPANY: McWendy King
YOUR POSITION: Head of Franchise Operations
THE PLACE: Wichita, KS

McWendy King is one of the largest fast-food restaurant companies in the United States, with over 5,000 units. The restaurant chain has a traditional fast-food menu with hamburgers, chicken, and roast beef sandwiches as well as other specialty sandwiches, salads, french fries, shakes, and so forth. McWendy King owns and directly operates roughly 50 percent of its restaurants, with the rest run by franchisees. Unlike in some other franchise systems, McWendy King franchisees are small-business operators who own just one or two outlets. This gives the franchised restaurants the advantage of being run by local businesspersons who are involved in the daily operations of their outlets. Such owner/operator involvement and control are not as evident in McWendy King's major competitors.

One store manager of a company-owned unit in Peoria, Illinois, wished to experiment with the development and sale of pizzas at his restaurant. After talking with his district manager, the store manager drafted a proposal and presented his ideas to the company's headquarters in Wichita. Company representatives were impressed with the insights, competitive analysis, profitability projections, and operational considerations presented. The executives believed the idea had merit, and they decided to test it in the Midwest region, working closely with the store in Peoria.

Headquarters worked for months developing the perfect fast-food pizza that could be produced as quickly as possible and would require a minimum of equipment investment for the company and franchise restaurants. The company then tested the product in company-owned restaurants in the Midwest region. The final conclusion was that the pizza product would achieve success, but not in the 12-inch size originally offered. Instead, research suggested that if only one size was offered, it should be 16 inches to accommodate small families and those who like to reheat the product for later meals.

McWendy King presented the concept, with all the financial information, to the franchisees. The company's presentation indicated that each store would need

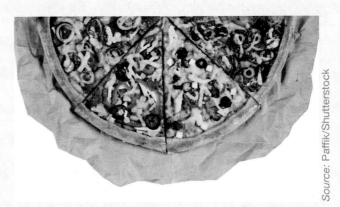

McWendy King franchisees were aware that the company was testing the pizza concept, but were not informed along the way of the operational considerations and costs.

to invest approximately $41,000 in equipment and employee training. In addition, because the 16-inch pizza box was too large to fit through the current store drive-through windows, all the stores would have to make structural modifications. The cost to redo each drive-through window was roughly $15,000.

The franchisees were aware that the company was testing the pizza concept, but were not informed along the way of the operational considerations and costs. Unlike the company units that had flat or declining sales, the franchise units, because of the tighter owner control, operated with significantly higher sales. With emotional responses, the franchisees rejected the idea of making such sweeping changes in order to add pizza to the menu. They suggested that the company look into other less costly alternatives for expanding the McWendy King menu.

QUESTIONS

1. As the head of franchise operations, what should you have taken into consideration in evaluating operational changes for the system?

2. Identify and evaluate compromise alternatives to resolve the situation; consider both quality and productivity for each alternative.

3. What is the role of communications between the corporate and franchise organizations?

---

supply-chain management: Occurs when managers connect all members of the distribution system to satisfy customers; is an important component of operations.

Managing the Supply Chain

Supply-chain management is an important component of operations. It occurs when managers connect all members of the distribution system to satisfy customers.[8] Supply-chain managers are involved with purchasing of raw materials, managing inventory, routing and scheduling, managing finished products, and distributing them to customers.

TABLE 16.2 Functions of Supply-Chain Management

Function	Description	Example
Purchase	The buying of all the materials needed by the organization	The procurement manager of a factory purchases the month's first shipment of supplies
Inventory control and management	Determining how many supplies and goods are needed and managing quantities on hand, where each item is, and who is responsible for it	The inventory control manager of a retailer determines how much stock needs to be ordered for next month
Outsourcing	Occurs when business activities are contracted to independent companies	A consumer electronics firm outsources the manufacturing of its products to Asia
Routing	Sequence of operations through which the product must pass	The operations manager of an automobile factory determines the order of operations for constructing a vehicle
Scheduling	Assigning the work to be done to departments or to specific machines or persons	A fast-food restaurant assigns different tasks to different employees

More companies are placing increasing importance on supply-chain management, prompting many universities to begin offering degrees in this field.[9] The supply chain is a complex system that requires different controls and monitoring systems to ensure compliance. Because the supply chain deals with so many different members, mistakes are not uncommon. We have all seen major news headlines of a supply-chain disaster. For instance, European customers were outraged when it was found that horse meat had been introduced into frozen beef products, resulting in a major backlash.[10] For these reasons, it is important for managers to understand the different functions of supply-chain management as well as their importance. Table 16.2 summarizes the different functions of supply-chain management.

Purchasing

Purchasing, also known as procurement, is the buying of all the materials needed by the organization. Consider a hypothetical small business called Fleet Athletic Shoes, Inc., which manufactures athletic shoes, selling primarily to sporting goods and department stores. Fleet Athletic Shoes must purchase not only leather and other raw materials, but also machines and equipment, manufacturing supplies (oil, electricity, and so on), and office supplies to make its shoes. People in the purchasing department locate and evaluate suppliers for these items. They must also be on the lookout for new materials or parts that will do a better job or cost less than those currently being used. The purchasing department's objective is to obtain items of the desired quality in the right quantities at the lowest possible cost. Moreover, there is a public relations dimension to purchasing: The individuals who work in this area must maintain good relations with suppliers.

The purchasing function is sometimes very complex. The average automobile, for example, has more than 16,000 different parts, each of which is associated with at least one

Source: Mascha Tace/Shutterstock

The supply chain is a complex system that requires different controls and monitoring systems to ensure compliance.

purchasing: The buying of all the materials needed by the organization; also known as procurement.

supplier. The importance of the task of purchasing is further revealed by the amount of money spent by various organizations. Further, the nature of the purchasing task is changing and becoming highly competitive. The European Commission has shown an interest in green procurement practices (GPP) of public authorities in member states. GPP is a voluntary tool that EU states can use and is intended to create purchasing practices that will have less of an environmental impact.[11]

Not all organizations elect to purchase all the materials needed to create their products. Often, they can make some materials more economically and efficiently than can an outside supplier. Coors, for example, manufactures its own cans at a subsidiary plant. On the other hand, firms sometimes find that it is uneconomical to make or purchase an item, and instead arrange to lease it from another organization. Some airlines, for example, lease airplanes rather than buy them. Whether to purchase, make, or lease a needed item generally depends on cost, as well as on product availability and supplier reliability. Once the purchasing department has procured the items needed to create a product, some provision has to be made for storing the items until they are needed.

Inventory Control

Inventory refers to all the materials a firm holds in storage for future use. Every raw material, part, and piece of equipment has to be accounted for, or controlled. **Inventory control** is determining how many supplies and goods are needed and keeping track of quantities on hand, where each item is, and who is responsible for it.

Inventory managers spend a great deal of time trying to determine the proper inventory level for each item. The answer to the question of how many units to hold in inventory depends on variables such as the usage rate of the item, the cost of maintaining the item in inventory, the cost of paperwork and other procedures associated with ordering or making the item, as well as the cost of the item itself. Several approaches may be used to determine how many units of a given item should be procured at one time and when that procurement should take place.

Economic Order Quantity (EOQ)

To control the number of items maintained in inventory, managers need to determine how much of any given item they should order. One popular approach is the **economic order quantity (EOQ) model**, which generally identifies the optimal number of items to order

Inventory managers spend a great deal of time trying to determine the proper inventory level for each item.

while minimizing certain annual costs that vary according to order size. We should note here that the purchase price per item is not generally included because it does not change or vary with order size unless a quantity discount is a factor. The optimal order quantity (Q_o) can be obtained by using the following formula:

$$Q = \sqrt{\frac{2DS}{H}}$$

where D equals the annual demand in units; S equals the ordering cost (in dollars); and H is the carrying cost (in dollars per unit/year). Carrying and ordering costs typically are estimated values. Thus, the EOQ should be viewed as an approximation rather than an exact quantity.

For example, let's say Fleet Athletic shoes expects to sell 5,000 units (pairs) of its RXII model next year. The company buys shoelaces from a supplier at 10¢/unit (pair) of laces. The carrying costs are 5 percent of the purchase price and ordering costs are $10. How many units of laces should the shoe manufacturer order from its supplier per order?

$$Q = \sqrt{\frac{2DS}{H}} = \sqrt{\frac{2 \times 5,000 \times 10}{.05 \times .10}}$$

$$= \sqrt{\frac{100,000}{.005}} = \sqrt{20,000,000}$$

$$= 4,472.1 \text{ units of laces}$$

Thus, the optimal order quantity is 4,472 pairs of laces per order. Notice that if Fleet Athletic Shoes orders only 4,472 units next year, there will be an eventual shortfall of 528 units. This provides an excellent illustration of how EOQ provides only an approximation of the number of units to order, rather than the exact number.

Just-in-Time Inventory Management

The **just-in-time (JIT) inventory management** concept minimizes the number of units in inventory by providing an almost continuous flow of items from suppliers to the production facility. It eliminates waste by using smaller inventories, which require less storage space and less investment. To illustrate, let's say that Fleet Athletic Shoes buys 500 units of shoelaces from a supplier per day. Traditionally, its inventory manager might order enough for one month at a time: 11,000 units per order (500 units per day times 22 workdays per month). The expense of such a large inventory could be considerable because of the cost of insurance coverage, recordkeeping, rented storage space, and so on. The just-in-time approach would reduce these costs because shoelaces would be purchased in smaller quantities, perhaps in lot sizes of 500, which the supplier would deliver once a day. For such an approach to be effective, the supplier must be extremely reliable and relatively close to the production facility.

just-in-time (JIT) inventory management: Minimizes the number of units in inventory by providing an almost continuous flow of items from suppliers to the production facility.

Material-Requirements Planning (MRP)

Another technique firms use is **material-requirements planning (MRP)**, a planning system that schedules the precise quantity of materials needed to make the product. The basic components of MRP are a master production schedule, bill of materials, and an inventory status file. At Fleet Athletic Shoes, for example, the inventory-control manager will look at the production schedule to determine how many shoes the company plans to make. She will then prepare a bill of materials—a list of all the materials needed to make that quantity of shoes. Next, she will determine the quantity of these items that Fleet already holds in inventory (to avoid ordering excess materials) and then develop a schedule for ordering and delivery of the right quantity of materials to satisfy the firm's needs. Because of the large number of parts and materials that go into a typical production process, material-requirements planning must be done on a computer. MRP can be and often is used in conjunction with just-in-time inventory control. Some potential benefits, if these

material-requirements planning (MRP): A planning system that schedules the precise quantity of materials needed to make the product.

systems are correctly implemented, are reduced inventory, reduced delivery lead times, realistic commitments, and increased efficiency.

Manufacturing-Resource Planning (MRPII)

Manufacturing-resource planning (MRPII) is another computerized system that helps a company control all of its resources, not just inventory needed for production. It includes data from all divisions within the organization to help executives plan all elements of the firm's operations. Thus, it is sometimes called the "closed loop" MRP because it incorporates all aspects of the company (accounting, marketing, etc.) rather than just the manufacturing component. Here, Fleet Athletic Shoes might, based on marketing research information, utilize MRPII to allocate resources including personnel and materials to various regional areas in order to meet projected swings in demand for the company's products. This is accomplished, by MRPII, through adopting a focal production plan and using a "unified" database to plan, update, or change *all* organizational activities.

Managing Inventory

After a facility is running, operations managers oversee the transformation process and control the inputs and outputs. There are three different types of inventory to manage. **Finished-goods inventory** includes those products that are ready for sale, such as a fully assembled automobile ready to ship to a dealer. **Work-in-process inventory** includes those products that are partially completed or are in transit. At McDonald's, for example, a hamburger being cooked represents work-in-process inventory because it must go through several more stages before it can be sold to a customer. **Raw materials inventory** includes those materials that have been purchased to be used as inputs for making other products. Nuts and bolts are raw materials for an automobile manufacturer, while hamburger patties, vegetables, and buns are raw materials for the fast-food restaurant.

Managing operations must be closely coordinated with inventory management. The production of televisions, for example, cannot be planned without some knowledge of the availability of all the necessary materials—the chassis, picture tubes, color guns, and so forth. Also, each item held in inventory—any type of inventory—carries with it a cost. For example, storing fully assembled televisions in a warehouse to sell to a dealer at a future date requires not only the use of space, but also the purchase of insurance to cover any losses that might occur due to fire or other unforeseen events. For this reason, managers must keep a careful eye on the inventory of materials and components when they develop a production plan.

Outsourcing

As we discussed in Chapter 5, outsourcing occurs when business activities are contracted to independent companies. Because outsourcing is so common, especially overseas where labor costs are often lower, it is an important component of supply-chain management. Working with third companies often results in greater productivity at lower costs, but it also introduces challenges as well. Firms must monitor their partners' activities to ensure they are complying with the firms' standards. Many countries have drastically different standards than those in the United States. For instance, in China working additional hours is not uncommon among factory workers, even if it violates the maximum number of hours that employees are supposed to work. Apple supplier Foxconn, for example, received negative attention after the public learned about unsafe working conditions and abusive labor tactics. Apple was forced to respond immediately because, as the hiring company, it is expected to ensure compliance among its suppliers and business partners.

Despite the difficulties, outsourcing has been able to provide competitive advantages for many major companies. Nike, for instance, has its shoes manufactured in Asia. This generates lower labor costs and other benefits that are passed on to the end consumer. Additionally, outsourcing can also allow businesses to receive help from experts in areas in which they are weak. Many organizations might outsource their accounting needs or janitorial responsibilities to third parties that specialize in these areas.

Routing and Scheduling

Routing

After all materials have been obtained and their use determined, operations managers must then determine the maximum or optimum level of production. As part of this process, management must consider the **routing**, or sequence of operations through which the product must pass. For example, before employees at Fleet Athletic Shoes can begin sewing together the leather in the shape of a shoe, it must be cut and stretched into the appropriate sizes. Likewise, the material used in the soles of the shoes must be cut to size before it can be attached to the leather uppers. Routing, therefore, establishes the order of operations through which each shoe at Fleet Athletic must pass on its journey, from being sheets and stacks of leather, rubber, and other raw materials to a finished and ready-to-wear shoe.

Once management knows through which departments or work stations the product must pass and in what sequence, it can then schedule the work.

routing: Sequence of operations through which the product must pass.

Scheduling

Once management knows through which departments or work stations the product must pass and in what sequence, it can then schedule the work. **Scheduling** is assigning the work to be done to departments or to specific machines or persons. At Fleet Athletic, cutting leather for the company's high-top basketball shoes might be scheduled to be done by the "cutting and finishing" department on machines designed especially for that purpose.

Many approaches to scheduling have been developed, ranging from simple trial and error to highly sophisticated mathematical procedures. One popular scheduling technique is the **Program Evaluation and Review Technique (PERT)**. Managers using this technique first identify all the major activities required to complete a project. To produce a McDonald's Big Mac, for example, involves removing meat, cheese, sauce, and vegetables from the refrigerator, grilling the hamburger patties, assembling the ingredients, placing the completed Big Mac in its package, and serving it to the customer (see Figure 16.2).

scheduling: Assigning the work to be done to departments or to specific machines or persons.

Program Evaluation and Review Technique (PERT): A popular scheduling technique where managers first break down a project into events and activities, and then lay down their proper sequence, relationships, and duration in the form of a network.

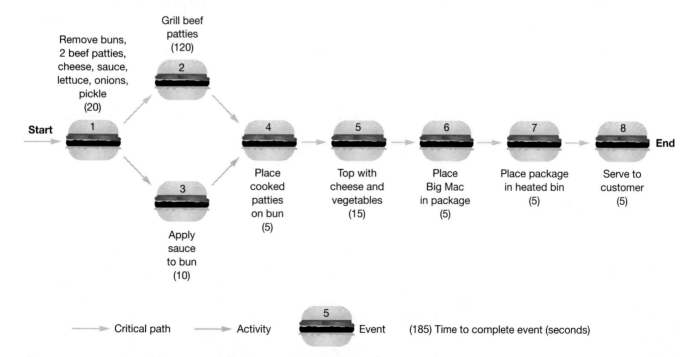

FIGURE 16.2 **A Hypothetical PERT Diagram for a McDonald's Big Mac**

FIGURE 16.3
A Hypothetical Gantt
Chart for Studying
for Midterm Exams

Project Activity	Week	1	2	3	4
Study Accounting 202	[-------------------			]	
Study Finance 112	[-------------------------			]	
Study Economics 202	[--------------]				

V shown above week 2

[Start of an activity	[-] Actual progress of activity
] End of activity	V Point in time where the project is now

Each complete activity is called an *event*. A scheduler arranges each event in a sequence, ensuring that an event that must occur before another event in the process does so. For example, at McDonald's, the cheese, pickles, lettuce, onions, and sauce cannot be put on a Big Mac before the hamburger patty is completely grilled and placed on the bun. The scheduler depicts the sequence of a project graphically as a path, with arrows to connect events that must occur in sequence, as in Figure 16.2. Finally, the time required for each activity is estimated and noted near the corresponding arrow. The scheduler then totals the time to complete each path. The path that requires the longest time from start to finish is called the *critical path* because it determines the minimum amount of time in which the process can be completed. For example, if any of the activities on the critical path for production of the Big Mac fall behind schedule, the sandwich will not be completed on time, causing customers to wait longer than they usually would. Thus, PERT allows managers to identify critical activities that can be performed concurrently so as to minimize completion time.

Gantt chart: A bar chart that shows the relationship of various scheduling activities over time; a popular technique used for scheduling purposes.

Still another popular technique used for scheduling purposes is the **Gantt chart**, a bar chart that shows the relationship of various scheduling activities over time. Usually, the scheduling activities are listed vertically and the time frames are listed horizontally. One of the main strengths of the Gantt chart is its simplicity.[12] Consider, for example, a student who is preparing for midterm exams in Accounting 202, Finance 112, and Economics 202. Figure 16.3 illustrates how a Gantt chart could be used in this situation. The student would list courses down the page and the activity time frames across the page. We can see from the chart that the student has studied for Accounting 202 for one and a half weeks, Finance 112 two and a half weeks, and has completed studying for Economics 202. The "V" shows where the project is currently.

Managing Quality

quality: The degree to which a good or service meets the demands and requirements of the marketplace.

Quality reflects the degree to which a good or service meets the demands and requirements of the marketplace. Quality, like cost, is a critical element of operations management, for defective products can quickly ruin a firm. A defective shoe, for example, could result in an athlete's injury and expose Fleet Athletic Shoes to lawsuits and declining sales. Quality is so important that we need to examine it in the context of operations.

quality control: The activities an organization undertakes to ensure that its products meet its established quality standards.

Quality control refers to the activities an organization undertakes to ensure that its products meet its established quality standards.[13]

total quality management: A management view that strives to create a customer-centered culture which defines quality for the organization and lays the foundation for activities aimed at attaining quality-related goals.

To control quality, many organizations establish total quality management (TQM) programs. **Total quality management** is a management view that strives to create a customer-centered culture which defines quality for the organization and lays the foundation for activities aimed at attaining quality-related goals.[14] TQM is not merely a technique, but a philosophy anchored in the belief that long-run success depends on a uniform commitment to quality in *all* sectors of the organization. The concept of TQM results largely on five principles: quality work the first time, focus on the customer, strategic holistic approach to improvement, continuous improvement as a way of life, and mutual respect and teamwork. TQM is an outgrowth of an emerging American perspective on quality that can be traced to changes in Japanese management practices immediately following WWII. Toyota has become famous for its TQM approach.

Establishing Standards

Quality control involves comparing the quality of products against established quality standards. Product specifications and quality standards must be established so the company can create a product that will compete in the marketplace. Fleet Athletic Shoes, for example, may specify that each of its shoes has soles of a specified uniform thickness, that the toe and heel of each shoe be reinforced to a specified level to ensure adequate support, and that each shoe be able to last through a specified number of miles of use. Production facilities must be designed that can produce products with the desired specifications.

Quality standards can be incorporated into service businesses as well. Fast-food restaurants, for instance, might set the standard that it wants to get customers through its drive-thru within a certain amount of time. The less time spent in the drive-thru, the more satisfied customers tend to be—and satisfied customers often translate to increased sales. At the same time, restaurants must make sure that they are not sacrificing quality for speed. It has been estimated that Wendy's is one of the quickest drive-thru restaurants, whereas McDonald's has recently scored highest in terms of accuracy of orders.[15]

Quality control is also important for customer payment methods in both goods and service operations. Ensuring the security of customer's personal information is paramount to customer loyalty and repeat visits. A few years ago, Target stores discovered the consequences of lax security measures in this area. At the beginning of the holiday shopping season, hackers installed malicious software onto the debit and credit card swiping machines in the stores. This resulted in over 70 million customers' personal information being stolen over a two-week period. The fact that the security breach occurred over such a long period of time is evidence that Target did not have appropriate controls in place. In addition to reducing its profit forecasts by 20 percent, Target has incurred other costs related to the incident.[16]

One of the challenges of developing quality standards is that standards tend to vary by country. For instance, while the United States might have one set of quality standards, the European Union may have stricter environmental standards for products sold in the region. It can be hard for global companies to recognize the various quality standards of different countries. For this reason, the **International Organization for Standardization (ISO)**, a set of international management standards, was developed to provide common standards that would apply globally. **ISO 9000** deals with quality, including providing a framework for companies to document records, train employees, test products, and fix defects. Companies from across the world have been certified by the ISO, including General Electric Analytical Instruments.[17] **ISO 14000** provides a number of comprehensive environmental standards for businesses to ensure that they are limiting their negative environmental impact and improving environmental performance. Another standard that has gained in popularity is ISO 26000. Intended as a guideline, ISO 26000 is a corporate social responsibility standard. Organizations choosing to adopt ISO 26000 must monitor and control their societal, environmental, cultural, legal, political, economic, and organizational diversity and comply with international standards for behavior.[18] Table 16.3 summarizes these three standards.

Inspection

Inspection reveals whether a product meets quality standards. Some product characteristics may be discerned by fairly simple inspection techniques—for example, weighing the contents of cereal boxes or measuring the time it takes for a customer to receive his or her hamburger. Other inspection techniques are more elaborate. Automobile manufacturers use automated machines to open and close car doors to test the durability of latches and hinges. The food-processing and pharmaceutical industries use various chemical tests to determine the quality of their output. Fleet Athletic Shoes might use a special computer

International Organization for Standardization (ISO): A set of international management standards developed to provide common standards that would apply globally.

ISO 9000: An international management standard that deals with quality, including providing a framework for companies to document records, train employees, test products, and fix defects.

ISO 14000: An international management standard that provides a number of comprehensive environmental standards for businesses to ensure that they are limiting their negative environmental impact and improving environmental performance.

inspection: Reveals whether a product meets quality standards.

TABLE 16.3 ISO Standards

Standard	Type	Description
ISO 9000	Quality Management	Provides a framework for companies to document records, train employees, test products, and fix defects
ISO 14000	Sustainability	Provides comprehensive environmental standards for businesses to ensure that they are limiting their negative environmental impact and improving environmental performance
ISO 26000	Corporate Social Responsibility	Standards requiring members to monitor and control their societal, environmental, cultural, legal, political, economic, and organizational diversity and comply with international standards for behavior

that can accurately simulate long-term usage of a shoe to determine how many miles a runner can expect the shoe to last.

Inspection tests may be classified as performance tests or destructive tests. The repeated opening and closing of car doors to determine the life expectancy of hinges and latches is a destructive test because the test lasts until the product fails. Performance testing, on the other hand, does not destroy or damage the product. Many software companies, for example, use performance tests to find and eliminate bugs in their programs, even asking customers worldwide to help with the tests. For example, Facebook asked its employees and mobile partners for help in beta testing its pre-release Facebook for Android. Facebook wanted its app to function on a wide variety of Android devices. By engaging the help of mobile partners such as Sony, Ericsson, and Huawei, Facebook was able to test its app and gather feedback on ways to improve it.[19]

Organizations normally inspect purchased items, work-in-process, and finished items. The inspection of purchased items and finished items takes place after the fact; the inspection of work-in-process is preventive. In other words, the purpose of inspection of purchased items and finished items is to determine what the quality level is. For items that are being worked on—an automobile moving down the assembly line, a booster rocket at an intermediate stage of completion, or an athletic shoe being assembled—the purpose of the inspection is to find defects before the product is completed so that the corrections can be made.

Sampling

An important question relating to inspection is how many items it should include. If Fleet Athletic Shoes produces more than 500 shoes a day, should they all be inspected or just some of them? At Alaska Airlines, hundreds of employees taste test the food to make sure it is satisfactory for passengers.[20] Whether to inspect 100 percent of the output or only part of it is related to the cost of the inspection process, the destructiveness of the inspection process, and the importance of the item to the safety of consumers or others.

Some inspection procedures are quite expensive, use elaborate testing equipment, destroy products, and/or require a significant number of hours to complete. In such cases, it is usually desirable to take a sample of the output and test that. If the sample passes inspection, the inspector may assume that all the items in the lot from which the sample was drawn would also pass inspection. By using principles of statistical inference, management can employ sampling techniques that assure a relatively high probability of reaching the right conclusion—that is, rejecting a lot that does not meet standards and accepting a lot that does. Nevertheless, there will always be a risk of making an incorrect conclusion—accepting a population that *does not* meet standards (because the sample was satisfactory) or rejecting a population that *does* meet standards (because the sample contained too many defective items).

Human life and safety depend on the proper functioning of certain items, such as the navigational systems installed in commercial airliners. For such items, even though the inspection process is costly, the potential cost of flawed systems in human lives and safety is too great not to inspect 100 percent of the output.

Continuous Improvement

As part of the TQM philosophy, organizations must constantly look for ways to eliminate defects and improve operations. One strategy that many organizations have adopted for quality improvement is known as Six Sigma. **Six Sigma** involves improving existing processes and developing new processes to meet Six Sigma standards, which requires organizations to produce no more than 3.4 defects per million opportunities. Building upon previous research, engineers at Motorola popularized the concept of Six Sigma after realizing that their current methods of measuring defects were insufficient. Motorola built on this concept in the mid-1980s and used it to improve Motorola's operations. The organization estimates that their Six Sigma initiatives saved it more than $16 billion.[21] Since then Six Sigma has been adopted by thousands of companies. In 1995, General Electric's CEO Jack Welch announced that Six Sigma would be a top priority for the firm during the subsequent five years. Each of General Electric's businesses was held responsible for achieving Six Sigma results. Six Sigma was later expanded and continues to be applied at General Electric.[22]

One strategy that many organizations have adopted for quality improvement is known as Six Sigma.

Six Sigma: Involves improving existing processes and developing new processes to meet Six Sigma standards, which requires organizations to produce no more than 3.4 defects per million opportunities.

Managing Productivity

The importance of productivity has increased dramatically in recent years and continues to escalate as a critical concern. For instance, productivity became such a concern that Yahoo! eliminated the company's work-from-home policies to get employees back into the office.[23] One of the primary objectives of the operations function is to increase productivity by using resources efficiently. Before we continue, let's establish what productivity is and how it is measured.

Measuring Productivity

Productivity measures the relationship between the outputs produced and the inputs used to produce them. It is usually expressed as a formula:

$$\text{productivity} = \frac{\text{output}}{\text{input}}$$

productivity: Measures the relationship between the outputs produced and the inputs used to produce them.

In general, productivity measurements can be classified in two ways: partial productivity or total productivity. **Partial productivity** reflects output relative to a single input or some combination of inputs. For instance, labor productivity is a very common concern. Examples of labor productivity include labor hours, machine hours, and number of workers necessary to produce at a given level of output:

partial productivity: Reflects output relative to a single input or some combination of inputs.

$$\frac{\text{output}}{\text{labor hours}} = \text{output per hour}$$

$$\frac{\text{output}}{\text{machine hours}} = \text{output per machine hour}$$

$$\frac{\text{output}}{\text{number of workers}} = \text{output per worker}$$

Total productivity reflects all the inputs used to obtain an output(s). For example, if we know that all inputs consist of labor, machines, and materials, we can use the following formula to express the total productivity measurement:

$$\frac{\text{output}}{\text{labor costs + machine costs + material costs}} = \text{output per total inputs}$$

Please note that this ratio requires that the inputs and outputs be measured using a common unit such as cost or value. In the above example, the output(s) would need to be converted to a dollar value.

The Importance of Productivity

Productivity is important on three levels. Organizations do not have unlimited resources, so they must determine how to allocate their limited resources to different departments or divisions within the firm. Consequently, each department or division must use its allotted resources as efficiently and effectively as possible. Moreover, the most productive departments are those most likely to be given larger allocations of the firm's resources.

From the perspective of an entire organization, productivity is a critical factor in competitiveness. For instance, if a company can achieve the same level of output as its competitors using fewer resources, then it has a competitive advantage. It can charge the same price for its products and generate higher profit margins than its less productive competitors, or it can charge a lower price and thereby increase its sales at the expense of its less productive competitors. Walmart has adopted an everyday-low-price (EDLP) strategy, undercutting its competitors' prices. Its efficient distribution systems and agreements with suppliers make the firm more productive, saving it costs and providing it with a competitive advantage over its rivals.

Productivity is also important from a national perspective because there is a close relationship between a country's productivity and its standard of living. High productivity levels are largely responsible for the high standards of living enjoyed by the citizens of the industrialized nations. Moreover, if productivity levels are not in alignment with wage and price levels, the nation's economy may be adversely affected. High wages and prices combined with low productivity, for example, may result in inflationary pressure. Modest gains in productivity can also convince employers to avoid hiring new workers, contributing to greater unemployment.[24]

In 1960, the United States accounted for 51 percent of the free world's total output, but its share had fallen to 22 percent by 1980. In contrast, Japan accounted for only 19 percent of the free world's total output in 1960, but its share climbed to 24 percent by 1980.[25] Moreover, over the last couple decades, the United States has lost its dominance of industries such as TVs, cameras, and minor appliances to foreign competitors, particularly in Asia. However, the United States has gained dominance in a surprising industry: oil and natural gas. The United States is now one of the world's largest producers of these commodities due to its extensive shale formations.[26]

Improving Productivity

Many factors affect productivity, including methods, capital, quality, technology, and management. For example, a student studying for a comprehensive final exam may take a speed-reading course (method) and try to better organize the material (management) with the aid of a laptop (capital and technology). The incentive of getting good grades and the personal pride of doing a good job are also important. The point is that all of these factors are potential sources of productivity improvements.

Some key steps toward improving productivity are listed below:

1. *Develop adequate productivity measurements.* For example, if Fleet Athletic Shoes measures only the number of shoes made, it may be ignoring other indicators of productivity, such as wasted materials or product quality, that provide a better picture of true productivity.

2. *Consider the "entire" or "whole" system when deciding on which operations to concentrate.* For most products, the production process is a closely integrated sequence of events that must take place in exact order to achieve the desired results. If just one of these steps, regardless of its apparent importance, is not performed satisfactorily, the whole production process may be thrown off course. Only by considering the entire system as a whole is it possible to detect relatively minor difficulties that may be causing major problems.

3. *Develop productivity improvement methods (such as work teams) and reward contributions.* Florida State University has a Prudential-Davis Productivity Awards Program that provides monetary rewards to individuals and teams within the school that have enhanced the productivity of their departments.[27]

4. *Establish reasonable improvement goals.* If goals are set too high, workers may be frustrated when they cannot achieve them. However, if goals are set too low, the company is not likely to reach its potential in terms of productivity because it is not challenging its workers enough.

5. *Make productivity improvements a management, particularly top management, priority.* Commitment from management is critical to the achievement of any goal, particularly those concerning productivity improvements.

6. *Publicize productivity improvements.* Publicizing improvement not only tends to instill a sense of pride in those workers most responsible for the improvements, but also creates somewhat of a challenge to other workers to see if they too can do something that will help the company's overall productivity.

7. *Use decision-support systems.* Specialized computer systems allow managers and other workers to consider the effects of a wide range of possible factors on organizational productivity. As a result, outcomes of decisions can be predicted more accurately than they otherwise could.

8. *Link incentives with productivity increases.* For example, rather than merely giving automatic annual year-end bonuses to employees, Fleet Athletic Shoes could base its bonuses on work teams or individual employees successfully meeting preset productivity goals.

9. *Provide adequate training.* Accenture provides more than 40 hours of training per employee. The company also has a global learning portal that employees can access while on the job.[28]

Employees' attitudes have an important influence on productivity. For instance, it is believed that workers who are committed and have a positive attitude about their jobs and company will have a high overall productivity level, all other things being equal. Some of the ways to increase productivity through employees' attitudes include providing sufficient job training, increasing job autonomy, providing financial incentives, and eliciting and integrating employees' input on productivity issues. Eaton considers employee feedback to be essential in improving its operations. The company conducts a biannual employee engagement survey for all of its employees.[29]

Unfortunately, when faced with the challenge of improving productivity, managers frequently focus on updating equipment rather than developing employees. Tom Peters and Robert Waterman revealed in their book *In Search of Excellence* that the best-run organizations view their employees "as the root source of quality and productivity gain." These firms achieve high productivity through high employee performance by respecting employees as individuals, trusting them, and "treating them as adults."[30] It is evident, then, that a key way to improve productivity is through employees.

Workers who have a positive attitude about their jobs and company are more likely to have a high overall productivity level.

■ *Define* operations management *and identify the activities associated with it.* Operations management is the development and administration of the activities involved in transforming resources into goods and services. Operations managers oversee the transformation process, the planning and designing of operations systems, and the managing of inventory, quality, and productivity.

■ *Determine the elements involved in planning and designing an operations system.* Operations planning is necessary before actual production can occur. Product design depends on what customers want and on the organization's technical abilities. Facility layout is the arrangement of the physical layout of an organization. Layouts may be fixed-position layouts, process layouts, or product layouts. The decision where to locate operations facilities is a crucial one that depends on proximity to the market, availability of raw materials, availability of transportation, availability of power, climatic influences, availability of labor, and community characteristics. Technology is also vital to operations, particularly computer-assisted design, computer-assisted manufacturing, flexible manufacturing, and robotics.

■ *Specify how managers manage the supply chain.* Supply-chain management is an important component of operations. It occurs when managers connect all members of the distribution system to satisfy customers. Supply-chain management involves purchasing, inventory control and management, outsourcing, and routing and scheduling. Inventory refers to all the materials a firm holds in storage for future use. Inventory control is determining how many supplies and goods are needed and keeping track of how many of each item are on hand, where each item is, and who has responsibility for each item. The economic order quantity (EOQ) model generally identifies the optimal number of items to order while minimizing certain annual costs that vary according to order size. The just-in-time (JIT) inventory concept minimizes the number of units maintained in inventory by providing an almost continuous flow of items from the suppliers to the production facility. Material-requirements planning (MRP) is a planning system that schedules the precise quantity of materials that are needed to make the product. Manufacturing-resource planning (MRPII) is another computerized system that helps a company control all of its resources, not just inventory needed for production. There are three types of inventory: finished-goods inventory, work-in-process inventory, and raw materials inventory. Some companies may choose to outsource certain business functions, which occurs when business activities are contracted to independent companies.

After all materials have been obtained and their use determined, operations managers must then determine the maximum or optimum level of production. As part of this process, management must consider the routing, or sequence of operations through which the product must pass. Once management knows through which departments or work stations the product must pass and in what sequence, it can then schedule the work. Scheduling means assigning the work to be done to departments or to specific machines or persons. The Program Evaluation and Review Technique (PERT) and the Gantt chart are common types of scheduling methods.

■ *Assess the importance of quality in the operations management process.* Quality is a critical element of operations management because low-quality products can harm a firm. Quality control refers to the activities undertaken to ensure that products meet established quality standards. Total quality management (TQM) is a management view that strives to create a customer-centered culture which defines quality for the organization and lays the foundation for activities aimed at attaining quality-related goals.

To control quality, a company must first establish what standard of quality it desires and then determine whether its products meet that standard through inspection. The International Organization for Standardization (ISO) is a set of international management standards developed to provide common standards that would apply globally. ISO 9000 and 14000 are two common ISO standards for quality and sustainability. Inspection reveals whether a product meets quality standards. An important question relating to inspection is how many items should be included in the inspection process. In some cases, it is usually desirable to take a sample of the output and test that. Finally, an important part of quality control is continuous improvement. One strategy that many organizations have adopted for quality improvement is known as Six Sigma. Six Sigma involves improving existing processes and developing new processes to meet Six Sigma standards, which requires organizations to produce no more than 3.4 defects per million opportunities.

■ *Define* productivity, *explain why it is important, and propose ways to improve it.* Productivity measures the relationship between the outputs produced and the inputs used to produce them.

Partial productivity reflects output relative to a single input or some combination of inputs; total productivity reflects all the inputs used to obtain an output(s). Productivity is important because it relates to a firm's (or nation's) efficiency in using resources and competitiveness. There are many ways to improve productivity, including developing adequate productivity measurements, developing productivity improvement methods, establishing reasonable improvement goals, publicizing productivity improvements, linking incentives to productivity increases, providing adequate training, and motivating employees to be more productive.

■ *Evaluate operations issues in a franchise operation.* Evaluate the scenario described in the "Business Dilemma" box and come up with a compromise solution to the problem. Your solution should enable all outlets to maintain quality and productivity standards.

Key Terms and Concepts

capacity 488

computer-assisted design (CAD) 490

computer-assisted manufacturing (CAM) 490

economic order quantity (EOQ) model 494

finished-goods inventory 496

fixed-position layout 489

flexible manufacturing 491

Gantt chart 498

industrial robot 491

inputs 483

inspection 499

International Organization for Standardization (ISO) 499

inventory 494

inventory control 494

ISO 14000 499

ISO 9000 499

just-in-time (JIT) inventory management 495

manufacturing 485

manufacturing-resource planning (MRPII) 496

material-requirements planning (MRP) 495

operations 485

operations management (OM) 483

outputs 483

partial productivity 501

process layout 490

product layout 490

production 485

productivity 501

Program Evaluation and Review Technique (PERT) 497

purchasing 493

quality 498

quality control 498

raw materials inventory 496

routing 497

scheduling 497

Six Sigma 501

supply-chain management 492

total productivity 502

total quality management 498

work-in-process inventory 496

Ready Recall

1. What is the purpose of operations management?
2. Distinguish between the terms operations, production, and manufacturing.
3. Compare and contrast a manufacturer versus a service provider in terms of operations management.
4. In what industry would the fixed-position layout be most efficient? The process layout? The product layout? Use real examples.
5. What criteria do businesses use when deciding where to locate a plant?
6. What is flexible manufacturing? How can it help firms improve quality?
7. Explain why organizations using the just-in-time inventory concept must have zero defects in their inventory.
8. Describe the methods a firm may use to manage inventory.
9. When might a firm decide to inspect a sample of its products rather than test every product for quality?
10. Explain why productivity is important to the organization or a nation. Include some steps that can be taken to improve productivity.

Expand Your Experience

1. Compare and contrast operations management at McDonald's with that of Honda of America. Compare and contrast operations management at McDonald's with that of Citibank, a banking firm.

2. Find an existing company that uses JIT, either in your local community or in a business journal. Why did the company decide to use JIT? What have been the advantages and disadvantages of using JIT for that

particular company? What has been the overall effect on the quality of the company's goods or services? What has been the overall effect on the company's bottom line?

3. Interview some local operations managers and ask them what induced their companies to locate in your area. Compare and contrast the different criteria and report the results to your class.

Strengthen Your Skills

Operations Management and Services

Instructions: Read the following scenario and answer the questions. Use concepts from the chapter to defend your answer.

Scenario:

John Manor, the recently hired chief operating officer of Southern States Airlines, has decided to hire you as a consultant. He explained his problem: Over the past few months, there have been several inefficiencies in service operations such as long lines at the service desk and a lack of communication between employees and customers. This has resulted in a multitude of unhappy customers. From your experience in the industry, you are aware that smaller airlines tend to have better operations and happier customers. Mr. Manor explained that the employees do not seem fully aware of the issues that exist. He wants them to engage and feel empowered in their positions, and wants you to incorporate this into your recommendation. The following is a list of major issues that your recommendation needs to cover:

- Service employees are dismissive of customer questions about flight delays. This is due to a lack of information resulting from inefficient communication channels, and a lack of training in how employees should respond to inquisitive consumers.
- Issues with lost luggage exist because so many people are involved in the process of transporting the luggage. Service desk employees have no way to track lost luggage immediately.
- Service employees fail to acknowledge customers waiting to ask questions. They are often too involved in conversations with other service representatives.
- Flight attendants fail to provide adequate service and follow up with customers on drinks, picking up trash, etc.
- Pilots often refuse to give customers adequate information of flight delays after boarding the plane.

QUESTIONS:

1. What is your analysis of the problems in the transformation process for Southern States Airlines? How do you recommend the inputs be improved such that the outputs are of higher quality?
2. What is your recommendation for including the employees in the solution to these problems?
3. What kind of operations management methods would you recommend for the luggage problem?
4. What are your recommendations for the use of technology in this scenario?
5. How can improvements in communication and the flow of information contribute to the overall betterment of the transformation process? How would these improvements be implemented?

Case 16: Ford Motor Company—Managing Quality and Production in Just-in-Time Manufacturing

Henry Ford established Ford Motor Company in 1903 in Dearborn, Michigan. At this time, only the rich could afford to purchase vehicles, and Ford wanted to make a vehicle that the common person could afford. The Model A was the first vehicle produced by the company. This model was followed by several more over the first five years of the company's existence. In 1908 the most famous model, the Model T, made its debut and was the catalyst for the company's operations efficiency and mass production.

In the early years, the production of vehicles was designed so that one worker built an entire vehicle over the course of about 8.5 hours. Henry Ford, whose purpose was to mass produce an affordable vehicle, was always search-ing for ways to make the production process more efficient in terms of time and cost. In order to accomplish this, he set the vehicles up at assembly stations and designated each worker with a specified task. The workers would then go to each stand and perform their specific duty on each vehicle. This reduced worker production time from 8.5 hours to 2.5 minutes. However, some workers were faster than others, creating a bottleneck in the production process. By 1913, Ford had perfected the system with a moving assembly line. Workers remained stationary while the vehicle came to them when it was ready for their specialized task. This further reduced the amount of inputs (not only time, but parts as well) needed to produce the

With the assistance of Six Sigma, Ford implemented many new innovations in operations management to improve quality.

final output throughout the transformation process. The assembly line served as the model for the cost-effective, mass-production assembly-line concept still used today.

Although the mass-production assembly line has proven successful, there have been many new innovations in operations management to improve quality. One of these is known as Six Sigma. Six Sigma is a process that emphasizes quality in manufacturing and requires mass amounts of training. Over the years, Ford Motor Company became known for its mass-manufacturing capabilities, but the quality of its final products was lacking. In 2000, it wanted to reposition the company as a consumer products company through the Six Sigma system. The company identified the top quality complaints from customers and developed Six Sigma projects to address these quality issues. There are three criteria by which Ford chooses each project: its relation to customer satisfaction, its potential to reduce quality deficiencies by 70 percent, and its ability to save $250,000 in costs. Furthermore, in order to ensure quality and control in its Six Sigma projects, Ford utilizes a define, measure, analyze, improve, and control (DMAIC) cycle to evaluate issues and their solutions. Overall, the company has been able to meet these standards success-

fully. Quality and efficient manufacturing have become so important to Ford that it adopted the following vision statement: "People working together as a lean, global enterprise to make people's lives better through automotive and mobility leadership."

In order to remain competitive on a global scale, the company has used computer-aided design (CAD) to derive a model of the Ford Focus that could be recognized globally. This is all a part of a continued attempt at reducing the amount of component parts and labor needed to make vehicles. Many companies entering the global market tend to design vehicles specific to the tastes of those native to the country or region. This drives up costs and reduces the quality of the final product. Former Ford CEO Alan Mulally conveyed the "One Ford" philosophy in order to produce a vehicle that could be recognized and liked no matter where it is sold. This vehicle incorporates recognizable Ford features, such as the curve of the roof of the vehicle to the function of the accelerator, known as Ford Global DNA.

Today, Ford Motor Company is the second-largest American automaker and is expected to produce additional vehicles to meet consumer demand. In order to meet this demand, the company is increasing its capacity. Ford increased the number of shifts at most of its factories from two to three; about 90 percent of Ford's plants around the world currently run on a three-shift or three-crew model. It plans to reduce the core platforms on which it bases its vehicles from 15 to 9, which will significantly boost efficiency. Ford is also adopting new technologies such as 3D printing, robotics, and virtual reality tools to speed up the design and development of new vehicles. With its success at operational efficiencies, Ford appears to be gaining business.[31]

1. Describe some of the different processes Ford has used to improve its operational capacity.
2. How has Six Sigma improved the quality of Ford vehicles?
3. Why does Ford consider it important to develop a global car?

Notes

1. Trader Joe's website, http://www.traderjoes.com (accessed October 1, 2013); Beth Kowitt, "Inside the Secret World of Trader Joe's—Full Version," *Fortune*, August 23, 2010, http://archive.fortune.com/2010/08/20/news/companies/inside_trader_joes_full_version.fortune/index.htm (accessed January 1, 2018); "2010 World's Most Ethical Companies," *Ethisphere*, http://m1.ethisphere.com/wme2013/index.html (accessed October 1, 2013); Lisa Scherzer, "Trader Joe's Tops List of Best Grocery Store Chains," *Yahoo Finance!*, July 24, 2013, https://finance.yahoo.com/blogs/the-exchange/trader-joe-tops-list-best-grocery-store-chains-182739789.html (accessed January 1, 2018); Nancy Luna, "Trader Joe's Expanding to Texas," *Orange County Register*, May 5, 2011, https://www.ocregister.com/2011/05/05/trader-joes-expanding-to-texas-2/ (accessed January 1, 2018); Progressive Grocer, "Trader Joe's Opens Fewer-Than-Average Stores in 2017," October 16, 2017, https://progressivegrocer.com/trader-joes-opens-fewer-average-stores-2017 (accessed January 1, 2018); "Trader Joe's: Groceries for the 'Overeducated and Underpaid,'" Technology and Operations Management, a course at Harvard Business School, December 9, 2015, https://rctom.hbs.org/submission/trader-joes-groceries-for-the-overeducated-and-underpaid/ (accessed January 1, 2018); John Boyle, "As Earth Fare Grows, Some Workers Feeling 'Squeezed,'" *Citizen Times*, September 3,

2016, http://www.citizen-times.com/story/news/local/2016/09 /03/earth-fare-grows-some-workers-feeling-squeezed/ 88412772/ (accessed January 1, 2018); Sheiresa Ngo, "15 Secrets Trader Joe's Shoppers Should Know," *Business Insider*, May 8, 2017, http://www.businessinsider.com/15-secrets-trader -joes-shoppers-should-know-2017-5/#3-shoppers-can-win -prizes-3 (accessed January 1, 2018); "Trader Joe's: Food for Thought," Technology and Operations Management, a course at Harvard Business School, December 9, 2015, https://rctom .hbs.org/submission/trader-joes-food-for-thought/ (accessed January 1, 2018).

2. Caryn Ginsberg, "The Market for Vegetarian Foods," *The Vegetarian Resource Group*, http://www.vrg.org/nutshell/ market.htm (accessed December 31, 2017); Jaag Korteweg, founder of De Vegetarische Slager, November 2017 (J. Wienen, Interviewer); Nielsen, "Green Generation: Millennials Say Sustainability Is a Shopping Priority," November 5, 2015, http://www.nielsen.com/us/en/insights/news/2015/green -generation-millennials-say-sustainability-is-a-shopping -priority.html (accessed December 31, 2017); The Vegetarian Butcher, "About Us," 2017, https://www.thevegetarianbutcher .com/about-us/since-1962 (accessed December 31, 2017); Niamh Michail, "Vegetarian Butcher Slams Dutch Food Authority for Double Standards over 'Misleading' Meat Name Ban," *Food Navigator*, October 5, 2017, https://www .foodnavigator.com/Article/2017/10/05/Vegetarian-Butcher -slams-Dutch-food-authority-for-double-standards-over -misleading-meat-name-ban (accessed December 31, 2017); Bryan Walsh, "The Triple Whopper Environmental Impact of Global Meat Production," *Time*, December 16, 2013, http:// science.time.com/2013/12/16/the-triple-whopper -environmental-impact-of-global-meat-production/ (accessed December 31, 2017).

3. Paul B. Finney, "A hunt for space," *International Business 6*(June 1993), 38–44.

4. Ross Toro, "How 3D Printers Work (Infographic)," *Live-Science*, June 18, 2013, http://www.livescience.com/37513 -how-3d-printers-work-infographic.html (accessed January 20, 2018).

5. Joseph P. Ziskowsky, "Robotics—The first step to CIM and the factory of the future," *Robotics and Factories of the Future*, ed. Suren N. Dwivedi (Berlin: Springer-Verlag, 1984), 154–160.

6. Gregory L. Miles, with Neil Gross and Mark Maremont, "It's a dirty job, but something's gotta do it," *Business Week* (August 20, 1990), 92–97.

7. John Markoff, "Making Robots More Like Us," *The New York Times*, October 28, 2013, http://www.nytimes.com/2013/ 10/29/science/making-robots-more-like-us.html (accessed January 20, 2018).

8. O. C. Ferrell and Michael Hartline, *Marketing Strategy* (Mason, OH: South-Western Cengage, 2011), 215.

9. Melissa Korn, "The Hot New M.B.A.: Supply-Chain Management," *The Wall Street Journal*, June 5, 2013, https:// www.wsj.com/articles/SB1000142412788732442390457852359 1792789054 (accessed January 20, 2018).

10. Ibid.

11. European Commission, "What Is GPP?" http://ec.europa. eu/environment/gpp/what_en.htm (accessed January 20, 2018).

12. Everett E. Adam, Jr., and Ronald J. Ebert, *Production and Operations Management* (Englewood Cliffs, NJ: Prentice-Hall, 1992).

13. Ross Johnson and William O. Winchell, "Business and Quality," pamphlet (Milwaukee: American Society for Quality Control, 1989).

14. Marshall Sashkin and Ken Kiser, "What is TQM?" *Executive Excellence 5*(May 1992), 11.

15. SeeLevel HX, "2017 QSR Drive-Thru Mystery Shopping Study Results," 2017, https://www.seelevelhx.com/drive-thru -study-results/ (accessed January 20, 2018).

16. Paul Ziobro and Danny Yadron, "Target Now Says 70 Million People Hit in Data Breach," *The Wall Street Journal*, January 10, 2014, https://www.wsj.com/articles/no-headline -available-1389359240 (accessed January 20, 2018).

17. General Electric, "ISO Certifications and Accreditations," https://www.geinstruments.com/company/iso-certification-and -accreditations (accessed January 20, 2018).

18. "ISO 2600—Social Responsibility," International Standard-ization, https://www.iso.org/iso-26000-social-responsibility .html (accessed January 20, 2018).

19. Facebook, "Introducing the Facebook for Android Beta Testing Program," June 27, 2013, https://www.facebook.com/ notes/facebook-engineering/introducing-the-facebook-for -android-beta-testing-program/10151529228878920/ (accessed January 20, 2018).

20. Mandi Woodruff, "So THIS Is Why Airline Food Tastes So Bad," *Business Insider*, http://www.businessinsider.com/so-this -is-why-airline-food-tastes-so-bad-2012-6 (accessed January 20, 2018).

21. "The History of Six Sigma," iSixSigma, https://www .isixsigma.com/new-to-six-sigma/history/history-six-sigma/ (accessed January 20, 2018).

22. Roger Hoerl, "An inside look at Six Sigma at GE," *Six Sigma Forum Magazine 1*(3), 35–44.

23. Claire Cain Miller, "Will Yahoo Increase Productivity by Banning People from Working at Home?" *New York Times*, February 25, 2013, https://bits.blogs.nytimes.com/2013/02/25/ will-yahoo-increase-productivity-by-banning-people-from -working-at-home/?mtrref=www.google.com&gwh =5875A5078920C48E67D3B4F3D0B29C68&gwt=pay (accessed January 20, 2018).

24. Christopher Rugaber, "U.S. Worker Productivity Rises at Modest Pace," *Time*, November 14, 2013, http://business.time .com/2013/11/14/u-s-worker-productivity-rises-at-modest-pace/ (accessed November 22, 2013).

25. Adam and Ebert, *Production and Operations Management*.

26. Matthew Rocco, "U.S. to Surpass Russia as the Largest Oil and Gas Producer," *FOX News*, October 3, 2013, http://www .foxbusiness.com/industries/2013/10/03/us-to-surpass-russia-as -largest-oil-and-gas-producer/ (accessed January 20, 2018).

27. Florida State University, "Prudential-Davis Productivity Awards," http://hr.fsu.edu/?page=FacultyStaff_Training_Events (accessed November 22, 2013).

28. Accenture, "Accenture Connected Learning," https://www.accenture.com/us-en/careers/your-future-training-counseling (accessed January 20, 2018).

29. Eaton, "Employee Engagement," http://www.eaton.com/us/en-us/company/sustainability/workforce/talent-management.html (accessed January 20, 2018).

30. Thomas J. Peters and Robert H. Waterman, Jr., *In Search of Excellence: Lessons from America's Best-Run Companies* (New York: Warner Books, 1982), 14–15, 260–277.

31. Matthew Goyette, "100 Years After Ford: Where the Conveyor Belt Has Taken Us," *Apriso*, July 24, 2013, http://www.apriso.com/blog/2013/07/100-years-after-ford-where-the-conveyor-belt-has-taken-us/ (accessed November 22, 2017); Scott M. Patton, "Consumer-Driven Sigma Six Saves Ford $300 Million," *Quality Digest*, 2000, https://www.qualitydigest.com/sept01/html/ford.html (accessed November 22, 2017); Joseph O'Reilly, "The Evolution of Inbound Logistics—The Ford and Toyota Legacy: Origin of the Species," *Inbound Logistics*, January 2008, http://www.inboundlogistics.com/cms/article/the-evolution-of-inbound-logistics-the-ford-and-toyota-legacy-origin-of-the-species/ (accessed July 30, 2013); Joseph Szczesny, "Ford Boosting Production as Sales Heat Up," *The Detroit Bureau*, May 23, 2013, http://www.thedetroitbureau.com/2013/05/ford-boosting-production-as-sales-heat-up/ (accessed November 22, 2017); Deepa Seetharaman, "Ford Adds Production to North America to Meet New Car Demand," *Chicago Tribune*, May 21, 2013, http://articles.chicagotribune.com/2013-05-21/marketplace/sns-rt-us-autos-ford-capacitybre94l04e-20130521_1_ford-fusion-ford-focus-ford-motor-com (accessed November 22, 2017); Ford, "Innovation—The Making of a Global Vehicle: Design," 2012, http://corporate.ford.com/innovation/innovation-detail/making-of-global-vehicle (accessed July 31, 2013); Ford, "Our Company," https://corporate.ford.com/company.html (accessed November 22, 2017); Ford, "New Goals for Advanced, Flexible Manufacturing," 2017, http://corporate.ford.com/innovation/100-years-moving-assembly-line.html (accessed November 22, 2017); Ford, "Car Workers Buddy Up with Robots—Man and Machine Work Hand-in-Hand as Ford Applies Industry 4.0 Automation," *Ford Media Center*, July 14, 2016, https://media.ford.com/content/fordmedia/fna/us/en/news/2016/07/14/car-workers-buddy-up-with-robots--man-and-machine-work-hand-in-h.html (accessed November 22, 2017); Lucas Mearian, "3D Printing Is Now Entrenched at Ford," *CIO*, August 21, 2017, https://www.cio.com/article/3214471/3d-printing/3d-printing-is-now-entrenched-at-ford.html (accessed November 22, 2017).

Entrepreneurship and Small Business

Source: Monkey Business Images/Shutterstock

After reading this chapter, you will be able to:

- Define *entrepreneurship* and *small business*.
- Summarize the importance of small business in the U.S. economy and the reasons certain fields attract small business.
- Analyze why small businesses succeed and fail.
- Specify how you would go about starting a small business and what resources you would need.
- Determine why many large businesses are trying to "think small."
- Critique a small business's strategy and make recommendations for its future.

Louisville Slugger Hits the Ball Out of the Park

The story and success of the Louisville Slugger baseball bat is a prime example of how entrepreneurship can change an entire industry. It all started over a century ago when an 11-year-old boy, Bud Hillerich, used his ability to innovate to bring significant changes to baseball. Bud was the son of Frederick Hillerich, who owned a woodworking shop. Bud, who was an apprentice in his father's shop, also played amateur baseball. Bud took his knowledge of woodworking and his love of baseball and applied it to developing bats for himself and several teammates. What might have started out as a simple invention would lead to a business that remains popular to this day.

In 1884, Bud made a bat for Pete Browning, a star on the professional Louisville Major League Baseball team. Browning debuted the bat at the next game three days later and got three hits. Bud wanted to create a business out of selling bats, but Bud's father initially thought there was no future in making baseball bats. Despite his father's opposition, young Bud kept promoting his idea and finally convinced his father to pursue the endeavor. Ten years later when Bud took over the business from his father, he renamed it "Louisville Slugger," and registered with the U.S. Patent Office. Afterward, Bud started patenting his process for making bats.

In 1905, the "The Flying Dutchman" Wagner, a superstar with the Pittsburgh Pirates, signed an endorsement with Louisville Slugger, becoming the first athlete to endorse a product. By 1911, salesman Frank Bradsby had brought his professional sales and marketing expertise to the company. With his help, by 1923 the Louisville Slugger was selling more bats than any other bat maker in the country. Among the baseball legends who used Louisville Slugger bats are Babe Ruth, Lou Gehrig, Hank Aaron, and many other sports icons.

Currently, the Louisville Slugger has sold more than 100 million bats, making it the most popular bat brand in baseball history. Louisville Slugger continues to dominate the game in both the wood and aluminum bat categories. Sixty percent of all Major League Baseball players use Louisville Slugger bats. On average, each of the players will order approximately 120 bats in a season. The company has become so skilled in developing bats that it can carve a bat in 45 seconds and have it completed in six hours or less. In recent years, the company has expanded beyond making

Source: Thomas Kelley/Shutterstock

bats into selling gloves, helmets, catcher's gear, equipment bags, training aids, and accessories. In addition, Louisville Slugger also offers personalized, miniature, commemorative, and collectible bats.

Over time, the bats have become lighter. Both Babe Ruth and Hank Aaron used similar bat models, yet Aaron's was nine ounces lighter. This is due to the hollowing technology invented by the Japanese. With this newer technology, Louisville Slugger now has the capability to custom build bats to the players' specifications. The players are given options on what type of wood they want for their custom bats, as well as the weight, length, and cosmetics of the bat, including grips, color, knobs, and end caps.

Louisville Slugger has predominately used ash wood from Pennsylvania. Today, half of the professional bats made are from the northern white ash and half from maple. The best timber comes from the northeastern United States where the conditions are favorable for the growth of these trees. To help manage the enormous amounts of bats that Louisville Slugger produces, the company owns 6,500 acres of timberland in Pennsylvania and New York.

Today, Louisville Slugger makes 1.8 million bats a year. This breaks down to 3,000 full-size bats each day, with approximately 5,000 full-size bats each day during peak periods. Even with the large amounts of bats produced every day, the company maintains 8,000 different variants, with 300 of the variations being the most popular among baseball players. If Bud had listened to his father and continued making butter churns, the world would have never known of Louisville Slugger.[1]

Introduction

Although many management students go to work for large corporations upon graduation, others may choose to start their own business or find employment opportunities in small businesses with 500 or fewer employees. There are approximately 29 million small businesses operating in the United States today, each representing the vision of its entrepreneurial owners to succeed by providing new or better products.[2] Small businesses are the heart of the U.S. economic and social system because they offer opportunities and express the freedom that people have to make their own destinies. Today, the entrepreneurial spirit is growing around the world, from Russia and China to Germany, Brazil, and Mexico.

In this chapter, we examine the world of entrepreneurship and small business. First we examine several definitions of small business, the role of small business in the American economy, and industries that provide small-business opportunities. Then we analyze why small businesses succeed or fail. Next, we discuss how an entrepreneur goes about starting a small business. Finally, we look at entrepreneurship in larger businesses.

The Nature of Entrepreneurship and Small Business

An **entrepreneur** is a person who creates a business or product, manages his or her resources, and takes risks to gain a profit. **Entrepreneurship** is the process of creating and managing a business to achieve desired objectives. In the past, entrepreneurs were often inventors who brought all the factors of production together to produce a new product. Thomas Edison, whose inventions include the record player and lightbulb, was an early American entrepreneur. Entrepreneurs have been associated with such uniquely American products as Levi's 501 blue jeans, Dr Pepper, and Apple iPods. More recent entrepreneurial ventures have included Microsoft, Starbucks, and Google. Of course, smaller businesses do not have to evolve into such highly visible companies with large market shares to be successful, but those entrepreneurial efforts that result in rapidly growing businesses become more visible with their success. Successful recent entrepreneurs are Mark Zuckerberg (Facebook), Tony Hsieh (Zappos), and Jack Dorsey (Twitter and Square). See Table A.1 for more examples of great entrepreneurs over the last few decades.

The entrepreneurship movement is accelerating, with many new, smaller businesses emerging. Computing power that was once available only to the largest firms can now be acquired by a small business. Technology such as websites, podcasts, online videos,

entrepreneur: A person who creates a business or product, manages his or her resources, and takes risks to gain a profit.

entrepreneurship: The process of creating and managing a business to achieve desired objectives.

TABLE A.1 Great Entrepreneurs of Innovative Companies

Company	Entrepreneur(s)
Hewlett-Packard	Bill Hewlett, David Packard
Walt Disney Productions	Walt Disney
Starbucks	Howard Schultz
Amazon.com	Jeff Bezos
Dell	Michael Dell
Microsoft	Bill Gates
Apple	Steve Jobs
Walmart	Sam Walton
Google	Larry Page, Sergey Brin
Ben & Jerry's	Ben Cohen, Jerry Greenfield
Ford	Henry Ford
General Electric	Thomas Edison

ENTREPRENEURSHIP

Source: Rawpixel.com/Shutterstock

Entrepreneurship is the process of creating and managing a business to achieve desired objectives.

small business: Any business that is not dominant in its competitive area and does not employ more than 500 people.

Small Business Administration (SBA): An independent agency of the federal government that offers managerial and financial assistance to small businesses.

social media, cell phones, and even expedited delivery services enable small businesses to be more competitive with today's giant corporations. Small business can also develop alliances with other businesses to produce and sell products in domestic and global markets.[3] Indeed, John F. Welch, Jr., former chairman of giant General Electric, says, "Size is no longer the trump card it once was in today's brutally competitive world marketplace—a marketplace that . . . demands value and performance.[4]

Defining Small Business

What is a small business? This question is difficult to answer because size is relative. In this book, we define a **small business** as any business that is not dominant in its competitive area and does not employ more than 500 people. A local Mexican-food restaurant may be the most patronized Mexican-food restaurant in your community, but because it does not dominate the restaurant industry as a whole, it can be considered a small business. This definition is similar to the one used by the **Small Business Administration (SBA)**, an independent agency of the federal government that offers managerial and financial assistance to small businesses. Table A.2 shows additional standards that the SBA uses to determine which businesses qualify to receive its help.

The Role of Small Business in the American Economy

No matter how you define small business, one fact is clear: Small businesses are vital to the soundness of the American economy. Over 99 percent of all U.S. firms are classified as small businesses, and they account for approximately 40 percent of the U.S. gross national product (GNP). Small businesses are largely responsible for fueling job creation, innovation, and opportunities for minorities and women.[5]

Job Creation

The energy, creativity, and innovative abilities of small-business owners have resulted in jobs for other people. In fact, two-thirds of net new jobs are created every year by small businesses, and they contribute approximately half of annual GDP.[6] Table A.3 indicates that businesses employing fewer than 20 people account for 89 percent of all businesses, and 99.7 percent of all businesses employ fewer than 500 people. Many small businesses today are being started or growing because of encouragement from larger businesses. For example, DIRECTV is partnering with New York movie studio startup A24. The deal provides the startup with financing to produce independent films, and DIRECTV receives exclusive rights to these films.[7] Whether through formal joint ventures, supplier

TABLE A.2 Small Business Administration (SBA) Qualifying Factors for Assistance

- Operate for profit
- Be engaged in, or propose to do business in, the United States or its possessions
- Have reasonable owner equity to invest
- Use alternative financial resources, including personal assets, before seeking financial assistance

Source: U.S. Small Business Administration, "SBA Financial Assistance Eligibility," http://www.sba.gov/content/sba-financial-assistance-eligibility (accessed October 15, 2013).

TABLE A.3 Number of Employer Firms by Employment Size

Firm Size	Number of Firms	Percentage of All Firms
0–19	5,205,640	89.4
20–99	513,179	8.8
100–499	87,563	1.5
500+	19,076	0.3

Note: This table measures employer firms, those with paid employees. About three-fourths of all businesses are considered nonemployers.

Source: Small Business Administration, "Firm Size Data," 2014, https://www.sba.gov/advocacy/firm-size-data (accessed January 19, 2018).

relationships, producing or marketing cooperative projects, or other types of partnerships the rewards of collaborative relationships are creating many jobs for small-business owners and their employees.[8] Another example is Hipstamatic, a small photography company with several product lines. Hipstamatic has worked with several large companies such as Nike, Levi's, and *W* magazine to create exclusive cameras used in marketing and promotion activities. As Hipstamatic builds its portfolio of partnerships, the company is becoming a reputable figure in the business world.[9]

Innovation

Perhaps the strength of small businesses is their ability to innovate, bring significant changes and benefits to customers, and stimulate the economy.[10] Mary-Cathryn Kolb cofounded the company Brrr°, which designs and licenses a high-performance synthetic-blend fabric designed to keep the fabric cool and avoid moisture. The Brrr° label was sold in Neiman Marcus and Dillard's. This is just one example of a small company's ability to innovate and contribute to the benefit of customers and the economy.[11] According to the U.S. Office of Management and Budget, more than half the major technological advances of the twentieth century—including air conditioning, the ballpoint pen, the instant camera, insulin, the zipper, and xerography—were developed by individual inventors and entrepreneurs. Xerox, Ford Motor, Procter & Gamble, Levi Strauss, and Apple Inc. all began as innovative small companies and grew into multibillion-dollar enterprises.

Successful firms are built on innovation, which takes many forms. William Wrigley Jr. founded his eponymous company in 1891 selling baking powder, soap, and other necessities. In order to generate interest, Wrigley offered free gum with product purchases. This small activity turned out to be one of the defining and long-lasting contributions to the identity of the company. He quickly found that the gum was popular among customers and began developing innovative new recipes. Despite solidified stereotypes among the public about gum chewing and harsh economic conditions, Wrigley used his entrepreneurial insight and risk-taking perspective to build his business. He invested all the money he had in an advertising campaign for his new line of chewing gum and proved successful. Brands such as Wrigley Spearmint® and Juicy Fruit® are still well-known staples of the multibillion-dollar company.[12] Ray Kroc, a small business owner, is another example of an innovative entrepreneur. He developed a new way to sell hamburgers and turned his idea into one of the most successful fast-food franchises in the world—McDonald's. Additionally J. Darius Bikoff founded Glaceau, well-known for its enhanced water drinks, after a water contamination scare. He built his small business offering slightly flavored drinks in health food stores into a nationally recognized company that was acquired by Coca-Cola. Brands such as VitaminWater and SmartWater are popular today.[13] Small businesses have become an integral part of our lives, and the entrepreneurs that lead them provide fresh ideas and usually have greater flexibility to change than large companies.

Opportunities for Minorities and Women

Small businesses also provide opportunities for minorities and women that are sometimes unavailable in larger firms because of prejudice and other factors. The United States is home to over 9.1 million women-owned businesses and comprise 31 percent of privately held companies. Similarly, there are 8 million minority-owned businesses in the United States. One explanation for this strong growth is a result of the many resources available to women and minority entrepreneurs on both the federal and local levels. For example, the Small Business Administration (SBA) offers special programs to women and minority groups who meet the qualifications. If applicants are accepted, they then have access to financing and business development programs, as well as to opportunities such as exclusive contracts and partnerships with other businesses. Additionally, women and minorities are encouraged to become entrepreneurs through incentives such as tax breaks.[14]

Many women will start their own business for financial or lifestyle reasons.[15] Some start their own business as a means of supplemental income or to have the ability to work full-time on their own terms. As women continue to balance work and family responsibilities, many find that starting their own business is the best way to achieve both of these goals simultaneously. The flexibility of owning one's own business is a driver for more women to become entrepreneurs. In Atlanta, launchpad2X provides programs for women entrepreneurs.

Immigrants have an unusually high tendency toward entrepreneurship. They are less likely to fear the risks associated with starting a business, they tend to have a competitive advantage in bringing their native perspective to the United States, and some immigrants are likely to start a business out of necessity due to lack of education or inability to secure traditional employment. Recent reports have shown that from a sample of 100,000 immigrants who do not own a business, 620 will begin their own business in any given month. Conversely, only 280 from the same sample size of native non-business owners start their own business. Immigrant business owners are also more likely to hire more people and contribute a greater percentage of wealth to the economy.[16]

Women and minority small-business owners often face problems associated with lack of experience and education. This is being addressed by a number of government, industry, professional, and collegiate groups that offer managerial and financial assistance as well as training programs for women and minority entrepreneurs. For example, the Small Business Administration has organized an Office of Women's Business Ownership, and

One reason why women and minority entrepreneurs have experienced strong growth is because of the many resources made available to them on both the federal and local levels.

there is a National Association of Women Business Owners. Additionally, the Women's Business Ownership Act of 1988 established a training and assistance program for businesswomen, while banning discrimination against women applying for business loans. Such programs are helping to boost minority business ownership as well as enhancing the opportunities minorities have to thrive in the world of business.

Industries That Attract Small Business

Small businesses are found in nearly every industry, but retailing, wholesaling, services, and manufacturing are especially attractive to entrepreneurs because they are relatively easy to enter and require low initial financing. Small-business owners also find it easier to focus on a specific group of consumers in these fields than in others, and new firms in these industries suffer from heavy competition, at least in the early stages, than do established firms. Figure A.1 describes some of the industries that attract small business.

Traditionally, small businesses have been strongest in low-technology areas such as retailing and wholesaling. But the growth of small businesses in computer and information processing, scientific equipment, medical goods, electronic components, and chemical and allied products demonstrates that small business is moving into the high-technology area at a rapid pace.[17]

Retailing

Retailers acquire goods from producers or wholesalers and sell them to consumers. Main streets, shopping strips, and shopping malls are lined with independent music stores, sporting-goods shops, dry cleaners, boutiques, drugstores, restaurants, caterers, service stations, and hardware stores that sell directly to consumers. Chipotle Grill, Walmart, Sears, Starbucks, and Best Buy are all examples of retailers.

Retailing attracts entrepreneurs because gaining experience and exposure in retailing is relatively easy. An entrepreneur opening a new retailing store does not have to spend the large sums of money for the equipment and distribution systems that a manufacturing business requires. All that a new retailer needs is a lease on store space, merchandise, enough money to sustain the business, knowledge about prospective customers' needs and desires, the ability to use promotion to generate awareness, and basic management skills. When Sharon Munroe wanted to open up a retail consignment store in Austin, Texas, she figured that it would be impossible to get a loan from the bank. Munroe estimated her cash flow projections beforehand and spent more than $30,000 to open her store Little Green Beans, which covered rent/operating costs, public relations, marketing,

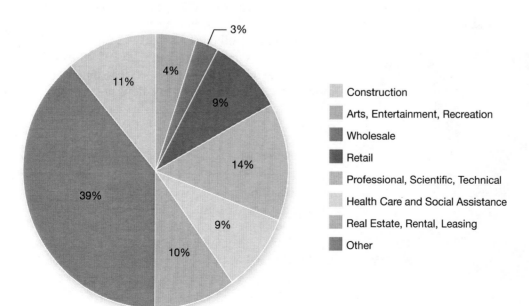

FIGURE A.1

The Relative Proportion of Small Business by Industry in the United States

Note: Based on 2013 data.

Source: U.S. Small Business Administration, *United States Small Business Profile*, 2017, https://www.sba.gov/sites/default/files/advocacy/United_States_1.pdf (accessed January 19, 2018).

IT, and miscellaneous expenses. She was able to avoid inventory costs by agreeing to split the profits of the sales with her consigners.[18]

Wholesaling

Wholesalers supply products to industrial, retail, and institutional users for resale or for use in making other products. Wholesaling activities range from planning and negotiating for supplies, promoting, and distributing (warehousing and transporting) to providing management and merchandising assistance to clients. Wholesalers are extremely important for many products, especially consumer goods, because of the marketing activities they perform. Although it is true that wholesalers themselves can be eliminated, their functions must be passed on to some other organization such as the producer, or to another intermediary, often a small business. McKesson Corp., W.W. Grainger, Liberty USA Inc., and Eby Brown Co. are all examples of wholesalers.

Success in today's highly competitive global economy requires finding the right partners to warehouse, transport, track inventories, communicate, and deliver products. Many small businesses have the flexibility to solve distribution problems for large businesses. For example, Zoom Systems quickly built an international distribution business with its large vending machines. The company's machines can now be found in airports and other heavy-traffic locations. High-profile companies such as Best Buy, Apple, and Macy's entered into partnerships with the distributor to increase the reach of their distribution capabilities. The vending machines dispense small, high-priced items such as cell phones, iPods, headphones, and more.[19] Moreover, small businesses are often closer to the final customers and know what it takes to keep them satisfied. Some smaller businesses start out in manufacturing but find their real niche as a supplier or distributor of larger firms' products.

Services

Services include businesses that do work for others but do not actually produce tangible goods. Real-estate and insurance and personnel agencies, barbershops, banks, television and computer repair shops, copy centers, dry cleaners, and accounting firms are all service businesses. Services also attract individuals—such as beauticians, morticians, jewelers, doctors, veterinarians—whose skills are not usually required by large firms. Many of these service providers are also retailers because they provide their services to ultimate consumers. Wells Fargo, KPMG, the Walt Disney Company, and the Ritz-Carlton all operate in the service industry.

One of the best-known examples of a small service business that expanded dramatically is H&R Block, Inc., the tax preparation company. With $5,000 borrowed from an aunt, Henry W. Bloch started United Business Services with his younger brother Richard after World War II. The firm provided bookkeeping, management advice, and income tax preparation for small businesses. By 1954, the bulk of the business was tax preparation, so in 1955 the brothers dissolved United Business Services and formed H&R Block, Inc. The company now prepares more than 23.2 million tax returns per year and is valued at $3 billion.[20]

Manufacturing

Manufacturing goods can provide unique opportunities for small businesses, which can often customize products to meet specific customer needs and wants. Such products include custom artwork, jewelry, clothing, furniture, and computer software. Started in 1988, the Malcolm Baldrige Award recognizes achievements in quality and performance in businesses of all sizes. It is designed to spur competitive business practices in American industry. One previous winner of the Mal-

Lululemon takes advantage of the growing market for yoga clothing.

Source: fizkes/Shutterstock

colm Baldrige Award in the small business area is Momentum Group, a California-based small business that creates and distributes contract textiles. Momentum Group incorporates quality in every aspect of its operations, such as adopting process upgrades that reduce sample production time while increasing yields and being the first to offer a textile product line of fabrics that has a reduced environmental impact.[21] IBM, Cummins, Samsung, and Toyota are examples of manufacturers.

"Small" is often equated with responsiveness and flexibility in production. Moreover, technological developments have made it possible for small businesses to compete with larger companies. Computer-control devices help maintain quality, while computerized databases give small businesses access to information resources comparable to those of large firms with extensive research and development departments. Electronic networks can allow small firms to interact with other firms to exchange information and expertise. Finally, computers and advanced software allow smaller firms to perform computer-aided design, which was available only to large firms with significant resources a few decades ago.[22]

Reasons for Small-Business Success

There are many reasons why small-business entrepreneurs succeed. Entrepreneurs are often obsessed with their vision of success and are willing to work hard and long hours. The ever-present risk of failure may place a degree of excitement and concern on each decision. The small business is more flexible in responding to the marketplace through innovative products and staying close to the customer. Small businesses usually have only one layer of management—the owner(s)—so they can make decisions without consulting multiple levels and departments within the organization. Flexibility and rapid decision making mean that new product development can occur more rapidly in small businesses than in larger ones.

Entrepreneurs go into business for themselves for many reasons, but most say it is so that they can use their skills and abilities, gain control of their life, build for their family, and simply enjoy the challenge. Other reasons include being able to live in a location of their choosing, gain respect and recognition, earn lots of money, and fulfill others' expectations. Some say that it was the best alternative available at the time.[23] Small businesses sometimes emerge because of a distinctive competency to meet a consumer need not being addressed by other firms. For example, Merry Maid took a simple service (housecleaning) and offered standardized service in cities across the country. Table A.4 shows some of the reasons entrepreneurs start their own businesses; many of these reasons provide a strong drive to succeed.

Independence and Autonomy

Independence and autonomy are linked to success and probably are the leading reasons that entrepreneurs choose to go into business for themselves. Being a small-business owner means being your own boss. Many people start their own businesses because they

TABLE A.4 Reasons Entrepreneurs Start Businesses

1. Desire to be one's own boss
2. Desire to choose the people one works with
3. Desire to fulfill a market or societal need that is not sufficiently being met
4. Desire to make a profit from an invention
5. Desire to contribute to a social and economic good
6. Desire to engage in competition and risk taking
7. Desire to realize one's vision
8. Desire to create something
9. Desire to have a flexible work schedule
10. Desire to generate or supplement income

The development of the home office, with computer, copy machine, telephone, and fax machine, has fostered the development of many home-based businesses.

believe they will do better for themselves than they could do by remaining with their current employer or by changing jobs. They may feel stuck on the corporate ladder or feel that no business would take them seriously enough to fund their ideas. Sometimes people who venture forth to start their own small business are those who simply cannot work for someone else. Such people may say that they just do not fit the "corporate mold." More often, small-business owners just want the freedom to choose whom they work with, the flexibility to pick where and when to work, and the option of working in a family setting.

Many small businesses start in the entrepreneur's home and then expand to a separate office or facility. Working out of the home has accelerated in popularity as a result of the explosion of telecommunications technology, and the downsizing of many major companies. The development of the home office, with computer, copy machine, telephone, and fax machine, has fostered the development of many home-based businesses. Not all people are suited to working at home, however—there are often complaints of a sense of isolation and missed interaction with coworkers. Other complaints relate to overworking—not being able to confine work activities to normal hours, family problems, and an inability to generate the increased productivity expected. Nonetheless, the home work environment provides the autonomy that many successful small-business owners desire.[24]

Taking Advantage of Market Opportunities

Small businesses that utilize industry databases, conduct market surveys, and develop a marketing plan are more successful in business. Learning allows the entrepreneur to see opportunities. Success in finding a market opportunity is often attributed to luck, but successful entrepreneurs review alternatives and capitalize on their discoveries, not random events. In other words, even with a limited budget, entrepreneurs engage in "luck-shaping market strategies" because they do their homework well. They pay attention to facts, assess unexpected occurrences, and notice patterns that increase the chance that something predictable will happen.[25]

Causes of Small-Business Failure[26]

Despite the importance of small businesses to our economy, there is no guarantee of small-business success. According to the Small Business Administration, approximately half of all new ventures last up to five years and one-third of those surpass 10 years or longer. This is due to many factors, such as high-stress level, lack of capital, management inexperience or incompetence, inability to manage economies of scale, etc. In the first few years of a venture, the founders often fulfill multiple duties including operations, marketing and sales, finding investors, and more. It is vital to the success of a new business to ensure a strong founding team. Businesses that have a founding team comprised of two or more members are more likely to succeed than those that are established by a single founder. Furthermore, the team should have at least one visionary and one who excels at operations or management. This combination increases the chances of survival even further. It is important to note that there is a happy medium when it comes to the number of members on a founding team. Having more than four members often causes more problems, such as inability to resolve conflict and decreased efficiency in decision making.

Small businesses fail for many reasons. A poor business concept—such as insecticides for garbage cans (research found that consumers are not concerned with insects in their

You're the Manager . . . What Would You Do?

THE COMPANY: Signet Marketing Consultants
YOUR POSITION: Owner and Chief Executive Officer
THE PLACE: Wilmette, IL

Signet Marketing Consultants was founded by Dan Signet, an engineering major and graduate of the Minnesota State University MBA program. It publishes promotional calendars and business planners. The company originated as a printing firm where Dan could use his education to provide creative, high-quality printing services. To differentiate and grow, Dan decided to specialize in customized desk-pad calendars imprinted with promotional advertising for a company or product. The company sells these calendars directly to businesses for use in their own promotion.

The company grew and, through its success, Dan made major financial commitments to add a new, large, high-speed press and to purchase, redesign, and rebuild a specialized collating machine to further automate the assembly process. The sophistication of the company's marketing efforts improved dramatically. Signet began identifying customers by their Standard Industrial Code (SIC) number and sales volume. It also installed a toll-free phone line to encourage direct calls from potential customers. Customers who call to inquire about Signet's services receive a sample calendar with alternative advertising ideas related to their area of business and a follow-up phone call within several days after they receive the materials.

Realizing that the commercial printing business had matured and that competition was increasing, Signet decided to sell his printing operations and focus all his efforts on the marketing of these specialty calendars. A long-term contract with the buyer of the printing plant assured Signet the opportunity to maintain production at that plant. Now Signet could focus all of his energy on creating and selling new calendar products.

Dan revised his customer base in order to aggressively pursue *Fortune* 500 service companies. He expanded the product line to include wall planners, pocket calendars, diaries, and desktop calendars. In addition, more aggressive marketing efforts were developed. Signet built new office facilities and eventually grew to a staff of nine full-time employees. Between 2015 and 2018, the business grew rapidly and profits were very high.

After carefully assessing the characteristics of the calendar buyers, Signet identified a new market opportunity. Signet had historically worked closely with marketing/advertising people within large companies who distributed the calendars to customers through

Signet developed the "Total Service" program to provide all services needed for an entire calendar promotion.

Source: andy0man/Shutterstock

their sales forces. Managing and implementing such a calendar program required extensive time on the part of the company initiating it. Therefore, Signet developed and marketed a "Total Service Package" as an option for customers. Signet employees handled the entire calendar promotion, including conception, design, production, and delivery. Of course, the process for Signet employees became very stressful and time consuming and required great attention to detail and approval-seeking from the client. Dan has been lucky to have such a loyal, productive, and cohesive group of employees. In many ways, their culture has been like that of a small family.

The "Total Service" program has been enormously successful, with Signet shipping to some 20,000 locations for single customers. The only problem facing Dan Signet and his employees is that they are outgrowing their facilities. He wonders if he should hold business at its current level or sell the current building and purchase a new, larger facility and hire and train additional staff.

QUESTIONS

1. What do you perceive as the key to Signet's success?

2. As owner of Signet, do you feel that selling the printing portion of the business was the correct decision to help the company achieve its objectives?

3. Evaluate Signet's opportunity and the considerations involved in expansion of its operations to grow its overall sales.

garbage)—will produce disaster nearly every time. Expanding a hobby into a business may work if a genuine market niche exists, but all too often people start such a business without identifying a real need for the goods or services. Other notable causes of small-business failure include the burdens imposed by government regulation, insufficient funds to withstand slow sales, and vulnerability to competition from larger companies. However, three major causes of small-business failure deserve a close look: undercapitalization, managerial inexperience or incompetence, and the inability to manage growth.

Undercapitalization

undercapitalization: The lack of funds to operate a business normally and the shortest path to failure in business.

The shortest path to failure in business is **undercapitalization**, the lack of funds to operate a business normally. Many entrepreneurs underestimate the amount of capital they will need in order to become successful. Estimates are often short-sighted, focusing only on the amount needed to open the doors and operate for the first few months. New ventures do not usually make a profit for the first three to five years, so having enough capital for only the first few months is a fast path to failure. Writing a business plan, which will be discussed more later in the chapter, before beginning a new business will help alleviate this problem. The business plan forces the founders to formulate their idea, the market they are going to address, and the finances needed to accomplish this. Generally, a business plan encompasses a five-year period from the time it is written, so it helps the founders practice having foresight and planning for the future. Without sufficient funds, the best small-business idea in the world will fail.

Managerial Inexperience or Incompetence

Poor business management results in many business failures. Just because an entrepreneur has a brilliant vision for a small business does not mean he or she has the knowledge or experience to manage a growing business effectively. A person who is good at creating great product ideas and marketing them may lack the skills and experience to make good management decisions in hiring, negotiating, finance, and control. Moreover, entrepreneurs may neglect those areas of management they know little about or find tedious, at the expense of the business's success. Some businesses fail when their owners "burn out." It is important for a team to be composed of members whose skills vary and complement one another in order for all aspects of the business to be properly and sufficiently addressed. To manage a small business takes significant time, effort, and planning. The stress and strain can lead to closure or sellout.

While many entrepreneurs successfully learn these skills on the job, they may still find that, as the company grows, it is necessary to give up some control by bringing in more experienced managers to run the company. The founders of many small businesses, including Michael Dell of Dell Computers, found that they needed to bring in more experienced managers, in specific areas, to help manage their companies through intense growing pains.

Source: REDPIXEL.PL/Shutterstock

To avoid "burn out," it is important for a team to be composed of members whose skills vary and complement one another in order for all aspects of the business to be properly and sufficiently addressed.

Inability to Manage Growth

Depending on the type of business and industry, some small businesses may be likely to experience extremely fast growth. While this is an indication of success, the inability to deal with economies of scale can contribute to the downfall of the venture. The mobile and Internet game company Zynga is experiencing the consequences of the inability to manage growth. Since 2008, the company was wildly popular thanks to a partnership with Facebook. The game Farmville contributed to Zynga's success and was continually contributing to user growth. In order to facilitate the rapid growth, founder Mark Pincus solicited investments totaling $408 million. Soon after, Facebook raised the fees for hosting Farmville, popularity in Zynga's games decreased, and one of the company's acquisitions turned bad. Currently, the company has laid off most of its staff and is posting losses in the millions. In the end, the inability to foresee and manage growth can hurt the business's reputation with customers, strain the company's finances, and do irreparable damage.[27]

Starting a Small Business

To start a business, an entrepreneur must first have an idea. Sam Walton, founder of Walmart stores, had an idea for a discount retailing enterprise and spawned a global retailing empire that changed the way traditional companies look at their business. Next, the entrepreneur needs to devise a business plan to guide planning and development. Finally, decisions must be made as to the form of ownership, the financial resources needed, and whether to buy an existing business, start a new one, or buy a franchise.

The Business Plan

A key element of business success is a **business plan**—a meticulous statement of the rationale for the business and a step-by-step explanation of how it will achieve its goals. The business plan should include an explanation of the business, an evaluation of the competition, estimates of income and expenses, and other information. It should establish a strategy for acquiring sufficient funds to keep the business going. Indeed, many financial institutions base their decision of whether to loan a small business money on its business plan. However, the business plan should act as a guide and reference document, not a shackle to limit the business's flexibility and decision making.

Table A.5 presents the fundamental components of a business plan. The executive summary outlines the main focus of the plan. It should be two to three pages in length and consist of an introduction, the major aspects of the plan, and implementation considerations.

business plan: A meticulous statement of the rationale for the business and a step-by-step explanation of how it will achieve its goals.

TABLE A.5 The Components of a Business Plan

I. Executive Summary
II. Situation Analysis
   A. Nature of the business
   B. Target market
   C. Measures of performance
III. Strengths, Weaknesses, Opportunities, and Threats
   A. Operations
   B. Financial
   C. Management
   D. Political, legal, and regulatory forces
   E. Economic factors
   F. Competitive factors
   G. Technological factors
IV. Business Resources
   A. Financial
   B. Human
   C. Experience and expertise
V. Financial Projections and Budgets
   A. Delineation of costs
   B. Estimate of sales and revenues
   C. Expected return on investment
VI. Controls and Evaluation
   A. Measures of performance
   B. Monitoring and evaluating performance

The situation analysis examines the difference between the firm's current performance and past stated objectives. In a brand-new firm, it assesses where the entrepreneur is now in his or her development. The situation analysis may also include a summary of data relating to the creation of the current business situation obtained from both the firm's external and internal environment. Depending on the situation, details on the composition of the target market segment, marketing objectives, current marketing strategies, business trends, sales history, and profitability may also be included.

In the analysis of strengths, weaknesses, opportunities, and threats, the business plan must address both internal and external elements. Internally, the firm must look at the strengths and weaknesses of its major functional areas: operations, finance, management, and marketing, as well as the opportunities and threats of those elements in the business's operating environment. Externally, the plan describes the current state of the business environment, including the political, legal and regulatory, economic, competitive, and technological factors. It should also make predictions about the future directions of those forces and their possible impact on the implementation of the business plan. Because of the dynamic nature of these factors, managers need to periodically review and modify this section of the plan to adjust for changes.

A business's human and financial resources, as well as its experiences and expertise, are major considerations in developing a business plan. Therefore, the business plan outlines the human, financial, and physical resources available for accomplishing goals and describes resource constraints that may affect implementation. This section also describes any distinctive competencies that may give the firm an edge, and it takes into account strengths and weaknesses that may influence the firm's ability to achieve implementation.

The financial projections and budgets section outlines the returns expected through implementation of the plan. The costs incurred are weighed against the expected revenues. A budget must be prepared to allocate resources in order to accomplish business objectives. It should contain estimates of the costs of implementing the plan.

The controls and evaluation section detail how the results of the plan will be measured. Next, a schedule is developed for comparing the results achieved with the objectives set forth in the business plan. Finally, guidelines may be offered outlining who is responsible for monitoring the program and taking remedial action.

Forms of Business Ownership

sole proprietorships: The most popular form of business organization; businesses owned and managed by one individual.

While developing a business plan, the entrepreneur also has to decide on an appropriate legal form of business ownership, of which there are three basic ones: sole proprietorship, partnership, and corporation.

Sole Proprietorships

Sole proprietorships, businesses owned and managed by one individual, are the most popular form of business organization. Common examples include most restaurants, barbershops, flower shops, dog kennels, and independent grocery stores. Indeed, many sole proprietors focus on services—small retail stores, financial counseling, appliance repair, child care, and the like—rather than on the manufacture of goods, which often requires large amounts of capital not available to sole proprietors.[28]

Sole proprietorships are typically small businesses employing fewer than 50 people. There are more than 23 million sole proprietorships in the United States (more than 70 percent of all businesses), but they account for just 20 percent of the profits in the United States.[29]

Sole proprietorships have the advantages that they are easy and inexpensive to form; they permit a high de-

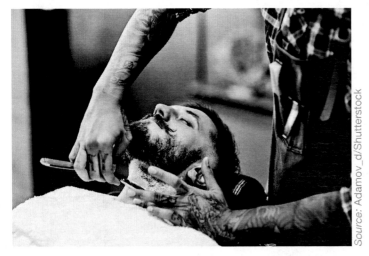

Many sole proprietors focus on services, such as a barbershop, rather than on the manufacture of goods.

Source: Adamov_d/Shutterstock

gree of secrecy; all profits belong to the owner (taxed as the owner's personal income); the owner has direct control over the business; there is minimal government regulation; and the business can be easily dissolved. Disadvantages are that sole proprietors generally must use personal assets to borrow money, often find it difficult to obtain external sources of funds, and generally must be jack-of-all-trades managers to handle diverse activities. Moreover, the survival of the business is tied to the life of the owner and his or her ability to work.

Partnerships

The Uniform Partnership Act defines a **partnership** as "an association of two or more persons who carry on as co-owners of a business for profit." There are three basic types of partnership. A **general partnership** involves a complete sharing in the management of a business, with each partner having unlimited liability for the business's debts. Professionals such as lawyers, accountants, and architects often join together in general partnerships. A **limited partnership** has at least one general partner, who assumes unlimited liability, and at least one limited partner, whose liability is limited to his or her investment in the business. Limited partners are barred from participating in the management of the business but share in the profits in accordance with the terms of a partnership agreement. Limited partnerships exist for risky investment projects where the chance of loss is great, such as oil-drilling and real-estate ventures.

The third type of partnership is a joint venture, established for a specific project or for a limited time. The partners in a joint venture may be individuals or organizations, as in the case of the international joint ventures discussed in Chapter 5. Control of a joint venture may be shared equally, or one partner may control decision making. While joint ventures are usually used by companies to easily enter other countries, other organizations enter into these partnerships with local organizations to make operations easier and less costly or even to further a cause. The American Bird Conservancy (ABC), for example, has entered into joint ventures with Central Hardwoods, Appalachian Mountains, Oaks and Prairies, and Rio Grande to further conservation initiatives. Through the combination of the efforts and distinct capabilities of each organization, such as science-based strategies, the joint ventures have been able to conserve bird habitats, land, and other animals.[30]

Partnerships offer the advantages of being easy to organize and having higher credit ratings because of the partners' combined wealth. Other advantages include the ability to specialize and make decisions faster than large businesses, less subjection to government regulations, and the fact that profits are paid directly to owners. On the other hand, partnerships can be disadvantageous due to large amounts of liability. General partners have unlimited liability for the debts of the partnership, and each partner is responsible for the decisions of others, which can be complicated if partners disagree. Furthermore, the distribution of profits may not reflect the amount of work done by each partner. Financial issues can also arise as selling a partnership interest at a fair price is difficult. Investors also tend to favor corporations over partnerships. Finally, the death of a partner terminates the partnership.

partnership: An association of two or more persons who carry on as co-owners of a business for profit.

general partnership: A partnership which involves a complete sharing in the management of a business, with each partner having unlimited liability for the business's debts.

limited partnership: Has at least one general partner, who assumes unlimited liability, and at least one limited partner, whose liability is limited to his or her investment in the business.

Source: PhotoStock10/Shutterstock

Limited partnerships exist for risky investment projects where the chance of loss is great, such as oil drilling.

Corporations

A **corporation** is a separate legal entity, or body, created by the state. Its assets and liabilities are distinct from those of the owners of the corporation. As a legal entity, a corporation has many of the rights, duties, and powers of a person, including receiving, owning, and transferring property. Corporations can enter into contracts with individuals or with other legal entities. They can sue and be sued in court. The owners own shares of **stock** in the corporation, which can be bought, sold, given as gifts, or inherited. As sole proprietorships or partnerships grow, many may choose to incorporate.

corporation: A separate legal entity, or body, created by the state; its assets and liabilities are distinct from those of the owners of the corporation.

stock: Shares of ownership in a corporation which can be bought, sold, given as gifts, or inherited.

Source: Kheng Guan Toh/Shutterstock

Corporations are a legal entity with the rights, duties, and powers of a person, with the shareholders having limited liability.

The corporate form of business boasts several advantages: The owners are not responsible for the firm's debts and have limited liability, ownership (stock) can be easily transferred, corporations usually have a perpetual life, external capital is more easily raised than in other forms of business, and expansion into new businesses is simpler because of the company's ability to enter into contracts. However, corporations also have disadvantages: They are subject to double taxation, which is tax on the company's income as well as stockholders' profits received as dividends. Additionally, forming a corporation can be expensive and complicated, much information must be made available to the public and to government agencies, and owners and managers may be different individuals with diverse goals.

limited liability company (LLC): The assets and liabilities of the company are separate from the owners', and if the company fails, all that is lost is the initial investment put forth by the owners.

Small-business owners are likely to form a **limited liability company (LLC)** in order to reduce the risk for themselves and their stockholders. Under an LLC, the assets and liabilities of the company are separate from the owners', and if the company fails, all that is lost is the initial investment put forth by the owners. While a creditor can sue an LLC for its debts, stockholders are not responsible to pay these debts from their own personal assets. Sometimes owners will pledge their personal assets to secure a loan for the LLC. This kind of activity is unusual for other kinds of corporations.[31]

Financial Resources

To make money from a small business, the owner must first provide or obtain money to get the business started and to keep it running smoothly. Even a small retail store will probably need initial financing to rent space, purchase or lease necessary equipment and furnishings, buy initial inventory of merchandise, and use as working capital. Often, the small-business owner has to contribute a significant percentage of the necessary capital. Few new business owners have the entire amount, however, and must look to other sources for additional financing. Many small-business owners combine funds from a variety of sources to finance their business ventures.

Equity Financing

The most important source of funds for any new business is the owner. Many owners include among their personal resources: ownership of a home, the accumulated value in a life-insurance policy, or a savings account. A new business owner may sell or borrow from the value of such assets to obtain funds to operate a business. Additionally, the owner may bring useful personal assets, such as a computer, desks and other furniture, or a car, as part of his or her ownership interest in the firm. The owner can also provide working capital for the business by reinvesting profits or simply by not drawing a full salary.

venture capitalists: Persons or organizations that agree to provide some funds for a new business in exchange for an ownership interest, or stock.

Small businesses can also obtain financing from investors. They may sell stock in the business to family members, friends, employees, or other investors. **Venture capitalists** are persons or organizations that agree to provide some funds for a new business in ex-

Lessons from *Shark Tank*

Shark Tank, a reality television show that airs on ABC and CNBC, features entrepreneurs who pitch their business ideas to a panel of investors. These investors include such successful entrepreneurs as real-estate mogul Barbara Corcoran, inventor and television personality Lori Greiner, businessman Robert Herjavec, founder of FUBU clothing line Daymond John, businessman and owner of the National Basketball Association's Dallas Mavericks Mark Cuban, and "Eco-preneur" Kevin O'Leary. These investors make the decision of whether to invest their own money with these entrepreneurs, based on whether they believe their ideas hold promise. Pitches range from ideas that are not yet realized to those that have already achieved sales and need more money for growth.

Some believe this show is having a positive impact on entrepreneurial-minded individuals, motivating some to start their own businesses while others gain insight on how to pitch their ideas to investors. Clear and quick articulation of the business opportunity, a thorough understanding of the business market, knowledge of cost and profitability metrics, and idea protection are lessons that many viewers have learned from watching the show. These lessons are important for potential entrepreneurs who will someday want to present their ideas to venture capitalists.

The "sharks" have invested more than $66 million in business ventures that were pitched on the show. Entrepreneurs who are passionate about their idea and well researched are more likely to be successful. However, many entrepreneurs on the show do not get the funding they desire. Yet even when the sharks choose not to invest, being on the show provides exposure for the entrepreneur.

Source: Kathy Hutchins/Shutterstock

The TV program *Shark Tank* is promoting entrepreneurship in America.

The sharks also offer advice on steps the entrepreneurs should take to make their businesses or ideas more viable, such as the following tips:

- Pursue profitability. Do what works.
- Take ownership for your success.
- Keep on persisting.
- Refuse to be intimidated.
- Work hard if you want to be successful.

Shark Tank has also given people a better and more optimistic view of the nature of American business. Whereas the media often give attention to technology-based businesses residing in Silicon Valley, this reality show offers insight into regular people who are trying to create something they are passionate about.[32]

---

change for an ownership interest, or stock. Venture capitalists hope to purchase the stock of a small business at a low price, and then sell the stock for a profit after the business has grown successful. Although these forms of equity financing have helped many small businesses, they require that the small-business owner share the profits of the business, and sometimes control as well, with the investors.

Debt Financing

New businesses sometimes borrow over half of their financial resources. In addition to financial institutions, they can also look to family and friends as sources for loans of long-term funds or for other assets such as a computer or automobile in exchange for an ownership interest in the business. In such cases, the business owner can usually structure a favorable repayment schedule and sometimes negotiate an interest rate below current bank rates. If the business fails, however, the emotional losses for all concerned may greatly exceed the money involved. Anyone lending a friend or family member money for a venture should state the agreement clearly in writing.

The amount a financial institution is willing to loan depends on its evaluation of the business's likelihood of success and of the entrepreneur's ability to repay the loan. The institution will often require the entrepreneur to put up collateral, a financial interest in the property or fixtures of the business, to guarantee payment of the debt. Additionally, the small-business owner may have to offer some personal property as collateral, such as the owner's home, in which case the loan is called a mortgage. If the small business fails to repay the loan, the lending institution may eventually claim and sell the collateral (or the owner's home, in the case of a mortgage) to recover its loss.

Banks and other financial institutions can also grant a small business a line of credit—an agreement by which a financial institution promises to lend a business a predetermined sum on demand. A line of credit permits an entrepreneur to take quick advantage of opportunities that require a bank loan.

Small businesses may obtain funding from their suppliers in the form of trade credit—that is, suppliers allow the business to take possession of the needed goods and services and pay for them at a later date or in installments. Occasionally, small businesses engage in bartering—trading their own products for the goods and services offered by other businesses. For example, an accountant may offer accounting services to an office supply firm in exchange for computer paper and printer cartridges.

Additionally, some community groups sponsor revolving loan funds to encourage the development of particular types of businesses. State and local agencies may guarantee loans, especially to minority businesspeople or for development in certain areas.

On the federal level, the Small Business Administration offers four types of financial assistance to qualifying businesses: direct loans, usually made only to businesses that do not qualify for loans from financial institutions; guaranteed loans, which ensure that a direct loan made by an institution to a qualified small business will be repaid; participation loans, a combination of guaranteed loans and direct loans in which the SBA guarantees an institution's loan for part of the firm's needs and makes up the balance in a direct loan; and Specialized Small Business Investment Companies (SSBICs), which are financing companies partially funded by the SBA that make loans to minority-run businesses. However, the SBA makes loans only to businesses that have been in operation for three years. It does not offer start-up money for new ventures.[33]

Approaches to Starting a Small Business

Starting from Scratch versus Buying an Existing Business

Although entrepreneurs often start new, small businesses from scratch much the way we have discussed in this section, they may elect instead to buy an existing business. This has the advantage of providing a network of existing customers, suppliers, and distributors and reducing some of the guesswork inherent in starting a new business from scratch. However, an entrepreneur buying an existing business must also deal with whatever problems the business already has.

Franchising

Many small-business owners find entry into the business world through franchising. A license to sell another's products or to use another's name in business, or both, is a **franchise**. The company that sells the franchise is the **franchiser**. Dunkin' Donuts, McDonald's, and Jiffy Lube are franchisers with national visibility. The purchaser of a franchise is the **franchisee**.

The franchisee acquires the rights to a name, logo, methods of operation, national advertising, products, and other elements associated with the franchiser's business in return for a financial commitment and the agreement to conduct business in accordance with the franchiser's standard of operations. Depending on the quality of the franchise, the initial fee and start-up costs can range from $1,000 to more than $2 million. In addition, the franchisee pays the franchiser a monthly or annual fee based on a percentage of sales or

franchise: A license to sell another's products or to use another's name in business, or both.

franchiser: The company that sells the franchise.

franchisee: The purchaser of a franchise.

profits. In return, the franchisee often receives building specifications and designs, site recommendations, management and accounting support, and, perhaps most importantly, immediate name recognition.

The practice of franchising first began in the United States when Singer used it to sell sewing machines in the nineteenth century. It soon became commonplace in the distribution of goods in the automobile, gasoline, soft-drink, and hotel industries. The concept of franchising grew rapidly during the 1960s, when it expanded to more diverse industries, particularly restaurants. Growth slowed in the 1970s, but franchises again grew steadily throughout the 1980s. During this period, many U.S. franchises, including McDonald's, Kentucky Fried Chicken (KFC), and Holiday Inn expanded internationally.

Franchises continue to grow at a fast pace today. Subway, a submarine sandwich franchise, is the world's largest fast-food chain, surpassing McDonald's. In 2013 alone, the franchise opened over 1,700 new locations and plans to open 10,000 more by the end of 2017. Anytime Fitness, a 24/7 fitness center, is another example of a company that has successfully used the franchising model to expand. Placed in convenient locations, with low membership rates and all-hours access, the franchise has grown internationally with over 3,000 locations in more than 20 countries.[34]

Help for Small-Business Managers

Because of the crucial role that small business and entrepreneurs play in the U.S. economy, a number of organizations offer programs to improve the small-business owner's ability to compete. These include entrepreneurial training programs and those sponsored by the Small Business Administration. Such presentations provide small-business owners with invaluable assistance in managing their businesses, often at little or no cost to the owner.

Entrepreneurs can learn critical marketing, management, and finance skills in college classrooms and seminars from Harvard to the University of Washington. Knowledge, experience, and judgment are necessary for success in a new business. While knowledge can be communicated and some experiences can be simulated in the classroom, good judgment must be developed by the entrepreneur. Local chambers of commerce and the U.S. Department of Commerce offer information and assistance helpful in operating a small business. Additionally, many urban areas—such as Chicago; Jacksonville, FL; Portland, OR; St. Louis; and Nashville—have a weekly business journal/newspaper that provides stories on local businesses as well as on business techniques that a manager or small business can use.

The Small Business Administration offers many types of management assistance to small businesses, including counseling for firms in difficulty, consulting on improving operations, and training for owner/managers and their employees. Among its many programs, the SBA funds Small-Business Development Centers (SBDCs). These are business clinics, usually located on college campuses, that provide counseling at no charge and training at only a nominal charge. SBDCs are often the SBA's principal means of providing direct management assistance.

The Service Corps of Retired Executives (SCORE) and the Active Corps of Executives (ACE) are volunteer agencies funded by the SBA to provide advice for small firms. Both are staffed by experienced managers whose talents and experience the small firms could not ordinarily afford. Together, SCORE and ACE have about 12,000 counselors working out of 350 chapters throughout the country. The SBA has also organized Small Business Institutes (SBIs) on almost 500 university and college campuses in the United States. Seniors and graduate students and faculty at each SBI provide on-site management counseling.

Entrepreneurship in Large Businesses

The continuing success and competitiveness of small businesses through rapidly changing conditions in the business world have led many large corporations to take a closer look at what makes their smaller rivals tick. More and more firms are emulating small businesses

3M's successful intrapreneurship program has contributed to the development of several new products, including Post-it Notes.

intrapreneurs: Similar to entrepreneurs, employees who take responsibility for, or "champion," developing innovations of any kind within the larger organization.

in an effort to improve their own bottom line. Beginning in the 1980s and continuing through the present, the buzzword in business has been to *downsize*, reduce management layers and corporate staff, and to focus work tasks to make the firm more flexible, resourceful, and innovative like a smaller business. Many well-known U.S. companies, including IBM, Apple Inc., General Electric, Xerox, and 3M have downsized to improve their competitiveness, as have German, British, and Japanese firms. Other firms have sought to make their businesses "smaller" by making their operating units function more like independent small businesses, each responsible for its profits, losses, and resources. Of course, some large corporations, such as Southwest Airlines, have acted like small businesses from their inception with great success.

In an attempt to capitalize on small-business success in introducing innovative new products, more and more of even the largest companies are trying to instill a spirit of entrepreneurship. In these large firms, **intrapreneurs**, like entrepreneurs, take responsibility for, or "champion," developing innovations of any kind *within* the larger organization.[35] Often, they use company resources and time to develop a new product for the company. At 3M, for example, an employee who develops an idea for a new product forms a team of interested coworkers from technical, operations, marketing, and finance areas. The team designs the product and develops a plan to manufacture and market it. If the new product achieves sales of $5 million, the intrapreneur who developed it is promoted to project manager for the product. Such intrapreneurship has contributed to the development of Post-it Notes, light pipes, and Scotch-Brite scrubbing sponges, all successful products for 3M.[36] LinkedIn, DreamWorks, and Google are also encouraging their employees to become intrapreneurs.[37] A company can foster intrapreneurship by supporting employees, letting employees learn from failures, rewarding innovation, breaking down barriers to internal communication, employing teams for long-term projects, and eliminating paperwork and red tape that may hinder timely action.

Summary and Review

- *Define* entrepreneurship *and* small business. An entrepreneur is a person who creates a business or product and manages his or her resources and takes risks to gain a profit; entrepreneurship is the process of creating and managing a business to achieve desired objectives. A small business is one that is not dominant in its competitive area and does not employ more than 500 people.

- *Summarize the importance of small business in the U.S. economy and the reasons certain fields attract small business.* Small businesses are vital to the American economy because they provide products, jobs, innovation, and opportunities. Retailing, wholesaling, services, and manufacturing attract small businesses because they are comparatively easy to enter, require relatively low initial financing, provide an opportunity to focus on a specific group of consumers, and may experience less heavy competition.

- *Analyze why small businesses succeed and fail.* Small businesses often succeed because of their owners' vision and hard work; independence and autonomy; ability to pinpoint market opportunities overlooked by other firms; and the flexibility, innovation, and rapid decision making afforded by small size. Small businesses fail for many reasons: undercapitalization, management inexperience or incompetence, neglect, disproportionate burdens imposed by government regulation, and vulnerability to competition from larger companies.

- *Specify how you would go about starting a small business and what resources you would need.* First, you must have an idea for developing a small business. Next, you need to devise a business plan to guide design and development of the business. Then you must decide what form of business ownership to use: sole proprietorship, partnership, or corporation. Small-business owners are expected to provide some of the funds required to start their businesses, but you can also obtain funds from friends and family, financial institutions, other businesses in the form of trade credit, investors (venture capitalists), state and local organizations, and the Small Business Administration. In addition to loans, the Small Business Administration and other organizations offer counseling, consulting, and training services. Finally, you must decide whether to start a new business from scratch, buy an existing one, or buy a franchise operation.

■ *Determine why many large businesses are trying to "think small."* More large companies are emulating small businesses in an effort to make their firms more flexible, resourceful, and innovative like a

smaller business, and generally to improve their bottom line. This effort often involves downsizing (reducing management layers, laying off employees, and focusing work tasks) and intrapreneurship, in which an employee takes responsibility for (champions) developing innovations of any kind within the larger organization.

■ *Critique a small business's strategy and make recommendations for its future.* As the manager of Signet Marketing Consultants (described in the "Business Dilemma" box), you should be able to analyze your company's strategy, including its strengths, weaknesses, threats, and opportunities, and make recommendations for the future.

Key Terms and Concepts

business plan 523

corporation 525

entrepreneur 513

entrepreneurship 513

franchise 528

franchisee 528

franchiser 528

general partnership 525

intrapreneurs 530

limited liability company (LLC) 526

limited partnership 525

partnership 525

small business 514

Small Business Administration (SBA) 514

sole proprietorships 524

stock 525

undercapitalization 522

venture capitalists 526

Ready Recall

1. Why are small businesses so important to the U.S. economy?
2. Which fields tend to attract entrepreneurs the most? Why?
3. What elements contribute to the success of small businesses?
4. What are the principal reasons for the high failure rate among small businesses?
5. What decisions must an entrepreneur make when starting a small business?
6. List the advantages and disadvantages of each form of small-business ownership.
7. What types of financing do small entrepreneurs typically use? What are some of the pros and cons of each?
8. List the types of management and financial assistance that the Small Business Administration offers.
9. Describe the franchising relationship.
10. Why do large corporations want to become more like small businesses?

Expand Your Experience

1. Interview a local small-business owner. Why did he or she start the business? What factors have led to the business's success? What problems has the owner experienced? What advice would he or she offer a potential entrepreneur?
2. Write a business plan for a small-business idea that you have, using Table A.5 as a guideline.
3. Using business journals, find an example of a large company that is trying to emulate the characteristics that make small businesses flexible and more responsive. Describe and evaluate the company's activities. Has it been successful? Why or why not?

Do you have entrepreneurial qualities?

The following are some characteristics that successful entrepreneurs have in common. Rate yourself on a scale of 1–5, 5 being the highest, to see how your inherent characteristics match up against other entrepreneurs.

	Not at all		Neutral		Very much
1. How comfortable are you in taking risks?	1	2	3	4	5
	Always		**Sometimes**		**Rarely**
2. How often do you avoid uncertainty?	1	2	3	4	5
	A little		**Moderately**		**A lot**
3. How independent are you?	1	2	3	4	5
	Rarely		**Sometimes**		**Frequently**
4. How often do you make decisions based on instinct?	1	2	3	4	5
	Not well		**Fairly well**		**Very well**
5. How well do you handle rejection?	1	2	3	4	5
	Not at all		**A little**		**A lot**
6. How much do you enjoy public speaking?	1	2	3	4	5
	Not at all		**A little**		**Very much**
7. How persuasive are you?	1	2	3	4	5
	Not at all		**A little**		**Very much**
8. How effective are you in building relationships quickly?	1	2	3	4	5
	Rarely		**Sometimes**		**Frequently**
9. How often do you think of new ways to solve problems?	1	2	3	4	5
	Rarely		**Sometimes**		**Frequently**
10. How often do you generate new ideas?	1	2	3	4	5

Source: Adapted from U.S. Small Business Administration, "Is Entrepreneurship For You?" http://www.sba.gov/content/entrepreneurship-you (accessed November 18, 2013).

Add your score and find the range into which you fall below.

10–20: If your score falls in this range, you are probably not suited to be an entrepreneur at this point in time. However, by practicing the traits listed above, you can develop your skills to become more suited to starting your own business.

20–40: If your score falls in this range, you may be able to handle the complexities involved in starting your own business. However, you may experience some difficulties. Work to strengthen your weaknesses and you will soon be able to deftly participate in the activities of entrepreneurship.

40–50: If your score falls in this range, you currently possess the characteristics of an entrepreneur. Beware of becoming complacent, however. Continue to practice dealing with uncertainty, the power of persuasion, and building relationships to sustain these qualities.

In 1962, a couple opened up a small one-room restaurant in Albuquerque, New Mexico. They called their restaurant El Pinto. Using family recipes, the entrepreneurs Jack and Connie Thomas were one of the first restaurants to market their food as New Mexican. The restaurant became a popular dining spot for locals, and it soon gained a reputation for its flavorful salsa. Jack and Connie built their home next to the restaurant so that they could be close to both their family and business. Over the years, the two expanded the restaurant to include a patio and an additional dining room.

Fast-forward 50 years and El Pinto looks very different from its humble origins. Today El Pinto is owned by Jack and Connie's twin sons, Jim and John Thomas, who bought out their parents more than 20 years ago. The two men share the entrepreneurial spirit of their parents. After taking control of the restaurant, they began further expansion. The business now consists of 12 acres of land, a restaurant that can seat more than 1,200 guests, and an 8,000-square-foot manufacturing facility used to develop salsas for commercialization. The restaurant itself consists of a cantina, five patios, and three dining rooms. The restaurant has a tequila bar that sells 160 varieties of tequilas. Despite this expansion, the traditions of El Pinto remain the same. For instance, the owners continue to use their grandmother's recipes for their menu items.

El Pinto's popularity as a restaurant is not limited to New Mexico. The restaurant has a wall with photos of famous people who have patronized the business, including President Obama, President Bush, Hillary Clinton, Mel Gibson, Bill Cosby, Toby Keith, and Snoop Dogg. El Pinto has been voted the Best New Mexican Restaurant in Albuquerque. Under the leadership of Jim and John Thomas, the business has gone from under $1 million from when the twins bought out their parents to a multimillion-dollar restaurant and manufacturing facility.

Outside the Southwest, consumers are more likely to recognize El Pinto not from the restaurant but from its salsa. During the 1990s, El Pinto's loyal customers began requesting products of the company's famous salsa and sauces. Jim and John Thomas saw an opportunity to expand their business even further. At night, the two experimented with salsa recipes to find the best ones for bottling. In 2000, the salsa product line was launched. The chiles for the salsa are grown organically on land the brothers lease in Mexico. Using organically grown chiles, the company manufactures the products on the premises in its own facility. The El Pinto product line includes enchilada sauce, green chile sauce, hot salsa, chipotle salsa, and special-edition products such as super-hot Scorpion salsa. Its products can be found nationwide at Walmart, HEB,

By operating both in the service (restaurant) and manufacturing (salsa production) industries, the entrepreneurs running El Pinto have taken advantage of multiple opportunities for expansion and growth.

Source: Foodio/Shutterstock

Albertson's, Kroger, and Costco. Currently, the site is able to produce 4,000 cases of salsas and sauces per day.

Traditionally, El Pinto salsa products have come in 16-ounce jars. Yet in the past few years, El Pinto has begun to experiment with other sizes. The company conducted market research on whether there would be demand for a 3-ounce jar of salsa. One major issue with salsa is that many salsa companies recommend eating the salsa within a week after opening. Otherwise, the salsa will start to deteriorate. However, 16-ounce jars can be hard to consume in a week. Small sizes, on the other hand, could allow consumers to consume and transport the product more easily. El Pinto feels that consumers could use the smaller sizes for snacks or lunches without feeling pressured to finish off a large container within a week.

El Pinto introduced its 3-ounce salsa in package sizes of four with limited distribution to test the market. Although other companies offer similar package sizes of salsa, including Chi-Chi's, the smaller-size package is a relatively new concept that appeals to those who desire smaller portions. El Pinto has since expanded into other small sizes. The company released its limited-edition Scorpion salsa in 2-ounce and 3-ounce packages. El Pinto also sells green chiles and red chiles in 4-ounce cups that come in packages of 12.

The Thomas brothers have plans to expand their manufacturing capabilities. An investment of $7 million will allow El Pinto to expand its manufacturing facility to more than 20,000 feet. The expansion will open additional employment opportunities for the community—the business is one of the largest employers in the North Valley of the city of Albuquerque. Today, the business uses 120 tons of chiles a year—a far cry from the amount produced with the 35-gallon kettle and pump at the original production site.

By operating both in the service (restaurant) and manufacturing (salsa production) industries, the entrepreneurs running El Pinto have taken advantage of multiple opportunities for expansion and growth. Their ability to innovate with new product ideas, restaurant improvements, and different package sizes has made their small business into one of the highest-grossing restaurants in New Mexico.[38]

1. Describe some ways in which the entrepreneurs of El Pinto engaged in innovation.
2. How did the Thomas brothers take advantage of a market opportunity?
3. What are the management challenges El Pinto faces in the future?

Notes

1. Louisville Slugger Museum and Factory, "About Us—FAQs," 2017, https://www.sluggermuseum.com/about-us/faqs (accessed December 26, 2017); Louisville Slugger, "Our History," 2017, http://www.slugger.com/en-us/our-history (accessed December 26, 2017); "Baseball Bat," http://www.madehow.com/Volume-2/Baseball-Bat.html (accessed December 26, 2017); David Mielach, "Louisville Slugger's Unlikely Home Run," *Business News Daily*, July 8, 2012, https://www.businessnewsdaily.com/2806-louisville-slugger-story.html (accessed December 26, 2017).

2. U.S. Small Business Administration, *United States Small Business Profile*, 2017, https://www.sba.gov/sites/default/files/advocacy/United_States_1.pdf (accessed January 19, 2018).

3. John A. Byrne, "Enterprise; How entrepreneurs are reshaping the economy—And what big companies can learn," *Business Week/Enterprise 1993*, Special Issue, 11–18.

4. Byrne, "Enterprise," 12.

5. U.S. Small Business Administration, "Frequently Asked Questions," September 2012, https://www.sba.gov/sites/default/files/FAQ_Sept_2012.pdf (accessed January 19, 2018).

6. Small Business for Sensible Regulation, "Quick Facts," http://www.sensibleregulations.org/resources/facts-and-figures/# (accessed November 12, 2013).

7. Shalini Ramachandran and Ben Fritz, "DirecTV to finance films," *The Wall Street Journal*, September 30, 2013, B4.

8. Darryl Hartley-Leonard, "The entrepreneurial spirit," *Inc.* 15, Special Advertising Section (December 1993).

9. Hipstamatic, "About—Partnerships," http://hipstamatic.com/about/partnerships/ (accessed January 19, 2018).

10. Michael Gleckman, "Meet the giant killers," *Business Week/Enterprise 1993*, Special Issue, 69.

11. Gene Rebeck, "Mary-Cathryn Kolb," *Delta Sky*, December 2017, p. 28.

12. Wrigley, "The Story of Wrigley," http://www.wrigley.com/global/about-us/the-story-of-wrigley.aspx (accessed January 19, 2018).

13. Business Insurance Quotes, "10 Mom-and-Pop Businesses That Turned into Empires," *Business Insurance*, http://www.businessinsurance.org/10-mom-and-pop-businesses-that-turned-into-empires/ (accessed January 19, 2018).

14. https://www.sba.gov/contracting/government-contracting-programs/8a-business-development-program/about-8a-business-development-program (accessed January 19, 2018); BizFilings, "A Guide to Starting and Running a Woman-Owned Business," http://www.bizfilings.com/libraries/pdfs/starting-woman-owned-business-guide.sflb.ashx (accessed January 19, 2018); U.S. Small Business Administration, "United States Small Business Profile," 2017, https://www.sba.gov/sites/default/files/advocacy/United_States_1.pdf (accessed January 19, 2018).

15. Score for the Life of Your Business, "Small Biz Stats and Trends," http://www.score.org/node/148155 (accessed November 12, 2013).

16. Catherine Rampell, "Immigration and Entrepreneurship," *Economix*, July 1, 2013, https://economix.blogs.nytimes.com/2013/07/01/immigration-and-entrepreneurship/ (accessed January 19, 2018); Elaine Pofeldt, "First-Generation Immigrants Dive into Entrepreneurship," *Forbes*, June 26, 2013, https://www.forbes.com/sites/elainepofeldt/2013/06/26/first-generation-immigrants-dive-into-entrepreneurship/#67b8fe0b74d8 (accessed January 19, 2018).

17. Gleckman, "Meet the giant killers."

18. Darren Dahl, "The Cost of Starting Up a Retail Shop," *Inc.*, August 8, 2011, www.inc.com/articles/201108/business-start-up-costs-retail-store.html (accessed January 19, 2018).

19. Mark Morford, "Great Leap Forward for Instant Gratification," SF Gate, October 4, 2006, http://www.sfgate.com/entertainment/morford/article/Great-leap-forward-for-instant-gratification-2468803.php?ipid=amp-related-link (accessed January 19, 2018); Zoom Systems, "Company Overview," http://www.zoomsystems.com/about-us/company-overview/ (accessed November 13, 2013).

20. A. David Silver, *Entrepreneurial Megabucks* (New York: Wiley, 1985), 146–149; H&R Block, "Corporate Overview," http://investors.hrblock.com/corporate-overview (accessed January 19, 2018); H&R Block, "H&R DIY Products Surpass 100M Tax Returns Prepared," June 22, 2017, https://www.hrblock.com/tax-center/newsroom/filing/filing-online/100-million-diy-returns/ (accessed January 19, 2018).

21. National Institute of Standards and Technology, "Momentum Group—Malcolm Baldrige National Quality Award 2016 Award Recipient, Small Business," https://www.nist.gov/baldrige/momentum-group (accessed January 19, 2018).

22. Peter Coy, "Start with some high-tech magic," *Business Week/Enterprise 1993*, Special Issue, 24–25.

23. Michael Oneal, "Just what is an entrepreneur?" *Business Week/Enterprise 1993*, Special Issue, 108.

24. Sue Shellenbarger, "Some thrive, but many wilt working at home," *The Wall Street Journal*, December 14, 1993, B1; and

Sue Shellenbarger, "I'm still here, home workers worry they are invisible," *The Wall Street Journal*, December 16, 1993, B1.

25. Tom Ehverfeld, "B school bohemians," *Inc.* 15 (September 1993), 59.

26. U.S. Small Business Administration, "Frequently Asked Questions," September 2012, https://www.sba.gov/sites/default/files/FAQ_Sept_2012.pdf (accessed January 19, 2018); Les Mckeown, "Starting a Company? 3 Things You Can't Mess Up," *Inc.*, March 11, 2013, http://www.inc.com/les-mckeown/3-fundamentals-of-startup-success.html (accessed January 19, 2018).

27. Brian Patrick Eha, "Zynga Layoffs: What Happens When Startups Grow Too Fast," *Entrepreneur*, June 4, 2013, http://www.entrepreneur.com/article/226921 (accessed January 19, 2018); Josh Constine, "Why Zynga Failed," *Techcrunch*, October 5, 2012, http://techcrunch.com/2012/10/05/more-competitors-smarter-gamers-expensive-ads-less-virality-mobile/ (accessed January 19, 2018).

28. Adam J. Wiederman, "The Rise of the Sole Proprietor, and the Future of Employment," *Daily Finance*, July 24, 2013, https://www.aol.com/article/finance/2013/07/24/sole-proprietors-future-employment/20674277/ (accessed January 19, 2018).

29. Rosemary Peavler, "Forms of Small Business Entities," *About.com*, http://bizfinance.about.com/od/incometax/a/busorgs.htm (accessed December 6, 2013); Adam J. Weiderman, "The Rise of the Sole Proprietor, and the Future of Employment," *Daily Finance*, July 24, 2013, http://www.dailyfinance.com/2013/07/24/sole-proprietors-future-employment/ (accessed January 19, 2018); Scott A. Hodge, "The U.S. Has More Individually Owned Businesses than Corporations," Tax Foundation, January 13, 2014, https://taxfoundation.org/us-has-more-individually-owned-businesses-corporations/ (accessed January 19, 2018); Caron Beesley, "Sole Proprietorship—Is This Popular Business Structure Right for You?" Small Business Administration, February 27, 2013, https://www.sba.gov/blogs/sole-proprietorship-popular-business-structure-right-you (accessed January 19, 2018).

30. American Bird Conservancy, "Joint Ventures," http://www.abcbirds.org/abcprograms/alliances/JVs.html (accessed November 19, 2013).

31. O. C. Ferrell, Geoffrey Hirt, and Linda Ferrell, *Business: A Changing World*, 9th ed. (McGraw-Hill Irwin: New York, NY, 2011), 135.

32. Andrew Medal, "5 Important Startup Lessons from 'Shark Tank,'" *Entrepreneur*, May 29, 2015, https://www.entrepreneur.com/article/246716 (accessed January 1, 2018); Gary Golden, "This Student Entrepreneur's Pitch Impressed Daymond John so Much That He Got a 'Shark Tank' Invite," *Inc.*, August 31, 2017, https://www.inc.com/gary-golden/how-a-20-year-old-college-entrepreneur-perfected-h.html (accessed January 1, 2018); Laura Woods, "The Best Advice 'Shark Tank' Investors Have Given Entrepreneurs," *Business Insider*, January 20, 2017, http://www.businessinsider.com/the-best-advice-shark-tank-investors-have-given-entrepreneurs-2017-1/#-1 (accessed January 1, 2018); Steven Key, "3 Lies You Heard on 'Shark

Tank,'" *Entrepreneur*, September 3, 2013, https://www.entrepreneur.com/article/228162 (accessed January 1, 2018); Naomi Schaefer Riley, "'Shark Tank' Offers Valuable Business Lessons," *The New York Post*, November 26, 2013, http://nypost.com/2013/11/26/shark-tank-offers-valuable-lessons-about-american-business/ (accessed January 1, 2018); Alice Daniel, "Inside the Shark Tank," *Success*, http://www.success.com/article/inside-the-shark-tank (accessed January 1, 2018); Alison Griswold, "Successful Companies That Didn't Get a 'Shark Tank' Deal," *Business Insider*, November 18, 2013, http://www.businessinsider.com/successful-companies-that-didnt-get-a-shark-tank-deal-2013-11 (accessed January 1, 2018); Carol Tice, "The Shark Tank Effect: Top Success Stories from the First Three Seasons," *Entrepreneur*, September 13, 2012, http://www.entrepreneur.com/slideshow/224405#0 (accessed January 1, 2018).

33. Inc., "Small Business Investment Companies (SBIC)," https://www.inc.com/encyclopedia/small-business-investment-companies-sbic.html (accessed January 19, 2018).

34. Franchising.com, "SUBWAY Franchising News," November 14, 2013, http://www.franchising.com/subway/news.html (accessed November 19, 2013); Venessa Wong and Steph Davidson, "Subway at 40,000: Fast Food's Global King Keeps Growing," *Bloomberg Businessweek*, August 26, 2013, https://www.bloomberg.com/news/articles/2013-08-26/subway-at-40-000-fast-foods-global-king-keeps-growing (accessed January 19, 2018); Brandon Southward, "Meet the World's Fastest-Growing Fitness Chain," *CNN Money*, July 31, 2013, http://fortune.com/2013/07/31/meet-the-worlds-fastest-growing-fitness-chain/ (accessed January 19, 2018).

35. Gifford Pinchot III, *Intrapreneuring* (New York: Harper & Row, 1985), 34; Anytime Fitness, "Get to a Healthier Place," 2016, https://www.anytimefitness.com/wp-content/uploads/2016/04/Anytime-Fitness-Media-Guide-2016-1.pdf (accessed January 19, 2018).

36. Russell Mitchell, "Masters of Innovation: How 3M Keeps Its New Products Coming," *Business Week*, April 10, 1989, 58–63.

37. Dan Schawbel, "Why Companies Want You to Become an Intrapreneur," *Forbes*, September 9, 2013, http://www.forbes.com/sites/danschawbel/2013/09/09/why-companies-want-you-to-become-an-intrapreneur/ (accessed January 19, 2018).

38. El Pinto, "The Salsa Twins Story," http://www.elpinto.com/salsa-twins-story#.WksSdFQ-dAY (accessed January 1, 2018); El Pinto, "12 Count Single Serving El Pinto 4 Oz. Medium Green Chile," https://www.elpinto.com/index.php?option=com_virtuemart&category_id=29&flypage=flypage.tpl&manufacturer_id=1&page=shop.product_details&product_id=97 (accessed January 1, 2018); El Pinto, "Gov. Susanna Martinez Announces El Pinto Foods Growing to Create up to 25 New Jobs, $7 Million Investment to Support 20,000 Sq. Ft. of Manufacturing Facilities," January 31, 2017, https://www.elpinto.com/el-pinto-blog (accessed January 1, 2018); El Pinto, "History," http://www.elpinto.com/history#.WksM0VQ-dAY (accessed January 1, 2018); El Pinto, "History," https://www.elpinto.com/index.php?page=shop.cart&option=com_content&Itemid=53&view=category&layout=blog&id=34

&limitstart=5 (accessed January 1, 2018); El Pinto, "Biggest Little Tequila Bar in Albuquerque," http://www.elpinto.com/tequila-bar-albuquerque#.WksNj1Q-dAY (accessed January 1, 2018); El Pinto, "Looking for Scorpion Salsa?" https://www.elpinto.com/looking-for-scorpion-salsa#.WksUYVQ-dAY (accessed January 1, 2018); Steve Ginsberg, "El Pinto's Thomas Twins Seek Salsa's Superstar Status," *Albuquerque Business First*, August 23, 2009, https://www.bizjournals.com/albuquerque/stories/2009/08/24/story7.html (accessed January 1, 2018); El Pinto, "Family," http://www.elpinto.com/family#.UflCLPXLQ4k (accessed January 1, 2018); El Pinto, "El Pinto Fires Up the History Channel," http://www.elpinto.com/press-releases (accessed January 1, 2018).

Glossary

Abilene Paradox   A situation occurring when members of a group publicly agree on a course of action even though there is an underlying consensus agreement that an alternative course is preferred. (page 413)

Ability tests   Paper-and-pencil quizzes, usually multiple choice, that measure an applicant's knowledge of specific work content or cognitive ability. (page 274)

Acceptance theory of authority   The theory that, in formal organizations, authority flows up, because the decision as to whether an order, or communication, has authority lies with the person who receives the communication. (page 52)

Accommodating style   A style exhibiting low assertiveness and high cooperation. (page 408)

Action research   Encompasses and further defines the steps of the Lewin change model and involves an ongoing process of joint (consultant with clients) problem discovery, diagnosis, action planning, action implementation, and evaluation. (page 313)

Adhocracy   A decentralized, informal, but complex organization that tries to maintain flexibility in the face of rapid environmental changes by using a matrix or network formal structure. (page 256)

Adjourning stage   The stage in which task forces, project teams, or committees complete their task and disband. (page 401)

Administrative management   The universality of management as a function that can be applied to all organizations. (page 41)

Administrative model of decision making   A descriptive approach, recognizing that people do not always make decisions with logic and rationality, that outlines how managers actually do make decisions; also known as the organizational, neoclassical, or behavioral model. (page 203)

Affiliative power   Power that is derived by virtue of a person's association with someone else who has some source of power. (page 330)

Affirmative action programs   Legally mandated plans within organizations that attempt to increase job opportunities for traditionally underrepresented areas of the workforce. (page 289)

Antigroup roles   Behaviors that disrupt the group, draw attention to individual rather than group functioning, and detract from positive interactions. (page 405)

Assessment center tests   Programs that typically simulate managerial tasks. (page 274)

Association of Southeast Asian Nations (ASEAN)   Comprised of ten Southeast Asian countries with the goal to promote economic growth and overall progress in the area via trade and security. (page 148)

Authentic leader   A leader who is passionate about company objectives, models corporate values in the workplace, and forms strong relationships with stakeholders. (page 343)

Authority   The right to give work orders to others in the organization; associated with a position within an organization, not with the individual occupying that position. (page 226)

Avoidance   The act of strengthening a desired behavior by allowing individuals to avoid negative consequences by performing the behavior. (page 373)

Avoiding style   A style displaying low assertiveness and low cooperation. (page 408)

Balance sheet   A snapshot of the organization's financial position at a given moment; indicates what the firm owns and what proportion of its assets are financed with its own or borrowed money. (page 465)

Balanced Scorecard   A management control system customized for a company's industry, technology, mission, and strategy. (page 466)

Behavior modification   An application of reinforcement theory that involves change in behavior and encouraging appropriate actions by relating the consequences of behavior to the behavior itself. (page 373)

Behavioral approach   A view of management that emphasizes understanding the importance of human behavior, needs, and attitudes within formal organizations. (page 45)

Behavioral approach to job design   The design of jobs based on the view that workers are independent parts of the production process whose individual characteristics should be taken into account in forming jobs. (page 230)

Behavior-based appraisal   A subjective evaluation of the way an employee performs job tasks. (page 280)

Birth   The initial stage of the product life cycle when the product is introduced. (page 183)

Body language   The broad range of body motions and behaviors, from facial expressions to the distance one person stands from another, that send messages to a receiver. (page 428)

Bottom-up budgeting   Flows up from lower levels of an organization for review by top management and involves those more directly engaged in the actual tasks covered by the budget. (page 464)

Boundary-spanning roles   Group behaviors involving interaction with members in other units of the organization or outside the organization. (page 405)

Bounded rationality   The idea that people have limits, or boundaries, to their rationality. (page 203)

Brainstorming   A technique in which group members spontaneously suggest ideas to solve a problem. (page 212)

Budgeting   The principal means of controlling the availability and cost of financial resources. (page 463)

Budgets   Formal, written plans for future operations in financial terms. (page 463)

Bureaucracy   A theory of management by office or position, rather than by person, based on rational authority. (page 44)

Bureaucratic control   Attempts to control the firm's overall functioning through formal, mechanistic structural arrangements; sometimes called hierarchical control. (page 459)

Business ethics   Principles, values, and codes of conduct that define acceptable behavior in business. (page 95)

Business-level strategy   The area of responsibility usually assigned to the divisional-level managers. (page 178)

Business plan   A meticulous statement of the rationale for the business and a step-by-step explanation of how it will achieve its goals. (page 523)

Cafeteria benefits program   Allows an employee to choose which benefits he or she wants from a menu of different options. (page 283)

Capacity   The maximum load that an organizational unit can carry or operate at a given point in time. (page 488)

Capital budgeting   Concerned with the intermediate and long-term control of capital acquisitions, such as plants and equipment. (page 463)

Capitalism   An economic system wherein the natural laws of supply and demand and free competition within the marketplace will efficiently regulate the flow of resources within a society. (page 33)

Cartel   A group of firms or nations that agree to act as a monopoly and not compete with each other. (page 135)

Cash cows   Those businesses that tend to generate excess cash over what is needed for their continued growth due to their high market share in a slow-growing market. (page 181)

Centralization   The pattern of concentrating authority in a relatively few, high-level positions. (page 237)

Certainty   The condition that exists when decision makers are fully informed about a problem, its alternative solutions, and its respective outcomes. (page 198)

Chain of command   An organizing concept that ensures that all positions are directly linked in some way to top management. (page 235)

Channel   The medium or method used to transmit the intended information and meaning (such as leaving an email or telling a person face to face). (page 424)

Channel richness   A channel's ability to transmit information, including the ability to handle multiple cues simultaneously, encourage feedback, and focus personally on the receiver. (page 429)

Charisma   The ability to inspire admiration, respect, loyalty, and a desire to emulate, based on some intangible set of personality traits; a personal source of power. (page 329)

Clan control   Seeks to regulate overall organizational functioning through reliance on informal, organic structural arrangements; also referred to as decentralized control. (page 460)

Classical approach   An approach to management that stresses the manager's role in a formal hierarchy of authority and focuses on the task, machines, and systems needed to accomplish the task efficiently. (page 36)

Classical approach to job design   The design of jobs based on the principles of division of labor and specialization. (page 230)

Classical model of decision making   A prescriptive approach—asserting that managers are logical, rational individuals who make decisions that are in the best interests of the organization—that outlines how managers should make decisions; also known as the rational model. (page 202)

Closed system   An organization that interacts little with its external environment and therefore receives little feedback from or information about its surroundings. (page 51)

Cluster chain   An exchange in which one person or a selected few share information with only a few others. (page 433)

Codes of ethics   Formalized rules and standards that describe and delineate what the organization expects of its employees. (page 105)

Coercive power   An organizationally based source of power derived from a leader's control over punishments or the capacity to deny rewards. (page 328)

Cohesiveness   The tendency of group members to unite in their pursuit of group goals and to be attracted to the group and each other. (page 406)

Collaborating style   A style displaying both high assertiveness and high competition. (page 409)

Collective bargaining   A process of negotiation through which management and unions reach an agreement regarding employee pay, work conditions, and hours. (page 288)

Committee   A permanent formal group that does some specific task; may be either a functional or cross-functional group. (page 395)

Communication   The process through which information and meaning are transferred from one person to another. (page 423)

Compensation system   The basis on which an organization gives money, goods, or services to its employees in exchange for their work. (page 280)

Competing style   A management style involving a stance of high assertiveness with low cooperation. (page 396)

Competitors   Other organizations that produce similar, or in some cases identical, goods or services. (page 75)

Complexity   The level of differentiation among structural units, including the specialization of jobs, geographical dispersion, and height of the firm. (page 244)

Comprehensive model of planned change   A step-by-step plan for implementing major change. (page 305)

Compressed workweek   A four-day (or shorter) period in which an employee works 40 hours. (page 379)

Compromising style   A style that reflects a moderate concern for both your goals and the other person's goals. (page 409)

Computer-assisted design (CAD)   The use of computer systems to assist in the creation, modification, analysis, or optimization of a design. (page 490)

Computer-assisted manufacturing (CAM)   The use of computer software to control machine tools and related machinery in the manufacturing of products. (page 490)

Conceptual skills   The intellectual abilities to process information and make accurate decisions about the work group and the job tasks. (page 13)

Confidence   A person's faith that his or her decisions are reliable and good. (page 209)

Conformity   Adherence to the group's norms, values, and goals. (page 412)

Conglomerates   Firms that pursue unrelated diversification strategies. (page 180)

Congruence model of change   An outgrowth of the systems approach to organizational theory, emphasizes the interrelationships between the various parts of an organization and how change in one part will cause reactive changes in other parts. (page 304)

Consideration behaviors   Patterns of being friendly and supportive by listening to employees' problems, supporting their actions, "going to bat" for them, and getting their input on a variety of issues. (page 333)

Consumerism   The activities undertaken by independent individuals, groups, and organizations to protect their rights as consumers. (page 113)

Content theories   A group of theories that assume that workers are motivated by the desire to satisfy needs and that seek to identify what their needs are. (page 365)

Contingency approach   An approach to management theories that emphasizes identifying the key variables in each management situation, understanding the relationships among these variables, and recognizing the complex system of cause and effects that exists in each and every managerial situation. (page 53)

Contingency plans   Alternate courses of action to be undertaken if certain organizational or environmental conditions change. (page 186)

Contingency theory   The suggestion that successful leadership requires matching leaders with primarily stable leadership styles to the demands of the situation. (page 337)

Continuous technology   A method of production in which raw materials flow continuously through a system that transforms them into finished products. (page 252)

Contract manufacturing   Occurs when a company hires a foreign company to produce a specified volume of the firm's product to specification; the final product carries the domestic firm's name. (page 144)

Contracting for leadership style   A process whereby employees may not initially agree with a manager's assessment of their developmental level, thus requiring a leader's skill in arriving at an assessment consensus and an agreed-upon leadership style. (page 337)

Controlling   Those activities that an organization undertakes to ensure that its actions lead to achievement of its objectives. (page 8)

Coordination   The linking of jobs, departments, and divisions so that all parts of the organization work together to achieve goals. (page 253)

Corporate governance   The formal system of oversight, accountability, and control for organizational decisions and resources. (page 78)

Corporate strategy   The scope and resource deployment components of strategy for the enterprise as a whole. (page 178)

Corporation   A separate legal entity, or body, created by the state; its assets and liabilities are distinct from those of the owners of the corporation. (page 525)

Cost leadership   A business-level strategy aimed at achieving the overall lowest cost structure in an industry. (page 183)

Countertrade agreements   Exporting that involves bartering products for other products instead of for currency. (page 143)

Cross-functional groups   Groups that cut across the firm's hierarchy and are composed of people from different functional areas and possibly different levels. (page 394)

Customer division structure   The organization of divisions by customer. (page 240)

Customers   Those who purchase an organization's goods and/or services. (page 74)

Decentralization   When authority is dispersed to several positions at various levels in the organization. (page 237)

Decision   A choice made from alternative courses of action in order to deal with a problem. (page 197)

Decision making   The process of choosing among alternative courses of action to resolve a problem. (page 197)

Decision styles   Determined from patterns among an individual's predispositions, such as which situations to avoid, what kind of jobs an individual enjoys, which things he or she dislikes, how an individual communicates, how an individual approaches problems, and how he or she makes decisions. (page 204)

Decisional roles   Activities that deal primarily with the allocation of resources in order to reach organizational objectives. (page 11)

Decline   The product life cycle stage marked by decreases in the product's market share. (page 184)

Decoding   The process of interpreting and attaching personal meaning to the message. (page 424)

Delegation   The assignment of work activities and authority to a subordinate. (page 236)

Deontology   Focuses on human rights and values and on the intentions associated with a particular behavior. (page 102)

Departmentalization   The grouping of related jobs to form an administrative unit—department, area, or center. (page 238)

Devil's advocate   When a member of the team argues for an alternative position; can be helpful in avoiding groupthink because it encourages team members to carefully consider alternative courses of action. (page 215)

Diagonal communication   The flow of information, often in matrix structures, between individuals from different units and organizational levels. (page 433)

Differentiation   A business strategy in which the strategic business units offer a unique good or service to a customer at a premium price. (page 183)

Direct investment   The purchase of overseas production and marketing facilities; a company may control the facilities outright, or it may be the majority stockholder in the company that controls the facilities. (page 145)

Distinctive competence   What a firm does well relative to its competitors. (page 174)

Distortion   A deviation between the sent message and the received message. (page 431)

Diversification   A strategy of acquiring or developing other businesses, which must ultimately be justified by its ability to build stockholder wealth. (page 179)

Divestment   A strategy of selling off businesses that the company no longer wishes to maintain, either because they are failing or because the company has changed its corporate strategy and does not wish to be in those businesses any longer. (page 180)

Division of labor   The idea of breaking an entire job into its component parts and assigning each specific task to an individual worker; also called specialization. (page 34)

Divisionalized form   A multidivisional structure or hybrid; typically a very large corporation that has organized its departments into divisions. (page 256)

Dogs   Businesses that have only minimal profits or even losses due to their low market share in slow-growing markets. (page 181)

Downward communication   The traditional flow of information from upper organizational levels to lower levels, such as job directions, assignment of tasks, performance feedback, and information concerning the organization's goals. (page 433)

Dumping   Occurs when a country or business firm sells products at less than what it costs to produce them. (page 138)

Economic dimension   The overall condition of the complex interactions of economies throughout the world. (page 72)

Economic forces   The relationship of people to resources. (page 33)

Economic order quantity (EOQ) model   Identifies the optimal number of items to order while minimizing certain annual costs that vary according to order size. (page 495)

Effectively   Using resources in a way that produces a desired result. (page 3)

Efficiently   Accomplishing the objectives with a minimum of resources. (page 3)

Embargo   The suspension of trade in a particular product by the government. (page 138)

Emotional intelligence   The capacity to be aware of, control, and express one's emotions, and to handle interpersonal relationships judiciously and empathetically. (page 332)

Employee-centered leaders   The most effective managers, who engage in both dimensions of leadership behaviors by getting employees involved in the operation of their departments or divisions in a positive and constructive manner, setting general goals, providing fairly loose supervision, and recognizing employees' contributions. (page 333)

Empowerment   The process of providing employees with the ability to contribute input and take on responsibilities for organizational decisions. (page 330)

Encoding   The process of transforming information into understandable symbols, typically spoken or written words or gestures. (page 424)

Entrepreneur   A person who creates a business or product, manages his or her resources, and takes risks to gain a profit. (page 513)

Entrepreneurship   The process of creating and managing a business to achieve desired objectives. (page 513)

Entropy   The tendency of systems to deteriorate or break down over time. (page 51)

Environment   All of those factors that affect the operation of the organization. (page 65)

Equity theory   A theory stating that the extent to which people are willing to contribute to an organization depends on their assessment of the fairness of the rewards they will receive in exchange. (page 370)

Escalation of commitment   The tendency to persist with a failing course of action. (page 208)

Ethical issue   An identifiable problem, situation, or opportunity that requires a person or organization to choose among several actions that may be evaluated as ethical or unethical. (page 97)

Ethics audit   A comprehensive evaluation of a firm's ethics and compliance program and its ethical decisions used to determine whether the program is effective. (page 107)

European Union (EU)   An economic and political union of 28 member nations that are located primarily in Europe. (page 147)

Exchange controls   Restrictions on the amount of a particular currency that may be bought or sold. (page 138)

Exchange rate   The ratio at which one nation's currency can be exchanged for another nation's currency or for gold. (page 140)

Expectancy   A person's expectation that effort will lead to high performance. (page 371)

Expectancy theory   A theory stating that motivation depends not only on how much a person wants something but also on the person's perception of how likely he or she is to get it. (page 360)

Expert power   Power or influence derived from a person's special knowledge or expertise in a particular area. (page 329)

Exporting   The sale of goods and services to foreign markets. (page 142)

External environment   All of the factors outside the organization that may affect the managers' actions. (page 65)

Extinction   Weakening an undesired behavior by not providing positive consequences. (page 374)

Facilitators   Leaders who help the group overcome internal obstacles or difficulties so that it may achieve desired outcomes. (page 410)

Feedback   The receiver's response to the sender's communication. (page 425)

Feedback (or post-action) control   Monitors the firm's outputs, the results of the transformation process. (page 462)

Finance managers   Managers who focus on obtaining the money needed for the successful operation of the organization and using that money in accordance with organizational goals. (page 17)

Financial audit   A periodic and comprehensive examination of a firm's financial records. (page 465)

Finished-goods inventory   Includes those products that are ready for sale, such as a fully assembled automobile ready to ship to a dealer. (page 496)

Fixed-interval schedule   A pattern of reinforcement at specified periods of time, regardless of behavior. (page 374)

Fixed-position layout   A company has a central location for the product and brings all resources required to create the product to that location. (page 489)

Fixed-ratio schedule   A pattern offering reinforcement after a specified number of desired performance behaviors, regardless of the time elapsed between them. (page 374)

Flexible benefits program   Works by giving employees credits to spend on benefits that meet their needs, rather than forcing them to sign up for a package that is not catered to them. (page 283)

Flexible manufacturing   Computers can direct machinery to adapt to different versions of similar operations. (page 491)

Flextime   A work schedule that allows employees to choose their staffing and ending times as long as they are at work during a specified time period. (page 379)

Focus   A business strategy in which the business concentrates on one part or segment of the market and tries to meet the demands of that segment. (page 183)

Foreign Corrupt Practices Act (FCPA)   Outlaws direct payoffs to and bribes of foreign governments or business officials by American companies. (page 136)

Formal groups   Groups created by the organization that generally have their own formal structure. (page 394)

Formal organization   The arrangement of positions, as shown on an organizational chart, that dictates where work activities are completed, where decisions should be made, and the flow of information. (page 226)

Formalization   The degree to which the organization's procedures, rules, and personnel requirements are written down and enforced. (page 244)

Forming stage   The stage when group members meet for the first time or two, become acquainted, and familiarize themselves with the group's task. (page 399)

For-profit companies   Organizations owned either privately by one or more individuals or publicly by stockholders. (page 20)

Framing   The tendency to view positively presented information favorably and negatively presented information unfavorably. (page 208)

Franchise   A license to sell another's products or to use another's name in business, or both. (page 528)

Franchisee   The purchaser of a franchise. (page 528)

Franchiser   The company that sells the franchise. (page 528)

Franchising   A form of licensing in which a company—the franchiser—agrees to provide a franchisee a name, logo, methods of operation, advertising, products, and other elements associated with the franchiser's business, in return for a financial commitment and the agreement to conduct business in accordance with the franchiser's standard of operations. (page 144)

Free-riding   The tendency of some individuals to perform at less than their optimum in groups, relying instead on others to carry their share of the workload. (page 397)

Functional groups   Groups that perform specific organizational functions, with members from several vertical levels of the hierarchy. (page 394)

Functional structure   The grouping of jobs according to similar economic activities, such as finance, production and operations, and marketing. (page 238)

Gantt chart   A bar chart that shows the relationship of various scheduling activities over time; a popular technique used for scheduling purposes. (page 498)

General environment   The broad, complex factors that affect all organizations. (page 66)

General partnership   A partnership that involves a complete sharing in the management of a business, with each partner having unlimited liability for the business's debts. (page 525)

Geographic division structure   The organization of divisions by geographic region. (page 239)

Global business (globalization)   A strategy in which organizations treat the entire world or major regions of it as the domain for conducting business. (page 131)

Global dimension   Pertaining to the general environment, those factors in other countries that affect the organization. (page 73)

Goal   The final result that a firm wishes to achieve. (page 165)

Goal-setting theory   A theory that recognizes the importance of goals in improving employee performance. (page 372)

Gossip chain   The spreading of information by one person to many others. (page 433)

Grapevine   Informal communication channels, found in virtually all organizations. (page 421)

Grid OD   A six-phase overall organizational intervention that comprehensively and systematically attempts to enhance personal management style, team functioning, intergroup problem solving, overall organizational functioning, and the ability of the organization to continually improve how it solves its own problems, resolves conflicts, and makes decisions. (page 316)

Gross domestic product (GDP)   The market value of a nation's total output of goods and services for a given period. (page 139)

Group   Two or more individuals who communicate with one another, share a collective identity, and have a common goal. (page 391)

Group-maintenance roles   Behaviors that help the group engage in constructive interpersonal relationships, and help members fulfill personal needs and derive satisfaction from group participation. (page 405)

Groupthink   A phenomenon occurring when cohesive "in-groups" let the desire for unanimity, or consensus, override sound judgment in generating and evaluating alternative courses of action. (page 215)

Growth   The product life cycle stage characterized by dramatic increases in the product's market share. (page 183)

Hawthorne studies   A group of studies that provided the stimulus for the human-relations movement within management theory and practice. (page 46)

Holding company   An organization composed of several very different kinds of businesses, each of which is permitted to operate largely autonomously. (page 240)

Horizontal communication   The exchange of information among individuals on the same organizational level, either across or within departments. (page 421)

Horizontal coordination   The linking of subunits on the same level. (page 253)

Human-relations movement   A practice whereby employees came to be viewed as informal groups of their own, with their own leadership and codes of behavior, instead of as just unrelated individual workers assigned to perform individual tasks. (page 48)

Human resource management (HRM)   All activities that forecast the number and type of employees an organization will need and then find and develop employees with necessary skills. (page 267)

Human resource planning   Involves forecasting the organization's future demand for employees, forecasting the future supply of employees within the organization, and designing programs to correct the discrepancy between the two. (page 268)

Human resources managers   Managers concerned with developing and carrying out systems that are used to make decisions about employees, such as selection, training, and compensation. (page 17)

Hybrid structure   A combination of several different structures; the most common form of organizational structure. (page 241)

Import tariff   A tax levied by a nation on goods bought outside its borders and imported into the country. (page 137)

Importing   The purchase of goods and services from a foreign source. (page 143)

Income statement   Shows the profitability of an organization over a period of time—a month, a quarter, or a year; helps managers focus on the organization's overall revenues (from sales and investments) and the costs incurred in generating those revenues. (page 465)

Incremental change   A relatively small change in processes and behaviors within just one or a few systems or levels of the organization. (page 300)

Individual values   Sets of principles that describe what a person believes are the right way to behave; also known as moral philosophies. (page 101)

Industrial robot   A machine designed to move materials, parts, tools, or specialized devices through variable programmed motions, for the performance of a variety of tasks. (page 491)

Informal groups   Groups that arise naturally from social interaction and relationships and are usually very loosely organized. (page 394)

Informal organization   The relationships among positions that are not connected by the organizational chart. (page 227)

Information overload   The condition of having too much information to process. (page 440)

Information power   Power that is a result of having access to important information that is not common knowledge, or of having the ability to control the flow of information to and from others. (page 329)

Information technology (IT) managers   Managers who implement, maintain, and control technology applications. (page 17)

Informational roles   Activities—including reporting, preparing data analyses, briefings, delivering mail, emailing, websites, and making telephone calls—that focus on data important for the decisions the manager needs to make. (page 10)

Infrastructure   The physical facilities that support its economic activities, such as railroads, highways, ports, airfields, utilities and power plants, schools, hospitals, communication systems, and commercial distribution systems. (page 140)

Initiating-structure behaviors   Defining and structuring leader-employee roles through activities such as scheduling, defining work tasks, setting deadlines, criticizing poor work, getting employees to accept work standards, and resolving problems. (page 333)

Innovation   The act of introducing a new product, method, process, or approach. (page 307)

Inputs   Resources such as labor, money, materials, information, or energy that are transformed by a process to become an output. (page 483)

Inspection   Reveals whether a product meets quality standards. (page 499)

Instrumentality   A person's expectation that performing a task will lead to a desired outcome. (page 371)

Integrity tests   Tests that measure an applicant's attitudes and opinions about dysfunctional behaviors, such as theft, sabotage, physical abuse, and substance abuse. (page 274)

Intergroup team building   Designed to facilitate functioning between two or more groups by helping the groups understand and deal with areas of conflict; debilitating interaction patterns; perceptual discrepancies; norm, goal, and value differences; and lack of coordination. (page 316)

Internal controls   Processes that are developed to provide assurance that an organization reaches its objectives relating to operational efficiency, accuracy of financial reporting, and regulatory compliance. (page 453)

Internal environment   All factors that make up the organization, such as the owners, managers, employees, and board of directors. (page 66)

International business   The buying, selling, and trading of goods and services across national boundaries. (page 131)

International Monetary Fund (IMF)   Basic mission is to oversee the international monetary system and help ensure stable currencies and exchange rates throughout the world. (page 141)

International Organization for Standardization (ISO)   A set of international management standards that were developed to provide common standards that would apply globally. (page 499)

Interpersonal roles   Activities that involve interacting with others who may be external or internal to the organization at a higher or lower level than the manager. (page 10)

Interpersonal skills   Skills such as communication, listening, conflict resolution, and leading that are necessary to work with others. (page 13)

Intrapreneurs   Similar to entrepreneurs, employees who take responsibility for, or "champion," developing innovations of any kind within the larger organization. (page 514)

Intuition   The immediate comprehension that something is the case, seemingly without the use of any reasoning process or conscious analysis. (page 206)

Inventory   All the materials a firm holds in storage for future use. (page 494)

Inventory control   Determining how many supplies and goods are needed and keeping track of quantities on hand, where each item is, and who is responsible for it. (page 494)

ISO 14000   An international management standard that provides a number of comprehensive environmental standards for businesses to ensure that they are limiting their negative environmental impact and improving environmental performance. (page 499)

ISO 9000 An international management standard that deals with quality, including providing a framework for companies to document records, train employees, test products, and fix defects. (page 499)

Job analysis The systematic process of gathering information about important work-related aspects of a job. (page 268)

Job-centered leaders Less-effective managers, who are mostly directive in their approaches and more concerned with closely supervising employees, explaining work procedures, and monitoring progress in task accomplishment. (page 333)

Job design The process of grouping tasks into jobs. (page 229)

Job enlargement A behavioral approach to job design aimed at increasing the number of tasks that comprise a job. (page 231)

Job enrichment A behavioral approach in which jobs are designed to increase the number of similar tasks involved, especially tasks that require information processing and decision making. (page 231)

Job evaluation methods Techniques that determine the value of an organization's jobs and arrange these jobs in order of pay according to their value. (page 282)

Job redesign Focuses on changing the nature of how tasks are performed and often entails job rotation, job enrichment, and/or job enlargement. (page 316)

Job rotation A behavioral approach to job design involving a deliberate plan to move workers to various jobs on a consistent, scheduled basis. (page 231)

Job sharing A working arrangement whereby two employees do one job. (page 380)

Job specialization The division of work into smaller, distinct tasks. (page 229)

Joint venture When a company that wants to do business in another country finds a local partner (occasionally, the host nation itself) to share the costs and operation of the business. (page 144)

Just-in-time (JIT) inventory management Minimizes the number of units in inventory by providing an almost continuous flow of items from suppliers to the production facility. (page 495)

Knowledge workers A person who works primarily with information or one who develops and uses knowledge in the workplace. (page 54)

Labor contract A formal, written document that describes the relationship between employees and management for a specified period of time. (page 288)

Leader-Member Exchange (LMX) Theory A description of how leaders develop "unique" working relationships with each of their employees, based on the nature of their social exchanges. (page 341)

Leadership The process of influencing the activities of an individual or a group toward the achievement of a goal. (page 327)

Leadership enhancers Aspects of the task, subordinates, or organization that amplify a leader's impact on employees. (page 341)

Leadership neutralizers Aspects of the task, subordinates, or organization that have the effect of paralyzing, destroying, or counteracting the effect of a leadership behavior. (page 340)

Leadership substitutes Aspects of the task, subordinates, or organization that act in place of leader behavior and thus render it unnecessary. (page 339)

Leading Influencing others' activities to achieve set goals. (page 7)

Learning organizations Refers to companies that facilitate the learning of their members and continuously transform themselves. (page 55)

Least Preferred Coworker (LPC) Scale A measurement of a leader's style consisting of a series of adjective continuums. (page 337)

Legitimate power The influence that comes from a person's formal position in an organization and the authority that accompanies that position. (page 328)

Licensing A trade arrangement in which one company—the licensor—allows another company—the licensee—to use its company name, products, patents, brands, trademarks, raw materials, and/or production processes in exchange for a fee, or royalty. (page 144)

Life and career planning Involves the use of structured counseling and group discussions, often accompanied by skill and interest testing, to assist employees in planning career paths and integrating life and career goals. (page 316)

Limited liability corporation (LLC) The assets and liabilities of the company are separate from the owners', and if the company fails, all that is lost is the initial investment put forth by the owners. (page 526)

Limited partnership Has at least one general partner, who assumes unlimited liability, and at least one limited partner, whose liability is limited to his or her investment in the business. (page 525)

Listening Accurately receiving and understanding information. (page 429)

Lower or first-line managers Managers concerned with the direct production of items or delivery of service. (page 16)

Machine bureaucracy A highly structured, formal organization that emphasizes procedures and rules. (page 255)

Maintenance factors Those aspects of a job that relate to the work setting, including adequate wages, comfortable working conditions, fair company policies, and job security. (page 372)

Management A set of activities designed to achieve an organization's objectives by using its resources effectively and efficiently in a changing environment. (page 3)

Management control Includes all activities an organization undertakes to ensure that its actions lead to achievement of its objectives. (page 453)

Management control system A planned, ordered scheme of management control that allows managers to readily assess where the firm actually is at a point in time relative to where it wants or expects to be. (page 453)

Management science The field of management that includes the study and use of mathematical models and statistical methods to improve the effectiveness of managerial decision making. (page 39)

Management theory A systematic statement, based on observations, of how the management process might best occur, given stated underlying principles. (page 36)

Managers Individuals who make decisions about the use of the organization's resources, and are concerned with planning, organizing, leading, and controlling the organization's activities so as to reach its objectives. (page 3)

Manufacturing The activities and processes used in making tangible products; used interchangeably with the term *production*. (page 485)

Manufacturing-resource planning (MRPII) A computerized system that helps a company control all of its resources, not just inventory needed for production. (page 496)

Marketing managers Managers who develop marketing strategies and make decisions about how to implement those strategies. (page 17)

Maslow's hierarchy of needs The order in which people strive to satisfy the five basic needs as theorized by Maslow—physiological, security, social, esteem, and self-actualization. (page 365)

Mass technology The production of large numbers of the same product. (page 252)

Material-requirements planning (MRP) A planning system that schedules the precise quantity of materials needed to make the product. (page 495)

Matrix structure A structure in which members of different functional departments are chosen to work together temporarily on a specific contract or project. (page 242)

Maturity The product life cycle stage when the product's market share either slows or has no growth. (page 183)

Mechanistic organizations Structures that are highly formal, complex, and centralized. (page 246)

Middle managers Managers who receive broad statements of strategy and policy from upper-level managers and develop specific objectives and plans. (page 16)

Mission A definition of an organization's fundamental purpose and its basic philosophy. (page 164)

Mission statement A formal written declaration of the organization's mission; often includes the firm's philosophy, its primary products and markets, the intended geographic scope, and the nature of the relationships between the firm, its stakeholders, and society. (page 162)

Morale The sum total of employees' attitudes toward their jobs, employer, and colleagues. (page 362)

Motivation An inner drive that directs behavior toward goals. (page 361)

Motivational factors Those aspects of a job that relate to the content of the work, including achievement, recognition, the work itself, involvement, responsibility, and advancement. (page 368)

Moving A transition period during which the behaviors of the organization or department are shifted to a new level. (page 304)

Multidivisional structure The organization of departments together into larger groups called divisions. (page 238)

Multinational corporation (MNC) A corporation, such as IBM, ExxonMobil, and Nestlé, that operates on a worldwide scale, without significant ties to any one nation or region. (page 145)

Munificent environment An environment in which the organization has a large market for its product and has funds needed to continue operations readily available, and other stakeholder groups are satisfied or pleased with the organization's performance. (page 250)

Negotiated budgeting Involves a degree of give and take between upper and lower levels of management to develop the most appropriate form of budgetary control for a given situation. (page 464)

Negotiation Occurs when two or more parties discuss a problem with the intent to resolve differences and come up with a solution. (page 409)

Network organization A structure, primarily a command unit, that does not make a good or provide a service but instead coordinates agreements and contracts with other organizations to produce, distribute, and sell products. (page 243)

Noise Anything acting as an information filter, such as knowledge, attitudes, and other factors, that interferes with the message being communicated effectively. (page 425)

Nominal group technique A process that involves the use of a highly structured meeting agenda and restricts discussion or interpersonal communication during the decision-making process. (page 213)

Nonfinancial controls Provide a company with a method to measure nonfinancial performance such as ethics and compliance activities as well as those related to sustainability. (page 466)

Nonprofit organizations Institutions such as governments, social cause organizations, and religious groups that cannot retain earnings over expenses, do not have equity interests, and cannot be bought or sold. (page 20)

Non-programmed decisions Decisions made in response to situations that are unique, relatively unstructured, undefined, and/or of major consequence to the organization. (page 197)

Nonverbal communication Information conveyed by actions and behaviors rather than by spoken or written words. (page 427)

Norming stage The stage when conflicts are largely resolved and harmony ensues. (page 400)

Norms Prescriptions for appropriate behavior of group members that help reduce the disruption and chaos that would ensue if groups members didn't know how to act. (page 401)

North American Free Trade Agreement (NAFTA) Went into effect on January 1, 1994, and effectively merged Canada, the United States, and Mexico into one market of about 400 million consumers by eliminating most tariffs and trade restrictions on agricultural and manufactured products among the three countries. (page 146)

On-the-job training A technique in which the employee learns the job tasks while actually performing the job. (page 277)

Open system An organization that continually interacts with its environment and therefore is well informed about changes within its surroundings and its position relative to these changes. (page 51)

Operating budgeting Deals with relatively short-term financial control concerns, including having sufficient cash on hand to cover daily financial obligations such as routine purchases and payroll. (page 463)

Operational goals Short-term goals that are addressed to first-line managers and usually apply to specific work operations that lead to the production of goods or services. (page 168)

Operational plans Plans that are intended to achieve operational goals. (page 172)

Operations The processes used in the making of both tangible and intangible products. (page 485)

Operations control Regulates one or more individual operating systems within an organization. (page 461)

Operations management (OM) The development and administration of the activities involved in transforming resources into goods and services. (page 469)

Organic organizations Structures that are less formal, fairly simple, and decentralized. (page 246)

Organization of Economic Cooperation and Development (OECD) An international economic organization comprised of 30 countries that accept the basic principles of free-market economies and representative democracy; recommends and promotes policies to improve the well-being of consumers and societies across the world. (page 142)

Organizational change Any modification in the behaviors or ideas of an organization or its units. (page 297)

Organizational chart A graphic display of the official lines of authority and communication within the organization. (page 226)

Organizational control A broad-based form of control that guides all organizational activities and oversees the overall functioning of the whole firm. (page 459)

Organizational culture The values, norms, and artifacts shared by members of an organization. (page 18)

Organizational development A system-wide application of behavioral science knowledge to the planned development and reinforcement of organizational strategies, structures, and processes for improving an organization's effectiveness. (page 306)

Organizational power A person's ability to satisfy or deny satisfaction of another's need, based on a formal contractual relationship between an organization and the individual. (page 328)

Organizational structure The way managers group jobs into departments and departments into divisions. (page 237)

Organizations Groups of individuals who work together to achieve the goals or objectives that are important to these individuals. (page 3)

Organizing The activities involved in designing jobs for employees, grouping these jobs together into departments, and developing working relationships among organizational units/departments and employees to carry out the plans. (page 6)

Orientation The process of familiarizing newly hired employees with fellow workers, company procedures, and the physical properties of the organization. (page 276)

Outputs The amount of goods, services, or ideas produced by a machine, factory, company, or an individual in a period. (page 483)

Outsourcing Involves transferring manufacturing or other functions (such as data processing) to countries where labor and supplies are less expensive. (page 145)

Partial productivity Reflects output relative to a single input or some combination of inputs. (page 501)

Partnership An association of two or more persons who carry on as co-owners of a business for profit. (page 525)

Path-goal theory A model concerned with how a leader affects employees' perceptions of their personal and work goals and the paths to goal attainment. (page 338)

Perception The process through which we receive, filter, organize, interpret, and attach meaning to information taken in from the environment. (page 430)

Perceptual organization The natural and essential process of organizing, interpreting, and attaching value to the selected stimuli. (page 431)

Perceptual selection The choosing of stimuli from the environment for further processing; also known as filtering or screening. (page 431)

Performance appraisal A formal measurement of the quantity and quality of an employee's work within a specific period of time. (page 278)

Performance gap The difference between an organization's desired and actual performance levels. (page 298)

Performance or work-sample tests Examinations that verify an applicant's ability to perform actual job behaviors identified from a job analysis. (page 274)

Performance standards Targets set by management against which actual performance is compared at a future date; the first step in the control process. (page 456)

Performing stage The stage in which members have reached a level of maturity that facilitates total task involvement. (page 400)

Peripheral norms Norms that are accepted by some, but are not important for organizational success. (page 402)

Personal power A person's ability to satisfy or deny satisfaction of another's need, based on an interpersonal relationship between individuals or on his or her personal characteristics. (page 319)

Personality inventories Programs that measure the thoughts, feelings, and behaviors that define an individual and determine that person's pattern of interaction with the environment. (page 274)

Physical examinations Tests that qualify an individual's placement in manually and physically demanding jobs. (page 275)

Pivotal norms Standards that are critical for group success. (page 401)

Plan A set of activities intended to achieve goals, whether for an entire organization, department, or an individual. (page 161)

Planned change The deliberate structuring of operations and behaviors, often in anticipation of environmental forces. (page 299)

Planning Determining what the organization will specifically accomplish and deciding how to accomplish these goals. (page 6)

Political forces The relationship of individuals, their rights, and their property to the state. (page 33)

Political model of decision making Based on the idea that certain individuals or groups will be able to influence others to achieve their goals. (page 203)

Political-legal dimension Within the general environment, the nature of the relationship between various areas of government and the organization. (page 68)

Politics The maneuvering by an individual to try to gain an advantage in the distribution of organizational rewards or resources. (page 413)

Portfolio analysis A technique allowing for managers to visualize their businesses as a set or portfolio using certain common criteria, such as profitability or growth potential. (page 180)

Positive reinforcement The act of strengthening a desired behavior by rewarding it or providing other positive outcomes. (page 373)

Potential new competitors Companies not currently operating in a business's industry but which have a high potential for entering the industry. (page 75)

Power A person's capacity to influence the behavior and attitudes of others. (page 327)

Preliminary (or feed-forward or steering) control Monitors deviations in the quality and quantity of the firm's resources to try to prevent deviations before they enter the system; its focus is on inputs to the product or service production process. (page 461)

Primary stakeholders Those who have a formal and/or contractual relationship with the firm, such as customers, suppliers, employees, regulators, investors, and communities. (page 80)

Problem The difference between a desired situation and the actual situation. (page 197)

Process consultation A consultant focuses on the dynamic task-related processes—how a client or group sets goals, gathers information, solves problems, and allocates work—and assists the client organization in diagnosing how to enhance these kinds of processes. (page 315)

Process layout Firms organize the transformation process into departments that group related processes. (page 490)

Process theories A set of theories that try to determine "how" and "why" employees are motivated to perform. (page 370)

Product division structure The organization of divisions by product. (page 239)

Product layout Requires that production be broken down into relatively simple tasks assigned to workers positioned along the line. (page 490)

Product life cycle The cycle of birth, growth, maturity, and decline of a product. (page 183)

Product-development teams A special type of project team formed to devise, design, and implement a new product. (page 395)

Production The activities and processes used in making tangible products; used interchangeably with the term *manufacturing*. (page 485)

Production and operations managers Managers who schedule and monitor the work process that turns out the goods or services of the organization. (page 17)

Productivity Measures the relationship between the outputs produced and the inputs used to produce them. (page 501)

Professional bureaucracy An organization that has a functional structure, is medium sized, and works best in stable environments, but has primarily professional employees and a decentralized informal structure. (page 256)

Program Evaluation and Review Technique (PERT) A popular scheduling technique where managers first break down a project into events and activities, and then lay down their proper sequence, relationships, and duration in the form of a network. (page 497)

Programmed decisions Decisions made in response to situations that are routine, structured, and fairly repetitive. (page 197)

Project teams Groups similar to task forces, but usually responsible for running an operation and in control of a specific work project. (page 395)

Promotion The advancement of a current employee to a higher-level job within the organization. (page 284)

Protestant ethic An interpretation of the purpose of life, stating that, instead of merely waiting on earth for release into the next world, people should pursue an occupation and engage in high levels of worldly activity so that they can fulfill their calling. (page 33)

Punishment The act of weakening or eliminating an undesired behavior by providing negative consequences. (page 373)

Purchasing The buying of all the materials needed by the organization; also known as procurement. (page 493)

Quality The degree to which a good or service meets the demands and requirements of the marketplace. (page 498)

Quality control The activities an organization undertakes to ensure that its products meet its established quality standards. (page 498)

Quality-assurance teams Fairly small groups formed to recommend changes that will positively affect the quality of the organization's products. (page 396)

Quantitative approach A viewpoint of management that emphasizes the application of mathematical models, statistics, and structured information systems to support rational management decision making. (page 39)

Quantum change A large-scale planned change in how the firm operates. (page 300)

Question marks Those businesses that are viewed positively in the sense that they are located in attractive, fast-growing markets, but for which there is a question as to their ability to compete, given their low market share. (page 181)

Quota The maximum number of units of a particular product that may be imported into a country. (page 138)

Ratio analysis Managers take information from the two financial statements (balance sheets and income statements) so that they can measure the company's efficiency, profitability, and sources of finances relative to those of other organizations. (page 465)

Raw materials inventory Includes those materials that have been purchased to be used as inputs for making other products. (page 496)

Reactive change A situation in which organizational members react spontaneously to external and internal forces but do little to modify these forces or their behaviors. (page 299)

Receiver The person to whom the information and meaning are sent. (page 424)

Recruiting The process of attracting potential new employees to the organization. (page 270)

Referent power Personal power that results when one person identifies with and admires another. (page 329)

Refreezing Stabilizes the organization at a new state of behavioral equilibrium. (page 304)

Reinforcement theory A process theory that assumes that behavior may be reinforced by relating it to its consequences. (page 373)

Related diversification A firm's acquisition of a business that has some connection with the company's existing businesses. (page 180)

Relationship-oriented behaviors Behaviors such as being considerate, supportive, and helpful to employees by showing trust and confidence, listening to employees' problems and suggestions, showing appreciation for contributions, and supporting employees' concerns. (page 333)

Relevant norms Norms that are important, but not as critical as the pivotal norms. (page 401)

Resources People, equipment, finances, and data used by an organization to reach its objectives. (page 3)

Responsibility The individual's burden of accountability for attainment of the organization's goals. (page 234)

Reward power Organizational power that stems from a person's ability to bestow rewards. (page 328)

Risk The condition that exists when decision makers must rely on incomplete, yet reliable information. (page 198)

Risk propensity A person's willingness to take risks when making decisions. (page 209)

Role A description of the behaviors expected of a specific group member. (page 404)

Role negotiation Entails structuring interactions between interdependent persons or groups to clarify and negotiate role behaviors and expectations. (page 316)

Routing Sequence of operations through which the product must pass. (page 497)

Satisficing The decision maker's decision to choose the first alternative that appears to resolve the problem satisfactorily. (page 203)

Scalar chain The principle of organizing whereby authority should flow through the organization from the top down, one level at a time. (page 235)

Scarce environment An environment wherein money is tight, the market is stagnant or declining, or stakeholder groups are making conflicting or difficult demands. (page 250)

Scheduling Assigning the work to be done to departments or to specific machines or persons. (page 497)

Scientific management A theory within the classical approach that focuses on the improvement of operational efficiencies through the systematic and scientific study of work methods, tools, and performance standards. (page 36)

Screening (or yes/no or concurrent) control Regulates operations to ensure that they are consistent with objectives; the focus is on the transformation process that converts inputs into outputs. (page 461)

Secondary stakeholders Groups that have a less formal connection to the organization, such as environmentalists, special interest groups, and the media. (page 80)

Selection The process of collecting systematic information about applicants and using that information to decide which applicants to hire. (page 272)

Self-directed work team (SDWT) An intact group of employees who are responsible for a whole work process or segment that delivers a good or service to an internal or external customer. (page 396)

Self-reference criterion An unconscious referencing to the way things are done in one's own culture and experiences in making global business decisions. (page 149)

Semantics The different uses and meanings of words, often influencing the effectiveness of a message. (page 437)

Sender The person who wishes to relay or share particular information and meaning, and initiates the communication process. (page 424)

Servant leader A leader who leads by example and forms strong relationships with employees. (page 344)

Simple structure A structure with few departments, arranged by function, headed by an entrepreneur/owner, and with few technical support staff. (page 255)

Situational leadership theory A leadership model whose premise is that a leader's style should be contingent on subordinates' competence and commitment. (page 335)

Six Sigma Involves improving existing processes and developing new processes to meet Six Sigma standards, which requires organizations to produce no more than 3.4 defects per million opportunities. (page 501)

Small-batch technology The production of small numbers of goods in response to a specific customer request. (page 252)

Small business Any business that is not dominant in its competitive area and does not employ more than 500 people. (page 514)

Small Business Administration (SBA) An independent agency of the federal government that offers managerial and financial assistance to small businesses. (page 514)

Social audit A systematic examination of the objectives, strategies, organization, and performance of the social responsibility function. (page 121)

Social forces The relationship of people to each other within a particular culture. (page 33)

Social learning theory A theory stating that employees learn not only through direct experience but also through observation and personal qualities. (page 376)

Social responsibility The obligation a business assumes to maximize its positive impact and minimize its negative impact on society. (page 108)

Socialization The process by which an individual learns the norms, values, goals, and expectations of the organization. (page 403)

Sociocultural dimension The aspect of the general environment that includes the demographics, attitudes, and the values of the society within which an organization operates. (page 67)

Soldiering The systematic slowdown in work by laborers, with the deliberate purpose of keeping their employers ignorant of how fast the work can be done. (page 37)

Sole proprietorships The most popular form of business organization; businesses owned and managed by one individual. (page 525)

Southern Common Market (Mercosur) A political and economic agreement among the countries of Bolivia, Argentina, Brazil, Venezuela, Uruguay, and Paraguay. (page 149)

Span of control The actual number of subordinates over which a position has authority. (page 234)

Stable environment   An environment in which stakeholder demands, and specifically customer desires, are well understood and relatively stable over time. (page 250)

Stakeholder   A person or group that can affect, or is affected by, an organization's goals or the means to achieve those goals. (page 5)

Stakeholder map   A representation of the organization's stakeholders and their stakes. (page 81)

Stakeholder orientation   The degree to which a firm understands and addresses stakeholder demands. (page 80)

Stars   Those businesses that have high market shares and operate in industries experiencing major growth. (page 181)

Statistical process control (SPC)   Another form of screening control; employs "control charts" to continuously track performance variation over time. (page 461)

Stereotyping   A type of perceptual organization in which we categorize people into groups based on certain characteristics, such as race, sex, or education level, and then make generalizations about them according to their group. (page 431)

Stock   Shares of ownership in a corporation that can be bought, sold, given as gifts, or inherited. (page 525)

Storming stage   The stage when conflict usually occurs and in which group members begin to assert their roles, jockey for leadership positions, and make known their feelings about a task. (page 400)

Strategic alliance   A partnership formed to create competitive advantage on a worldwide basis. (page 144)

Strategic business unit (SBU)   A separate division within a company that has its own mission, goals, strategy, and competitors. (page 180)

Strategic control   Ensures that the organization effectively understands and responds to the realities of its environment. (page 463)

Strategic goals   Goals set by higher managers that deal with such general topics as the firm's growth, new markets, or new goods and services. (page 167)

Strategic management   All the processes an organization undertakes to develop and implement its strategic plan. (page 172)

Strategic plans   Plans that are intended to achieve strategic goals. (page 169)

Strategy   A course of action for implementing strategic plans and achieving strategic goals; a general statement of actions an organization intends to take or is taking that is based on the fit of the organization with its external environment. (page 172)

Substitutes   Goods or services that may be used in place of those furnished by a given business. (page 75)

Subsystem   Any system that is part of a larger one. (page 51)

Suppliers   Organizations and individuals who provide resources to other organizations. (page 73)

Supply-chain management   Occurs when managers connect all members of the distribution system to satisfy customers; is an important component of operations. (page 492)

Survey feedback   Involves gathering data through questionnaires and personal interviews. (page 314)

SWOT analysis   The evaluation of the organization's internal strengths and weaknesses and the opportunities and threats associated with the business's external environment. (page 175)

Synergy   The ability of the whole system to equal more than the sum of its parts. (page 51)

System   An arrangement of related or connected parts that form a whole unit. (page 51)

Systems approach   An approach to management theory that views organizations and the environments within which they operate as sets of interrelated parts to be managed as a whole in order to achieve a common goal. (page 51)

Tactical goals   The intermediate goals of the firm, which are designed to stimulate actions necessary for achieving the strategic goals. (page 167)

Tactical plans   Plans that are designed to achieve tactical goals. (page 172)

Task environment   Those factors that have a direct effect on a specific organization and its managers, including customers, suppliers, competitors, substitutes, and potential new entrants to the industry. (page 66)

Task force   A temporary group of employees responsible for bringing about a particular change. (page 395)

Task-oriented behaviors   Behaviors—such as planning and scheduling work, coordinating employee activities, and providing necessary supplies, equipment, and technical assistance—designed primarily and specifically to get tasks completed. (page 333)

Task-specialist roles   Behaviors oriented toward generating information and resolving problems. (page 404)

Team   A small number of people with complementary skills who are committed to a common purpose, set of performance goals, and approach for which they hold themselves mutually accountable. (page 391)

Team building   Involves using structured group experiences to help ongoing work teams function more effectively through better decision making, goal setting, and intragroup communications. (page 315)

Team structure   Occurs when groups of employees are used to determine ways to allocate tasks and assign responsibilities. (page 244)

Technical skills   The knowledge and ability to accomplish the specialized activities of the work group. (page 13)

Technological dimension   Within the general environment, the knowledge and process of changing inputs (resources, labor, and money) to outputs (goods and services). (page 70)

Techno-structural redesign   A large-scale intervention that involves redesigning the organizational structure to better address environmental contingencies and better utilize information and process technologies. (page 316)

Termination   The separation of an employee from the organization. (page 284)

Theory X   The assumption that people are naturally lazy, must be threatened and forced to work, have little ambition or initiative, and do not try to fulfill any need higher than security needs at work. (page 49)

Theory Y   The assumption that people naturally want to work, are capable of self-control, seek responsibility, are creative, and try to fulfill higher-order needs at work. (page 49)

Third-party peacemaking   Involves a consultant who facilitates conflict resolution between two individuals. (page 316)

360-degree feedback Used to get multiple perspectives (employee, co-workers, customers, and/or suppliers) on an employee's performance. (page 279)

Top-down budgeting Top managers establish budgets and hand them down to middle-and lower-level managers for review and implementation. (page 464)

Total productivity Reflects all the inputs used to obtain an output(s). (page 502)

Total quality management A management view that strives to create a customer-centered culture that defines quality for the organization and lays the foundation for activities aimed at attaining quality-related goals. (page 498)

Trading company Acquires goods in one country and sells them to buyers in another country. (page 143)

Training The process of instructing employees in their job tasks and socializing them into the organization's values, attitudes, and other aspects of its culture. (page 276)

Training and experience form An application device that presents a small number of the important tasks of a job and asks the applicants whether they have ever performed or been trained in each of the activities. (page 273)

Trait appraisal A subjective evaluation of an employee's personal characteristics, such as attitude, motivation, cooperation, and dependability. (page 279)

Transactional leadership A more traditional approach in which managers engage in both task- and consideration-oriented behaviors in an exchange manner. (page 345)

Transfer The reassignment of a current employee to another job at the same level as the original job. (page 284)

Transformational leadership A style that goes beyond mere exchange relationships by inspiring employees to look beyond their own self-interests and by generating awareness and acceptance of the group's purposes and mission. (page 346)

Transition state The period during which the organization learns the behaviors needed to reach the desired future state. (page 310)

Triple bottom-line approach Focuses on the social, environmental, and economic impact of a company's operations equally and simultaneously; also known as people, planet, profit. (page 468)

Turbulent environment An environment wherein customer or other stakeholder demands are continuously changing or the primary technology of the firm is constantly being improved and updated. (page 241)

U.K. Bribery Act All organizations with business operations in the United Kingdom can be held liable for bribery, even if the bribery did not occur within the United Kingdom. (page 136)

Uncertainty The condition that exists when little or no factual information is available about a problem, its alternative solutions, and their respective outcomes. (page 199)

Undercapitalization The lack of funds to operate a business normally and the shortest path to failure in business. (page 522)

Unfreezing Involves disrupting the forces maintaining the existing state or level of behavior. (page 304)

Unions Employee organizations that work with employers to achieve better pay, hours, and working conditions. (page 288)

Unity of command The principle that a subordinate should report to only one immediate superior. (page 235)

Unrelated diversification The action of diversifying into any business that is potentially profitable for the organization. (page 180)

Upper managers Managers who spend most of their time planning and leading because they make decisions about the overall performance and direction of the organization. (page 16)

Upward communication Communication flowing from lower to higher levels of the organization, such as progress reports, suggestions, inquiries, and grievances. (page 432)

Utilitarianism A philosophy where believers seek the greatest satisfaction for the largest number of individuals. (page 102)

Valence The value of each potential outcome that describes its importance. (page 371)

Variable-interval schedule A pattern whereby the period of reinforcement varies between one reinforcement and the next. (page 374)

Variable-ratio schedule A pattern whereby the number of behaviors required for reinforcement is varied. (page 374)

Venture capitalists Persons or organizations that agree to provide some funds for a new business in exchange for an ownership interest or stock. (page 526)

Verbal or oral communication Words spoken through various channels to convey information and meaning. (page 426)

Vertical coordination The integration of succeeding levels of the organization. (page 253)

Virtual organization Occurs when organizational members in different geographic areas use information technology to collaborate on projects and objectives. (page 244)

Wage and salary survey A study that tells the company how much compensation is paid by comparable firms for specific jobs the firms have in common. (page 282)

Webb-Pomerene Export Trade Act Allows selected American firms desiring international trade to form monopolies in order to compete with foreign cartels. (page 136)

Whistle blowing Occurs when employees expose an employer's wrongdoing. This might occur internally or externally. (page 107)

Work-in-process inventory Includes those products that are partially completed or are in transit. (page 496)

World Bank Formally known as the International Bank for Reconstruction and Development, it was established and supported by the industrialized nations in 1946 to loan money to underdeveloped and developing countries. (page 141)

World Trade Organization (WTO) A global association of member countries that promotes free trade. (page 141)

Written communication Information and meaning transferred as recorded words, such as memos, reports, and electronic mail. (page 426)

Zero-based budgeting (ZBB) A method of budgeting in which managers thoroughly reevaluate organizational activities to determine their true level of importance. (page 464)

Name Index

Company Index

Subject Index